The *Coutumes de Beauvaisis* of Philippe de Beaumanoir

The *Coutumes de Beauvaisis* of Philippe de Beaumanoir

Translated by F. R. P. Akehurst

University of Pennsylvania Press
Philadelphia

University of Pennsylvania Press
MIDDLE AGES SERIES
Edited by Edward Peters
Henry Charles Lea Professor
of Medieval History
University of Pennsylvania

A complete listing of the books in this series
appears at the back of this volume

Copyright © 1992 by the University of Pennsylvania Press
All rights reserved
Printed in the United States of America

Library of Congress Cataloging-in-Publication Data
Beaumanoir, Philippe de Remi, sire de, ca. 1250–1296.
  [Coutumes de Beauvaisis. English]
  The coutumes de Beauvaisis of Philippe de Beaumanoir / translated by F. R. P. Akehurst.
    p.   cm. — (Middle Ages series)
  Translation of: Coutumes de Beauvaisis.
  Included bibliographical references and index.
  ISBN 0-8122-3105-8
    1. Customary law—France—Beauvais.   2. Law—France—Beauvais—Sources.
  I. Title. II. Series.
  KJV264.B433B4313   1992
  349.44—dc20
  [344.4]   91-31497
                                                          CIP

FRONTISPIECE: The first page of a Paris manuscript of the *Coutumes de Beauvaisis*. Paris, Bibliothèque Nationale, MS fr. 18671. Reproduced by permission of the Bibliothèque Nationale, Paris (Phot. Bibl. Nat. Paris).

*To the memory of
my Mother and Father*

Contents

List of Abbreviations   xi
Introduction   xiii
Map   xxxiii

Prologue   3
1. Judges   14
2. Summonses   33
3. Permissible Delays   47
4. Attorneys   57
5. Advocates   69
6. Complaints   76
7. Answers   92
8. Latecomers   103
9. Inspections   106
10. Superior Jurisdiction   112
11. Ecclesiastical Jurisdiction   118
12. Wills   133
13. Dower   155
14. Inherited Real Property   165
15. Custodianship   180
16. Minors   194
17. Tutors   201
18. Illegitimacy   204
19. Consanguinity   216
20. Good-Faith Holders   219
21. Partnerships   223
22. Corporations   237
23. Property   244
24. Customs   249
25. Highways   263
26. Measurements   273
27. Prices   279

28. Horses   288
29. Services   291
30. Offenses   302
31. Larceny   334
32. Novel Disseisin   340
33. Fraud   351
34. Contracts   355
35. Writings   381
36. Safekeeping   395
37. Loans   400
38. Rentals   405
39. Proofs   418
40. Auditors   443
41. Arbitrators   458
42. Liquidated Damages   470
43. Sureties   474
44. Redemption   486
45. Avowals   506
46. Religious Houses   525
47. Subinfeudation   530
48. Freehold   536
49. Necessity   540
50. Communes   543
51. Seizures   551
52. Trespass   560
53. Reclamation   571
54. Creditors' Remedies I   576
55. Creditors' Remedies II   585
56. Incompetents   589
57. Marital Maintenance   593
58. Jurisdiction   599
59. Private War   610
60. Truces   619
61. Appeals   627
62. Default of Judgment   652
63. Defenses   659
64. Judicial Battles   670
65. Jurors' Delays   677
66. Recusal   684

Contents   ix

67. Judgment   689
68. Usury   704
69. Misadventure   710
70. Unenforceable Gifts   720
Conclusion   725

Glossary   727
Index   735

Abbreviations

The following works are cited in the notes by the short form indicated:

Beugnot. *Les coutumes du Beauvoisis par Philippe de Beaumanoir, jurisconsulte français du XIIIe siècle*, ed. le comte Beugnot. 2 vols. Société de l'Histoire de France. Paris: Renouard, 1842.

Bordier. Bordier, Henry-Léonard. *Philippe de Remi, sire de Beaumanoir: Jurisconsulte et poète national du Beauvaisis 1246–1296*. 1869. Reprint. Geneva: Slatkine Reprints, 1980.

De Laurière. Ragueau, François and Eusèbe de Laurière, eds. *Glossaire du droit françois*. New ed. Niort: Favre, 1882.

De Lépinois. De Lépinois, Eugène. *Recherches historiques et critiques sur l'ancien comté et les comtes de Clermont en Beauvoisis du XIe au XIIIe siècle*. Beauvais: Pere, 1877.

Est. Les Etablissements de Saint Louis, ed. Paul Viollet. 4 vols. Société de l'Histoire de France. Paris: Renouard, 1881.

Glanvill. Ranulf de Glanvil(le) (supposed author). *The treatise on the laws and customs of England commonly called Glanvill*, ed. and trans. G. D. G. Hall. Medieval Texts. London: Nelson, 1965.

Olim. Beugnot, le comte, ed. *Les olim ou registre des arrêts rendus par la cour du roi, sous les règnes de Saint Louis, de Philippe le Hardi, de Philippe le Bel, de Louis le Hutin et de Philippe le Long*. 4 vols. Paris: Imprimerie Royale, 1839–44.

Ord. Ordonnances des rois de France de la troisième race, ed. Eusèbe de Laurière et al. 21 vols. Paris: Imprimerie Royale, 1723–1849.

Salmon. *Philippe de Beaumanoir: Coutumes de Beauvaisis*, ed. Am[édée] Salmon. 2 vols. 1899–1900. Reprint. Paris: Picard, 1970.

Introduction

The esteem in which modern scholars hold Philippe de Beaumanoir's *Coutumes de Beauvaisis* is evidenced in such descriptions as admirable,[1] significant,[2] most important,[3] the best,[4] "l'oeuvre juridique la plus originale et la plus remarquable du moyen âge français,"[5] and so forth; indeed it is hard to find any disparaging remarks about it (I have found none). It is all the more surprising, therefore, that no translation of it has been published up to now, except in Japanese.[6] Only three printed editions have been produced of the original Old French version, in 1690,[7] in 1842,[8] and in 1899–1900 (reprinted in 1970).[9] The present translation therefore fills a very real need.

It is all the more important to stress from the outset that Beaumanoir's treatise is limited both in place and time: it deals only with the customs of the Beauvais region (or to be more precise, the county of Clermont), and it was valid in its entirety perhaps only for the two or three years during which it was being written, ending in 1283. Customs described in the *Coutumes de Beauvaisis* cannot be assumed to have been in force in any other region, or at any other time (although they may have been). While many customs were identical in several adjoining castellanies, others were different in a province as close as Normandy, where for example the royal writs introduced by the Angevin monarchs were still in force in Beaumanoir's time, yet totally unknown in Clermont. What the *Coutumes* offer us is not the common law of France, but the customs of a small region. They also provide the incalculably valuable testimony of an important public official who was familiar with the laws, who had meditated on their worth and cohesiveness, and who left on his book the stamp of a personality which today's readers cannot but find attractive and surprisingly modern. It has become unfashionable in literary studies to look for "the author behind the work." The reader who does not sense the man Philippe de Beaumanoir behind this book is missing one of the greatest pleasures it holds.

Features of the *Coutumes de Beauvaisis* which have won for it the accolades quoted above include comprehensiveness, clarity, and independence. The comprehensiveness may be an illusion, since there remain questions to which Beaumanoir provides no answers: the actual course of the procedure, the rhythm of cases, the formality of the proceedings— much that an observer of 1283 could see for himself—all remain rather obscure. Yet Beaumanoir does cover much more law than other custumals, which seem preoccupied with property, its ownership and change of ownership. The law is clearer, also, in Beaumanoir, for he gives definitions which non-specialists of his own time could probably understand fairly readily, many of which are still transparent to us today. And for Beaumanoir, the living law is the customs, as seen applied in cases that he recounts, rather than the law of Rome which, in spite of its growing prestige, is sometimes hard to reconcile with the customs of the time. Other custumals take pains to cite the Roman law most like the custom under discussion,[10] but Beaumanoir never does this, and it is easy to imagine that the customs he describes have gradually grown up and evolved, that they somehow reflect the will of the people. This is probably a delusion, and scholars have discovered many influences of Roman and Canon law;[11] but the customs of Beauvais hang together, and the modern reader can learn a considerable amount about the society of Clermont and its county just by reading Beaumanoir. He often gives his defense of a custom, usually based on reasonableness or, as he says, the fact that "it would be a bad thing"[12] if the law were otherwise.

While Beaumanoir's law is thus at once limited and broad, allegedly merely remembered but in fact logically defensible and defended, it can often be used to explain some actual or literary event or procedure elsewhere and at a different time. Nowadays Beaumanoir is frequently cited as an authority, even for events which occurred decades before his time.[13] This recourse to Beauvais law can be dangerous, since the law is not always and everywhere the same; but even if the law is not available to us for the region where an event occurred, the fact that the event *would* have been (un)lawful in Beauvais allows us to guess that it was also (un)lawful where it did occur.

Beaumanoir's Life and Times

The jurist's grandfather was Pierre de Remi (before 1190–c. 1229), who distinguished himself at the Battle of Bouvines (1214).[14] Pierre's arms consisted of a red shield with three gold cinquefoils, two above and one below. Pierre's son Philippe (c. 1205–c. 1266), father of the jurist, generally signed himself Philippe de Remi. He acquired land to consolidate that which he had inherited from his father, and eventually built a house called Beau Manoir, whose name he then took. This Philippe held his land in Remi as a fief from the Abbey of St. Denis. He was a *bailli*[15] of the Gâtinais[16] for several years. He had three children: Girard, who left a daughter before disappearing, probably to the Holy Land; Péronne, who married; and Philippe the younger (b. c. 1247–52, d. 1296), who took the name of Philippe de Beaumanoir, which was how he referred to himself in the *Coutumes de Beauvaisis*. It is probable that he was never the lord of Beaumanoir, which passed to his niece on her marriage. Philippe the younger did, however, have property in the area, and he built a house called le Moncel in the commune town of Pontpoint, near Pont-Sainte-Maxence. It was in building this house that Philippe ruined his finances, and after his death le Moncel passed eventually to the king, Philippe le Bel, who used it as a hunting lodge. Both Philippe de Remi and Philippe de Beaumanoir, father and son, used seals with the arms already used by Pierre de Remi. Philippe de Beaumanoir's seal, however, includes a bar (*lambel*), showing he was a younger son.

The jurist Philippe de Beaumanoir became *bailli* of Clermont in 1279. At about that time, the count of Clermont, Robert of France (b. 1256, count 1270–1318), sixth son of Louis IX (Saint Louis, b. 1205, reigned 1226–70, canonized 1297), was the victim of an accident: during a tournament in 1277 he was struck violently on the helmet and was never quite right afterwards, although he lived until 1318.[17] In September 1283, the *bailli* Philippe de Beaumanoir had to make public amends for an improper arrest made in the grange of Trambloi, which belonged to the Cistercian abbey of Chaalis. Soon afterwards he left Clermont, where he had been an employee of the count, to become a part of the royal administration of Philippe III le Hardi (1270–85) and his successor Philippe IV le Bel (1285–1314). He served these kings in turn as *sénéchal*[18] of Poitou (1284–87) and of Saintonge (1287–88), then *bailli* of Vermandois (1289–91), Touraine (1291–92), and finally of Senlis (1292–96). (It was normal for the *baillis* to change posts every few years.) The high point of Philippe's career may have been as *bailli* of Vermandois, for that post carried the highest pay (five hundred livres per year) and was the largest jurisdiction. While there he also undertook a mission to Rome on behalf of Philippe le Bel in the fall of 1289. There are numerous documents which bear his name, but the records of the Parlement in Paris show no appeals against his judgments. He seems to have died after a longish illness in January 1296.

Philippe de Beaumanoir had two wives, Saintisme who died in 1292 after having borne him two (or possibly four) children, and a second wife whom he married at the end of his life, Mabile de Boves, who survived him. She too was dead by the end of the century. Philippe was buried with his two wives in the church of the Augustins in Compiègne, which disappeared at the time of the Revolution. He was survived by a daughter (and possibly by two leper children).

Two lengthy romances, *Jehan et Blonde* and *La Manekine* have been attributed to Philippe de Beaumanoir the jurist. Recent scholarship suggests that the literary works should rather be attributed to Philippe de Remi, the father of the jurist, who was also, of course, a *bailli* in his own right.[19] There are also some minor works, of lyric and narrative genres, which form part of the poetic oeuvre, and which should perhaps now be attributed to the father, Philippe de Remi.

The life of Beaumanoir neatly fits into the second half of the thirteenth century. Born under Louis IX, he served both that king's son, Philippe III le Hardi, and his grandson, Philippe IV le Bel. The language of the period could be called Late Old French, for the period of Middle French was soon to begin.[20] The great crusades were over by 1250. In architecture, the Gothic style was triumphant everywhere, and the great cathedrals were recently built or a-building. Beauvais Cathedral, in Philippe de Beaumanoir's own county, suffered a disastrous second collapse of its ambitiously lofty choir vaulting in 1284. The universities were flowering, but not yet very numerous; the University of Paris had obtained its statutes in 1215, and Robert de Sorbon (1201–74) left it his library and his name. The library had grown to 1,000 volumes by 1289. The troubadours, those poets of love and war in the Old Occitan language, were in decay, with the self-styled last of the troubadours, Guiraut Riquier, dying in 1292. The province of Toulouse where Occitan was the native language was annexed to the French portion in 1271, following the Albigensian Crusade earlier in the century.

The beginning of Beaumanoir's half-century, in 1253, was to witness the death of an important figure from the preceding period: Thibaud de Champagne, a great lyric poet or trouvère and also a great nobleman, leader of a crusade, and king of Navarre. Teaching in Paris in 1252–59 and again in 1269–72 was the Doctor Angelicus, Thomas Aquinas; and a student there in 1243–48 was Saint Bonaventure, the Seraphic Doctor (c. 1217–74, canonized 1482), who became the minister general of the Franciscan Order in 1257 and lived in Paris at various times thereafter. Roger Bacon wrote his

Opus maius in Paris in 1266–68. In the literature of the north of France, one of the great figures known today from the second half of the thirteenth century is Jean de Meung, who in about 1267–78 added a much longer and more scholastic continuation to the delicately allegorical *Romance of the Rose*, left unfinished in about 1230 by Guillaume de Lorris. Other great figures in literature include Adam de la Halle (c. 1235–after 1285), originally from Arras, who wrote poems and plays and probably studied in Paris; and Rutebuef (dates uncertain, but in Paris c. 1256), the first unabashedly Parisian poet, who left a considerable corpus of works, including a miracle play and some occasional poems.

Among the Italians, Dante was about fifteen years Beaumanoir's junior, Marco Polo was almost exactly his age and living in China when Beaumanoir was composing his book, and Brunetto Latini briefly resided in Paris in 1260–66, and in that city composed in French his *Trésor*. In 1282 the guild system of government which was to dominate Florentine politics for two centuries was established. For Venice, one of the richest cities in Europe, the second half of the thirteenth century was marked by a continuing war with Genoa. In Spain an important event at this time was the publication, probably in 1255, of the *Libro del fuero*, also known as the *Espéculo de la leyes*, which was attributed to Alfonso X (el Sabio, b. 1221, reigned 1252–84), and subsequently revised into the *Siete partidas*, a monumental law code in Castilian.

By the time Beaumanoir was writing his book on the customs of Beauvais, several other authors had undertaken the same task for their own regions of France. The first region to produce a *coutumier* was Normandy, where the first part of the Latin text of *Le très ancien coutumier de Normandie* was written in about 1199–1200,[21] followed by a French translation from about 1248–70.[22] Also in Normandy, a larger compilation called the *Summa de legibus Normannie in curia laicali* was written in about 1254–58.[23] The French translation of the *Summa de legibus* was produced in about 1280.[24] An anonymous compilation of the customs of the Orléans region was written probably by 1258[25] and later included, along with a similar compilation from the Touraine from about 1246,[26] in the *Etablissements de Saint Louis*, the whole collection being put together by 1273.[27] The title of this collection is deceptive, since only the first few pages concern an actual ordinance promulgated by Louis IX, the rest being the work of anonymous legists. From about the same period comes *Li livres de jostice et de plet* (c. 1254–60).[28] At this time also (c. 1253), Pierre de Fontaines was writing his *Conseil*.[29]

While similarities exist between these earlier compilations and the *Coutumes de Beauvaisis*, Beaumanoir's treatise is not clearly derived from any of them. Its mixture of procedural and substantive law, the impression it leaves of the competence and experience of its author, and its solid grounding in case decisions and dicta make it unique. Whereas *Li livres de jostice et de plet* reads like a law student's notes[30] and the *Conseil* of Pierre de Fontaines is written for a noble pupil,[31] Beaumanoir's work addresses a wider audience, and does so in a practical manner.

There are some compilations of customs from the southern part of France, but written in Latin. The customs of Toulouse were copied in order to be approved by Philippe le Hardi in 1283, and two manuscripts from 1285 have survived.[32] The customs of St. Gilles survive in an abbreviated form, perhaps compiled in the early thirteenth century, but in a manuscript copy from the fifteenth century.[33]

After Beaumanoir, the writing down of customs continued, and there is a *Coutumier de Champagne*, whose editor dates it in the last decade of the thirteenth century,[34] and *La très ancienne coutume de Bretagne*, which dates from about 1312–25.[35] Of a slightly different type is the *Livre Roisin*, compiled by one Jean Roisin, from the Lille region, soon after 1283.[36] A century after Beaumanoir, another wave of compilations included the *Grand coutumier* of Jacques d'Ableiges, from about 1387–89,[37] and *La Somme rurale* of Jean Boutillier from 1395.[38] The books of customs mentioned here, from before and after Beaumanoir's time, by no means exhaust the list. Several of them were among the first books printed in France, although Beaumanoir's treatise had to wait until 1690 for its first printed edition. It was this edition that was known to Montesquieu.[39]

There are also some treatises in Latin written in England. It has sometimes been asserted that Philippe de Beaumanoir may have visited England, although this hypothesis is now generally rejected.[40] He may, however, have been aware of what was going on across the Channel. First in time of these Latin documents is the *Leges Henrici Primi* from about the year 1118.[41] Henry II's justiciar Ranulf Glanville may be the author of a treatise commonly called *Glanvill*, written in about 1187–89,[42] of which a mid-thirteenth-century French version exists in four manuscripts.[43] The English jurist Henry of Bracton produced the great treatise *De legibus et consuetudinibus Angliae* before 1250.[44] In England also the treatise *Fet asaver* composed in Anglo-French in about 1267 was one of the two most copied law tracts of its age.[45]

By Beaumanoir's time, a good deal of work had been done on Canon law. Gratian's *Decretum* was completed in about 1140,[46] and the *Glossa ordinaria* of Joannes Teutonicus was composed in 1215–18.[47] Roman law as compiled and promulgated in 533 in the *Corpus juris civilis* of Justinian,[48] and later revived in Italy in the twelfth century, had already benefited from the work of the great teachers Irnerius and his four pupils, the Doctors, a century before Beaumanoir. Accursius's *Glossa ordinaria* on the *Corpus juris civilis* was completed by 1234.[49] There were schools of Roman law in Orléans and Montpellier in Beaumanoir's own century. Where Beaumanoir owes something to Canon law or Roman law, the borrowing is done with great discretion, so that Roman laws are not identified as such, but so artfully patched into the customs of Clermont that the seams are invisible.

The *Coutumes de Beauvaisis*

While not totally without order, Beaumanoir's treatise is not very systematically arranged, according to our modern standards.[50] The treatise begins with a pious Prologue, in which the author modestly declines to name himself but declares that he will do so at the end of the book (§6), and this promise is fulfilled in the Conclusion (§1982). There follows an enumeration of the chapters (§10). The first chapter then deals with the position of *bailli*, Beaumanoir's own post in the administration of Robert, count of Clermont, while he was writing the *Coutumes*. Beaumanoir rather naturally claims that a *bailli* must be an extraordinary person, with unusual personal qualities. The conduct of the *baillis* was regulated by an ordinance of Louis IX, and there are records of inquiries into their affairs.[51]

The other chapters of the book discuss the procedural and substantive law of the county. The several chapters on procedure, both civil and criminal, do not all occur together. Beaumanoir begins his book logically enough by discussing the early stages of a law suit (Chapters 2–9), but then he goes off into jurisdictional problems (Chapters 10–11) and substantive law until Chapters 39–40, where he discusses witnesses and their interrogation. Another group of chapters (51–53) contains information on seizures of property and how to get it back by applying to the court. More substantive law follows, until the author turns to the problems of appeals (Chapters 61–62) and of the judicial battle (Chapters 62–64), before giving warnings and instructions concerning judgments (Chapters 65–67). There is finally a chapter on misadventures (Chapter 69), and the book ends somewhat lamely with a chapter on gifts, which repeats much information given earlier.

There is some general legal information which is neither procedural nor substantive: Beaumanoir discusses the distinction between real and personal property (Chapter 23), between custom and usage (Chapter 24), and how to deal with force and trickery (Chapter 33). He sets forth the regulations concerning arbitration (Chapter 41), the defense of necessity (Chapter 49), and other matters where a strict application of the laws is to be tempered by mercy (Chapter 69). In addition, he shows how minor children and orphans are to be looked after, especially in court (Chapters 15–20), and who has the responsibility for safeguarding religious establishments (Chapter 46) and the chronically ill (Chapter 56). Comparatively late in the book (Chapter 58), he finally gives the definition (which might have been useful much earlier) of high and low justice.

The substantive law which Beaumanoir exposes in his treatise is of great interest. In terms of modern law, much of it can be classified under familiar headings: Criminal Law (Chapters 30–31), Property (Chapters 12–14 and 44), Creditors' Remedies (Chapters 54–55), Contracts (Chapters 34–35 and 42), Business Associations (Chapters 21–22), Agency (Chapter 29), Commercial Law (Chapters 36–38 and 68), and Family Law (Chapter 57). Other less familiar areas of the law include Feudal Law (Chapters 28, 32, 45, and 47–48), the law governing the waging of private war (Chapters 59–60), and what might be called the law of administration (Chapters 25–27 and 50). Of course many topics are covered in passing, to which separate chapters are not devoted. Beaumanoir does not discuss torts (in the modern sense) as such, but it is clear that remedies did exist for trespassing and damage to chattels (§§1350, 1557–61), for example, as well as for defamation (§§844–48) and battery (§841).

Lawyers are not unaccustomed to a certain lack of order in general books on the law. It has probably always been recognized that the law is a "seamless web" and that everything in it is somehow connected to everything else, so that no matter where you begin to study it you will eventually be led into all other areas. A medieval practitioner might well have learned law in the random manner it was presented by the cases he saw, rather than according to some more logical order. Beaumanoir is not trying to write a school book, to teach the law to students; he does not begin with easier topics and go forward to more complicated ones; he does not begin with basic principles and go on to the application of them. Instead, he is writing for those who might be involved in litigation in his own jurisdiction of the Beauvaisis (§1), and he gives them much very practical advice not merely on the law but on procedure, and on pitfalls to avoid (e.g., §1755). In that sense, therefore, his book is arranged with a certain logic, since the first event with which a person might have to deal is the summons, delivered by a court official or two gentlemen, and the information on such is contained in the very second chapter. Beaumanoir then takes his reader through the first few steps of a suit, before going on to discuss possible issues of substantive law which might be involved in the suit.

As an example of Beaumanoir's composition, we might examine Chapter 6: "Complaints." In an introductory section, Beaumanoir discusses the form of complaints and answers in ecclesiastical courts, and declares that the secular mode of pleadings is simpler and more quickly done. He then lists the kinds of substantive law that require pleadings. The discussion takes up these items in the order listed, and gives details on each kind of pleading. At the end of the list, Beaumanoir sums up with a generalization on pleadings: you must say what you are asking for, and why, and offer to prove your contentions. The chapter does not end here, for the author goes on to explain how you can find yourself in a suit without ever having made a complaint; and how you can accuse someone of something without it leading to a suit. The discussion also includes matters of jurisdiction, recording the pleadings in writing, amending the pleadings, problems of multiple plaintiffs and multiple defendants, res judicata, and the oaths sworn by the parties. Along the way there are several comparisons between ecclesiastical and secular procedures. Near the end of the chapter, Beaumanoir returns to make a different analysis of the various kinds of suits, this time according to the Canon law categories of personal, real, and mixed actions (but see also Justinian, *Institutes*, 4.6) and includes another section on jurisdiction. Finally he cites a case that deals with a problem of high and low justice (and is not, therefore, from Beaumanoir's own jurisdiction, where both kinds of justice were administered by the same person). The various kinds of substantive law dealt with in the early part of the chapter all have their own subsequent separate chapters, but not in the order of the list given in Chapter 6. The composition of this chapter is thus not incoherent or random, but it is not completely coordinated with the rest of the book. It gives practical advice for litigants wishing to make a complaint, as well as some advice on pitfalls to avoid; and the same material is analyzed twice, in detail for those who are not professional lawmen, and more briefly by comparison with ecclesiastical procedure for those who may already be familiar with that body of law.

For the modern reader, this mode of exposition is also ideal, since on the one hand not much knowledge is presumed, and on the other a comparison may be made with something about which there is information from another, independent source.

Beaumanoir's style is to some extent dependent on his subject matter. In the chapters on procedure, the cases he cites as examples are relatively rare, but in the chapters on substantive law the cases may demonstrate either a general principle or a minor distinction. When the jurist is producing examples or a hypothetical, he begins his remarks with the words "Or veons . . . ," which I have translated as "Let's see." A glance at the first sentences of a number of consecutive paragraphs will show that Beaumanoir is at some pains to vary his opening words, while wasting no time in getting to his subject matter.

While some individual sections (such as §1492) are somewhat incoherent, others are models of order and precision (such as §1605). We have no information concerning the order in which the chapters were written, although even in the earliest chapters specific allusions are made to some of the very late ones—references that could easily have been added after the chapters were otherwise long completed. Certainly information is sometimes repeated, after only a few sections (for example from §224 to §257), suggesting that the jurist had forgotten his earlier section on the same topic. This is really a proofreading error, however, rather than a compositional defect, and it has been asserted that Beaumanoir did not revise his work once it had been completed in 1283.[52]

Beaumanoir is not uncritical of the law as he found it and administered it, or of the people he had to look after in his capacity as *bailli*. He never forgets, however, that he is there to uphold the customs. He is plainly against the institution of serfdom (§1453), which exists only in an attenuated form in the Beauvais region (§1457). On the other hand, he warns of the problems involved for those who might try to free their serfs (§1445). Reading between the lines, one may surmise that he is impatient with the gentlemen who are supposed to be judging cases by acting as jurors in his court (§§1853, 1862). These men seem to have many opportunities for shirking their responsibilities (Chapter 65). He insists, however, that in the Beauvaisis judgments are made by juries, not by judges acting alone (§24).

Perhaps as a way to get over this difficulty, Beaumanoir suggests that when the facts and the law are clear, the judge should act on his own and expedite matters, and not overwork the jurors (§31).

Beaumanoir and the Common Law

A much-debated problem in Beaumanoir studies is what the jurist meant by the common law, or *droit commun*. The expression appears many times in the text. It has been asserted that by this expression Beaumanoir meant Roman law, as incorporated into customary law[53] or royal ordinances;[54] another interpretation is that *droit commun* is the law of a wider area of jurisdiction than that of local customs: either the whole of France,[55] or the whole of the barony presided over by the feudal lord who held directly from the king of France (§724). Readers will be able to judge for themselves while reading the translation, where the expression *droit commun* has been translated systematically, and I hope not confusingly, as "common law." This expression is of course not to be understood in its modern meaning in American law.

A related issue is the way in which law is actually made or found in the Beauvaisis. Beaumanoir cites nearly a hundred different cases, some of which he says he saw, others of which he says were tried by him, and yet others of which are from outside the county jurisdiction. Do these cases make law, in the sense of setting precedents, or do they merely illustrate what the law already is? Although a few royal laws or *establissements* are cited by Beaumanoir, and the *bailli* is admonished that he must apply these laws, very little exists in the thirteenth century of what we would today call legislation, or statutes. The law, or custom, is in the mind and memory of those who have to apply it and make judgments by it. When there is no doubt, Beaumanoir recommends a summary procedure without going through a trial by peers (§31). When there is a perceived public danger, the judge can act swiftly and independently (§§884–85). When the case is complex, or obscure, it should be put to the jurors (§31). In every case Beaumanoir cites, the question put to the jurors is one of law, not fact. These jurors give a judgment of what the custom is, and this makes the outcome of the case inevitable. Their judgment, however, is not necessarily based merely on memory, since questions of public policy are considered in coming to a decision (§1414). The judgments also often contain obiter dicta (as the expression is used in modern American law), or remarks about how the case would have come out if the facts had been different. The status of these cases, then, is a complex one, and cannot be easily defined.

Beaumanoir the *Bailli*

Beaumanoir's first chapter is devoted to the office of the *bailli*. Here, the jurist defines the ideal *bailli*, whose ten qualities (which do not include "learned in the law") make him a successor to the knight who has often been seen as the defender of the oppressed in the Middle Ages. Included in the other sixty-nine chapters are many pieces of advice to the *bailli* or any other judge, whose task is not merely to supervise his lord's estate and preside over his lawcourt, but to be in some sense a reformer and even a legislator. Beaumanoir observes that he has himself improved the administration of Clermont in several ways: he has obliged all citizens to join the hue and cry that helps identify and capture wanted persons (§§1571, 1904) and has reformed the corrupt system of placing live-in guards on property to force the compliance of the occupant (§1604). These remarks and the other advice given to judges must have been very helpful to the person who replaced him as *bailli* in 1283.

Much other advice in the *Coutumes* is addressed to the litigators whom Beaumanoir identified in his introduction. When he is giving a warning, the paragraph may begin on a monitory note: "Bien se garde . . . ," which I have translated "[Someone] should be careful. . . ." It is often points of procedure which are signaled this way, for it is apparent that an unwary party could easily be outmaneuvered by a seasoned litigator, as is still true today. An appeals procedure was available, but the very procedure for obtaining an appeal was full of traps and dangers, and Beaumanoir displays great familiarity with these difficulties, such as could only have been obtained by long experience on the bench or at the bar (§1755).

Some surprise has been shown at the appointment of so young a man as Beaumanoir to the post of *bailli*. By one reckoning, he must have been about thirty-two in 1279, by another he may have been only twenty-seven. We have no knowledge of where he received his formal legal training (although there is great interest in this problem), or indeed if he had any. For modern lawyers, the idea that a person untrained in law might practice at the bar or sit on the bench is disturbing; but it must be remembered that the task of the *bailli* was not the same as that of the modern judge. In fact he was little more than a facilitator: he did not need to prove the facts, for they *proved themselves*. As long as two witnesses could be produced whose stories agreed, and who were not successfully challenged for bias, their testimony was taken as proof of the facts (§1230). Nor did the *bailli* really need to know the law: it was the task of the jurors to recall the custom that was appropriate to the case. Thus all the *bailli* needed to do was to apply the given law to the given facts and come to a conclusion. No doubt this is a simplification, and indeed another important task of the *bailli* was to listen to the pleadings and try to make sense of them, so that the issues were clear (§43); but for much of the time that task must have required more patience and common sense than legal knowledge (§§15, 33). And it is clear from the *Coutumes de Beauvaisis* that Beaumanoir did in fact know a great deal of law by the end of his tenure as *bailli* in Clermont. The task of his successor must have been rendered substantially easier if he had a copy of the *Coutumes* to consult. By writing down those customs, Beaumanoir was providing a written law for his district that he hoped would not be as changing and changeable as merely remembered customs were (§7). That which is not written down, he observes, is soon lost (§7). Other persons, such as Pierre de Fontaines for the Vermandois, had written down the customs of an important region.[56] The written law of the *Corpus juris civilis* had great prestige; was Beaumanoir hoping to give the same authority to customs by setting them down in writing?

Note on This Translation

All translations are imperfect, just as all language is an imperfect mirror of the reality it reflects. A translation such as this one, of a technical book from a past century, must be reasonably comprehensible to the modern reader without extensive notes; it must give an accurate rendering of the specialized material; and it must not create resonances which are improper, but which arise because modern words have different connotations and values from the medieval ones they render.

Apart from the difficulty of translating faithfully and elegantly, there is for the modern translator the problem of modern usage. It has recently become necessary, in order to avoid insulting a large part of the readership, to avoid the use of the masculine to include the feminine. The possessive that corresponds to the subject "one" must now be "his or her" (although I have always liked "one's") or even "their," which strains the assent of those trained in languages where agreement must frequently be observed. How to translate a medieval book where most of the activity described is couched in terms of men and what they (masculine) do? I have tried to use sex-neutral language where it does not do absolute injustice to the original: to translate an indefinite subject I have often used "persons" instead of "men"; but I fear that it would have sounded very strange to Beaumanoir's ear to hear what were essentially men designated that way.

It is not just a question of gender, however. How much of the charm of the original will be destroyed if some of the rough edges are sanded smooth, or even chamfered? Is it perhaps the work of a *traditore* to make intelligible to non-lawyers a work that was probably comprehensible in its author's time only to the lawyers and litigants for whom it was intended?

It was inevitable that some modern legal jargon would find its way into this translation. It is useless to try to hide that the translator is himself a lawyer, and that it would be relatively an easier task to translate Beaumanoir into modern law lingo. But in fact modern lawyers are mostly quite uninterested in the history of the law, except insofar as it affects the present, and I shall not expect many of them to read this book. It is unlikely to be prescribed in law schools, for it deals not only with what is described as "no longer good law" but with what is not even any longer good law in the foreign country where it was once, in a very circumscribed area, the law. Where I have chosen, then, to use a modern word in its specialized, legal sense I have signaled this fact in a note. The notes and parentheses will seem repetitive to those who read very much of the book; but I am anticipating that the translation will be dipped into and consulted, rather than read right through, so that even within a chapter the same notes and parentheses will have to be repeated.

I have not achieved a completely uniform correspondence of modern English words to Old French ones. For instance, the frequently occurring word *eritage* designates "real property" or "realty," which can include not merely land but also, for example, the power to levy tolls (although the tolls thus levied are not realty but personalty). Usually, however, *eritage* means "land," and that is how I have often translated it. Likewise, an *essoine* is a legal excuse not to appear in court, often because of illness; and thus it can often be translated as "illness," although there are other legal excuses or *essoines*, such as bad weather or a rising creek. Occasionally Old French possesses a generic term not available in English: the *levees* of a fief, for example, would include money rents but also payments in kind from tenant farmers, certain taxes, harvests reaped or dug up from the ground, wood cut in the forests, or the price received for any of these non-monetary items (the proceeds). To call these things "revenues" or "interest" or "profits" or "income" ignores the fact that they may not be received in the form of money; but to call them "harvests" or "crops" or "fruits" implies that they are never money. Even the word "yield" has modern connotations of quantity rather than origin. These words have therefore sometimes been translated "crops," sometimes "fruits," sometimes "income," according to what they probably were.

Where I am not sure I have translated correctly, and where it is important to guide the reader who is making a comparison with the Old French text, I have given the Old French term, exactly as it appears in the French edition, in square brackets, thus [. . .]. Where I have added a word or two to make the translation read more coherently, I have done so in curly brackets, thus { . . . }.

While Beaumanoir's book is not a complete account of the law of his time, it may have seemed complete to those familiar with the working of the courts in his time. He was at least trying to be comprehensive. What he supposed his readers to know, however, is often difficult for us to recuperate. It is as if we had from some culture a written text which we could read and decipher, but without being able to reconstruct the sound of the language. In many ways Beaumanoir's book forms a seamless web, that is to say that it forms a coherent system in which every part is connected to all the other parts. What is said in one chapter is illuminated or clarified by what is said in several other chapters; but one cannot read all the chapters at once, and one must start somewhere. I have tried to help by making references in notes to other parts of the book that will shed light on the passage being read. The chapter headings are also quite explicit, and may guide the reader to a fuller treatment of a subject which he or she finds puzzling.

The Old French text I have used is the edition of Salmon (*Philippe de Beaumanoir: Coutumes de Beauvaisis*, ed. Am[édée] Salmon [2 vols., 1899–1900; rpt. Paris: Picard, 1970]). I have followed Salmon's system of numbering the sections (or paragraphs) consecutively from start to finish. The previous editor, Beugnot (*Les coutumes du Beauvoisis par Philippe de Beaumanoir, jurisconsulte français du XIIIe siècle*, ed. le comte Beugnot [2 vols., Société de l'Histoire de France, Paris: Renouard, 1842]), numbers these sections within each chapter. Salmon established a stemma suggesting that the original manuscript, dictated by Beaumanoir, was copied twice, and that all surviving manuscripts were copied directly or indirectly from one of these two copies, which he calls α and β. There is thus an α group and a β group of manuscripts. By comparing and collating the manuscripts of the α group, Salmon has reconstructed the α manuscript, as far as possible, and that is what he prints. Where the manuscripts disagree, he gives variants, and these are sometimes helpful in providing an alternate reading which makes more sense than Salmon's base text. Where I have chosen a variant reading rather than Salmon's basic text I have indicated the fact in a note. I have also indicated in a note places where the Salmon text seems to me faulty because of a typographical error, in which cases I have also consulted Beugnot's text.

Since I have cited in the notes some of the manuscripts by the sigla assigned by Salmon, I list here the manuscripts referred to by those sigla:

A. Paris, Bib. Nat. MS fr. 11652.
B. Berlin, Staatsbibliothek MS Hamilton 193.
C. Paris, Bib. Nat. MS fr. 4516.
D. Paris, Bib. Nat. MS fr. 8357.
E. Rome, Vatican, MS Christine 1055.
F. Rome, Vatican, MS Ottoboni 1155.
G. Paris, Bib. Nat. MS fr. 24059.

I am grateful to Dr. Lowanne Jones, who has read most of the chapters, and to William Davis, Esq., who has read many of them. Their comments have allowed me to avoid many obscurities and inaccuracies. Any errors that remain are my own.

I wish to express my thanks also to the University of Minnesota for awarding me a sabbatical leave in 1988–89, and to the College of Liberal Arts of the University of Minnesota, which awarded me a Bush Foundation Fellowship to supplement my sabbatical funds. I am also grateful to the Camargo Foundation, which welcomed me in Cassis (Bouches-du-Rhône) from January to May 1989, and where much of the translation was refined.

Notes

1. "What historian of feudalism could ignore that admirable analyst of medieval society, Philippe de Beaumanoir . . . author, in 1283, of the *Coutumes* of Beauvaisis?" Marc Bloch, *Feudal Society*, trans. L. A. Manyon, 2 vols. (Chicago: University of Chicago Press, 1964) 1: 119.

2. "The *Coutumes de Beauvaisis* is the longest and most significant work on customary law to survive from thirteenth-century France." Fredric Cheyette, "Beaumanoir," *Dictionary of the Middle Ages*, 13 vols. (New York: Scribner's, 1982–89) 2: 144.

3. "For other regions there is . . . and, most important, Beaumanoir's *Coutumes de Beauvaisis*." Joseph R. Strayer, "Law, French: in North," *Dictionary of the Middle Ages*, 13 vols. (New York: Scribner's, 1982–89) 7: 458.

4. "The best work by a French feudal jurist was Beaumanoir's Coutumes de Beauvaisis." Robert S. Hoyt, *Europe in the Middle Ages*, 2d ed. (New York: Harcourt, Brace and World, 1966) 395.

5. "Les plus important des auteurs du XIIIe siècle est Philippe de Remi, sire de Beaumanoir. Son ouvrage . . . est l'oeuvre juridique la plus originale et la plus remarquable du moyen âge français." Auguste Dumas, *Histoire du droit français* (Aix-en-Provence: Librairie de l'Université, n. d.) 147.

6. Hiroshi Hanawa, trans., "Traduction des 'Coutumes de Beauvaisis' (Philippe de Beaumanoir)," *Kobe Law Journal* 15 (1965–66): 533–592, 730–796; 16 (1966–67): 602–668, 785–840; 17 (1967–68): no. 3: 72–126, no. 4: 43–98; 18 (1968–69): 97–125; 19 (1969–70): 455–527; 20 (1970–71): 32–164, 210–324, 458–534.

7. *Assises et bons usages du royaume de Jérusalem, tirés d'un manuscrit de la Bibliothèque Vaticane, par messire Jean d'Ibelin . . . ensemble les Coutumes de Beauvaisis par messire Philippes de Beaumanoir, bailly de Clermont en Beauvaisis et autres anciennes coutumes*, ed. Gaspard Thaumas de la Thaumassière (Paris: Morel, 1690).

8. *Les coutumes du Beauvoisis par Philippe de Beaumanoir, jurisconsulte français du XIIIe siècle*, ed. le comte Beugnot, 2 vols., Société de l'Histoire de France (Paris: Renouard, 1842). This edition is referred to subsequently in these notes and in the notes to the translation as Beugnot.

9. *Philippe de Beaumanoir: Coutumes de Beauvaisis*, ed. Am[édée] Salmon, 2 vols. (1899–1900; rpt. Paris: Picard, 1970). This edition is referred to subsequently in these notes and in the notes to the translation as Salmon.

10. Citation of Roman law is systematic in, for example, *Les établissements de Saint Louis* (see n. 22 below), where in the middle of the text one finds such insertions as: "*et selonc droit escrit ou Code, De transactionibus, l. Si causa cognita in fine, et en la Digeste, De re judicata, l. A divo pio . . .*" *Est.* 2: 3.

11. Jean Gaudemet, "L'influence des droits savants (romain et canonique) sur les textes de droit coutumier en occident avant le XVIe siècle," *Actes del III Congreso internacional de derecho canónico, Pamplona 1976: La norma en el derecho canónico, 1* (Pamplona, 1979) 165–194. See also P. van Wetter, "Le droit romain et Beaumanoir," *Mélanges Fitting* (Montpellier: Société anonyme de l'imprimerie générale du midi, 1908) 533–582.

12. See, for example, at the end of §1710.

13. Thus, for example, Emanuel J. Mickel suggests that the arrest of Ganelon may be justified because he threatened to attack Roland, since for Beaumanoir threats constitute a kind of proof if what was threatened subsequently happens. But Beaumanoir's book is written at least a century after the *Roland* and in a different province. See Emanuel J. Mickel, *Ganelon, Treason, and the "Chanson de Roland"*

(University Park and London: Pennsylvania State University Press, 1989) 34 and §1159 below.

14. The biographical information concerning the jurist Beaumanoir and his family which is used in this introduction has been gleaned from two articles in *Actes du Colloque International Philippe de Beaumanoir et les Coutumes de Beauvaisis (1283–1983)*, ed. Philippe Bonnet-Laborderie (Beauvais: GEMOB, n.d. [c. 1985]). The articles are: Robert-Henri Bautier, "Philippe de Beaumanoir, rapport général au colloque," pp. 5–17, and Louis Carolus-Barré, "Origines, milieu familial et carrière de Philippe de Beaumanoir," pp. 19–37.

15. In the thirteenth century, the *bailli* was the administrator of a county or an area of similar size. His duties were broad, for he was the administrator of the whole area and the chief judge. The *baillis* were generally chosen from among the minor nobility, although where there was more military responsibility, such as in the south, more noble men were appointed.

16. The Gâtinais was a district south-southeast of Paris, including the town of Lorris, and whose old capitals were Montargis and Moret-sur-Loing.

17. For this injury, see Louis Carolus-Barré, "Les grands tournois de Compiègne et de Senlis en l'honneur de Charles, prince de Salerne (mai 1279)," *Bulletin de la Société nationale des antiquaires de France* (1978–79): 91.

18. The *sénéchal* was a royal administrator, the equivalent in southern France of the *bailli* in the north.

19. Bernard Gicquel, "Le *Jehan et Blonde* de Philippe de Rémi peut-il être une source du *Willehalm von Orlens*?" *Romania* 102 (1981): 306–323.

20. Guiraud claims that linguists are agreed that the beginning of Middle French may be placed at about 1328 (accession of the Valois kings) but himself follows Walter von Wartburg in placing the beginning of Middle French at about 1350. Pierre Guiraud, *Le moyen français*, Que sais-je? (Paris: Presses Universitaires de France, 1963) 12. Brunot and Bruneau seem to place the beginning of Middle French a little earlier, perhaps about 1285: Ferdinand Brunot and Charles Bruneau, *Précis de grammaire historique de la langue française*, 4th ed. (Paris: Masson, 1956) xi.

21. Ernest-Joseph Tardif, ed., *Coutumiers de Normandie: Textes critiques publiés avec notes et éclaircissements*, 2 vols., [Tome I.] Premiere partie: *Le très ancien coutumier de Normandie: Texte Latin* (Rouen: Cagniard, 1881); Deuxième partie: *Le très ancien coutumier de Normandie: Textes français et normand* (Rouen: Lestringant; Paris: Picard, 1903); Tome II. *La Summa de legibus Normannie in curia laicali* (Rouen: Lestringant; Paris: Picard, 1896): 1, première partie, p. LXII. This multi-volume work will be referred to in the rest of the notes as Tardif.

22. Tardif, 1, deuxième partie, p. LXIX.

23. Tardif, 2: CXCIV.

24. Tardif, 2: CXXXVII. For an edition of the Old French translation of the *Summa de legibus Normannie*, see *L'ancienne coutume de Normandie*, ed. William Laurence de Gruchy (St. Helier, Jersey, British Channel Islands: Charles le Feuvre, 1881).

25. *Les Etablissements de St. Louis*, ed. Paul Viollet, 4 vols., Société de l'Histoire de France (Paris: Renouard, 1881) 1: 80. This edition will be referred to subsequently in these notes and in the notes to the translation as *Est.*

26. *Est.* 1: 24.

27. *Est.* 1: 2.

28. *Li livres de jostice et de plet*, ed. Rapetti (sic), glossary by P. Chabaille, Collection de documents inédits sur l'histoire de France publié par les soins du Ministre de l'instruction publique, Première série, Histoire politique, 81 (Paris: Firmin Didot, 1850) XIV.

29. *Le conseil de Pierre de Fontaines, ou traité de l'ancienne jurisprudence française*, ed. M. A. J. Marnier (Paris: Durand, libraire and Joubert, libraire, 1846) XX.

30. Rapetti, ed., *Li livres de jostice et de plet* (see n. 28 supra) xxviii–xix.

31. *Le conseil de Pierre de Fontaines* (see n. 29 supra) 2–4.

32. *Coutumes de Toulouse*, ed. Ad. Tardif, Recueil de textes pour servir a l'enseignement de l'histoire du droit (Paris: Picard, 1884).

33. *Les coutumes de Saint-Gilles (XIIe–XIVe siècles)*, ed. E. Bligny-Bondurand (Paris: Picard, 1915). For other compilations of customs from southern France, see Jean-Marie Carbasse, *Bibliographie des coutumes méridionales (Catalogue des textes édités)*, Recueil de Mémoires et Travaux, publié par la Société d'Histoire du Droit et des Institutions des Anciens Pays de Droit Ecrit, 10 (Montpellier, France: Faculté de Droit et des Sciences Economiques, 1979) 1–89.

34. *L'ancien coutumier de Champagne (XIIIe siècle)*, ed. Paulette Portejoie (Poitiers: Oudin, 1956) 10–11.

35. *La très ancienne coutume de Bretagne*, ed. Marcel Planiol, Bibliothèque Bretonne Armoricaine, 2 (Rennes: Plihon et Hervé, 1896) 7.

36. *Li livre Roisin, coutumier lillois de la fin du XIIIe siècle*, ed. Raymond Monier (Paris: Domat-Montchrestien; Lille: Raoust, 1932) XXXV.

37. Jacques d'Ableiges, *Le grand coutumier de France*, eds. Ed. Laboulaye et R. Dareste (Paris: Durand and Pedone-Lauriel, libraires, 1868). For the date of this compilation, see Léopold Delisle, "L'auteur du Grand coutumier de France," *Mémoires de la Société de l'histoire de Paris et de l'Ile de France* 8 (1881): 151.

38. Jean Boutillier, *La Somme rurale*, ed. Louys Charondas de Caron (Lyon, 1621).

39. Charles-Louis de Secondat, baron de Montesquieu, *De l'esprit des lois*, in *Oeuvres complètes*, ed. Roger Caillois, 2 vols., Bibliothèque de la Pléïade (Paris: Gallimard, 1949). See especially Chapter XXVIII.

40. See, for example, Robert-Henri Bautier, "Philippe de Beaumanoir, rapport général au colloque," *Actes du Colloque International Philippe de Beaumanoir et les Coutumes de Beauvaisis (1283–1983)*, ed. Philippe Bonnet-Laborderie (Beauvais: GEMOB, n.d. [c. 1985]) 14.

41. *Leges Henrici Primi*, ed. L. J. Downer (Oxford: Clarendon, 1972) 36.

42. Ranulf de Glanvil(le) (supposed author), *The treatise on the laws and customs of the realm of England commonly called Glanvill*, ed. and trans. G. D. G. Hall, Medieval Texts (London: Nelson, 1965) xxxi.

43. Ranulf de Glanvil(le) (supposed author), *The treatise on the laws and customs of England commonly called Glanvill*, ed. and trans. G. D. G. Hall, Medieval Texts (London: Nelson, 1965) lviii.

44. Henry de Bracton, *De legibus et consuetudinibus Angliae*, ed. George E. Woodbine, 4 vols., Yale Historical Publications, Manuscripts and Edited Texts 3

(New Haven, CT: Yale University Press; London: Milford for Oxford University Press, 1915–42). English version: *On the Laws and Customs of England*, translated, with revisions and notes, by Samuel E. Thorne, 4 vols. (Cambridge, MA: Belknap, 1968–77).

45. George E. Woodbine, ed. *Four Thirteenth-Century Law Tracts: A Thesis Presented to the Graduate School of Yale University in Candidacy for the Degree of Doctor of Philosophy* (New Haven, CT: Yale University Press; London: Henry Frowde, Oxford University Press, 1910) 7.

46. Gratian, *Decretum Magistri Gratiani*, in *Corpus juris canonici*, ed. Emil Friedberg, 2 vols. (Leipzig: Tauchnitz, 1879–81; rpt. Graz: Akademische Druck-u. Vrelagsanstalt, 1959).

47. Joannes Teutonicus's *Glossa ordinaria* was published in various editions of Gratian's *Decretum* during the fifteenth and sixteenth centuries. It may be consulted, for example, in Gratian, *Decretum* (Venice: Apud Iuntas, 1605).

48. Flavius Justinianus, *Corpus Iuris Civilis*, ed. Theodor Mommsen and Paul Krueger, 3 vols. (Berlin: Weidmann, 1868). Partial translations include Justinian's *Institutes*, trans. Peter Birks and Grant McLeod (London: Duckworth, 1987), and *The Digest of Justinian*, ed. Alan Watson (English text), Theodor Mommsen and Paul Krueger (Latin text), 4 vols. (Philadelphia: University of Pennsylvania Press, 1985).

49. The *Glossa ordinaria* of Accursius was often printed with the *Corpus juris civilis* in the sixteenth and seventeenth centuries. An example is the *Corpus juris civilis cum glossa ordinaria*, 5 vols. (Lyon, 1549–50).

50. References to the *Coutumes* will be made in the text to Salmon (see note 9 above), by section number.

51. Henry-Léonard Bordier, *Philippe de Remi, sire de Beaumanoir: Jurisconsulte et poète national du Beauvaisis 1246–1296* (1869; rpt. Geneva: Slatkine Reprints, 1980) 384–401.

52. Salmon (see note 9 above), p. XL.

53. P. Van Wetter, "Le droit romain et Beaumanoir," *Mélanges Fitting*, 2 vols. (Montpellier: Imprimerie Générale du Midi, 1908) 2: 533–582.

54. Salmon (see note 9 above) 4, n. 1.

55. Beugnot (see note 8 above) 1: 13 n. b., and see also E. Petot, "Le droit commun en France selon les coutumiers," *Revue Historique du Droit Français et Etranger* (1960): 412–429.

56. See note 29 above.

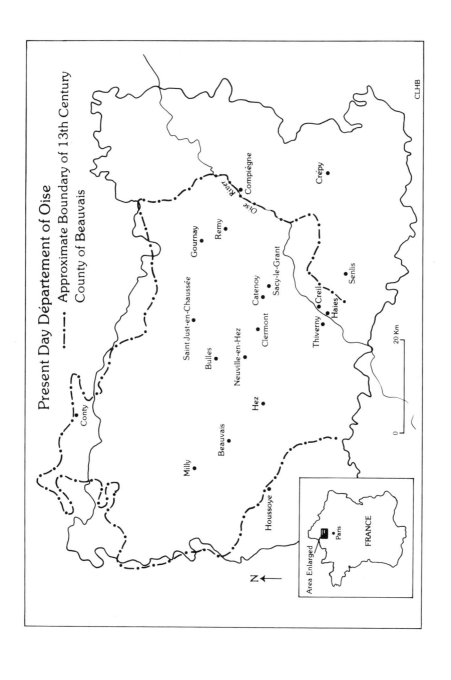

Present Day Département of Oise

—·—· Approximate Boundary of 13th Century
County of Beauvais

CLHB

Compiègne

Crépy

Oise River

Gournay

Remy

Saint Just-en-Chaussée

Catenoy

Sacy-le-Grant

Senlis

Clermont

Thiverny

Creil

Haies

Bulles

Neuville-en-Hez

Conty

Hez

Milly

Beauvais

Houssoye

N ←

Area Enlarged

Paris

FRANCE

0

20 Km

HERE BEGINS
THE BOOK OF THE CUSTOMS AND USAGES OF
BEAUVAIS AS THEY WERE CURRENT AT THE TIME
THIS BOOK WAS MADE, THAT IS TO SAY IN THE
YEAR OF OUR LORD'S INCARNATION 1283.

Prologue.

1. The great hope we have in the help of him by whom all things were made and without whom nothing could be made,—the Father, the Son, and the Holy Spirit, which three very holy and very precious things are a single God in Trinity,—gives us a desire to devote our heart and understanding to plan and think how to make a book by which those who wish to live in peace can be quickly taught how to defend themselves from those who wrongfully and for evil reasons attack them in lawsuits, and how they can distinguish right from wrong, according to the usage[1] and custom[2] in Clermont in the county of Beauvais. And because we are from this district, and we have undertaken to protect and to enforce protection of the rights and customs of the said county by the will of the very great and very noble count Robert, son of the king of France, count of Clermont, we should be more willing to write [*trouver*] concerning the customs of the said district than of any other; and we distinguish three main reasons which should persuade us of this.

2. The first reason is that God commanded us to love our neighbor as ourselves, and the people of the said district [*païs*][3] are our neighbors by reason of proximity and nationality, and even some by kinship. And it seems very profitable for us, by our work, with the help of God, to be able to make this book for them, by which they can be instructed how to pursue the right and abandon the wrong.

3. The second reason is so that we can, with the help of God, do something which will be pleasing to our lord the Count and his personal counsel, for, if God pleases, he may be instructed by this book concerning how he should preserve and enforce preservation of the customs of his lands in the county of Clermont, so that his vassals[4] and the common people can live in peace under his rule, and so that by this teaching the tricksters [*tricheeur*] and dealers in sharp practice [*bareteeur*] may all be revealed in their sharp practice and trickery, and thrust down by the law and justice of the count.

4. The third reason is that we should remember better what we have seen habitually done and ruled in our district than in other districts whose customs and usages we have not learned.

5. Yet we do not expect to find in ourself the wit needed to complete this book and this undertaking. It has often been observed that many men have begun good works who did not have the wisdom to complete them; but God who knew their hearts and their understanding sent them his grace, so that they easily completed what seemed difficult to them in the beginning. And in the Holy Scripture it is written: "Begin, and I will complete the work."[5]

6. And in the confidence that he will complete the work and that we can earn his good will by the toil and labor which we put into it, we have begun, intending to confirm a great part of this book by judgments which have been made in our time in the said county of Clermont; and another part by well-known usages and well-known customs habitually followed and customary for a long time without challenge; and another part (doubtful cases in the said county) will be confirmed by the judgments of neighboring castellanies; and another part by the law which is common to all in the kingdom[6] of France. And if anyone hungers to know who it was that began this book, we will not write our name until the end, if God permits us to reach the end. For sometimes good wine is refused when you name the area where it grew, because people do not believe that that area can grow such wine; and we are also afraid that if our name were known so soon, our work would be valued the less because of the small wisdom in us.

7. But because we see people acting according to local customs and forsaking old laws for these customs, it seems to us and also to others that it is good and profitable to write down and register the customs which are current now, so that they can be observed without change from now on; because owing to memories which fade and people's life which is short, what is not written down is soon forgotten. And this is clear from the fact that the customs of France are so varied that you could not find in the kingdom of France two castellanies which used the same customs in all cases. But you should not for this reason fail to learn and remember the customs of the district where you are resident, for from there you more easily learn and remember the others, and in any case in several instances they are identical in several castellanies.[7]

8. And just as the person who has a job to do (which he cannot do without the help of the king of France), and who has not deserved so much from the king that he does not fear that he will fail to receive that help if he asks it without support, is glad to seek the aid and the benevolence of the king's counsel to help him make his request to the king, just so we need incomparably more to request the help of those in the company of the King of Paradise to help us make our request to the Lord of heaven and earth. And we call on the Blessed Virgin Mary, who prays to her son better and more boldly than all others, and then on all the saints, together and separately, in whose prayers we have confidence, that God will help us in this work and in all our other works. And we will now begin our book in the following manner.

Here ends the prologue of this book.

*   *   *

Here begins the division of this book.

9. Since it would be hard for those who want to consult this book on some matter which is relevant to what they want to do for themselves or their families to have to search through this book from end to end, in this section we will set out briefly and give a name to all the chapters which will be contained in this book, in the order in which they will appear, and designate them by a number in this division and each chapter when it appears by the same number, so that in this way you can easily find the material you want to study.

10. Everyone should know there are seventy chapters in this book, which speak of the following matters:[8]

First chap. Speaks of the duties of the *bailli*, what *baillis* should be like, and how they should behave in office.

Second chap. Speaks on summonses and summoners, and of those who do not heed summonses, and how you should make a summons.

Third chap. Speaks of adjournments sine die and continuances that you can take by custom.

Fourth chap. Speaks of attorneys and those who are appointed to represent others, and of who can appoint an attorney, and which letters of appointment are valid and which are not, and of how attorneys should perform their duties.

Fifth chap. Speaks about advocates, how they should be accepted and how they should perform their duties, and which ones can be excluded.

Sixth chap. Speaks of complaints, how you should word your complaint before a judge, and requests and reports; and the cases where drunkenness or ignorance can be a defense; and on the oath to speak the truth.

Seventh chap. Speaks of the defenses which defendants can raise against the complaints made against them, which clerks call exceptions; and on answers and denials.

Eighth chap. Speaks of those who come too late to make their complaint, and of how long a peaceful possession is sufficient in a suit on personal property, and in a suit on real property.

Ninth chap. Speaks of the cases in which an inspection day may be given, and how you should raise defenses in a secular court, and how an inspection should be made, and of the counsel day for witnesses who request it.

Tenth chap. Speaks of the cases in which the count of Clermont is not obliged to send cases back down to his vassals, but retains cognizance for reasons of sovereignty.

Eleventh chap. Speaks of the cases in which the cognizance belongs to Holy Church and of those in which it belongs to the secular court, and of the cases when the one should help the other, and of the difference between holy places and places of religion, and of the cases when Holy Church should not give protection, and of the arrest of clerks.

Twelfth chap. Speaks of wills, which are valid and which are not, and of what you can leave in a will, and how you can contest or reduce a will; and what should be enforced for the good of men's souls; and how the executors should administer the execution of a will, and the form of making a will.

Thirteenth chap. Speaks of dowers, how they should be handed over to women, and how widows should hold them, and how they should participate in a distribution after the death of their husbands.

Fourteenth chap. Speaks of inheritance laterally and by descent, and of distribution of realty, and bringing back realty to the hotchpot, and of gifts which are not to be allowed, and of paying homage to your lord.

Fifteenth chap. Speaks of custodianships and guardianships, and the difference between them, and of when children come of age in Beauvais.

Sixteenth chap. Speaks of minor children, how and in what cases they can gain or lose in suits; and how they can cancel their obligations; and how their age can be proved; and how a distribution can be made against them.

Seventeenth chap. Speaks of tutors who are appointed for minor children, to take care of them and administer their business.

Eighteenth chap. Speaks of which heirs are legitimate heirs for holding real property, and which are excluded for bastardy, and how bastardy can be proved; and of which marriages are valid and which are not.

Nineteenth chap. Speaks of the degrees of kinship, so that everyone can know how close and how distant his relatives are, for this may be necessary for {private} wars and for redemptions of real property.

Twentieth chap. Speaks of those who hold real property in good faith and shows how they should be kept from loss, and how those who wrong-fully and for a bad reason hold other people's property should be punished, and how certain partitions cannot be made in some cases.

Twenty-first chap. Speaks of partnerships and of how partnerships are formed according to custom, and how you can win and lose in a partnership, and how a partnership is dissolved; and of removing children from your custodianship.

Twenty-second chap. Speaks of another kind of partnership called capital property partnerships, which can be dissolved and which cannot, and how you should proceed in such partnerships.

Twenty-third chap. Speaks of what things are personalty and what things are realty according to the custom of Beauvais.

Twenty-fourth chap. Speaks of what a custom is and what a usage is, and the difference between custom and usage, and which usages are valid and which are not; and of abandoning land instead of paying quit-rent; and of buildings.

Twenty-fifth chap. Speaks of what width the roads should be, and how they should be kept at the proper width without disrepair and without narrowing, and of who has the jurisdiction over them; and of the safe-conduct of merchants and pilgrims, and of things found in the road, and of crosses and other public amenities.

Twenty-sixth chap. Speaks of weights and measures, and how you should weigh and measure, and how those who give false measure should be punished.

Twenty-seventh chap. Speaks of the income which can come to lords from the property held from them, for example relief and sales taxes; and also speaks of the price of land.

Twenty-eighth chap. Speaks of how you should supply your lord with a farm-horse in dues for your fief, and the loss you may suffer if you do not do what you should.

Twenty-ninth chap. Speaks of services performed for pay or on authorization or at will, and on accountings rendered by employees and the other services performed because of holding a fief; and of how to get back what you overpaid.

Thirtieth chap. Speaks of offenses {crimes} and what punishment should be given for each offense, and what penalties are at the lord's discretion; and of boundary markers; and of banished persons and false witnesses, and of how long securities should be kept, and of conspiracy; and of the cases where a sworn oath is sufficient testimony; and what losses must be made up to others; and how to conduct prisoners through someone else's lordship; and of those who are appealed against or imprisoned on suspicion of crime; and of those who seduce the wife or daughter of another; and of insults and fights.

Thirty-first chap. Speaks of larcenies which are clear and open, and of those which are in doubt, and of how larceny is proved.

Thirty-second chap. Speaks of novel disseisin and force and nuisance, and how you should deal with them, and of the obedience which a tenant [*ostes*] owes his lord.

Thirty-third chap. Speaks of not enforcing what is done by coercion or fraud or by excessive intimidation.

Thirty-fourth chap. Speaks of agreements, and of which have to be kept and which do not; and of deals and leases; and of things which are enforced without any agreement, and of how payment is proved without witnesses; and what intimidation is; and of frauds.

Thirty-fifth chap. Speaks of obligating yourself in a writing and of how you should validate a writing and how you should challenge a writing and the form of making a writing.

Thirty-sixth chap. Speaks of things deposited for safekeeping, how they should be kept and given back to those who deposited them.

Thirty-seventh chap. Speaks of things lent and how the borrowers can make use of them.

Thirty-eighth chap. Speaks of things rented or farmed out, and leases.

Thirty-ninth chap. Speaks of proofs and of excluding witnesses; and of alibis and of the danger in threats, and how to speak against witnesses, and of which cases may be put to proof.

Fortieth chap. Speaks of examiners and auditors, and of inquiries [*aprises*], and of examining witnesses, and the difference between inquiries and inquests, and on challenging witnesses.

Forty-first chap. Speaks of arbitrators and the power they have, and which arbitrators are valid and which are not, and how an arbitration comes to an end, and the kind of cases which can go to arbitration.

Forty-second chap. Speaks of prenegotiated penalties, in which cases they are to be paid and which not; and of the difference between physical penalties and money penalties.

Forty-third chap. Speaks of sureties, and how they should be discharged, and on the payment of damages to be enforced in secular courts, and who can be a surety; and what days in court each should have.

Forty-fourth chap. Speaks of redemption of real property, and exchanges, and of how no sharp practice is to be permitted.

Forty-fifth chap. Speaks of avowals and disavowals, serfdom and freedom, and the danger in disavowing and how you should sue those who disavow.

Forty-sixth chap. Speaks of the guardianship of religious houses, and how you should punish those who mistreat them, and of the two swords, one spiritual, the other temporal; and of the damages which can be suffered by a religious house which disavows its true lord.

Forty-seventh chap. Speaks of how fiefs can be held more or less directly from their lords according to the custom of Beauvais, and on how the holders of fiefs should keep from dividing them in contravention of the custom.

Forty-eighth chap. Speaks of how commoners can hold freehold fiefs in faith and homage, and how they should fulfill the obligations.

Forty-ninth chap. Speaks of laws and the times when a custom should not be observed for reasons of necessity.

Fiftieth chap. Speaks of people in towns and of their rights, and how they should be protected and justice administered so that they can live in peace.

Fifty-first chap. Speaks of the reasons why lords can make seizures and take possession of property, and how they should act to the advantage of their subjects while maintaining their rights.

Fifty-second chap. Speaks of prohibited actions and seizures of property made for offenses or damages, and how you should deal with them; and of forced sales of property and of sales taxes.

Fifty-third chap. Speaks of reclamations, and in which cases you may permit reclamations, and in which not; and how a reclamation may be requested and how it may be made in those cases where it is appropriate.

Fifty-fourth chap. Speaks of how creditors should be paid and kept from loss, and how you should attach things in a house; and how you put a guard on someone and what the guards should be like.

Fifty-fifth chap. Speaks of follow-up suits {for debt}, and shows which ones are rightfully brought and which are not, and how the lords should proceed.

Fifty-sixth chap. Speaks of those who should not hold property, what you should do with the mad and insane; and of the guardianship of leper-houses and poor houses, and who has the guardianship and jurisdiction over them.

Fifty-seventh chap. Speaks of incompatibility between married persons, how their lords should deal with it, and the reasons why one person can be separated from the other.

Fifty-eighth chap. Speaks of high and low justice, and the cases which fall into one or the other; and of those going armed through another person's jurisdiction; and how a settlement may not be accepted in serious crimes; and how lords can commandeer fortresses from their subjects.

Fifty-ninth chap. Speaks of {private} wars, how wars come about according to custom, and how wars are ended, and how you can use the right of war as a defense.

Sixtieth chap. Speaks of truces and guaranteed peace [*asseurement*], and of who can be excluded from them, and of the danger of breaking truces and guaranteed peace.

Sixty-first chap. Speaks of appeals and how one should appeal, and how to word your appeal, and in what cases an appeal lies and of pursuing your appeal; and of banished persons; and of the arms you use in fighting a battle.

Sixty-second chap. Speaks of appeals for default of judgment and how you should petition your lord before you have a good appeal against him for default of justice.

Sixty-third chap. Speaks of what are valid defenses for those who are appealed against to avoid the battle, and of the cases where the wager of battle should not be accepted.

Sixty-fourth chap. Speaks of the presentations which should be made in suits where there is a wager of battle with respect to the arms and the words, and of the oaths and the things that follow, up to the end of the battle.

Sixty-fifth chap. Speaks of the delays permitted by custom and the delays permitted to jurors before they can and must be compelled to give a judgment.

Sixty-sixth chap. Speaks of recusing judges and of cases where a single witness is believed, and how lords should zealously execute judgments which have gone unappealed.

Sixty-seventh chap. Speaks of judgments and the way to make judgments and how you should judge, and who may judge, and how the lord may send an observer to find out the kind of hearings his vassals are giving, and how you can have a judgment reversed, and how employees must be sent back to give an accounting.

Sixty-eighth chap. Speaks of usury and mark-ups and how you can avoid paying usurious charges.

Sixty-ninth chap. Speaks of cases of misadventure which arise out of ill-luck, in which pity and mercy should temper justice.

Seventieth chap. Speaks of outrageous gifts which should not be enforced, and of those which can be enforced, and which you cannot and should not contest.

{End of the division}

Notes

1. Usages, and their relation to customs, are discussed in Chapter 24, where it appears that a usage is a kind of personal or group privilege, such as an easement, not amounting to a custom, and probably not enforceable for the general public by a court.

2. A custom is defined as an established rule of procedural or substantive law, in force for as long as anyone remembers without challenge, or which has been approved by a judgment. See §683.

3. I have used the translation "district" for *païs* where the latter means "jurisdiction," or "judicial district," by analogy with U.S. federal or state districts.

4. I have used the translation "vassal(s)" for *homme* when it concerns the count's noble subordinates. The French word *vassal* appears nowhere in the *Coutumes*, and yet this word so well describes the relationship of these men to the count, and is so ordinary a word, that I have often used it instead of the ambiguous "man."

5. The source of Beaumanoir's quotation is not apparent. Salmon gives no footnote. Beugnot's footnote is to 1 Samuel 3:12 (in some Bibles, 1 Kings 3:12). Here God is speaking to Samuel: " . . . Incipiam et complebo," which might be translated "I shall begin and I shall complete [it]." This refers to God's treatment of the house of Eli. The subject of both verbs is "I" (God), which is not the same as in Beaumanoir's sentence, where the first verb is an imperative. Another possible source is Philippians 1:6, " . . . Qui coepit in vobis opum bonum perficiet usque in diem Christi Iesu," which might be translated: "Whoever among you commences a good work will continue it until the day of Jesus Christ." Here, the subject of both verbs is a third person, and not God. Perhaps Beaumanoir is remembering something else.

6. One manuscript tradition has here "the customs of France" and another "the kingdom of France."

7. This sentence does not seem very coherent in Old French. Beaumanoir seems to be saying that there is a common core of customs, and that by learning those of your own district you can easily master the differences between the customs of your own and of other districts.

8. Rather than give explanatory notes in the rest of this chapter, I have provided in the individual chapters explanations of the material in these chapter headings.

1. Judges

Here begins the first chapter which speaks of the duties of the bailli.

11. Although there are not in us all the virtues which there must be in a man who takes on a judgeship, that will not keep us from beginning this chapter by discussing the estate and the duties of *baillis*. And we will say briefly what are the virtues they should have, and how they should behave, so that those who perform the duties can take their example from it.

12. In our opinion, a man who wants to be an honest judge and a just one should have ten virtues, one of which is and should be the lady and mistress of all the others, for without it the other virtues cannot be controlled. And this virtue is called wisdom, which is the same thing as being wise. Therefore we say that the person who wants to hold the office of a judge and do justice should be wise for otherwise he would not be able to perform the duties of a judge.

13. The second virtue that the *bailli* should have is that he must love God our Father and our Savior very much, and also for the love of God he must love Holy Church. And this must not be the love that some serfs have for their lord, those who love their masters because they fear them and are afraid of them, but {it must be} a complete love, as the son should love his father, for all good things come from loving and serving God; and he who does not give his heart to the love of God above all things has no wisdom in him. And we would find a great deal to say concerning the reasons why we should love Him, and of the good things which come from loving Him. But we would have to depart for a long while from the subject which we have begun, and in any case Holy Church shows and teaches {these things} to us every day.

14. The third virtue which a *bailli* should have is that he should be kind and gentle without ill-will [*felonie*] and without severity [*crueus*]; but not

kindly when among criminals nor towards the cruel, nor towards those who commit offenses, for to such people he should show the face of severity and ill will and of the force of justice, for their evil to be less. For as the doctor, out of pity for his patient's suffering, exposes him to the danger of death by not treating the wound he should cure him of,[1] just in the same way the *bailli* who is kindly towards the criminals in his jurisdiction puts those who want to live peaceably in danger of death. And a *bailli* can do no greater good (all things considered) than to weed out evil men from among the good by strictness of justice. Therefore when we said that he should be kindly, we meant kindly towards those who are on the side of good and towards the common people and in cases which come about more by ill luck than by ill will. And as we have said that wisdom is the supreme virtue of those which a *bailli* should have, he should not be considered wise who is stern [*fel*] and severe to everyone. And it often happens that simple people who have good and honest disputes allow their disputes to be lost because they dare not maintain them before such a *bailli* because of his sternness, out of fear of losing even more.

15. The fourth virtue which a *bailli* should have is to be indulgent and ready to listen without getting angry or upset about anything, for the *bailli* who is in too much of a hurry to reply or who gets upset and angry at what he hears cannot remember {memorize} what is said before him in court. And since he cannot remember it, he cannot recall it from memory;[2] and without remembering and recalling from memory properly no one should undertake to be a judge. Therefore the *bailli* should be indulgent and listen so that he allows those who are before him in court to say everything they want, one party against another, without cutting off their arguments. And if he does this, he will be able to judge them better and more wisely, or have them judged if it is a court where the decisions are made by a jury. And as we were saying above that the *kindness* of a *bailli* should not extend to evil men, we also say that his *indulgence* should not extend to them, but he should listen carefully to them, because by listening to them carefully they often reveal the evil which is in their hearts {Beaumanoir's syntax} so that afterwards the *bailli* knows better how to proceed than he did before. And we also do not mean that the *bailli* should be too indulgent in a matter which brings ill repute [*porte despit*] or damages to his lord or to himself; thus if either is done wrong or defamed, he should take vengeance [*vengier*] swiftly and wisely, punishing according to what the offense requires, so that by the vengeance [*venjance*] which he takes others will have an example of

proper behavior towards their lords and towards their *bailli*. For the *bailli* as long as he is acting in an official capacity [*tant comme il est en office de baillie*] represents his lord's person; and for this reason a person who offends against the *bailli* offends against his lord. And the greater control that the *bailli* has over the authority of his lord, the greater care he must take to do no wrong, and to make an effort to possess the virtues which are enumerated in this chapter.[3]

16. The fifth virtue that a *bailli* must have is that he must be bold and vigorous without any laziness. For a *bailli* who is lazy leaves many things undone and permits to continue things which should have been stopped, and he has others do things which he should have done himself, and also by his laziness stretches out and delays many things which he should have hurried along; and through this the *bailli* who is lazy may bring on himself ill repute [*vilenie*] and a bad reputation [*disfame*] and loss, and for this reason we recommend to them that they should avoid the vice of laziness. And when we say that a *bailli* should be bold, it is a virtue without which the *bailli* cannot perform his official duies; for if he were a coward, he would not dare to anger the rich man who was in a suit against a poor man, or he would not dare, out of fear of his lineage, to order the punishment of someone who had deserved to be put to death, and he would not dare to arrest criminals and quarrelsome persons, for fear that they might defend themselves {resist}; and all these things which he would refrain from doing out of cowardice are things which he is supposed to do. Therefore he should be bold without cowardice and without fearing anything, or otherwise he is not doing what he is supposed to or what his office requires. And yet when he does something where boldness is needed, he should do it wisely. For there are two kinds of boldness: one wise, and the other foolhardy. The wisely bold man is the one who wisely and deliberately shows his boldness; the foolhardy man is the one who takes no thought of the consequences of what he undertakes, and the one who acts boldy at the wrong place or time, such as if I went alone and unarmed to attack several people where my boldness could not avail me; and this is called foolhardiness.

17. The sixth virtue which a *bailli* should have is generosity. And from this virtue flow two others which he may greatly need in order to keep up his position and advance himself and to be loved by God and his fellow men [*du siecle*]: they are courtesy and moderation [*courtoisie et neteés*]. For generosity is worthless without these two and they are worthless without

generosity. And it is very necessary for generosity to be used wisely and temperately; for there are two kinds of generosity, one of which is controlled by the virtue of wisdom, and it is called wise generosity [*sage largece*]; the other kind of generosity is so mixed with foolishness that the one cannot be separated from the other. So we can understand that the wisely generous man is the one who takes account of how much he has, whether through inheritance or purchases or salary, and then he spends and gives to good people what he can dispense with without wasting his fortune and without acquiring more by dishonest means; for the avaricious heart acquires however it can, and it can never have enough, and in such a heart honesty cannot be found. And you often see that people pile up on the one hand possessions and on the other enemies, so that when the Wheel of Fortune turns, they go down more in an hour than they went up in ten years, and so they lose God and the world [*le siecle*]. And in the same way avarice lodged in the heart of a *bailli* is worse and more dangerous that it is in other people, for in order to satisfy his avarice the avaricious *bailli* has to do and permit many things which are contrary to his station. Therefore we recommend that he should be generous in such a way that he can keep up his generosity without ruining himself, and that he should avoid foolish generosity, for the foolishly generous person throws his possessions away. The foolishly generous man is the one who spends his substance rashly [*folement*], gaining neither profit nor respect, and who lives a life which he cannot maintain with what he has; and sometimes it happens that when the foolishly generous person has spent everything he becomes something less than good and he does not care where his possessions come from, provided that he can keep up his mad spending. And for this reason the wise *bailli* should bestow his generosity temperately, he should give alms and he should use {his wealth} to honor his associates and good neighbors, and to maintain himself courteously and honestly and moderately. For some people lose the grace which should come to them from generosity when they give in a vile and ugly way [*vilainement et ordement*], and for this reason it is appropriate to be courteous and moderate in one's generosity.

18. The seventh virtue which a *bailli* should have is obedience to the will of his lord in all his commands, except the commands by which he could lose his soul if he carried them out, for the obedience which he owes should be understood to mean applying law and maintaining honest justice. And the *bailli* would have no excuse towards God if he knowingly did wrong at the command of his lord; and it is better for the *bailli* to leave his

service than knowingly to do wrong while obeying a command or for any other reason. However, the *bailli* does not have to decide on the rightness of the commands which his lord gives him with respect to personal property or chattels or real property, or in any other case except loss of life or limb. Instead he must obey the commands, for if the party against whom the command is directed complains, he can go to the lord and demand that justice be done to him, and thus he has a legal remedy and the *bailli* has obeyed the command; but in case of loss of life or limb if the command were carried out, it could not be mended, and for this we do not recommend that *baillis* should obey such commands but instead they should leave the service if the lord will not countermand his order; for it is not good to serve a lord who is more concerned about doing his will than about maintaining law and justice.

19. The eighth virtue which a person who undertakes to perform the duties of a judge must have is to be very knowledgable. First he must know good from evil, right from wrong, peaceful men from quarrelsome men, the honest from the deceivers, the good from the bad. And especially he must know himself; and he must know the wishes [*la volontés*] and the habits [*les manieres*] of his lord and of the members of his council, and he must know his own household, and take careful account of how they are, for although the *bailli* himself may do or intend nothing but good, yet he may receive ill repute [*vilenie*] and loss [*damage*] through the offense of someone from his household. And when we say the *bailli's* household, we mean the provosts and the officers who are below him, and the people who live in his house. And we will now speak briefly about the good things which can accrue to a *bailli* by having the above-mentioned knowledge. If a *bailli* knows good from evil, he will know better how to do good and avoid evil and in this way he can keep his position [*maintenir son estat*] and come to the love of God and his fellow-men [*du siecle*]. If he knows right from wrong, he will know how to do the right to his subordinates [*sougiés*], and how to subdue [*bouter arrieres*] those who are wrong; and this is part of his duty. If he knows the peaceful from the quarrelsome, he can keep the peaceful in peace by the threats he makes to the quarrelsome and the controls [*les contraintes*] he imposes on them; and it is certainly part of a *bailli's* duties to frighten and control the quarrelsome, so that the peaceful may live in peace. If he knows the honest from the deceitful, he will be able to (and he should) attract the honest men about him and give them comfort and cheer if they have need of comfort and good cheer, and he can subdue

the deceitful and punish them according to lawful justice for their trickery. If he knows the good from the bad, he will be able to (and he should) weed out and clear out the bad from the good in the way that you remove the weeds from the wheat; and he is supposed to do this. If he knows himself, he will know what he is like; and if he detects in himself some evil vice, he will be able to get rid of it more easily, and it is a terrible thing when a person who should put others on the right road by his example remains evil himself, and no one who is full of evil vice is able to carry out properly the duties of a *bailli*. If he knows the wishes and habits of his lord, it is a great advantage for maintaining himself in office if he knows that the habits and the wishes are good and honest; and he can easily win the good will of his lord if he knows and follows his wishes. And if he knows that the wishes and habits {of his lord} are bad, he should take his leave and depart from his service as soon as he can, for it has long been said: "He who serves a bad lord should expect a bad reward." If he knows the wishes and habits of his lord's council, and they agree with the good habits of his lord, he can easily find favor with them, so that he can be guided and supported by them. And if the council is contrary to the wishes and the habits of his lord, so that the council recommends one thing and the lord has something else done, we recommend that he should leave his service; for no *bailli* can stay in office and perform the duties of the office when his lord is opposed to his council. For a powerful man [*riches hons*] who wants to do everything himself, without taking advice, cannot continue to dispense honest justice nor honestly govern a large fief [*grant terre*]; and for this reason, the *bailli* who remains in such service is not wise. If he knows his household, that is to say his provosts and the members of his household and his officers, he can (and should) remove from his service those who are full of evil vices, so that he will be protected from blame and ill repute [*vilenie*] that could come to him from their improper acts. And when they act improperly, the *bailli* should punish them for their offenses more severely than any other kind of people, for three reasons: the first, so that the people the *bailli* has to govern realize that he does not wish to support them in their wickedness; the second reason is so that the other officers will refrain from wrongdoing when they see that if they did wrong they would be severely punished by their master; the third reason is because the common people live more in peace when the provost and the officers do not dare to oppress them wrongfully. For when the *bailli* allows the provosts and officers and his household members to be full of wickedness, they are like wolves amongst the sheep, for they take away and seize the things the common people need to live on; and sometimes the blame for this falls on the *bailli*, even though the takings do not find their way into his purse.

20. The ninth virtue that a person who undertakes the duties of a *bailli* must have is clever and eager skill in management [*soutil engieng et hastif de bien esploitier*] without doing wrong to other people, and secondly to be a good accountant. And good management [*bien esploitier*] means taking care that the value of his lord's land does not diminish through his negligence but that it should instead always increase through his wise stewardship, for he is not a good *bailli* in whose hands his lord's land diminishes through his folly; but a man is a good *bailli* in whose hands his lord's land increases without doing wrong to other people. And it is very necessary for him to know how to do the accounts well, for it is one of the greatest dangers in the position of a *bailli* to be negligent or careless in his accounts, and for two reasons: the first is that if he makes a mistake against his own interest he has to bear the loss; and the second reason is that if he makes a mistake to the detriment of his lord, and it is noticed, he can be (albeit mistakenly) thought dishonest; and to avoid blame and loss, he has to know very well how to keep accounts.

21. The tenth virtue which a person who undertakes a judge's office must have is the best of all and without it the others can do nothing, for it is the one which illuminates all the others; it is the one without which nothing is worth anything; it is the one which is so joined with the virtue of wisdom that wisdom can in no way exist without it. And this virtue is called honesty [*loiautés*], for whoever is honest is wise in maintaining honesty; and the sense of the person in whom dishonesty is lodged should not be valued at all. And a person who is not honest would have been better to be an imbecile than to know anything about the world, for the more he knows the more bad things come from his knowledge, and (to tell the truth) a dishonest person should not be called wise but a confidence man [*bare-teeur*]. And it often happens that when someone has honesty lodged in him and he has little intelligence and few other virtues he is nevertheless toler-ated and esteemed for love of this virtue all by itself; and if anyone had all the other virtues and it were known that honesty was lacking in him, he would not be believed nor liked nor esteemed, and for this reason you can see that honesty is worth more all by itself than all the other virtues without honesty. And in the same way dishonesty can do more harm when it is

lodged in a man who should maintain lawful justice than in other persons, for there are many dishonest people of low estate [*basses*] who in their dishonesty cannot do much harm because they have little power; but dishonesty, when it is lodged in the heart of a man who has a great fief to govern, can cause very much evil [*puet semer trop de venim*] {literally, "can sow much venom"}; for all sorts of evils can flow from him and for this reason we recommend that everyone and especially *baillis* should be honest and if they do not want to be honest we recommend to their lords that as soon as they know them to be dishonest they dismiss them from their service and punish them according to their dishonest dealings; and no one should be so bold as to serve another, if honesty is not lodged in him.

22. We have spoken of the ten virtues which a person who undertakes the duties of a *bailli* should have; and the *bailli* who had them could obtain the love of God and of his lord. And because it is difficult to have them all the *bailli* should take care that at least honesty be not lacking. And if he can be wise and honest he has in these two virtues alone all the others which have been described.—We have spoken of the virtues which *baillis* should have in general. Now let us examine a few things they must do in particular.

23. There are some places where the *baillis* give the judgments, and other places where jurors who hold fiefs from the lord give the judgments. Now we say that in the places where the *baillis* give the judgments, when the *bailli* has heard the arguments and they are declared ready for judgment, he should call to advise him the wisest men and give the judgment according to their advice; for if the judgment is appealed and reversed, the *bailli* is excused from blame when it is known that he acted by the advice of wise men. And in the place where a judgment is given by jurors, the *bailli* must in the presence of the jurors receive the arguments of those who plead, and should ask the parties if they want a judgment, according to the arguments they have made. And if they say yes, the *bailli* must force the jurors to give a judgment. And how he should force them to do so will be set forth in the chapter concerning the delays permitted by custom {Chapter 65}. And if the *bailli* or the jurors do not wish it, the *bailli* is not required to be present when the judgment is arrived at nor at the pronouncement of the judgment, unless it happens that the *bailli* is a vassal of the lord whose *bailli* he is, for in that case it would be appropriate for him to be a peer along with the others.

24. Although we have spoken of the places where the *baillis* give the judgments, there is no such place in the county of Clermont; instead, all the judgments must be made by jurors, the lord's vassals. And there is a great difference between the appeals made against the judgments of *baillis* and the appeals made against the judgments of jurors; for if you appeal the judgment of *baillis* in the court where they are the judges, they do not have to defend their judgment by a wager of battle. Instead, the record of the case [*li errement du plet*] on which the judgment was made is taken to the court of the sovereign lord of the *bailli* who gave the judgment. There the judgment is sustained or overturned. And it is not the same way for those who appeal against the jurors who have given a judgment, for the appeal is conducted by a wager of battle; and on this kind of appeal and how you can and should make your appeal we will speak sufficiently in the chapter on appeals {Chapter 61}.

25. It is true that not everything which is brought before the *bailli* needs to be submitted to a judgment. For when the complaint is on some case which concerns his lord's lands, or his reputation or slanders against him, or his loss, and the case is brought by the vassals who would like to gain some advantage in such a case against their lord, the *bailli* should not submit it to a judgment, for the men should not judge their lord, but they should judge each other and the disputes of the common people; and if someone who makes a claim against the lord requires a hearing [*que drois lui soit fes*], the *bailli*, with the advice of his lord and his lord's council, should do for him what he believes is reasonable; and if he is not satisfied with what the *bailli* does for him, he should bring his complaint to the count and the members of his council [*ceus de son conseil*]; and they must reverse or change anything the *bailli* has done which is excessive.

26. And this is the way we mean to be used in all the cases which concern the profit or the advantage of all the vassals {in a body} against their lord. But there are various cases in which the lord pleads individually against one of his men, or one of the men against their lord, such as if the lord demands a fine for some offense that has been committed on his land or he is asking his man for some land or some personal property which is in his possession and saying that it belongs to him by the custom of the locality. And the other defends himself and says that by saying that the fine is not so great or that this piece of land or personal property that the lord is asking him for should be his own and he asks for a hearing [*et en requiert droit*].

The *bailli* can and should submit all these disputes to the judgment of the jurors, for in such disputes the count should treat his vassals according to the custom which his men apply among their own vassals. But if the quarrel concerns the reputation of the lord, such as for slander which has been said or hands raised against the *bailli* or the provost or the officers, the *bailli* should not submit the fine for these offenses to the judgment of the jurors, nor is there a fixed fine for these offenses which are committed against the lord; for if there was a sum certain of money taxed for such an offense, then everyone would know how much it would cost him to assault the *bailli* or the provosts or the officers, and there would be a good number of them beaten when vassals were more strictly penalized than they would have liked and they knew a sure way to get off. And for this reason it is imperative for those who undertake to serve great lords that there should be no fines for such offenses except at the lord's discretion; and his will should be a long prison term and loss of property, but not loss of life or limb if the offense did not include loss of life or limb.

27. A *bailli* has no power to put up boundary markers nor to divide between his lord's land and that of others unless he has special intructions from his lord to do so. And if the lord is willing, it is helpful for the people who live on the borders to get a writing from the lord saying that he wanted and permitted his *bailli* to put up certain boundary markers, because what is permitted is forgotten in a short time if there is no certain memorial in a writing or by living witnesses.

28. It is part of a *bailli*'s duty to sell the rents paid in kind and the products [*les rentes et les issues*] of his lord's land at the customary price, if he cannot get more. But once they are sold, and the due date established, if the debtors ask for an extension of time to pay, he cannot give it to them without the permission of his lord.

29. Whoever enters on the duties of the *bailli* must swear by the saints that he will safeguard the rights of his lord and others, and that he will accept no payment to do right or wrong, and that he will maintain proper and honest justice. Once he has taken this oath he must act in such a way as not to perjure himself. For a person who perjures himself is well on the way to having ill repute. Yet although we have said that it should be in his oath that he must take nothing, the lord excuses him from this part of his oath to the extent of accepting wine and food; and not in an outrageous manner,

such as wine in vats and barrels, or live pigs and cattle, but things ready to eat and drink on the same day, such as wine in jugs or firkins [*baris*] or meat ready to send to the kitchen. And *baillis* are permitted to take such things because a person who for such {small} gifts took away the rights of others would be very dishonest. He would also be dishonest if he did this for greater gifts; but in any case it is more to be feared that he would do wrong for a great gift than for a small one; and in particular the *bailli* is given leave to take the above-mentioned things to eat and drink.

30. The *bailli* who wants to maintain proper justice and who has the virtues enumerated in this chapter is without love and without hate. This means he must do no wrong, and must not allow wrong to be done when he can remedy it; and the courtesy he can show to a person who is his friend in doing justice is to give him his judgment speedily [*haster son droit*] if he is right, and if he is wrong, to help him to leave his wrongdoing with the smallest loss and the least ill repute that he can, provided that in doing so the *bailli* does no wrong to other people nor acts fraudulently [*par voie de barat*].

31. Because it would be very time consuming and tiresome to the jurors to send to the jury all the cases which come before the *bailli*, he should take great pains to expedite what is pleaded in his court when he knows what to do with a case according to custom and when he sees that the matter is clear and obvious. But when there is doubt and when there is a big dispute, the cases should be sent to the jury; and it is not appropriate to send to the jury a case which has been judged before, even though the judgment was given to other parties, because you should not make different judgments on the same case.[4]

32. It is a good thing for a *bailli* to have frequent sittings at six- or seven-week intervals at most, for judgments are given more quickly that way. And you also remember them better and the sitting is less encumbered [*chargiee*] and comes more quickly to an end. And we also recommend that the *bailli* should not cancel a sitting which he has announced unless he has a good reason or a legal excuse [*essoine*], such as sickness or orders from the lord, or other important and unexpected business comes up; for when you cancel a sitting you can cause great loss to those who have arranged for their counsel, their family, and their lawyers, and the judgments are delayed. And in any case, when a *bailli* has to cancel it is great courtesy to announce it

early; for when they get early notice, the loss is reduced for those who have things to do.

33. The *bailli* should perform his duties so justly that none of the parties who have to plead in his court are advised by him. For there is no doubt that a *bailli* who informs one party of something by which the other party can suffer loss is acting improperly. But it is sometimes true that the parties plead in so disorderly a fashion that their arguments cannot be declared ready for judgment and judgment cannot be given on their arguments. And when the *bailli* sees this he should show them their error and put them back on the right course of pleading so that they can obtain a judgment.

34. A *bailli* should take care not to be an advocate for a person who is appearing in his court, nor should he appear on his behalf, for he would hurt his reputation and could also be challenged and removed by the other party from the duties of judge in this dispute; for no one should be a judge and advocate in any dispute. If the suit were not in his court but in some other lord's court, but neverthless the suit *could* come to his court by removal, he should also not be an advocate; and to put it briefly, no judge in his own jurisdiction should be an advocate or counsel in a proceeding which *could* come to his own court for judgment. But outside of his jurisdiction he can help anyone he wants whether as an advocate or as counsel.

35. If the *bailli* or any other judge has to plead in his own dispute in the very court whose judge or *bailli* he should be, he should set up another judge or another *bailli* in place of him for everything pertaining to his own dispute. For no one should be both judge and party in his own suit except the king, for the king can be a judge and a party in his own suit and in anyone else's suit.

36. We do not agree that if the count of Clermont (or some other man who has jurisdiction and a jury system in his court) is a plaintiff in his own court he should be both a juror and a party. Instead he is merely a party and the jurors do the judging. And this is clear because if the jurors gave a judgment which the lord did not like, if the lord wanted to challenge it the challenge would have to be through an appeal to the sovereign's court and the appeal would be through a wager of battle. An exception is made for those who are sons of the king, for if the count of Clermont appealed

against his vassals for false judgment, the record of the case would be taken to the king's court and there the appeal would be won or lost; and he would have this advantage because he is the son of a king, and the son of a king should not fight his own vassal in a case concerning real or personal property or chattels. But if he appealed against his vassal for murder or treason, in such a case he would have to fight his vassal, for these cases are so serious that no exception should be made for the accuser; and we will refrain from speaking on this matter of appeals until we give it its own chapter which will be called On Appeals {Chapters 61, 62}.

37. *Baillis* and provosts, when they have a legal excuse, can appoint substitutes. Substitutes are those people who represent the person of the *bailli* or the provost in the execution of their duties, but the *bailli* and the provost must be careful what sort of people they put in their place when they cannot preside. For if these persons were to do something wrong, those who had appointed them would be blamed and the substitutes themselves would be punished.

38. The judge who wants to put someone in his place to do his duties must name a man who is very honest and of good reputation and wise. And he should appoint him by a writing or {present him} at the sitting, or in the lower court. Otherwise, if anyone disobeyed their commandments, he could not be fined, for he could defend himself by saying that he did not know that the substitute was there in place of the judge. But he would have to swear this if he wanted to be excused for not obeying, for it is hard to believe than anyone would claim to be a *bailli* or a provost, or a substitute for a *bailli* or a provost, if he really was not. For the fine of anyone who claimed to be such and was not and who took official action would be at the lord's will.

39. You should not appoint as a substitute a man whom the person who names him could not punish if he were to discover his wrongdoing: such as a clerk or a crusader, for he could not punish them if they did wrong, since they are under the cognizance of Holy Church.

40. Those who are not worthy to be *bailli* or provost should not be put in their place: such as people who are deaf, mute, blind, mad, or with legal excuses from many other duties, nor those who can be challenged and recused by the parties on some suspicion; and for all the reasons why you

can challenge *baillis* and provosts you can also refuse those who are replacing them; and what these reasons are is set forth in the chapter which speaks of recusing judges {Chapter 66}.

41. Sometimes it is appropriate for the *bailli* or the provost to be required to name a substitute, such as when the party suspects him for some reasonable cause, which he states, or when the *bailli* or the provost is the adverse party of the person who has to plead whether as plaintiff or defendant. And if the *bailli* or the provost insisted on remaining the judge in such cases and would not appoint a substitute at the request of a party, we do not recommend that that party should proceed. For nothing that the *bailli* or the provost did against him would stand once he had recused him for good reasons. And if the *bailli* or the provost compels him to proceed, by arresting him or attaching his goods, he has a good reason for complaining to the lord; and everything that was done under this compulsion will be cancelled. We also agree that in cases where the *bailli* or the provost who for good reasons should not have presided nevertheless *did* preside by force, they should make good the loss which a party has suffered through the force which the *bailli* or the provost used on him because he did not want to reply in their court for the good reasons which he had advanced in order that they should not be his judge.

42. It is part of the duties of the *bailli* if he sees the jurors give a bad judgment [*varier en jugement*] through error or for a bad reason,—such as out of love or hatred, or for a bribe [*louier*] or because they have not properly understood the dispute,—to correct them courteously and wisely so that they are instructed by him to give an honest judgment. And he should recall the pleading from memory for them; and if the jurors do not want to believe the *bailli's* recall from memory, or one of the parties disputes it, the *bailli* should have the dispute pleaded over again in the presence of those who are to participate in the judgment; for the jurors if they do not want to are not obliged to give a judgment in a dispute which has not been pleaded before them, unless by the agreement of both parties. Nevertheless because it would be a nuisance to the jurors and to those who had to plead if all the jurors had to be present at all the pleadings of every dispute, it is enough if a part of the jurors are at the hearing, two or more of them who are above suspicion, along with the *bailli* or provost, and in any case they should be the kind of jurors who can recall from memory to the other jurors what was pleaded when they assemble to deliberate the judgment.

43. Although the *bailli* must receive the arguments of those who are pleading and make the parties declare they are ready for judgment, nevertheless he is not present at the deliberations unless the jurors wish it, and no one should be with the jurors when they are deliberating unless he is summoned by the jurors. And sometimes when they disagreed too much to make a judgment and we could not make them agree, we have left them to argue and we have gone off to hear cases while they were arguing about the judgment. And the *bailli* can do this.

44. It sometimes happens that there is a suit between the count and all his vassals, such as when one of the vassals asks for a case to be remanded to his court and it should not be,—or he says that he has jurisdiction in his land by reason of his fief, which the count does not recognize but says instead that it belongs to him, for reasons of superior jurisdiction,—or he says that he has the cognizance of some suit such as concerning a writing or a dower or a guaranteed peace or some other case which he says he should have and the count says it belongs to him. In all such cases the *bailli* should not send the suit to the jurors for they are themselves parties; and they should not give a judgment in their own dispute. Therefore if such a case arises between a count and his vassals, and the vassals request a hearing, they must get such a hearing from the count and his council; and if the count refuses to give them a hearing, or gives them a bad judgment, they can take it to the king as sovereign by one of the two methods of appeal;[5] but the danger in appeals will be discussed in the chapter on appeals {Chapter 61}.

45. In suits which arise between the count on the one side and any of his men individually on the other side, in which all the men cannot be parties, such as for some real estate or some forfeiture, or some dispute, in which judgment should be given according to the custom of the area, in such a case the *bailli* can give the count a hearing by the jurors. For as it is proper for the count's men to govern [*mener*] *their* men by the judgment of their peers, so also must the count govern his vassals by the judgment of his other vassals who are *their* peers, in disputes in which not all the vassals are parties against him, as is said above.

46. It is not necessary for the *bailli* to have a full hearing for everything that happens. Instead he should deal speedily with wrongdoing and according to the offense; and in any case he should take care not to put anyone to

death without a trial. And there is no need to wait for a {regular} sitting when some case arises where justice should be given swiftly, but he can take three or four of the jurors, or more if he wants, those who are above suspicion, and have the judgment given without delay. For many wrongdoers have escaped and done many evil deeds because of judges who delay too much.

47. There are some wrongdoers whose actions are not so well proved or so publicly known that you can dare to condemn them to death. The *bailli* should ask these kinds of people if they want to wait for an honest inquest, and if they do not want to wait he can put them in prison and not let them out if their bad reputation is against them.

48. A *bailli* should not wait to be told by his provosts and officers what prisoners he has and for what reason each one is held. And he should have the prisoners held according to the accusation for which they are imprisoned. For it is not reasonable for the prisoners to be held in more severe conditions than the cases require. But those who are held for crimes should be put in dungeons and in irons and those who are held for less serious offenses, for which the punishment involves no loss of life or limb, can have a less severe captivity.

49. It is a good and honest thing for the *bailli* not to allow a woman to be put in prison for a false accusation or for any case except for a case of crime. And we say the same thing about those women whose company is desired for their youth or their beauty. And if it happens that the case requires women to be put in prison, they should be given a guard who is above suspicion, so that they do not sin through force or fear.

50. If the *bailli* is informed that someone is causing annoyance to Holy Church, for example if they will not be quiet in the church but speak so that the service could be interrupted, or if they are excommunicated and they try to enter the church [*moustier*] in spite of the priest, or if they try to commit some serious sin in a holy place, such as the cemetery or the church, as soon as this has been reported to the *bailli* by people who are believable, he should arrest and imprison such a person as part of his duty until he has been reconciled with Holy Church for the wrongdoing; for Holy Church should be protected from wrongdoers by the temporal sword. For the spiritual sword would not be much feared by wrongdoers if they did not

believe that the temporal sword would get involved; this in spite of the fact that the spiritual sword is incomparably more to be feared.

51. The laws [*establissement*] which the king makes for the common good must be strictly kept through the precautions of the *baillis*; and among others they must be careful to keep the law which was made against blasphemous oaths.[6] For it is the law that those who swear falsely by God and Our Lady should be put on the ladder for an hour in the presence of the common people so that he will be shamed and after this he still owes a fine because he has broken the law {Beaumanoir's change of number}; and the fine is not fixed except at the sovereign's will, according to the oath and according to the wealth of the person who swore blasphemously.

52. Because the seal of the court is authentic and believed concerning what is witnessed by it in a writing, the *bailli* is not wise who does not keep it carefully, so that no letter is sealed with it which he has not seen himself and knows whether it should be sealed or not. And for this reason the recent law which was made is a good one. For our king Phillip {III le Hardi, or "the Bold"} has ruled that in each good town where there is an assize two men are chosen to hear the deals and the contracts on which a {sealed} writing from the judge is requested.[7] And what is witnessed by the seals of these two men the *bailli* seals {also}, to give it even greater value as testimony, and he charges for the seal a half-denier per pound; and the money belongs to the lord. And if the *bailli* uses the seal of the court otherwise than he should, he can get evil repute and bad things can come to him, such as losing his office and paying damages; and if he did it knowingly or in bad faith he would be punished according to the offense.

53. It is part of the duties of the *bailli* that after he has left the office he should remain living for a space of forty days in the place where he was the *bailli*, so that improperly confiscated items (if there are any) can be requested back from him, and so as to instruct the new *bailli* on the state of the disputes. And if he cannot be there continuously because of some reasonable cause, he should be summoned to the court with the knowledge of the common people, and there, if anyone wants to make any accusation against him, it should be heard by the lord whom he served, or by a capable man sent by the lord. For out of respect for the fact that he held this same office, he does not have to answer to the *bailli* who comes after him unless the new *bailli* is specially assigned {to hear complaints against the old *bailli*}, and then the old *bailli* would have to answer to the new one. And if the

bailli leaves his office and goes off without doing what is said above and there are complaints about him in the place where he was in charge, wherever he has gone he should be sent back to the place where he was in charge until he has given a good account to his lord and given back the things he took contrary to his oath and paid a fine for these takings to the lord, that is to say for every denier two deniers fine, and in any case he must make restitution before anything else. And what we have said about *baillis* we also mean to apply to provosts and officers and all those who hold such offices.

54. Unless he has special orders the *bailli* cannot hear a case concerning his lord's land, nor put up boundary markers nor set the boundaries between his lord's land and another's, nor sell nor lease any of his lord's things except in the way that the woods and the districts and the farms were accustomed to be sold formerly by the *baillis* who were before him, for his plain duty is to keep the laws and the customs of the place and the revenues of his lord's land, without making any improper innovations.[8] And if he does more than he should with his lord's lands without special orders, what he does is null and void.

55. If the *bailli* knows there is in his jurisdiction a man or woman of religion who has left the abbey after making their vows, and the person is sought by the supervisor of the house [*qui a l'eglise a gouverner*] which he left, he can have them arrested and sent back to their abbey either by force or by another means if he finds them outside of holy places [*hors de lieu saint*].[9]

56. We have spoken in this chapter of the duties of *baillis* and how they should perform them. And along with what we said they will see many other things in the chapters which come after this one, things which they must do as disputes arise, and about which we will speak if it please God.

Here ends the chapter on the duties of baillis.

Notes

1. This passage is obscure, and there is some disagreement among the manuscripts. I have given a rendering which is supported by the second term of the comparison (a doctor who does not treat his patients' wounds is like a *bailli* who does not stamp out evil in his community).

2. The judge's memory of events, exposed in a *record* or recall from memory (not a written record, see §§1150–53, 1208, 1226, 1233, and 1818), was of considerable importance in a judicial system with few written records.

3. When Beaumanoir was *bailli* of Clermont, the count was a semi-invalid, having been injured in a tournament in 1279 (see Preface). Thus, Beaumanoir had unusual authority.

4. This is the principle of stare decisis, familiar to the common law.

5. The two methods are appeals for denial of a hearing (*defaute de droit*) and for false judgment.

6. *Ordonnances des rois de France de la troisième race*, ed. Eusèbe de Laurière et al., 22 vols. (Paris: Imprimerie Royale, 1723–1849) 1: 99. Subsequent references to this work will be given as *Ord.*, followed by a volume and page number.

7. This law of Phillip III has not been found in the records.

8. For innovations see §§1517–18.

9. For holy ground see §324–25.

2. Summonses

Here begins the chapter on summonses and it is the second chapter of this book.

57. When someone complains of some wrong which has been done him for which he is seeking relief in the courts, he has to have the person against whom he wishes to lodge a complaint summoned to the court of the lord who can give him a hearing; and for this reason we will in this chapter deal with summonses of gentlemen and of others who are not gentlemen. And we will say how each one must be summoned, and how they must obey the summonses which are made to them for reasons either of real or of personal property, or a dispute which concerns the person, either in word or in deed. And we will explain the cases in which, when they are summoned, they can, according to the custom, take a continuance[1] and the ones where they cannot, and the cases in which they can take an adjournment sine die; and what loss they can incur if they do not appear as they should in response to the summonses which are issued to them.

58. When the lord wants to summon a gentleman concerning what the latter holds from him as a fief, he should use two of his vassals who are peers of the person he wants to summon. And if he has no vassals he should borrow them from his lord and his lord is obliged to lend them to him. And he should say to them that they should go and summon his vassal so that he will appear before him in such and such a place; and he should instruct them that they should explain to the man the reason why he is summoned; and then these men should serve the summons, and the summons should be for an appearance not less than fifteen days later.

59. The person summoned should take notice of the form of the summons and why he is summoned. If he is summoned simply,—such as if the summons servers say: "We summon you to appear fifteen days from today in such and such a place before our lord from whom you hold such

and such a fief," and they say no more; or if they say: "We summon you to come to court for anything he might ask[2] of you,"—in these two kinds of summonses the man can take a continuance three times for fifteen days[3] each time and on the fourth occasion he can take an adjournment sine die. And if his lord confiscates his fief claiming that he cannot take these continuances, then when his vassal comes to court he must be reseised[4] completely, if he requires it, before responding to any complaint made against him.

60. If he is summoned for fraudulent concealment of a fief or because he has made his fief or a part of his fief into a sub-fief, or for reasons of the service he owes for his fief, there is no continuance but he can adjourn sine die one time. And he should be sure that he has a good reason to adjourn, for he will have to swear it is so in court if his lord wishes, and if he does not want to swear it, he will be found in default.

61. The lord must reseise his man completely of anything that he has taken into his possession and which was formerly in the possession of or vested in his man (unless he takes it by the judgment of the man's peers) before the man makes response in court to anything that the lord asks him. And when he has been reseised, the lord can make any complaint he wants against him in the presence of his peers.[5] And the man must make his defenses against it, and then they should await a hearing by the above-mentioned peers.

62. If someone is summoned for a partition,—such as if brothers and sisters cause to be summoned for the purposes of partition their brother who holds everything, or if the land has descended laterally[6] to several persons of the same degree of lineage and one of them has taken possession of the whole,—for such summonses there is no continuance, and if a person who is summoned in such a case *takes* a continuance or defaults, the lord should take possession of all the things of which those who caused the summons to be made are requesting partition; and he should hear their complaint and should make a partition and divide everything among them, retaining the share of the defaulter for when he requests it. And we apply this to all partitions of personal or real property[7] whether held in fief or in villeinage,[8] which passes by direct or lateral line. And what the shares should be will be explained in the chapter which speaks of direct and lateral descent {Chapter 14}.

63. When the lord has his man summoned for a case of ownership of land, either in the lord's own suit or in another's, the person summoned has three continuances, each of fifteen days, and he can take one adjournment sine die. But as soon as his legal excuse is no longer valid, he should inform his lord, so that the lord can summon him again if he wants; and if he does not make it known that his legal excuse is ended, and it is proved against him that he has been about his business or going about cheerfully after taking the adjournment,[9] he should be found in default unless it is after he has informed his lord that he no longer has a legal excuse.

64. Now let's see[10]: when someone is summoned on a case of owner-ship of real estate and he does not appear, but instead is in default, how many times he must be allowed to default.[11] We say that he must be found in default three times, not including the appearances that he can continue or adjourn according to custom. And people have sometimes said that these defaults had to be one after the other, but it is not so. For if he continues one or two times and then defaults and then is summoned again and continues this appearance, nevertheless the default that he made is counted as one: that is to say that in this circumstance if he takes his continuances between his defaults, it still happens that each default is counted as one and each continuance counts as one, so that when he has had three continuances and one adjournment and three pure defaults,—or just three defaults if he does not take his continuances or adjournment,—the lord should place the plaintiff in seisin of the property in such a way that the plaintiff must give a surety for the income [*levees*], {so that} if the person who previously had seisin of the land summons him in a suit on ownership[12] within a year and a day and wins the dispute, then he can recuperate the income. And if it is the lord who was the plaintiff on his own account he should demonstrate the defaults to his vassals who are peers of the defaulter, and through their judgment he should take seisin for himself; for if he took it without a judgment he would always have to reseise his man, as I have stated above. But if he has seisin through the judgment of his men, and the person who has lost seisin because of his defaults wants to bring a case on ownership, the lord will retain seisin until the end of the suit.

65. Those who are summoned to help their lords against their enemies or to help their lords to defend their houses must not take continuances nor seek any delay.[13] And if they take a continuance or seek a delay they are not keeping their faith towards their lords. And when they fail their lords in

such need, they deserve to lose their fief; and they cannot use as a defense that they have a legal excuse when they are in the district and the war is not against the person from whom their lords hold their homage, nor against the count who is their sovereign, nor against the king who is over all. Because if they have a legal excuse they can send enough gentlemen to represent them, each person sending one for himself, armed and equipped as befits the rank of the person who sends him.

66. When any men are summoned to help their lord or to guard his house as I have said, the lord should give them reasonable expenses from the first day they leave their home; and {this applies} also if they are summoned for the count's army or the king's army, in which their lords can lead them.

67. If someone is summoned to help his lord to defend against his enemies, unless he wants he is not required to leave the fief or sub-fiefs of his lord, against the enemies of his lord; for it would be clear that his lord was attacking and that he was not defending himself, since he was leaving his own land and lordship. And his man is not required to help him to attack another outside of his fiefs unless it is in the sovereign's army as I said above.

68. The count has an advantage over his vassals in summoning his vassals, for his vassals, as I said before, can only summon through peers, when they want to be the plaintiff, but the count can summon them through his sworn officers, one or more; and the officers are believed merely on their oath when they say that they delivered the summons to the person himself or to his dwelling, for everyone must have a place where there are people who will inform him of the summonses and the commands of his lord.

69. Those who are going to deliver a summons can make their summons wherever they find the person, and if they do not find him by chance they should go and deliver the summons to his residence where he resides; and if it is a man who has no residence, and who stays sometimes here and sometimes there, they should summon him at the place where he stays the most often; and if they do not find him they should tell the neighbors that as soon as they see him they should tell him he is summoned for such and such a day; then he will be in default if he does not come after the neighbors have told him that he has been summoned.

70. If someone summons his vassal at the request of a person who is not under the jurisdiction of the lord in whose court he is seeking a hearing, it is no great wonder if the man issuing the summons wants to have a surety that the person will pursue the case for which the summons is made. But if he is poor or from another district, so that he cannot provide a surety, it is enough for him to give his word [*sa foi*].

71. Those who are summoned for a case of dower cannot take a continuance, but they can adjourn one time if they have an honest legal excuse. And if they take a continuance or they default, the lord should immediately find out if the husband of the woman who is requesting dower was, on the day he married her, the holder of and receiving the income from the place which she is requesting in dower, whether he had inherited it or acquired it some other way, and as soon as the lord knows the truth he should install her in her dower.

72. Now, let's see,—when someone is summoned before the lord under whom he is a resident, and on the same day he is summoned before one of his other lords because of land which he holds from him, and the cases are such that there is no continuance,—which one he should best go to. I say he should best go to the summons of the lord under whom he is a resident, for he owes him much more obedience than he does to the other lords from whom he holds only land, since the lord under whom he has his dwelling has jurisdiction over his person and the cognizance of the real and personal property and chattels that he holds from him. Nevertheless if he is summoned in this way he can go to *both* appearances, for he can go in person before the lord under whom he is a resident, and before the other lord he can send his attorney; for it is as a defendant that he is summoned to appear concerning the land which he holds, and in all disputes concerning land and personal property, I can be defended by an attorney.[14] But if I am the plaintiff, I am not admitted to plead [*oïs*] through an attorney, according to our custom, unless it is by the sovereign's special permission, as you will hear in the chapter concerning attorneys {Chapter 4}.

73. In all cases where reseisin is appropriate, the person should be reseised so completely that all the things that were harvested,—or their value if the things themselves cannot be had,—must be given back to the person who is reseised, before he responds to anything he is asked in the dispute, for reseisin would be worth little if it were not made completely to the person who had been disseised.

74. A person who has reached the point in his suit where he has an inspection day [*jour de veue*]¹⁵ should be very careful not to default nor to take a continuance after the inspection day; for if he takes a continuance it is considered a default, because he cannot take a continuance; and by a single default he loses seisin of everything in the dispute of which an inspection has been made.

75. A person making an inspection should show all the things which are being asked for in the suit, in every place and in every room, because if he wins the dispute he only wins what has been produced for inspection, and for this reason it is good for him not to be negligent in showing everything that is in dispute.

76. I said before that the lord must always reseise his man when, without a judgment, he seizes something he finds in the man's hands, and it is true. But this does not mean that, if the lord finds something which is improperly [*par mesfet*] out of the possession of his vassal, or of someone who *should* be his vassal, he cannot take it before obtaining a judgment; and I will tell you how this can be.

77. If the man of some lord makes his fief or a part of it into a sub-fief, contrary to custom and without his lord's permission, as soon as his lord learns of it he can take it as his own because of the offense. And if the person who should have held it from him asks to be reseised, his lord is not obliged to comply. For he can say to him that he did not take from his possession the thing he confiscated, so that the man cannot ask to be reseised of it. And if the man who made his fief into a sub-fief asks to be reseised of it, the lord can reply that he is not obliged to comply, for he took nothing from his possession, but took what he found converted into a sub-fief from the domain which he used to hold from him; and thus the lord will not reseise his man, but the land will come back to his own personal holdings as a forfeiture.¹⁶

78. The second situation where a lord is not obliged to reseise the person who should be his man is when he reaps benefits from the fief for lack of a holder [*par defaute d'homme*]. For anything that the lord can harvest before there is a holder is his by right.

79. The third situation where the lord is not obliged to reseise his man is when there is a suit for redemption [*rescousse d'eritage*],¹⁷ and he holds in his hands the fruits at the request of the person seeking redemption.

80. Pierre sued Jehan, from whom he held his fief, saying that the said Jehan had summoned him to appear in the most distant town he could find in the county, where the said Jehan had neither fief nor sub-fief, and because he had not obeyed the summons and had not gone to his appearance the said Jehan had confiscated his fief. He requested that the said Jehan be disseised of his fief, and a ruling that he could not summon him in such a place.

81. To this Jehan responded that he admitted that he had summoned him in such a place, and declared he could summon his man anywhere in the county because the fief that Pierre held from him was separated [*desmembrés*] from the county. And on this issue they requested a judgment.

82. It was judged that Pierre was to be reseised completely, and that he was not required to go to such a summons, and that according to custom no one can or should summon his man outside of his own fief or sub-fief, for poor men who hold small fiefs would be much harmed {if they could be thus summoned}.

83. We have seen several arguments of those who were summoned before their lords at the request of a third party for debt, and afterwards those who were summoned gave entire satisfaction[18] to those at whose request they were summoned, so that they did not appear in court against them, and those summoned did not make an appearance. Nevertheless the lord wanted to find them in default because they had been summoned to appear, although no one had appeared against them.[19] And those summoned said in their defense that no one had appeared against them, and said they did not owe a penalty. And because we saw this argument many times, we sought a jury opinion [*meismes en jugement*] on whether those summoned owed a penalty for default in such cases.

84. It was judged that those who were summoned for debt at the request of a third party in the manner described, where the party did not appear against them, owed no penalty; but if the party appeared against them and they did not come then the default was clear.

85. In[20] summonses to appear which are issued for cases of use of force, or of novel disseisin, or for cases of serious crime or fighting, the person summoned must certainly come to his appearance, or he would be in default. For once the summons has been made for any of these things, the

parties cannot let the matter drop without the permission of the lord. Indeed the person who had the summons issued must pursue the matter for which the appearance was scheduled; and, if he does not want to pursue it, he receives the same fine as the person whom he caused to be summoned would have had if he had been found guilty. And if he pursues it and the person summoned defaults, he should be punished for the defaults. And if there are three defaults, he is guilty of the matter on which he was summoned. And if neither one of them proceeds after the court date has been set, the lord should pursue the one who had the summons served and the one on whom it was served until he knows whose default is holding up the suit, and then he can extract a penalty from the person who is defaulting.

86. It sometimes happens that one man summons another and later the person summoned comes to court and the one who had him summoned does not come. Now let's see what is to be done in such a case. If the person who had the summons served does not come before midday, the person summoned should be allowed to leave; and if the one who did not come has him summoned again, he need not respond until he has had his damages for the previous appearance. And if both are resident under the same lord, we agree that the lord can exact a fine for the default of the person who caused the summons to be served, even though we have not seen this happen very frequently. For it happens rarely that someone has another person summoned and then himself defaults, and the person who does so and does not come to the appearance which he has had set should suffer the same loss as would be suffered by the person whom he had had summoned if he did not appear.

87. When someone is summoned to defend his lord or to go to battle for the common good of the kingdom, he should take care to do his part; for if he flees he has lost his honor and everything that he holds as a fief; and he should not afterwards be heard to give testimony in court nor to appeal against another unless he had reasonable cause for his flight: such as if so many others were fleeing before him that by staying he could have done no good. In such a case the first to flee should be blamed, for they are wicked and the others are, because of them, in greater danger of death or shame; and sometimes, however strong and vigorous the others are, they lose heart from the defection [*mauvestié*] of those who should be helping them. And many men have thus been killed and vanquished and many lands have been lost and many a town demolished and razed; and those who go on such

business {battles} know that those who flee are in greater danger than those who attack or defend themselves vigorously. And in all the skirmishes [*besoignes*] that we have heard spoken of, more of those who fled were killed than of those who stayed. For a man who abandons the place where he should be fighting his enemy gives great courage to him; and it has long been said that a person who flees finds plenty of people to pursue him.

88. What we have said about those who flee from battles we apply also to those who are placed in garrisons, in towns or in castles to guard or defend them, at the command of their lord, either by the faith they owe him or by an oath; for neither for death nor for life nor in any way in the world should they give up to the enemies of their lord the thing that their lord gave them to guard, but they should defend and look after it up to death, except in one case: it's the case of very great famine with no expectation of help. For if there is so great a famine that they have for lack of food eaten nothing for three or four days and they have no horses or anything else left to eat and several persons have already died of famine and it is obvious that no help in the form of men or food can come to them, you should not be surprised if they vacate the place with their lives, for staying could not do any good, and they may later be able to help their lord more than if they had waited until they died.

89. Everyone should take great pains to behave wisely and honestly in the occupation [*office*] in which he is, for it is a great honor to God and the world, and if someone does otherwise and it goes badly for him, it is only fitting.

90. Now, let's see,—if a woman at the time of her widowhood or when she is still a virgin, being of age and emancipated, incurs a debt in the jurisdiction where she lives and afterwards marries in another region before the debt is paid, and her own land or some of her personal property remains in the jurisdiction which she left when she married,—whether the person to whom the debt is owed can have attached the thing which is in the jurisdiction where she contracted the debt in order to have himself paid, or if he must pursue the husband or the woman before the lord where the husband has his domicile. We say in this case that the creditor can have the property attached where the debt was incurred; and the husband must pay it there since there is some of the wife's property there, for it would be a bad thing if you had to go and plead in another place to have a debt paid which

was incurred in your own area and the person who had left had something to pay with in the place which he had left. Nevertheless if the woman had taken everything away and the creditor had no surety, he would have to sue the husband where the latter had his domicile (or, if there were sureties, *they* would have to sue him where he had his domicile to be reimbursed).

91. If someone summons to the ecclesiastical court a man who is not in the jurisdiction of the person summoning, such as if the official {ecclesiastical judge} of Beauvais has summoned a man who is from the diocese of Soissons, the person summoned should go or send someone to the hearing and show the judge that he was wrongly summoned because he is not in his jurisdiction and that he is not obliged to answer in that place. And the reason why he should go or send someone is because if he did not go or send anyone he would be sentenced to excommunication. And excommunications are to be feared however they come about, whether rightly or wrongly; and for that reason he should go or send someone; for in some cases he might be required to answer there: such as if he owned something in the diocese of Beauvais and this thing was being asked of him because of a will, or if he had pleaded against someone and the person against whom he pleaded in Beauvais had made a counterclaim against him, or if his predecessor had pleaded there or begun a suit before he died, in all such cases he would be required to answer, and for this reason it is good for him to go or to send an attorney to maintain that he is not under that jurisdiction, or to answer if he is asked something to which he is required to answer.

92. In the secular courts the custom is the opposite of what we have described above; for if the *bailli* of Clermont has someone summoned who is in the jurisdiction of another count of another lord outside his county, and the person summoned owns nothing in the county of Clermont, he is not required to obey the summons; but if he does own something in the county and he is called to appear with these words: "Be on such and such a day in Clermont to appear against such and such a person to respond concerning such and such a thing which you own in the county of Clermont," then he must go, for he must defend his possession where it is located. Nevertheless if it is personal property which he owns in the county of Clermont and it is not the subject of a contract in writing, he can say, when he arrives in court, that he wants to answer only where he has his residence, and then he does not have to answer; but if it is a case on land, the suit remains before the lord from whom he holds the land.

93. What we have said about appearing in response to a summons to the ecclesiastical court, even though you are not in the jurisdiction of the lord who issues the summons, we apply also to summonses by judges who have their power from the pope. If they make a summons in a way they should not,—such as if they are deceived by a writing which was obtained falsely and in bad faith, or if they issue a summons to someone more than two days journey beyond the boundaries [*metes*] of the diocese where they are,[21] or if they do any other improper thing in their summons,—nevertheless the person summoned should appear or send someone. And when he arrives he should complain to the judge for the improper summons and require a ruling. And if the judge refuses to rule or finds against him, he can appeal to the pope. And concerning these appeals in the ecclesiastical courts, if the suit is before the dean you can appeal to the bishop and from the bishop to the archbishop and from the archbishop to the pope. But against a judge sent by the pope you can appeal only before the pope himself. And in the secular courts appeals are also from level to level, from the vassal [*sougiet*] to the lord, and from lord to lord up to the king, in cases which do not proceed by a wager of battle, for in courts to which you appeal by wager of battle, if the battle is fought, the dispute is at an end, so that no other appeal is proper. But before the battle has been fought the appeal could go from level to level to the king, even though the appeal proceeded by a wager of battle, that is to say on the part of one of the parties; such as if one of the count's vassals had a judgment made in his court and a party appealed to the count's court for false judgment and the jurors who had given the judgment wanted to uphold their judgment by a wager of battle, and the appellant made a motion [*proposoit resons*] to reject the wager of battle and to have the judgment declared false on the record of the pleadings [*les erremens du plet*] and they requested a judgment on the issue of whether the appeal would proceed by wager of battle or on the record of the pleadings, and then the count's jurors judged that the appeal would be by a wager of battle, and the appellant appealed against the count's jurors for false judgment: in such a case the appeal would come from level to level up to the king.

94. It should be known that the person who is summoned, when he comes to his appearance, should present himself [*se doit presenter*][22] before the lord who had him summoned (or his substitute), in the place where he hears cases, and should declare himself ready to face those with whom he has business; and if he does not find the lord nor the person who is

presiding over the court, he should go to the place where he normally hears his suits, and should wait until midday. And then if no one comes on behalf of the lord who has the power to preside over the court, he can leave without being found in default for that day. We nevertheless recommend him to tell some honest people about his wait, so they can testify on his behalf if need be.

95. When a summons is made for an appearance without mentioning the time, the person summoned should understand that it is for the morning before midday. And if he does not come before that time and announce his presence, he is in default. But if the appearance is for the afternoon or the evening, the time for announcing his presence lasts until sunset; and a person who announces his presence while the sun is still shining cannot be in default for an appearance which was set for the afternoon or evening.

96. In the ecclesiastical courts, no summons is issued for feast days and no suits are heard; and if a summons is made for a feast day without anyone realizing it, there is no pleading when a person comes to the appearance; and the same is true for the grain harvest [*la seson d'aoust*] or grape harvest time, for Holy Week [*en la semeine peneuse*], for Easter week [*la semaine de Pasques*], the week of Pentecost, and the week of Christmas. But we do not keep this custom in the secular court; the lords make their summonses for any day they want. Nevertheless if a person were summoned for Christmas Day or Easter or Pentecost, unless it were on account of the lord's great need, or for something very dangerous, and the person summoned did not come, we don't agree that he should pay a default penalty; and the same is true for Holy Week, for such days should be free and unencumbered with suits; and what is pleaded on other feast days should be taken as proper since it would be a burdensome thing to poor men who have to plead in minor disputes that their suits should be carried on on the days when they must earn their bread and do their work [*labourages*] {literally, "plowing"}. And this is a good reason for someone to give summonses for feast days and to hear suits. But at all events if you want to hear suits on such days you should hear them after the service of Our Lord has been celebrated, so that God does not fail to be celebrated because of these suits, or otherwise it would not be right to hear suits on such days.

97. If it is apparent that some lord hates one of his poor subjects and that in order to harass him he calls him to a court appearance on the days

when he should be working and doing his work, if this situation is made known to the count he should not permit it, but instead require his man to give an immediate hearing to his poor subject and on a day when he will not lose work time. Nevertheless you can summon your commoner-subject any day you want from one day to the next. But a lord holding directly from the king, when he sees that one of his men wants to enforce this custom too cruelly against his poor subjects can by the power of his office suspend [*restraindre*] this custom and take a look at the complaint that his man has against his subject; and unless he sees the complaint is good he can by his power forbid him to maintain the suit. For when customs began to be observed, people began to keep to them for the common good, and not to act harshly and cruelly. Nevertheless in cases of crime there should be no indulgence, but you should act as the case requires and custom permits, except in cases where it is reasonable to be merciful. And what those cases are is explained in the chapter which speaks of cases where pity and mercy are appropriate {Chapter 69}.

Here ends the chapter on summonses.

Notes

    1. For continuances [*contremens*] and adjournments [*essoines*] see Chapter 3.

    2. "To ask" is another way of saying "to state a complaint." The plaintiff or person stating a complaint is also called the "*demanderes*."

    3. In the French way of counting days, fifteen days is two weeks (fourteen days), so that the new appearance falls on the same day of the week as the first. Eight days are likewise the equivalent of a week.

    4. To reseise is to place in seisin of a thing from which one was disseised. See Chapter 32 for a fuller treatment of seisin, which means, broadly speaking, possession.

    5. These peers are like jurors.

    6. Where there is no descendant or ascendant heir, land escheats to lateral branches of the family, such as brothers, sisters, nephews, etc. See Chapter 14.

    7. For personal and real property, see Chapter 23.

    8. For fief and villeinage, see §§467 ff.

    9. Here the meaning of "sickness" for *essoine* seems indicated, since the man is going around in good health (cheerfully) after his *essoinement*. The commonest legal excuse [*essoine*] for an adjournment was sickness, so that gradually the two words became synonymous. Cf. Villon's use of *essoine* to mean "calamity, disfigurement" in his *Ballade des dames du temps jadis*.

10. *Or veons* 'let's see' is the way Beaumanoir typically introduces an example or hypothetical.

11. Once the defendant has defaulted a certain number of times he loses his case.

12. *Saisine* 'seisin' and *propriété* 'ownership' are not at all the same thing, and are sued on separately. For example, a lord who rents his land to another person will retain ownership while giving up seisin. While seisin in many respects resembles possession, it is not quite the same and sometimes the two must be distinguished; therefore I have adopted the translation "seisin" for *saisine*. For suits on novel disseisin (invented perhaps by Henry II of England), see Chapter 32.

13. Here feudal law intersects with judicial law, since men are summoned to military service in the same way that they are summoned to court for a lawsuit.

14. For attorneys see Chapter 4.

15. For inspection days see Chapter 9.

16. This paragraph is a bit muddled. One would expect Beaumanoir to discuss whether either the *original* fief-holder or the *new* sub-fief holder could get back the confiscated fief; but Beaumanoir appears to discuss *twice* what the original fief-holder can do and not to mention what the new fief-holder can do.

17. For redemption see Chapter 44.

18. That is, they paid what they owed or otherwise discharged the debt.

19. The lord would receive a penalty from each defaulter.

20. Here I read *Es* 'in the' for *Mes* 'but.'

21. Lawyers will recognize here an early forerunner of the hundred mile rule, Fed. R. Civ. P. 4(f).

22. To present oneself is to make some official declaration of one's presence. In modern procedures, we might say something like "sign in," but this is not what the litigant literally did in the thirteenth century.

3. Permissible Delays

Here begins the third chapter of this book which speaks of adjournments sine die and continuances.

98. Having spoken in the chapter before this one of summonses, it is right that we should speak afterwards in this chapter of adjournments [*essoines*] and continuances [*contremans*],[1] how you should make them and in what disputes they are permitted; and we have already spoken about them in several places, in the chapter on summonses {Chap. 2}; and we shall say here what we have not mentioned before. And since after summonses comes the taking of adjournments [*essoinement*] and continuances, according to the issues for which the summonses were made, it is right that we should speak about them before beginning other material.

99. There are several kinds of legal excuses [*essoines*] for which or for any one of which you can adjourn [*essoinier*] the appearance which you are to make before your lord, such as bodily sickness; for whoever has a sickness because of which it is clear that he cannot go to his court appearance [*a son jour*] without distress [*grant grief*], can take an adjournment in good faith [*loiaument*].

100. A person who is summoned before his sovereign lord, if he is summoned before some other lord at the same time (or so close that he cannot easily go from one place to the other) should obey the summons of his sovereign, and he can boldly adjourn all the other appearances.

101. A person who is to appear in court to swear an oath as a witness or in his own case before his ecclesiastical judge, can, if he is summoned to another court, take an adjournment; for the disputes which cannot be ended without an oath of truth [*serement de verité*] would otherwise be too long delayed.

102. When someone has set out to go to his court appearance and he meets some obstacle on the way,—such as if his horse dies or is injured so that he cannot proceed, and he cannot get another horse, and he is not the sort of man who should go on foot; or if he finds such a great flood that he dares not pass it because of the danger of death; or the weather becomes so bad that it is dangerous to travel through the fields, such as at a time of great frost or great snow or storm,—in all such cases he can in good faith adjourn his hearing.

103. A person who is summoned on the day he is to become betrothed or married to a woman, or on the day when he gives in marriage one of his children or his brothers, or his sisters or nieces or nephews, or any other person of his lineage whom he may give in marriage, he may adjourn in good faith.

104. When a person is summoned and he dares not go to court because his wife or children are in danger of death, he can adjourn in good faith.

105. And again a man may adjourn his case who dares not go to his court appearance through fear for his life, such as when he is threatened or in a private war either on his own account or through his lineage.

106. In all cases where a man could seek an adjournment he can instead, if he wishes, seek a continuance, if he has not already taken his three continuances, for if he had taken them he could no longer continue his case.

107. A person who adjourns can no longer obtain a continuance after the adjournment; therefore a person who wants to take all his continuances must take them before he takes an adjournment; and the reason is that the person who adjourns must, when his legal excuse is no longer valid [*quant il est hors de son essoine*], seek a new court appearance, and the day which is given to him at his request cannot be continued or adjourned. And if he does so he is in default.

108. There is a great difference between continuances and adjournments. For in all disputes where a continuance is permitted, you can take three continuances before coming to court, and each of the three continuances is for fifteen days; and it is not necessary to swear an oath nor to give

the reason for taking a continuance. But you can only have one adjourn-ment between two court appearances, and the adjournments must be sine die, for no one knows when the legal excuse for the adjournment will be no longer valid, in the case of most adjournments. And when the party comes to court, on the request of the adverse party he must swear that his legal excuse for adjournment was valid [*li convient son essoine jurer*].

109. In all disputes in which a continuance is possible, a person with a legal excuse can have one adjournment; but you cannot necessarily have a continuance in all the disputes where you can have an adjournment; for there are few or no disputes in which you cannot have an adjournment, if you have a legal excuse. But you can only have a continuance if the summons is a simple one, such as if the summoners say: "Such and such a person summons you to appear in court for any complaint he may make against you," or they say: "Such and such a person summons you to court for a case concerning land." Only in these two kinds of summons can a person take a continuance if he wants, and in other cases he cannot.

110. Each time that a person who has been summoned leaves the court in a case where there can be a continuance he has his three continuances anew, and he can take an adjournment if he has a legal excuse, until the inspection day [*jours de veue*] has been taken,[2] but after the inspection day there is no continuance and instead you lose possession by default as I have said elsewhere {§74}.

111. When someone is seeking a continuance the person who asks for it on his behalf should speak in this manner to the person presiding over the court: "Sire, Pierre, who was to appear before you today against Jehan, continues his appearance until fifteen days from today." And then if the party who issued the summons wants to challenge the continuance, he must do so immediately saying: "Sire, in a case like this there is no continuance of today's hearing, and we will give the reason at a time and place when the other party is present; and we will show why he should be found in default for this appearance." Then the judge should write down that the continu-ance is disputed, and hear the arguments of the parties on the issue of the challenge to the continuance when they come to court, and give a judgment [*faire droit*] according to what the parties say. And if the party does not challenge the continuance on the day when it is claimed, he cannot later have the continuance turned into a default; but instead, the continuance is

held to be proper [*soufisans*], even though there would have been no continuance permitted in this dispute if a party had challenged the continuance.

112. A person who claims an adjournment for someone else should speak in this manner to the person presiding over the court: "Sire, Pierre adjourns today's appearance which he had before you against all those with whom he had business; and when his legal excuse is over, he will let you know, so that you can assign him another appearance date if you wish or if a party asks you to do so." And if any party wants to challenge the adjournment he should do so immediately in the manner described above where the method of challenging continuances is discussed.

113. It is obvious that if someone has several disputes in the same court on the same day he cannot appear for one dispute and continue or adjourn another; for since he comes to court he must proceed in each dispute that he has in the court on that day. For it would be a bad thing for him to be able to adjourn or continue the other suit after he had appeared or registered his presence [*se seroit aparus ne presentés*] in court on that day.

114. There is no purer default than that of a person who appears in court, and does not register his presence before midday; and therefore if he does not register his presence and the adverse party requests a default, he should have it exactly as if the other had not made an appearance at all; for his coming to court would be hardly worth it if he did not register his presence {and readiness} to appear and proceed in the disputes he had to take care of that day.

115. There are people who announce their presence before midday and then go away from the court without leave; or {again} when the adverse party is about to speak they say they are waiting for their counsel, in order to cause annoyance to those against whom they have to plead. But those who act this way should beware; for if they wait so that the time passes and the person presiding over the court wants to leave at the time when he normally leaves, they are found in default, for announcing their presence would not be very useful if they did not want to proceed in the dispute.

116. When a woman pleads or is complained against she can adjourn sine die if she is pregnant, provided she is close to term, such as about two

months away, even though the suit was in the town where she is residing [*ele est couchans et levans*], and that everyone can see that she goes out to church. For she can leave the church when she wants for her private needs [*pour son privé essoine*] if she must. But she could not do this if she had come to court to plead; instead she would be in default if she did not proceed with the pleading according to the business of the day. And when she adjourns because of pregnancy she must arrange to appear within fifteen days after her confinement, unless she is still lying sick, as it sometimes happens that women are confined for more than their month.

117. It sometimes happens that those who have come to court to plead have a legal excuse of sickness, which comes upon them before the time when it is proper for them to leave. And if the suit which such people have is as *defendant*, they can leave an attorney [*procureeur*] to act for them;[3] and if the excuse of sickness is so sudden that they do not remember, or they are not able, to leave an attorney, they should not lose for this reason. For the pity that everyone should have one for another excuses them. And if a *plaintiff* has such an excuse of sickness, his suit should remain in the posture it was in when his sickness overcame him, since as a plaintiff he cannot leave an attorney.

118. When a suit is begun against someone, and during the suit he becomes mad, so that he cannot maintain his suit, the judge should, at the request of the other party, give a guardian ad litem [*defendeur*] to the madman, whether the suit is for land or personal property. For one person's madness should not cause loss to another, especially [*meismement*] when the suit was begun before his madness. And for this reason he should have a guardian, for you cannot know the day when he will be cured. But it is not this way for minor children, for although the suit was commenced during the life of their father and the father died during the suit, and before a judgment had deprived him of what he was in possession of [*ce dont il est saisis*], the children remain in possession [*en la saisine*] and until the children reach majority the suit remains in the posture it was in when the father died.

119. A person who takes an adjournment or a continuance because he has summoned someone else in another court is not taking his adjournment or continuance in good faith, because he should not interrupt his own defense in order to attack someone else.

120. If it happens that a man is summoned to appear before his lord, and this lord is below the count, and the count needs the person who was summoned on that day, he can take an adjournment in good faith. For the will of the sovereign excuses him, even if it was some other lord than the count who was lord to the lord before whom he was summoned to appear.

121. A person who appeals by wager of battle cannot take a continuance but he must come as he should for each scheduled appearance. But he can take a single adjournment if he has a legal excuse; and he should swear in court that this excuse was a legal one, and he should summon the party against whom he appealed as soon as his reason for adjournment is no longer valid. And if he does not do so, and he is seen doing other things, the appellee can use this as a defense and have him declared in default; and by this default the appellee should be liberated from the wager and the appellant stands charged before the judge of false appeal; and if the appeal was not for a serious crime and the apellant is a gentleman, the fine is sixty pounds and he loses the suit, and if he is a commoner the fine is sixty sous and he loses the suit. And if the appeal was for a case of serious crime and the appellant is in default for not pursuing his appeal as he should, he is at the mercy of the lord and may lose life and property.

122. It is true that, each time he leaves the court, an appellee can take three continuances and after that he can adjourn sine die if he has a legal excuse. But when he has had himself summoned again and comes to court, he must swear, if the other party requests it, that the excuse was legal and he must name the excuse. And he must beware that the excuse is such that he does not perjure himself, and that it is accepted by the court, for if he were found in default by a judgment he would be found guilty in the appeal.

123. It could happen that a person takes an adjournment sine die in some case and after his excuse is no longer valid he requests to be summoned again; but before the date of the appearance comes he has so great a legal excuse that he cannot make his appearance nor proceed in his suit. Now we should see what to do in such a case, for according to our custom only one adjournment can be taken: we say that if the second legal excuse is that of sickness, without fraud or sharp practice, the lord, by virtue of his office, for the sake of pity, should preserve him from loss.

124. A person who is summoned to go with the king's or the count's army, or to guard the person or the house of his lord, even though there may be still two or three months until the commencement of his service [*au jour de la muete*] can take an adjournment in good faith. For when such summonses are made, the period between the day of summons and the day of the commencement of the service is not to be used for being in court but for procuring equipment and making preparations.

125. Although a person who adjourns can do so sine die, there are some people so stupid that they take an adjournment for fifteen days. And since they announce a day certain when they will come to court, the scheduled date should stand [*li jours doit tenir*], for they are certainly permitted to give up the right which they had to take an adjournment sine die.

126. A person who adjourns because of the death of his children who die of natural causes or otherwise while they are still nursing can swear in good faith that he has a legal excuse. For such children {'s deaths} distress [*courroucent*] the hearts of fathers; and if the child is dead of an unnatural death, through poor care [*mauvese garde*], such as by suffocating [*estaindre*] or burning or drowning, he can take a legal adjournment even more properly, for his distress excuses him.

127. A person sending a messenger should be careful whom he sends to take a continuance; for if he instructs him to take a simple continuance for fifteen days and the messenger takes an adjournment sine die he has lost his continuance and can be found in default if he will not swear he had a legal excuse when he does appear in court. And if the messenger was supposed to take an adjournment after three continuances and he takes a continuance for fifteen days, he puts his principal [*mestre*] into default, because you cannot take four continuances. And from the foregoing you can know that it is the words which are said in court which are adhered to and not the intention of those who gave the words to their messengers.

128. Some adjournments are long. So now let us see how long the other party must wait if someone takes an adjournment for a legal excuse of sickness: it is our opinion that he should wait for a year and a day; and if the adjournment lasts longer than a year, a party can have the other person summoned again, for a sickness longer than a year and a day should not

delay the adverse party any longer. And if the party summoned cannot appear, as a defendant he can send an attorney; and as a plaintiff he might well have good cause for the count to give him the privilege of acting through an attorney as it happens in special cases [*causes piteuses*].[4] For those who are suffering from a very long illness should have someone to see to their business.

129. When someone has to swear that his excuse was a legal one, he must swear that so help him God and all the saints he had a good faith legal excuse why he could not come to the hearing, and that he did not seek this legal excuse purposefully nor through fraud or sharp practice; but unless he wants, he need not name what his excuse was in any suit, except in the case of crime;[5] and when he has sworn such an oath he should be believed and nothing can be done against it.

130. According to our custom those who are to plead in a suit where a continuance is possible must take the continuance before sunset on the day before the hearing. And if the continuance is not taken in this manner and the day of the suit arrives, a continuance is not to be permitted if a party wants to challenge it; instead the person who tried to make such a continuance is found in default.

131. It is true that a messenger who is sent to take the continuance on the day before should not go away until the next day and should come to the court and recall from memory[6] the continuance he made the evening before. And if a party does not want to believe him, he must prove he took the continuance the day before by the court's recall from memory or that of the person who is supposed to receive continuances (for some people have their mayor [*maieur*] or their officer do this). And if the person taking the continuance found no one in the court who could officially recall from memory, or anyone else from whom he could take the continuance, if he can prove by two good men [*preudommes*] that he came to the place where he was supposed to take the continuance and told them that he had come to take the continuance, but he did not find anyone to take it from, that is enough for his principal {to have the continuance}. And this proof must be made by the person who had the continuance taken, when he {finally} comes to court, if someone is trying to have him found in default; for the person who is sent by me to take a continuance should not and cannot plead anything for or against me but merely take the continuance; and if a party

challenges it, it should be written down as challenged; and when I appear in court then the dispute over the challenge to the continuance can be heard.

132. We saw a knight who had to plead before us in several disputes, and some of the disputes were as plaintiff and the others as defendant. He sent an attorney for those in which he was a defendant, and for those in which he was a plaintiff he took an adjournment. And his opponents said that he should be in default for this day in court, for it was two contradictory things to take an adjournment on the one hand and to send an attorney on the other.

133. The knight replied to this that he had sent an attorney to the suits in which an attorney should and could be accepted on the defendant's behalf; and because by custom an attorney cannot be accepted on behalf of a plaintiff, he had taken an adjournment in these suits because he could not be there; and they requested a judgment on these arguments [*s'apuierent a droit*], that is to say whether he could do things in the manner described above.

134. It was judged that he could not on the one hand adjourn and on the other hand send an attorney on the same day and in the same court. And for this reason he was found in default for everything he had to do on that day, for if you want to take a continuation or an adjournment it must be for everything you have to do in that court on that day. And a person who has various suits should be very careful how he takes an adjournment or a continuance because he might lose one suit because of the other; such as if he had taken all his continuances in one dispute and he had not had them in the other suit, if he took a continuance he would be in default in the suit in which he had already had all his continuances; and if he appears in court he can no longer take the continuances he could have taken in the dispute in which he had *not* taken his continuances, and thus it often happens that one suit shortens or prolongs another. And a person who has several suits to pursue in the same court should decide on the best course: either to go to court for the whole day, or to take a continuance, or to take an adjournment for everything he has to do on that day.

135. We have said above that the continuance should be taken on the day before, and it is true. Nevertheless if the messenger who is going to take the continuance, and who set off early enough to arrive in time, has a legal

excuse for sickness on the way, so that, because of his excuse, he cannot arrive in time to take his continuance, in that case the continuance may be taken on the day of the suit, for the legal excuse of the messenger should save his principal from default.

Here ends the chapter which speaks of continuances and adjournments.

Notes

1. Adjournments [*essoines*] and continuances [*contremans*] postpone a court appearance. The *essoine* is for an indefinite period (*sine die*) and is appropriate when the litigant has some legal excuse [*essoine*] such as sickness (§§ 99–104). *Essoine* will therefore be translated as "adjournment" when it concerns the postponing of the court appearance and as "legal excuse" when it concerns the reason why the postponement is taken. Note that the Old French *ajourner* does not mean "adjourn" but rather the opposite, "to summon to a hearing, to set a court date." The difference between *essoine* and *contremans* is clearly stated by Beaumanoir in §108 infra. Glanvill spends a lot of time on *essoines* but does not use the term or concept of *contremans*.

2. For the *jours de veue* see Chapter 9.

3. See Chapter 4.

4. For the special cases see §168.

5. But see §122; the *essoine* must be specified by an appellee on request of the appellant.

6. For *recort* 'recall from memory, repetition' see §§1150, 1208, 1226, 1233, 1818.

4. Attorneys

Here begins the fourth chapter of this book which speaks of attorneys [procureeurs] *and those who are appointed to represent others* [establis].

136. It is true that after a summons has been served and the person summoned has taken as many continuances and adjournments as custom allows,—of which things we have spoken in the preceding chapter,—the person who is summoned has to come to court or send a competent attorney [*procureeur soufisant*].[1] And for this reason in this chapter we will speak about attorneys and those who are appointed to plead for others and what letters of appointment [*procuracions*] should be given.

137. According to the custom of the Beauvais region anyone can send an attorney in a case where he is a *defendant*; and if he has a good letter of appointment the attorney can act in the case as his principal [*ses sires*] would if he were present.[2] But no *plaintiff* is heard through an attorney, except privileged persons such as religious houses or people who are kept busy by the commands of the king or the count so that they cannot take care of their business; for the sovereign can certainly give a dispensation [*grace*] to such people for them to be heard as plaintiffs through an attorney.

138. Now let us see what attorneys should bring with them to court and what power they have and how you can proceed against them and which letters of appointment are effective and which are not.

139. When the attorney comes to court he should register his appearance in the name of the person for whom he appears against all those with whom his client has business on that day; and he should place in the judge's hands his letter of appointment. And those who have business with him should require that the letter be seen and read in order to know that its effect is that the attorney should be accepted by the court. For if the letter of

appointment does not have the effect that the attorney who brings it should be accepted, it is of no value, and the person who sent the attorney is in default. And because it is dangerous to send an attorney with an inadequate letter of appointment, you will hear the contents of a general letter of appointment which cannnot be reasonably challenged in the secular courts:

140. "To all those who read or hear this letter, the *bailli* of Clermont sends greetings. And be it known to all that, in our presence [*pour ce establis*], Pierre of such and such a town has appointed Jehan of such and such a town his general and special³ attorney, in all suits commenced or to be commenced, for or against him, against whatever party, religious or secular, as plaintiff or as defendant, before whatsoever judges, ecclesiastical judges [*ordinaires*], delegates [*delegas*], subdelegates [*subdelegas*], arbitrators [*arbitres*], conservators [*conservateurs*], auditors [*auditeurs*], examiners [*enquesteurs*], *baillis*, provosts, mayors [*maiurs*], aldermen [*eschevins*], and whatever other judges, in ecclesiastical or secular courts, and the officers of the same who have their powers, and gave to the said Jehan full power and special instructions [*mandement*] to act for him, to defend him, to make and amend contracts [*convenir, reconvenir*], to respond, to duplicate, triplicate, to hear interlocutory and final judgments [*oïr interlocutoires et sentences desfinitives*], to appeal, to pursue his appeal, to swear by his soul any kinds of oaths, to make pleadings [*faire posicions*], to receive what is given him by judgment, to request second production [*requerre seconde producion*] {of witnesses}, or to call witnesses even after second production [*avec la sollempnité de droit et de faire icele sollempnité*],⁴ and to do on his behalf all the things the said Pierre would or could do if he were present, and this in suits concerning land, personal property, and chattels. And he also gave to the said Jehan the power to appoint instead of him a substitute attorney whenever he wished, which substitute would have the same power as the said Pierre, if he were present. And the said Pierre promised before us that he guarantees up to the value of all his possessions everything that the said Jehan or his substitute [*sousestabli*] does or says, in witness to which appointment I have at the request of the said Pierre sealed this letter of appointment with the seal of the *bailli*'s court in Clermont. This was done in the year . . . , et cetera."

141. If it happens that someone does not want to give such a general letter of appointment, it can be made special, that is to say that the attorney

will have in his letter of appointment a power only in the case for which he is sent, and about which the letter of appointment speaks.

142. And you can appoint an attorney who will have no power except for what is to be done on a single day, if the letter of appointment states this in this manner.

143. No letter of appointment is worth anything unless the person who appoints the attorney obliges himself to uphold everything that is done or said by his attorney.

144. Every gentleman, according to our custom, can seal with his own seal a letter of appointment in his own case and as a defendant. But this letter would not be valid for anyone else, for the seal of any gentleman is not authentic [*autentiques*]⁵ and is not believed in a court except against the gentleman whose seal it is.

145. A person who wants to appoint an attorney and has no seal, or is a commoner who is not supposed to have a seal, must have his letter of appointment sealed with the seal of the *bailli*'s court or by his ecclesiastical judge, or by some other authentic seal; for if the letter of appointment could only be made by the seal of the *bailli*'s court or by the ecclesiastical judge, those who are out of the district and need someone to defend them for the possessions they have in the county would be in bad straits. And for this reason those who are out of the area can send back letters of appointment sealed by an archbishop or a bishop, or a king or a prince or some other judge who has a well-known and approved [*bien conneu et bien aprouvé*] seal.

146. Letters of appointment for attorneys which are made for those who are resident in the county last only for a year and a day; for much danger could come about through old letters of appointment forgotten in the hands of attorneys. But it is different for those who go out of the district and leave behind an attorney with general powers, for the power of the letter of appointment lasts as long as the person is out of the district unless he cancels it by a firm order or by appointing a new attorney. For a later letter of appointment which comes into court cancels an earlier one if it does not mention it.

147. The person who came to court bringing a good letter of appointment to proceed in the case and when he had shown the letter wanted to take a continuance for fifteen days for the court appearance of his principal [*mestre*] did not understand the custom. And he could not do this because he personally represented the principal through his letter of appointment and could proceed in the case; and if he had not proceeded after he had shown the letter of appointment, his principal would have been found in default.

148. An inspection day [*jours de veue*] was set in a case concerning real estate. The defendant sent an attorney to the inspection, an attorney who had a good letter of appointment for the whole suit. Nevertheless the other party wanted to challenge him and said that an inspection should not be made by such an attorney because the letter of appointment did not make special mention of the inspection day. The attorney said that his letter of appointment gave him sufficient authority [*estoit bien soufisans*] to make the inspection, for it was a general appointment for the whole case and allowed him power to lose or win the whole case. And on this issue they requested a judgment.

149. It was judged that the inspection could indeed be made by such an attorney, for a general appointment for a case includes all the special powers which are required for the suit. That is to say,—if I am an attorney in a suit on real estate in which my principal is the defendant and the letter of appointment is general for the whole suit,—I can make a special request and demand an advice day [*jour de conseil*] and an inspection day, and each and every thing which can be obtained in a suit for real estate; for the requests that I make as an attorney are for the defense of the person who is my principal.

150. A person who makes a response to an attorney who has an invalid letter of appointment should beware. For if he loses the suit, he loses, and if he wins, the person who sent the incompetent[6] attorney can have the judgment voided; for he is required to be bound only in accordance with the provisions of the letter of appointment which was delivered in court.

151. The judge should retain in his own keeping all the letters of appointment which are brought to court so that he will always be in possession of the instrument which gives the attorney his authority [*saisis*

du pouoir au procureeur]. For then if the attorney loses, through the authority of the letter of appointment the judge can have the judgment executed.

152. A person accused of a crime cannot be defended by an attorney; but instead he must come to court in person. But if there is an appeal and he has a legal excuse, he can have a substitute to fight for him as we will explain in the chapter on appeals {Chapter 61}.

153. When the letter of appointment is valid and in the possession of the judge, the other party must proceed in the suit just as he would if the person who sent the attorney were there himself.

154. Those who are attorneys representing the people [*le commun*] of some town which is not a chartered commune should be appointed to be representatives by the lord who has jurisdiction over the town and by the agreement of all the people; the agreement should be made in the presence of the lord or of a person sent on the lord's behalf to take notice of the agreement. And the lord or his envoy should ask each person separately if he agrees that those who are named to be the attorneys for the town *should* be the attorneys for the town and should have the power to win or lose in the cases for which they have been appointed attorneys. And all those who consent should be written down as consenting, and all the names of those who do not consent should be written down as not consenting, so that when the suit is ended, whether it is won or lost, everyone will know who can win or lose in that suit. For those who do not consent to the suit should neither win nor lose.

155. The attorneys for the people of a town can be established in another manner, {and this occurs} if the lord or a person he sent has all the people assembled before him and then says to them: "Some people are agreed that such and such persons should be attorneys for you all in the cases which you have or expect to have against such and such persons—*and he should name the cases*—and if there is any one of you who disagrees then he should say so." Then if no one disagrees, those who were named previously remain the attorneys and can win or lose in the cases for which they are the representatives.

156. No one can cause to be voided what his attorney did unless the attorney exceeded the authority granted to him by his letter of appoint-

ment. For example if it is stated in the letter of appointment that he is entitled to act in cases for personal property, or to request jurisdiction of a case [*court requerre*] or to receive the verdict [*justice tenir*] and he commences some case on real estate, then if he loses this case his principal can have the judgment voided; for he did not give him authority to act in this way. And for this reason anyone who pleads against an attorney should make sure that the attorney has the authority to act and that the party does not get involved in a suit which the attorney's principal cannot lose. Indeed as soon as he sees that the attorney is exceeding his authority he should challenge the attorney. And if he does not challenge him and accepts him as an attorney until the end of the suit or until they have declared the arguments ready for judgment [*se soient apuié a jugement*], if he loses the suit he cannot have the judgment voided, for the attorney's principal can say, if he likes, that he accepts as proper that which was done on his behalf.

157. When a town which has a communal charter is going to court, it is not necessary for the whole commune to go to the suit; but it is sufficient if the mayor and two of his assessors [*jurés*] go, for these three can win or lose for the entire town.

158. Attorneys are not expected to take care of their principals' business at the attorneys' cost; instead they should have an appropriate salary according to the matters in which they act as attorneys, even though nothing had been agreed about giving them anything, for no free man is obliged to serve another for nothing.

159. An attorney should make sure that he does what he is supposed to do in his official capacity, for it is possible for him to act in such a manner that he would have to make good his principal's loss: that is to say, in any case where his principal lost through the attorney's dishonesty [*tricherie*] or through his indolence [*fole perece*]. And dishonesty would be if he took money from the other party to allow his principal's suit to be lost, or if he lost on purpose out of hatred for his principal or out of love for the other party, or for some other similar case where dishonesty could be found. And the attorney could be obliged to make good his principal's loss on account of his indolence, such as if he failed to go to the court appearances assigned for his principal's business and then his principal lost through his default. And it is right that the principal should have an action against his attorney in such a case because he expected him to go to the court appearance.

160. According to our custom, no one can be an attorney for another person in a case of serious crime. Instead the person who is making the accusation, and the person accused, should come to court in person without sending an attorney.

161. There is a custom amongst the attorneys in the ecclesiastical courts which is not the custom in the secular courts. For the attorney {in the ecclesiastical courts} has to give a deposit, that is to say a security, that his lord will accept what is done. And this deposit is a security or a sum of money which the attorney promises to pay if his lord did not want to do what was judged against him. But we do not do this in the secular courts; instead we look at the letter of appointment that the attorney brings, and if it is valid the judge retains it in his own keeping and enforces what is done by the attorney. And if it is not valid in this particular suit, the attorney's principal is in default just as if he had not sent anyone to represent him.

162. If someone has appointed an attorney until a certain time, this authority is valid until the time stated in the letter of appointment. And if he had been made an attorney without an ending date and the lord was in the district, the letter would be believed for only a year and a day. But it would be different if the lord was out of the district, for in that case the letter would be valid until the lord came back or sent another attorney, as is mentioned above.

163. It should be known that when someone has made an attorney by a general letter of appointment,—that is to say that the attorney has authority in all the things where an attorney can have it,—and afterwards the principal appoints an attorney specially in another suit, the general attorney is not for this reason dismissed. But if the principal makes the second one a general attorney without mentioning the first attorney in the second letter of appointment, then the first one should no longer be accepted. Instead the later one should be given all the business, and the first attorney stops being one as soon as the second letter of appointment comes into court. But if the second attorney says nothing, or hides his letter of appointment, and the first attorney (who knows nothing about it) acts in accordance with his own letter of appointment, what he does should be enforced, for otherwise a lot of tricks could be played by those who appointed attorneys, for then they could say: "My attorney was not the person that you say lost my suit; my attorney was the person whom I had subsequently appointed." And for

this reason no one should believe any attorney until the letter of appointment is in the hands of the judge presiding over the court.

164. You can see, by what is said above, that the later attorney ousts [*boute . . . hors*] the first if his letter of appointment gives him authority equal or superior to that in the first. Nevertheless, Pierre, who was the first attorney, who collected and made use of [*leva et exploita*] the possessions of the person who appointed him an attorney, before the later attorney made his appearance, is not required to give an account of what he did as an attorney to Jehan, who was later made the attorney, unless the following is contained word for word in Jehan's letter of appointment: "I require that Pierre who was my attorney give account to Jehan my later-appointed attorney." For then it is seen that the lord wants the second attorney to be the adminstrator [*amenistreres*] of his property both for the past time and for the future; and in such a case if the first attorney gives an account to the later attorney, so that the second believes everything is paid up [*tel qu'il s'en tiegne a paié*], the lord who made the first one an attorney cannot accuse him of anything further. Instead the second attorney must be responsible for everything. And if the first attorney is not required to give an account to the later one (because no mention was made of it in the later letter of appointment), each of the attorneys is required to give accounts for his period of administration [*de son tans*] whenever the lord who made them an attorney (or his heirs if the lord is dead) wants to have an account rendered.

165. It sometimes happens that an attorney has business for his lord in different courts and in various suits, and yet he has only one letter of appointment; and it may be that his lord is away so that he cannot obtain another letter. What will he do, then, when the first court to which he comes to plead retains his letter of appointment? He should request the court to transcribe his letter of appointment word for word and to seal this transcript with the seal of the court or some other authentic seal. And he can use this transcript which is given to him (or his own letter of appointment which is given back to him if the court keeps the above-mentioned transcript) in the second court. And if he has business in a third or fourth court, he can use the same method in each court by means of transcripts sealed with an authentic seal.

166. Although someone has appointed an attorney until a certain date and has promised him a certain sum of money to be his attorney until the

time mentioned in the letter of appointment, he has not given up his right to make someone else his attorney and dismiss this one. But if he dismisses him without his having done anything wrong [*sans son mesfet*], he has to pay him his whole salary; and it is this way with all other services, for anyone can dismiss from his service a person in his employ, whenever he wants, provided that he pays him as much as if he had served the full term, since he does not leave the service because of some wrongdoing.

167. An attorney cannot make peace [*pes*] nor set up a stipulated penalty [*mise*] nor a pay off [*ordenance*] nor another transaction [*concordance*] in his lord's suit unless the authority is specially given to him by the words of his letter of appointment. And if he does so the lord is not obligated unless he wants to be. And if the attorney gives assurances to the other party that his lord will be obligated and he cannot afterwards make his lord agree to the obligation, the attorney must give to the other party what he agreed or something of the same value. And thus he can suffer a loss because of his rash promises. For this reason attorneys must be aware of what authority they have and act only within their authority.

168. It is not customary for a commoner to appoint an attorney in any case; but a gentleman, a person in religion, a clerk, and women can do so as defendants but not as plaintiffs, except for religious houses and those to whom special permission is given by the king (or, in his own domains, by the lord who holds directly from the king) and those who go to foreign lands for the common good, for they can appoint attorneys both as plaintiffs and as defendants.

169. When some group, such as the people of a town, wants to commence a suit which touches the whole community, it is not necessary for the whole group to go to court, and also you should not make individual responses to each person, for when one person had lost, the others could begin the suit for the amount to which they were involved, and thus a suit against a community would never end. Therefore, if some town wants to commence a suit which concerns the whole community, they must appoint for all of them one, or two or three or more persons if they want, and should give them the authority to win or lose for all of them. And this should be done before the lord from whom they hold their land and who has jurisdiction over them, or before the lord who holds directly from the king, in whose court they intend to plead, especially when they reside in his

jurisdiction or the jurisdiction of his vassals. And all those who agree should be written down so that they cannot deny that the representatives were appointed with their agreement. And then those who are appointed representatives in this manner are attorneys for the town and can win or lose the suits for which they are appointed. And if they are given a general appointment for all suits which have been brought or which are to be brought, they can proceed in the suits which are to be brought or which have been brought until they are removed from their office by those who appointed them for this purpose.

170. It is a good thing for attorneys to behave honestly and wisely in their official duties so that they are not dismissed for doing improper things [*par leur mauveses euvres*]. Neverthless if they have a valid letter of appointment, the court should be patient with them so that their lords do not lose; but the *bailli* should inform the person who appointed them that he should look for another attorney and should tell him the reason why the present one is not competent. And if the lord will not change him, then the *bailli* can remove him by virtue of his office; and the principal should suffer whatever the loss is for his default, because he would not send a competent attorney.

171. It is not right that when a town community appoints an attorney (which some people call a representative [*establi*]), or when something necessary or appropriate is done for the town, that what is done can be void because not all {the citizens} were there to give their agreement. It is enough that two-thirds of the people, and the most competent ones, were present at the agreement. For it is not right, and it should not be allowed, that the minority and the poorest citizens should be able to prevent what the majority and the most competent citizens agree to. And what we have said about representatives who are made for the people of a town refers to towns which are not chartered communes. For the chartered communes have their mayors and their assessors [*jurés*], who are appointed to represent the commune, and can win or lose through the power which is given to them by the terms of their charters.

172. The powers of the representatives who are appointed as attorneys for the needs of a community last until the tasks for which they were appointed are finished, unless they are removed in order to appoint others to their office by those who appointed them, or by the greater part of the

most competent citizens, and in the presence of the lord under whom they are domiciled, or of their sovereign, if they are expecting to plead in his court.

173. When the letter of appointment allows the attorney to appoint other attorneys, he can do so; and they are called sub-representatives. And when sub-representatives are appointed, they must bring to court the letter of appointment authorizing their appointment and their own letters of appointment from the attorney who appointed them. And then you must answer to them as to a real attorney. But those who are thus appointed sub-representatives may not appoint others, for it is enough to be able to subappoint attorneys the second time.

Here ends the chapter on attorneys.

Notes

1. A *procureeur*, as this chapter explains, is a person appointed to deal with the affairs of another in a lawsuit. In most cases, a *procureeur* can do everything a *defending* party can do, and does not need the presence of the person who appointed him. *Plaintiffs* cannot normally appoint a procureeur to represent them. The *procureeur* is appointed by means of a *procuracion*. I have chosen to translate these words by "attorney" and "letter of appointment" respectively. It must be understood, however, that the word *attorney* does not bear the same meaning as it does in modern American usage, where it is a synonym for *lawyer*. Nothing in Beaumanoir's time quite corresponds to the modern notion of lawyer. Nor does it correspond to the British "solicitor" or "barrister," although it includes something of both. Some of a barrister's functions are performed by the person termed in Old French *avocat*, discussed in Chapter 5.

2. The person employing an attorney in modern society is termed the "client." However, Beaumanoir's word is generally the same as that for "lord" (*mestre, sire, seigneur*). I have therefore used for the employer a word used in modern agency law, "principal," since the *procureeur* acts in many ways as his "agent."

3. Beaumanoir uses the terms *general* and *especial* with their modern legal meanings of "general, overall, all-encompassing" and "special, particular, restricted," respectively.

4. Parties or their attorneys were normally given two days to present all of their witnesses, but exceptionally, if they were unable to obtain them all in the two days, they could request a third day on affirming their good faith, *cum solemnitate juris*; see L. Tanon, *L'ordre du procès civil au XIVe siècle au Châtelet de Paris* (Paris: Larose and Forcel, 1886) 42–43.

5. The meaning of *autentiques* appears to be more like "recognized, well-known, official" than the modern "authentic." For the sake of brevity, however, I will use the modern word "authentic" to translate it.

6. "Incompetent" here does not refer to the attorney's professional or personal abilities, but only the lack of authorization from his principal.

5. Advocates

Here begins the fifth chapter of this book which speaks about the duties of advocates [l'office as avocats].

174. Because many people do not know the customs concerning how to proceed in a suit [*comment on doit user*], nor what is necessary for maintaining their dispute, those who have to plead are permitted to seek a counsel and various persons to speak for them; and those who speak for others are called advocates.[1] And in this section we will talk about what their duties are and what they should do.

175. A person who wants to be an advocate [*se veut meller d'avocacion*], if he is so required by the judge or the party against whom he is pleading, must swear that as long as he performs the duties of an advocate [*maintenra l'office d'avocat*] he will perform them well and honestly, that he will not knowingly uphold any but a good and honest dispute, and that, if he starts to maintain some suit which, when he takes it on, he thinks to be a good one, and which he later recognizes to be a bad one, then as soon as he recognizes it {is bad} he will abandon it. And after he has sworn this oath in a court he is no longer required to swear it again from then on. But until he has done so he cannot be received as an advocate if a party challenges him.

176. According to our custom advocates can receive from the party for whom they plead the salary which has been agreed on, but it must not exceed thirty pounds for a single suit; for they may not take more than thirty pounds by reason of the law [*establissement*] of our king Phillip {III le Hardi or "the Bold"}.[2] And if they do not make an agreement with those for whom they plead, they must be paid by the day, according to what they know, and according to their station [*estat*] and according to whether the suit is big or small, for it is not right that an advocate who drives one horse should have as big a daily fee as a person who drives two horses or three or more, nor that the person who knows little should have as much as the

person who knows a good deal, nor that the person who pleads in the little suit should have as much as the person who pleads in the big suit. And when there is a disagreement between the advocate and the person for whom he pleaded because they cannot agree about a salary which was not agreed on in advance, an estimate should be made by the judge according to what he sees to be reasonable, according to what is said above.

177. An advocate, after he has been of assistance to someone in his dispute or who has been his counsel in his dispute, should be careful not to leave the party's service by his own fault to help the other party against him. For he could be excluded if the person he first helped wanted to challenge him; and it is quite right that a person who was my counsel or the advocate in my dispute should not be able to be against me in this same dispute. And for this reason advocates should be careful whom they begin to help, and how; for if they make an agreement for the whole dispute and the person who called them to be their counsel wants to drop them from the suit, the advocate does not for that reason fail to have everything that was agreed upon, since he is not failing in his part of the bargain. And if he was hired by the day, the person who hired him can dismiss him when he wants and pay him for as many days as he worked; and then the advocate cannot afterwards be counsel to the other party in this dispute.

178. We have said that no one should be allowed to become an advocate until he has taken the oath if a party challenges him. But we mean here the people who perform the duties of an advocate for a salary, for there are other people who can certainly plead for others without swearing the oath which advocates have to swear; for example, if someone pleads without expectation of payment for someone in his lineage, or for one of his vassals whom he is supposed to help, or for his lord, or for some poor religious house [*aucune religion pauvre*] or for some other poor person, for the love of Our Lord; all such kinds of people can be heard for others and they are not for that reason called advocates, and they do not need to swear the oath which the advocates do.

179. The advocate who is supposed to help a party for a salary, if he takes money from the *other* party, with the understanding that he will not support one party or the other as counsel or as advocate, if this is proved against him, he should lose the title of advocate [*il doit perdre l'office d'avoca-cion*] {Beaumanoir's syntax}. Because it is a patent evil [*aperte mauvestiés*] to have an agreement to help someone and then not to perform, because of

greed; and those who are found guilty of this are no longer worthy to have this title [*d'estre en tel office*] nor any other.

180. When the advocate pleads on someone's behalf, he should say to the person presiding over the court, at the beginning of his speech: "Sire, I will speak for Pierre, subject to his corrections and those of his counsel." For if he does not mention the possibility of correction, and he is not confirmed by Pierre for whom he speaks, he gets a fine from the lord. And if he mentions the possibility of correction, then Pierre, for whom he is pleading, has the possibility of taking away something he said that was too much, or having him say more if he has said too little, providing that this is before he has publicly confirmed what he said [*avoué sa parole*]; for after he has confirmed what has been said for him, unless he confirms it with corrections, he cannot later add or subtract anything. But if he confirmed it subject to correction, he should say or have someone else say immediately what he wants to correct, before he declares the arguments ready for trial [*il s'apuie en jugement*],[3] for after the arguments have been declared ready for trial [*couchiés en jugement*] nothing further can be added or taken away.

181. However many persons someone has as counsel, one only should be chosen to speak for him, and he should consult the other counsel as to what he should say. For if all or several of the counsel spoke for a party, the judge would be confused [*empeechiés*] by the multitude of arguments, and the suits would be too long. And for this reason it is right for just one to speak; but if he is making a correction, the remark can be made by him {the advocate} or any of the others, at the wish of the party who is pleading.

182. However wise a man is, if he has a big dispute, we do not advise him to state his own arguments [*conte sa parole*] because of two dangers: one danger is that everyone is more easily upset and confused in his own dispute than in another's when he is not given or told all he asks for; and the second danger is that when he says something against his own interest he cannot correct it, which he can certainly do in the mouth of his advocate when the latter speaks subject to correction.

183. A person fulfilling the duties of an advocate must be able to wait and listen without getting upset, for a man who is upset soon loses the thread [*pert legierement son propos*]. He must be patient and not get upset, and he must listen well to what is said against him in order to understand it better and remember it.

184. A person who is an advocate, and all manner of people who have to plead on their own behalf or for others, demonstrate a talent, when they are making their speech, if they include all they have to say in as few words as they can, provided that the whole dispute is contained in the words. For a man's memory retains more easily a few words than many, and they are more acceptable to the judges who hear [*reçoivent*] them; and it is a great hindrance to the *bailli* and the jurors to hear long arguments which do nothing for the dispute, for when they are said, the *bailli* or the judge who has to accept [*recevoir*] them has to extract only the arguments which are needed for the dispute, and the others are considered merely superfluous [*oiseuses*].

185. An advocate can certainly hire himself to a litigant for a dispute, but nevertheless he is not for this reason (unless he wants to be) prevented from being against him in another dispute; for if he does not want to, he is not obliged to help him except in the suit for which he contracted to be of service to him. And if the advocate thought at the beginning that the dispute was a good one, and then later he discovered it to be a bad one, so that he gave up helping him {his client} in order to preserve the oath he made that he would not maintain a bad dispute as soon as he recognized it as such, he should not for this reason go to the aid of the other party, against whom he had begun to be of service in this same dispute; instead he should not interfere either on one side or the other. And since an advocate could believe a dispute *which was in fact a good one* to be a *bad* one, when his conscience assails him he should withdraw; but this should be done courteously, and in such a way that the person who was relying on him can find another advocate.

186. Now we have to know, if the advocate acts in this manner, whether he will be paid by the person to whom he promised his help for the whole suit, since he is leaving him before the end of the dispute. We say yes, provided he swears on the saints that he stopped helping him (because he recognized that the suit was a bad one) to save his oath; and having sworn this, he should be paid according to the work he did before he recognized that the suit was a bad one, and according to the money he was supposed to receive for the whole suit, following an estimate made by the jurors.

187. All those who can be excluded from testifying because of their serious crimes, can and should be excluded from being advocates; but those

people who could be excluded from testifying for something other than a serious crime cannot be excluded from being advocates; just as anyone can be an advocate in his own suit and yet he is not allowed to testify, or just as those who are members of my household, or my serfs, or my bastards, can be my advocates and yet they could be excluded from testifying in my dispute.

188. A person who is not under the jurisdiction of the judge of the court where he wants to be an advocate, such as a clerk in a secular court, should not be accepted as an advocate unless the judge gives him permission, for if he did wrong or if his words were not affirmed by his client, he could not be punished by a fine nor indeed for his wrongdoing at all, unless he were sent back to his ecclesiastical judge. Nevertheless a party may not exclude him if the judge wants to permit him to speak, and if the judge does not want to, the clerk can still make requests or plead for himself or for his house, or for his lineage, or for the common profit, or for a pauper *pro bono* [*pour Dieu*], but he must swear an oath that he receives no payment and does not expect to do so.

189. A *bailli* can on his own motion exclude an advocate so that he is not heard as an advocate before him, if he is in the habit of saying bad things [*vilenies*] to the *bailli* or to the jurors, or to the party against whom he has to plead, for it would be a bad thing if this kind of person could not be excluded from being an advocate.

190. A woman cannot act as an advocate for another person for a fee, but without a fee she can speak for herself or for her children or for someone in her lineage, but this must be with the permission of her husband if she has one.

191. A person who is under ordinary or aggravated excommunication [*renforciés*] can be excluded from acting as an advocate by a party or by a judge until he has been absolved, because all those who speak to him knowing about his excommunication are themselves excommunicated, and you have to reply to and speak to advocates.

192. A man in religion should not be received to speak as an advocate in a secular court unless it is on the business of his house and on the authority of his sovereign who has specially appointed him to do so.

193. A *bailli* should take notice of which advocates usually plead before him; and he can remove them unless he finds them competent [*soufisans*],[4] as was said in this very chapter, and also if they are disobedient to his commandment in things in which they should obey him, for example if I have begun some business where he should not interfere, and he interrupts it and acts in an annoying way, in order to speak about some of *his* business, and I command him to be quiet and he will not be quiet, then I can exclude him from being an advocate before me. And also if a party requests that I nominate a counsel for him, such as a party who cannot get a counsel out of {people's} fear of the person against whom he is pleading, or their fear of being badly paid, and I command an advocate to be his counsel, the advocate must obey the commandment if he can be sure of receiving his salary from the party according to the day's work. Nevertheless the advocate can for various good reasons excuse himself from going to be a counsel or an advocate to the person whom he is commanded to help,—such as if he is obligated to the other party, or if he is his relative [*amis de char*], or if he is a great friend of his [*a grant affinité d'amour*] and everyone knows it, or if he has some marital relationship [*aliance*] with him or some partnership [*compaignie*], or if he has hatred towards the party whom the *bailli* commands him to help or towards one of his close relatives and for good cause, or if he helped him another time and he did not pay him his fee and still will not pay him, or if the suit touches him personally or any of his relatives, or his relatives through marriage, or if he swears that he believes the dispute to be a bad one for which reason he does not want to be his advocate,—for all these reasons he can excuse himself and request the *bailli* to rescind his order, and the *bailli* should do so if he sees any of the above-mentioned causes.

194. If someone comes to court to plead and cannot obtain a counsel because all the advocates are excused for a good reason from being on his side, the suit should not, according to the custom of the secular court, be stopped or postponed for that reason. Instead, the party must be required to proceed. For this reason everyone should take care to come to court accompanied by his counsel; and if he does not want to proceed he should be declared in default just as if he had not come to court.

195. Advocates and counsel can take salaries and services [*service*] for their counsel or for their being an advocate; but the judges and the jurors

cannot do this, for services [*services*] and counsel can be sold but judgments cannot and should not be sold.

Here ends the chapter on advocates.

Notes

1. Advocates spoke for their parties in court, as modern barristers do in British courts. Attorneys, on the other hand, replaced their parties in some or all functions, including sometimes speaking for them in court (see Chapter 4). The attorney had discretion to manage his party's business; the advocate merely said what he was told to say. For a description of the attorney's possible functions, see §140.

2. Ordonnance of the 23d October, 1274. *Ord.* I: 301.

3. The declaration by both parties that the issues have been defined, the arguments raised, and the pleadings finished, is marked by a declaration called *appuyer en jugement* or *couchier en jugement*. This does not mean that a judgment immediately follows, for no proofs have been made at this point, no witnesses called, and no documents produced. Thus it would be erroneous to translate "ready for judgment" and I adopt here the expression "ready for trial" since this best approximates modern procedure where the pleadings, which are of course in writing, precede the trial proper.

4. "Competent" here does not mean "skilled" but rather "officially adequate, authorized, certified."

6. Complaints

196. Churchmen [*li clerc*] have a very beautiful way of speaking in Latin; but the laymen who have to plead[1] against them in secular courts do not even understand very well the words they speak in French, even though they are proper and suitable for pleading. And for this reason, we will discuss in this chapter, in such a way that laymen can understand it, what is most often said in secular courts and what is most needful. This is concerning complaints which are made and which you can and should make in secular courts, which complaints are called by the clerks *libelles*; and a complaint is the same as a brief. And afterwards we will discuss the defenses which the defendant should state in his answer to the plaintiff, the defenses which the clerks call exceptions [*excepcions*]. And afterwards we will discuss the defenses which the plaintiff raises to destroy the defenses which the defendant raised against his complaint, which the clerks call replies [*replicacions*]; and to go further than the replies is not necesssary in the secular court, because each party only pleads at the bar [*barroie*] once. And we call pleadings at the bar the reasons the defendant raises against the complaint [*ce qui li est demandé*] and the reasons the plaintiff raises against the defenses of the defendant; but in the ecclesiastical courts they plead as many times as they reserve the right to by what they call an objection [*protestacion*] and as many times as they can find something to say against each other; and for this reason they file triplications against the plaintiff's responses, and then they file quadruplications to the defendant against his triplications. But all this is unnecessary in the secular courts, except for the defenses which the defendant raises in his answer to the complaint and the reasons the plaintiff raises against these defenses. And we will discuss only these three things: in this chapter the complaints which the plaintiff should make, and in the next chapter which comes after this one the defenses of the defendant and the

reasons the plaintiff raises against the defenses; and first we will speak of the complaint, because it is the commencement of the pleadings [*plet*].

197. There are several complaints which are made, on issues of personal property and chattels, on seisin of real property, on ownership of real property, on contracts [*convenances*], on dower, on custodianship or guardianship [*de bail ou de garde*] on behalf of minor children, on the use of force, on novel disseisin, on nuisance, on crimes against the person: so it is right that we should say briefly how a complaint should be made before a judge on each of these things.[2]

198. A person asking for personal property or chattels should speak in this manner: "Sire, I demand of Jehan over there such and such personal property and such and such chattels," and he should name them if they are big things or with few parts. For they might be such that it would be enough for him to state his request in general: such as if he were asking for things shut up somewhere and which he had not seen, or some crops harvested when he was not there, or a share of all the personal property in a house, for in such cases he would not be able to name everything. And for that reason it would be enough to say: "I ask for all the things which are shut up in there," or a *part* of them if he is not asking for them all,—or *the personal property in the house which belonged to this person,*—or *the crops from the real property belonging to that person.* And if he is only asking for a part, he should say which part, a half or a third or a quarter, or less if he is asking for less. And then he should give a reason why he should have it, such as that the right passed to him laterally or by descent, or by purchase or gift, or for some other good reason; for to ask for something when you give no reason why you should have it is not valid, and the defendant is not obliged to answer; for it means nothing to say: "Jehan owes me ten pounds: make him pay me," if I do not say why and what he owes them to me for.

199. There are people who need to word their complaint just for seisin of real property, so that they do not mention in their complaint the issue of ownership [*propriété*], because if they mentioned ownership in their complaint it would be a suit on ownership; and the suit would be longer and more dangerous, for after seisin has been won or lost you can start a suit on ownership. Therefore a complaint on seisin should properly be made in the following way: "Sire, I ask to have the seisin of this real property which is in

such and such a place and which belonged to so and so, and I say the seisin is mine for this reason." And he should state the reason: such as that it passed to him laterally or by descent, or he is asking for it as an executor of a will, for this is how seisin of real property passes. And if no one is preventing the seisin, he does not need to make a request, for he can enter the thing of which law or custom gives him the seisin, without speaking to the lord, except that if it is a fief he must pay the homage to the lord within forty days of entering into seisin.

200. A person wishing to make a complaint for ownership of real property must word his complaint differently, for he should say: "Sire, I ask for this real property which Jehan is keeping from me—or which I see Jehan holding—and the property is in such and such a place, and it belonged to so and so, and the rights to the real property belong to me for this reason." And he should state the reason and offer to prove the reason if it is denied. And also in all complaints, whatever they are, you must offer to prove the reason stated if it is denied by the other party; for a reason you put in your complaint would be invalid if it were denied and you did not prove it.

201. A person wanting to make a complaint on a contract should speak in this manner: "Sire, here is Jehan who made this contract with me," and he should describe the contract, what is was for and why; for it may or may not be that Jehan will be obliged to keep it, if he admits it or it is proved against him. And those contracts which may be broken are described in the chapter on contracts {Chapter 34}. And if the contract is in writing, he should have the writing read to the judge instead of a complaint; and this is adequately discussed in the chapter which speaks of written obligations.

202. Dower complaints are rather short, for the woman should say: "Sire, I request my dower," or "I request my dower to be divided off and separated for me from the land which belonged to this man who was my husband, which he held and took the crops from [*estoit tenans et prenans*] on the day he married me," or "which {land} passed to him by descent from his father or his mother, from his grandfather or his grandmother, during the marriage between him and me," and offer to prove what she says if a party denies it; and she should specify what share she wants, such as a half if she was the decedent's first wife, a quarter if she was his second wife, or an eighth if she was his third wife.

203. Sometimes you have to make a complaint on a question of custodianship or guardianship on behalf of minor children; and you should make the request in the following manner: "Sire, I request the custodianship,—or the guardianship if it is a father or mother, to whom the guardianship falls when one of them dies,—which I should have by right and reason [*par droit et par reson*] as the next of kin to the child on the side from which the fief descends."³ But in a request on a question of guardianship, you do not need to say that you are from the side of the family from which the real property moves, for a father gets the guardianship of real property that passes through the child's mother, and the mother of the father's; and if the guardianship passes to a more distant relative than father or mother, it is to the next of kin, and he is guardian of the real property⁴ and the possessions of the children whichever side he is from. And how custodianship and guardianship should be performed, and the difference between them, is explained in the chapter on custodianship and guardianship {Chapter 15}.

204. Now let's look at the complaints that should be made for use of force. You should say: "Sire, there is Jehan, who wrongfully and for no reason, himself or someone else at his orders, came into such and such a place and did me the following violence," and he should state the violence and all about the act, and offer to prove it was as he stated, if it is denied by the adverse party. And when he has told all about the act, he should ask to be compensated for the insult [*vilenie*] and paid for the loss, if he suffered any loss by the violence.

205. A complaint for novel disseisin must be made differently, since novel disseisin was recently created by law [*de nouvel establissement*]⁵: and you should follow the law in making your complaint. Therefore you should speak thus: "Sire, that is Jehan who has disseised me recently of such and such a thing," and he should name the thing of which he has been disseised; and if he was done violence at the disseising, he can state it in his claim; and when he has recited all the facts, he should offer to prove them if they are denied by a party, and should request to be entirely reseised.

206. The complaint made for nuisance [*tourble dessaisine*] must be made differently from the complaint for disseisin, for there is a difference between novel disseisin and nuisance. Therefore you should speak in this manner: "Sire, there is Jehan who is disturbing and preventing [*empeeche*]

my seisin in which I was without challenge," and he must describe the manner of the interdiction: such as if he has forbidden him to farm it [*qu'il n'en esploite*], or if he has threatened those who wanted to work there, or if he has had it attached[6] by the lord, or any other interdiction like these. And he must offer to prove the interdiction if it is denied by the party, and ask for the interdiction to be removed, so that he can enjoy the seisin which he had formerly been in. And force and novel disseisin and nuisance, how you should plead them and what the difference is between them, are described in the chapter which speaks of these three things {Chapter 32}.

207. Other complaints can be made which are more dangerous than the ones we have described above: these are complaints made on cases of crime. And there are several of these complaints, and they can be made in two ways: the first, by a simple complaint in the form of an accusation against the person whom you are accusing [*a qui l'en met sus*] of the crime; and in these complaints you have to become a party and speak in this manner: "Sire, that is Jehan who committed a murder, or a treason, or a homicide, or a rape, or arson, or a robbery," and he should name the occurrence of which he is accusing him and offer to prove it, if the party denies it, and ask for justice to be done.

208. The second kind of accusation is done another way, for the person accusing does not have to become a party. Instead he can speak in this manner: "Sire, I denounce Jehan, whom you see here, for such and such an act which you should avenge,[7] like a good judge; and the act is so clear and well-known [*notoires*] that there is no need for anyone to be a party against him," and he should say how the fact is clear; such as that it was done before a great company of people, or if he boasted he would do it, or in any other manner that makes the fact clear, for facts which are so clear should be avenged by the judge as part of his duties [*par l'office*], even though no one will be a party against the accused. And how you should proceed in a case of crime, whether by accusation or by denunciation, is explained in the chapter on offenses {Chapter 30}.

209. Many complaints are and can be made on many issues which we have not discussed in particular. But from those which we have spoken of you should understand that in all complaints and requests to a judge, where they concern the lord or a third party, you should state the thing you are asking for, and how much, and the reason why you want to have it, and ask

for a hearing [*que droit soit fes*] and offer to prove what you claim, if it is denied by the adverse party.

210. It happens sometimes that a person pleading does not make an outright complaint against a party, but makes a request to the lord: such as if he asks him to accept him as an enfieffed man {as a vassal}, or to release his land or his possessions which he has attached, or to place him in seisin of something he is asking for, or to have given back to him something someone has taken away from him or stolen or removed by force. In all such requests, and any others made to the lord or to a judge, the lord or the judge should make certain whether the request touches a party: such as if Pierre holds the land that Jehan is asking for, or if he attached Pierre's property at Jehan's request; and when he sees that the request touches a party, he should not grant the request until the party has been summoned. And when he appears, Pierre should repeat the request he made to the lord or the judge; and Jehan should ask the lord not to grant Pierre's request, and say why not, and Pierre should give his reasons why the lord should grant his request. And thus a suit can begin between the parties without a complaint having been made against each other, and they can win or lose as if they *had* made a complaint. And if the lord grants the request made to him without calling the party it affects, his action is invalid, and must be cancelled if a party complains about the request; for no one should suffer loss from a request made behind his back [*en derriere de lui*] until he has been heard and called into court [*apelés en jugement*].⁸ But reasonable requests which are made, which are not challenged and which no one can challenge because there is a clear custom in favor of the person making the request,—such as if you are requesting to be seised of the possessions of a decedent as an executor or an heir, or some other thing which is as clear as this,—the lord or the judge should grant such requests until there is someone who challenges them for some reason; for lords and judges should maintain what is given by clear custom until what is said against it is proved, for clear things should take precedent over murky [*orbes*] ones.

211. The customs concerning pleading in the secular courts are different from those used in the ecclesiastical courts, for in the latter you serve [*baille*] your party with your complaint in writing if it is for forty sous or more; and in some places if it is twenty sous or more. And all the pleadings are served, with a copy to the witnesses; and the whole suit is carried on in writing. But according to our custom in Beauvais we do not do any of that, for you do

not plead in writing, but you have to make your complaint or your request without writing, and repeat it each time you go to court, if a party requests it, until the pleadings are declared ready for trial [*couchiees en jugement*]. And the jurors must remember what they are to give a judgment on. But since memories fade, and it would be hard to remember so many issues as there are in many disputes, it is true that the *bailli* or the judge can write down in brief form what the parties are seeking a trial [*jugement*] on. And also if the parties have to prove several issues [*articles*] against each other, they can write down what they intend to prove; and such writings are called rubrics [*rebriches*]. And the adverse party is entitled to a copy of the rubric, if they request it, for each party must give the judge in writing what they intend to prove; and you must give the adverse party the same thing, so that if the rubrics agree, they can be given to the auditors who will hear the witnesses {Chapter 40, §1226}; and if they disagree on the rubrics, and say they are not written in consonance with the {oral} pleadings, they should be written and reconciled by the lord and the jurors who are to judge, and who were present at the pleadings; and then a day should be appointed for them to bring their witnesses and to have auditors appointed to hear their witnesses and ask them questions concerning the pleadings, on the basis of the rubrics of the pleadings, and put all this in writing. And the parties should not find out [*savoir*] anything that their witnesses say, nor what the other party's witnesses say; but the auditors should close up and seal {the record of} what is done, and bring it to trial [*apporter en jugement*]; and the duties of auditors are discussed in the chapter on auditors and examiners {Chapter 40}.

212. Sometimes someone is accused of a crime in court without there being any wish to have him brought to trial [*justiciés*],—such as when witnesses are called against me and I challenge one of them by saying he is a perjurer, or that he made peace on a serious crime without going to court [*soi espurgier*], or that he killed someone, or that he had committed some theft,—in order for him to be excluded from testifying. When such a thing occurs, if the person wanting to exclude him proves the accusation, he wins only that the witness is not heard to testify against him, unless the witness offers to defend himself by a wager of battle against the accusation of treason, theft, or some other serious crime for which you might be sentenced to death. For then the person who wants him prevented from testifying would have to prove him guilty of what he had accused him of, and then the accuser would have to become a party, in danger of losing his

life, if he did not prove it {if he did not win the battle}, as the other would be if he were found guilty. But before the wagers were given on either side, if the person who made the accusation of a serious crime to prevent a witness from testifying saw that he wanted to defend himself and be free of the accusation, the accuser could certainly withdraw on the payment of a fine for the defamation and insult he had said about him; and the fine[9] is simple. And also if the accused person wants to withdraw from being a witness, he may, if he wishes, say no more than: "If anyone wanted to be a party and accuse me, I would defend myself, but although the accusation against me is not true, I would rather refrain from testifying than enter a wager of battle." And there is still another way, for he can say to the person who called him as a witness: "I am not anxious to do battle in your suit, nor to begin pleadings in my own; and if you will defend me {fight on my behalf} I will answer truthfully, but if not I want to take no part." Then the other man must uphold [*face bon*] his witness or do without his testimony; and for the witness this is the best and the least dangerous way, for if he were accused of a crime and the person who called him as a witness could not uphold him by a wager of battle, but he or his champion was defeated, no one would be condemned to death, but he would be excluded from testifying, and the champion would have his hand cut off, if the battle was fought by a champion.[10]

213. If several plaintiffs make a complaint against someone for personal or real property, and each one asks for the whole thing, the person against whom the complaints are lodged should keep still [*demourer en pes*] until it is known who can rightly make the complaint, for it cannot be that each of several plaintiffs has the right to the same whole thing: such as if I have a horse and three men are suing me for it, and each one says it is his, I do not have to answer any of the three until they have argued [*pledié*] against each other to find out who is entitled to complain. But it would be different if each was asking for a part, and said which part, for then I would have to answer each of them concerning what he was asking for, provided the parts did not exceed the whole of what I was being asked for; for if each of them was asking for half the horse, one of them would have to be excluded before I answered, for nothing can consist of three halves. In any case I could never be required to answer several plaintiffs each of whom was asking for the whole thing, or {together} more parts than there were in the thing: namely, if I were being sued for my action or my contract, such as if I sold, or gave, or exchanged, or contracted something separately to several persons, none

of whom knew about the others. In that case each person could ask me for whatever part I had contracted to give him; and it would be right for the person to whom I had first promised the thing to take it, and afterwards I would have to give sufficient consideration to the others in return for what they had given me [*soufisant chose par retour des autres choses*]; and I would fall into ill repute, for it is not without deception [*tricherie*] to sell a whole horse to each of three persons and to receive the money from each. And what we said above about a person not having to answer several plaintiffs who are each asking for the whole of something, we also apply to cases where the person is being sued on something other than his act or his contract.

214. Some complaints are on personal property or chattels, some are on real property, and the others are against the person; and no complaint can be made which does not derive originally from one of these three. And we should know that by general custom and common law [*droit commun*],[11] complaints against the person or for personal property or chattels must be made before the lords in whose domain the persons complained against have their domicile [*sont couchant et levant*], except in certain cases,—such as when you have agreed [*obligies*][12] to have your property sued on [*justicies*] anywhere, or before the lord in whose jurisdiction they are situated, or when the complaint is for use of force or novel disseisin, which is under the cognizance of the sovereign, or when things are attached by some lord and several persons are claiming them, or when they are left in a will, or when you go to live in another place and you have left debts in the castellany you left, or when you are suing for conversion [*chose emblee*] or homicide, or when you are summoned before your lord and before the day of the appearance you take up residence in the jurisdiction of another lord,—in all these cases a person's property can come under the jurisdiction of the lords where they are situated, although you are not a resident there. In a case on real property, however, there is no doubt that the complaint must be made before the lord from which it moves {is held}, wherever your residence is.

215. As we have said that you do not answer a complaint by several plaintiffs where each plaintiff is asking for the whole, save in the cases where exceptions are allowed, you are also not obliged to answer if you are accused of a crime by several persons, until all abandon the accusation except one, who becomes the accusing party. And when several persons want to be a party and they cannot agree on {which} one of them, the lord

before whom the suit is to be should choose the most suitable to pursue the accusation, such as the person most closely involved in the dispute, and should make the others refrain, and if the accused can win against the person accusing him, no one can afterwards accuse him of the same act. And there is adequate discussion of this in the chapter on appellee's defenses {Chapter 7}.[13]

216. When a person has made his complaint requesting something before a judge, and said why he wants to have what he is asking for, and he loses what he asked for by the good reasons of the defendant, the plaintiff can never sue again for the thing he lost, even if he asked for it the second time for different reasons than he used in his first request, for it would go against the judgment; unless he had come into a new right to the thing after the trial: such as if I pleaded against someone from my lineage for some real property and lost my suit in a trial, and afterwards my relative died without heirs of his body and the real property came to me laterally as the next of kin, in such a case you can see that I had acquired a new right after the trial; and by this case you can understand others which could arise, where a new right could be created and acquired.

217. It is true that if you see you have not stated your complaint properly you can amend it whenever you want, provided it is before the pleadings are declared ready for trial [*couchiees en jugement*]; but if you complain against the defendant about a fact other than the first fact, as many times as you change the complaint the defendant has a new counsel day [*jour de conseil*]. And if I have a counsel day for a complaint against me and when I appear again in the court the complaint has been changed, it is right that I should have another counsel day, for I had to answer only on the complaint which was made to me in the cases where a counsel day can be given.

218. You should know that on all complaints on real property there should be a counsel day and afterwards an inspection day, and the same for every complaint which involves another's act, unless I am accused of having the act done, or that I procured the doing of it, for that which I command to be done is certainly my own act.

219. When someone makes a complaint against me before the lord in whose jurisdiction I am, and the plaintiff is from another jurisdiction, if I

request it he should give a surety that he will seek a hearing in the court of my lord and that he will not take me to some other court for the same matter, unless by an appeal for default of judgment or false judgment. And the surety must be sufficient and such that he comes under the easy jursidiction of my lord, before whom the plaintiff wishes to plead. But if he wants to swear by the saints that he can have no surety in this jurisdiction, he can use an adequate surety from another jurisdiction; and if he wants to swear that he cannot obtain a surety, he can merely swear that in the suit he is bringing he will seek a hearing in this court and will not take it to some other court except by the above-mentioned appeals.

220. If two or more men are making a complaint against Jehan, and one is asking for payment of a debt he owes him, such as for money lent or goods sold, and the other is asking for paymemt of a gift or a promise made to him, and Jehan does not have enough to pay the debts and promises asked of him, he should be made to pay all the debts; and afterwards, if he has anything left, he should be made to pay the agreed-on gifts and proper promises, for certain gifts and promises could be agreed on which would not be enforced: such as if it is clear that a man likes to get drunk, and when he is drunk he promises to give a hundred marks or a hundred pounds to someone and you cannot see why he would give such a gift if he were in command of himself, then such a promise is not to be enforced; and also if he makes promises when he is in a frenzy, or out of his right mind, or in prison, or because of coercion or intimidation, they are not enforced; even if his promises had been paid, he could ask for them back for reasons of deception or coercion or intimidation. And on this matter of force and intimidation, we will give a chapter later, which will speak plainly of things done by reason of force or intimidation {Chapter 33}.

221. Just as we have said that drunkenness can cancel gifts or promises, it also does so for deals and contracts in which deception is clearly seen, for otherwise deceivers who pursue drunkards in taverns to deceive them would have won everything. But in such cases you should neverthless look very closely into the act or the contract, for if there is found no clear trickery, nor too great a deception, the contracts should be enforced, so that those who bargain cannot easily use drunkenness as a defense when they have made a deal or a contract which they regret; and everyone should that drunkenness cannot be used as a defense in a serious crime.

222. A complaint which is self-contradictory is invalid, and the defendant is not obliged to answer it except to show how the complaint is self-contradictory, such as if I ask for payment of ten pounds for a horse I sold to Jehan, and afterwards ask for the horse to be given back to me because I lent it to the said Jehan, then this complaint is self-contradictory; for it cannot be that Jehan holds the same horse by purchase and on loan; then I have to decide whichever I think right, the sale or the loan; and this case is enough to show the complaints which can be made about other things which are self-contradictory.

223. If a man has several heirs who each take a share, the creditors cannot ask for payment of all the debts from one heir and leave the others alone; they must ask each of the heirs according to the quantity of possessions he took: such as if he took half the things, he must pay half the debts, and if he took more, he must pay more, and if less, less.[14]

224. In some cases, because the plaintiff cannot make a specific complaint, the defendant must answer certain questions asked of him, without whose answers the plaintiff cannot make a specific complaint: such as if I want to ask Jehan for a piece of plowland [*couture de terre*], or all of Pierre's real property, or various other things which were given or sold to me and which I am expecting to come into for some reason, and I send to ask Pierre if he holds everything I am asking for, or which part he holds, he must tell my messenger what he holds, so that I know how much I can ask him for in my pleadings. And if he will not tell him, he must be declared in default; and by his default he can lose seisin of what he holds of the property. And if he said in bad faith that he held only a half and it is clear that he held the whole thing, I must be given seisin of the half and maintain my suit on what he said he held {i.e., the other half}, for it is right for you to lose when you knowingly tell a lie about something about which you should tell the truth.

225. When a complaint is made against someone and he dies during the suit, you can sue the heirs for the suit which was commenced against their predecessor, except in cases of crime; for if the predecessor was accused of a case for which he could be condemned to death if found guilty, and he died before he was convicted, the suit is void, and the heirs take the property which passes from him; and you should not say to them: "You shall not have them because the person because of whom you have this suit com-

mitted an offense [*cil de qui vous avés cause l'ait mesfet*]," because he was not condemned in his lifetime, for you should believe each person innocent [*bons*] until the opposite is proved. You can nevertheless make a complaint against the heirs to get the real or personal property which the predecessor acquired wrongly, but not the possible death sentence [*perius du cors*] and the fines of the predecessor for offenses. For the heirs need not answer in cases where they are sued for their predecessor's offenses, except inasmuch as they are involved; but they do have to answer to creditors [*deteurs*]¹⁵ who advanced property [*crurent le leur*] to their predecessor and for the sureties their predecessor offered for credit [*detes*]; and they must discharge the sureties [*les doivent aquitier*] and pay the creditors, however little is left over for them to take, since they agreed to be heirs.

226. Plaintiffs and defendants, in any cases except those of serious crimes, must swear to tell the truth, so that the plaintiff must swear that he will ask for only that to which he believes he has a right, and that if he has to call witnesses, he will call good and honest [*loiaus*] witnesses as far as he knows; and the defendant must swear to admit to anything asked of him in the matter which is true, and that he will not knowingly put forward a defense which is not good and proper [*soufisans*], and that if he has to call witnesses to prove his defenses, he will call good and honest ones as far as he knows; and the oath the witnesses must swear is discussed in the chapter [*titre*] on proofs {Chapter 39}.

227. A plaintiff who will not swear that his complaint is true should not be admitted to complain, for he falls under the suspicion that his complaint is false. And if the defendant will not swear that the defenses he raises are true, they should not be allowed. And if the parties agreed not to swear, the judge should not permit it. His duty is to take the oaths of the parties in order to seek out the truth in the dispute, for the pleadings are at an end concerning what they agree on under oath, and the pleadings must be continued concerning what they disagree on, and the witnesses called. But the matter of oaths only concerns the courts where you are pleading according to the king's laws,¹⁶ for according to the old customs they are not required. Nevertheless if the men in the lower courts want to proceed under the old custom in small suits, in order to be able to have a wager of battle, the lord from whom they hold is showing mercy [*aumosne fet*] by not allowing them to, and by suppressing the wager and requiring the suit to be conducted according to the laws. For it is not a godly thing to allow wager

of battle in a little suit for personal or real property; but custom allows it in cases of serious crime and in other cases, even in the courts of knights, unless they are made to desist by their sovereign.

228. There are three kinds of complaints: the first are called personal, which the clerks call personal[17] actions; the second are real[18] complaints; the others are mixed, that is to say real and personal.

229. Personal complaints affect the person, such as on contracts, purchases, sales, defamation, obligations, and many other cases which can affect the person.

230. Real complaints are when you are asking for real property, such as land, woods, pasture, vines, water, jurisdiction, lordship, bakehouses, mills, houses, quit-rents, rents, and other things accounted real property.[19]

231. Mixed complaints are those which begin as personal and later become real: such as if Pierre asks Jehan for an acre of vineyard which he sold him or gave him or contracted to warrantee [*convenança a garantir*] him, such complaints are mixed, for they are personal insofar as they touch the person, and real because at the end of the complaint they involve real property.

232. The reason why we have explained this distinction is that according to our custom complaints which are purely personal must be made to the lords under whom the defendants are residents and complaints that are real or mixed must be made to the lords from whom the real property is held: and it is good to know which lord to go to if you want to make a complaint.

233. Pierre was lord of a town, and held the high justice by law on his lands and on others' lands, and Jehan had real estate in the form of rental property [*en ostises*] in the town. And two of his tenants came to him with a suit on the real property, and since Jehan had the low justice and the suit was on a real complaint, he had jurisdiction to take cognizance of this suit over who had the rights to the land. One of the parties happened to call witnesses to prove his contentions, and the other party challenged one of the witnesses and accused him of being a false witness and offered to prove him so by a wager of battle, and the witness offered to defend himself and

Jehan took the wagers. When Pierre, who had the high justice in the town, both on John's land and elsewhere (and he was quite aware of it), heard of this, he said the wager should be brought to his court because it was a case of high justice, and those who have only low justice on their land should not allow wagers of battle in their court. Jehan answered this by saying that because the suit had begun before him, and concerning the land which was held from him, although there was a wager of battle, that was how the land would be won or lost; for which reason he said the suit was real, so that he could keep it in his court. And on this issue they requested a ruling, namely in which court the wager would be held.

234. It was judged that as soon as the accusation of falsity had been made, it was a personal action, and a subdivision [*esbranchemens*] of the real suit, and it was said that cognizance of the wager of battle should go to the person having the high justice, and not to the person who had only the low justice. And for this reason they agreed that Pierre (who had the high justice) would have the wager of battle in his court, and when this was over, that is to say when the witness had been either upheld or excluded from his testimony as invalid, the suit on the land would go back to Jehan's court. And in this manner the rights of the high justice were preserved for Pierre and of the low justice for Jehan, along with the cognizance of the real complaint which was made in his court.

Here ends the chapter on complaints.

Notes

1. The pleadings, where the parties plead, are the preliminary parts of a trial. Today they are made in writing, but in Beaumanoir's time they were made orally; see §211 below. The first item is the *demande* or "complaint," which is still called a complaint in modern courts, and the complainant is also call the *demandere*. I shall use the word "plaintiff" to designate this party, and "defendant" to designate the other, called *li defenderes*. Beaumanoir uses longer expressions, such as *cil qui demande* but I shall simply translate "plaintiff." The defendant then states his *defenses* in what modern usage calls an "answer." Unless there is a counterclaim, modern pleadings stop with the answer. The plaintiff may respond to a counterclaim with a "reply." The complaint may seem more like a request, and the word *demande* fits well with that meaning. Since the modern word is "complaint," I shall generally use it even though the complaint is actually in the form of a request.

2. Many of the types of complaint enumerated in this section are the subjects of individual chapters. See the table of chapters and the index.

3. Land is said to "move" from an overlord to a lesser lord when the second holds it from the first, and from a predecessor to a successor holder.

4. A guardian who is more distant than father or mother would by definition not be holding a *fief* as a guardian, but a *vileinage*. See §§513, 516, and 517.

5. This law is from January 7th, 1277; see *Ord*. II, 542.

6. Attaching real property is rather like arresting a person.

7. "Vengeance" and "avenge" are the words commonly used to describe punishment for a crime against the person. They do not have the connotations of illegal self-help which attach to the modern usage of the word. See Romans 12:19.

8. See U.S. Constitution, 14th Amendment.

9. A simple fine is ten sous for a gentleman.

10. For this practice, see Chapter 61 §1721.

11. There is some argument as to what is meant by *droit commun* in Beaumanoir. It may mean Roman law (as contained in the *Corpus Juris Civilis*) or that the custom is the same in the whole of France. In the latter case, the expression *coustume general* which is used in this same sentence and linked to *droit commun* by the word *et* 'and' must be a synonym for *droit commun*.

12. For example, by a clause in a contract. *Obligies* and *justicies* in this sentence show an unusual form (probably Picard dialect) of the past participle feminine plural, which would normally be *obligiees* and *justiciees*. But compare *marie* in §503.

13. An accusation of a crime is termed an appeal, so that even in the court of first instance the accused is an appellee.

14. Heirs who inherited personal property had to pay the decedent's debts; but they could also refuse this inheritance, and avoid paying any debts. See §368.

15. *Deteurs*, which ought to mean "debtors" clearly means "creditors, persons to whom money is due." This meaning is confirmed by F. Godefroy, *Dictionnaire de l'ancienne langue française et de tous ses dialectes du XIe au XVe siècle*, 10 vols. (Paris, 1880–1902) 2: 685 s.v. Deteor. For a paragraph where *deteur* and *creancier* are used indifferently of the same person, see §527.

16. Law of 1260, *Ord*. I, 86.

17. From the Latin *persona* 'a person.'

18. From the Latin *res* 'a thing.'

19. For definitions of real and personal property, see Chapter 23, especially §§671–673.

7. Answers

Here begins the seventh chapter of this book which speaks of the defenses which are called exceptions, which defendants can raise against the complaints made against them, and on replies and denials.

235. In the previous chapter we spoke of the complaints that plaintiffs can make. It is right for us to speak in this following chapter of the defenses which the defendant can raise, if he has them, against the complaint made against him; and these defenses are called exceptions. And we will speak of the arguments the plaintiff puts forward to destroy the defendant's defenses, and these are called replies.

236. We should know that all the arguments advanced to defend oneself come down to one of two things: namely {first of all} those arguments made to postpone [*alongier*] the complaint made against you, and these arguments are called *dilatory* exceptions. To say dilatory exceptions is the same as saying arguments which serve only to delay the suit. And {second of all} the arguments which come down to the other purpose are called *peremptory* exceptions. By these peremptory exceptions we mean the arguments which are so powerful by themselves that the whole dispute can be won through them, and they are called peremptory because they make the complaint perish.

237. Let us see first what the arguments are whose only effect is to delay the dispute: when someone says in his defense that he was not properly summoned, for which reason he will not answer; or when someone has won seisin, and before he has been reseised of all the things of which he was disseised, someone lodges a complaint against him on ownership, and he will not respond until he has been entirely reseised; or when someone is complained against [*emplediés*] concerning real property, or some other thing, and he asks for a counsel day or an inspection day, in cases where an inspection day can be had; or when you ask for a first day to make proof and

a second day when you cannot bring all your witnesses to the first day; or when you take a continuance or an adjournment sine die, in cases where they are permitted by custom;[1] or when you challenge the judge for some suspicion you raise, or because the defendant says he should not be the judge in this suit, but another lord should [*ançois se fet requerre par autre seigneur*]; or when you challenge attorneys by speaking against their letter of appointment, or by saying that the suit is the kind which should not be pursued through a lawyer, that is, that an attorney is not heard for the plaintiff; or when the plaintiff is claiming debt or contract, and the defendant alleges an extension, or that the due date has not yet come; or when someone says he is a minor, so that he will not answer; or when the defendant says that the plaintiff complained against him with this same complaint in another court, and he will not answer; or when the king or the pope gives an extension for debts for the good of Christianity and the defendant alleges this extension; or when the suit is delayed because one of the parties is suing for default of judgment or false judgment. For all such arguments that the defendant raises, the dispute can be delayed but not lost; and by many other arguments also, which you can recognize by those which are stated above, which are only used to delay suits; and they are all called dilatory exceptions.

238. The arguments on which the whole dispute hangs, and which are called peremptory exceptions, are quite different: such as when I am sued for a hundred pounds which were lent to me, and I allege payment or substantial payment [*qui le touche*]; or if I am sued on a contract, and I say I performed it or I simply deny it; or if I am asked for a piece of real property, and I say it came to me as a direct heir by descent from my predecessor, or if I raise the defense of long tenure without challenge which means I do not have to answer, or if I show a writing saying that what is being asked of me should remain mine; or if I am being asked for something and I say that I bought it from a person able to sell it, or was given it by a person whose it was to give, or I exchanged it with someone empowered to exchange it. All these and similar arguments are peremptory exceptions, for each one separately, provided it is proved, is enough for the defendant to be rid of the complaint made against him.

239. A person wishing to allege arguments which serve only to delay the suit should raise them before raising those which can make the whole suit end [*perir*], or he would have waived them: such as if I denied the

complaint and afterwards wanted a counsel day or an inspection day, or alleged an extension or due date, or requested another judge, it would be too late, for I would have proceeded so far that nothing would be left except to hear the plaintiff's witnesses. And what we said about denial {being a waiver} is also true for other arguments raised to show why what is asked of us should remain ours, for the suit is commenced on the main issue [*le tout*] so that you cannot come back to the reasons you may have to delay the suit. Nevertheless, certain dilatory arguments can be raised later, such as challenges to witnesses, requesting days to call witnesses [*producions*], continuances and adjournments for bona fide reasons, allegations of force, or intimidation, or threats: all such arguments can certainly be raised after you have given a plain answer in the suit, along with others which can come about during the suit, which can come about by the way the suit goes [*par l'aparance du plet*].

240. All arguments, whether dilatory or peremptory, must be raised before the deliberation begins [*avant que le jugemens soit enchargiés*], for once the jurors have received the pleadings [*paroles*] of the parties and the latter have declared them ready for judgment [*il se sont apuié a droit*], they cannot add or take away anything, except for reasons which could arise during the jury's deliberation, such as if I had claimed that the land belonged to me as a custodian,[2] and my opponent said he was the custodian, and the child died during the deliberation, I could discharge the jurors from the judgment they had to make and tell them not to give a judgment on the custodianship I had raised but on the lateral succession which I took while they were deliberating. And the jurors would be rid of the deliberation on custodianship and the suit would be on lateral succession. And from a case like this you can see that you can raise timely new arguments after the deliberation has been commenced, but this means when they arise while the suit is in progress.

241. It is true that if I ask in my complaint for some real property because I say I bought it, and the defendant raises an argument why I should not have it, and the decision is against me, I cannot ask for this land because of purchase or for any other reason during the suit; but after I had lost it by a judgment, another reason might arise for me to be able to ask for it, such as if it were given or sold to me or exchanged, or I took it as an heir at someone's death; and if I asked for it for any of these reasons I could not be told that I was going against the judgment, because I would be asking

for it for new reason which had arisen after the judgment. If I asked for it for the arguments I could have raised before the decision, or for those on which the judgment was given, I would be going against the judgment; and I should not be heard; and I would pay a penalty to the lord, which is sixty pounds for a gentleman residing [*qui mandroit*] on his fief and sixty sous for a commoner residing on his villeinage.

242. There is a good defense for an heir who is being asked to pay a penalty for his father's or his predecessor's misconduct, for he does not have to answer, nor does he for any case of crime that could be brought up against them, because they were not found guilty during their lifetimes. And it may be believed that if they had been accused they would have been better able to defend themselves and with more certainty than their heirs could do it for them, and it should be believed that all those who die before they are condemned for serious crimes, or before they pay a penalty for misconduct, although they died while the suit was in progress, die pardoned for the misconduct for which they were being tried, as far as this world is concerned, and the heir is not obliged to carry on the suit as he would have if it had been for personal or real property or for contract. For the heir would have to answer on these issues, and concerning all the things an heir was sued for because his predecessor had acquired them improperly he would have to answer for the portion he had taken, and if he could not raise the defenses of unchallenged possession or the fact that his predecessor had good reason to hold the property, he would lose what he had taken, and the income from the property since the death of his predecessor; but he would not have to give back anything earned by his predecessor unless the latter had been sued while still alive; for if he had been sued in his lifetime, and died while the suit was in progress, and his heir kept fighting the suit and lost, the heir would have to give back the earnings from his predecessor's time and his own; and if there are several heirs, each one need only answer for as much of the improperly acquired property as he took. But once they have admitted to being heirs, they are liable for all of their predecessor's debts, however much property they took.

243. All complaints and all arguments raised by the defendant against the complaint, and all the arguments the plaintiff raises (called replies) to destroy the defendant's arguments, must be proved if they are denied by the adverse party. And if the allegations are not proved, they are invalid, and are nullified [*esteinte*] as if they had never been spoken.

244. All arguments raised for adjudication [*proposees en jugement*], whether by the plaintiff or the defendant, and which are not challenged by the adverse party by denial, or by arguments as to why they should not be valid, are taken as true and proved; and judgment should be given on the arguments raised when they have not been challenged by a party.

245. A person being asked for something lent him or contracted from him, cannot if he denies the fact go back after his denial and allege payment or some other reason why he should be considered not liable, if the thing lent or the contract he denied can be proved against him; for inasmuch as he denies, he claims that the thing was never done, and inasmuch as he alleges payment afterwards, he admits the thing was done; so that he is contradicting himself.

246. You should know that according to the custom of the secular courts there should be no waiting period for things which have come to judgment unless the judgment has been appealed: all judgments should be executed without delay. Nevertheless some cases must be excepted, such as cases which arise out of bad luck or misadventure. It is not a mistake to put off the judgment until you know whether the sovereign will want to have mercy. And also when a woman is condemned to death by a judgment and she says she is pregnant and she can be seen to be of an age when it might be true, or when she is visibly pregnant, the judgment should not be made nor executed until she has been imprisoned long enough to have the child or for it to be known that she lied. And also judgments made on security given or for life interests [*rentes a vie*] cannot be executed because the due date is in the future; and it is sufficient in that case to give seisin to the person who won the judgment.

247. When an admission is made in court, what was admitted cannot later be denied, even if the admission was made outside the suit [*hors plet*], for if it were made in the street outside the trial, the adverse party could use it to his advantage by proving it had been admitted before good people {credible witnesses}.

248. There is no reservation {of defenses} in the secular courts as there is in the ecclesiastical courts, for in the latter they can plead one of their arguments and reserve the right to raise the other arguments if the first one should fail, and they may have judgment on the first one before raising the

others if they wish. But you cannot do this in the secular courts, once you have answered the complaint and the suit has commenced on the main issue [*sur toute la querele*]. But it is true that as long as you are raising dilatory exceptions, that is the arguments that are only used to delay the suit, you can make reservations; for example if I say of the complaint made against me: "I claim an inspection day by law; and if the law says I do not have an inspection day, I reserve the right to make my arguments," in such a case a reservation is valid. For if I raised the arguments whose only purpose is to delay the suit (called dilatory exceptions) and at the same time the arguments on the main issue (called peremptory exceptions) I would have waived the dilatory exceptions. And for this reason there is a reservation as long as the dilatory exceptions last; but when all the dilatory exceptions are over, and you have to answer on the main issue and raise your peremptory exceptions, you should raise them all and keep nothing back, and ask for a judgment on each argument one after the other, for once you have raised your peremptory arguments in court you cannot add any others by making a reservation. And for this reason it is said that in the secular courts you only argue once.

249. We call arguing [*barroier*] the arguments that one party raises against the other when the dilatory exceptions are over, as when each party raises arguments in law or fact or custom to support his allegations [*conforter s'entencion*]. And you can argue dilatory exceptions several times, for example if I say I should have a counsel day and give a reason, and the adverse party says I should not and gives reasons why not, and each person raises several arguments; this is how you plead dilatory exceptions. And as we have shown you can plead on a counsel day, you can also argue other dilatory exceptions, when one person who is seeking a delay says why he should have it and the adverse party challenges it and says he should not have it. And when these issues [*barres*] are being decided, the principal issue of the dispute is in abeyance; the judgment is on whether the party seeking the delay will have it or not, and if he does not win the decision, he is still in good time to answer on the main issue.

250. No argument raised by either party in which an open lie is patent should be accepted in a trial: for example if I ask for a piece of land and say I took it by descent from my father, and it is well known that my father never had any land, the person pleading against me on the land needs raise no other exception than my lie; so he can say: "Sire, he says he has rights in the

land from his father; order an inquest; you will find that his father never owned any land." Then if the plaintiff does not prove that his father did own land, his complaint is refused and the defendant is cleared. And from this lie you can understand the others which are brought to trial according to what the cases are.

251. It is not right or godly that long trials and great costs be devoted to small disputes. And this is what we have done as a *bailli*: when some suit begins on a small matter, one party against another, and the plaintiff offers to the other party that he will swear on the saints that things are as he says they are (or that if the defendant wants to swear the opposite the plaintiff will declare himself satisfied), we have obliged the defendant to choose which he prefers: either to believe the plaintiff on his oath or to swear his own oath that the complaint is false; and if they pursued the suit such an oath would be sworn if one of the parties requested it; and if one of the parties wants to drop the suit and believe the adverse party on his oath, we do not agree that it should be refused.

252. It can happen that you pay Pierre what you owed Jehan, because you thought it was owed to Pierre, or because you thought Pierre was still Jehan's agent and administering Jehan's affairs, or because Pierre had an agreement to take it to Jehan: in all such cases and ones like them you can sue Pierre for what you gave him. If Pierre admits receiving it or it is proved against him, he must give it back.

253. And it also happens sometimes that you think you owe something and you do not. Thus if I think I owed Pierre ten pounds which I do not owe him, and I give him ten pounds as payment, and afterwards I realize I did not owe him, I could ask for them back, and he should give them back unless he can prove that I owed him and that he accepted them for a good reason.

254. A good argument was raised by a man who did not want to bring back to the hotchpot[3] the portion he was given on his marriage by both his father and mother when only one of them died; but he did want to bring back what he took from the parent who had died. And to make this clearer: if my father and mother make me a marriage gift from their common personal property, and afterwards my father dies and I want to share in what he left, I am obliged to bring back only half of the personal property I

took, because my mother who is still alive warrants me the other half as long as she lives. And the same thing happens when they give me a gift from the real property they acquire during the marriage [*leur conquès*]. But if I receive as a marriage gift some real property from my father, I must bring it all back to the distribution, if I want to participate in it; and if my marriage gift came from my mother's real property, I need bring nothing back until she dies.

255. Since the custom is that a person given a marriage gift by his father and mother can (if he wants) refuse to bring back the gift, and not participate in the distribution (unless the gift made to him was too outrageous and deprived the other heirs too much), if my father and mother have given me a marriage gift, and either my father or mother dies, and I don't want to declare myself satisfied, but want to bring back the gift and participate in the distribution because I see that this will be to my advantage, and then afterwards, when I have brought back and shared in the hotchpot, the other parent dies and I don't want to bring back and share, perhaps because the father who died first had a big estate so that I profited by bringing back, and my mother who died second had a small estate so that I would lose by bringing back,—now let's see whether I can be permitted to abstain {from the second hotchpot} or if I will have to bring back for the distribution whether I want to or not, at the request of the other heirs. In my opinion, I say that when I brought back and shared at the death of my father I waived the custom of not bringing back; and for this reason I must bring back after the death of my mother, whether I want to or not, if the other heirs and I disagree.

256. A good exception was raised by the plaintiff against the lord who wanted a trial sent back down to his court,[4] when he said that the defendant had already answered his complaint and begun the suit by denying and admitting and raising contrary facts to counter his complaint, for it should be known that suits are commenced by the answer, which is why the lord does not have to send the suit back down [*ne rent pas sa court*].

257. There are two kinds of denial made in secular courts, each of which is adequate: the first is to deny directly and simply what is proposed against you, and the second is to propose contrary facts against what the adverse party says and offer to prove them. For it is the same as a denial if a man asks me to give back a shoed horse which he lent me and I reply: "Sire, he sold

me the horse he is asking for for such and such a sum and I offer to prove it." The words of this defense contain a denial of the loan, and I do not have to answer the loan issue directly since I make this other exception. By this case you can understand many others; and it must not be said that the complaint should count as admitted to, because I did not make a denial, if I answered with a contrary fact to the complaint made to me and offered to prove it, for this is the same as a denial.

258. A party should not be found in default for not having his witnesses, or his counsel, or his advocates because of the actions of his adverse party; and when such a complaint comes into court, the party who maliciously or by force, or through threats or for money or requests, takes away from the other party what they need, should be forced to give back to the other party the help they have taken away; and if it is witnesses who do not dare come because they were threatened, they count for the person who wanted to call them as if they had testified for him, for the person who kept them away should suffer this loss.

259. A good exception was raised by the defendant who did not want to answer concerning a writing which was brought to trial against him until he had seen it and had time to read, to see if he would admit it as genuine or say it was false. But it is true that a plaintiff who wants to make use of a writing need not give it to the defendant unless he wants; but he should give it to those holding the court and they, when they have read it, can and should give it to the defendant and order him to give it back again right away without any damage.

260. A person with several arguments, whether against the defendant or against the plaintiff, should say the arguments he likes least to start with and the best ones at the end, and each one in as few words as possible, provided the whole argument is stated; for a few words are better remembered than a great number, even in a court where the suit is not in writing. And you should state the best arguments last because people remember the last arguments better than the first. Nevertheless the jurors would be crazy [*fou*] if they did not remember all the arguments on which they have to give a judgment, for otherwise they could not give judgments well and in good conscience. And if they do not remember them well from hearing them once, they should have them repeated so many times that they do remember them; then they can make an honest judgment.

261. We have seen a ruling [*nous avons veu jugier*] that no one has to bring a writing or a charter or a record [*erremens*] which are against him, unless he agreed to do so; and this agreement must be proved if the person who does not want to bring the writing or the record tries to deny it, or unless it is a joint writing or record, such as writings which are made for a property distribution [*pour parties*] or orders by several people, for such writings must be brought into court by whoever has them when any of those for whom they were made has need of them.

262. The man received good counsel who did not want to answer a complaint because he was in prison, before he was released from prison, for no one {in prison} needs to answer except for a case of crime. But in a case of crime he has to answer on the case for which he was put in prison, and no other, until he is found not guilty [*espurgiés*] of that one. Nevertheless, along with crimes we make an exception for cases involving the king and those who hold directly from him against their vassals, and the cases we mentioned in the chapter before this one; for in cases which involve them such as for debts or misconduct, even though they are not as serious as cases of crime, they can keep defendants in prison until the debts are paid or until the penalties for the offenses are set and paid according to the offense, unless they have renounced this right by a privilege. For all lords should rule their subjects according to their own or their predecessors' privileges, unless they have acted in contradiction to the privileges for so long that they are destroyed; for many privileges are curtailed because people have been allowed to act in contravention to them for as long as is needed to acquire property, that is, according to our custom, thirty years against the church, and ten years against laypersons, and forty years religious house against religious house when the suit is in a secular court. And those who have no privilege are still in the jurisdiction and under the customs of the castellanies where they reside.

Here ends the chapter on exceptions and replies.

Notes

1. For continuances and adjournments see Chapter 3.
2. The custodian looks after the land in the interest of a minor child. See Chapter 15.

3. On bringing back to the hotchpot, see Chapter 14, especially §480. The word "hotchpot" is commonly used in modern American law to designate the augmented estate of a decedent in which earlier gifts to beneficiaries (for example, gifts to children on their emancipation or marriage) have been included or "brought back." A beneficiary who has received during the life of the decedent more than s/he would take if s/he brought it back in and then received a fair share of the hotchpot can (ignoring any moral considerations) benefit more by retaining the gift and refusing to participate in the partition.

4. This might happen if a plaintiff brought a suit in a court higher than the lowest one having jurisdiction. See Chapter 10.

8. Latecomers

Here begins the eighth chapter of this book which speaks of those who come too late to make their complaint according to our custom.

263. Those persons wishing to make a complaint in court against a party should know that it is possible to appear too late to make a complaint, for there is a time established after which you can lose your {chance} to complain because of the time which has elapsed; and we will say how.

264. If a man sues another for personal property or chattels, whether there is a writing or not, and he has refrained from making his request for the space of twenty years since the debt was due, the person being asked for the things need not answer unless the plaintiff has a good reason [*resnable cause*] why he let the time pass without suing. And there are several such reasons as you will hear.

265. The first reason is that the plaintiff has been out of the district on a crusade, or prisoner of the Saracens, or sent abroad for the public good or at the order of the sovereign, and he came to court to make his complaint within a year and a day of his return.

266. The second reason is if his father or his predecessor contracted the business {for which the debt is due} and then died, leaving him a minor and he did not have a tutor [*tuteur*] who would take care of the debt for him, and within a year and a day of reaching his majority he appeared in court and made his complaint.

267. The third reason is if the defendant has been out of the district or in prison, so that he could not be summoned for the debt.

268. The fourth reason is if the defendant has been in such poverty that he could not pay, but an order for payment was obtained before the twenty years had passed.

269. The fifth reason is that the defendant was a minor and he is being sued for a debt of his ancestor so that twenty years had passed before he came of age and could be sued.

270. A person wanting to make use of the reasons listed above to force someone to answer him beyond the twenty-year period must account for all of the twenty years, for if he only got rid of ten of them, and there remained ten in which the complaint could have been made, it would not avail him.

271. The waiting time for real property is not as long, by our custom, for if a man sues another for real property, and the defendant can show ten years of unchallenged tenure, where the plaintiff saw it and knew about it, and was living in the area and not a minor, and could have sued for the thing if he wanted and he did not for ten years, the occupant is not obliged to answer the complaint, unless the plaintiff can eliminate the time [*corrompre la teneure*] for a valid [*vive*] reason, as is described above.

272. When divisions of property [*parties*] are made between brothers, or between sisters, or between brothers and sisters, by their family [*amis*] or by a judge, and they do not complain [*se suefrent . . . pesiblement*] about their share for a year and a day, the division should stand and not be called in question later.

273. Pierre sued Jehan for a hundred pounds for a piece of land he said he had sold his father and never been paid for, according to him; and since Jehan was the heir and was in possession of the land, Pierre asked the judge to make the said Jehan pay the aforesaid hundred pounds.

274. Jehan answered that he did not want to be made to pay what was asked, for he said that his father, after being seised of the land he bought, lived nearly a year, and Pierre saw it and knew it; and they lived in the same town, and it was hard to believe that Pierre would have disseised himself of his land without receiving any money or a good surety, when he did not ask him for anything for that year. Jehan also said that when his father felt ill, he had his will announced in public in the parish [*en plaine paroisse*], saying that whoever he owed should come forward and he would pay him, and Pierre saw this and knew it, and never did the said Pierre come forward to ask for payment of his debt. Jehan said also that after his father's death he had held this piece of land which was in dispute for nearly a year, and was

never before sued for it; for which reasons he did not wish to have to answer the said Pierre. These reasons having been admitted [*conneues*], they requested a judgment.

275. It was judged that Jehan did not have to answer Pierre's complaint for this debt for the reasons given above. And by this you can understand that you can indeed come too late to make a complaint.

Here ends the chapter of those who come too late to make their complaint.

9. Inspections

Here begins the ninth chapter of this book which speaks of the cases in which an inspection day may be given, and those in which it may not.

276. It is true that every time that seisin or ownership of real property [*eritage*] is sued on, the person seised of the property must have an inspection day if he requests it. But if he begins the suit[1] without asking for an inspection day, he cannot have it later; for a counsel day and an inspection day must be requested before a suit is begun, and the suit is not begun by asking for a counsel day, nor an inspection day, nor an advisory day, in the cases where they should be given.

277. Pierre sued Jehan saying that the said Jehan had had his personal property [*muebles*] and chattels [*chateus*] attached outside the castellany of Clermont, and outside the count's lands, by the king's men; and because he was a resident under the count, and the cognizance of his suits for personal property and chattels belonged to the count, he asked for the said Jehan to be made to release [*desarester*] them, as he was ready to answer in the count's court for whatever Jehan wanted to sue him for.

278. Jehan requested an inspection day of the place where the personal property had been attached, and Pierre contested it because he said that in a suit for personal property and chattels there is no inspection day; and they requested a ruling on whether there was an inspection day or not.

279. It was judged there was no inspection day, and by this judgment you can see that in a suit for personal property or chattels only there is no inspection day. And by this judgment you can see that if you joined your request for personal property and chattels with a request for real property [*eritage*], such as if Pierre had said: "I ask Jehan for such and such a piece of land which he is holding wrongfully and the personal property and chattels

which are on the property—*or which have been derived* [issu] *from the property*," Jehan would have an inspection day if he requested it, for he would not have to answer concerning the personal property and the chattels until he had lost the case on the land.

280. Each time a person wants to sue for personal property or chattels, he must say why the thing should be his. And if he says the reason is dependent on the ownership of real property, and the real property is held by someone other than the plaintiff, and it is not admitted to be the plaintiff's property, his complaint is worthless, because first he must sue on the land on which the personal property depends, before anyone has to answer concerning the personal property. And when he has won on the real property, he can sue for the personal property and the arrears.[2] And if it were not so, everyone would want to sue just on the personal property, because custom allows more delay in suits on real property than in suits for personal property, and thus the suits would be back to front, which is not to be allowed if a party contests it. But if the party does not contest it, but answers the complaint on the question of personal property and chattels, the judge should hear the pleadings and give a trial according to the arguments of the two parties, for a person can waive what he could have taken advantage of; and once he has answered and begun the suit [*plet entamé*] on the complaint made against him, he cannot raise a defense which would relieve him of having to answer, because it is too late once the suit has been begun [*entamés*].

281. A defendant in the secular court should be careful, once the dilatory exceptions are over, and he has to answer on the main issue, to raise all his peremptory exceptions, if he has several, and to ask for judgment on them one after another, for if he asks for judgment on {just} one and the judgment is against him, he can no longer raise the others; instead, he loses the dispute, even if he had reserved the right to raise the others if the judgment were against him, for once you have declared the main issue ready for judgment [*couchiés en jugement*] any reservation is too late. And if it were otherwise, suits would be too long and it would be a bad thing if someone demanded payment of a debt from Pierre and Pierre alleged payment, and the payment was denied, and he offered to prove it, and he failed to make a proof, if he could say afterwards: "I never owed that debt," or: "He forgave me that debt," or: "He cancelled that debt," for in that way the suits would always be starting over.

282. When a defendant raises defenses which contradict each other, the judge should not accept them, even if the other party was so stupid as not to contest them: such as if Jehan asked Pierre to pay him twenty pounds he owed him for a horse, which he had delivered to him, and Pierre answered: "I don't owe you anything, for I never had a horse from you, and {as for} the twenty pounds you are asking for, I am ready to show that I have already paid them." These two defenses that Pierre raised in his answer would contradict each other: for how would he prove payment if he denied the debt was owed? In such a case the judge would have to force Pierre to abandon one of these defenses, and say: "Sire, I never had the horse, not did anyone in my name, so that I do not owe this debt," or else say: "Sire, I had the horse and owed the twenty pounds, but I made full payment." And by this contradiction we have described which the judge should not accept, you can understand, if you have any common sense [*sens naturel*], all other cases which contain a contradiction.

283. If someone is assigned an inspection day, the person making the inspection must be accompanied at the inspection by someone sent by the court to oversee the inspection; so that, if there is a disagreement about the inspection, it can be recalled from memory by the person who was sent. And for this repetition, one person is sufficient who is credible and sent by the court, or an officer under oath, because an inspection day does not win or lose a dispute, but is a delay permitted by custom to clarify what the dispute is about.

284. If the plaintiff who is to furnish the inspection defaults {is not there}, the suit must be brought again and another inspection day given, if the defendant requests it.[3] And if the plaintiff who is to furnish the inspection is ready to furnish an adequate inspection, and the person who is to receive the inspection defaults, the inspection is counted as done; for it is in the power of the person who can have an inspection day to ask for it or waive it, and proceed without an inspection. And it is right, if he requested it and did not go and receive it, that the other party, who was ready to furnish it, should not be delayed in his suit because of the default of the person who should have received the inspection.

285. We saw a suit where Pierre was asking Jehan to assign [*asseïst*] ten pounds' worth [*livrees*][4] of land which he was supposed to assign him from

his own land, and also asked for the arrears, since he had been under the obligation to assign him the land for five years.

286. To this Jehan answered: "I admit that I agreed to assign you ten pounds' worth of land from my own land five years ago, and I offered to do it then and there, and there has not been a year since when I have not been ready to do so if you had asked me to as you are doing now; and I am ready to assign you the land. But the fifty pounds you are asking for in arrears I am not obliged to give you, for you did not deliver the land to me for a lease [*a ferme*], nor for rent [*a louage*], nor under any agreement whereby I am required to give you money. And until the land is assigned to you and you are seised of it, I can take the profits from it as from my own land, and I owe you nothing but land, and I will pay you in land. And I want to be clear of any payment because the delay was not caused by my failure to make the payment, but in your failure to take delivery of it." And on this issue they asked for a judgment.

287. It was judged that Pierre would not get the money for the arrears but merely have the land assigned to him. And by this judgment you can see that you can lose by delaying your request for what you are entitled to, for if the land had been inspected and handed over and delivered to the said Pierre the first year, and Jehan had subsequently entered on to the land, he would have been liable for the arrears; and he would also have been liable for them if he had been in default in assigning the land.

288. When an inspection day is given to a party requesting it and the inspection cannot be made on that day for some good reason,—such as if the person furnishing the inspection takes an adjournment sine die for some valid legal excuse, or such as if the land is covered with water or snow, or the weather is such that it is dangerous to go into the fields, or the lord who is going (or sending an observer) to observe the inspection defaults or has a legal excuse,—in all such cases another inspection day must be assigned as many times as the impediments [*essoine*] occur. But in all this neither party loses anything except that the suit is prolonged.

289. Some inspections should be carried out as soon as the lord hears of the problem, without permitting a suit between the parties; such as when someone complains about an obstruction of public land,—for example a

road or a fountain or a well that has been blocked or narrowed, or the course of a river where someone wants access to the water [*point d'eaue*],— in all such cases the sovereign lord who holds directly from the king should not permit a suit between the parties. Instead, as soon as someone complains, the lord who is to settle the matter should announce an inspection day, and inform the person who must have caused the obstruction to be there; and afterwards, whether the person is there or not, if the lord sees that the obstruction is recent, he should have it removed and the place put back in the state it was in before the obstruction. And the person causing the obstruction must pay a penalty of sixty sous, for such obstructions involve novel disseisin {see Chapter 32}; and the reason why the lord should act in the above-said manner is because he has in his authority the preservation of public property for the public good.

290. It happens sometimes that the person furnishing an inspection shows[5] more or less than he should; and when he shows what he should and more along with it, the inspection is not on that account invalid, for the person furnishing the inspection can remove what was excessive on the day of the pleadings. And we have seen this approved in a judgment. And when you show less than you should, the person receiving the inspection can lose only what is shown. And when someone shows a part of what he is asking for in the suit, and another piece of real property along with it by mistake, the inspection is not on that account invalid as regards what was supposed to be shown and was shown, and the inspection of the surplus which was not part of the suit should be counted as a nullity.

291. An inspection day can be assigned in cases other than ownership of real property: such as when you are pleading on seisin or possession of land only, or for a partition required by the court. And such suits should have an inspection day.

292. If the witnesses, who are called to prove some issue in the suit for which an inspection day was given, request to see the place, they should have an inspection day, for they cannot testify as well or as certainly before the inspection as after it.

293. Each time witnesses are examined and they are asked a question they are not prepared to answer, if they ask for a day to prepare they should have it, provided they swear they are not prepared. And this preparation

should be from one day to the next unless it must be extended for some good reason stated by the witness, and the person hearing the witnesses should look into the reason, as we will explain in the chapter on auditors {Chapter 50}. And in speaking of this delay which the witnesses are allowed, we mean in inquests and suits which are conducted in accordance with the king's law, for according to the old custom there is no delay for proving what must be proved, but the proof must be made on the first day; and suits where there can be a wager of battle are also an exception. And of this we will not speak until we write a chapter on it, which will discuss appeals and how you should proceed in a suit where there is a wager of battle {Chapters 61 and 62}.

Here ends the chapter on inspection days and preparation days.

Notes

1. That is, by giving an answer. Once you have answered, you lose your right to raise dilatory exceptions. See Chapter 7 §239.

2. The arrears would be the personal property, or profits such as for sale of crops, derived from the land while it was wrongfully held.

3. It is the defendant who is entitled to an inspection, namely, to have shown to him exactly what it is the plaintiff is suing him for. Since this is generally land of which the defendant is in seisin, or possession, the plaintiff will be showing the defendant what the defendant is occupying at the time.

4. The land here is measured by the annual revenue, ten pounds, not by size or quality. This is made plain when the arrears are calculated as fifty pounds over a five-year period in the next section. See also Chapter 27.

5. The person making the inspection is pointing out to the other party and the jurors what he claims to be his, hence he "shows" it. If it turns out that the defendant, to whom the land was shown, loses his suit, the plaintiff will get only what he "showed" even if he claimed more. One imagines that the result of this rule is that the person "showing" will err on the side of exaggeration!

10. Superior Jurisdiction

Here begins the tenth chapter of this book which speaks of the cases in which the count of Clermont is not obliged to return cognizance to his vassals, but retains it for reasons of sovereignty.

294. For those who hold as freely as directly from the king,—and especially for my lord, who is a son of the king of France and count of Clermont,—it is a good thing to know when they should comply with the requests of their subjects {to have cases sent down to lower courts} and when they should keep cognizance for themselves, so that they maintain their rights but do not do wrong to their vassals; and for this reason, we discuss in this chapter [*partie*] the cases where the count has cognizance before his vassals, and before the vassals of his vassals, without sending the case back down to their cognizance, so that he can know clearly which cases he should send down and which not, and so that his men will know which cases they should ask to be sent down and which not.[1]

295. All those who hold fiefs in the county of Clermont have in their fiefs both high and low justice, and jurisdiction over their vassals, except where the count has it, such that in cases where the vassal complains concerning his overlord for default of judgment, the case is not sent down, but the overlord must answer in the count's court; and if he is defeated, he will lose the suit, if he is a party, and will pay a fine to the count of sixty pounds; and if the vassal who complains is a gentleman and he cannot defeat his overlord, he must pay a fine to the count of sixty pounds and will be sent down to his overlord's court, where he will be fined sixty pounds for suing his overlord in the count's court; and the fine is sixty pounds, and then his case on the main issue will be tried by his peers in his lord's court, to which his case has been sent down; and if he is a commoner who cannot defeat his lord for default of judgment before the sovereign, the fine is at the will of the lord to whose court he is sent down, excepting the death penalty:

this means that, if the lord wishes, the vassal has lost all he holds from him and the sovereign receives a fine of sixty pounds because he complained against his lord.

296. The second reason why the case is not sent down is if it is an appeal to the count's court for false judgment in the court below [*en leur court commune*], whether the appellant is in his jurisdiction or not.

297. The third reason why the case is not sent down but stays in the count's court for reasons of sovereignty is if some gentleman is summoned to the count's court to answer concerning a writing, even though he is a resident under some other gentleman, then the cognizance of the writing belongs to the sovereign lord, and in the summons the sovereign should enforce the contents of the letter to the extent that, if the writing is sealed with the seal of the person summoned, he should have fifteen days at least before his appearance. And the person serving the summons should speak as follows: "Pierre, you are summoned to appear against Jehan fifteen days from today in Clermont, concerning your writing." And then the person summoned cannot take a continuance [*contremander*] but he can take an adjournment *sine die* [*essoinier*] one time if he has a legal excuse.[2] And if he was summoned simply,—so that the person serving ths summons did not say: "I summon you to answer concerning your writing," but said: "I summon you to answer on whatever Jehan asks you," he could take three continuances for fifteen days each and the fourth time take an adjournment if he had a legal excuse, and he would have to swear his excuse was legal, if requested to do so by a party, at his first appearance in court after the adjournment. And for this reason it is right for the person serving the summons not to be negligent in naming the reason why he is giving the summons, whatever reason it may happen to be, for if he summons him to answer on the writing there is no continuance as described above. If he summons him to answer on an agreement for personal property or chattels without a writing, he can still not take any continuance, but the lord where he is a resident can have the case sent down if he asks for it before it is commenced before the sovereign. If he summons him for novel disseisin, for nuisance [*nouvel tourble*], or for redemption [*rescousse d'eritage*], or on dower, or a serious crime or a guaranteed peace, he cannot take a continuance on any of these cases, but he can take an adjournment sine die one time if he has a legal excuse.

298. The fourth reason why the case is not sent down is if someone has made an agreement in a writing sealed by the sovereign, such as the king, or the count, or in a writing sealed with the *bailli*'s court seal.

299. The fifth reason why the case is not sent down is if someone wants to have a truce or a guaranteed peace, for the count can better exert control over those who break a truce or a guaranteed peace than his subjects can. But this is when people request a truce or a guaranteed peace from the count, for if the tenants [*oste*] resident under some local lord want to obtain a guaranteed peace where their lord has jurisdiction [*la ou il chiet*], he can take cognizance; but this is not applicable to gentlemen, for no one has jurisdiction over them in such a case except the count.

300. The sixth reason why the case is not sent down is when someone makes a complaint for broken truce, when the truce was given by the count, or for a broken guaranteed peace, when it was given by the count, for it is right for the offense to be punished by him, since he had the truce or the guaranteed peace given; but if one of the count's vassals had the truce or guaranteed peace given in his court, the case must be sent down and he should be the one to punish the offense.

301. The seventh reason why the case is not sent down is if the count is demanding what is due him, or due to his provosts or his foresters in connection with his land, or suing concerning a surety assigned to him, or a penalty owed him, or someone who has broken out of his prison, or committed an offense against him or his people or trespassed on his land, or in any other case where the count may have a suit against him, for he is not obliged to go to the court of his subject for anything which involves him personally. For then, if the case were not tried by him, since he would not go and plead in the courts of his subjects, he would lose what was due to him.

302. Some vassals try to say that if one of their men [*ostes*] was in a fight [*fut mellee*] in the count's own domains, and left without being caught in the act, that the count cannot arrest him on the land of his vassal or on his own, nor have cognizance of the offense. But I do not agree, for then the count would have less {power} on his land than his men on theirs, and I will show how.

303. If the count's tenant commits an offense on the land of one of his vassals and he is neither caught nor arrested, and the vassal complains to the count for the trespass, the count makes him {the offender} pay a penalty for the offense if it is admitted or proved. And therefore it is right,—since the count does not plead in the court of his subject, as I said,—that concerning a trespass on his own land the count can take cognizance to exact his penalty and to give a truce or guaranteed peace if a party requests it. But if the party makes a complaint without asking for a truce or guaranteed peace, the lord under whom the person complained against is resident can have the case sent down if he asks for it, and yet the count has cognizance with respect to the fine due him, as I said above.

304. If the count prosecutes one of his gentlemen for a case of serious crime and it is denied, the count must demonstrate it by two honest witnesses at least; and if he will not admit or deny it, the count can make an official inquiry and he may find the fact so well-known that he does him no wrong if he punishes him for the offense. But the offense must be very clear and very well known, and if it cannot be demonstrated to be publicly known, but there are many presumptions {circumstancial evidence} found, he should receive a long prison term.

305. For small matters, if the count prosecutes his subjects for them, such as for five sous for commoners or ten sous for gentlemen, the count need not make proof except by one of his officers, and the officer has the power to issue a summons.

306. The eighth reason why the case is not sent down is if some woman has a party summoned to answer on dower, even though the land on which she is asking for dower is held by one of the count's men; for the woman requesting dower has this advantage, that if she wants she can plead before the lord from whom the land is held and, if she prefers to plead in the ecclesiastical court, she cannot be prevented, for she may choose any of these three courts. But once the suit is begun before whichever judge she chose, she cannot abandon it to go to one of the other judges, but her dower suit must be decided there. And if she goes to one of the other judges and a party wants to use as a defense that the suit has been brought elsewhere, it should be sent back.

307. The ninth reason why the case is not sent down is in cases for novel disseisin, or force, or nuisance [*nouvel tourble*]. I put these three cases together because they depend on each other, and yet there is a difference as you will hear in the chapter which deals with them {Chapter 32}.

308. The tenth reason why the case is not sent down is when the suit is commenced between the parties in any dispute any time before the {count's} court is asked to send the case back down.³ For this reason it is established that the count's officers should not summon the tenants [*ostes*] of the vassals of the county in person, but should go to the lord or the person appointed by the lord and say to him: "We order you in the count's name to have so and so who is your tenant before the count's people on such and such a day and in such and such a place." And then the lord should obey the order. This order was made to the officers because it often happened that the lords did not know that their subjects were summoned to the count's court, so that they came too late to request to have the case sent back down. For the subjects sometimes preferred to begin the suit rather than stay in prison so long that their lord found out, and thus the lords lost the opportunity to have the cases sent down.⁴

309. A suit is not commenced by a request for a counsel day in cases where such is appropriate, nor by asking for an inspection day, in cases where an inspection is appropriate. But when you admit or deny, or when you answer after an inspection day, the suit is commenced.⁵

310. Now let's see the cases in which a counsel day is appropriate if it is requested. If I am sued on real property, a counsel day is appropriate. If I am sued for the act of a third party, such as the debt incurred by my father and mother, or by any other relative whose heir I am, a counsel day is appropriate. In the case of real property mentioned above there are continuances and then an inspection day; and in the latter case {on debt} there is only a counsel day, and this is adequately dealt with in the chapter on continuances {Chapter 3}.

Here ends the chapter on the circumstances in which the count of Clermont does not have to send cases back down to his vassals' courts, but retains cognizance.

Notes

1. I have translated *ravoir sa court* as "send down [cases] to a lower court" or the like, but the Old French term means literally "to have back your court." In a system where the lord with jurisdiction and cognizance pocketed the fines, it must have been annoying for the count to appropriate cases for his own court, and the lower vassals (who may have acted as their own judges) would petition to have the case removed to their court. This chapter gives rules for this procedure, and explains when the cases will not be removed into the lower court. Glanvill uses similar terminology in Book VII, section 7, saying: "poterit dominus illius curie die placiti curiam suam ea ratione repetere quod nondum probata fuerit de recto defecisse; et ita eam per iudicium retro habebit," which G. D. G. Hall translates "the lord of that court may on the day appointed for the plea reclaim his court, on the ground that it has not yet been proved to have made default of right; in this way he shall have judgment to have his court again."

2. For *essoines* and *contremans* see Chapter 3.

3. Cf. §256.

4. For other circumstances where the baron does not send cases back down, see §§380, 428.

5. Cf. §237.

11. Ecclesiastical Jurisdiction

Here begins the eleventh chapter of this book which speaks of the cases in which the cognizance belongs to Holy Church or to the secular court, and of the difference between holy places and places of religion.

311. It would be a good and profitable thing, both for God and the secular world, for those who are involved in spiritual justice to deal only with what belongs to spirituality, and leave the cases which concern the world to the jurisdiction and efforts of those who deal with secular justice, so that everyone received a hearing from the spiritual judge or the secular judge. And for this reason we consider in this chapter [*partie*] the cases which belong to Holy Church, in which the secular courts should not become involved; and we will deal with the cases which belong to the secular jurisdiction, in which Holy Church should not get involved; and we will speak of a few cases where it is right and proper for one court to help the other: that is to say where the ecclesiastical courts should help the secular courts, and vice versa.

312. It is true that in all accusations concerning faith, that is to say concerning who believes truly and in good faith, and who does not, the cognizance belongs to Holy Church, for since Holy Church is the fountain of faith and belief, those who are expressly designated to keep the faith of Holy Church should have cognizance to inquire into the faith of each person, so that if there is a layperson who holds unorthodox views, he can be brought back to the true faith by their teaching; and if he will not believe them, and wants to maintain his wicked errors, he can be condemned like a heretic [*bougre*] and burned. But in such a case the secular justice should help Holy Church, for when someone is condemned as a heretic by the inquisition [*examination*] of Holy Church, Holy Church should give him over to the secular arm and the secular arm should burn him because the spiritual court should not put anyone to death.

313. The second case whose jurisdiction belongs to Holy Church is marriage. Such as when a man promises a woman (if Holy Church agrees) to marry her within forty days, if one of them refuses, the other can have them forced into the marriage, unless there is a good cause why the marriage should not take place. And the cognizance of all the cases which can arise from this, both before and after the marriage (and concerning which marriages are to be permitted and which are not), belongs to the bishop; and the secular courts should not get involved.

314. The third case which belongs to the ecclesiastical courts is concerning all the property and all the donations [*aumosnes*] given and donated [*aumosnees*] and contributed [*amorties*] to serve and sustain Holy Church, except the cases of temporal jurisdiction and guardianship, which belongs by a general custom to the king and by special custom to the barons in whose baronies the religious houses are founded. And there is no reason why secular justice should not help those who hold the property of Holy Church to defend and safeguard their temporal possessions, so that offenders may not do them harm or violence. Nevertheless, they can summon and excommunicate those who offend against them, if those who are summoned do not have a good defense. But because the members of Holy Church sometimes think they have a right to certain things to which they have no right,—such as when they sue for some real property which someone is in possession of,—the cognizance belongs to the person from whom the person in possession says he holds the land. But where something is admitted to be theirs, whether it be real or personal property, they can if they wish excommunicate the person standing in their way [*qui leur empeeche*].

315. When someone does wrong or violence to those who have the property of Holy Church, they have two ways to pursue their rights. The first is that if they wish they can plead before the ecclesiastical judge according to the procedure which is customary in the ecclesiastical courts; and if they prefer, they can plead in the secular courts before the person who is supposed to keep them from harm; and there they should await the hearing which will be given to them after they have applied there; and they should give good sureties, if the other party requests them, that they will not sue him in some other ecclesiastical court; instead they will accept whatever hearing the secular judge requires or will give them; for it would

be a bad thing if they could bring to the secular judge their complaint concerning what was done to them, and then, if the result was not to their liking, they could start over in the ecclesiastical court.

316. If it happens that some clerk or some religious house is pleading against someone in the ecclesiastical court, and in the very same case, while the case is pending in the ecclesiastical court, they try to plead in the secular court, the party they are trying to plead against is not required to answer until they have completely abandoned the case in the ecclesiastical court; and if they had had him excommunicated in the case by the ecclesiastical judge, they would have to have him absolved before the party was obliged to answer in the secular court.

317. The fourth case where jurisdiction belongs to Holy Church is concerning clerks: jurisdiction over all disagreements which can arise among clerks concerning personal property, and chattels, and over personal actions, and the belongings they have from Holy Church, except real property which they hold as secular fiefs or for quit-rent or rent from a lord, for whoever holds such property, the jurisdiction belongs to the lord from whom the property is held, as is said in this very chapter. And also whatever suits laypersons want to bring against clerks, the cognizance of them belongs to Holy Church, except concerning the above-mentioned real property.

318. The fifth case where cognizance belongs to Holy Church is concerning crusaders. Whoever has taken the cross for the overseas crusade is not required to answer in any secular court, unless he wishes, on any agreements or personal property, nor on chattels. Nevertheless, if the crusader is sued on a case of crime or real property, the cognizance belongs to the secular court; and he can make agreements concerning all other small matters in the secular courts if he wishes.

319. The sixth case where cognizance belongs to Holy Church is concerning widows. And as was said concerning crusaders, a widow, during her widowhood, is under the jurisdiction of Holy Church. Nevertheless, when a crusader or a widow begins a suit in a secular court, Holy Church should not get involved, and the case should be completed by the secular authorities.

320. The seventh case where cognizance belongs to Holy Church is concerning wills. For if the executors want to collect the property for distribution through the ecclesiastical courts, they may; and if they need the secular judge in collecting the property, they should not be denied his help, for any judges asked to do so should help the executors in the case of a will, so that the wishes of the deceased do not go unfulfilled through default of judgment.

321. If it happens that someone wants to plead against the executors and ask for something by reason of the will, the executors do not have to answer in the secular court, unless they wish to; but cognizance belongs to Holy Church and the executors should be required by Holy Church to pay out on the will. And when it comes about that the executors will not obey the orders of Holy Church, but allow themselves to be excommunicated, the secular judge should help the ecclesiastical judge, for the executors should be forced to act by the seizure of their temporal goods, so that the will is administered as it should be. Nevertheless, the secular judge does not exercise this distraint on the *orders* of the judge of Holy Church but at his *request*, for in cases which involve secular justice the secular judge is never required to obey the order of the spiritual judge, according to our custom, unless it is as a favor. But the favor should not be refused from one judge to another, when it is asked in good faith [*benignement*].

322. It is true that the prelates of Holy Church and the chapters of churches and several other religious houses have lands on which they have lordship and the power to administer justice. And those who hold land in such a manner can have *baillis*, provosts and officers to do what pertains to the secular jurisdiction; and if there arises a case which pertains to the spiritual arm, in these places the jurisdiction belongs to the bishop. But the secular courts which they possess in these places must be held from the count of Clermont in the places which lie in the county of Clermont, or from the bishop, if the places lie in the county of Beauvais, not because of the bishopric, but because of the county of Beauvais which belongs to it. And by this you may know that everything which is held as a secular court must be held from a secular lord; and those who hold as barons {directly from the king} hold in this manner, as far as their barony stretches, and if they do not do what they should and it concerns their jurisdiction [*resort*] when they have been sufficiently summoned[1] you can take the matter to the

king; and the king has cognizance of it, for the whole secular jurisdiction of the kingdom is held from the king as fiefs or sub-fiefs. And for this reason you can come into his court {on an appeal} for default of judgment or false judgment when those who hold from him do not do what they should. But before you reach him, you must sue in the courts of the lower lords, from stage to stage, and this means,—supposing I have both high and low justice in my lands, and I hold it from the count of Clermont, and the count of Clermont holds it from the king, and I do not do what I should in my jurisdiction, so that someone wants to sue me for default of judgment or false judgment,—2 I must be sued before the count, for if I were sued directly before the king, the case would be sent back down to the count if he asked for it.3

323. There are yet other cases the jurisdiction of which belongs to Holy Church, such as the protection of holy places, for this protection [*garde*] must be so zealously protected [*gardee*] that anyone offending against it must be *de facto* excommunicated; and the person offending must be admonished by Holy Church and, if he does not heed the admonition, he must be publicly excommunicated.

324. There is a difference between holy places and places of religion, and because there are several cases which, when they occur in places of religion, belong to the secular jurisdiction, yet which if they occurred in holy places would belong to Holy Church, we will explain which places are holy places and which are places of religion, according to our understanding.

325. Holy places are those which are dedicated and established for the services of Our Lord, such as religious houses, churches, chapels, cemeteries, and the buildings of privileged abbeys [*mesons d'abbeies privilegiees*]. All such places must be observed so zealously [*dignement*] that all those who seek sanctuary there [*i queurent a garant*], however they have offended, and whatever offense they are accused of, whether they are clerks or laypersons, must receive sanctuary as long as they stay there, except in three cases in which no place however holy should be a sanctuary for those who are guilty, but the secular authorities can arrest them wherever they are found and Holy Church should not get involved. And we will explain which cases those are.

326. The first case in which Holy Church does not provide sanctuary to a person convicted of it is sacrilege: sacrilege is committed by a person stealing a holy object from within a holy place or outside a holy place, or who steals something not sacred from within a holy place. Holy objects are those which have been blessed and provided for the service of Our Lord. Therefore anyone committing such a larceny can be arrested by the secular authorities both within and without the church. And sacrilege can be committed in other manners, such as when someone strikes another in anger in a holy place, or beats him or draws blood or kills him: such offenses are sacrilege and Holy Church provides no sanctuary for them. But it is true that when the sacrilege is such that there is no larceny or death, the bishop of the jurisdiction in which the holy place lies receives the fine; and when there is larceny or a man dies, the jurisdiction belongs to the secular lord in whose jurisdiction the holy place lies.

327. The second case in which Holy Church does not give sanctuary to a person found guilty is the case of a well-known highway robber working from ambush; for when he is pursued for such an act and he flees to the holy place for sanctuary, the place does not give him protection from being arrested and dealt with as a thief and a traitor.[4]

328. The third case in which Holy Church does not afford sanctuary to the guilty is that of persons causing property damage, such as those who purposely burn houses or spoil vines or trample [*gastent*] wheat. Whoever is guilty of such offenses should be arrested wherever he is found and dealt with according to the offense. And there are many good reasons why the holy places do not give sanctuary to those who are guilty of the three offenses described above, and we will here give three of those reasons, one for each of the offenses.

329. The reason why the holy place does not give sanctuary to a person committing sacrilege is that Holy Church is the mother of every Christian, and Holy Church should protect every Christian who comes to her for sanctuary, just as a mother would protect her child in good faith if she could; and just as a child which robbed or struck its mother should be punished according to the offense, and the mother should not protect it from this, in the same way, and a hundred thousand times as much, a person offending against Holy Church should not be protected by Holy Church.

330. The reason why Holy Church should not protect highway robbers is that every Christian, by the common law,[5] must come and go safely on the highways. And both the spiritual and the temporal law should protect all Christians so zealously that whoever commits robbery against this law offends against both jurisdictions; and for this reason there should be no sanctuary for such offenders.

331. The reason why holy places do not afford sanctuary to persons destroying property as described above is that Holy Church could not be served nor the people preserved if property was destroyed, and it would be a bad thing if an evil man burned a city and then found sanctuary by entering a holy place. In the same way, what is laid waste in such manner does no good to anyone, so that a holy place should not give sanctuary to such offenders.

332. We have spoken about holy places: now let us consider places of religion. We call places of religion the houses surrounded by walls which belong to religious establishments. But all such places are not the same, for some, by special privilege given by a prince with power to do so, are so powerful that they can give the same sanctuary to those seeking sanctuary there (as soon as they are inside the gates) as would be obtained in a church; but not all religious houses have such privileges. Therefore as regards all courtyards and houses of religious establishments which are not privileged as described above, the jurisdiction over all cases of crime and all other offenses belongs to the baron in whose barony the place is established, except for the religious houses which have high and low justice in their lands, for these houses have the cognizance of offenses committed in their jurisdiction.

333. There are yet other cases which belong to Holy Church, such as when there is a dispute over bastardy, to exclude bastards from taking anything as heirs. The cognizance of this belongs to Holy Church, and a person whom Holy Church designates as legitimate and from a legal marriage cannot and must not be excluded as a bastard in a secular court, and the secular judge must give full credit to what the ecclesiastical judge testifies to in such matters.

334. The other case which belongs to Holy Church is sorcery; for sorcerers and witches err against the faith, and whoever errs against the

faith must be admonished by Holy Church to forsake their errors and make amends to Holy Church. And if they do not heed the admonition, Holy Church should condemn them, so that by the power and judgment of Holy Church they are condemned and held miscreants; and then, at the request of Holy Church, the secular judge should arrest such people. And the error may be so great that the person arrested has merited death, such as if it is observed that the sorcery they used could kill a man or a woman; and if you see there is no danger of death, they should be put in a painful prison [*griés prisons*] for their error until they make amends and completely abandon their error.

335. Now let us consider what sorcery is: sorcery is, for example, when a man or woman claims to a young man that she [*ele*] will obtain for him a young woman in marriage, whom he could not obtain in marriage through his relatives or for money, and assures him she will obtain her for him by force of words or through herbs or other acts which are wicked and evil to recall.

336. Those who undertake to perform such sorceries and those who believe them are deceived, for no words have the power to cause such effects as these do except through the power of the devil [*anemi*], especially in persons in whose words there are no powers to do evil. For we see that if a man or a clerk who was not ordained a priest said a mass, and all the words of the sacrament, nevertheless whatever he said or did he could not perform the sacrament even if he said the exact same words that the priest says. Thus you can see that the words in the mouth of an old woman which are said in order to do evil have little power; but it happens that sometimes the devil (who does all he can to deceive men and women to attract their souls into everlasting sufferings), when God permits him to, performs the things for which the sorcery was said, since the person's words give him an opportunity to work against the faith in this manner; and sometimes God allows him to do so because of the weak belief of those who practice these things. But if no one was ever to avoid this error except for the fact that no one ever saw anyone make use of it who succeeded at it, nevertheless everyone should despise it and speak ill of it in his heart.[6]

337. It is true that any time someone does harm or injury to Holy Church and Holy Church cannot or will not mend it itself, if it asks the secular court for help, the secular court should help and succor it as a son

would a mother; for all Christian men and women are sons and daughters of Holy Church, and are supposed to protect and safeguard Holy Church any time it has need and complains to them as if to its children.

338. It is true that all spiritual matters,—such as commandments of the church, and holy things, and the disputes which arise from personal actions between clerks and members of religious houses, and the penitences which should be imposed because of sins confessed to Holy Church,—all such matters and the cases which can arise from them should be handled [*corrigié*] by Holy Church.

339. We have spoken of matters the juridiction of which belongs to Holy Church, and later we will speak of more which come to mind, but just here we will speak of the cases which belong to the secular jurisdiction and in which Holy Church should not become involved.

340. It is true that in all cases where there can be a wager of battle, or danger of losing life or limb {as a punishment}, the secular courts should be in control, and Holy Church should not get involved, except concerning privileged persons such as clerks, who remain in any case in the jurisdiction of Holy Church.

341. All cases of serious crime between laypersons should be handled by the secular courts, and Holy Church should not get involved; and because it would be tedious to explain and define the cases of crime, they will be described in the chapter on offenses {Chapter 30}.

342. The third case which should be handled by the secular courts is that of agreements and obligations made between laypersons and proved by witnesses or a writing. But it is true that in such cases on agreements and obligations, if the parties meet to plead in the ecclesiastical court of their own free will, and they begin the proceedings, the ecclesiastical court has cognizance of the suit and can hear it right up to the final verdict [*sentence desfinitive*]; and when one of the parties loses the suit, the court can force the loser to pay the judgment on pain of excommunication, but not otherwise, for according to our custom the secular justice is not required to enforce judgments from the ecclesiastical courts in such cases.

343. The other matters which should be heard in the secular courts are all the suits which can arise from homage for fiefs and sub-fiefs, and from

other land held in villeinage or servitude, when these things are held from laypersons; for Holy Church hears such suits in respect to things held from it.

344. All fights, and insults said by or against laypersons, and in secular jurisdictions, should be handled by the secular courts. But it is true that when the fights take place in holy places the fines should be exacted by Holy Church as is said above.

345. When a clerk holds land,—as part of his inheritance or by purchase,—from a secular lord and someone sues for all or part of it, the jurisdiction belongs to the secular lord from whom it is held.

346. If a clerk is a merchant, his merchandise does not go free of tolls and taxes because of his privilege as a clerk; instead his merchandise must pay market taxes, tolls and other customary payments which are due according to the custom of the place. But the clerk who lives on allowances [*benefices*] from Holy Church or from his inheritance without engaging in any trade is not required to make any customary payments.

347. When there are acts {of violence} or threats between clerks on the one hand and laypersons on the other, if the laypersons ask for a guaranteed peace,[7] they must sue for it in the ecclesiastical court; and if the clerks are asking for it, they must sue in the secular court. And we will explain how the secular court should obtain the guaranteed peace for them: for when a guaranteed peace is made, it must be made by one and the other party, and a clerk cannot create an obligation nor[8] a guaranteed peace in a secular court. Therefore when a clerk is requesting a guaranteed peace from a layperson he must guarantee him first, and oblige himself to a guaranteed peace before his ecclesiastical judge. And when the ecclesiastical judge has certified in writing that such and such a clerk has undertaken to keep the lawful peace with respect to such and such a layperson and his people, then the secular judge should require the layperson to make a guaranteed peace between him and his people and the clerk and his people; and a certain guaranteed peace cannot be made any other way between such persons.

348. At common law, all tithes should belong to Holy Church; and for this reason, when there is a suit over tithes, the jurisdiction belongs to Holy Church, except for certain tithes which are held specially on a secular fief, for these should be administered by the lords from whom they are held.

349. No one has, because of a tithe he has on my land, however he holds it, from Holy Church or from a secular fief, any lordship or power to administer justice on the land because of his tithe, and no one can legally remove anything {as a tithe}; and if I want I can take away everything I have there, before he may remove anything or enter the land. Nevertheless, I should not fail to leave him honestly his lawful tithe. And if I do, I sin and I am required to give him the tithe I withhold, as if I had done a wrong; for tithes were all established and given of old in order to sustain Holy Church, but some of them have subsequently passed into secular hands, some by exchange, others by gift from Holy Church.

350. When some clerk is suspected of a crime, secular judges must arrest him and hold him in prison, provided they do not put him to death in the prison; and if the ecclesiastical judge requests it, they should hand him over and report the reason why he was arrested and then the ecclesiastical judge can deal with him according to the law of Holy Church.

351. We have seen that when we arrested some clerk for a crime in the county of Clermont, the bishop wanted us to convey him to Beauvais; but we would never do so, but said they had to send someone for him to the prison where he was held, at their cost and with a valid attorney [*certain procureeur*].

352. If a clerk is arrested by the secular authorities for a case of serious crime9 and his ecclesiastical judge wants him, before he is handed over he must pay for his expenses and what he owes for the imprisonment; and if he has nothing to pay with, his ecclesiastical judge must pay on his behalf if he wants to have him. But if the clerk is arrested for something other than a serious crime, he should be handed over to his ecclesiastical judge without making any payment.

353. A clerk should not wear a striped garment or be without a visible tonsure, once he has received the tonsure from his bishop; nevertheless, if he does, he has not renounced his privilege as a clerk. Therefore if such a man is arrested in such a dress by the secular authorities and his ecclesiastical judge asks for him, if the secular judge knows he is a clerk, he must hand him over; and if he does not know, the ecclesiastical judge must prove in the secular court that he is; and when he has proved this, the clerk should be handed over; and if a person arrested in such a dress cannot prove he is a

clerk, and nor can his ecclesiastical judge, he must remain in the jurisdiction of the secular court like a layman.

354. I do not recommend to secular judges that they should quickly give a hearing to a man they have arrested in a secular dress and who claims to be a clerk, until they know the truth of whether he is a clerk or not, and if he can prove himself to be a clerk or not, or after he has been requested by Holy Church as a clerk. For if he were tried after the claim was made, of after he had said: "I am a clerk," and he was later proved to be a clerk by Holy Church, those who had tried him would be strictly excommunicated with no absolution save from the pope. But if he was arrested in secular clothes, and he did not say : "I am a clerk," and no warning was received concerning Holy Church, and he was punished by a judgment for his offense, Holy Church would have no further complaint to make concerning secular justice, even if Holy Church wanted to prove afterwards that the person condemned had been a clerk. For if Holy Church could arrest the secular authorities in such a case, no sure justice would ever be done in such cases, and much justice would not be done at all, which no one should wish to happen, because justice is for the common good of all.

355. It sometimes happens that laypersons are arrested in clerks' habits, such as when thieves or murderers or other evil folk have tonsures made by each other, or by a barber to whom they claim to be clerks. When such people are arrested, they should be handed over to Holy Church and Holy Church should find out the truth. And if they are found to be clerks, they should be punished according to the form of Holy Church, that is to say by life imprisonment, if they are found guilty of a serious crime. And if they are found to be laypersons, by their admission or by some other sure method, if they were arrested for a case of crime, Holy Church should not hand them over to the secular authorities, for those who gave them back would be outside the rules [*irregulier*] if the accused were punished for such a crime. Therefore they can and should put them in prison for life, as if they were clerks. But if they are arrested for something other than a serious crime, they can and should hand them over to the secular authorities; and once they have been handed over by Holy Church as laymen, they cannot be requested a second time by Holy Church as clerks.

356. When the secular authorities are trying to arrest offenders for a crime and they resist arrest [*se requeuent a prendre*], so that they cannot be

arrested without killing them, if the arresting officers kill them they should not be accused of anything, whether those who resisted were clerks or laymen, even if the clerks said: "We are clerks." And this is quite right, for in arresting clerks for crimes, those who arrest them are officers of Holy Church; and this is made clear by the fact that they must turn them over to their ecclesiastical judge; and if they refrained from arresting them dead or alive when they defended themselves, a clerk would never allow himself to be arrested by the secular authorities without defending himself, and even less by the ecclesiastical judge if he tried to arrest them, for they would know very well that if he killed them he would be outside the rules; therefore they could not be arrested, and many evils could arise because of that. And if the secular authorities did not dare to arrest them dead or alive when they defended themselves, even if there was no clerk among them and they were all laymen, the arresting officers would be afraid there *was* a clerk, so that many offenders could escape because of this fear. And for this reason it is for the common good of all for the secular authorities to be able to arrest clerks and laymen for crimes, and kill them if they defend themselves, rather than let them escape.

357. There is a custom in the ecclesiastical courts which is not current in the secular courts: for if Pierre summons Jehan and asks him to give him ten pounds which he promised to return, Jehan can ask Pierre to return the horse he lent him, even though Pierre had Jehan summoned, and Jehan did not have the said Pierre summoned. And in the ecclesiastical court this custom is called a counterclaim [*reconvencion*]. And if the said Pierre who had Jehan summoned will not answer concerning the loaned horse, because he was not summoned to answer Jehan, as Jehan was summoned to answer to him, Jehan would not have to answer on the ten pounds. But it would be different in the secular court, for the person summoned would answer, and the defendant could not make a complaint without having the other summoned on something other than the dispute on which he himself had been summoned. But if he raised defenses, such as if he alleged payment or said he had handed something over in payment for the debt, the plaintiff would have to respond. Thus you can see that there is no counterclaim in the secular courts as there is in ecclesiastical courts.

358. A clerk demanded twenty pounds from a layman in a secular court, in payment for a horse, and the laymen admitted the debt. But he said that in trying to pay this debt he had given the other person money and other

goods, and asked the clerk to give him an accounting, and said he was ready to pay whatever remained unpaid after the accounting was given. The clerk replied that he would not answer on the accounting that was asked of him, but that, since the defendant had admitted that he owed the twenty pounds, he required that he be made to pay; and if he wanted to sue him for anything he should summon him before his ecclesiastical judge.

359. As the judge before whom this plea was made, we said to the clerk that if he did not respond concerning what the layman said he had given him since the time when the twenty-pound debt was incurred, we would not make him pay the twenty pounds, for it was not a counterclaim when he said he had given him the things in trying to pay the debt; but if he had asked the clerk for somehing owing from *before* the time the debt was made, or if he was asking him for horses or other animals, or wheat or wine or agreements which did not at all involve the dispute over the twenty pounds, we would have made him pay the twenty pounds and told him to go and make his complaint against the clerk concerning these things before his ecclesiastical judge, for then the laymen would have been making a counterclaim, which is not done in the secular courts as is said above.

360. When a man in the jurisdiction of one lord makes a complaint against a man from another jurisdiction, and the latter wants to make a complaint against the former on some matter, the person having the other summoned is not required to answer, even though both are laymen, unless it represents a defense in the current dispute, for this would be a counterclaim, which is not valid in the secular courts, as we explained above.

Here ends the chapter which teaches which cases belong to Holy Church and which ones belong to the secular courts, and the occasions when one of these courts must help the other when asked to do so.

Notes

1. For summoning a lord for default of judgment see Chapter 62.
2. The punctuation of Salmon has not been followed here in the translation. In that edition, the second ,— follows the word "jurisdiction" in the line above.
3. On sending cases back down to the lower courts see Chapter 10.

4. For the definition of *traïson*, see Chapter 30, §826. The main meaning of this word is "stealth" rather than *lèse majesté*.

5. For the notion of common law, see the Preface, pp. xxiii.

6. This last sentence in §336 is rendered somewhat obscure by the multiple negatives in Old French.

7. For guaranteed peace see Chapter 60.

8. I read Salmon's *en* as *ne* in this sentence, p. 1: 166, bottom line (also *en* in Beugnot, 1: 172, top line).

9. That is, the sort of crime for which the punishment might be death.

12. Wills

Here begins the twelfth chapter of this book which speaks of wills, which are valid and which are not.

361. After speaking in the previous chapter about the cases which belong to Holy Church and to the secular courts, we will speak in this following chapter about wills, for it is needful for every jurisdiction to lend aid in upholding wills which are legally made, for the salvation of the souls of those who make them; and so that everyone may know how you can and should make a will, we will discuss who has seisin of the will, and which wills are valid and which are not, and how you can and should make them, and how they should be executed.

362. Jehan asked the court to be put in possession of the personal property [*muebles*] and purchased real property [*conquès*] and of a fifth of the inherited real property [*eritage*] of the late Thomas,[1] because the said Thomas had made him his executor in his last will, and it said in his will that his devises [*devis*] should be paid out of these things.

363. To this Pierre answered that possession of these things should go to him, that is to say to the son and legal heir of the said Thomas; and when he was in possession, if Jehan could properly ask him for something for the purposes of execution of the will or anything else, he would have the right to do so. They asked for a ruling on who would get possession: either Pierre as heir or Jehan as executor.

364. It was judged that Jehan as executor would be placed in possession, once the will had been admitted or proved, for it would be a very dangerous thing if wills were blocked or delayed by the heirs of those who make wills.

365. Every gentleman or commoner who is not a serf can, according to our custom, leave in his will his personal property, his purchased property,

and a fifth of his inherited real property, to whomever he wants, except that he cannot leave more to one of his children than to the others; but a serf can leave in his will only five sous.

366. It is a settled custom that a man can leave all the above to his wife, or the wife to her husband. But if a wife in good health made such a legacy to her husband because of violence or threats, and it was proved by the woman's heirs, the legacy would be invalid.

367. If a legacy is made to the church of purchased property or the fifth of the inherited real property which may be left, the lord from whom the property is held may not prevent it, but he can order the house to which the legacy was made to relinquish possession and transfer the property to secular hands within a year and a day; and if the house does not do so, the lord can make a seizure of the property and appropriate the fruits [*issues*][2] until the church has obeyed the order.

368. If someone leaves his personal property, his purchased property, and a fifth of his inherited real property to one or several persons, and the testator owes debts which he orders to be paid or has committed wrongs for which he orders restitution to be made, and he does not say where the money is to come from, those who take[3] under the will will have nothing coming unless there is a surplus once the debts and restitutions are paid; for it would be a bad thing if the legal heirs of the testator, who take only four-fifths of the inherited real property, had to pay the debts and restitution payments, and the others took their legacies unencumbered; and for this reason you should use the personal property first to pay debts and restitution payments. And if the personal property is not enough, you should use the purchased property; and if that is not enough, the person to whom the fifth of the inherited real property was left will pay the rest or leave his fifth to the heirs, and they must pay it all. And if the testator gave instructions to pay the debts and payments out of the four-fifths remaining to the heirs, he could not do so, for it would seem that he was able to leave more than a fifth of his inherited real property, unless the restitutions and debts were so great that everything went to pay them; for if the personal property and the purchased property cannot pay off the debts and restitutions, the inherited real property must be used even if the debts and payments are so great that nothing remains for the heirs.

369. If someone leaves a fifth of his inherited real property and the property is in several parcels, he can leave the fifth as a single parcel if he wants, provided the parcel is not worth more than a fifth of the whole; and if the testator made no provision, and the judge is petitioned by the legatee or the heirs, because the former wanted to take a fifth out of each parcel, the judge should not permit it, for this is to the advantage of both parties and judgments have been made on this matter.

370. No legacy is valid unless it is made by a person of sound mind and memory, and unless he says it aloud.[4]

371. When a will is made there must be present persons who can give testimony concerning it if there is any argument about it, or it must be sealed with an authentic seal or several seals of noble persons, for example gentlemen or men in religion who have seals.

372. It sometimes happens that lords lose revenue by the wills that their subjects make, and you will know that this is true because we will recount a case we saw.

373. A knight married a lady, who had a child by a former husband. During the marriage, the knight purchased a fief and did homage for it to the count. Afterwards the lady, in her last will, gave her husband all her personal property and her purchased property, for him to hold the said purchased property for life; and afterwards she died at a time when her oldest son was not old enough to do homage for his mother's purchased property, and for that reason we seized for lack of a vassal[5] half of the said purchased property, which the child was to take from his mother.[6] And the knight appeared before us and requested us to surrender possession of the land, because as he had purchased the land he had done faith and homage for the whole thing, and since his wife had left him her portion to hold for life, and such a gift was permitted by the custom of Beauvais, it was wrongful of us to make a seizure of it for lack of a vassal.

374. We sought advice on this matter from the king's counsel and others, and the advice was that since the custom allowed a man to give his wife, and a wife to give her husband, personal property and purchased property and a fifth of his inherited real property, it would be wrongful of us to prevent it. And for this reason we surrendered possession of it and

allowed him to have the use of it. And by this you can clearly see that the lord lost by the will that was made, for if the wife had not given it in her will to the husband, it is clear that the lord would have held half of the purchased property until the child came of age or until someone from the child's lineage came forward to ask for the custodianship.

375. Now let us see whether there would have been two homages if the testamentary gift had been made to the husband for ever.[7] We say no, only one. And this is clear because, according to the advice we received, by his one homage the knight held it all after his wife died until his stepson came of age; and when he came of age, he did homage for the ownership of the property because he was the legal heir to the property, and this did not prevent his stepfather from enjoying what he took under the will.

376. Now let's see,—if the legal heir, who has done homage for the property but does not reap the benefits, falls into default or owes some fine to his lord,—whether the lord can confiscate benefits from the fief he holds from him, if another person is reaping the benefits under the will. We say that if the defaults or fines [*entrepresures*] are in connection with a matter which concerns the fief,—for example if he disobeyed, or if the lord summoned him on service and he did not serve him as he should, or if someone sued him for ownership of the property and he would not appear in court, but defaulted more times than he was permitted,—for all such cases the lord can take possession of the fief he holds from him and reap the benefits until his men give a verdict on the above-mentioned fines. And the person who should be reaping the benefits under the will can take the heir to the secular court and have him forced to free his property which is encumbered because of his action, and if the heir has nothing with which to pay or if he leaves the district, the person who has a life interest in the benefits under the will,—when the heir has defaulted the requisite number of times,—can ask the lord to accept his homage for the time he is to hold the fief under the will, and the lord must do so. And when he has accepted him as his vassal for the benefits [*il l'a receu a homme des fruits*], he should give back to the vassal what he reaped in the way of benefits after he was asked to accept his homage. But when the person who has only a life interest in the benefits dies, and the legal heir comes back to reap the benefits from the property, the lord can still take possession of the property a second time because of the disobedience which occurred at a time when someone else was reaping the benefits under a will; for even though someone else is reaping the

benefits from a fief for which I am the vassal, I am required to do the service for the fief because of the homage which I did and for the property I am waiting to get, and I can win or lose the property in a suit or because of an offense; but I cannot lose the interest someone else has in it under a will or dower. And this is even stronger in the case of dower than in the case of a will, for I cannot make a seizure of benefits held in dower because of the offense committed by my vassal against me; and whatever the heir does, it is not appropriate for the person holding in dower to pay me homage or other fees; the person holding in dower should reap the benefits freely and without obligation.

377. For this reason, if a person who is my vassal owes me a debt or we have an agreement which he does not keep, I should not make a siezure of the benefits going to another person under a will, for any reason except something which involves the fief, as is explained above in this very chapter.

378. I should take care that what is held from me is not held by a stranger[8] under a will or in dower, except as is permitted by custom, even if the heir of the thing were willing to remain silent; for I can become involved when I see a clear disadvantage to myself. And it is to my disadvantage if what is held from me passes into the possesson of someone over whom I have no jurisdiction, such as I *would* have if my vassal held it. Therefore if someone leaves more than half of the property he holds from me in dower to his wife, I do not have to permit it, unless I want to; and also, if someone leaves under a will the benefits of more than a fifth of his real property, which is not purchased property, I need not allow it, unless I want to, even though no one but me opposes it. But I must permit what is allowed by custom to be given in a will or in dower.

379. Although we have said that the custom of Beauvais is that whoever wants to sue someone on personal property or chattels must do so before the lord in whose jurisdiction he has his residence, nevertheless in some cases you can sue for personal property and chattels before the lord in whose jurisdiction they are situated; for example, in seeking partitions in direct or lateral descent, and in things left in a will, for if something is left to me in a will I can have it attached as my thing by the lord in whose jurisdiction I find it, and if no one wishes to contest this, the cognizance belongs to the lord in whose jurisdiction it is, except for the executors of wills, for the latter are not required to plead on anything connected with

the will, unless they want to, before any judge except the baron[9] of the land or the bishop; and the said executors must be given the possession of what is contained in a will before any suit, for the will must be executed by them.

380. When a person who can legally do so contests[10] a will because he says it is not legally made, the things mentioned in the will must be carefully kept in the possession of the baron in whose jurisdiction they are situated, without the case being sent down to anyone else's lower court. And when the suit is finished, the baron should deliver the things to the person to whom the judgment awards them.

381. Not everyone can contest a will, and those who can are those who can give a good reason why they are wrongfully injured on account of the will which was made contrary to law or custom; for other people would sometimes contest it out of hatred for the deceased, or for the heirs or executors, and for this reason no one should be admitted to contest a will unless he feels himself injured by the will.

382. We have said in this very chapter that anyone can leave in his will a fifth of his inherited real property, and {all} his personal property and {all} his purchased property. Nevertheless, if the rest of his real property is not sufficient to maintain his children, and there is a lot of personal property and chattels and he leaves none of it to his children, but leaves it all to strangers, we do not agree that such a will should be adhered to, but enough should be taken away from the will for the children to be reasonably maintained according to their station, except in two cases. The first is if it is said in the will that the legacy is made to make restitution for a wrong, for in such a case nothing would be given to the heirs, even if the whole of the property was used up, for it is a serious debt to have someone else's property wrongfully, and no heir should be enriched by his father's wrong, and no one should be believed more readily concerning his wrongs than a person who admits them in his will. The second case in which nothing should be given back to the heirs is if the testator mentions in the will that the heirs have wronged him, so that he does not want to leave them anything in his will; for if I see my daughter or my mother or the woman who should be my heir leading so dishonest a life that it is a scandal to her and her lineage, I have a good reason to write her out of my will. And scandal means scandalous sin of the body, or an inappropriate marriage they make against my will, or such profligacy that you see that whatever falls into their hands is lost; and it would be a bad thing if I had to leave

something in my will to my daughter or my mother or someone else who was married to my enemy; and if I want to exclude them from my will, I should say in my will: "I do not want so and so who is my heir to take any of my personal property, or my purchased property nor the fifth of my inherited real property, for he [*il*] has offended against me in such a way that I believe I shall do my soul more good by leaving it to someone else." But it is true that I cannot for any of the above reasons take away from my heirs their share in the four-fifths of my inherited real property that law and custom gives them.

383. There is yet another reason why I can exclude my heirs from inheriting my personal property, or my purchased property, or the fifth of my inherited real property: it is if the four-fifths of the real property are of such value that they can suffice for the maintenance of my heirs, or if my heirs have so much of their own or from the other side of the family that it is enough for their maintenance, or if I was once poor and they were rich and I asked them for help and they refused, or if they raised their hands against me in ill will. For all these reasons I can exclude them from my will. Thus you can see that what we have said about helping the heirs who have been excluded from a will, when everything has been left to strangers, means when they are poor and have done nothing wrong, and out of a proper pity.

384. If someone leaves all his personal property and his purchased property to one or two persons, and the heirs are put back in the will out of pity, it seems to us to be proper for the person who was to take under the will to be counted among the heirs, and take as much as any of the heirs under the will, each one alike; for it does not seem that the deceased had *no* reason to give them something when he remembered them in his will.

385. When a will is seen to provide that someone be disinherited, or a legacy is made without regard to pity,—for example if I leave all my property to rich persons and nothing to my poor heirs or poor near relatives,—it is not wrong to go against the will, and have it declared invalid; for it is apparent that the testator was wrongly motivated, against reason, unless he says in his will why he did this, and the stated cause is seen to be reasonable.

386. There are two things which cannot be left by will: one is a servile dwelling which pays fees [*masure taillable*][11] to the lord, because a legacy should not be made of real property which owes a servitude to the lord; and

the second is a serjeanty [*serjanterie a eritage*], for it cannot be divided even among heirs, but one of the heirs must take all of it because the service which is due from it to the lord is not divisible. Nevertheless we have seen servile dwellings left in a will by the lord's leave; but if the matter were taken to court, we believe it would not be permitted; but of all other real property, whether in fief or in villeinage, a fifth may be left in a will, provided the rights of the lords are preserved and except that, if the property is left to Holy Church, the lord can command them to surrender possession of it within a year and a day, in the way which is described elsewhere in this same chapter.

387. You should give help to those who are disinherited by the exhortations of their stepmothers and stepfathers, for it sometimes happens that a woman, in order to follow her second husband's wishes, leaves to him, or to his children by another wife, her personal property, her purchased property, and a fifth of her inherited real property, thereby disinheriting her heir; and although our custom in Beauvais certainly permits this, we do not believe it is right, and we believe it would be right and merciful to contest such wills and make them invalid, especially when they exclude the heir without cause; and we believe that if this were taken to the highest level, appealing either from the bishop to the pope or from the barons to the king, such a will would not be upheld.

388. I cannot benefit under part of a will and contest it in another part, saying that the will was not legally made; for example if I took something which was left me in a will and now I want to object to someone else's taking what was left to him in the will: I cannot do that, for as soon as I took what was left me in the will it was clear that I approved the will, and for this reason I can no longer contest it.

389. If there are several heirs and only one of them contests the will, and the others stay silent for a year and a day after the death of the testator, and the person contesting the will manages to have the will declared illegal, the other heirs get no advantage from the suit, but it goes only to the one who maintained the suit at his own expense; for inasmuch as they kept silent for a year and a day, and they saw the person contest the will and did nothing, it is clear that they approved the will; and the person contesting the will, who was an heir like them, was not obliged to plead for them, and for this reason he receives all the advantage.

390. What we said above, that someone taking something under a will cannot later contest the will, is true; however, if I am an heir of the person who made the will, if someone else is asking for something under the will, and I can raise against him other issues than that the will was not properly made, I can raise them: for example that he refused [*quita*] what was left him in the will, or that he did not want to take it while there was still something left to distribute, for in such a case or ones like it I am not contesting the will.

391. Executors, once they have undertaken to be executors, cannot say the will was not properly made. And for this reason heirs who are disinherited by a will which was not properly made should take care not to accept to be the executors, for they would have given up their right to contest the will. And there is a good reason why those who are executors cannot contest a will for which they are the executors, because they represent the person of the deceased, and because of what they promised to do when they became executors.

392. If someone makes a will and names in his will executors who are not present, and he dies before they have accepted to be executors, they may undertake to execute the will or not as they choose. Nevertheless, if they refuse, the will should not be thereby rendered invalid, but the bishop or the lord of the land should have it carried out with the costs taken out of the estate funds, for every judge should make an effort to have properly made wills carried out and fulfilled.

393. When someone makes a will and he names two or three executors, and the will does not state that one may act without the other, and one of the executors dies before the will is executed, the will is not thereby rendered invalid; instead, at the request of the surviving executor, the count or the bishop should name a colleague for him; and if he does not request this, he can go ahead with the work of the execution all alone, so that the wishes of the deceased are carried out.

394. Each time the executors meet or make a journey, they can take their reasonable expenses out of the estate funds according to their condition, and also the costs they incur in suing to safeguard the estate funds. And if they act outrageously, they commit great sin, for the person who made them executors believed them to be honest, and inasmuch as he

trusted them and they accepted to execute his will and then did not do their duty, they are thieves in God's eyes.

395. The heirs of the deceased may ask the executors for an accounting of the property they had in their possession in order to execute the will, and for two reasons: the first is so that they know that the wishes of their predecessor were carried out; the second is because if there are funds remaining after the execution, they must be given to the heirs. And if the heirs have not asked for an accounting, the count or the bishop should ask for it, and make the executors do their duty.[12]

396. When a will is made in such a away as to leave a certain quantity of funds for the payment of debts and the restitution of wrongs, and the person to whom the payments should be made are not named, the executors should have it announced in all the churches in the towns where the deceased used to go that those who want to ask for debts and restitutions to be paid should come to such and such a place on such and such a day. And when they come to the place, their demands should be written down, and those which the executors suspect are not true must be proved by those asking. And when the announcement has been made three times in public in the churches and they have received the proof of the unclear requests, they should see how much they have to pay out, and the quantity of funds in the estate, and if they have enough funds to pay everything they should do so; and if they have too little, they should calculate how much each should receive in the partition of the estate, for it would be a bad thing if they paid one everything and another nothing. And if anyone waits too long to make his request for what is owed him from the will, so that the funds are all paid out, the executors need not answer, for their power lasts only as long as the estate funds last.

397. If the executors are pleaded against before the judges of the ecclesiastical court or before those of the secular court for some matter touching the will, they can keep in their possession funds from the estate up to the value of what they are being sued for and their costs in the suit, so that they can pay what is judged against them. And the executors could commit a fraud in this situation which could cost them: for example, if they paid out the entire estate during the suit so that they could get out of it by saying: "We have nothing left from the estate." But if they had paid out the estate before the suit was begun, they could say that and be dismissed from

the suit; and again if the suit was for a legacy, and they paid out the estate funds to cover debts and restitution payments, whether before the suit was begun or after, the executors could not be blamed; for {even} if the legacy was quite clear and {its validity} admitted to the person suing, he would take nothing until the debts and restitution payments were paid, and for this reason the executors should not refrain from paying debts and restitution payments because of a pending suit on a legacy. But if the suit is for payment of debts or restitution, they should keep back sufficient funds as was said above.

398. When the executors have paid out what was in the will, and they have some remaining funds from the estate, and they have had an announcement made three times (as was said above) that if anyone wants to claim something from them he should come forward, and they have dealt with claimants by paying them or raising good defenses, so that they have been inactive for a year and a day since the announcement, they may give the residue to the heirs, and they should be forced to do so; for if there were no time limit, they could say in bad faith: "We want to retain these funds in case someone should sue us, so that we have the power to defend ourselves if someone attacks us." And even before the year and a day, when the debts and the clear payments have been made, and the executors are not being sued, if the heirs who will get the residue from the estate want to give assurances to the executors that they will reimburse them for costs and damages, we agree that by these assurances they may take what remains of the estate.

399. No one who writes the will, or who is an advocate for it for the executors when they have to plead, or who is their counsel in finding grounds why the will is good, or who has held the will good in a suit, or before honest men, or who having come of age since the death of the testator has promised to enforce it, can contest the will nor say that it was not legally made, for in all these cases the people have approved the will by the help they gave.

400. If the testator makes his heirs who are not of age (or those who are of age but who are not emancipated) promise that they will enforce the orders of his will, and if the heirs see that he made the will illegally, their promise should not do them harm, for a person under age can use as a defense that he was not of age to make a promise or an agreement, and the

person who was of age but not emancipated can use as a defense that he was afraid that if he did not do the testator's will or agree to do so, the other would die in anger or in hatred, or that he would sell what he was to leave him if he escaped death.[13] But nevertheless, as far as God is concerned, we believe that a person who was of age does wrong if he goes against what he swore and promised.

401. A person who was still in his mother's womb when the person whose heir he is made his will can have it revoked if it was made illegally, for his rights should be preserved as others' are.

402. It sometimes happens that a testator has no children, but his wife is pregnant and has been so for so short a time that it is not known; and the testator makes his will differently than he would have if he had expected to have children, and dies before he learns that his wife is pregnant, so that he does not revoke his will. And when such cases arise you should pay great attention to whether the heir is much hurt by the will; for example, if the testator left all his personal property and his purchased property and he had no other property sufficient for his child, and then provision must be made for the child out of the estate, so that he can have enough according to his condition, for you may well believe that the testator would not have made such a will if he had had an heir of his body.

403. If the executors sell real property through the power of the will, for example the fifth which can by custom be left in a will, the family of the deceased can redeem[14] it from the buyer just as if the testator had sold it, for those who inherit are not deprived by the will of the power of redemption.

404. There is a difference between gifts given by will and those made inter vivos,[15] for it is clear that everything which is promised in a will, whether it is a gift or charity or restitution, can be revoked by the testator, or reduced or increased at his will while he is still alive, but this cannot be done for gifts given or promised inter vivos, for they have to be given. And the reason is that you cannot ask the testator for anything given in a will as long as he lives, because he is permitted to amend or revoke it if he wants as is said above.

405. A will made without a writing can be valid if it is witnessed by the oath of two valid witnesses with no suspicion that they might benefit from

the will. For if they expected to benefit, their testimony would not be valid. And formerly a non-written will was not valid unless it was witnessed by five witnesses, as we have heard from the law lords [*seigneurs de lois*]. But our custom has done away with this law, and permits wills to be proved by two valid witnesses, in the same way as everything else can be proved according to our custom.

406. It sometimes happens that men go out of the district and leave their will made and set up [*ordené*], in the hands of their executors, before they leave; and before they return they want to make another and new will, in the place where they are; and in making the later will, they do not revoke the former will which they made when leaving their district; and afterwards they die and the two wills come forward. Now we need to know if the former will will be upheld in such cases, or if it is revoked by the later will. According to our custom, and also in our opinion, we decide in the following manner: that where the later will does not expressly revoke the former one, and no contradiction is found in the later will from which it appears that the deceased's wish was to revoke the earlier one, both the former and the later will should be held to be valid wills; and it is clear, since no contradiction or revocation is found in the later will, that the latter is only an addition to the will; for example it happens sometimes that you make your will according to your estate at the time you leave home, and when you are away, you make it according to the things you brought from home or that you purchased, or even the things left behind which can be left in a will and were not left in the first will. In all such cases the earlier *and* the later wills would be valid.

407. Since we have said above that the earlier will would not be valid if a contradiction was found in the second one, it is right for us to explain what contradiction cancels the earlier will when it is not revoked specially.

408. A contradiction is as follows: when the testator leaves in the later will the opposite of what he left in the earlier one, for example if he says: "I want my executors to take the ten pounds that Phelippe owes me and give it to the poor," and in the first will it is stated that he has forgiven Phelippe the debt of ten pounds. In such a case it appears that the later will is the opposite of the ealier one, and for this reason Phelippe must pay the ten pounds. Or if in the earlier will he left a certain person ten pounds, and in the later will he leaves the same person a hundred sous,[16] the person can

only claim the hundred sous from the second will, for he cannot use the first will since the testator mentioned him in the second will, and it is clear that he is reducing the ten pounds to a hundred sous. And you must understand that if a contradiction is found in the later will in several items found in the first will, we do not mean to say that the first will is false except in regard to the items where the contradiction is found; for example, if it is directed in the first will that someone left me a fifth of his real property or some other thing certain in restitution or in charity, and in the later will he does not mention me but he does not leave to anyone else what he left me, I can ask for it under the first will, even though there is a contradiction found in the later will against several of the persons named in the earlier will. For a contradiction to the detriment of another person but not against me should not do me harm. But if he had left to someone else in the later will what he left me in the earlier will, I could not ask for it, for it would be clear from the later will that he did not want me to have it.

409. If someone makes two wills at two different times and both are valid in whole or in part for the above-mentioned reasons,—for example if he chose different executors in the second will from those he chose in the first,—this is not a contradiction which takes away the validity of the first will, for the deceased may well have wanted the execution of the will accelerated by being taken care of by two pairs of people. But the conclusion of the second will may be such that it revokes the power of the first pair of executors, for example if it says generally: "I wish my executors to have control over all my possessions in order to accomplish my last will." By such words the power of the first will and the power of the first executors would be taken away. And for this reason, when such a case arises, you should pay great attention to the meaning of the words which are contained in the will.

410. Every time words are used, either in a will or not, and the words admit several constructions, the construction should be taken which is most favorable to the speaker, for it should not be supposed that someone will purposefully use words which could be to his detriment (unless he says something so clearly and in such clear words that another construction cannot be found in them). Therefore if someone makes a will and there are in the will words which are obscure or have two constructions, it should be judged according to the construction which it should have for the good of the soul; and if the word is said in another suit, it should be ruled that the person who said it did so with the intention that it would help him to win

his suit. And obscure words should be made clear, if that is possible, before they are submitted to the jurors. But since they cannot be made clear in a will because the testator is deceased, he should be given the benefit of the doubt [*doit on jugier selonc la meilleur partie a son oes*]. And as for the words where there are several constructions or which are obscure, we had better not write them down, lest someone use them to work mischief, but they can be easily known and recognized as the cases arise. And we will say no more.

411. Not everyone can make a will, for those who are under age in another person's custodianship or guardianship cannot make a will, since they have nothing; and madmen and the insane cannot make a will, for they have no sense which could make what they wanted be upheld; but if a madman or a person who had gone crazy or insane made a will before it happened, it is valid, even if they revoked it when insane or crazy, for what they do when in that condition should not work against the good will [*bonne volonté*] they had before.[17] And those who cannot speak, either because they are mute by nature or because they are so sick they cannot speak, cannot make a will; and those who are condemned in a verdict for their offenses cannot make a will, for they have nothing; and those who are banished from the kingdom for serious crimes cannot leave in a will anything they have in the kingdom, for they forfeit everything they have as if found guilty of the crime, since they did not dare wait for a trial. A man in religion cannot make a will, for all he has belongs to the church, except prelates and those in the other orders in which you can own property, for example canons and secular priests, for such people can hold real property and do what the church requires, and for this reason they can make a will. But they should heed their conscience as to how they dispose of property which has come to them from their churches; for it is better for them to leave their property to their churches than to anyone else, unless they see their churches in good condition and they are moved by pity to leave what they have saved to someone else.

412. It sometimes happens that those who are making their will are mistaken into thinking that what they leave belongs to them when in fact it belongs to someone else; for example, if someone leaves a parcel of land which he thought was his and it was someone else's. In such a case you should inquire why he was motivated to leave it,—to make restitution for a wrong, or in charity, or out of family feeling, or in payment for a debt he owed,—and if it is seen that it was left as payment for a debt or in restitu-

tion of a wrong, the value of the thing should be paid, even if there was nowhere to take the money from except from what he had left to charity; but if
the legacy had been made to charity or out of friendship, the legacy would
be invalid, for you cannot give away someone else's thing as a present or to
charity, and a gift to charity that a testator made in his will should not be to
the detriment of a person to whom he owed a debt or restitution.

413. When someone leaves in a will some holy place or holy thing
thinking it is his when it is not, the legacy is invalid. And if someone owns a
holy place or a holy thing, he can leave it in his will to an appropriate place
or person. For if someone left the ornaments of an altar to a layperson who
had no chapel in which to make use of them, it should not be permitted; for
the things which were established for the service of God should not be let
out of the possession of those who are appointed to perform the service of
God.

414. If someone leaves me in his will something that is my own, the
legacy is invalid, for he cannot leave me what is already mine; and we have
put this in our book because of doubts we have seen concerning those who
left to their wives (or wives who left to their husbands) certain things from
their personal property or purchased property, saying something like: "I
leave to my wife the piece of land in such and such a place," or: "I leave my
horse," or some thing of his. When he died, the wife said she owned half of
the thing left her in her own right, and because he had left her the whole
thing in his will, she wanted to be compensated {from elsewhere} for the
half which was not his, but rightfully already belonged to the wife.[18] The
executors answered that she should consider herself satisfied because she
had taken all she would have taken however it came to her, either under her
own right or under the will. And on this issue they requested a judgment.

415. It was judged that nothing would be given to the wife in compensation, and that the will only extended to what the testator owned; and by
this judgment you can see that a person who leaves me what is already mine
leaves me nothing.

416. If someone makes a will and afterwards orders the opposite of
what he ordered or left in his will, the testament is in that regard invalid, for
example if he left me in his will twenty pounds which I owed him, and after
the will was made, he forced me to pay the twenty pounds, it is clear that he

is revoking his will as far as concerns me; or if he left me a piece of land, and after the will was made, he sold it to me or someone else, I cannot later ask for it under the will, for it is clear that it was not his last wish that I should have that land in the will.

417. If a thing is left as a whole to several persons by mistake,—for example if the testator says in his will: "I want Pierre to have my horses," and afterwards in the same will he says: "I want Jehan to have my horses,"—the horses should be divided equally between Pierre and Jehan, for it is clear that the deceased wanted them both to gain by the will, and neither party can have them all; and the wishes of the deceased should be followed as closely as possible.

418. When a testator leaves something to someone , and he gives the name and forgets the surname,[19] or he gives the name and surname and several people come forward who have the same name and surname,—for example if someone said Pierre of Clermont, and there were several people called Pierre of Clermont,—you should inquire in such cases who the deceased meant; and you can discover this through presumptions, for example if the deceased had dealings or traded with or took the service of one of them, and not the others, then you would know he was the one. And if such presumptions are not found, you should look at others, for example if one is poor and the other rich, you should believe that he left the thing to the poor man rather than to the rich one; and you should give the legacy to the person you think the deceased had in mind.

419. When a thing certain is left in a will and the thing is destroyed before the testator dies, of after his death but before it is delivered to the person to whom it was left, with no fault of the executors,—for example if a horse is left and it dies, or a house and it burns, or wine and it is spilled,—the loss is borne by the person to whom it was left, and no compensation should be given. And if the legatee sues the executors for compensation and claims that the thing was destroyed by their fault, if the fault was that the executors had converted the thing to their own gain, they would be re-quired to compensate for the loss. But if they had been keeping the thing in good faith until they had paid the debts and restitution, and it was de-stroyed during that time, they would not be required to compensate for the loss because the debts and restitution should be paid before the legacies, as we have said elsewhere in this very chapter.

420. If a testator leaves all his animals [bestes] without further specification, and he has a flock [fouc]²⁰ of sheep, you should understand that that is what he left. And nevertheless because of the general nature of the term, we believe the legatee would take everything which is called an animal [beste]: horses, cows, pigs, and other animals, if he had them. But if he said: "I leave my *flock* [fouc] of animals," only the sheep should be understood, because you do not say a flock of cows or a flock of horses, but you can say herd [fouc] of pigs and flock of sheep. And for this reason, if he said: "I leave my flock [fouc] of animals," it would mean the sheep, and if he said "My flocks of animals," and there were several flocks [fous] of sheep or {herds} of pigs, they would all be meant; and if he reduced one {flock} or increased others, after making the will, the will would still be valid as their numbers grew or shrank. And if the testator removed so many animals that the remainder could not be called a flock [fouc], the legacy of the flock would be invalid. And by flock [fouc] should be understood so many animals that a shepherd/swineherd [garde] is needed, for it is not a flock unless there is a special shepherd/swineherd for it; and for this reason there are in the towns shepherds [bergiers] and swineherds [porchiers] who look after the animals of all those who have so few animals that they don't want to hire a special shepherd or swineherd [garde]. And for this reason, even if it is called a flock {or herd} when they are all together, each individual owner cannot say that he has a flock of animals.

421. For everything which is named specially in a will, if it spoils or increases in value after the will is made, the increase or decrease in value accrues to the person to whom it was left, for it is right that the person who can have the loss should get the gain; for example if someone leaves a parcel of land which he purchased or which is a fifth of his inherited real property and, after the will was made, he builds a house or plants a vineyard on the said land, without revoking the will, the person to whom the land was left should take the the the land as it is after the testator's death. And against this, if there was a house or a vineyard on the land when the will was made, and the person making the will demolished the house or cut down the vines, the person taking under the will could not ask for anything except the land as he found it. And by what we have said you can understand the same for other things which can increase or decrease in value after the will is made, as you have been told before.

422. Under our customs you can make a conditional will, for example if someone said: "I leave my personal property and my purchased property

to my wife provided she looks after my children and behaves honestly and keeps her good reputation; and if she does not, I wish her to be required to give to my heirs what I leave her." If a legacy is made this way and the wife does not fulfill the condition,—for example if she behaves foolishly[21] or sends the children away,—she must give back what was left to her. And for this reason every time a will is made conditional, the person who wants to take his legacy under the will must give security to the executors of the deceased that he will fulfill the condition as it is stated in the will, except for conditions which are against God, for example if someone said in error in his will: "I leave a hundred pounds to Pierre provided that he avenges me on Jehan who beat me"; because such legacies and such conditions are invalid; for, if he had beaten Jehan, he could not ask for what was promised him because of his evil deed; and a will should not be made in cruelty but in mercy. And some people have also left things to their wives, or to their husbands, on condition the survivor did not remarry; but this condition is against God; and for this reason we are of the opinion that the survivor is not required to fulfill the condition, unless he promised to do so to the testator, or vowed himself to chastity. And legacies should not be lost for this reason, for reasons of love and charity provide that one can leave things to the other, and the evil conditions should be removed. And by the conditions in wills which we have named you can understand the others which should be fulfilled or not fulfilled.

423. It is true that if the heir of the deceased wants to give good security to the executors that he will pay on their advice everything in the will, he should not be prevented from taking possession of the deceased's estate; for if the executors took the property to pay out on the will, and there was a residue, they would have to give it to the heir.

424. The heir may have the executors made to give an accounting of what they did with the will which they undertook to administer, for two reasons: the first is because everyone should want the wishes of his predecessor to be carried out; the second is so that if there is a residue when everything has been paid, it goes to the heir; and when he may have a right to something, it is proper for him to know what it is, and he could not know unless an accounting was made concerning the will.[22]

425. Because simple people do not know the form for making a will, and they often need to do so in a place where they cannot easily obtain counsel, it is right that we should put in our book the general form of

making a will, so that those who want to make a will can find an example of how to do so:

426. *"In the name of the Father and of the Son and of the Holy Spirit, Amen. I, Pierre, of such and such a place, make known to all those present and to come that, for the good of my soul, in my right mind and with good memory, I make and ordain my will in the following manner: first, I wish and ordain that all my debts be paid and restitution made for all my wrongs, which are admitted or proved before my executors."* And he should name and specify in his will all the debts and the wrongs which he can remember, for it is a great help and relief to the executors and those who are named in the will: to the executors because they are without difficulty made certain of the truth by the testimony of the testator; and to those who are named in the will because they are relieved from making proof. And what is not mentioned in the will {where it says}: *"my debts and wrongs which are admitted or proved before my executors,"* must be proved by two valid witnesses, as you would have to do before a judge in other disputes, for the executors are the judges in the disputes arising from a will, on this issue and others according to the power given to them in the will; and if the testator names in his will any of his debts or wrongs, those others who wish to make an honest proof should not suffer loss. Afterwards you should say in the will,—when the debts and wrongs are paid and specified, or described in general terms {by the words} *admitted or proved before my executors,*—what you want to leave and distribute for the good of your soul in charity;[23] and then when you have said how much and to whom, you should specify the funds from which these bequests will be paid, for example out of personal property or out of purchased real property or out of a fifth of your inherited real property, or out of all three, if one or two are not enough. And afterwards you should name your executors and give them the power to execute your will by saying: *"And to take care of all the above things, I have selected as executors Phelippe, Guillaume and Jehan,"* and you should give their surnames, and give them full powers to receive and pay out property, and full possession of the property from which the will should be paid; and because of the danger that one or two of the executors may have such a legal excuse that they cannot attend to the work of the will, you should give the power to them jointly and severally if the others cannot be there. And after that you should put the time when the will was made, and seal it with your seal and the seals of your executors, if they are people who have seals. And if the testator has no seal, he must have it sealed with an authentic seal, for example the seal of

the *bailli's* court, or of the ecclesiastical court, for the seal of a simple priest is worth only one witness; but if two priests affix their seals, it is enough if they testify in the writing that they were present when the will was made, or that they heard it repeated by the testator and he asked them to affix their seals. And if the testator is laid low by sickness, so that he cannot wait for people to come who can witness by their seals, if the will is attested viva voce, it is enough as we have stated elsewhere in this chapter.

427. If someone makes a will and the executors have such legal impediments that there is a delay in the execution of the will, the will should not for that reason be nullified; but it is reasonable that, as soon as the news of it reaches Holy Church or the lord of the district, they should have the will executed by honest persons for the good of their souls.

428. Although the count who holds directly from the king has the cognizance of wills when they are brought before him, nevertheless, if there is a dispute over a will, he cannot prevent the suit going to an ecclesiastical court, provided this is done before the suit is begun before the count. And if a suit over a will is brought to an end in a secular court, however it is administered, and for whatever parties, the ecclesiastical court can inquire how the case went, so that if there is something to be set right, it can be set right by the ecclesiastical court, for it is they who, more than other people, have authority over what is done for the salvation of souls.

Here ends the chapter on wills, which are valid and which are not.

Notes

1. For definitions of real property and personal property, see Chapter 23. Purchased real property, Old French *conquès* means real property which was not inherited by the person holding it, but acquired through such means as gift or purchase for money. It may be sold or left in a will, whereas only up to one-fifth of inherited real property may be left in a will. See §365.

2. The *issues* includes all personal property derived from real property, such as rents, crops, timber, taxes.

3. The normal word for inheriting property in English is "take," and I have used this systematically to translate the Old French *en porter.*

4. It is not clear whether the testator must make his will orally or must say that he is of sound mind and memory.

5. If there was no legal heir who was of age, the lord from whom land was held could make a seizure of the land and take the fruits until the heir came of age or until a member of his lineage did homage for the land in custodianship.

6. Marriage partners share equally in real property purchased during the marriage. Thus half of the property mentioned in this paragraph belongs to the husband and the other half to his wife, and she leaves him her half as a life interest. When the husband dies it will pass to her son.

7. The words "for ever" translating *a tousjours* are words with a special meaning in law, because they signify an outright gift of the ownership of real property, and not just transfer of possession or of a life interest.

8. By "stranger" Beaumanoir means a person from another jurisdiction.

9. The "baron" is the highest vassal, holding his fief directly from the king.

10. I have followed Beugnot, which includes here the word *s'apert* (taken from MS C) "appears in court," for Salmon seems to lack a main verb in this sentence.

11. For the *masure*, see Eugène de Lépinois, *Recherches historiques et critiques sur l'ancien comté et les comtes de Clermont en Beauvoisis du XIe au XIIIe siècle* (Beauvais: Pere, 1877) 305.

12. The substance of this section is repeated in §424.

13. If a person who had left something in a will sold the thing before he died, the bequest was nullified. See §416.

14. For redemption, see Chapter 44.

15. I use here the common legal term for gifts between living persons.

16. A hundred sous is equivalent to five pounds.

17. The translation of *bonne volonté* by "good will" appears to preserve an ambiguity.

18. This passage is somewhat obscure, but the wife, already in possession of her own half, seems to be asking for the half her husband had owned and which he left her in his will, *and* another "half" to make up for the wife's own half (which the husband thought he owned and left her in his will but did not). The executors point out that if he *had* owned it all, she would have ended up with both halves, which was what she now had, and she should be satisfied with that.

19. The "surname" is what American English calls a "family name." British English preserves the term "surname."

20. In Old French, the word *fouc* can mean "flock" (of sheep) or "herd" (of pigs), but not "herd" (of cows or horses). Likewise in this paragraph, the word *garde* is a generic word for persons looking after all sorts of animals, and no such word exists in English. I have been obliged to put in many of the Old French words in square brackets, because the Old French does not translate easily into English here.

21. Under the expression "behaves foolishly" there is a connotation of adultery.

22. The substance of this section is also given in §395.

23. This clause which makes specific bequests suggests that those taking under the will are supposed to pray for the testator's soul in return for what they receive.

13. Dower

Here begins the thirteenth chapter of this book which speaks of dowers which, by reason of their marriages, women should have after the death of their husbands.

429. After speaking in the preceding chapter of wills, it is right that we should in this following chapter speak of dower,[1] because after those who are married have set out their last will and testament and they have departed this life, their wives, who remain distressed [*esbahies*] and cheerless [*desconfortees*], must be kept from harm that might be done to them, after the death of their husbands, in the matter of what they have acquired through their marriage; and for this reason we will say what dower they should have and how they should hold it according to our customs.

430. As a general custom,[2] a wife takes in dower half of all the inherited real property legally possessed by her husband on the day of the marriage, unless the husband had had a former wife by whom he has children, since then she only takes in dower a quarter of her husband's inherited real property: for the children of the first wife take the half which their mother would have taken in dower, and if the man has had two wives and children by each wife, the third wife takes only an eighth; and from this you can undertsand that the fourth wife takes a sixteenth. But however many wives the husband had had, if he has no children by them, the dower of the succeeding wife is not decreased, for the inherited real property of the husband remains what it was when he married a wife by whom he had no issue.

431. In a suit on dower there is no continuance or counsel day, but there is an inspection day;[3] and so that the wife is not caused a loss by delay, the judge should take possession of all she is asking for in dower as soon as she asks him to, and then determine in the presence of the parties if there is dower or not.

432. According to our[4] custom, if a man has children by his wife and she dies, the man may if he wishes sell his inherited real property in spite of his children, even though the mother of the children would have taken half of it in dower; for according to our custom dower does not devolve to children in such a way that the father cannot do what he wants with his property after his wife's death.

433. If it happens that a man sells his property during his wife's lifetime, and the wife does not wish to waive her dower rights in it, the man can warrant the sale during his lifetime in spite of his wife. And, if the wife dies before the husband, he warrants it for ever; but if the husband dies first, the wife takes her dower; and as soon as she dies, the property goes back to the person who purchased it, even though she had children by the man who sold it. And this shows clearly that according to our custom a mother's dower does not devolve to her children.

434. I saw a case in which it appears clearly that dower does not devolve to children, for a gentleman had three wives: by the first and second he had daughters, and by the third both sons and daughters; afterwards the gentleman died; the daughters of the first wife asked for half of his inherited real property because their mother had had inchoate dower in it; the daughters of the second wife asked for a quarter of the property because of their mother's inchoate dower, and the male son [fius masles] of the third wife asked for the firstborn's share of all his father's inherited real property, that is to say two-thirds of the fiefs and the principal dwelling and the homage of his sisters for the other third,[5] even though they were older than he was from previous marriages. And on this they requested a judgment.

435. It was judged that the male heir of the last wife would take the firstborn's portion, that is to say two-thirds of the fiefs and the principal dwelling and the homage of his sisters for the other third.

436. A woman who has a house on her dower land must provide it with an adequate roof and doors.

437. If a woman has a wood on her dower lands, she may not cut trees until they are seven years old.

438. If a woman has a vineyard on her dower land, she must maintain it in such a way that it is not spoiled [essiliés].

439. According to our custom, the wife takes in dower the principal dwelling, even though it is a castle, and all its surroundings, even though they are held from several lords; and the case of the castle I have seen challenged and then approved by a judgment.

440. When her husband dies, a wife has the choice of leaving all the personal property and debts to the heirs and taking her dower free and clear. And if she wishes, she can take a share of the personal property; and if she takes a share, she must pay her share of the debts; and once she has made her choice, she cannot change to the other, but she must abide by her choice, whether she gains or loses.

441. Now we must see if she must give security [*fera seurté*] to the heirs to pay her share of the debts if she takes a share of the personal property.

442. It was judged in Creeil, which is part of the county of Clermont, that she was not obliged to give security, for the heir has a defense against the creditors [*deteurs*] since he is only obligated for his share.⁶ But it is a good thing,—if it is reported to the judge that she has only a small amount of property to pay her debts with and she is not being careful with her personal property, or that she wants to leave the district,—that her portion should be attached until she has given good security to the lord. But if she wishes, she need answer only in the ecclesiastical court during her widowhood.

443. When a widow remarries, she returns completely to the jurisdiction of the secular court.

444. When a woman who holds in dower dies, the dower property goes to the heirs in the condition it is in at the death of the woman, even though there is on it timber old enough to be cut, or grapes ready for harvest, or wheat or small grains ready to be reaped, or meadows ready to be mown.⁷ But if there are rents or money payments owing, and their due date is past before she dies, such debts go the the heirs of the woman or to carry out her will, if she designates them for that purpose.

445. The general custom of dower, which is that the widow takes half of what the husband held on the day of their marriage, as I said above, began in a law [*establissement*] of good king Phillip {Augustus}, king of France, who was reigning in the year 1214.⁸ And he ordered this law to be

observed in the whole kingdom of France, except as concerns the crown and a few baronies held from the crown, which are not divided into halves for dower, and the wives take only what has been agreed on at the time of the marriage. And before this law of king Phillip, no woman had anything in dower except what had been agreed on at the marriage. And that the custom was that way of old is made clear by a promise that the priest makes the man say when he marries him, for the man says to the woman: "I endow thee with the dower which was agreed on between my family and thine."

446. If a married man takes land by lateral inheritance, for example from his uncle or aunt, from his brother or sister, or from a more distant relative, and the man dies, the widow has no dower rights in such property; but if the man inherited something laterally before he had married her, it is clear that she has a dower right in it, as she does in the other inherited real property of the husband.

447. If property descends directly to a man while he is married, for example from his father or mother or his grandfather or grandmother, or from a more distant ancestor, and the man dies after he takes it but before his wife dies, she has a dower right to half of the property; but if the inheritance does not come until after the man has died, even though she had children by him, she cannot ask for any part of it in dower, for her husband had never held it; instead it descends to the heirs, and if the heirs are not of age, the guardianship of the heirs and the property goes to the mother, and she would also have guardianship of all other laterally passed property that was taken by her underage children.[9]

448. In one case a widow would have a dower right in property which her husband had never held or reaped benefits from: that is to say, if a man marries and he has a mother who holds land in dower through the father of the husband, if this husband dies, and then his mother who held in dower dies also after him, the wife would have dower rights in half of what the mother held in dower, for it had already descended to the husband from the father during the marriage, since the mother had only a life interest, and for this reason it is included in the second dower as if the mother had died before her son.

449. There are three cases in which the heirs do not {on the widow's death} take the dower property just as [*aussi vestu comme*] they find it. The

first case is when a widow farms out the dower land to sharecroppers, half and half. For in such a case, if she dies before the crops are harvested, the sharecropper [*li gaaigneres*] takes his half of the crop, unless the heirs want to give him back his reasonable costs he has invested; for after her death the widow cannot warrantee a deal she makes on her land, and it is not reasonable for the other party to lose what he invested in good faith. Nevertheless, the other party might make an unwise investment, for example if he took the land to farm it for a term of years, or to improve it with marl [*marler*], or to plant a vineyard, for in that case the heirs are not required to keep the agreement after the death of the widow or to repay such costs.—The second case is if a woman has farmed out her land for a payment of grain or money, and she dies before the crops are harvested; in that case the heirs should take only what the farmers owe, unless they see that the thing was given at an unreasonable price, for then the heir can take all the fruits by paying a reasonable profit [*li gaaignage*].—And the third case where the heirs do not take what is on the dower land is when wood has been cut or grapes cut from the vines, or if wheat or small grains have been reaped before the widow's death, for these are personal property which has been separated from the real property. But various frauds might have to be put right, for example if the wood was cut down too soon, before it was seven years old, or the grapes cut before they were ripe [*en verjus*], or the grain reaped while it was still too green, and then the woman died before the time when these crops should have been harvested. In this case the heirs could take the crops if they were still on the land. And the heirs of the deceased widow would have to restore the loss incurred in the things which were harvested too soon, even if the items had been removed from the dower lands before the widow died, for it would be a wrong, and for this reason the heirs {of the husband} would have an action for damages for such wrongs against the heirs of the woman (or the executors, if the executors had enough of the woman's possessions that they could make restitution for such damages).

450. I saw another judgment made in which it is clear that heirs are not endowed with the dower rights of their mother, and the judgment concerned a knight who had two wives: by the first he had a son, and by the second a son and a daughter. The knight died, and so did his wife; the children made a distribution according to the custom of the area, and then the male son of the second wife died; his sister wanted to take the inheritance laterally because she was his sister by the same father and mother, and

because their mother had had dower rights in what she and her brother had taken in the distribution, and there was no other heir but herself to the dower rights. The male heir by the first wife answered that he should take the inheritance laterally for two reasons: the first being that sisters do not share in lateral inheritance;[10] and the second reason being that dower rights could not be inherited according to the custom of the county; and since the property descended from his father, of whom he was the son and male heir, he requested to take the property laterally; and on this issue they requested a judgment.

451. It was judged that the male heir would take the inheritance laterally and that the sister would take nothing; and by this it is clear that according to the custom of the county dower rights are not inheritable.

452. When we said, for various reasons, that dower rights are not inheritable according to the custom of Beauvais, we were talking about property held in fief; for property held in villeinage *is* distributed according to dower rights; for example if a man has three wives, and children by each wife and afterwards the father dies, the children of the first wife take a half of all the villeinages because their mother had inchoate dower in them; and the children of the second wife take half of the remaining half, that is to say a quarter of the whole, because their mother had dower rights in that amount; and the children of the third wife take a half of the remaining quarter, that is to say an eighth of the whole, because their mother had inchoate dower in that amount; and when these distributions have been made there remains an eighth of the property. Or if there are only children from two wives, the first take a half and the second a quarter, and there remains a quarter of the land to divide up. And you should know that the remaining quarter, if there are only two sets of children, or the eighth if there are children from three wives, should be equally divided among all the children, whether from the first or the second or the third wife, as much to one as to the other, for no children have any right as firstborn in the part of their father's property which was not encumbered with dower (that is to say as concerns villeinage property, for we will speak of fiefs and how they are divided in the chapter on direct and lateral inheritance).

453. According to the custom of Beauvais, although ladies take fortresses [*fortereces*] in dower, we mean fortresses which are not castles [*chastel*], which are called castles because they are the principal ones in the

county, such as Clermont or Creeil, for none of these would be taken in dower.

454. Nevertheless as soon as the lord of a castle dies, the widow should remain in possession of the castle residence until the heir has provided her with an adequate dwelling according to the dower of the land and the place where the dower is situated, even though the widow has other residences on her land. And we saw a judgment on this matter for the lady of Milly[11] in the king's court. For when her husband died, his heirs by his first wife claimed that she should not take the castle of Milly in dower for two reasons: the first was that their mother had had inchoate dower in it, and the second reason was that it was a castellany. But neither of these arguments prevented her from taking it by a judgment, and by this it is clear that heirs do not inherit dower rights in Beauvais in property held in fief; for if such rights were inherited as they are in {the Ile de} France, she would not have taken it in dower, since the lord of Milly had had another wife and children by the first wife; and the children of the first wife would have taken the castle because of their mother's dower rights.

455. Even though according to the customs of Beauvais the second or the third wife takes her {dead husband's} residence in dower, it nevertheless does not go to the children she had by the husband through whom she takes the residence in dower. When she dies, the residence goes to the oldest male heir of the deceased husband to the exclusion of the others.

456. We have seen several suits between widow ladies on the one hand and the executors or heirs of the deceased on the other, on the the question of whether, when the widow waived her share of the personal property and debts, she could nevertheless take her best ceremonial dress [*robe a parer*] and her best bed with its bedclothes, and the best of each kind of precious object, for example the finest goblet, the finest ring and the finest chaplet; and in some places, where it was permitted out of kindness, we have seen a woman take as much personal property as the heirs and executors had left, or even more. And we have seen cases where a woman wanted to take her share in the personal property and debts, but she wanted to take also what was mentioned above, before the division. But, thanks be to God, this dispute came before us in Clermont, and it was judged that when the lord dies, whether the widow wants to take her share of the personal property and debts, or renounces her share because the debts are large and the

property small, she takes (in addition to her share) only her everyday dress, which she used to wear every day when her husband was taken sick, and her bed in which she normally slept; and then all the other personal property whatever must be brought to the distribution, if she takes a share in the personal property and debts. And if she waived her right to a share, everything must be given to the executors appointed by the deceased, or to the heirs when the payments in the will have been made. And we mean this ruling to apply to free commoners as well as to gentlemen.

457. No one should doubt that when personal property is to be divided among widows and the heirs and executors of their husbands, and there is sown wheat or *tremois*,[12] or vines advanced so that their grapes appear, that these crops are also part of the division just like the other personal property, for they are personal property according to the customs of Beauvais. And concerning any costs involved before such crops can be harvested, each party must contribute according to the share he or she is to receive of the personal property, for it would not be right for the executors to have the wheat reaped or the grapes harvested as part of the costs of execution, when the widow would take a share of the crops, and for this reason each person should contribute his or her share.

458. If it happens that the deceased dies before the wheat is sown, but the fields have their furrows or some of their furrows, or the vines are dug or pruned or sprouted [*provignies*], but the grapes have not yet appeared, in that case the crops which grow there later are not brought to the distribution, but only the work [*labourages*] done in the past: for example if the plowing [*jaschieres*][13] has been done while the lord is still alive, and the widow's dower lands are assigned to her as empty fields, if the plowing was done with her money and her husband's, it is only right that what she contributed should be returned to her by those who take the fields already plowed.

459. It is true that when the dower lands are to be separated from the portion going to the heirs, the custom is that the widow who is taking the dower makes the division of the land, and when she has done so, the heir takes whichever part he wants; and for this reason the lady, if she places the empty fields [*terres vuides*] in one portion and the already worked ones [*les pleines*] in the other, should make the reservation that, if the executors or

the heirs take the worked fields, her share of the personal property[14] should be restored to her; for if she allowed the distribution to take place without making this reservation, she would have no reimbursement for the {work done on the} worked fields, so that it would seem that she had taken that into account in making the division.

460. Dower rights are acquired by a wife as soon as a legal marriage is contracted and carnal knowledge [*compaignie charnele*] occurs between her and her husband, and not otherwise.

Here ends the chapter on dower.

Notes

1. Dower was part of the common law in colonial America, and it gave the widow a third of her husband's inherited property which he held at any time during the marriage. During the husband's lifetime, the wife's rights to dower are called inchoate dower, and after his death the widow has consummate dower. Dower is only a life interest, that is to say that the widow does not own the property, but merely enjoys the benefits derived from it during her lifetime. Dower is not to be confused with dowry, which is property a bride brings to a marriage.
2. By general custom, Beaumanoir usually means a custom observed in France as a whole; but the custom described in this section which allows children to take their dead mother's dower property does not apply in Beauvais. See §434.
3. For continuations, see Chapter 3; for counsel days see §§218 and 249; and for inspection days, see Chapter 9.
4. Beaumanoir is now discussing dower in Beauvais, and not the general custom of France.
5. For the firstborn's share, see §465.
6. See §223.
7. Some of this property would be considered personal property of the woman, which she could leave in a will, or could pass to *her* heirs, not her husband's, under ordinary circumstances. See §673.
8. This law has not been found.
9. See §517.
10. See §470.
11. Milly is in the department of the Oise, near Marseille-le-Petit. The judgment is mentioned in Le comte Beugnot, ed., *Olim.*, 4 vols. (Paris, 1839–44) 2: 208, xvi, where it is dated 1282.

12. *Tremois* is three-month-old wheat sown in the spring, also called spring wheat.

13. Here *jaschieres*, which also has a meaning of "fallow" must mean the first plowing that is done to a field after it has lain fallow; in Modern French the verb is *jachérer*.

14. That is, the personal property resulting from the crops which would grow in the worked fields.

14. Inherited Real Property

Here begins the fourteenth chapter of this book which speaks of inheritance laterally and by descent, and of distribution of realty,[1] and bringing back realty to the hotchpot,[2] and of gifts which are not to be allowed, and of paying homage to your lord.

461. There are many and varied customs in the kingdom dealing with the distribution[3] of realty which passes by descent [*en descendant*] or laterally [*par escheoite de costé*],[4] and for this reason we will speak of them in this chapter and will say how distribution of fiefs and villeinages[5] should be made; and we will say what the difference is between direct and lateral descent; and we will speak of things which must be brought back to the distribution by those who want to share in it,[6] and how outrageous gifts should not be permitted; and how heirs should approach their lord to render their homage.

462. Taking by descent [*descendemens*] is when realty passes from a father to children or from a grandfather to the children of his children; such as it happens when a man has children and they have children and the children in the first generation die before the grandfather {scil. their own father}, so that the realty passes from the grandfather to the grandchildren; or when realty passes from the mother or the grandmother. All realty which passes to people this way should be said to be by descent.[7]

463. Lateral passing is when realty is passed laterally, because of a decedent's lack of children, or even of children who are the issue of his children, so that the realty passes laterally to his closest relative, for example, his brothers, or his sisters if there are no brothers, or to his uncles if he has neither brothers nor sisters, or to his aunts if he has no brothers or sisters or uncles, or to his first cousins, male or female, if he has no closer relative, or to his closest relative within the fourth degree of kinship.

464. When realty passes by descent to sisters, among all the fiefs the oldest takes the principal dwelling [*le chief manoir*]⁸ and the rest is divided equally between them; and the younger sisters do homage to the oldest sister for the share [*partie*] that they take; and the oldest sister does homage to the lord for the share she receives in the realty, and for the homage of her sisters.

465. If realty passes by descent to children, where there are male heirs, the oldest male heir takes the principal dwelling before the rest is divided, and afterwards he takes two-thirds of each fief; and the third which remains should be divided equally among the younger children, the same amount to each whether they are brothers or sisters; and they owe homage to their oldest brother for their shares.

466. If a villeinage passes to children by descent or laterally, the oldest has no right of firstborn, instead the oldest and the younger ones take equal shares.

467. We call a villeinage the realty which is held from a lord subject to payment of a quit-rent [*a cens*] or rent [*a rente*] or a portion of the yield [*a champart*], for no such payment is required for realty which is held as a fief.

468. There is a great difference between a fief which you take by descent and a fief which you take laterally, as appears in several distinctions which you will hear.

469. The first distinction is that when heirs take a fief by descent there is a privilege of the firstborn, for the oldest male heir takes two-thirds and the homage of his younger siblings, as I said above; when they take laterally there is no privilege of the firstborn: each person takes the same as the others, and each one owes homage to the lord for his own share.

470. The second distinction is that a sister takes a portion of the third of a fief which passes by descent, and she takes nothing from a fief which passes laterally when there is a male heir who is as close kin as she is to the decedent; but when there is no male heir as close as she is, she can take laterally.

471. The third distinction is that no fief that passes by descent owes any inheritance tax [*rachat*] to the lord in the county of Clermont except the

fiefs and sub-fiefs of Bulles and Conty;[9] for these owe inheritance tax to the lord, and from son to father [*de fil au pere*]. And all fiefs which pass laterally owe an inheritance tax to the lords.

472. Marie, a gentlewoman, sued Jehane, her younger sister, claiming that she should receive her sister's homage for half of the fief which had passed to them by descent from their father and mother, and asked to have the principal dwelling excluded from the partition; to this Jehane replied that between sisters there was no right of firstborn, for which reason she wanted to have the house [*la meson*] and the other realty divided half and half, and to do homage to her lord for her own share; and on this they requested a judgment.

473. It was judged that Marie, the older sister, would take the dwelling before partition, and for half of the rest of the estate she would receive the homage of her younger sister, from which it appears that a sister has a right of firstborn only in the dwelling.[10]

474. It is certain that as long as any direct descendants have survived, whether male or female, no one who is on the lateral line (however closely related he is to the decedent) can take realty or personalty, except through execution of the decedent's will; that is to say that if it happens that I have brothers and I have children, and my children have children, and all the children die before me except the last of them who are already in the fourth degree of lineage by direct descent, they would take my realty and my personalty (whatever personalty I had not left for the good of my soul) before my brothers or other persons in a lateral line, however close the latter were to me in lineage. For no one who is lateral to me should take my realty as an heir as long as an heir can be found who is my direct descendant, however distant he may be through the deaths of fathers and mothers. For the heir who takes by descent still represents the person of his or her father and mother in taking whatever could pass to the father and mother by descent.

475. It is said above that sisters do not participate in the partition of a fief which passes laterally when there is a male heir as close as they are on the side from which the realty passes; but it is true that if it is a villeinage they do participate in the partition whether there is a male heir or not, and the sister takes as much as the male heir; for however villeinages pass they are distributed equally among those taking, whether they are male or female.

476. Fiefs which pass by descent include only one right of firstborn among the living heirs, and that this is true can be shown by the following judgment:

477. During his lifetime a knight married off his oldest son and gave him some of his realty; afterwards the knight died. He had other children and the oldest, who was married, considered that it would not be in his interest to take his right as firstborn in the estate of his father, because if he wanted to take {anything by inheritance}, he would have to bring back what his father had given him when he was married; and when his younger brother saw afterwards that his oldest brother was not claiming his right as firstborn in their father's estate, he himself petitioned to have the right of firstborn in the estate against those younger than himself. To this the younger brothers replied that he had no right as firstborn in the estate because their older brother, who need not take as a firstborn unless he wished, had taken so much from the father's estate that he was satisfied with respect to his right as a firstborn; and for this reason the younger brothers requested that what remained should be divided equally among them, giving as much to one as to the other. And on this issue they requested a judgment.

478. It was judged that because the oldest son had taken so much from the father that he was satisfied with respect to his right as firstborn, the next-born son after him could not claim the right; instead they would divide their father's estate equally, and each one would do homage to the lord for his share. And in this case the lord acquired the homage of the younger brothers, for if the oldest who was married during his father's lifetime had demanded the right of the firstborn in the estate, he would have received the homage of his younger brothers; and because he did not demand it and none of the others could demand the right of the firstborn, the homage of the younger brothers came to the lord. And by this judgment you can understand that children whom the father and mother marry have the choice of remaining silent if they wish or of bringing back what they took and participating in the distribution of the estate.

479. A person who wishes to participate in the distribution of an estate and who has received something from the father and mother must bring back everything that he took unless he no longer has it in his possession, so that he cannot bring it back. And in that case he must bring back the value

of what the thing was worth at the time it was given to him, whether realty or personalty; and when he has brought it back he should participate in the distribution of the estate as if he had never taken anything.

480. If someone has taken realty and he does not want to bring it back in because he has built on it or improved the site, and he wants instead to bring back in the value of what it was worth when he took it, that is not enough; he must bring back the realty with the improvements, for the improvement which is made to real estate which can come back into the hotchpot must be to the advantage of each of those who can have a share.

481. When someone takes some realty during the lifetime of his father and mother, and he has not maintained the property, so that it is no longer worth as much in the distribution with the rest of the property, he must bring back what it was worth when it was given to him; for the waste which he has permitted in the realty must not be to the detriment of anyone else.

482. It is said above that a person whom his father and mother have married may refrain if he wishes from participating in the distribution, and can abide by what was given to him. Neverthless, this gift that the father and mother gave might have been so outrageous that it could not be allowed to stand; for a father and mother may not give so much to one of their children that the rest are left orphans and disinherited. Therefore it is to be understood that the gift must be reasonable according to what they possess, so that the other heirs are not disinherited, for it may well happen that a father and mother love one of their children so much more than the others that they wish him to inherit everything they had; thus the others would be left without land. Nevertheless, custom does allow the person whom the father and mother marry to have more than he would have had in the distribution, provided it is not outrageously more. And whether it is outrageous must be decided by the judge at the request of the other heirs after the death of the father and mother, for as long as they are living they can and should warrantee to their children possession of what they were given when they married.

483. When some fief passes, whether by descent or laterally, the new owner should not wait for the lords from whom they are to hold the fief to summon them to offer their homage, for the lord is not required to inform them that they must appear; instead they must appear within forty days of

the fief's passing by descent or laterally; and they should not reap any benefits [*riens lever*] from the fief which derive from the realty, until their homage has been offered to the lord. And if they do not act in this manner, the lord from whom the fief should be held can make a seizure of the fief and take for himself whatever benefits he can reap [*lever des issues*] until the heirs offer their homage.

484. Supposing that someone is holding his fief without doing homage and the lord does not make a seizure of the fief (either because he does not know about it, or because he considers that he is not required to make known to the person who has taken the fief that he should pay his homage) and the latter holds the fief and reaps the benefits [*lieve*] for a great while; {if} after he has held it for a great while without an overlord, the lord wants to make a seizure of the fief, he can, if he wishes, hold it himself for as long without a vassal as the person who should have been his vassal held it without an overlord, except for those who hold as custodians. For if a lord allowed a custodian to take the harvests [*despueilles*] of the fief for which he should be the lord's vassal, and he wanted to hold the fief himself as long without a vassal as the other person had held it without a lord, and the heir to the realty came of age before that time was ended, the lord could not refuse the heir the fief because of the improper behavior of the custodian.

485. There is one case where the lord is required to give notice to those who should be his vassals that they should come to pay homage at a certain place and time; and it must be at least fifteen days from the notice. When a lordship [*seignourages*] changes from one person to another,—such as happens when a man to whom homage is due dies, and the succession and the right to the homage passes to his heir,—in this case the heir should inform those who were vassals of his father that they should come to pay their homage in the manner described above; and also when the lordship changes in some other manner, for example by gift or by sale or by passing laterally. And by this it should be understood in brief that when some lord acquires land, he should inform his vassals to come and pay homage; and when those who hold from the lord acquire land, they should present their homage to the lord in the manner described above in this very chapter.

486. It is true that each lord who acquires land should make and present his homage to his lord before he summons his own vassals to come pay him their homage; for until he has done his duty towards his lord he

should not benefit or take profit from his fief, as is said above in this very chapter.

487. During their marriage a knight and a lady bought a fief which was part of the knight's realty; they had children. Afterwards the mother died, and the children asked for half of the fief because of their mother's purchase [*aqueste*]; and within a year and a day of the death of their mother the knight who was their father redeemed it from his children for money;[11] and the lord from whom the fief was held required two homages for this fief, one for the half that the knight had in his own right by his purchase, and the other for the other half which he had redeemed from his children for money. The knight responded that there should be only one homage, for his children had no rights in the realty after he had taken it back for money; and whereas he was the lord of the entire fief, and no one took anything except him, he was not required to pay two homages. And on this issue they requested a judgment.

488. It was judged that there should be only one homage. But it is true that if the children had taken half because it was purchased property of their mother's, and the father had not redeemed it for money, there would have been two homages.

489. Because we have seen in court several demands by lords to have from their vassals two homages for fiefs which were purchased during a marriage, when one parent died and there were surviving children, even though the father or mother agreed with the children that the fief should remain whole and not be split in half, we had this declaratory judgment announced at the assizes in Clermont as follows:

490. If a gentleman and a gentlewoman, married to each other, pur-chase a fief and they have children, then afterwards the father or the mother dies, and the remaining parent and the children agree to make the distribu-tion in such a way that the purchased fief passes undivided to one of the parties, the lord from whom the fief moves cannot prevent [*debatre*] it. For a father or mother (or children among themselves if they have neither father nor mother) may partition the inheritance in the way most profitable to them, without dividing or splitting up their fief; except that[12] if a younger sibling takes, with the permission of the oldest, any whole fief, or more than a third of any one fief, then his or her homage is lost to the oldest brother

and goes directly to the lord. And if it happens that each party takes whatever share comes to him by custom without making any deals,—either father or mother with the children or the children or lateral takers among themselves,—there are as many homages as there are parts of fiefs and they are all due to the lord, except that the younger siblings give homage to their oldest brother where fiefs pass by descent; for, as we have said in this very chapter, they should take a third of the fiefs and pay homage to their oldest brother.[13] And if they have a third of several fiefs and they agree to have as their third a whole parcel, even though the whole fief is not worth more than the overall third they took, the oldest son can nevertheless not keep the homage; instead it goes to the lord. And we have confirmed all the issues discussed above by judgments.

491. Pierre should have had Jehan as a vassal for a fief which came to him laterally; and on the fief there were two dowagers still living, of which the first had half the fief and the second half of the other half, so that Jehan who was the legal heir had left only a fourth of the fief to hold and benefit from [*tenant et prenant*]. And because he saw that he would have to pay an inheritance tax [*racheter*] on the whole fief, both the part in dower and the part he could get benefits from, he elected not to pay homage or inheritance tax. And Pierre, because the land was without a vassal holding it, took possession of the quarter fief which he found vacant, for he could not disturb the dowagers. And when the dowagers died five or six years later, Jehan saw that the fief was vacated of the dowagers, and he went to Pierre who was the lord of the place and asked him to accept his homage and his inheritance tax. Pierre answered that he wanted to hold the parts that had been in dower as long as he had held the rest, for the dowagers had prevented him from taking benefits. And on this issue they requested a judgment, namely whether Jehan would take the whole or if his lord would hold what the dowagers had held for as long as he had held the quarter fief for lack of a vassal.

492. It was judged that Jehan would pay homage {and take} the whole thing because Pierre, who was the lord of the fief, had taken possession of what he found vacant for lack of a vassal. But if Pierre had refrained from reaping benefits, and Jehan had taken the quarter without paying homage, and Pierre had waited until the dowers fell vacant, he could have taken possession of the whole thing and held it as long without a vassal as Jehan had held the quarter without a lord. And by this you can see that the lord lost by taking possession and reaping benefits too soon.

493. Some have doubted that once realty has passed from the father and mother to the children, by their grant or their gift or in any other way, it can later come back to the father and mother; but it can. When a child dies without heirs of his body, his realty and purchased real property and personalty pass to his father or mother as next of kin, even though he may have brothers and sisters; and it would be a bad thing if the father and mother lost both their child and their property, for you are in any case more easily consoled for one loss than for two, and fathers and mothers will be more easily persuaded to make gifts to their children. And when it is said that realty does not pass by ascent, it means that if I have a father and I also have children and I die, my realty passes down to my children and not up to my father; even if my children were dead and they had left children, my realty would go to them rather than to my father. And however many degrees distant they were as descendants they would take before my father. But if I have no heirs of my body, no one who is lateral to me takes my property before my father or mother, as is said above.

494. If I have realty which came from my father and my father dies and then I die without heirs of my body, my realty which came from my father does not pass to my mother, but it passes laterally to my closest relative through my father, even if he were at the fourth degree of lineage; for my mother is a stranger to the realty which comes to me from my father, and my father is a stranger to the realty that passes to me from my mother. But as to my personalty and my purchased real property, wherever it came from, no one takes them laterally as next of kin before my father or my mother.

495. It would be different if I had neither father nor mother, nor heirs of my body, and I had a grandfather or grandmother, and I died; for the realty which I had taken through my father or mother would go back to my grandfather or grandmother on whose side of the family it had come down, rather than to my brothers or sisters; for my brothers and sisters would not be in my direct line of descent. But my personalty and purchased real property would be inherited laterally by my brothers and sisters because they would be a point closer to me, even though it was laterally. And yet we believe that custom here gives them more than the law does, for we understand that according to the law, nothing should go out of the direct line of descent as long as there is a living survivor, whether an ancestor or a descendant. And this custom, which takes the personalty and purchased real property away from the grandfather or the grandmother and gives them to the brothers and sisters, would not take them away from the

children of children, who are at that same degree of lineage down the direct line as are the grandfather and the grandmother going up the line.

496. If I have neither father nor mother, and no heirs of my body, and no brothers or sisters, but I do have a grandfather or grandmother and also nephews and nieces, and I purchase some real property and then die, my personalty and realty pass to my grandfather or my grandmother and not to my nephews or nieces, even though they are of the same degree of lineage. And by this example you can understand that the law tries [*drois se prent pres*] to prevent anything from leaving the direct line of descent, either ascending or descending.

497. According to the custom of Beauvais, I can make a third of my fief into a sub-fief and keep the homage of it, for example if I married one of my children. But if I split off more than a third, the homage of the third and the extra passes to the lord. And I could do this in such a way as to lose even more, for example if I kept the homage for the portion which was more than third, for then I would have to pay a penalty of sixty pounds for the offense. And I would have to warrantee to my children what I had given them, or the same value, if the lord wanted to hold it as long without a vassal as my children had held it without doing homage to him, which is something he could do if he wanted.

498. If it happens that someone gives a third of his fief inter vivos[14] to his children and keeps the homage, and then dies, and those who were married and who took the third wanted to stay out of the distribution and not bring {the gift} back in to divide it with their unemancipated [*en celle*] brothers and sisters, the two-thirds of the fief which the father had retained when he gave the third to his children should not be divided in three a second time; instead the heirs should consider how much the father gave and how much remained, and take out a third from the whole for the younger brothers and sisters. And if they take more than a third, either the ones who were married first or the unemancipated ones, the homage of all the younger siblings' share goes to the lord.

499. Now let's see,—[15] if a person has sixty pounds' worth [*livrees*] of land in a single fief and he has four children and he marries one of the younger children and gives him twenty pounds' worth of land from the fief; and, after he has received the homage for it, he dies, and the child with the

twenty pounds' worth does not want to bring them back in, but stay with what the father and mother gave him when he married,—if the gift will stand. We say no, when there is no other fief or realty but this one, for the other two younger children would take nothing if the gift were permitted.[16] And if they took, it would have to be from the oldest's share of forty pounds' worth of land; and he would lose the homage for the others' portions, which would go to the lord. And because the others would be caused too much loss, such unfair gifts should not be permitted. But if there were some other realty, {whether} fiefs or villeinages, from which the unemancipated younger siblings could take shares as great or almost as great (within forty or fifty sous' worth [*soudees*]) as that which their brother or sister had already had, the gift would not be canceled, for if the loss is not too great or too evident, the marriage gift which a father and mother give should stand.

500. There are places where an uncle divides an inheritance with a nephew, but this is not our custom; for according to our custom whatever is taken at a distribution passes to the closest kin, whether direct or lateral, on the side from which the realty comes. And everyone should know that the uncle is closer than the nephew, for the nephew is one degree further down, since he is the son of the brother or sister, and the uncle is at the same level as the nephew's father was.[17]

501. We saw a case where some realty passed laterally to several first cousins who were sons of brothers and sisters {of the deceased}. The cousins descended from the brothers did not want their cousins who had descended from the sisters to take any of the realty, for they said that if their father and the mother of their cousins had both lived, and the realty had passed in their lifetimes, the brother, who had been their father, would have taken the whole since the realty was a fief and sisters do not share in a fief which passes laterally.[18] And since their cousins' mother would have taken nothing if she and their own father had been both living, and their cousins had no claim to the realty except through their mother, they said that it was wrong for them to ask for a share in the distribution. The cousins who were children of the sister countered this by saying that the argument put forward by their cousins born of the brother was not a good one; for, they said, things should be judged according to how they stand now, and at present they were all proven first cousins, and of the same degree of kinship, and male heirs; and although their mother would have taken nothing if she

and her brother had been both living, nevertheless if the brother had died and the realty had passed while she was still living, it would have passed to her; and since she could be the legal heir under at least one circumstance, and they were her children, male heirs like those who had been born to their mother's brother, they said that it was not lawful for them to be excluded from taking as first cousins in the distribution; and on this issue they requested a judgment.

502. It was judged that they would all participate as first cousins in the distribution of what passed laterally. And by this judgment you can see that those who are of the same degree of lineage all share equally in realty passing laterally, if they are male heirs and they are from the side of the family from which the realty comes, and the women do not, unless they are closer kin, except in taking villeinages and personalty, for they take a share of these along with the males; and they also share in what descends from their fathers and mothers, or from their grandfathers and grandmothers, as was said above in this very chapter.

503. If a father and mother had married their child and given him as a marriage gift some real property they had purchased jointly and the child later died without heirs of his body, after his father or his mother had died, the father or mother who survived him would take the half of the real property they had purchased and given him; and the closest kin to the deceased parent would take the other half, since the father and mother had the same rights in the property they had given their child: thus each can take in his or her own right only half of the property if the child dies without an heir. But if the father and mother are both living when their child dies without an heir, everything they gave their child comes back to them unless the child has alienated [*aloué*] it while still alive, and excepting what he can legally devise and has left in his will: that is, his personalty and his purchased real property [*conquès*] and a fifth of his realty, as is said in the chapter on wills {Chapter 12}; and except for the portion which the son's wife takes, if the son who dies without an heir was married: that is, her dower, half the personalty and half the purchased real property. And if it was a daughter who was married [*qui fust marie* {for *mariee*}] by the father or the mother or both, and she dies without heirs of her body, her husband takes a half of the personalty and half of the purchased real property; and this would be true even if there was no personalty except what she brought to the marriage from her father or mother, because of the marriage partnership.[19]

504. In addition, if anyone is the custodian of a child and the child acquires something while in their custodianship, everything which they acquire belongs to the custodian; except that whatever is given to them or left to them in a will should be kept for them until they are of age; and this does not apply to those who are under guardianship (and not under custodianship),[20] for if they purchase something it should be theirs, and they should be given an account of their personalty and villeinages which are held for them while they are minors.

505. Everyone should know that if someone purchases real property, as soon as the purchased property passes to his heirs, it becomes realty, as soon as the purchased property has passed a single degree {to an heir}. Thus although a person who has purchased real property can leave it all in his will, his heir who takes this purchased property can leave only a fifth of it in a will; and also no person of his lineage can redeem real property for money if the person who purchased it sells it.[21] But when the heir sells it, there can be a redemption. And by this it can be seen that realty is legally *that real property which has passed to an heir one degree by descent or laterally [c'est drois eritages puis qu'il descent ou eschiet un seul degré de lignage]*.

Here ends the chapter on taking realty by descent or laterally.

Notes

1. Real estate, and the inheritance of real estate, is an area of the law which is full of jargon, or specialized vocabulary, that can be misleading. The reader is advised to consult the original text if in doubt. Since in the rest of this book the word *eritage* tends to refer to only one kind of real estate, namely land, the word "land" is often used to translate *eritage* except in this chapter, where the translation "realty" is used. For a definition of what is included by Beaumanoir in his word *eritage*, see Chapter 23, especially §672. Section 505 of the present chapter also states that, properly speaking, realty is that real property which has passed once by reason of the death of its former holder. Only one-fifth of such realty may be left in a testament, the rest passing by operation of law to the legal heirs. A parcel of land purchased (not inherited) can be left in its entirety by a testator; and such property is called not *eritage* but *aqueste* or *conquès*, which I have generally translated as "purchased real property." For the difference between realty and personalty (real and personal property) see Chapter 23.

2. The word "hotchpot" is commonly used in modern American law to designate the augmented estate of a decedent in which earlier gifts to beneficiaries

(for example, gifts to children on their emancipation or marriage) have been included or "brought back." A beneficiary who has received during the life of the decedent more than he or she would take if he or she brought it back in and then received a fair share of the hotchpot can (ignoring any moral considerations) benefit more by retaining the gift and refusing to participate in the partition. Hotchpot is a concept known to Roman law as *collatio*; see Justinian, *Digest*, 37.6.

3. Two English words are used to describe splitting up realty: "partition" and "distribution" (Old French *partie*). The first is used to designate a physical division of land which has had multiple owners, and where one or more of the owners is having his or her share split off from the rest of the parcel. The second is used to designate how a decedent's realty is divided between multiple takers, and may or may not include a physical division of land. Since the word *distribution* is commonly used in American law to describe the execution of a will for both realty and personalty, it is retained here to translate *partie*; but it must be borne in mind that in this chapter it refers only to splitting up realty and distributing it to the heirs of some decedent. Note that *partie* also means "share," as in §464.

4. In modern American law, "escheat" refers to what happens when an estate passes to the state because no heirs can be found. The Old French *escheoite* has another meaning, for it refers to passing of land from a decedent to a person not his direct descendant (e.g., to his brother rather than to his son). For this reason the word "escheat" has not been used in the translation.

5. As defined in §467, a villeinage is real property which is not held as a fief, for homage, but for a rent or other payment in money or kind, or as a sharecropper.

6. See note 2 above.

7. Beaumanoir fails to mention in §462 that living parents can inherit from their children who die without heirs of their body: "When the child dies without heirs of his body, his realty [*eritages*] and purchased real property and personalty pass to his father or mother as next of kin . . ."; §493 below.

8. A possible translation for *chief manoir* would be "homestead," but this word has other meanings besides what is meant here, so I have chosen to translate it as "principal dwelling." In §472 Beaumanoir uses the word *meson* as a synonym for *chief manoir*.

9. Bulles and Conty are north-northeast of Clermont.

10. According to §465, an oldest male heir would take the dwelling and two-thirds of the realty. From what Beaumanoir says here, however, it appears that the oldest sister also receives, as a right of firstborn, the homage of the younger sisters for their share of a fief which passes by descent.

11. For redemption, see Chapter 44.

12. Salmon here gives *essieuté qui* which looks like a misprint for *essieuté que*. Beugnot gives *exepté que*, 1: 234.

13. Section 465.

14. That is, while both are living,

15. These are the words by which Beaumanoir introduces an example or a hypothetical.

16. The oldest of the four would take two-thirds (see §465) and the three others

would have shared the remaining third, except that the married brother wants to keep it all.

17. Beaumanoir appears to mean that where the deceased had two brothers, and one of the brothers had a son and then died, leaving two relatives related to each other as uncle and nephew (and to the deceased as brother and nephew), the nephew does not, according to the Beauvais custom, take the share his father (the decedent's dead brother) would have taken if he had been still living. In modern law, we would say that the nephew does not take by representation.

18. See §470.

19. In Beauvais, marriage is considered as a kind of partnership because the two married persons mingle their assets and behave in other ways as partners. See Chapter 21.

20. For custodianship and guardianship, see Chapter 15.

21. For redemption, see Chapter 44.

15. Custodianship

Here begins the fifteenth chapter of this book which speaks of custodianships and guardianships, and the age of majority of children, and when they come of age in the Beauvais region.

506. We will discuss here those who take custodianship[1] for minor children and the difference between custodianship and guardianship,[2] and at what age children are old enough to hold land and do things for which they can be held responsible; and we will discuss all these things in this chapter because one depends on the other.

507. Custodianship occurs when someone dies leaving a minor child, who cannot and should not pay homage to the lord for what they took by descent as a fief from their father or mother, their grandfather or grandmother, or from some higher degree. When this happens, the next of kin to the child who belongs to the side from which the fief descends[3] can take the custodianship if he wishes and pay homage to the lord as a custodian and be in his homage; and he should retain the custody until one of the children comes of age. And when one of the children comes of age he should do homage for his share and become the custodian of his minor brothers and sisters.

508. No one is obliged to become a custodian if he does not want to; and a person who takes it should be careful for as soon as he has taken it and done homage to the lord, he must pay to the lord an inheritance tax [*rachat*] for the fief of the sum of one year's value, at his own cost, and he must protect and look after the minor children at his own expense according to their estate; and when the first reaches his majority, he must give him what he held in his custody free and clear and unencumbered.

509. It is true that no one is obliged to be a custodian or a guardian of children, nor be anyone's heir, if he does not wish; but as soon as he has

consented, such as by profiting from anything that will be part of the custodianship or guardianship, or if anyone has profited as an heir from anything that passes by descent or laterally, he will not be able to have second thoughts; indeed if he holds as a custodian he will have to pay the lord and look after the children and give the property free and clear to the first to reach majority. And if he has the guardianship of the child, he administers the children's property; and if he takes as an heir, he must pay the debts of the person to whom he agreed to be the heir so that however little he took as an heir he will have to pay everything owed by the person whose heir he became.

510. However a fief comes to minor children, whether by descent or laterally, the custody goes to the next of kin to the children, provided he is from the side of the family from which the fief passed: that is to say, that if the father and mother die, and the fiefs pass to the minor children, and there are fiefs from the father and from the mother, the next of kin to the children on the father's side, man or woman, will take custodianship of the fiefs from the father, and the next of kin on the mother's side will take the custodianship for what comes to the children from the mother; and these two who take the custodianship will be made to surrender the property free and clear at the majority of the child, as is said above, not equally, but each according to what he held of the real property because of his custodianship.

511. Pierre had the custodianship of children, and the fief was so small it did not suffice to feed and clothe the children; the same children had some villeinages, of which Pierre was the administrator as guardian of the children; and Pierre wanted to use the profits from these villeinages to provide the children with what they needed over and above what the fief was worth, and the relatives [ami] of the children did not want to permit it, but asked the count to make Pierre give security that he would return to the children, when they came of age, all the profits from their villeinages; and they also requested that the said Pierre be required to feed and clothe the children as a custodian; and that he not be allowed to renounce the custodianship which he had taken on. And on these issues they requested a judgment.

512. It was judged that since Pierre had taken on the custodianship, however little it was worth, he had to support the children and surrender the fief free of debt when thay came of age, and guarantee all the profits from the villeinages by good security, given to the near relatives of the

children or to the lord, if the relatives did not want to take it. And by this judgment you can see that there is great danger in taking on a custodianship, and for this reason no one is obliged to do so unless he wishes; so that each person should consider well and take advice on whether the custodianship is worth anything, considering the costs, and whether it will bring a profit or a loss to take it on.

513. For villeinages there is no custodianship; but when villeinages pass to minor children and there is no fief, so that no one takes on the custodianship, the next of kin to the children can, if he wishes, have the guardianship [*garde*] of the children and manage the villeinages for the children on giving security to the relatives,—or to the court if the relatives require it,—that he will give a good account to the children when they come of age, deducting the expenses and reasonable costs of {caring for} the children. And in taking such a guardianship, it does not matter which side of the family the next of kin taking the guardianship is from, whether from the side the villeinage descends from or the other.

514. When the lord accepts anyone as his vassal because of custodianship, he should first take a good surety for the inheritance tax he will receive from the man, or a sure contract to pay it on time, if he wants to believe him without a security. And if he accepts him as a vassal, quite simply and without taking a security or other contract, he waives the right he had to the inheritance tax. For, since he has received him simply, he should guarantee him his fief freely and cost free, and should ask him for nothing more except what pertains to the service and obedience for the fief, unless the person taking the custodianship enters this homage by fraud or trickery,—for example if he claims falsely to the lord that the fief passed to him by descent, and that in such cases there is no inheritance tax, or by some other trick to make a false claim to the lord;—for this the lord could sue him and make seizure of the fief until he had his inheritance tax.

515. It is true that whatever the person holding the custodianship does, the heir on reaching his majority should find his fief free and clear without fail. Thus we can see that the custodian cannot forfeit the fief or obligate it except during the time of the custodianship. But as long as that lasts, he can forfeit it or obligate it to his lord or someone else.

516. There are several differences between custodianship and guardianship: the first is that a custodian delivers the fief free and clear to the child,

and a guardian must give an account when it is for a villeinage, for their should be no guardianship of a fief except in one case which you will hear after this.

517. When father and mother have children and the father dies, or just the mother, and there is a fief which passes from the decedent, the one remaining, whether mother or father, is the guardian of the children and the fief passing from the decedent, without paying an inheritance tax, except in the case of the fiefs of Bulles and Conti where there is always an inheritance tax, as I said above in the chapter on the passing of realty by descent or laterally {Chapter 14}.⁴

518. The second difference between custodianship and guardianship is that, if my minor children are with me and they take something from their mother who has died, they win or lose with me until they are given a proper distribution and emancipated. And those who are under custodianship can demand nothing but their fief, free and clear, when they come of age; the person who holds in custodianship keeps all the profits from the fief and all the personal property of the person leaving the fief except what is left in his will, or all the personal property if there is no will. And I have seen cases where the decedent died intestate and the archbishop tried to take all his personal property, but according to our custom he did not take them; I have given seisin to the heirs several times when I was *bailli*, to the knowledge of the bishop's court.

519. A person taking under custodianship must maintain the buildings on the property, if there are any, in the state they were in when he took them, so that the heir does not find his buildings deteriorated when he comes of age.

520. A person holding under custodianship must not allow any waste of the property: that means that if there are vines, he must not cut them down or tear them out, or leave them to grow wild without pruning, for a vine is wasted which is no longer tended, according to the custom of the district. And if there are woods on the property, they must not be cut until they are seven years old; and if there are trees sixty years old or more, they must be kept for the heir without harm. And if there are fruit-bearing trees, they must not be cut or harmed. And if someone acts in contravention to these things, the lord should take a hand and compel the custodian to desist from doing them. And if he has already done it and the lord did not

know, when the knowledge comes to the lord, he should penalize him by having him give a good security that he will make good the loss to the heir, for lords are obliged by the common law to look after the rights of those not yet of age. And because those who hold as custodians cannot take away the things mentioned above, you can understand that those who hold as guardians can do so even less, for guardianship is so called because it should guard the rights of minors in every way.

521. If a custodianship becomes available and no one volunteers to take it on because there are too many debts, or because the children are near the age of majority, so that the efforts of the person taking the custodianship would not be rewarded, or because no one wants to take it, in that case the lord can hold the fief without a vassal until the child comes of age and does homage for it. And the lord will not have to pay anything owed by reason of the fief which he holds with no vassal; the creditors [*deteur*] must wait until the child is of age and becomes the heir; and then they can sue him and ask for what is due; and thus the debts owing to creditors [*creanciers*] can be put off because no one steps forward to take on the custodianship.

522. It is certain that according to our custom a male heir is of age when he is fully fifteen years old, and a woman when she is twelve. But this does not mean they cannot remain as long as they please under the custodianship or the guardianship where they are, provided it is without fraud or sharp practice; for if they made some contract with those who have them in custodianship or guardianship, by which contract it was clear that they had made it to cut down the rights of the lord, the lord would not have to permit it. But as long as they say nothing, without making contracts, and of their own free will, the lord cannot compel them {to take the fief} and you can see this by a case which follows.

523. Pierre held in custodianship a fief for his nephew and niece who were brother and sister. The sister turned twelve before her brother turned fifteen, so that if the sister had wanted, she could have taken the custodianship away from her uncle and kept it until her brother was fifteen. And when the lord, who would have been happy to have his inheritance tax, saw that she did not take on the custodianship, he made seizure of the fief. Then Pierre came forward and said: "Sire, you do me wrong by making seizure of what I hold from you in custodianship, and for which I am doing my duty towards you." The lord answered that he should no longer be in the

custodianship because the sister, who was next of kin, had come of age; and Pierre said it was true that she was of age, but if she did not want to take on the custodianship he could not compell her to do so, and the lord should not make seizure of the fief because it *was* held by a vassal. And they submitted this issue to the council of wise men [*sages hommes*].

524. The council of wise men of the county considered this issue, and they said the lord could not compel the sister to take the custodianship of her brother, and {the lord} must permit Pierre her uncle to hold it until she did offer to take it or until the brother took the fief as an heir who was of age. And by this it can be seen that anyone can remain in the custodianship or guardianship of someone else for as long as he likes and the custodian or guardian likes, except for the frauds which can be entered into to deceive the lord as is said above.

525. If someone holds in custodianship and he has vassals because of the custodianship, the vassals are not obliged to pay a service horse [*roncis de service*],⁵ to the person who holds the custodianship. This kind of service should therefore be held back until the heir comes of age; and the reason is that the person serving {by giving the horse} should be free of it for the rest of life, and the person holding under custodianship holds only for a certain time; and if he could profit from the services, the heir would find his fief diminished by what appertained to the services which had already been paid to the person holding the custodianship; and the person holding the custodianship cannot do this except in one case which follows; and the heir suffers no loss by it, as you will hear.

526. Pierre held a custodianship, and because of it he had vassals. One of the vassals called Jehan had a custodianship and Jehan's custodianship was going to last a shorter time than Pierre's because the heir was closer to coming of age. And because the custodian was therefore not going to give homage to the heir, for whom Pierre held in custodianship, he had to pay the service to Pierre, even though Pierre was holding as a custodian. And in such a case you can see that you can receive the service, even though you are holding through a custodianship; and the heir suffers no loss.

527. When someone holds in custodianship and there are debts, the creditors should sue the person who holds the custodianship; and if the person who holds the custodianship is competent and valid and can be

sued, and the creditor, by negligence or choice, does not sue for debt the person holding the custodianship until the heir is of age, and then sues the heir, the latter has a good reason for not having to pay the debt; for he can say to the creditor: "You had notice that I was under custodianship and the custodian was capable of assisting me, and you have let pass the time of custodianship without going to court for your debt, for which reason I do not wish to have to answer." And in such a case he does not have to answer, but the creditor must seek payment of his debt from the person who held the custodianship; but in some cases the heir would have to answer the creditor, even though he had been under custodianship, and you will hear which cases.

528. If someone is under custodianship and the person holding it is impoverished before the debts are paid, the heir is not clear and must answer the creditors; but he can sue the person who held the custodianship to indemnify him; and, if he has that much, he must be compelled to indemnify the heir.

529. The second case is when the creditor is out of the area all the time the custodianship lasts, and when he comes back the heir is in possession; in such a case the creditor can sue whichever he wishes, the heir or the person who had held the custodianship. And if he sues the heir, the heir can sue for indemnification by the person who held the custodianship.

530. The third case is if there is a confiscation of the property for an offense [li baus mesfet], so that the person holding in custodianship loses the property and whatever other property he had, so that the creditors cannot sue him. In such a case the heir is compelled to answer them, for the misconduct of the person holding in custodianship is no reason for the creditors to lose what is owed them.

531. Now let's see what an heir can do in such cases, for he cannot sue a person who lost all he had. I say that if the lord takes the fief into his possession because of the forfeiture of the person holding the custodianship, the lord should pay the debts of the heir up to the value of the profits from the fief between the day the lord took possession and the day the heir pays homage as heir, or could do so having come of age; for the lord would not have to pay the profits for the time after the heir had come of age and had not yet paid homage, for he could claim he was holding for lack of a

vassal. But he would have to pay the heir the value of the profits for the time he took it because of the forfeiture of the person holding the custodianship; and if there were more debts than profits, the lord would not have to pay the extra; and if there were more profits than debts, the lord would keep them because of the forfeiture. And in this manner no one is hurt by the forfeiture except the person who forfeited; except that, if there are more debts than profits the heir loses whatever exceeds the profits, for he has no one to sue for it.

532. When a custodianship falls vacant and there is no one to take it on because it includes too many debts, or because the custodianship will last too short a time because the heir is too close to coming of age, the lord can take possession of the fief for lack of a vassal and he takes all the profit from the fief until the heir comes of age without paying off any debts. And in such cases the heir may suffer a loss, because there was no one who would take on the custodianship, for he has to pay the debts the person taking the custodianship would have paid.

533. It is true that when a custodianship falls vacant and there is no one who will take it on or undertake the support of the children, and there is no villeinage from which the children might be supported, the lord who takes the fief for lack of a vassal must give them food and clothing according to the size of the fief; for it would be a work without mercy to let the children die of want [*par defaute*] after they had inherited a right to a fief. And it is the common law,—and reason agrees,—that all minor children, who have no one who will take on their custodianship or guardianship, are and should be in the guardianship of the lord; and so their lord should give them support, which comes from them [*qui tient d'aus*], so that he can do it.

534. The guardianship which lords have over minor children is not to be understood as meaning that if the lords hold nothing of theirs or which should be theirs, they give them no support except as charity. But they should protect them from harm and hurt [*tort ne grief*]; and if they have personal property and villeinages, the lord should ensure that they are spent reasonably on feeding them properly, and the rest kept for their profit.

535. When a custodianship falls vacant, it is not divided, but the next of kin takes it all. And if the next of kin are brothers and sisters, the oldest male

takes it without dividing it with the others; and if there are only sisters, the oldest takes it, and the younger sisters have nothing.

536. Some people say that the children of commoners are always of age, but it is not true: for if it were true, then a child still at the breast could disseise himself of his property, and no law or custom agrees. The common practice is to take what he does under fifteen years of age, or a woman under twelve, in abandoning his property as nothing which he cannot repudiate later. Thus it is obvious that a male heir is not of age until he is fifteen nor the woman until she is twelve, as I said above of gentlemen.

537. It is said that commoners have no custodianship, but this is to be understood as when they have no fief. For if they have a fief, they can have a custodianship and the next of kin takes it, as I explained to you above concerning gentlemen. But if there is only villeinage, there is no custodianship. Nor would there be among gentlemen if there were only villeinages; that would call for a guardianship, as I said above.

538. If a custodianship comes to a man who lives outside the district or the castellany where the property is situated, and he has no property in the said castellany which is adequate to pay the debts he owes because of the custodianship, and he wants to take the profits of the property, they should be attached at the request of the creditors or the family of the heir until he has given sufficient security that he will disencumber the custodianship property; for otherwise the heir could be much harmed [*deceus*]. But the lord does not have to attach the property unless he is asked to do so by the family or the creditors of the heir, for if they want to say nothing, the lord should not prevent his vassal from taking unchallenged what he holds from him.

539. It is true,—when someone holds in custodianship and the creditors to whom the debts are due because of the custodianship give an extension or make a new deal or a new contract for the payment of what is due them, and meanwhile the heir comes of age,—if the creditors try to sue the heir, in that case he need not answer. They must instead sue the person who held the custodianship, for it is clear that they were dealing with him [*s'en tinrent a li*] as soon as they gave him an extension, or as soon as they changed the debt from the way it was before.

540. If a debt is owed for so long in the future that the custodianship ends before the due date, the creditor can ask the heir for payment, for he could not ask the person holding the custodianship for anything, as the due date had not arrived; and for this reason the heir must satisfy the creditor. Nevertheless, the heir can sue the person who held the custodianship for indemnity, for although the due date did not fall during the custodianship, it is still true that the debt was owing and the custodian must give the heir unencumbered property.

541. It is true that when the heir comes of age after being in custodian-ship he takes his property as he finds it: that is to say that if he pays his homage when the crops have been harvested, he can ask for nothing back, provided they were not harvested too soon by trickery. And if there are crops of wheat or small grains [mars], or timber, or other things, the heir should take them free and clear; and the person who held in custodianship cannot ask for anything, for he is no longer master of the thing as soon as the child comes of age. But if there are crop-bearing lands which in the time of custodianship were given out for crop sharing, without fraud or sharp practice, the heir should be bound by the share agreement, for the share-cropper should not lose in this case.

542. Pierre took on a custodianship for which he had to pay homage. He mortgaged to his lord the fief he held in custodianship instead of giving a security for his inheritance tax; and he died before the lord was paid, and the custodianship came to Jehan who was the next of kin after the said Pierre. Then Jehan came before his lord and offered him heart and hands, and offered to give a security for his inheritance tax. The lord said he agreed; but he also wanted Pierre's mortgage that he had made when he held the custodianship paid off before Jehan took any profits from the property. To this Jehan answered that the said Pierre could not encumber the property he held except during the tenancy of the custodianship; for which reason he requested the property to be given to him free and clear of the said mortgage, since he was ready to give a good surety for his inherit-ance tax; and on this issue they requested a judgment.

543. It was judged that the mortgage that Pierre had taken was no longer valid, and that the lord would deliver the fief to the said Jehan for his custodianship free and clear of the above-mentioned mortgage. And by this

judgment you can understand clearly that no one can mortgage what he holds in custodianship to the detriment of the heir or of the person to whom the custodianship may pass; but while it lasts you can take profits from it without causing loss to anyone.

544. Pierre held a niece of his in custodianship and because of it held great lands. The family made an agreement to marry the girl at ten years of age. When she was married, her husband took the girl's uncle to court and demanded that he surrender to him the property which was to be his wife's, which he had held in custodianship, and said that since the young woman was married, however old she was, she had come of age to hold the land by reason of the marriage; for which reason he asked the lord from whom the fief was held that if Pierre did not want to deliver it then the lord should deliver it and take him as a vassal for his wife's property. Pierre answered this by saying that the custom of Beauvais was that a woman was not of age until twelve years old, and because the custom was clear, he did homage to the lord for his custodianship and paid the inheritance tax, and he was obliged to deliver the land to the young woman free and clear when she came of age; and for this reason, if the young woman was married as a minor, he should not lose what custom gave him up to a certain time; and on this issue they requested a judgment.

545. It was judged that Pierre would hold the custodianship until the young woman was twelve years old. And by this judgment we can see that marriage does not shorten the time of holding for those who hold in custodianship. But it would be different if it had been guardianship; for if I had a daughter and her mother were dead, and I held for this daughter a fief which came through her mother, and my daughter was married while still a minor, she would take the property coming from her mother as soon as she was married. And in this case you can see one of the differences between custodianship and guardianship.

546. In one case a woman may be returned to custodianship as a minor, even though she had come of age and paid homage for her fief. For example when a woman is twelve years old and she takes her land and pays her homage, and afterwards marries a man still a minor,—under fifteen years old by the Beauvais custom and under twenty years old by the custom of France,—in that case the woman's fief goes back into custodianship, for the man still a minor she has married cannot pay homage until he comes of age;

and she, since she is married, has no power to control her fief. Therefore it is right for the person who had the custodianship of her fief to get it back and keep it until the woman's husband comes of age, or else the lord could hold it as a fief without a vassal. And if this were to be pleaded in court, this is how we believe it should go; nevertheless we have seen the woman allowed to keep the fief, but we believe it was through indulgence [*debonaireté*] and not by law.

547. It is true that a father and mother who free a child from their custodianship do not on that account lose their guardianship; but they can have them removed from their custodianship by a judge for two reasons: the first is so that no one can sue them for any offense the child may commit; and the second reason is so that if the child has something from father or mother, or by gift, or from someone else's will, he will not be in partnership [*compaignie*] with the father or mother. And these are the two reasons for voluntarily taking your child out of your custodianship.[6] But this does not mean that you cannot afterwards keep them in your guardianship, for by custom the guardianship of children put out of custodianship belongs to the next of kin.

548. Because many marriages could be made which were not appropriate, by those men and women in the custodianship of another, it is right that the person having the custodianship or guardianship should give a good security to the close kin on both sides that he will not marry them off without their advice; and if he will not give the surety, the guardianship of the children should be taken away from him, and they should be placed in the guardianship of some honest man or woman [*preudomme ou ... preudefame*] of the lineage, who will give such a surety. And if no one can be found in this manner who will take them, the lord of the area [*terre*] should have them placed in safe guardianship if he is asked to; and when things are done this way inappropriate marriages are not so quickly made.

549. Briefly, the guardianship of minor children should not be confided to anyone with a bad reputation for a serious offense, nor to imbeciles [*fol naturel*], nor to blind persons. And the administration of their possessions should not be confided to rash spendthrifts nor to poor persons, unless they give a surety for giving a good account, nor to a person who is so deaf he hears nothing, nor to a leper, for all these people cannot administer other people's things very easily.

550. Guardianship or custodianship of minor children is such that as long as they are in someone else's custodianship or guardianship, they cannot do anything which can be enforced against them without the permission of the person holding the custodianship or guardianship. And if they did it on their own authority, and they were rooked [*conchié*] or deceived, they could annul it when they came of age, as is said in the chapter on minor children {Chapter 16}. Thus you can see that if someone who is under the power of another, takes delivery of what is owed him, the person paying is not free of debt, for the person holding the custodianship can sue the person who made the payment, and he would have to answer. Nevertheless, the person suing this way would have to swear on the saints that the minor child who received the money did not hand it over to him or at his command, and that he cannot obtain it from the child because he has spent it or paid it out, or he does not know what the child did with it and cannot find out; but if he should obtain the thing that was given to the minor child safe and sound, it would be a bad thing to make the debtor pay twice. But if the thing is destroyed or damaged or lost when in the child's possesson, the debt must be paid over again; and the person who paid rashly [*folement*] must suffer this loss. Even if the debt were acknowledged in a writing, he would have to give back the writing,[7] for minor children have no power to hand over or receive their own property or give orders concerning it.

Here ends the chapter on custodianships and guardianships, and on the coming of age of children.

Notes

1. In translating the word *bail*, the word "custodianship" has been preferred to "custody" since the latter has connotations of arrest and incarceration, although it is still used to mean the care of children whose parents are no longer, for whatever reason, living as a couple. Likewise, "custodian" sounds a bit like a janitor. On the other hand, "guardian" and "guardianship" do not have unfortunate resonances to the modern ear and can be used for *garde*. Generally, "guardianship" would have been an excellent translation for *bail* if it were not the obvious choice to translate *garde*. Note that those having *bail* and *garde* do not correspond to the notions of the Latin *tutor* and *curator* (see Justinian, *Institutes*, I, 13 and 23) and that "tutor" and "curator" also have connotations which make them unsuitable for use in our

translation. Other possibilities such as "supervisor" and "foster parent" were also considered and rejected.

2. Beaumanoir promises to make this clear, but in fact he does not. He uses *bail* to refer to looking after fiefs and the minor children who inherit them, and (but for the exception listed under §517) *garde* to refer to looking after villeinages and the children who inherit them.

3. As this paragraph shows, under Beauvais law the property that passed to a person from his or her father and that which passed from his or her mother are treated differently. See also §510.

4. See §471.

5. For the *ronci de service*, see Chapter 28.

6. See §§640, 641.

7. A person paying off a debt which he had acknowledged in a writing was entitled to get his writing back when he paid off the debt.

16. Minors

Here begins the sixteenth chapter of this book which speaks of children who are not of age, how and in what cases they can gain or lose through those who administer their business.

551. According to our custom, there are a few cases where you can plead against a minor child, for example when the father of the minor had taken something or seized it by force in the year when he died, and had not been in possession of it for a year and a day, you can sue the minor heir, provided that the thing has been held less than a year and a day, in the lifetime of the father and son together. But if a year and a day have passed since the father entered into possession of the thing, the heir need not answer in court until he comes of age; instead he will remain in possession of the thing until he comes of age and you can plead against him on the issue of ownership.

552. Again, if the father has bought some real property and he dies before a year and a day have passed, and the heirs are minors, persons who by right of lineage can and should redeem[1] property can redeem the property for money from the minor child. And in all cases where a minor must answer in court he must have a tutor [*tuteur*] to defend him. And if none of his near relatives want to step forward to be his tutor, the lord of the minor must give him a stranger[2] as a tutor. And if the lord can find no one to take care of it (for no free person is required to be a tutor if he does not want to), the lord himself must be his tutor, because by common law all minor children are in the guardianship of the lord in whose jurisdiction they are; and he must keep them from harm, or be their guardian himself.

553. Just as we have said that the minor need not answer concerning something he and his father have held peacefully for a year and a day, in the same way no one need answer a minor concerning something he has held peacefully for a year and a day. For a person entering a suit concerning ownership against a minor would put himself in a position where he could

lose but not win: for if the judgment in the suit gave the thing to the minor, a person of age who had fought the suit could not ask to get the thing back; but the minor could do so, and he could sue for the thing to be restored [*restablissement*] when he came of age.

554. A person who is no longer a minor and who notices that he has been wronged or deceived when he was a minor should take care to sue before he has been of age a year and a day, if he wants to have restitution [*restablissement*]. For if he lets pass a year and a day since he came of age and then makes his complaint, the defendant can count all the time he was in possession of the thing while the other was a minor, so that if the defendant had held the thing for nine years unchallenged while the plaintiff was a minor, and it was after the minor had been of age for a year and a day, he would have acquired ownership of the thing, because he could count ten years of possession, and you can acquire ownership by that length of possession according to our custom.

555. A minor can make a redemption for money of property sold out of his family, for otherwise he would lose the right, since real property which is purchased and held for a year and a day belongs to the person who holds it by purchase. And the time of a year and a day was established so that those who were out of the district could return to find the money and make the redemption within that time limit, and so that minors could within the time limit find someone to redeem the property for them.

556. When someone wants to prove he is of age in order to be released from someone's custodianship, or to be able to hold his fief which his lord is holding for lack of a vassal, he cannot call just any witnesses he pleases to make his proof; instead an inquest concerning his age must be made through his godfathers and godmothers, and through his nurses, and the priest and those who were present at his baptism, and the people of his mother's household when he was born.[3] For a person who wants to prove his age by witnesses other than the inquest of the persons named above makes himself very suspicious. Nevertheless, we have seen persons allowed to make proof by other witnesses; but the restrictions are made because it has been discovered for certain that some people, because they were allowed to call witnesses of their own choosing, were able to take real property as being of age, when they were not. And no wrong is done to minors if the truth concerning their age is sought through the persons named above.

557. If there are several children and some are of age and some minors, those who are of age cannot, by anything they do, lose the share of those who are minors, but they can win for them in a suit and not lose. And outside of a suit they can gain profits for them through a partnership, if they have common personal property or villeinages. But if all the real property is in fief, and they have a judge make a distribution of the personal property, the oldest can hold for the minors in custodianship, and hand over the shares to each as they come of age; and how the distribution should be made is explained in the chapter on direct and lateral inheritance {Chapter 14}.

558. If a minor sells something and swears to warrantee the sale and gives sureties, and afterwards, when he comes of age, tries to contest his sale or deal by a claim that he was a minor at the time, we do not agree that the deal is nullifed, if he was twelve years old or older when he swore the oath; for you can swear oaths at that age. But if he did not swear an oath but gave sureties that he would uphold the deal, and the sureties are sued because he does not want to uphold the deal he made as a minor, you should examine the deal and how it was made; and if you see it was made without fraud or bad faith, for the benefit of the minor, or because of his need, you should have the deal upheld and discharge the sureties. And if you see that the deal was made in bad faith, by deceiving or injuring the minor, and he contests it when he comes of age, he can make a complaint concerning the deception; and then the deal will not be upheld, and the sureties will not be obliged to stand surety, because the person who named them as sureties has nullified the deal because he was deceived when he was a minor.

559. Now let's see,—if someone buys some property from a minor and accepts sureties that the sale will be warranteed, and afterwards he erects a building on the property, and the minor later has the sale invalidated because he was deceived when he was a minor,—whether the buyer will be reimbursed for his investment. We say yes, because he was in possession of the land and held it in good faith, for otherwise he would not be reimbursed. Therefore in such a case, if the heir asks to get the thing back because he was deceived, he must give back the costs of building the house.

560. When a minor child commits a serious crime, you should look at the manner in which it was done and the discretion he has according to his age. For it can happen that a child of ten or twelve years is so wayward

[*pervers*] and full of wickedness that he will not do any good work; and if such a child commits a murder at his own will or at the encouragement of another, he should be brought to justice. But if he committed larceny, he would not be punished, for his age would excuse him. And we do not believe a minor child should lose life or limb for any serious crime, save only for the death of a man or woman.

561. If some deal is done for a minor child, and it is known for certain that it is to his advantage, and when he is of age he wants to cancel this deal because he does not want it, even though it is to his advantage, it is our opinion that he should not be able to cancel it; for you should pay more attention to doing things to the advantage of children than to acting according to their wishes, and you should not cancel deals which are made for the advantage of minor children, but you should cancel those which have been made to their detriment.

562. If someone manages to have himself accepted as a vassal, even though he has not yet come of age, he can win or lose in a lawsuit, since he has been put in possession of property and {furthermore} by his lord. Therefore the declaration of majority can be accelerated [*pueent estre li aagié aprochié*] at the will of lords on the request of the minors and their families.[4] Nevertheless if this was done in bad faith, for example if the relatives had it done in order to obtain some agreement which was to his disadvantage, he could make a complaint concerning the deception when he came of age; and if the deception were proved, his thing would be returned to the condition it was in when he was deceived.

563. If it happens that someone is close to coming of age, for example within a year or two, and he claims by his oath or by making proof that he is fully of age, and then he arranges some deal, and then afterwards wants to cancel it, he should not be listened to, since he claimed under oath or by proofs that he was of age. Instead, the deal must be upheld, unless he was deceived by a half or more. And because he swore concerning his majority, or proved it by witnesses, he can win or lose like a person who is of age.

564. Some people think that brothers who look after their minor brothers and sisters have only the guardianship and administration of them and that it is not a true custodianship. But it is, and it is clear that if the father and mother die and they have several children, of whom some are of

age and the others minors, the ones who are of age take all the personal property and do not make distribution to their brothers or sisters when they come of age, nor share the benefits of the lands in the minors' shares where they are fiefs.[5] And if the oldest son does homage for himself and his minor brothers and there are more debts than personal property, he has to pay all the debts, so that each minor takes his share free and unencumbered by debts, because they were in their brother's custodianship; excepting always the villeinages, for which an accounting must be made to the younger siblings, according to their shares, when they come of age.[6]

565. When a father and mother die and the oldest son enters the homage of the lord without naming what he is doing homage for, it is to be understood that it is for all the property his father held, and both for himself and for his brothers. And if a dispute arises later between him and his younger brothers because the oldest wants them to pay their share of the debts and the younger brothers say they are not obliged to because they have been in his custodianship, as it is clear because he has benefited from their shares, and he did homage to the lord simply and without making any reservations, in such a case the younger brothers are right, and they should take their shares free and unencumbered.

566. If the oldest brother sees that it is not to his advantage to take the custodianship of his younger brothers and sisters, because there are too many debts or because the children will soon be of age or because he does not want to take the custodianship, he should make a statement when he does homage saying to the lord that he is doing homage only for his own share: that is to say two-thirds of the fief and the homage of his younger brothers and sisters when they come of age. Then they will be in his guardianship in such a way that any benefit he reaps from their portions will be saved for the minors, and an accounting must be made to them when they do homage to their older brother. And the older brother, since he waived his right to the custodianship, cannot say that he should take the benefits from their shares while they are minors, for lack of a vassal,[7] because it was his choice to have the benefits as a custodian if he wanted; and it would be a bad and unreasonable thing for the oldest to be able to keep the benefits of the minors because of lack of a vassal, for no one can do homage for them, and no one is required to do homage for their shares except they themselves, as they come of age. But at that point if they did not want to do homage to their brother, he could hold {their property} for lack of a vassal, and keep the benefits until they had done homage to him.

567. Judges and lords of orphans and minor children should in no way permit any suspicious persons to be administrators or attorneys for the minors' business, nor guardians of their persons,—even though the relatives of the orphans and the minors wanted to permit it,—because the lord has the general guardianship of orphans and minors above everyone else: and as soon as a report of the loss has reached a lord he should take care that the orphans and minors are not caused any loss in any way.

568. Some people think that definitive partitions cannot be made which include minors who are in custodianship or guardianship, but they can. For it would be a bad thing if a man who was of age had to make a partition of land with a minor, and he had to wait until they were of age for his share to be set out and separated; for it might be that the minor was still in the cradle, and the person who was of age wanted to build on his portion, or make a vineyard or other improvements, or give or sell or exchange the property, or benefit from it in some other manner: and he could suffer great loss at having to wait until the other came of age. Therefore when such a partition is requested, it should be requested of the lord of the minor, and the lord should appoint a tutor for the minor and give him the power to make an appropriate partition by the oath of honest folk. And this tutor should be the closest relative of the minor, or the next one after that, if the closest one cannot or will not take care of it; and if the lord does not find anyone competent in the child's lineage, and who wants to be his tutor, the partition should not fail to occur for that reason, for the lord himself should appear or send a competent representative for the minor and have the partition made. And we recommend that those who have received such a partition with minor children obtain a writing from the lord who made the partition, which will testify to the partition, so that, if the child wants to repeal the partition when he comes of age, the person receiving the partition can, by means of the writing of the lord or by live witnesses, protect himself concerning what was done; and if the partition is carried out in this way, it is good for ever, with no repeal, and this is not true if it is done otherwise.

569. Every time a partition of land is to be made, whether among brothers and sisters, or among other people, it must be done in one of four ways, namely by the lord, or by arbitration, or by drawing lots, or by the agreement of those making the partition: *by the lord*, for example when they cannot agree and the lord steps in to have the partition made; *by arbitration*, for example when they agree that the partition will be made by the state-

ment and order of certain other named persons; *by drawing lots*, for example when they are agreed about what share {how much} each should have, but one wants one of the portions and the other does not want to let him have it; then lots must be drawn and each person takes the portion he draws; *by agreement*, for example when they agree among themselves what share {how much} each will receive and which portion he will take. And we have spoken of these four methods of partition so that if a dispute arises over a partition that was made, if one of the parties wants to use as a defense that the partition was made according to one of these four methods, it will be upheld without rescission.

Here ends the chapter on minor children.

Notes

1. For redemption, see Chapter 44.

2. By stranger is meant a person from outside the minor's family.

3. Cf. *Est.* 2: 126–128.

4. The note to this sentence in Salmon states that *aprochié* here means "sued." But this meaning does not make any sense in this paragraph. Another explanation of the meaning of the sentence is adopted here: that *li aagié* means not "those who have come of age" but "the attainment or declaration of majority, coming of age." Algirdas Julien Greimas, *Dictionnaire de l'ancien français jusqu'au milieu du XIVe siècle* (Paris: Larousse, 1968) 201 cites s.v. *eage, aage* the verb *eagier,* meaning "*déclarer majeur,*" or "declare somebody of age." Used as a noun, and misspelled *aagié* (the *aa-* and *ea-* are variants), both of which are plausible, this word, *li aagier,* will yield the translation I offer, which has at least the advantage of being coherent in the context of this paragraph.

5. This is the general rule of custodianship; see Chapter 15, especially §518.

6. For guardianship of villeinages, see §513.

7. A lord can take and reap benefits from lands for which there is no holder able to do homage. See §78.

17. Tutors

Here begins the seventeenth chapter of this book which speaks of tutors who are appointed for minor children, to take care of them and administer their business.

570. We have spoken previously of minor children, and of custodianships and guardianships for children; now let us discuss the tutors who are appointed by a judge to defend and protect [*garantir*] minor children, and uphold and protect their rights.

571. When a child or several children are left orphans and minors, and there is no near relative who has a right to their custodianship or guardianship, or if they *have* such relatives but they do not want to take them: all such children, whether of gentle or common birth, fall into the guardianship of the lord by common law according to the custom of the county. And if they have nothing, they must be fed by the lord's procurement; and he should sooner place a tax [*taille*] on his subjects than that the children should die for want of food. And if the children have rights in something, the lord should give them a kind of guardian called a tutor [*tuteurs*], and these tutors must look after the children and look after their property for the benefit of the children, and give a good and honest accounting at least once a year to the lord.

572. If a person who is a tutor for minor children has in his possession a lot of property for the children, the lord should take good security that the possessions will be safely looked after. And if he does not give security and the lord is afraid the heirs may be caused a loss by bad administration, he should take possession of the children's possessions and keep them safe for them so that they can have them when they come of age.

573. It could happen that minor children were left orphans in the jurisdiction of a lord who was poor and lowly [*au dessous*] and the children

had great wealth in their own right, and the lord would like to take these things for his own needs. But if this should happen, the relatives of the children should ask the count to make the lord give security for the children's possessions; and if the count was not asked to do so by the relatives, and he knew that one of his men had the possessions of such minor children, he himself should oblige the lord to give security, for the sovereign is supposed to make sure no harm is done to orphans.

574. The tutor of the minor children should be the attorney for the children's business, and it may not be argued against him that he should not be heard as a plaintiff for the children and as a defendant concerning personal property, because if he were not heard as a plaintiff for the children, the children could suffer great loss before they were of age to be plaintiffs. For the debts which debtors owed to the ancestors of the children would have to remain in the hands of the debtors until the children came of age, and the suits which the ancestors had brought on real or personal property would have to remain in the same state they were left in by the ancestors, and in this way the heirs would suffer loss. And it is better for the debts owing to minor heirs to be collected and kept safely in the possession of the lords or tutors until the children come of age, than for the debts to remain in the possession of the debtors.

575. What is pleaded on the children's behalf by the tutor appointed by the lord should be upheld, whether it is for or against the children, for if they could not lose in a suit and they could win, the defendants in suits against the tutors would not have a fair situation [*jeu parti*]; but when it is said that the tutors can lose in a suit, this means when the tutors are plaintiffs and the defendants win the suit.

576. It is true that if there is a suit on real property against the tutors acting for the children, the tutors need not answer; instead minors have the advantage of having possession of everything their predecessor held at the time of his death as their own real property; and even if a suit had been brought in the lifetime of the predecessor and he died while the suit was pending, the suit would remain at that same stage until the children came of age. But in cases on personal property and chattels, the tutors must answer for the children, for it would be a bad thing if the creditors who had advanced their property to the predecessors had to wait to be repaid until the children came of age. And for this reason it is appropriate for them to be

paid by the tutors, if the children have enough personal property; and if they do not have enough personal property, the benefits from their real property over and above what is strictly needed for their maintenance must be used to pay the debts; but they will not be required to sell their real property until they come of age. And then if there are debts to be paid, they must be made to sell as much as is needed to pay what is owing because of {the debts of} their predecessor, of whom they are the heirs; and they should be given forty days to make the sale.

577. A person who is a tutor to minor children need not do their business at his own cost; instead he must be paid an adequate salary out of the children's possessions according to their wealth and the work he does for the children. And the estimation of his salary should be examined by the count if it is brought before him first, or else before the lord where he has his residence. But if the count's vassals caused the tutor to have too large a salary, then when the children came of age, they would have an action for the excess against their tutor, and then the salary would be judged according to the work the tutor had done.

Here ends the chapter which speaks of tutors who are appointed for minor children, to look after them and protect them.

18. Illegitimacy

Here begins the eighteenth chapter of this book which shows which heirs are legitimate heirs for holding real property, and which are excluded for bastardy.

578. Some disputes arise among the children of a father who has had several wives, where claims are made that some of the issue are not legitimate heirs, but were born to an improper marriage, so that they must be held to be bastards and deprived of the portion they would have taken if they had been legitimate heirs. And for this reason it is right for us to explain briefly in this chapter which heirs are legitimate and which can be excluded for bastardy; and although the church has the cognizance of legal marriages, nevertheless suits are sometimes brought in the secular courts concerning real property held as secular fiefs, from which the true heirs want to exclude bastards. And because such suits arise from real property, the judges in the secular courts sometimes need to make a ruling on a bastardy issue which is argued before them.

579. You should know that all those conceived and born in a legal marriage are legitimate heirs, as are those who were conceived during a legal marriage, even though they were not born in one because their father died while the woman was pregnant. However a person might be born during a legal marriage who was not a legitimate heir, but a bastard: for example if a woman married a man other than the one who made her pregnant out of wedlock, for, although he was born during a marriage, that child was nevertheless conceived in bastardy. And such bastardies are sometimes so concealed that you cannot find out the truth, and sometimes the truth is discovered by the circumstantial evidence [*aparence*] of the time of the birth; for if the woman carries the child seven months after the wedding, she can conceal the fact, for it is not clear to everyone, since in that amount of time a child can be born and live, and it can also be that it was conceived two or more months before the marriage. But if she carries it for

less than seven months during the marriage and the child lives, it is clear that it was conceived before the marriage, and for this reason it can be held to be a bastard; and in this case nothing can save it from bastardy except one thing, which is if it is conceived by the same man who later married the mother. For, when a man has intercourse with a woman outside of wedlock and he marries her later when she is pregnant, the child in her womb becomes legitimate through the power of the marriage. Even if there were several children born before the father married the mother, but at the marriage ceremony the mother and children were placed under the palium [*paile*] of Holy Church,[1] they would become legitimate heirs and could inherit as legitimate heirs all kinds of inheritances both by descent and laterally.

580. The mother is not believed in any case against her children if she says they are bastards. For the hatred or love she has for their stepfather or the desire she might have for her other children to inherit her property could lead her to say that some of her children were bastards in order to give the inheritance to the others. And sometimes in their wickedness they have not refrained from saying this. Therefore when such cases arise, you should ask the mother all the questions by which you can find out the truth, and if you see that she is giving true indications, you should believe her more readily than anyone else; for no one can know the truth about such matters better than a mother. And you should examine why she is moved to say these things; for if you see that she is moved by honesty, for example, when a mother prefers to admit her wickedness than to allow to inherit those who should not, or perhaps when she was told on confessing her sins that she should speak out, because the truth could only be known through her, in such cases you should be prepared to believe her.

581. Even though it is well known that some married woman has carnal knowledge of several men,—and even if it is known because they have been seen lying together or by presumptions through which it can be believed that she has lain with other men than her husband,—and the woman has children while she is leading this kind of life, but she and her husband still live in the same household, in this case the children are not held to be bastards, for perhaps they are by the husband and perhaps not. And where there is any doubt, in this case or another, you should espouse the better opinion [*coron*] and the better course [*partie*] until the opposite is proved, and in this case it might be wrongly proved that they are bastards; and there

are quite a few people who hold the property of those who they think are their fathers or their relatives, and yet they are nothing of the kind, since the children are bastards and the fruits of adultery [*avoutre*]. And through such sin a man might marry his sister, and he and she and all the neighbors might think there was no relation between them. For example, if a married man had children by his wife, and children by another married woman, and afterwards the father and mother died, and the children intermarried, in this case the brother would be marrying his sister and they would not know it. And because of such dangers and many others which can arise, all such sin[2] is vile and criminal and forbidden, and especially by Holy Church because of the danger to the soul.

582. You should know that all those who are born more than thirty-nine weeks and one day after a marriage has ended [*dessevrés*] by the death of the husband are bastards; for a woman cannot carry a child more than thirty-nine weeks and a day, so that it is clear that it was conceived after the husband died, and thus it is proved a bastard by the circumstantial evidence [*aparence*] of the long time.

583. It can happen that a separation *a thoro*[3] of a marriage is made by Holy Church, and yet the children the partners had while they lived together are not proved as bastards: for example, if a man has arranged a separation from his wife because he has caught her in the sin of fornication, or she from him because she has caught him in it, in such a case Holy Church may well separate them and yet the children they had before the separation are not bastards. But if the woman has children after the separation, they are bastards. Nevertheless this kind of separation is not so strict that the man and the woman may not, if they wish to, get back together; and if they do and then have children, the children come from a valid marriage and can be legitimate heirs.

584. It is different with dissolutions of marriage made by Holy Church because of consanguinity, such as happens when a man marries his third or fourth cousin, or a woman nearer in lineage,—for once the fourth degree is passed, a marriage can be made,—and then afterwards, when they have been together long enough to have children, Holy Church finds out about it and dissolves the marriage: in that case the heirs are not legitimate, for as long as the parents were together they were in adultery. And yet, if the man and the woman knew nothing about the marriage [*mariage*],[4] either by the

banns which were announced in Holy Church or in any other manner, the
pope can confirm the marriage if he wants and out of pity for the children.
And if he will not, the marriage must be dissolved and the children held
illegitimate in that they are not held to be legal heirs,—which is a pity
because the marriage was not made in bad faith.—But it is this way because
some people might make such marriages in bad faith and afterwards, when
their lineages had taken notice and Holy Church wanted to separate them,
they would use as a defense that they knew nothing about their relationship, so that the children would be legitimate; and to avoid this danger, and
also the sin, every person should take great care not to marry except as he
can and should.

585. It is a good thing to know which marriages are to be avoided, for
there are many simple folk who do not know. And everyone should know
that he should not marry a woman who is related to him up to the fourth
degree of kinship; nor the godmother of a child, whether it be the man's or
the woman's;[5] nor a woman with whom he has raised[6] the child of someone else; nor his stepmother; nor the widow of anyone to whom he is
related up to the fourth degree of lineage; nor the cousin of a woman he has
known physically; nor his stepdaughter; nor the children of his fellow
godmother or godfather, once that relationship has begun; nor a woman
who is promised to another by present words;[7] nor a woman in religion or
a novice [*professe*]; nor the wife of a man still alive, even if he is out of the
district; nor a Jewess unless she is converted to Christianity; nor a woman
he knows to have had carnal knowledge of someone in his lineage, whether
in a marriage or outside of it. And whoever marries any of the above-
mentioned women is in adultery; and the children born to them are not to
be held legitimate, but as to the inheritance of property they are accounted
bastards. And in all these cases where there is a dispute the cognizance
belongs to Holy Church with respect to dissolving the marriage or holding
it to be legal.

586. Everyone should know that a marriage which is held legal by the
testimony of Holy Church cannot be contested or dissolved in a secular
court, nor the issue of it held to be bastards, even though Holy Church has
been gracious to the man and woman by permitting the marriage: for
example, if the marriage can be dissolved for some reason and Holy Church
permits and confirms it out of pity for the children who are already born, or
for some other charitable reason. And the heirs must be considered legiti-

mate, and can take inherited real property as legitimate heirs can and should, and can take all other property which can and should go to the legal heirs. And just as we should give credit to Holy Church when it declares a marriage is legal, we must also believe it when it declares marriages illegal. Therefore if there is a suit brought before us by some heirs who are excluding others from inheriting because they are bastards, and they bring before us the testimony of Holy Church that it has taken cognizance of the case and that by final judgment it has held the marriage into which they were born to be invalid,—or that it was proved against them that they were conceived out of wedlock,—we must give full credit to the testimony of Holy Church and give a judgment according to what it declares.

587. If Holy Church declares [*tesmoigne*] to a secular court that some heir is a bastard, so that because of this declaration [*tesmoignage*] the property he would have taken as a legal heir is delivered to another person who is a legal heir (since the former has lost it because of his bastardy) and then after this the person who was declard a bastard does something which causes Holy Church to declare that he is legitimate, it is too late, since another person has taken by a judgment in the secular court what would have gone to him were it not for the declaration of bastardy against him. For it is clear in this case that those who have cognizance on behalf of Holy Church were mistaken in their declaration, since if he was a legal heir, they were mistaken in testifying to his bastardy, and if he was a bastard, they were mistaken in testifying he was a legal heir; and the second declaration which they made contradicting the first is not to be accepted. But it would be different if the suit was only on seisin. For a person who had lost seisin by a judgment because it was testified against him that he was a bastard, and who later, in a suit on ownership, could prove that he was a legal heir and show how those who testified on the bastardy were mistaken, could make good his loss {of seisin} by winning in the suit on ownership.

588. And as we said that the declaration of Holy Church should be believed, when it testifies concerning the legality of marriages, we also mean that its testimony should be believed in all cases of which Holy Church has cognizance. But when the cases are of major importance or equivocal [*perilleus*], there must be more testimony than that of a single ecclesiastical judge [*official*], for the judge is but a single witness when he testifies in a secular court: unless the case is on some minor matter which can be easily handled and where he can easily be believed, such as concern-

ing an absolution, or that a suit is scheduled before him on such and such a day, or concerning a summons, or some order given in his court. What a judge testifies to is believed concerning these matters by the seal of the court, with no further testimony needed; and he is believed also when he testifies that someone is excommunicated.

589. If the ecclesiastical judge declares that someone is a bastard, and the bishop testifies that he is legitimate, you should not believe the judge but rather the bishop. And if the judge and the bishop testify the same way and the archbishop in the higher court over the said bishop testifies the opposite, you should believe the testimony of the archbishop. And if the archbishop testifies the same thing as the bishop, or confirms the decision, and the pope or his envoys testify the opposite, you had better believe the testimony of the pope than that of those below him. And we say the same thing about the secular courts, that you should rather believe what the higher court declares than the lower, and give a decision based on the better testimony.

590. Bastards born during a marriage are proved sometimes in the manner we have explained above in this chapter and sometimes in another way. For example if the husband is overseas or in some other foreign country, or in prison so long that ten months or more have passed, and after the thirty-nine weeks and a day have gone by, his wife has a child: in that case he can be proved a bastard by circumstancial evidence [*l'aparance du fet*]. But if a man were free and out of the district where his wife is, on business or because he is banished, or for a war, or because of poverty, and his wife had a child and you did not know by whom, neither by rumor nor because she had been seen lying with someone, in such a case the chilren would not be proved bastards by circumstancial evidence; for perhaps the husband was lying with her in secret when she conceived. But if the husband returns and finds his wife has had a child while he was away and he leaves his wife, and says the children are bastards, while affirming that he was out of the district night and day the whole time within which a woman can bear a child, in that case he must be believed; for it would be a bad thing if children who were bastards and the fruit of adultery inherited his property against his will; for it should not be believed that anyone would willingly have his own legitimate children declared bastards in order to divert his property to other heirs. And in any case, so that no one may be moved to do such a thing for a bad reason, for example, when hatred arises

sometimes between husband and wife for little reason, or because of jealousy or some other reason, you should look very carefully at whether the man had other than a good reason; and this may be discovered fairly clearly by the manner of the accusation and the surrounding circumstances.

591. And bastardy may be proved another way by circumstancial evidence: for example, when the husband cannot beget children because he does not have what nature must give him to beget children; such as happens when such a man takes a wife and does not reveal his proven disability [*essoine prouvé*], and the woman lives with him and does not seek an annulment of the marriage, but has carnal knowledge of another man than her husband, by whom she has children. In such a case, if the husband reveals his disability, the children are proved to be bastards by circumstancial evidence. But if the disability is kept secret until the husband is buried, and such a thing is proved in order to have them declared bastards, it should not be accepted as proof; for since he accepted the children as his for his whole lifetime, and made no mention of his injury [*mehaing*], they should be accepted as legal heirs, unless the mother accuses them as we have described above in another case.

592. Every time a court feels deceived, and because of the deception it does something or gives a judgment, and after the judgment it realizes it was deceived, it can repeal its judgment: but this applies to ecclesiastical courts, for in the secular courts what is judged must be enforced once the final judgment has been given and no appeal made, unless such great fraud or trickery is dicovered in the suit that the lord, by his authority, calls the parties back before him and repeals what was done by sharp practice; for an honest court certainly has authority to do this, whether it is a secular or an ecclesiastical court.

593. The ecclesiastical court should not deal lightly with suits brought to dissolve marriages, even though the husband admits to what the wife accuses him of, for it may be that they are colluding on the reason to dissolve the marriage because they want it dissolved, because they want to marry someone else or through hatred which has arisen between them. Therefore in such cases, Holy Church should not believe these declarations, but discover the truth of the matter by the fact that what is complained about is clearly demonstrated, or by the examination of other witnesses when the facts cannot be ascertained any other way: for example, if the wife

says that the man is not able to father children and he admits it because he wants the marriage dissolved, he should not be believed on his admission unless the thing has been proved by inspection [*veue*]; for example if he is seen to have what he claims not to have. And we say the same thing about other matters which can be proved by showing them or by circumstancial evidence; and in the other cases which cannot be so clearly shown, for example if one accuses the other of some adultery, an inquiry must be made on the issue, even though both admit it; for it would be a bad thing and dangerous for souls and heirs for marriages to be dissolved at every grudge [*mautalent*] which one partner had against the other.

594. Since we have said that the court should repeal a verdict when it sees after the judgment that it has been deceived, we will recount a case which we saw on this issue. A knight took a lady as his wife, and when they had been married so long that they had children, the marriage was denounced and was dissolved and held illegal by the judgment of Holy Church; and each one had permission to marry someone else. The knight took another wife and had children by her, and the lady took another husband and had children by him; and afterwards the second wife of the knight died, and the second husband of the lady died. And the knight and the lady were reproached by their consciences because their marriage had been dissolved in bad faith [*par mauvaise cause*]; they went before the ecclesiastical court and showed how it had been deceived into dissolving the first marriage; and the court, when the deception was realized, repealed the judgment it had given against the marriage and affirmed by a judgment [*sentence*] that the first marriage was good and legal and they could live together as in a good marriage, and they got back together [*se rassemblerent*]. And thus the knight had had children by two women whom he had married and who were both alive, and the lady had had children by two husbands both alive at the same time. Then the knight and his wife died. A suit was brought between the children of the first marriage and the children of the second marriages; for the children of the second marriages said that the children of the first marriage had been born during an illegal marriage, and that therefore they were bastards; and according to them this was proved by the fact that a judgment had been given against the marriage, and power to remarry, and, once this marriage had been dissolved, the children of the second marriages were born during a legal marriage, approved by Holy Church, and these marriages had lasted until they were ended by death; for which reason they requested to take the inherited real property as

legal heirs, and also that the others should be excluded as those having no rights to it for the already recited reasons. And the children of the first marriage said in their defense that they should take the inherited real property as legal heirs and older children from a legal marriage; and it was clear that Holy Church had repealed the judgment it had made against the marriage and admitted that it had been deceived into giving the judgment, and held that the marriage was a good and legal one, for which reason it was clear that they were the heirs. And on this issue they requested a judgment.

595. It was judged that the children of the first marriage were legal heirs and that they would take by descent from their father and mother, and that the children of the second marriages were legal heirs and would participate as younger siblings in the distribution of what descended to them from their father and mother. And by this judgment you can understand that each of the marriages was legal as long as it lasted, for the fact that Holy Church was mistaken in what it did against the first marriage should not harm anyone since it repealed its judgment, and the leave it gave to remarry made the second marriages legal, and the repeal of its first judgment against the first marriage reaffirmed it and held that it was legal.

596. All those who are bastards and are aware of it through the admission of their mother or by some other way should know they have no right to any inheritance by descent; and if they take possession of an inheritance because no one contests their right since no one knows the truth, nevertheless they are holding the property wrongfully and against God and to the danger of their souls. And if they want to do what they should by God, they must return the property to those whom they know to be the true and legal heirs.

597. It is true that a man or a woman can leave things in their will to bastard children, out of kindness, as they could leave things to strangers, that is to say their personal property and their purchased property and a fifth of their inherited real property. Nevertheless if a man or woman who has bastard and legitimate children has only personal property and pur- chased property, we do not agree that the property can be left to the bastards and nothing to the legitimate heirs, unless the heirs have offended against the father or mother, as we said in the chapter which speaks of that matter.[8] Therefore we say that in such a case the major part of the property

should be left to the legal heirs, and the bastards should be given something for their maintenance. But if man or woman has no legitimate children but does have bastards, they can leave them their personal property and their purchased property and a fifth of their inherited real property, in whole or in part. But if they die without leaving them anything, they take no more than a stranger would.

598. It sometimes happens that two people who are in a marriage separate voluntarily and with the leave of Holy Church without there being a bad reason, for example, when they want to make a vow of chastity or to enter a religous order. But such a separation cannot take place without the agreement of both parties, for the man cannot do it without the consent of his wife, and the woman cannot do it without the consent of her husband; and if they have children, the children do not cease to be legitimate, nor fail to take the succession of their father and mother.

599. Those who are known for certain to be bastards and the fruit of adultery cannot be in any way legitimate as far as taking property by descent from father or mother. But those who are merely bastards can be made legitimate by being placed under the palium [*paile*] at the wedding, as we have said above; and the fruits of adultery are those who are begotten in married women by someone other than their wedded husbands. Therefore if it happens that a man has children in concubinage [*en soignantage*] by a married woman and her husband dies, and the man who was keeping her during her husband's lifetime marries her, the children born after the marriage or who were begotten or born while she was a widow can be declared legitimate; but those who were begotten or born in adultery while she had another husband cannot be made legitimate as to taking by descent from their father or mother. But we have seen some men who, by the grace of the pope, were clerks and held the property of Holy Church; but the secular courts should not get involved in these matters, for the administration of Holy Church belongs to the pope and the prelates.

600. It should not be doubted that when a man lies with a woman out of wedlock and has children by her, and he marries her after the children are born or while she is pregnant, if the children are placed under the cloth [*drap*],—the cloth which is customarily placed on those who are solemnly married by Holy Church,—the children are legitimate since they are placed

there with the father and mother during the marriage ceremony; and then the children are no longer bastards, but heirs; and they can inherit like legitimate children born in wedlock. And by this grace which Holy Church and the custom bestow on such children, it often happens that the fathers marry the mothers for the sake of the children, so that less harm is done.

601. We are about to see a case in which my last-born son can take the firstborn's portion against my son (his older brother), and we will see how that can be. If a man has a son in concubinage by a woman, and then marries another woman by whom he has a child, and after that the woman he has married dies, and he marries the first woman, by whom he had a son in concubinage, and the son is put under the cloth with the father and mother to make him legitimate, in this case the last-born son is the firstborn as regards the inheritance, for he was born of the first marriage. And even though the other son is older in age, the time he was a bastard should not be counted for him, so that, when he is taken out of bastardy, he is a newborn as an heir. But if the heir from the first marriage was a female, and the former bastard, who was legitimated through the marriage of his father and mother, was a male heir, he would take the right of firstborn against his sister; for however many marriages there were with girls by each marriage, if there was a male in the last marriage he would take the firstborn's portion against all his sisters born of earlier marriages, according to our custom, because dower rights are not inherited as we said in the chapter on dower {Chapter 13}.

602. Where we say that according to our custom children do not inherit dower rights from their mothers, as they do in {the Ile de} France and other districts, we mean as concerns real property held in fief, for our custom agrees with the French custom with respect to villeinages: that is to say that children born of the first marriage take a half, and those of the second marriage take a quarter, of the third marriage an eighth, whether the children of each marriage are male or female. And when the father dies and the children of each marriage have received their portion according to what is said above, the remaining villeinages of the father should be divided among all his children, as much to one as to the other, for in villeinages there is no right of firstborn.

Here ends the chapter that shows which heirs are legitimate and which are bastards.

Notes

1. This custom is further explained in §600 below.
2. Here Beaumanoir evidently means adultery.
3. I.e., from the bed.
4. Beaumanoir means that they did not know they were too closely related to marry.
5. It is unclear what Beaumanoir means by this description. Perhaps it means that a widower cannot marry the godmother of his own child (by his first wife), or a widow cannot marry the godfather of her own child (by her first husband).
6. That is to say, held over the font at its christening, because he was the godfather and she was the godmother.
7. This is the equivalent of an unconsummated marriage, such as where the children were married in infancy.
8. Chapter 12, especially §382.

19. Consanguinity

Here begins the nineteenth chapter of this book which speaks of the degrees of kinship, so that everyone can know how close and how distant his relatives are.

603. So that everyone can know by what degree of kinship people are related to him, {and this} for several reasons,—for example so that marriage is not made within too close a degree of kinship or so that you can ask your relative to help you in your {private} war,[1] or so that you can ask for what is yours when you inherit it laterally through close kinship, or when you need to know how close in kinship you are to someone when you want to redeem for money some piece of property,[2]—we will discuss here in a short chapter the division of lineages and how a lineage is extended [*s'alonge*].

604. We should know that a lineage can be divided into four parts: the first part going up, such as to my father and mother, the second part going down, such as to my son or daughter, and these two parts are in direct line of descent; the third part is sideways and upwards, and the fourth part is sideways and downwards.

605. Now let us consider the degrees of kinship: my son is at the first degree going down, and my father at the first degree going up; and my brother is at the first degree sideways, and my uncle at the first degree going sideways and upwards.

606. My grandfather is at the second degree going up, and my son's son at the second degree of kinship going down; the son of my brother is at the second degree sideways and going down, and is called my nephew; and my uncle's son is at the second degree of kinship going up and is called my first cousin [*cousin germain*].

607. My great-grandfather is at the third degree of kinship going up, and the son of my son's son is at the third degree of kinship going down; and the son of my first cousin is at the third degree of kinship to me sideways and descends from my uncle and is called my first cousin once removed [*fius de cousin germain*]. And just as I worked down from the uncle, you can understand how things are going up, for there would be too great a number or words in telling about it, since a lineage extends outwards, with all the branches which come from it going up and down. And for that reason we will speak only of the four by which we have begun, for by the division of these four you can understand all the others.—So we'll say, then, that my nephew's son is at the third degree of kinship from me going down.

608. The father of my great-grandfather is at the fourth degree of kinship from me going up, and the son of the son of the son of my son is at the fourth degree of kinship from me going down; and the son of the son of my first cousin is at the fourth degree of kinship from me going down through my uncle, and the son of the son of my nephew is at the fourth degree of kinship from me going down and to the side.

609. My great-grandfather's grandfather is at the fifth degree of kinship going up and the fifth {generation of} children issued from me are at the fifth degree of kinship from me going down; and the son of the son of the son of my first cousin is at the fifth degree of kinship from me sideways going down through my uncle; and the son of the son of my nephew's son is at the fifth degree of kinship from me going down and sideways. And a marriage could take place at that degree of kinship, because it is beyond the fourth degree and the kinship is sideways; for if it could be that my great-grandfather's grandfather was still alive, he is at the fifth degree from me going up, and also the fifth {generation of} children of my issue were alive and there was a daughter among them, she would be at the eleventh[3] degree of kinship from him going down and yet he could not take her in marriage. Therefore you can see the difference between descending and sideways kinship, and the differences between them are discussed in the chapter on direct and lateral inheritance {Chapter 14}.

610. We have described as far as the fifth degree of kinship going up and going down, in the direct line of descent in which a marriage cannot

take place, and we have described as far as the fifth degree sideways, at which degree a marriage can be made. And by what has been said, you can understand who is of more distant kinship, for at each generation of children the kinship is extended by one degree. And everyone can tell by what was said at what degree of kinship every person is to him; and we will stop there.

Here ends the chapter on degrees of kinship.

Notes

1. For private wars, see Chapter 59.
2. For redemption, see Chapter 44.
3. Beaumanoir says eleventh, but according to one reckoning it is only the tenth.

20. Good-Faith Holders

Here begins the twentieth chapter of this book which speaks of those who hold real property in good faith and shows how they should be kept from loss.

611. Now that we have spoken of the degrees of kinship, let us consider those who hold property in good faith, so that those who knowingly hold other people's property wrongfully will know how they will be made to return it, and how those who hold in good faith should be kept from loss and indemnified.

612. You should know that those who are in good faith possession of real property are not required to return the benefits,[1] even if they later lose the property by a judgment. For example, if I had purchased a piece of property and I had been placed in possession by the lord and, afterwards, someone sued, showing by good evidence that the person who sold me the property had no rights in it, so that the sale was invalid: in such a case I am not required to give back the back benefits which I derived from the property before it went out of my possession. And if I hold the property through a gift, or by will or on a lease or in dower, or from someone whose heir I am, in all these cases I am not obliged to give back the benefits from the property. But if I have an improper reason for holding the property,— for example by force or in novel disseisin,[2] or by confiscation, or by concealment,—when the property is taken out of my possession, I should be compelled to return the back benefits, as a person who had no good reason to hold the property.

613. If a person builds on a piece of property he holds in good faith, and because he thought he had a right to the property, and afterwards another person rightfully obtains possession of the property, the cost of the building should be reimbursed to him, provided it was not on property which was still within the year-and-a-day redemption period; for in that case the costs of the building would not be paid back, except those which were

made to maintain the building which was part of the sale. For those costs can be included because they are to no one's loss. And if someone builds on a piece of land he holds in bad faith, the person who gets the land for good cause shown gets the building without giving back the costs; and for this reason it is very risky to build on someone else's land. And which reasons are good and which are bad is explained in the preceding paragraph [*peragrafe*].

614. Sometimes a definitive distribution [*certaine partie*] cannot be made among the heirs when the father or the person of whom they are the heirs dies, for example when the widow is left pregnant. For if the distribution will be taken by descent from the father and the wife is pregnant, you don't know how many children she will have,—for she may have two or three,—and if the children took a half of the personal property and purchased property, sharing with their mother, the children to be born might suffer loss if the other children spent their property unwisely. And for this reason we agree that enough for three children should be put into safe hands for the shares of the children to be born, so that if there are three they can have their share of their father's estate; and if there are fewer, the share of any extra children can be brought back and distributed among the common heirs. And if the living heirs will give good security to give back their fair shares to those still to be born, and each heir takes liability for all these shares, you can permit the distribution of the whole amount to be made among them.

615. It sometimes happens that when a man dies his wife is pregnant but has not been so long enough for it to be known except by what she says; and it sometimes happens that she herself does not know, for example when she has been so only a very short time. Now in such a case, when the deceased has living children, if they want to make a distribution before four and a half months have passed since the death of the father, the distribution should be made as explained above. But if four and a half months have passed and it is not clear that the woman is pregnant, and she will not swear that she thinks she is pregnant, then they can make a distribution among them of their father's estate. And if there is no heir apparent and it is not known if the woman is pregnant, if she will swear on the saints that she thinks she is more likely than not to be pregnant, no one will share in a distribution with her, but she will be left in possession of everything by giving good security that, if she turns out not to be pregnant, she will make

the distribution of the deceased's estate with those who are entitled to it. And if she will not or cannot give security, the judge in whose jurisdiction the property lies should take jurisdiction over the distribution until it is known if she is pregnant or not.

616. When a man dies without issue and his wife does not know if she is pregnant or not, and she will not swear that she thinks she is, at her request the judge should take the deceased's estate into his possession until four and one-half months have passed. And then if she will not swear, and it is not clear that she is pregnant, the distribution of the deceased's estate must be made to the heirs.

617. If a woman is left pregnant when her husband dies and she holds her husband's property by reason of her pregnancy because the guardian-ship of her minor children is hers, and she reaps the benefits during her pregnancy and the child is born dead, it is true that the deceased's estate passes laterally to his closest relatives. But they cannot ask to have back from the widow the benefits she reaped from the property during the time she was pregnant, for she reaped them in good faith because of the child which was in her womb, who was and should have been heir to the deceased.

618. If a woman is left pregnant when her husband dies and there are apparently no other children, the woman takes posession of the estate of the father, as we have said above. And afterwards, if she carries the child until it is born, so that it can be testified to that the child was heard to cry and afterwards it died, even though it did not live long enough to be taken to the church and be baptised, we believe that since there has been a live heir, the personal and purchased property of the deceased's estate go to the mother as the closest relative.[3] And some might believe they do not go to her, since the child had not been baptised, and we believe that they should; for as soon as an heir is born, we believe that the temporal estate of the father and mother passes to it by descent, and by baptism the spiritual inheritance of paradise passes to it.

619. In all lawsuits which arise for whatever reason, and in all cases of distributions to heirs, and in bringing property back to the {hotchpot for} distribution after the death of fathers and mothers,[4] before whatever judge the suits are heard, on request of a party the parties must swear they have a good and honest dispute, and that if they want to call witnesses, they will

call good and honest ones, and that they will answer truthfully to anything asked of them, and will not lie for the sake of father or mother or for their own advantage. And if the suit is for a distribution among persons who have to make a distribution among them or to bring things back, they must swear in addition to what is said above that they will bring back to the distribution (or designate things which are not in their possession [*baillie*]), except in cases of serious crime; for in cases of serious crime punishable by loss of life or limb, the accused is not required to swear unless the case is by wager of battle; for in cases of wager of battle the oath must be taken by the parties as is explained in the chapter on the procedure in wager cases {Chapter 64}.

620. A person swearing to bring back everything that is to be distributed among heirs (or who swears to the value of what he has, because he is to be taxed [*taillables*] by his lord or some chartered commune) should take care to tell the truth. For if he is found to have committed perjury, he must lose the extra over what he swore to, and it must go to the lord or the chartered commune who or which may exact taxes from him [*qui taillables il est*]. And if the oath concerns bringing back what should be distributed among heirs, and he hides something, what is hidden should go to the other heirs, and the person who should have brought it back and concealed it should lose his share in it. And it is right for the person to have to suffer loss who wants to deceive others and perjures himself.

Here ends the chapter on those who take benefits [poursievent] *in good faith from property.*

Notes

1. By "benefits," translating *levees*, we mean the income derived from property, in the form of rent money, taxes, crops, tolls, etc.
2. For force and novel disseisin, see Chapter 32.
3. The closest relative of the dead child, who has, momentarily, inherited from its dead father.
4. For bringing back property to the "hotchpot," see Chapter 15.

21. Partnerships

Here begins the twenty-first chapter of this book which speaks of how partnerships are formed and their dangers, and of removing children from your custodianship.

621. There are often various gains and various losses in the association which should be called a partnership according to our custom, and for this reason everyone should take care whom he joins in partnership and whom he accepts as a partner. And the partnerships we wish to speak of are those because of which the assets are divided when the partnership ends, and this kind of a partnership is formed in several ways. And for this reason we will discuss in this chapter how such a partnership is formed according to our custom, and the gains and losses which can arise from it; and we will speak of how you can and should keep a child out of your custodianship so that he cannot sue you for anything on account of a partnership.

622. Everyone knows that a partnership is created by a marriage, for as soon as a marriage is made, the assets of both persons are made common by the power of the marriage. But it is true that as long as they live together, the man is the administrator [*mainburnisseres*] and the woman must forbear and obey in everything that concerns their personal property and the benefits derived from their real property: even if the woman sees an obvious loss, she must bow to the will of her husband. But it is true that the husband cannot sell income-producing property which is owned by the woman, unless it is by the wish and permission of the woman herself, nor can he sell his own property, unless she waives her inchoate dower in it, so that she does not take the property in dower if she survives him. And we have discussed the partitions which must be made because of a marriage, when the marriage ends, in the chapter on dower.[1] And we will not speak about it any more here.

623. The second way a partnership is formed is through a business [*marcheandise*]: such as it happens that two or three merchants buy a

drapery or some other kind of business, and it often happens that each merchant pays as much towards the business as the other, and sometimes one contributes more and the other less. It is true that when such a business is set up, each one may, when he pleases, ask for his share in the business according to what he contributed and thus the partnership is dissolved. But as long as the business is all kept together without division, if they sell it or have it sold all in one lot, each one should share in the gain or loss according to what he contributed towards the purchase of the business: this means that if each put in as much as the others, they will all take an equal share, and if one put in half and the other two the other half, the one who put in a half will take half of either the gain or the loss, and the two others the other half; and by this you can understand who gets more and who gets less.

624. The third way a partnership is formed is by an agreement; and this kind or partnership is formed in many ways: for sometimes a partnership is formed up to a certain sum of money, and sometimes for a certain time, and sometimes for life. And in all these partnerships you must keep to the agreement and have it adhered to, except for certain reasons for which such agreements can be dissolved: such as when one of the partners falls ill [*en langueur*] so that he can no longer deal with the business for which they formed the partnership; or when he marries; or when he wants to give his children a piece of the business when they marry; or when he wants to go overseas or on some distant pilgrimage; or when he is so busy with his lord's or his sovereign's affairs that he cannot devote his time to the business; or when he shows that the business is bad for his soul, and that it is a sin to carry it on; or when he wants to enter religion; for all these reasons partnerships can be dissolved. And when the agreements are ended for such reasons, the business must be divided up according to the state of things when the partnership is dissolved. And it can also be dissolved when one of the partners can prove that his partner has acted as he should not concerning the partnership business, for it would be a bad thing if you had to remain in a bad partnership with someone, and invest your assets, if you could demonstrate the fault.

625. The fourth way a partnership is formed is the most dangerous, and the one by which I have seen the most people come to grief: for according to our custom a partnership is formed just by living together with a common board [*a un pain et a un pot*] for a year and a day after the personal property of both has been intermingled. We have indeed seen several rich

men who took in their nephews or their nieces or some of their poor relatives out of kindness, and when they had some personal property, they took charge of it to be kept and safeguarded for the person they took in partnership in good faith; nevertheless if they intermingled with their own any of the assets of those they took in, even in the slightest, after they had been there for a year and a day there was a partnership formed. So that we have seen approved in a judgment that a person who brought to the partnership only forty sous and who was there only two years and did no work, but was living with his uncle to be fed out of kindness, sued for a partition because of the partnership, and won a favorable judgment, and took more than two hundred pounds; and by this judgment you can see the danger in accepting such a partnership. And so that you may safeguard yourself from being deceived in this way, and yet not fail to act in a charitable manner (for example by not taking your poor relatives into your household for fear of this risk), we will explain how you can keep them in your household without danger.

626. A person who, out of kindness, wants to take his poor relatives into his household without thereby forming a partnership should just take in his person, without intermingling anything the person has with his own things, and if he is a minor, he should take him to the lord under whom he has his residence, and say, in the presence of two or three of the child's closest relatives: "Sire, I am taking this child into my household and I want you to know that I don't want him to be able to sue me for anything on the grounds of a partnership because I am supporting him; for I do not want to intermingle anything of his, however small, with my possessions, except as far as his things are handed over to me by you and by his relatives for a certain price in money, which money is all I am required to give him or put to his use." Whoever does things this way avoids the risk of forming a partnership.

627. And there is another way to have someone in your household without risk, for example when you do not intermingle any of the possessions, or when you hold them for a fixed rental. For example, it might happen if a man went to live in another's house and agreed to pay him a certain sum of money for his expenses and knew how to take care of his things [set bien au sien assener] so that he only paid the person in whose house he was what was agreed on. And in all these situations you cannot sue for anything on account of a partnership.

628. The fifth way a partnership is formed is among commoners, when a man or woman marries twice or three times or more, and has children by each marriage, and the children of the first marriage live with their stepmother or stepfather without a distribution and without an agreement to look after them: in such a case they can gain or lose on account of the partnership with their father and stepmother, or with their mother and stepfather. And when the children want a distribution, they take all the inherited real property which descended from their dead mother or father, and a third of the purchased property and personal property acquired during the time of the partnership. And if there are children from two marriages, in the partnership formed by the third marriage, the children of the first marriage should take as we said all the inherited real property which descended from their dead mother or father, and a third of the purchased property and personal property from the time of the second marriage; and from the time the third marriage was made and the children of the second marriage joined the partnership with them and their mother, they take a quarter of the purchased property and personal property acquired during the second marriage, and the children of the second marriage the second quarter, and the stepmother or stepfather the third quarter, and the father or mother from the third marriage the last quarter. Thus you can see that according to how many persons are living together who must form a partnership, the shares get smaller and smaller, except that all the children of a marriage, when they form a partnership in the second marriage or the third, are counted as only one person, for at the time of the distribution a single child would take as much as ten.

629. The partnership which we have spoken of above which is formed by custom among commoners is not made in this manner among gentlefolk: for when the children of a first marriage or a second stay with their father or mother and with their stepmother or stepfather, it is not called a partnership but a guardianship. And this guardianship is given to the father or mother by custom until there is a child who comes of age and wants to take his inheritance from his dead mother or father; then he takes it by the rules of succession, and also the guardianship of his younger siblings. And if there was personal property at the time their father or mother died, they should take a half of it; and if there were more debts that personal property and the father or mother has paid the debts during the guardianship, the children are not required to make any reimbursement, for a father or

mother must pay the debts of children while they are in their guardianship; but they are not permitted to encumber with debt the inheritance the children take from their dead father or mother.

630. When a gentleman or gentlewoman has a child in guardianship after the death of the child's father[2] or mother, and he holds villeinage property which should descend to the child by succession from his dead father or mother, all the profits and benefits from the villeinages should be kept for the child so that they are to his credit when he comes of age; for no one, whether custodian or guardian, can appropriate the benefits derived from villeinages belonging to the children in their care. And this means among gentlefolk, for among commoners when there is a partnership among them, the benefits from villeinages *do* accrue to the partnership, as long as the partnership lasts.

631. We have said that the guardianship of children among free persons [*franches persones*][3] belongs to the father or mother according to our custom, and it is true. Nevertheless I note [*voi*] various reasons for which, or for one of which, the judge, at the request of the child's relatives, should take the child out of the guardianship and partnership of the father or mother, when the children have only a father or a mother, and we will describe some of these reasons.

632. If it happens that a man or woman has his children in his guardianship, or some other children in his custodianship, and because of the custodianship or guardianship, he holds a lot of real property which should eventually pass to the children, and the relatives of the children from the other side of the family[4] (or from his own side of the family) fear that he may marry them off without consulting their relatives, they can ask the judge to have them removed from his care, or for him to give good security that he will not marry off any of the children without consulting the relatives. And if he will give the security, he cannot have the children taken away from him by this method; and if he will *not* give security, the children should be taken away from him and given to one of the other relatives who *will* give security. And the person taking them in guardianship must be given enough to maintain [*soustenir*] and care for [*mainburnir*] the children by the person who should have had them and did not want to give security. And because this thing has not been requested in many places, those who

had children in guardianship or custodianship have been seen to arrange improper marriages, out of foolishness or out of wicked greed for gifts or promises; and for that reason it is better to anticipate such dangers.

633. The second way in which you can remove children from the guardianship or custodianship of someone is when that person does not give the children sufficient maintenance according to their condition and to what he holds on their behalf.

634. The third way you can take children out of the guardianship or custodianship of someone is if the person who has them is the heir who would take the children's possessions if they died, and he has a bad reputation, and you know he has been accused of a serious crime which he was not honorably acquitted of, for it would be a bad thing to leave children in the care of a person who had a bad reputation because of his evil deeds.

635. The fourth way you can remove children from the guardianship or custodianship of a person is when the children have only a father or mother and the father or mother remarries, so that the children have a stepfather or stepmother, and it is clear that the stepfather or stepmother is treating the children badly [*menent mauvese vie as enfans*], or that they seem to hate them; in such a case the children should be removed from their care and put in someone else's care out of the power of the stepfather or stepmother.

636. The fifth reason is when the person in whose care they are acts so unwisely that there is in him no good sense [*conseil*] or discrimination [*areance*], for such people should not be allowed to have the care of children.

637. And in all these cases which we have described it is not necessary for those who are seeking to have the children removed from the care of those who have them to bring a full suit against them; it is enough for them to make a report to the judge. And the judge should in his official capacity investigate the case which is reported to him, and if he finds the report justified [*trueve le cas*] by his inquiry [*aprise*], he should remove the children as is stated above; for you should suppose that those who report such cases do so in good faith, and this is clear because of the fact that they do not gain anything by it [*il n'en metent riens en leur profit*]. And the count must have the lordship and cognizance of all these cases if his vassals do not act among

his subjects without delay, for all the cases which deal with the safeguarding of minor children should brook no delay; but the sovereign should act swiftly [*courre*] to help and safeguard them as soon as he sees that his vassal is not doing what he should.

638. It is explained above that no one can, for reasons of guardianship or custodianship, appropriate the benefits of villeinages belonging to the children. And in addition to this we say that a person who wants to reap the benefits {for the children} must give good security, if it is required of him, to give the profits to the children, or to put them to their use; and if he will not give the security, the judge should take possession of the said benefits and safeguard them until the children come of age.

639. We have explained how partnerships are formed by custom, and how you can remove children from someone's care. Now here let us speak of what risks there are in having children in your custodianship or guardianship, and how you can remove them from your care if you want to.

640. When a father and mother have their children with them in their guardianship and their care [*mainburnie*], and the children commit some offense, and there is a property fine for the offense, if you cannot arrest the person committing the offense you go after the father; and if the offender is arrested and must pay the fine, it is the father who has to pay the fine, for children in the care [*mainburnie*] of their father and mother own nothing, whether they are of age or not. And if the children commit some serious crime for which the punishment is death, if they are arrested, they are punished and the father and mother cannot be sued, unless the offense was committed by them or at their instigation, or they hid the children after the crime; for if they hid them afterwards, it would seem that they had approved of the crime. Nevertheless, they would not lose their lives, but they would be at their lord's mercy for all their property. Therefore the father and mother who want to avoid this risk can emancipate their children as they come of age, and no longer feed them or take care of them, {sending them out} to live by themselves, or to marry, or to serve out of their own household, or by giving them their share of the property to live on, all this without fraud. For it is clear that sometimes fraud is apparent in such gifts: such as when a father wants to take vengeance for some offense and he does not want to do it himself because he has too much to lose, he sends his children out of his household and gives them so little of his wealth that you

can see why he is doing so; for the reason is that he thinks that the authorities will only confiscate what he gives his children, when his children commit the offense {on his behalf}; and this way fathers who wanted to take vengeance through their children would have a cheap way to do things. Therefore if someone wants to send his children out of his care, he must give them a proper amount or emancipate them when it is clear that there is no bad faith, such as when the father is not in a {private} war and without a grudge and in times of peace. Nevertheless, it sometimes happens that a father sees that his child is so rash or quarrelsome or badly behaved [*de mauvaise maniere*], that he thinks that the more he gives him the more he will lose; and if such a notion moves the father to give the child little, and to send the child out of his care, it is not surprising, for it is better for the son, who is rash and badly behaved, to suffer loss through his rashness than the father, who is not at fault. And when children are removed from custodianship or guardianship in the manner described above and the children commit some serious crime, the judge should look carefully at the father's intention in removing the child from his guardianship, to see if it was done in bad faith or not, and according to what he finds, he should act in this matter.

641. The manner of removing a child from the care [*mainburnie*] of mother *and* father has been described above. Now let us see, when some children's father or mother has died, and they are living with the surviving parent, how they can be removed from their care. We say that, if the father or mother sends the child out of the household, giving them everything that they take from the deceased in personal or real property, without keeping anything back, the children are out of their care and their partnership; and a person acting in this manner should do it through a judge or the child's relatives.

642. It is right that those who bring nothing to a partnership can demand nothing from the partnership. Therefore if I have my motherless children living with me, and I take nothing of their portion which they inherit from their mother, and do not intermingle it with my own things, there is no partnership formed; and it is the same with other people who live with me: if they bring no personal property (or benefits from real property) which I intermingle with my own, they cannot sue for anything by reason of the partnership, however long they stay with me, for a person who brings nothing to a partnership can take nothing away from it.

643. When a widow who has children marries a widower who also has children, and all the children live with them in a partnership, and they bring to the partnership something from their dead father or mother, the partnership consists of four partners, so that each group of children takes a quarter and the father and mother a quarter each, except for gentlemen who hold in fief, because they have guardianship over their children, for among them there is no partnership, as is explained above in this chapter.

644. If a commoner has several children who form a partnership with him, because of the possessions of their dead mother which were intermingled with his, and he marries off one or two of them and gives them some of the common property of the partnership, and the others remain with him in the partnership for a year or two or longer after those who were in it are married, then when they want to make a partition with their father, this does not mean that the property that was given to the brothers or sisters who were married should not be taken out of the share of those who want the distribution [*partir*]. For those who were married and those who remained in the partnership formed in all a single partner, and the father would suffer too much loss if those remaining with him after the marriages took a whole share; for then the gift to those who were married would have been taken out of the father's share, which would not be right. And if the gift to those who were married was so great that the other children were left without [*deceu*], they can call the married children back into the partition of what they took from the partnership and from the estate of their dead mother; for the father could not give away the rights the other children had in the partnership and in the estate of their mother. Therefore a father or mother who marries off a part of the children, who form a partnership with their parent, should take care to give them only the share they are entitled to in the estate of their father or mother and of the partnership formed after their mother or father died; for if he gives them more, it must come out of his own funds, not from the share of the other children.

645. No one can sue for anything claiming a partnership, however much the assets are intermingled, unless they have been together at least a year and a day, except for a partnership formed by agreement or for business; for in these two cases the partnership is formed as soon as the agreement is made or as soon as the business is purchased.

646. There is one other kind of partnership, which cannot be dissolved or taken apart, but must endure, whether the parties in the partnership want it or not, except that it can be broken in one way which we will describe: it is the partnership formed by a community, and these partnerships are divided into two kinds. For one community exists by reason of a commune authorized by a lord in a charter. Such a partnership must operate according to the clauses in the charter, and they can gain or lose in common in the affairs which pertain to their commune. And if someone wishes to leave such a partnership, you must see how much he is worth and how much the other members of the commune are worth, and then see how much the commune owes whether in life interests [*a vie*] or in land or in money; and then you should look at how much each person would have to pay on the mark or on the pound if you wanted to pay off everything immediately, and then you should levy from the person wanting to leave his whole share; and then he must go and live outside of the commune property, and in this way he can leave the commune and the commune's fief, except that if he has real property which remains in the power and jurisdiction of the commune, that property can nevertheless be taxed [*taillié*] in the way it would be if it belonged to a stranger who had never been part of the commune.

647. The other kind of partnership which if formed by a community is made up of the inhabitants of towns where there is no commune, which are called *viles bateïces*. And this partnership is formed by the outlays and costs they have to make for things which they have in common, and which they cannot forego without loss, such as the upkeep of their churches [*moustiers*] and the repair of their roads, and the maintenance of their wells and fords, and the other things which are done by common accord, such as the expenses of lawsuits to maintain their rights and safeguard their customs; in all such cases and others like them such people form a partnership and each person must pay his fair share of the costs by law. And none of this kind of inhabitants can leave this partnership unless they go and live elsewhere and give up the public facilities [*as aisemens*] thus obtained; and if a person leaves in this manner, he will have to enter a partnership with the people of the place where he goes to live.

648. When you want to do something for the good of a town you do not have to refrain from doing it because there is no unanimity; it is sufficient that the majority [*la greigneur partie*],—containing the best [*souf-*

isans] people,—is[5] agreed. For if you had to have everyone's agreement, those who know little and have little wealth [*poi valent*] could disrupt things done for the common good and it would not be right to permit this.

649. Two partners had a partnership together in a deal [*marcheandise*] concerning wood. When the wood was sold and delivered, one of the partners went to those who owed for it and, without the knowledge of his partner, had them promise to pay other people to whom the partner owed a personal debt. When his partner found out that the payments in which he owned a half share had been promised without his consent to other people, to whom he personally owed nothing, he came before us before the due date for payment of the debts and demonstrated to us the deception practised by his partner; and once the truth was known to us, we ordered that those who had made the agreement {the bad partner's creditors} should expect only half of the payment, for the person making the agreement {the bad partner} had a right to no more than that, and that they should ask the person who made the agreement {the bad partner} for the other half; and we ordered those who had made the agreement {the purchasers of the wood} at the request of one of the partners to pay only half of what they promised to the other parties, and the second half to the {good} partner in the business; and in this way we had this deception undone. But if the due date for the debt had passed, and the payment made as it had been agreed, before the partner had showed us how he had been deceived, the payment would have stood; and the other partner in the business would have had no recourse against the debtors who had bought the wood, but would have had to sue his partner at whose request the payment had been made. For a person who accepts merchandise from someone and pays him (or someone else at his order) should be paid up, unless he is ordered not to by a judge or by someone asking for a share in the payment because of a partnership, *before the payment is made*. But when he is ordered not to make the agreed payment, he must pay each person his due or otherwise he will not be paid up and each of the partners could sue him for his share; and because of the risks that can arise, it is a good idea to be careful whom you do business with, and whom you pay, and with whom you form a partnership.

650. A partnership can be formed in many ways, as we have said; and we will add another, for a partnership is formed sometimes for a single purpose, and sometimes for two or three, according to what is agreed on.

For example when two partners take a farm for three years, or perhaps they take the farm and a wood business or some other particular business; because they form this partnership, they are not partners as to their whole assets, but only for the things for which the partnership was formed, and when the thing is over and they have made an accounting of the gain or loss they made from the business for which they were partners, the partnership is dissolved, and they cannot sue each other by reason of a partnership except concerning the business in which they had been partners.

651. You should believe that each partner in a partnership for one or several things does his best for the greatest good of himself and his partner until the opposite is proved. And for this reason what each of the partners does should be enforced, whether it concerns selling or paying for things necessary to the partnership, or accepting the payments made for the business. And if the person paying out or receiving acts otherwise than he should, his partner can ask him for his share, and can forbid him to interfere except in what his share in the business permits him to. And then, when such a dispute arises between partners, each one should be given his share in the thing for which they were partners, if it something that can be divided; and if the thing cannot be divided, such as a fish farm [*viviers*] or a safe passage [*travers*] or other such things, the lord before whom such a suit comes, or in whose jurisdiction the subject of the suit lies, should have them managed [*cueillir*] profitably at the expense of the partners, if he cannot get them to agree in any other way.

652. If there are several partners and one of them loses something belonging to the partnership,—such as if he sells something for less than it is worth; or if he has accepted money and it is taken or stolen from him, along with some of his own things; or if he is negligent without bad faith,—his partners cannot sue him because he himself lost in the action; for you should believe that no one knowingly and willingly does something to his own detriment, and for this reason you should take care whom you take on as a partner, for a person who loses through the negligence of his partner can only blame his own folly. But when he sees that the person has been too negligent, he can forbid him to do anything more and act in the manner described above.

653. A partnership is sometimes formed so that one partner pays all the money that the business costs and the other pays nothing, and yet he

takes half of the profit. And sometimes a partnership is formed in such a way that one person pays two-thirds and the other one-third, and the agreement is that they will share the profits fifty-fifty. And sometimes it is formed in such a way that one partner shares in the profits if there are any and, if there is a loss, he does not have to pay for the loss. And all these kinds of partnerships can be formed by agreement, for anyone can associate himself with someone and show kindness to the person with whom he is associated. And sometimes such partnerships are formed because one has more work to do in administering the partnership business than the other, so that it is reasonable for his share to be greater in proportion to the work he does.

654. If a partnership is formed for some fixed business without any agreement between the partners that that one partner will get more than the other, and one of the partners is incapacitated [*empeechiés*] in such a way that he cannot deal with the affairs of the partnership, and the other partner, because of the person's incapacity, must take care of all the administration of the business, it should not be at his own cost, but at the cost of the common property. And the business might be so great, such as the sale of wood or some other business [*marcheandise*], that the partner had to spend all his time on it, so that he could ask for a salary out of his partner's share because he had been his employee [*serjans*]; and such salaries should be paid at the estimation of a judge according to the condition of the person suing for it and the work he did to administer the share of his incapacitated partner; and it will still be this way if his partner had not told or ordered him to take care of the business. For if someone is my partner in something and he will not or cannot do the partnership's business, I have to take care of it in order to save myself from loss, and I can only take care of the whole thing, since the business is undivided. And thus it is sometimes necessary to be your partner's employee in spite of yourself; and it is reasonable for such a person not to have to lose because of it.

655. When a partnership is made for whatever purpose, and the partnership makes a loss, each of the partners must contribute for the loss according to the gain he would have taken as his share, unless the agreement says otherwise, as is explained above.

Here ends the chapter on partnerships formed by custom or by agreement, and on removing children from guardianship.

Notes

1. Chapter 13, which see also for inchoate dower.
2. The word *pere* is missing in Salmon, but is evidently meant to be there. The word *pere* appears in the corresponding place in Beugnot.
3. Beaumanoir probably means gentlefolk; see preceding paragraph.
4. That is, from the side of the dead parent.
5. I read *s'i* for *si* in Salmon.

22. Corporations

Here begins the twenty-second chapter of this book which speaks of capital property partnerships and how you should deal with them.

656. We have spoken of various types of partnerships in the preceding chapter; and we will speak in this following chapter of another kind of partnership which is called a capital property partnership [*compaignie en eritage*]: for example when several people can have shares in the jurisdiction of a town, or in a mill, or in a bakery [*four*] or in a winepress, or in a fishery [*pescherie*] or in any other kind of income-producing property [*eritage*] which is costly to keep up. And it sometimes happens that one of the partners [*parçoniers*] is willing to pay enough upkeep expenses [*mises*] according to what he earns in income from the business, and the other partners are reluctant to pay the expenses and yet they are happy to take the profits, so that sometimes the property deteriorates and loses value; and for this reason we will speak of how you should deal with such partnerships.[1]

657. When one of the partners sees that his partners do not want to invest enough to keep up the property, he should have the partners warned by the judge to put in their fair share [*avenant*] before a certain day, which must be chosen by the lord according to the haste needed for the work to be done. And if the day passes and the partners do not obey the command, the property will not deteriorate if the partner who asked for them to put in their fair share wishes; for he can report their default to the lord from whom the property is held, and the lord can give him leave to make the outlays which must be made to maintain the property, but then he will hold the property *without* the partnership of those who will not contribute, until they have paid their share of as much as they should have put in; and all the profits from the property will be his until the outlays he made have been repaid, without giving anything or discounting anything to the partners who would not contribute anything; and thus he holds the shares of his partners in mortgage until they have paid him; for if he merely subtracted

the costs from the income, he would have been lending the upkeep money in spite of himself, which no one need do unless he wants to; and it is better for the property to be mortgaged [*retenus*] and for him to take all the profits until the partners want to rejoin him, than for the property to be destroyed, so that it is worth nothing to any of the partners.[2]

658. Every time a suit is brought for the costs needed for the upkeep of property belonging to several partners, the lord who has jurisdiction over the partners should not permit a full lawsuit; instead he should simply look at what share each person earns from the property, and according to this measure he should compel each to pay his fair share or abandon his rights in the partnership; for if there were in such suits the kind of delay that there is in many disputes, the property would be worthless [*decheu*] before the suit was over. Nevertheless, if one of the partners says he has good reason why he should not contribute anything, and that the costs of upkeep of the property should fall on the other partners,—for example, it might be that some of them have rents from property which were given or sold or left to them, to be collected costfree every year; or for example if someone contributed his property as partnership property to be exploited; or for example if an agreement is made that one of the partners must pay all the costs and the other may take his share costfree; or it may be that one of the partners wants to use as a defense that he has always taken his share costfree, in the sight of the other partners and with their knowledge, without paying any of the costs, and his partners have several times paid the costs while he took his share costfree, and for so long that he has acquired the right to take his share freely and without debt,—in all these and in similar cases the partners who do not want to contribute anything to the costs and expenses of the property should be admitted to testify.

659. It is true that every time several partners have shares in some property and one of them asks to have his part cut out and divided off [*mise d'une part*], it must be done, except for certain property which cannot be divided by putting up boundary markers or other separators [*devises*], for example tolls and market taxes and wine taxes [*vinages*] and jurisdictions and mills and bakeries, and winepresses and fisheries and other enterprises [*rentes d'aventure*]. Therefore when several partners have shares in such property, the business should be rented out or farmed out; and then from the rental or farm income each partner can take what belongs to him. But

we mean here the partnership properties where one person has no more right to possession than another, for there are many properties where one partner has possession of the property and the others are paid by him: and the payments have to be made according to the long-established custom and according to how much each person should receive.

660. If someone holds property in partnership with others through a custodianship or in dower or as a lease, or for some other reason which allows him to reap the benefits of his share and yet the property is not his, and he does not want to contribute anything to the costs of the property because the costs would be greater than the benefits for the time during which he will hold the property, or he does not want to contribute out of foolishness or caprice, it should not be permitted; instead he must be compelled by his lord,—if the lord is asked to do so, or even without a request if he knows about the matter,—to pay his fair share towards the expenses of the property, as soon as he has reaped any benefit from the property or taken possession of it, for otherwise the person who has rights to the ownership of the property could suffer a loss by the action of the person who has only possession of it; and orphans and minor children could often suffer loss because of this.

661. We have spoken of property which cannot be divided unless it is rented out or farmed out; but if there is the same quantity of property and partners, so that each one can take a piece of the property, a division can be made. For example, if two partners own two mills of equal value, and each partner wants half of the two mills, the division can be made so that each partner gets a mill. And if one of the mills is worth more than the other, the person asking for the partition gets the lesser mill; and the partner who gets the better mill must give him year-by-year the extra yield of the other mill after the expenses are paid. And if one should have only a third of the two mills, and the other two-thirds, the person who has only a third should get the worse mill; and if it is worth more than a third, he must give the extra each year to the person who should receive the two-third share. And if there are three partners and one is to have half and the other two the other half, the two others can take one of the mills as their share and the other can take the other mill for his share, so that the recipient of the better mill gives the other the extra income, as is explained above. And what we have said about the division of two mills can be applied to a situation where there are several

bakeries, or several winepresses, or several safe passages, or several market taxes, or several jurisdictions, or several fisheries, belonging to several partners, when some of the partners want to make a partition.

662. If it happens that some capital property partnership which is divisible has been together without being divided up for as long as anyone can remember, and one of the partners wants to have it partitioned, and the other partners contest this because they want it to be the way it has always been, this long-standing situation which they allege does them no good, for all those who have a partnership together, whether in land or goods or other things, can refrain from making a partition as long as they have a partnership and they agree among themselves. And yet the long time does not prevent one of the partners from obtaining a partition when he wants it, unless there is an agreement that the partnership cannot be dissolved.

663. If there are several partners who own some property, and the partners are caused a loss because of the action of one of them,—for example if they have their shares in a mill and one of them does not do his duty towards his lord, so that the lord takes the grinding wheels [*fers*] out of the mill so that it will not grind flour, with the result that the partners suffer a loss,—in such a case the partners should recover their loss from the partner because of whom the grinding wheels were removed. Or if he is poor or out of the district, or somewhere where there is no jurisdiction over him, the partners in the property can take another approach: for they can ask the lord who removed the grinding wheels to have them put back, so that the mill will work, and when the profits from the mill are to be given out, the lord should take the share of the person who did not do his duty towards him. And a lord requested to do this should do so, for two reasons: the first is that the partners should not suffer loss because of the offense of their partner; the second reason is because it is for the common good of the lord and the district and the partners that property should be exploited according to its nature. And if the lord will not grant this request and the partners appeal to the sovereign, the sovereign should have the thing done; that means the appeal goes first of all to the lord of the lord who did not want to grant the request, and from lord to lord up to the king, if the others will not take action.

664. Many jurisdiction partnerships have not worked well because several lords were partners in the jurisdiction (in many towns the jurisdic-

tion is shared by two or three or four or more lords). And it happens that one or two have a great desire to administer justice well, and the others have not; or sometimes one of them likes a person who is to be tried better than the others do; or sometimes one of them wants to help the accused because he is asked or paid to do so, or for some other bad reason. And for this reason the king or those who hold directly from him, and from whom the partners hold their jurisdiction, must be very aware of how they administer justice in their jurisdictions, so that if justice is not done, the jurisdiction of the person failing to administer justice can be taken away from him and justice done by the sovereign.

665. We have sometimes held in prison offenders whose cases were asked to be sent to the lower courts by some of the partners in the jurisdiction in which the person should have been tried.[3] But we never would send the case back down unless all the partners in the jurisdiction joined in the request or sent competent attorneys. For if we had sent the case down to *one* of these lords and he did not administer proper justice, the other partners could excuse themselves, and I could only have recourse against the lord to whom the case was sent down. And for this reason it is a good thing for the case to be sent down to *all* the lords {in the partnership} and that they be commanded to act in such a way that there should be no reason for further interference because of their default; and then if they do not act adequately, they may be so inadequate as to lose their jurisdiction. And how they should act will be explained in the chapter on offenses, for it will be explained what punishments should be given for each offense.

666. All jurisdictions held by several partners must be administered in territory common to the lords; and they must hear pleadings and have the judgments made in common areas, where the administration of justice is held in common. For if one of the partners heard pleas which belonged to the group or exacted some punishment on his own land, or on someone else's, away from the common territory, he would be acting improperly towards his partners. Therefore if someone acts this way, he must return jurisdiction of what he did or the fines he levied [*esploita*] to the common territory, and pay a fine to the sovereign before whom the suit is brought.

667. When someone must plead before several lords who are partners in a jurisdiction, if the suit is against the lord, he need not answer unless the lords are all there or have sent a competent attorney to hold the court. And

again, if the lords are plaintiffs, they cannot make their complaint through an attorney. Thus if there were four lords who were partners in a jurisdiction, and three were present and made their complaint, and the fourth was not there, the defendant would not have to answer the three others on anything in the jurisdiction of the partnership. And for this reason it is a good idea for those who are partners in a jurisdiction to appoint someone who has power to administer justice for them all; and this {appointment} should be made so carefully that what is done before the appointees does not have to be done over; and how this can be done is explained in the chapter on attorneys {Chapter 4}.

668. Although we have said that the partners in a jurisdiction must be together to do justice in their court or to hold their court, they do not all have to be present at all the actions which can occur, and especially at the arrest of offenders. For each of the partners can arrest people or have them arrested throughout the common jurisdiction for all sorts of offenses, large or small. But once the arrest is made, the person arresting or having someone arrested cannot and should not make a release without his partners' presence. But he can set bail, if the offense is of the kind which allows bail, by assigning a date for the appearance of the person on bail, before himself and his partners; for, if he exacted a fine without calling in his partners, it would be improper.

669. It would be different in the places where the count shared jurisdiction with one of his vassals, for if he exacts a fine in the common territory of the jurisdiction he shares with his vassals, and the case concerns the matters on which he has superior jurisdiction [*le resort*] as a sovereign over his vassals,—for example, cases of agreements in writing, or dower, or wills, or for debts owed to himself, or novel disseisin,—for all these cases he is not required to plead in the common jurisdiction nor to give anything from the exacted fines to his partners;[4] for his partners can have no more sovereignty in the place where they share jurisdiction with the count than if their jurisdiction were entirely individual; for if they held their jurisdiction individually, the count would still have cognizance there over the above-mentioned matters because of his superior jurisdiction over his vassals.

Here ends the chapter on capital property partnerships.

Notes

1. To a modern reader, these so-called partnerships in real property seem more like corporations; but such a concept was still in the future for Beaumanoir, so I will continue to use the word "partnership," or occasionally "business," to translate the term *compaignie*. Likewise I have usually translated *eritage* as "real property" or "land" or just "property" in this book, and here I will sometimes translate it as "business," since it refers to the income-producing property which is exploited as a business by the "partners." Note that since judges kept the fines they levied, the lawcourts were treated like real property (that is, like income-producing property), and they could be held by a partnership also.

2. Here, as in many places, Beaumanoir shows a quite modern concern to avoid economic waste.

3. For sending cases back down, see Chapter 10.

4. For the count's superior jurisdiction, see Chapter 10.

23. Property

Here begins the twenty-third chapter of this book which teaches what things are personalty and what things are realty according to the custom of Beauvais.

670. Many suits have arisen several times about things in a distribution, where one of the parties wanted to take[1] certain things as personalty, and the other party said they were realty.[2] And to remove the doubts which can arise, we will deal in this chapter with what things are personalty and what things are realty according to our custom and according to what we have seen done.

671. Speaking generally, personalty is everything movable, that is to say everything which can be moved from one place to another; and there are a few things which, according to our custom, cannot be moved until they are ripe, and yet they are considered personal property as you will hear below.

672. Realty is things which cannot be moved and which have an annual worth to the lords to whom they belong: such as arable land [*terres gaaignables*], woods, pastures, vineyards, gardens, quit-rents [*cens*], rents, bakehouses, mills, winepresses, upright houses as long as their pegs hold, waterways, privileges,—provided they are held from lords,—rights to labor [*corvees*], homages, tolls [*travers*] and market dues [*tonlieu*]. All such things are realty.

673. Personalty is everything produced by realty, as soon as it is harvested, such as timber when it is cut down, wheat when it is sown. And in many places this is not true for wheat, places where it is realty until it is reaped [*soiés*]; but in Clermont we have seen it approved three times in judgments, and we will explain below the reasons why this was judged. And we have also seen judged that as soon as the vine has grown to the point where the grapes form, the harvest is counted as personalty, and

before that, the work done {is personalty}. And also for wheat before it is sown, the work done [*gaaignages*] on the land is counted as personalty.[3] Oats, wine, money, horses, all metals, and all like manner of merchandise are considered personalty.

674. It happened that a squire who had married a young lady sold his wheat while it was still in the ground, and before it was reaped he died; and the young lady {the widow} wanted to renounce the personalty and debts[4] and take her dower free and clear, and she wanted to take half the wheat which was in the ground, because of her dower. And the merchant who had bought it answered to this by saying that she should have none of the wheat, for her husband who had owned the wheat had sold it to him, the said wheat being personalty by the custom of the place; and if at the time of the sale of the wheat he had sold all his other personalty, she could not have canceled the sale; and as wheat in the ground was personalty by the local custom, and it was sold during the marriage, he requested that his deal be upheld. And on this issue they requested a judgment, namely whether *she* would take because of her dower rights, or *he* would take because of his purchase.

675. It was judged that the merchant would take because of his purchase, and by this judgment you can plainly see that wheat in the ground is personalty according to our custom; for if it had been realty, no one doubts that it would have vested in her as her dower.

676. We have also seen several times that in cases where decedents left their personalty by will, the executors, in order to execute the will, took the harvest of the crops which were sown when the testator died. And by this it is clear that they are personalty; for if they had been realty, the heirs would have taken them and not the executors.

677. We have said that wheat and oats in the ground are personalty and we have cited the cases we have seen by which it is clear that they are personalty. Nevertheless we have seen judgments which might seem to some people to be contrary to what we have said, for we have seen it judged that wheat in the ground is not personalty with respect to a dower, seeing that the woman should have taken in her dower the wheat that her husband had sold, since the dower passed to her before the sown wheat could be harvested [*levé*]. But the reason that the jurors considered was that because

the deal was made during the marriage, what the couple made should be for their common profit; and they also considered that it would be a bad thing if a man could not sell and promise his wheat in the ground. But it is true that when dower passes in a simple way and the woman who wants to take her dower free and clear has renounced the personalty and the debts, she takes her dower as she finds it; and so does a person who comes into land, when it has been held by a custodian,⁵ unless the property was held by shares [*muiage*] or halves, for then the dowager or the custodian takes only the share or the half. In these two cases, dower and custodianship, wheat in the ground does not follow the rule of being personalty, although it is in other cases.⁶

678. Nothing that can die should be considered realty, for what dies comes to an end [*faut*] and realty cannot come to an end [*faillir*]. And because someone might deny this and say: "My vineyard, which is supposed to be a good one, failed to produce [*a failli*] for two or three or four years," {we say} it is not enough to say this for it not to be realty; for because of the chance that realty will sometimes fail to produce, it is valued at a lower price: for example, when you see an acre of vineyard valued at only forty sous per year, and yet you see that it happens to produce ten (or fifteen or twenty) pounds' worth in a particular year (with the result that if you were sure that a crop could never fail you would value it at much too high a price); but no earthly thing is stable, and for that reason you cannot judge such things except as an estimate [*par avis*].

679. We have said that personalty is movable things, and that personalty is produced by realty; for as soon as the crops are taken from the ground [*levees*], or the stalk of things with roots has been cut, what could previously be called realty should afterwards be called personalty. Thus you can see that if rent money or wheat or oats are due on a certain day, then what is due and payable [*deu de terme passé*] (like rents and many other things) should be considered personalty once the day for payment of the said rents has arrived; and until the day when the rent is due it is realty.

680. In his will, a certain man [*preudhons*] left his personalty to be distributed in various places for the good of his soul, and he happened to die on Saint Remy's day before the hour of prime; and several rents in money and other things were due to be paid to him every year on Saint Remy's day. And when he died the executor demanded the rents due on

that day because the testator had lived until the day of payment had arrived.[7] And the decedent's heirs wanted to have the rents[8] because they said the day for payment had not passed, and until it had passed the things should not be said to be personalty; and they also said that a payment day was the whole day, for the renters could pay at any hour they wanted since they did not owe the rents at a certain hour but on a certain day. And on this issue the heirs of the decedent and the executors requested an opinion in the council of good men [*en conseil de bonnes gens*],[9] namely whether the rents due on that day would be personalty or realty.

681. The opinion was that the executors would take the rents due that day as personalty, for they {the men of the council} said that since the rents were not due at a certain hour, as soon as the day for payment dawned the day for payment had arrived, in the morning as much as in the evening; but if the hour of day had been specified, before which the rents had to be paid, such as at prime, terce, midday, nones, or vespers, and the testator had died before the hour, the heirs would have taken the rents as realty.[10]

Here ends the chapter which teaches which things are personalty and which things are realty.

Notes

1. In this chapter, the verb "take" is used to translate *en porter*, which means to receive as one's property because of the death of someone who had owned it. "Taking" here has no connotation of "stealing."

2. As will become clear in the next few sections, realty or real property includes land or something like land, or rights which produce income; personalty or personal property is the produce of the land or rights, whether in goods or money. Beaumanoir also uses the term *chateus*, which is like the modern term "chattels" and which is not discussed in this chapter. *Chateus* and *mueble* are not distinguished by Beaumanoir, although he often mentions both together. The reason for the argument at a distribution (where the property of a decedent is distributed to his heirs or those who take under a will) is that the heirs take realty by operation of law, but the personalty (and up to one-fifth of the realty) passes according to the wish of the decedent expressed in a *testament*. See Chapter 12.

3. If the owner died and the land passed after the plowing was finished but before the wheat was sown, the heir had to reimburse someone for the cost of the plowing.

4. A person who was entitled to a decedent's personalty also had to pay his debts; to avoid the latter, you also had to renounce the former. This means that this widow will receive only the realty which comes to her in dower, hence the argument as to whether the unharvested wheat is realty (and she takes it) or personalty (which she has renounced).

5. For land held by a custodian, see Chapter 15.

6. It is hard to reconcile the rule announced in this section with the result of the case recited in §§674–75.

7. That is, the executor considered the rents to be now due, and therefore personalty.

8. That is, they wanted the rents still not paid to be considered realty.

9. This opinion was given not by jurors but by *bonnes gens* who are supposed to remember what the custom is or give rulings on it.

10. Lawyers will recognize that the opinion contains some dictum, that is to say material which is not needed for the ruling in the case but which might guide some future court looking for a ruling.

24. Customs

Here begins the twenty-fourth chapter of this book which explains what a custom is and what a privilege is, and which privileges are valid and which are not.

682. Because all suits are brought according to customs, and this book generally explains things according to the customs of the county of Clermont, in this chapter we will briefly explain what a custom is and what should be held to be a custom, even though we have spoken of them specially in various chapters as appropriate in the cases we were discussing. And we will also speak of privileges [*usages*], and of which privileges are valid and which are not, and of the difference between custom and privilege.

683. Custom is approved by one of two methods, and the first of these methods is when the custom is generally observed throughout the county, and has been observed for as long as man can remember, without challenge: for example, when a commoner acknowledges a debt, he is commanded to pay it within seven days and seven nights, and the gentleman is given fifteen days; this custom is so clear that I have never seen it challenged. And the other way a custom can be acknowledged and held as a custom is if there has been a dispute and one of the parties cites a custom in his argument, and it is approved in the judgment, as has happened many times in distributions among heirs and in other disputes. And a custom can be adopted [*prouver*] by these two methods, and the count is obliged to uphold this custom and have it upheld by his vassals so that no one abolishes it. And if the count himself wanted to abolish it or permit it to be abolished, the king should not allow it, for he is supposed to observe and to cause to be observed the customs of his kingdom.

684. The difference between custom and privilege is that customs must be observed, but there are certain privileges which would be invalid if

someone wanted to bring a suit to challenge them and obtain a judgment on the matter. Now let us see which privileges are valid and which are not.

685. Peaceful use of a privilege[1] for a year and a day is enough to acquire possession: for example when a person has worked a field,—or a vineyard or other land,—and peacefully reaped the fruits for a year and a day, and someone wants to obstruct him from doing so, the lord should take away the obstruction, if requested to do so, and maintain the person in his possession until he loses ownership in the property by a lawsuit.

686. The second kind of {possession by} privilege is holding the land peacefully for ten years in the sight and knowledge of those who want to create the obstruction. This kind of privilege is valid for acquiring ownership and possession of real property, provided that you include an adequate reason why the property passed to you, for example by purchase or by gift, or by legacy, or by passing laterally or by descent, and provided the reason also includes some dues to the lord from whom you hold the property.

687. The third kind of privilege is thirty years, for a person who can say he has peacefully held some property for thirty years is not required to show how it passed to him; but he has ownership without showing any other reason, except for things held in dower or as a life interest, or as a farm or on a lease. For if the person suing for the property that had been held for thirty years tried to prove against the person in possession that he held it because his wife had held it in dower, and, before a year and a day after the wife was dead, the claimant presented himself to claim the property as the heir, no long tenure during dower could count against him if he could prove the dower. And also if he can prove the property was held on a lease, for example, when a man leases his land for ten or twelve years, and when the years have passed he leases it again to the same person: such possession of land is no defense against a person proving that it was held on a lease. And also if someone has sold a life interest in the fruits of his land, and the person buying this benefit as a life interest holds the land for thirty years or more and then dies, the deceased's heir cannot get possession of the property because of his father's tenure; nevertheless he does get possession until the life interest has been demonstrated, by giving good security that he will reimburse the profits from the land when the person suing for the land[2] has proved his contention. And also no one should be able to get ownership of

property which he held as a farm³ once you have proved that it was farmed out to the person holding it.

688. Now let's look at the kind of privilege which is invalid. When a lord sees one of his subjects holding land for which he pays no quit-rents, rents or obligations [*redevances*], the lord can take possession of it as his own, for no one, according to our custom, can hold property in allod, and allod is the name given to something you hold without owing any obligation to anyone.⁴ And if the count notices before any of his subjects that such allods are held in his county, he can seize them as his own; and he is not required to return them or to answer any of his subjects {who sue him over this matter}, because he is by law the lord of anything he finds held as allod. And if one of his subjects had taken possession of the property, he should not be allowed to keep it unless he can prove that it was his fief, or that it should have been held from him, which he had found concealed or subinfeudated [*esbranchié*];⁵ and if he cannot prove it, the allod should remain the count's, and the person holding it in allod cannot allege long tenure. And for this reason I recommend that all those who hold in this manner come to pay homage to the count, or pay some dues of the count's choosing, before he seizes the property; and if they do so, they should not lose the land, but you should be grateful to them for clearing up a situation in which their ancestors' manner of holding was not clear.

689. My lord Pierre de Thiverny sued the town of Les Haies,⁶ saying that the said town, wrongly and without good reason, habitually sent its animals to pasture in his pastures (over which he had lordship and jurisdiction) being people who paid him no quit-rent [*cens*]⁷ or rents or dues for this privilege; for which reason he required that they be prevented from making this use of his property, and that they be told by the court [*par droit*] they had no right to act this way. To this the said town answered, saying that it had maintained and preserved this privilege for as long as the memory of man could reach, and that it was a privilege accorded to them by the said lord Pierre; for which reason they requested to be allowed to make peaceful use of the privilege as they had been doing for a long time. And on this issue they requested a judgment.

690. The men of Creil, after having taken all their delays⁸ and sought advice in many places, pronounced the judgment that the said town of Les

Haies had no right to the use of the said lord Pierre's fields, that the longstanding privilege they had given as an argument was not valid, because they did not give for the said privilege any quit-rents, rents, or dues. And by this judgment you can see that no privilege which causes a loss to someone else is valid against the lord of the place where the privilege is enjoyed, unless you pay the lord or the count quit-rent or rents or dues.

691. There are privileges in varous places which would be worth nothing if they were contested and submitted for a judgment: for example, if some town or some individual has been used to sending his animals into my woods as soon as the trees are cut down, for this kind of privilege causes damage [*est essius*] and no damage should be permitted, unless people who are used to doing these things show in a charter that the privilege was given to them by the lord of the place and confirmed by the sovereign. For no one, except by the authority of the sovereign, can permit a privilege which causes damage.

692. No privilege which goes against the general custom of the district is valid unless it has been granted and confirmed by the sovereign, or if you do not pay the lord one of the things he is entitled to, namely quit-rent, rents, or obligations.

693. A habitual action [*usages*] by a subject against his lord's interest, and which deprives him of property, is invalid, for example when a man pays less rent than he should, or if he conceals some of the things the lord has a right to. As soon as the lord hears about such offenses, the lord can get redress in spite of the habitual nature of the action [*usages*]. But it is true that in such cases the subject keeps possession of the right to act the way he has been acting until the lord's rights are proved against him; but subjects should take care not to offend in such ways against their lord, for when the lords have recovered by a judgment what was concealed from them or held back from them for a long time, the subjects have to make all the back payments and pay a fine for each period in which they should have paid; that is to say, if the dispute was over ordinary quit-rents [*droit cens*], the petty fine [*simple amende*]⁹ by the custom of the district. But if the dispute was over other rents, for example in wheat or oats or wine or chickens, which do not bring on a fine according to the general custom if they are not paid by the due date, the subject will only have to make up the arrears for such rents.

694. If someone wants to move off land he holds for quit-rent or rents from some lord, he should pay for it up to the day he leaves it, and say to the lord from whom he holds it: "Sire, I have held such and such a property from you at such and such a quit-rent,—*or* at such and such a rent.—Here is the rent for this year,—*and if there are arrears he should pay them also,*—and from now on I no longer wish to hold it, but leave you the turf [*gason*]."[10] And all the while he says nothing about leaving the property, he still owes rent. And if it happened that he stopped paying the rent, the lord could give him a warning to pay the rents and arrears within a year and a day; if it is ordinary quit-rent, he could demand that he pay the fine along with the quit-rent. And if the tenant does not pay within a year and a day, the lord can seize the property for his own, and can still sue the former tenant for the arrears from when he was in possession of the property; for otherwise dealers in sharp practice could gain from their sharp practice, if they could hold the property and hold back their rent for a long time, and then say: "I am giving you back the property," without paying anything; for they might well owe more arrears than the property was worth, and thus the lords would lose through the trickery of their tenants, which would not be fair [*avenans*].

695. It is true that according to the general custom you can move off a property you hold from a lord whenever you want; but this means if you have paid what you owe for it up to the day when you leave it. But nevertheless agreements and obligations can bring this custom to an end: for example, when someone takes a forest to clear it, or a vine to be planted for a certain sum, and makes an agreement, giving sureties, or giving a promise, or giving land as a security [*par contreacens*][11] for the agreement, that he will pay the rents for the place he has taken *including a condition that he cannot leave it*; in such a case he cannot leave the property, but he must keep his agreement.

696. According to custom no man is imprisoned for debt, except for debts owed to the count or the king, unless he has agreed in writing that he may be arrested and imprisoned. But for those two kinds of debt you can arrest the person and attach his property, and no order to pay is required, neither in seven days nor in fifteen; for the prince has his right to take action against such debtors, as soon as the due date has passed, by arresting them and attaching their property.

697. Various kinds of debts can fall due for which no court order to pay need be obtained, according to the general custom. The first kind is when you have a written agreement. The second is when you owe workmen for their day's work, for it would be a bad thing if those who live by their labor had to wait for the due date of the order.[12] Therefore as soon as a workman appears before the judge, the latter should have him paid right away by confiscating some of the debtor's property and selling it. The third kind is when some payment is sued for, and the person sued denies it, and the plaintiff proves it against him: as soon as it is proved, you should have it paid, immediately and without an order. The fourth kind is when people have to make a distribution of personal property for reasons of direct or lateral inheritance, and one of the people takes possession of all or part of the property against the will of the others who are as closely related to the deceased as is the person who has taken possession. As soon as this is reported to the judge, he should take possession of everything and have the distribution made without delay; and if the person who has taken possession tries to allege various reasons why the others should not participate in the distribution, the judge should nevertheless take possession of everything during the suit, so that the person cannot during the interval dispose of any of the things the others are asking to be given if they are the winners [*ont reson*].

698. There are various privileges which are so common to all that they cannot be withheld, even though no taxes, rents, or obligations are given for them: for example, coming and going on the public highways, for no one owes any obligations for this privilege, since everyone has a right to it, and also taking water from a public river or well; such privileges cannot and must be forbidden to anyone; and also the church is available to all, to make their prayers at a convenient place and time, except those who are excommunicated, who should not go there until they are allowed to by the grace of Holy Church; and also the fords to water animals; and also many public amenities [*aisement commun*] which are situated in public places and have been there for a long time should not be forbidden to anyone. And because all such privileges are common to all, it is quite right that when expenses have to be paid to maintain them, all who have the benefit of the enjoyment [*aisement*] of the things should contribute their fair share. And in our opinion, no one should be exempted, even though some of our gentlemen do not wish to agree; for we do not see why their subjects should be made to maintain such public amenities for gentlemen, since the gentlemen make more than their fair share of use of them compared to commoners.

699. It may happen that for a long time someone permits his neighbor to go to his well, which is in his courtyard or within his fence [*dedans son enclos*]; nevertheless such a privilege is not valid so as to acquire such rights that the owner of the property cannot withhold the privilege and fence off [*enclore*] or fill in [*estouper*] the well when he wants to. Nevertheless we have seen those who were used to going to a certain well get seisin of the privilege; but they lost in a suit on ownership, because it would be a bad thing if I wanted to fence in my well or fill it in and I could not because of the right to use it [*aisement*] I had given my neighbor.

700. Those who have certain privileges in particular places, by charter or by the gift of lords, should take care to use these privileges as they should, for if they misuse them, that is to say if they use them otherwise than they should, they should lose their privilege for the offense. For example, it happens that a gentleman or a religious house has the right to take a cartload of logs every day from the lord's wood, and they send for two or three cartloads; if the user is found thus misusing his privilege and the lord in whose wood he had the privilege can prove that the misuse was by the consent or at the command of the person having the privilege, he would lose the privilege right away. But this would be hard to prove against a religious house, for you would have to prove it was against the wishes of the abbot and the chapter [*couvent*], if it is a house where there is a chapter; and if it is against the bishop he cannot lose the ownership of the privilege. Therefore {misusers of} privileges which are in the hands of the church [*amorti*] would merely pay a fine; and so would laypersons against whom it could not be proved that the misuse was on their orders. And the fine for such offenses [*prises*] is sixty sous and restitution of the damages. And those who perpetrated the misuse,—for example the carter and the laborers, who knew what the privilege was,—should be banished from the place where the privilege lies for a year and a day, so that they are corrected of their misuse by their banishment; and if they are caught there again afterwards, they should have to serve a long prison term and be banished forever from the said privilege.

701. Employees [*Cil qui servent*] should not do illegal work [*messervir*] on the orders of their employer [*seigneur*]. A person does illegal work who at his lord's orders causes loss to someone, or commits larceny or some other serious crime. And when someone's employee is caught committing a serious crime, he cannot protect himself by saying: "My lord made me do

it." And even if the lord admitted it, or the employee proved it against his lord if the latter denied it, the employee would be punished according to the crime, for no one who commits a serious crime is excused by saying that someone else made him do it, because no one may do harm on someone else's orders.

702. If a poor knight has a house near a forest and the lord gives to him and his heirs the privilege of gathering wood for his fires and construction, and of pasturing his animals,[13] and he or his heirs wanted to sell the house along with the privilege to a nobler and richer person, for example, a person for whom twice what the seller used would not be sufficient for his house and family, the question may be asked whether the lord of the place where the privilege lay should permit such a sale. We say no, for the seller cannot sell more than he has, and he has only a privilege according to his condition. Therefore, if he sells his privilege to a greater person, an estimate must be given to the buyer of what privilege the seller had; and the sale of such privileges should be made in this manner.

703. We have heard several cases where certain lords, when they asked their subjects for their quit-rents [*cens*] or rents and they were not paid on the due date, collected for the quit-rents or the rents and also a fine for missing the due date, and their tenants [*oste*] came before us and said that at no time in the world had they paid fines and they did not want to pay fines; and yet they did not produce a charter or a dispensation [*don*] from the lord. And since we saw that in this case the common law was against them, and most of the county of Clermont operating [*user*] differently, we would not listen to them with respect to simple quit-rents due in money on a day certain for land or peasant houses [*masure*]. And the judgment was announced to them that those who did not pay their quit-rents [*cens*] on time would have to pay the quit-rents and the petty fine, being five sous by the custom of Clermont and seven and a half sous by the custom of several towns in the county. But it is true that for rents paid in wheat and oats and capons and chickens we have not observed that fines are normally paid; instead when these things are not paid on the due date, if they are due for peasant houses, you can take off the doors and windows, or seize the personal property of the debtors; and if you don't find anything to seize, you can seize the property from which the rents are due and hold it until the rents and the arrears have been paid.

704. There is another kind of quit-rent which should be called surtax [*seurcens*] or *cens costier*, and there are many examples of this in the towns. For example when the holders of houses or land have sold their holdings for rent, and yet the ordinary quit-rent [*droit cens*] must still be paid to someone else; or for example, when someone gives another, on payment of the surtax, what he himself holds for an ordinary quit-rent from another lord; in the case of such surtax, there is no fine for a person who does not pay by the due date; instead, when he is not paid on time, the person who should receive the surtax must make a complaint to the lord who has the ownership, and then if the surtax is due from the subtenant [*ostise*] the lord should have the doors and windows removed until the surtax is paid. And if the surtax is on some other land, the land should be seized and the crops harvested until the surtax is paid. But it is true that in such cases of surtax the lord who has the ownership and to whom the quit-rent is due can first pay himself his ordinary quit-rent and the fines which are due. And according to the current custom, you cannot sell or give a new surtax on property which has not been thus held for a long time, without permission from the lord of the place; for it has been forbidden because some people so burdened their houses or their lands with such surtaxes when they needed money that they later abandoned the houses because they were too heavily encumbered; or, when they were falling down, they would not repair them; and the other lands sometimes remained uncultivated, because no one wanted to be the heirs to them because of the burden of the surtax. And for this reason many houses have fallen into disrepair and many lands been left waste, and for this reason the prohibition against new surtaxes is a good one.

705. You should know that when several people have a surtax on some house or some land, and the thing fails to produce [*dechiet*] in such a way that they cannot all be paid, the oldest tax should be the first paid, and then the others in order of precedence. And if there is a loss, it must be borne by the last persons, unless they want to take the land and pay the ordinary quit-rent to the lord and the surtaxes to those who have them.

706. There are various conventions [*usages*] for building and other things in the towns which are not found in villages [*viles champestres*]; for in the country, no one can build so close to me that the run-off from my roof [*li degous*] is in any way hampered [*ne me demeurt tous francs*]; and if I let the

run-off from my house fall on to my neighbor's land, I should be required to divert it. But other building conventions are current in the bigger towns because the lots are narrower, for my neighbor may support his construction beams against my adjoining wall, whether I want him to or not, provided that the wall is strong enough for my house not to be in danger. And if the wall is too weak and it is all on my land, my neighbor must support his house beams on his own land. And if he wants to build his house higher than mine, I cannot prevent it, even if it takes the light away from my house. And if the wall is between the two plots, each one can take advantage of the wall and can build on it in such a way that his gutter empties on to his own lot, and the water does not run off on to his neighbor's. And if the houses are the same height, they can have a common gutter which serves both houses; but if one wants to build his house higher, he can still do so, and each one must have his own gutter on his own side.

707. I am not allowed to have my laundry [*lavoir*] nor my kitchen sink in a place where the waste water will go into my neighbor's house or yard; but I must put it where it does not interfere with anyone; or I can put it facing the street if my lot is so narrow that I cannot conveniently do anything else, for it is a good thing to keep the streets clean in places where the waste can run away on your own ground.

708. When someone makes his garden or yard in a private place where the neighbors cannot see in, and one of the neighbors wants to build next to it, you cannot prevent him from building, but you can prevent him from building a door or a window which would spoil the privacy of the yard or garden; for some people would do it in bad faith to take away their neighbors' privacy. Therefore a person wanting light on that side must put in an opaque window [*verriere*]; then there will be light and the neighbor's place will not be spoiled.

709. We have said above that no one fails to build his house higher because it takes away his neighbor's light, and it's true. Nevertheless in the larger towns it is very necessary to see how each person can do things to his advantage and at the least detriment to others. And for this reason it could be so unreasonable for someone to take away his neighbor's light and ability to see out that it should not be allowed, even though he was building only on his own property, for example if the neighbor could not find a way

to see out anywhere, for otherwise the neighbor might lose his house because there was no light in it.

710. You cannot build under or over your neighbor's land any more than you can build on it at ground level. Therefore anyone wishing to excavate [*bonner*] must do so under his own land and not under his neighbor's. And if the place where he wants to do this is next to a street, and there are houses on both sides, and he excavates under the street next to him, he must not go past the middle of the street; for the privilege he has in this place must also go to his neighbor, if he wants to excavate. And a person working underground must take care not to do anything because of which the neighboring houses will fall down or the neighboring street sink, for he would have to make good the damage; for a person could do something on his own land which would cause the neighbor's house to fall down, and it is right for the person who does such damage to have to put it right.

711. It sometimes happens that you take something that belongs to someone else, without their leave or wish, and when you have it in your possession, you put it to a use which changes its nature and it becomes something else: for example, if someone takes lumber in someone else's forest, and puts it to use in making a house or a ship or many other things you can make with lumber; or, for example, if someone melts down silver money belonging to someone else and has a pot or a dish or a goblet made from them. In all these and similar cases, I cannot sue to have the thing which was made, because there is in the making something which did not proceed from what was mine; for I cannot sue for the house just because I can prove that some of my lumber was used to make it; and I cannot sue for the pot or the dish just because I can prove some of my silver went into it. How then can I get back what is mine? I should sue the person who took it from me on a charge of larceny, if I know that he took it from me with the intention of stealing it; but if I feel it was not taken out of a desire to steal,— for example, it happens that someone takes something belonging to someone else, thinking it is his own and it is someone else's; or when someone bought something from a person who had no power to sell it and the buyer thought it was the seller's; or it was bought in the public market or given by someone with no power to give it,—the person who is in possession of the thing can use all these defenses against a charge of larceny; but he is not excused from giving to the person who owned it the amount the thing was

worth and he must seek his warrantor,[14] for he needs him to recover his losses and to defend himself against the charge of larceny.

712. If a house or other thing is constructed with things which belonged to several people, and each one asks to have his things back again because he was not paid the price he sold them for, and because the buyer will not or cannot pay him, the house should not be torn down in order to give one man back his lumber and another his stone and another his tile: instead, those who supplied or sold the things must take their losses, if they sold the stuff without taking sureties to a person who cannot pay. But it is true that if each one finds his thing whole and before they have been built into the fabric, and it is after the due date when he should have been paid the price, and the buyer is still in possession of the thing, he can sue to get it back, unless the buyer makes full payment; for it would be a bad thing if I found the lumber I had sold, not yet built in and still in the possession of the buyer, and I could not get back either the price or my lumber. And by what we say about lumber you can understand how it is for other commodities which are sold.

713. You should know that any manufactured article in which there are several materials should be left whole, for it would be waste to take it apart; and if two or three or more persons are suing for it and prove that it is theirs, if it is personal property and it is of such a nature that it cannot be taken apart or divided, for example a horse, or a silver or gold ornament [*jouel*], the person owning most in the thing should have it, by giving compensation to the others according to what each person has in it.

714. If two persons mingle together their wheat or wine or money or merchandise which is fungible, without distinguishing signs or divisions or indications of what each person has, it should be understood that each person has a half; and each person can ask for that much when the time comes to make a partition. But it would be different concerning things mixed by mistake or by accident, for example, if my wheat was in a grainloft and the grainloft collapsed or let the grain fall through so that my wheat fell into another grainloft on to someone else's wheat, or as in many cases which happen every day of things getting mixed together. In such a case you should find out as nearly as you can how much each person had, both by the oaths of the parties and by any other means possible, and then give back to each person as nearly as possible what he had.

715. No privilege can or should be granted on another person's property without obtaining the leave of the person whose property it is and without the leave of the lord from whom the property is held, unless it is a privilege which has been enjoyed and customary [*acoustumés*] for a long time. And a new privilege can be asked for which the owner and the lord *must* agree to, for example in cases of necessity.

716. A case of necessity involves something which you cannot do without except with too great a loss or too great damage: for example, when a river has eroded the road which was on the bank, and my house or my vineyard adjoins the eroded place, as much of my property as is needed must be taken and used to remake the road which was eroded; or if I have a new house or a vineyard made in a place where there had never been any before, I cannot be refused a new road in order to have access to my house or my vineyard if I pay compensation [*damage*].

717. By what is said in this chapter you can know that you cannot go against what has been approved by custom, but you can go against certain privileges when they are misused or when they cause damage without dues being paid to a lord.

Here ends the chapter on customs and privileges, which privileges are valid and which are not.

Notes

1. Lawyers and landowners will recognize that by the word *usage* 'privilege,' Beaumanoir often seems to mean an easement. The word *aisement* appears later in the chapter, however, and I have translated it as "amenity" and "enjoyment." By *usage* Beaumanoir also means a longstanding habit of conduct, which may not have been granted as a privilege, and which indeed may be an offense against the lord (see §693). In other contexts, the usage is akin to our modern "adverse possession" (§§686–77). I have avoided using these technical terms from modern legal language, and used more familiar expressions like "privilege" and "habitual action," etc.

2. This would most likely be the heir of the person who sold the life interest to the deceased.

3. "Farm" here means property leased from another, for whatever purpose, not necessarily for agriculture.

4. One formulation of this doctrine is "Nulle terre sans seigneur," or "No land without a lord."

5. For illegal subinfeudation, see Chapter 47, §§1488–89.

6. Thiverny and Les Haies are on opposite sides of the river Oise, just south of the town of Creil.

7. "Quit-rent" is the way that the word *cens* is rendered in the English version of Marc Bloch's *Feudal Society*, trans. L. A. Manyon, 2 vols. (Chicago: University of Chicago Press, 1961) 1: 250. Not finding any better translation, I have adopted this one.

8. For the delays permitted to the jurors, see Chapter 65.

9. The *simple amende* varied from place to place in the county of Clermont, but was generally five sous.

10. The word *turf* here probably refers back to a time when the exchange of a piece of turf symbolized the exchange of the whole property.

11. For the *contreacens*, see §§1132–33.

12. Seven days and nights for commoners, two weeks for gentlemen. See §683 above.

13. A highly prized privilege was that of letting pigs eat the fallen chestnuts and beechnuts in forest lands.

14. The warrantor is the person who sold or gave the thing to the person accused of larceny, that is, the person who can (and must by law) explain the transaction, by putting himself in the place of the accused, who is thereby dismissed from the case. If the person waranteed has losses, the warrantor must reimburse him.

25. Highways

Here begins the twenty-fifth chapter of this book which speaks of what width the roads should be, and the safe conduct of merchants and pilgrims, and of things found in the road.

718. There was of old, as we have heard the law lords [*seigneurs de lois*][1] say, a law concerning how the width of the roads and highways should be maintained, so that the people could go from one town to another, and from one castle to another, and from one city to another, and so that merchandise could pass safely through the district under the protection of the lords.[2] And to protect and safeguard merchants safe passages [*travers*] were established; and by common law, as soon as merchants set out on a safe passage, the lord of the place, to whom the safe passage belongs, has them in his protection. And the lords should take great care that they can pass safely, for the people would have great shortages if merchandise could not pass through the country. And if someone does any harm to merchants or commits an offense against them, concerning which they complain, the judges should not operate according to the delays permitted by custom to those who are residents in the district; for before the merchants obtained a hearing on the offenses in a provost's court or at the assizes, they might lose so much by the delay that they would waive their right to a trial, and this would not be to the advantage of the lords or of the common people. Therefore they should be given speedy justice, and you should be lenient to them concerning their mistakes which they commit more out of ignorance than ill will.

719. It appears that when roads were laid out, they were divided into five types, according to width. The first type is four feet wide, called a path [*sentier*], and these paths were made so that you could go from one road to another or from one town to another; and no cart should go on a path at any time when it could cause damage to the land or things built nearby.— The second type of road that was made was eight feet wide, called a cart

track [*chariere*]; and on such a road carts can go one behind the other, but animals cannot go unless they are on a rope, nor carts two abreast, except when they cross.—The third type of road which was made is sixteen feet wide; and on these carts can go two abreast with a path on either side. And you can drive animals before you, without stopping, from town to town or from market to market, provided they do not stop to graze at a time or season when they can do damage to the surrounding property. And this kind of road was made for going from castle to castle or village [*vile champestre*] to village.—The fourth type of road that was made was thirty-two feet wide, and carts can go on this and animals can stop and graze or rest without offense, and all kinds of merchandise pass, for merchandise can go through cities and castles where tolls are due but they cannot pass on the roads described above, avoiding the toll payments; and sometimes they suffer great loss when they try to do so. Nevertheless they can pass everywhere that carts can go, provided they do not fail to pay tolls [*n'en portent le droit d'autrui*].[3]—The fifth type of roads which were made were those which Julius Caesar had made; and these roads were laid down in a straight line in places where a straight line can go without being obstructed by too high mountains or rivers or marshes, and they are sixty-four feet wide. And it should be understood that the reason why they are so wide is so that all products of the earth and living things which man and woman live on can be transported or carried along them, so that everyone can come and go and transport supplies for all his needs in the width of the road, and go through cities and castles to carry on his business.

720. We have spoken of the classification of roads because we see that they are all pretty much downgraded by the greed of those whose lands border them and by the ignorance of the lords who should maintain them at the proper width; and so that when there is a dispute concerning road width, you will inquire whether it should be a path, or a road, or a highway, or the widest of all which is called a royal road [*chemin royal*]; and according to what can be found out about what it was of old, it should be brought back up to the width described above; and no long habit of use which has been made to the contrary should be valid, for a use which is made against the common good should not prevent the thing from being restored to its former state.

721. According to common law all roads, even those of sixteen or thirty-two or sixty-four feet in width, belong in all ways to the lord who

holds the land directly from the king, whether the roads pass through their personal lands or the lands of their subjects, and they have jurisdiction and lordship over the roads. But with respect to roads, we have a different custom in Beauvais, for the general custom in Beauvais is that if I hold the land on both sides of the road, in which land I have jurisdiction and lordship, I have jurisdiction over the road as far as it runs through my lands; and if I have land on only one side of the road and someone else has the land on the other side, half of the road belongs to me and half to the person on the other side, so that if there is a fight on my side of the road, I exact all the fines for the offense, and if it is on the other side, the person whose lands border the road on the other side gets the fines; and if the fight is in the middle of the road, so that you cannot tell which side it was more nearly on, the offense should be jointly judged by the two lords whose lands border the road.

722. There are some persons who go against this custom: that is to say that in Beauvais there are people who have jurisdiction over roads passing through their land, and roads passing through other people's land, and these people are those who have highway jurisdiction [*voierie*], which they hold as a fief by doing homage to the lord. And these highway jurisdictions extend over a certain area, and all suits which occur within the highway jurisdiction area must be handled by the lord who owns the highway jurisdiction. And if no one can prove by a charter or by unchallenged habitual usage that he has highway jurisdiction on lands other than his own, the jurisdiction belongs to those whose land borders the road, as is explained above.

723. We have said that some people in Beauvais have highway jurisdiction on their own lands and on other people's lands, and similarly the count also has highway jurisdiction in various places on other people's lands, and also on his personal lands; and it is clear that in these places no one has jurisdiction except him, for otherwise he would have fewer rights on his lands than his men have on theirs. And where he has highway jurisdiction on his subjects' lands, he must have been in the peaceful habit of exercising jurisdiction instead of his men, or otherwise the men would assume jurisdiction on their lands by the general custom of the district, as is said above. And it is clear that such highway jurisdictions do exist, for in Clermont, in Creil, in Gournay, in Remy, and in Sacy-le-Grand there are tenants [*ostes*] who hold from the count's vassals and these vassals have lordship and

jurisdiction on the tenancies [*ostises*] held from them; and yet as soon as these men step out of their doors on to the roads, they are in the jurisdiction of the count, and all cases arising there must be dealt with by the count. And the highway jurisdictions extend outside the towns, and it would be hard to enumerate all the places, yet they are well known.

724. Although by the common law of Beauvais all roads belong to the person whose land borders them, nevertheless the holders cannot make them narrower or destroy them, for everything is held from the count; and the count should make them maintain the roads at their proper width for the common good, and the count should not permit the great roads of sixteen feet or more in width to be rerouted to other places and thus made worse. Therefore any one wanting to reroute roads must get leave from the count, and if the count sees that it is for the benefit of the district and the improvement of the road, he should allow it to be diverted. And if the count wanted to permit the deterioration of the roads, the king should not permit it; instead, at the request of the district or of some people who complained, without bringing a lawsuit, the king can command the count to have the roads in his lands kept up at their proper width.

725. If you want to mark off [*bonner*] a road, you should not make it wide in some places and narrow in others, instead it should all be of the same width. Nevertheless if there are in some places wide areas called *fros*,— such that it seems that they were left for animals to rest or graze, or because there is worse footing owing to the nature of the ground,—such places should not be changed, for they are very convenient for the common people, and they must be left at their old width without being made narrower.

726. When you see that a road is narrowed [*corrompus*] in various places and you want to put it right, where should you measure the proper width? You should not measure the width at the *fros*,[4] or at the entrances to the towns, for in many places at the entrances to a town the roads are wider than they should be in the open fields, for the convenience of the towns, such as for sending animals out into the fields, or to make repairs [*amendement*], or to go out for recreation [*aler jouer*]. Instead you should make the measurement out in the fields in a place where it is easier to see because of old markers which are found or old ditches which are discovered, and that is where the width should be measured. And if someone has plowed on to the

width of the road, his habit of doing so [*usage*]⁵ should not be a reason for him to continue, because it is against the common good, but no one should be fined where there were no markers or old ditches to mark off the road.

727. All fines for the deterioration of roads, such as causing erosion on [*esboueler*] the roadway, or making walls or ditches or buildings, or taking away dirt to the detriment of the road, are set at sixty sous, and the damaged roads must be restored to their former condition. But for doing something to improve the roads no one may be fined, but you should be grateful to everyone who makes improvements.

728. When someone has arable land on both sides of the road, and the road is less than sixteen feet wide, he can plow across the road to make a single furrow.⁶ But if the road is sixteen feet or more wide and it is marked, or there are old ditches, he cannot do so without being subject to a fine of sixty sous.

729. Since it has been said that no damage must be done to roads, it is a sure thing that damage is done by a person who interferes with the paving that was done to improve the road, or who takes away the stones or planks which were put there in the bad places, or who cuts the trees which were planted there for rest areas [*reposees*] or for shade, and even if the person who took away these things had jurisdiction over the road, the sovereign should not allow it, instead he should exact a fine and have the road repaired. And if the person cut down trees, we agree that the value of the trees should be added to the fine, so that he does not cut them down out of greed; nevertheless if the tree was dead [*sès*] or there were fallen branches [*bois esbouli*], the lord who has jurisdiction over the road could cut it down or uproot it without committing an offense.

730. When a road is in such bad disrepair in certain places that it cannot be repaired without too great a cost, the sovereign can have it relocated as near as possible to the place where it was and at the same width as it should be, with restitution to the person whose land is taken to relocate the road; and the costs should be recovered from all the landowners adjoining the road who derive the greatest convenience [*aisement*] from it.

731. A lord holding directly from the king may establish a new custom [*fausse coustume*] among his people for one or two or three years, according

to the need, in order to repair and restore the roads which are appropriate for the people of the district and for foreign merchants, but he cannot establish such a new [*nouvele*] custom in perpetuity, except by the king's permission.

732. If the lords in the towns who have jurisdiction over the roads see that there is a great need to repair them, and their subjects do not agree to this because of the costs, the lords should not on this account fail to have the roads repaired, provided it is not at great and excessive [*outrageus*] cost so as to harm his subjects. And he can and should force his subjects, whether gentlemen or commoners, to pay their fair share of the costs, and the estimate should be made under oath by good folk chosen by the lord.

733. It sometimes happens that those who are allocating the costs for roads, or the church, or some other public work, and who must put down a share from themselves, put down less from themselves than from the others; and the lord should set this right when he finds out and make them pay their fair share; and he must forbid them to take too excessive {collection} costs out of what they collect, according to their condition and according to whether the work is greater or smaller. And if they take out excessive expenses, or they collect too little from themselves according to their condition, and the others or some of the others complain, the lord should investigate [*metre conseil*], for otherwise they could burden others in order to lighten their own load.

734. It is said above that the assignment of costs which are incurred for the common good should be made on the oath of good people, and it is true; nevertheless, they cannot according to our custom allocate costs to clerks or gentlemen. Now let's see than how the latter are to be obliged to pay their fair share towards the costs, for no one who has land and residence in the area should be excused. The clerks should be forced to pay by their ecclesiastical judge and the gentlemen by the count, so that if they voluntarily contribute enough, they should be left alone; and if they will not put in enough, the lord should make an estimate of the gentlemen's share, and the ecclesiastical judge of the clerks' share; and it is not right to permit the poor to pay for the use that the rich have of public property, for the richer they are the more they need to have the roads and other public works kept in good repair.

735. If wagons or carts or packhorses or people with loads meet in the narrow parts of roads, the person who is least loaded and with the less delicate things should move to one side: such as if a cart was transporting stone and met another cart carrying a barrel of wine, the one carrying the stone should turn aside rather than the one carrying the barrel of wine, for the stone would not be as great a loss or at as great a risk as the barrel of wine would be; and from the example of the wine and the stone you can know how it would be for all other things, namely that the ones less at risk should move aside. And if the persons transporting the less delicate things are so overweening [*outrageus*] that they will not or disdain to cede the right of way to the others, and the delicate goods have an accident, because of their selfishness [*outrage*] or their stupidity [*niceté*], or because they would not turn off and they could have done so if they wanted, they must make restitution for the loss, even if they had had their own load damaged; for if I cause damage to myself and to someone else by my stupidity [*sotie*], the damage to me does not excuse the damage to the other person.

736. It is very dangerous to handle improperly things which are found in the road, and many bad things have occurred because of this. Improper handling occurs when people find a thing and know very well that it is not their own, but they hide it or take it [*l'aproprient a aus*]; and this is a kind of larceny, even though there are people so uncaring that they do not think so, but think the thing is theirs, even when someone asks them for it. But it is not theirs, and they should deal with the thing in the following way.

737. When someone finds something that has fallen in the road, he can pick it up and carry it openly, and if someone comes after [*siut*] him for it and makes out it is his, if he gives a good description of it [*en dit vraies enseignes*], the finder should give it back to him. And if no one comes looking for the thing found, the finder should take it to the person who has the high justice in the place where the find was made and hand over the thing to him; and then the judge should have announced at the church [*prone*] or in the market place that such and such a thing has been found, and if someone comes forward and proves it is his, he can get it back; and if no one can prove it is his, the lord keeps it as abandoned property [*epave*]. And thus you can understand that the finder receives nothing for his pains unless the lord or the owner gives him something [*fet aucune courtoisie*] of his own accord. And if the finder acts differently, he can receive shame and

loss, and if no one ever asks about what he found, he cannot keep it without wickedness and to the danger of his own soul.

738. Off a public road no one should take another's thing or pick it up, for it might be that someone had put it there on purpose, intending to come back for it. Nevertheless you may find something in such a hidden place, for example something lost long ago, that you can pick it up and take it to the lord, as is said above. And people keeping things they find this way can be prosecuted by the lord for concealment of abandoned property; and we believe that in such cases the fine should be in the same amount as the value of the object the finder wanted to keep.

739. When someone loses something and discovers the thing in some-one else's possession because it has been sold or given into safekeeping {by the finder} or in some other way, the person who has lost the thing can sue to get it back, if he wants, from the person who found the thing; and the finder must answer and give him back the thing, or its value if he cannot get it back. And if the loser prefers to sue the person who had the thing from the finder, or some later holder,—for things pass from hand to hand,—he can do so and the person in possession of the thing must answer. But if he requests it, he can have a day to find his warrantor, namely the person who delivered the thing to him; and if he cannot find him, or the warrantor cannot warrant him because of poverty or for some other reason, the plaintiff will nevertheless get back his thing from the person who has it, except in a few cases, such as if the person who has the thing bought it in the public market as a person believing the seller had the power to sell it and he does not know the seller, or he is somewhere where he cannot be called as a warrantor. In such cases the person suing to get back what he lost or which was stolen or taken from him cannot get the thing back unless he reimburses the money the buyer paid for it, for since he bought it without fraud and in the marketplace he should not lose his money because of the offense of another; but if he had bought it outside the market for less money than the thing was worth, by a third or a half, and he could not find his warrantor, the plaintiff would get his thing back without paying the purchase money, because there is a strong presumption against people who buy things this way.

740. And again if someone has lent money on the security of the thing which was taken or stolen or lost, and the owner sued the person who had

taken it as a security, and the lender could not find the person who gave it to him as security to be his warrantor, the owner will not get the thing back unless he pays the money that was lent on it; and if it was lent at interest, the owner will pay only the principal [*chatel*]. And if it can be discovered or if the judge sees a great presumption that the lender knew or believed that the thing was not honestly come by, in such a case we agree that the owner should get his property back without paying what was lent on it, for otherwise you could avoid paying for things and lend money on things with the expectation that they would not be redeemed. And there would be a great presumption against a person who had lent money on the security of a horse at the request of a poor man who brought the horse saying it was his and who could give no proof [*certaineté*]; but where it seemed from his condition or by the knowledge of the lender that he had no course of dealing in such merchandise, and that the horse was not his; and from this presumption you can understand others that could arise in such cases.

741. There is a custom in many places or erecting a stone or wooden cross at the crossroads or in other places outside consecrated holy ground, and this is a good custom for the remembrance of our lord Jesus Christ who for our redemption suffered on the cross his death and passion. Nevertheless, such crosses put up outside holy ground do not protect offenders, even though they go to them with the intention of getting protection for their offenses, for if such crosses could protect offenders, then murderers and highway robbers and quarrelsome people would find offenses very cheap, and many evils could be committed on purpose. And if such crosses afforded protection, a cross which you wore on your person would be a protection, and offenders would always have their warranty with them by reason of the cross they wore.

742. Along with the other things we have said about the public privilege that everyone must have of coming and going peacefully on the roads, all lords should take great care that pilgrims are not arrested or interfered with for petty reasons, for it is wicked to interfere with those who are doing good; and if anyone arrests or interferes with them wrongly or for petty matters, the sovereign should have them freed and their losses restored to them, and the same with all foreign persons going along the roads.

Here ends the chapter on the roads and things found on them, and on the safeguarding of merchants and pilgrims.

Notes

1. It is not clear what *seigneurs des lois* are. They might be those who sat in the higher courts such as the *parlement* in Paris, or teachers of law, generally Roman law, in the universities.

2. There is no extant written law to which Beaumanoir could be referring here.

3. This translation may seem very free, but it has the support of other passages in Chapter 30.

4. The *fros* are wide places in the road; see preceding section.

5. For habits of conduct and privileges, see Chapter 24.

6. This means that the plowman does not have to turn his team of oxen or horses, which is a difficult and time-consuming operation.

26. Measurements

Here begins the twenty-sixth chapter of this book which speaks of weights and measures.

743. We have spoken in the previous chapter of the width at which roads should be maintained, so that merchants and pilgrims and other people who need them can travel safely; and because many kinds of merchandise are sold by weight or volume, and especially things which should be delivered by volume, we shall speak in this chapter of volume measurements and of things which cannot be sold except by such measurements, and the dangers which lie in buying and selling because the measurements differ from town to town according to the local custom, and we will speak also of what measurements are used in general according to our custom.

744. Jehan sued Pierre saying that Pierre owed him a *quartier*[1] of wheat when he ground ten *mines* in his mill, and half a *quartier* for five *mines;* and as there was no half-*quartier* measure, and Pierre used to estimate it in the *quartier* measure by approximation, and a certain measurement could not be made that way, Jehan requested that a half-*quartier* measure be available at the mill so that he could pay for five-*mine* lots. Pierre answered that he had always had the habit of taking a half-*quartier* out of the *quartier* measure by estimation, and he did not want to do it any other way, but requested that his habit of measuring be confirmed.

745. It was judged that since Pierre admitted that Jehan owed him specific quantities for ten *mines* and for five *mines*, his longstanding habits of measuring did not mean that he need not supply a *quartier* measure and a half-*quartier* measure. And by this judgment everyone can know that everything which is paid by volume must be of the correct volume according to the custom of the place where it is to be paid.

746. It is certain that the measures are not all the same in the county of Clermont, but are different in several towns. Now we need to know,—if

Jehan sells Pierre in the town of Creil ten *muis* of wheat delivered in Clermont on a day certain,—by what measurement should they be delivered to Pierre, by the measurement of Creil where the deal was agreed, or the measurement of Clermont where the goods are to be delivered? My opinion is that he should take delivery at the measurement of Clermont. But if at the time of sale Jehan had said: "I sell you ten *muis* of wheat, to be transported to Clermont," I would have said that he should have delivered them in Clermont according to the measurement of Creil where the deal was made, for by the use of the word "transport" it seems that he is obligated to take the goods there.

747. If someone measures using a false measure, the measure should be burned and restitution made to all those who can prove they received goods measured by it; and if the person is a commoner, he owes a sixty-sou fine to the lord; and if he is a gentleman the fine is sixty pounds.

748. According to our custom everyone may have his own measure, provided it is correct according to the custom of the place where he wants to use it.

749. It has been said that everyone can have his own proper [*juste*] measure according to the place where he wants to use it, but this means that you cannot use measures to the detriment of long-established and customary markets; that is to say that no one can or should set up a new market, but eveyone can make measurements at home of things for his own use and to measure things grown on his own land which are for sale, but without making a marketplace [*estaple*] in a new location. And if you want to have a legal [*certaine*] measure and avoid risk, you should have your measure stamped with the count's stamp, and then you can measure things without risk.

750. For all grains, the measure throughout the county is twelve *mines* to the *mui*; but the *mines* are smaller or larger in one place than another, and for this reason if you buy or sell you should pay attention to where you are and what measure the deal is made in, so you are not deceived by the measurement units.

751. Measures for wine are not uniform; nevertheless twenty-four *setiers* make a *mui*, but the *setiers* are not all as large as each other; in many

towns in the county the wine is measured according to the Catenoy[2] measure, and there are other towns which use the Clermont measure, and there are towns which do not use the Clermont or any other measure, but have certain longstanding customary measures. And it is right to maintain the customary measurement units for each town, especially when the usage does not reduce the rights of the lord at all. For in many places a habit of conduct [usage] which is against the lord's interest is invalid, as you will hear in the chapter which explains which privileges [usage] are valid and which are not {Chapter 24}.

752. Land measurements are no more uniform than those for grain. Nevertheless, where the measure of grain is smaller, the measure of land is normally smaller as well, and where the measure of grain is greater, the measure of land is greater, which seems miraculous, even though the old land measurements were made according to the measurements of grain. For just as you count twelve *mines* of wheat to the *mui* in each town, you also count twelve *mines* of land for a *mui* of land. And you can see clearly that in just about every town you sow a *mine* of grain on a *mine* of land. For in Clermont a *mine* of land is of sixty *verges* at twenty-five feet per *verge,* and it takes one *mine* of grain by the Clermont measure to sow it; and in Remy the measurement of land is eighty *verges* of twenty-two feet and a hand [*pleine paume*][3] to the *verge,* and it takes a *mine* of grain by the Remy measure to sow it, and a *mui* of wheat in Remy measures fourteen and a half *mines* in Clermont, which is about as much bigger proportionately as the Remy measure is bigger than that of Clermont.[4] And as I have explained to you that the measurement of land follows the measurement of grain in these two towns, so in the other towns the measurement of the land corresponds to [*suit*] that of grain.

753. Woods, vines, thickets [*aunoi*], and pastures are not commonly measured by the unit of the *mine,* but by *arpents,* which are measured in two ways according to the custom: the first kind of measurement is when you give the name *arpent* to a hundred *verges* of the same *verge* which is used locally to measure arable land, so that in some places the *verge* is only twenty feet, and some places it is more and some places less, so that a hundred *verges* of the local *verge*-measurement make an *arpent.* And the other kind of *arpent* is one which contains a hundred *verges* of twenty-five feet per *verge,* and this is the king's legal *arpent.* And this *arpent* should have been used to measure all the above-mentioned land which is measured by the *arpent.* But

long-established habits change it in various places, so that for such measurements it is best to preserve the custom of each place.

754. When someone should deliver land to someone else by measuring a certain number of units, whether he is selling or giving the land, or transferring it some other way, he should deliver it according to the measuring units of the place where the land to be measured is situated, even though the deal or agreement was made in some other place where the units are greater or smaller. Nevertheless the deal is construed to conform [*raportee*] to the unit of the place where the land is situated, unless an agreement takes away this construction; for if an agreement is made to use greater units than the local custom provides, custom does not override the carrying out of the agreement.

755. If you have to measure some land and no one can remember it ever having been measured before, you should look at the custom of the closest pieces of land which *have* been measured; and if the land lies between two properties, so that on the one side an *arpent* of a hundred *verges* of twenty-five feet to the *verge* had been used, and on the other side a smaller *arpent*, you should choose the measurement with the larger *verge*, for it was made and established by the sovereign, and the other measurement units have only arisen from habit and because of the forebearance of lords who gave their lands for quit-rent [*cens*] or rent in olden times, and transferred them to their tenants using smaller units than the sovereign had established, and the tenants subsequently used the same unit when transferring the land that their lord had used to transfer it to them; and thus the legal measurement of the sovereign has been reduced [*corrompue*] in various places, as was said above.

756. Each lord who has jurisdiction and lordship in his land must safeguard the accuracy of the measuring units which have been used for a long time, whether for grain, for liquids, or for land; and if anyone reduces these measurements, the fine for a commoner is sixty sous; and he may not increase them either; but if he gives greater measure than he should and it is clear that he sells more by that measurement than he buys, his measure should be burned; but he should not pay a fine, for it can easily be seen that he did not do it in bad faith, but even lost by it. But if he had two measures, one too large and the other too small, and he normally bought according to the larger measure and sold according to the smaller one, in that case the fine would be at the discretion of the lord.

757. In some towns no one is permitted to have a grain measure unless it is marked with the lord's mark; and if they make measures which are not marked and use them to buy and sell in the towns where this custom is current, they must pay a fine to the lord, and the fine is sixty sous. And this is the custom generally in towns where there is a market.

758. It was reported to Pierre, who was the lord of a town, that there were taverners who were selling their wine using too small a measure. Pierre went round the taverns and confiscated the pots they used to measure with; and among others there was a taverner who, as soon as he saw Pierre going round the taverns and collecting the pots, took his measures and broke them, so that when Pierre arrived he found only the shards of the broken measures. Pierre asked the taverner why he had done this, and the taverner replied because he wanted to, and he would give no other reason, for he had no good reason to break them just as his lord was asking for them. Pierre arrested the taverner and put him in prison and had tested all the measures he had collected from the other taverns, and those he found accurate he gave back without damage; and he made the taverners whose measures were found too small pay a fine. And as for the one who broke his measures, he wanted him to pay a fine because he had broken them, and because by the breaking he stood convicted of the offense of measuring with too small a measure, for it was apparent and seemed clear by a presumption that he had broken his measures when he saw the lord coming because he felt they were inaccurate. To this the taverner replied that he did not want to have to pay the fine, because he was allowed to break his own pots when he wanted, especially since he had not been ordered not to, and it was not clear or proved that the measures were inaccurate or too small, and for this reason he did not want to be found guilty of the offense. And on these issues they requested a judgment.

759. It was judged that the taverner would pay a fine to Pierre and as great a one as if his measures had been found too small, that is to say sixty sous; for the presumption of his guilt was so clear that he should not gain by his bad faith. But if he had broken his measures before there was any word that the lord was asking for them, he should have suffered no loss. And by this judgment you can understand that you can give a judgment of guilty by a clear presumption where the punishment is only a money fine; for in cases where the punishment may be loss of life, you cannot be condemned by a presumption, but the thing for which you are condemned must be clear and evident. Nevertheless, you may find enough presump-

tions in a case of serious crime that there can be a sentence of life imprisonment, as is explained in the chapter which discusses witnesses and proofs {Chapter 39}.

760. By what we have said concerning the measurements used for land and things which are sold by volume, you can understand about things sold by weight. But there are not as many differences between weights as there are between volume measures, for they do not change in as many places. Nevertheless they do change, for weights are greater in one town than another. And in each town you should weigh according to the weights which have been in use for a long time, for a person caught weighing with a lower weight than was customary in the place would be punished like a person who had been measuring grain with a faulty measure, and so would a person found measuring cloth [*aunans*] with a short yardstick [*aune*]. For just as legal *mines* are used to measure wheat and oats and other grains, *setiers* and *quartes* are used to measure liquids, such as wine or oil or honey, and *aunes* are used to measure cloth and linen, and *verges* to measure land, and *toises* to measure buildings [*ouvrages*], and weights are used to measure wool and all things which are weighed. And although all these above-mentioned measures do not resemble each other, nevertheless a person committing an offense concerning any of these measures is punished as much for the one as for the other, for a person who sells cloth using a short yardstick is committing an offense just as much as a person is who delivers wheat using too small a *mine;* and you can understand from this how it works for weights and other measures.

Here ends the chapter on weights and measures.

Notes

1. Rather than use modern equivalents, I have retained Beaumanoir's words for most of the measurements in this chapter.
2. A small town near Liancourt in the *arrondissement* of Clermont. In Beaumanoir's time, it had a large fair on September 29 of each year.
3. *Pleine paume* was a third of a foot. Hands are still used to measure the height of horses.
4. If you take the *mine* of land, the *verge* and the *pied* to be square measures, the arithmetic works out very well.

27. Prices

Here begins the twenty-seventh chapter of this book which speaks of the income which can come to lords from the property held from them, and also speaks of the price of land.

761. Now it is right that after we have said that the lords should see to the accuracy of measures according to the custom of the place, we should speak in this following chapter on the revenues which can come to lords by reason of property which is held from them in fief or villeinage; and we will also speak of the assessment of land, and how it should be done when it has to be assessed, according to the custom of Beauvais, so that the lords will know what dues [*redevances*] they shoud levy from their tenants, and so that the tenants know what dues they owe their lords, and how to assess land when you need to.

762. When a fief passes to heirs laterally, there is relief [*rachat*] and the relief is as much as the fief brings in in one year.[1] And the lord who wants to levy this honestly should look at what the fief brings in in three years and take a third of that for his relief; for it often happens that a fief consists of arable land, which is all or nearly all in one parcel [*en une roie*], so that the greatest income comes only once in three years, that is to say in the year the largest parcel is in wheat; and if the fief passed in the year when it brought in the most, it would not be right for the lord to take his relief that year; and also if the fief passed in the year when the fields were fallow [*vuides*], it would not be right for the lord to have to be paid nothing, and for this reason you should look at what the honest income from the land is over three years and take a third, as I said above.

763. When a fief consisting of woodland passes laterally, if the wood is of less than seven years' growth the lord should not reasonably have to wait {for his relief} until the wood matures, and it is not reasonable for the heir to cut the wood at less than seven years of age. Therefore it is appropriate to

make an honest assessment of what the income per year is for each *arpent*, and whatever the yearly income is, the heirs who take the wood by lateral inheritance should pay the relief accordingly to the lord. And if the wood was seven or more years old, the price should not be set any higher for that reason; for if the lord exacted for his relief the income from the sale of the mature timber, the heirs would get nothing for seven whole years, unless they cut the wood too young, and thus the heirs would suffer a severe loss.

764. For a fief which passes by descent to the heirs, from father or mother, from grandfather or grandmother, or from a more distant relative, provided it passes by descent, there is no relief, except for the fiefs and subfiefs held in Bulles and Conty;[2] in whatever manner the latter fiefs pass, whether by descent or laterally, or by exchange, or by gift or legacy, they pay relief.

765. Some people say that when there is an exchange of fiefs without any money being involved, there is no relief, and they are right if the lord wants to permit the exchange uncontested; but he is not required to exchange one vassal for another without relief unless he wants. Therefore the exchange must be made with the permission of the lord; and the lord can exact what he wants up to the value of a year's income for permitting the exchange, or there will be no exchange. And yet when the lord sees that he will get a vassal who will serve him as well as the one he had, he should permit the exchange.

766. When real property is given, if it is a fief there is relief, and if it is in villeinage there are only possession charges [*saisine*],[3] and there are different kinds of possession charges. For there are some towns where you pay only two deniers for possession, and others where you pay three, and those where you pay three deniers in gloves [*.III. d. de gans*] and twelve deniers in wine, and some other towns where you pay more and and yet others where you pay less: and for this reason in cases of possession charges, you should look at the local custom of each town. And I think that the customs which vary and do not follow the custom of the castle of Clermont only came about by the customs given of old by men to their subjects; and yet these customs should be kept, which have been maintained for so long, especially when the tenants have borne them without challenge.

767. When property is sold, if it is a fief, the lord gets a fifth [*le quint denier*] of the sale price, that is to say that for every hundred sous he gets

twenty sous, and for ten pounds he gets forty sous, and so on in proportion. And when a property held in villeinage is sold, the lord gets a twelfth of the selling price, that is to say for every twelve pounds he gets twenty sous, for every twenty-four pounds he gets forty sous, and so on in proportion.[4]

768. When property is sold, whether it is in fief or villeinage, the seller and the buyer may, if they wish, cancel the agreement by common consent before the lord gives possession; for after possession has been given, the seller cannot come back to the property, except by another sale.

769. If a property is sold and an agreement is made that the sale will be firm [*tenir*], and the seller changes his mind and wants the sale canceled, he cannot call off the deal, except with the agreement of the buyer. Indeed the buyer can have him forced to give up possession for purposes of a sale through the lord from whom the property is held, even though the seller is a resident in some other jurisdiction.

770. Pierre sued Jehan before the lord from whom Jehan held his land, saying that Jehan had sold him the land for a certain price in money, and then when he was about to pay the money, he requested to have the said Jehan obliged to give up possession [*se dessaisist*] of the property. Jehan answered that he was not obliged to answer before the lord from whom he held the property because he was a resident in the jurisdiction of another lord, and by the general custom, the lord where he was a resident should have cognizance of agreements and personal property and chattels of his residents, and, since Pierre was only suing him on an agreement, he was not required to answer in that court. And Pierre said that yes he was, because the agreement derived from the real property. And on this issue they requested a judgment.

771. It was judged that Jehan would answer in the court of the lord from whom the land was held because the agreement derived from the land, for if the agreement was admitted or proved against him before the lord where Jehan was a resident, that lord could not have the judgment executed because the land was not held from him. And this kind of an agreement is called real [*reeles*],[5] and you have to answer before the lord from whom the subject of the suit is held.

772. Just as the buyer is not obliged to cancel a deal which has been promised [*convenanciés*] to him, unless he wants, in the same way a seller is

not obliged to cancel a deal with a buyer, unless he wants; but if he wants to sue him on the agreement, he must sue him before the lord where the buyer is a resident.

773. A proper assessment value for land, according to the common custom in the county of Clermont, is sixty sous per year for a *mui* of land, when the land is good enough for you to be able to find someone to cultivate it for a half-share [*qui la laboure a moitié*]; and if it is better than a half share's worth, the price should go up according to the extra value; and if it is less than half, the value should be reduced according to the lower amount. And the *mui* worth half a share that we designate as being worth sixty sous is measured as having twelve *mines* to the *mui*, and eighty *verges* of twenty-two feet per *verge* {to the *mine*}. But measurement units for land are different in almost every town, and for this reason you should look at which are bigger and which are smaller, and the value of the location [*terroir*], and the dues to be paid on the land, and you should estimate whether the land is worth more or less than a half share, estimated as explained above. And you can see a fuller account of the diversity of measurements if you look in the chapter on weights and measures {Chapter 26}.

774. The regular assessment for an *arpent* of woodland is ten sous per *arpent*; but you should look at the location of the wood, and the price it will bring when it is cut down, and what the yield [*revenue*] from it is, and how it is looked after; and according as you see that it is better than the regular value (above the costs), you should raise the price above ten sous, and if you see that it is worth less because of its poor site, or a bad market [*mauvese vente*], or low yield, you can and should lower the price.

775. It is true that as long as timber is attached to roots it is real property, and as soon as it is cut it is personal property; and I have seen this approved by a judgment in the following manner.

776. There was a knight who made a distribution to his children by his last will. One of his children took his share in forest land, and the timber was mature enough to be cut, and was sold while the knight was still alive, and good sureties accepted for the money; and at the moment when the knight died, the merchant had cut some of the timber, and the other part was still to be cut.[6] In his will the knight ordered that the devises in his will were to be taken out of his personal property by his executors. And when he had died, the heir who inherited the woods forbade the cutting of any more

timber until security had been given for the timber still to be cut in execution of the sale his father had made. The father's executors contested this, saying that the merchant did not have to stop cutting, and that the heir should take nothing from what his father had sold, and they gave two reasons: the first was that timber [*despueille de bois*] mature enough to be cut is personal property, and the personal property belonged to them and they should have it to execute the father's will. The second reason was that the father had in his lifetime sold the thing and accepted good security, by which it clearly appeared that what was owed as a debt belonged to them because it was personal property. And on these issues they requested a judgment, namely whether the purchase money for the wood still to be cut would go to the executors, or whether the heir would take from the purchase money the same proportion as that of the wood still to be cut (it being real property) at the time of his father's death.

777. It was judged that the executors would take nothing from the sale of the timber which was still to be cut at the time of the father's death, but that the heir would take it as inherited real property. And in the judgment an estimate was made of how much timber had been cut and how much was still to be cut at the time of the father's death, and the purchase money was assigned to each portion according to the father's sale, and the executors took as much of the purchase money as there was wood already cut, and the heir took the rest; and by this judgment is is clear that wood is real property as long as it is attached to its roots.

778. The price of vineyards, according to our custom, is forty sous per *arpent*, but this means those which can be shared half and half, or which a tenant would gladly cultivate for a half share; and if they are worth less, the price should be reduced according to the lower value.

779. The appraised price of pastures according to our custom is twenty sous per *arpent*, but this means when they are good and well-situated and in a good place. And if they are worth less because of their location, the price should be reduced; and generally the sites are so varied in value that you can hardly make an estimate except by looking at how much you could get {per year} from each piece of land in perpetuity [*a tous jours*], and after deducting the dues for the land, the land should be estimated at what is left after costs.

780. The proper estimate of income [*rentes*] in Clermont is: for land in mixed wheat [*bles moitoiens*], twenty sous per *mui*, in nothing but best

wheat twenty-five sous per *mui*, in nothing but rye fifteen sous per *mui*, and in oats fifteen sous per *mui;* and if the land measurement is greater than in Clermont, as it is in various towns, the assessment should be increased.

781. For income paid in capons [*chapons*], each capon is assessed at six deniers and a hen at four deniers.

782. The assessment of rent income is that if money is owed in a lump sum [*rente en gros*], such as surtax [*seurcens*][7] which is worth only the quantity of money paid each year, the assessment of this money does not increase or decrease, but is made at whatever it is worth per year and nothing else. But there is another kind of money income called small quit-rent [*menu cens*],—for example when you hold from your lord an *arpent* of vineyard (or some other real property you hold for quit-rent in money) which is worth forty sous in income, for one or six or twelve deniers in quit-rent, or more or less,—when an appraisal is made, this kind of quit-rent counts double in a court [*pour la justice*] and in assessing the sales taxes [*ventes*] which can come to a lord from such quit-rent lands [*censives*]; this means that if someone has ten pounds {of income} in that kind of rent, and his land value is appraised, the ten pounds will be assessed at twenty pounds; and however much he has in such quit-rents, whether a little or a lot, you should always count double when assessing land [*a pris de terre*].

783. If you want to appraise a building, such as a house or a winepress or a mill, you should look at the place where the building is situated, and its condition, and how much you could make from it in perpetuity [*a tous jours*] above the costs needed to maintain the building in the condition it is in when the estimate is made; for in everything which counts as real property, the costs must be deducted when they are appraised, since the value of real property means what the property is worth per year in perpetuity above the costs, and after deducting the outlays needed to keep up and maintain the property.

784. The assessment of yards and thickets and gardens should be made according to their location, and how much they are worth per year in perpetuity, over and above what must be paid out for such places; and there is no common value for such places, for the values are not uniform, and you will hardly find such a property where one is not worth more than another, and for this reason you have to assess such places according to their worth.

785. When an estimate is made of the value of fishponds, reservoirs, and pits where fish can feed and multiply, when they are fished every three years, you should look at what they are worth above the costs and the outlays and the guards and the fences, and then you should give as a value a third of the remainder.

786. When a bakehouse is assessed, it should be done in the manner described above for buildings, for it is a building; and when you assess the value of a bakehouse or a mill or a winepress, you should look carefully at whether the tenant has a monopoly [*banier*], or whether people can come there at will, or if the neighbors can build the same kind of buildings close by, so that they are worth less, for you should not assess as highly such property if customers only go there at will (or when they can be caused loss by some obvious circumstance) as when you see thay cannot be caused harm.

787. Labor obligation income [*corvees de rentes*] should be appraised as two sous per year for each day's work with two horses, and twelve deniers for a day's work with one horse. And if the labor is that of a man without a horse, such as it is in various towns, the {day's} labor of one man is worth four deniers per year.

788. There are several kinds of real property from which lords can derive benefits, and yet they cannot be assessed by land values, such as jurisdictions [*justices*],[8] the sales taxes of fiefs, homages held in sub-fief; for jurisdictions often cost more to keep up and supervise [*garder*] than they are worth, and sales of fiefs do not occur often, so that you cannot set a value on such things. And men paying homages held as sub-fiefs pay no dues except to the lords from whom they hold directly [*nu a nu*]; and therefore these dues should not be assessed to the lord from whom their lord holds, even though the homage may be reinfeudated [*aprochier*] and the fief held directly from the lord from whom it had been held in sub-fief, for many reasons which are explained in the chapter which shows how fiefs can, according to custom, be held directly or more distantly from a lord {Chapter 47}.

789. Sales taxes on villeinages, or on sharecropped fields, can be appraised by land assessment; for you can easily see, when someone holds several fields which are sharecropped, how much they bring in over ten or

twelve years, and then you can give a value to each year according to what you see they are worth in ten or twelve years. And if there is some kind of real property which we have failed to mention, the assessment of the value of the property should be made according to what we have said, and the costs and outlays made because of property should be deducted.

790. The assessment of income from wine should, according to custom, be made in three ways: that is to say for wine from *fourmentel* grapes, that from *moreillon* grapes, and that from *gros noir* grapes. *Fourmentel* wine, using Clermont measure, should be assessed at twelve sous per *mui* per year, *moreillon* wine at nine sous per *mui* per year, and *gros noir* or *gouet* wine at six sous per *mui* per year.

791. Tolls, market dues, and other real property which goes up and down every year can only be assessed by an estimation. And in making the estimate, you should look at how much income you would make on them in ten years above the costs, and then take a tenth of that for the income for a year; and there is no other way to make a precise assessment.

792. It happened that a gentleman had a debt and could only pay by selling real property. He made an agreement with his creditors that the creditors would receive some of the said squire's real property according to an assessment made by a judgment given by the jurors of Clermont. And when the matter was brought before the jurors, they ruled that the property would be assessed by the proper method of assessment provided by custom, as explained above in this chapter. When the assessment was finished, the creditors would be given twenty sous' worth of land[9] for every ten pounds owed, and the seller would pay the sales tax and arrange for the buyers to pay homage to the lords. And by this judgment you can see that when real property is to be assessed, for a sale or for some other reason, twenty sous' worth of land are assessed as equivalent to ten pounds in money. And just as twenty sous' worth of land are assessed at ten pounds, land held as villeinage, when assessed for sale, should be assessed at twenty sous' worth of land for twelve pounds; for fiefs should be assessed lower, on account of the services and other dues which you owe to the lord, and these services are onerous, as you will hear in the following chapter.

Here ends the chapter on the income which can come to lords, and on the assessment of property.

Notes

1. In the county of Clermont there is no relief (inheritance tax) on fiefs passing in a direct line, except in Bulles and Conty. See §764.

2. For Bulles and Conty, see Chapter 14, §471.

3. Here the word *saisine*, which normally means "seisin," or "possession" clearly refers to the payment made when possession changes, as is apparent from the next sentence.

4. It follows from this paragraph that in Beauvais a pound was worth twenty sous.

5. Real agreements (contracts) concern real property (from Latin *res, rem* 'a thing'). See §230.

6. For the understanding of this paragraph, it is helpful to bear in mind that heirs inherit real property (land, etc.), but the executors take possession of personal property (anything movable; see §673). The point under discussion is: When does a tree attached to land (and therefore real property) become movable (and therefore personal property)? The plain and reasonable answer here is: When it is cut down.

7. For *seurcens,* see §§704, 705.

8. Here *justice* 'jurisdiction' means the power to administer justice (and keep the fines levied on offenders).

9. This means land from which the annual income would be assessed at twenty sous. See §773.

28. Horses

Here begins the twenty-eighth chapter of this book which explains how you should supply your lord with a farm horse in dues for your fief, and the loss you may suffer if you do not do what you should.

793. According to the custom of Beauvais, a person summoned to supply a farm horse[1] in two weeks' time or longer may not take a continuance, but if he has a legal excuse he may adjourn once sine die.[2] Now let's see how he can perform without having his lord find him in default, for this is the dispute which has caused the most poor gentlemen in the county to suffer loss at the hands of their lords, because there is no judgment showing how to estimate accurately what horse they owe and of what value. And for this reason I want to show how those who are summoned in such cases can defend themselves and make an adequate offer to their lords.

794. It is certain that all those who hold in fief in the county of Clermont owe their lord for each fief a farm horse if the lord wants to take it. But if I hold my property from a lord and he does not call for my service until what I hold from him has passed into someone else's possession, the lord cannot ask me for the service any more, for I am no longer his man, and for that reason I do not owe him any service; and he cannot ask for service on my behalf from the man who is his man because of the thing I used to hold from him; but he can obtain service if he wishes, on the new holder's own account, because of his homage.

795. If I am summoned to supply a farm horse, then on the day I am summoned I must take a horse, sound in all its limbs, and offer him to the lord, and speak in this way: "Sire, you have summoned me to supply a farm horse; here is a farm horse, sound in all its limbs, which I offer you. I request you to take it, and if you don't want to, give me another date on which to bring another one." Then if he does not want to take the horse, he must give me a day on which to bring another fifteen days later, and he can

do this three times if he wants. And when I bring a horse the third time, I should offer the horse and some money, and speak this way: "Sire, you have summoned me to supply a farm horse; I have brought you one, two, and here is the third which is sound in all its limbs. I request you to take it, and if you do not like the horse, I offer you sixty sous in place of the horse, and here is the money. And if you do not want to take the horse or the money, I request you to consider me paid up for this service. And if you want to say that I have not offered you enough, I request you to tell me in a judgment by my peers what horse I owe you and of what value; and I offer to supply you without delay up to whatever they find in their opinion." And if I proceed in this manner, my lord cannot refuse me this hearing or find me in default without acting wrongly towards me. And if he takes or seizes something of mine, unless he does it by the judgment of my peers, he must always give it back into my possession before I answer any complaint he may make towards me.

796. If my lord has accepted a farm horse from me, and kept it continuously for forty days without sending it back to me, my service has been performed. And if he sends it back to me within forty days, sound in all its limbs, I cannot refuse to take it back again, and I will still owe him a farm horse. But if I have supplied him with a sound farm horse and he injures it while he has it in his possession and then sends it back to me, I am not obliged to take it back and I must be considered to have fulfilled my obligation.

797. When I have supplied my lord with a farm horse and he has considered the service performed, or when he has kept the horse for forty days without sending it back, I am free of this obligation for the rest of my life and I am no longer obliged to ride forth for my lord, either for his private war or to defend his house, unless I want to; but I should not fail on that account to go at his summons or to go to court.[3]

798. There are some fiefs called reduced service fiefs [*fiés abregiés*]. When you are called for service owed on such fiefs, you should offer your lord what is due by reason of the reduced service, and the lord cannot ask for more if the reduction is proved or admitted, and if it was properly granted by the count's permission. For I may not permit the full service held from me to be reduced without the count's permission, however many lords there are below the count one after another, even if they are all agreed

concerning the reduction. And if they do all agree, and the count finds out about it, he takes over the homage of the man holding the property; and the homage goes back to being full service, and the lord who reduced it owes a fine to the count of sixty pounds.

799. If someone reduces the service of a fief for his vassal, and makes an agreement to warrant it as a reduced fief, and the lord above him makes a seizure of the fief because he does not want to permit the reduction, the lord who permitted the reduction loses the homage as we have said above. And this is not the end of his obligations, for he must make restitution to the man whose service he reduced, by as much as he suffers loss by being brought back up to full service. And for this reason it is very dangerous to make reductions of service for a fief, unless it is by the consent of the lords step-by-step up to the count.

800. The king and those who hold directly from him should not require any service in the form of farm horses, because they can call up armed and mounted men any time they need them.

Here ends the chapter on supplying farm horses.

Notes

1. The *ronci de service* is an old established part of the service due from a vassal to his lord. Whereas it was originally a convenient way for the lord to be supplied with horses for use in battle, eventually the duty was commuted to a money payment. In Beaumanoir's time the duty was evidently still to supply an actual horse when it was asked for. See Marc Bloch, *Feudal Society*, trans. L. A. Manyon, 2 vols. (Chicago: University of Chicago Press, 1961) 1: 206.

2. For these delays, see Chapter 3.

3. This section suggests that the request for a farm horse means that the vassal will be thereby freed from some of his feudal obligations.

29. Services

Here begins the twenty-ninth chapter of this book which speaks of services performed for pay or on authorization or at will, and on accountings rendered by employees.

801. In the chapter before this one was discussed a kind of service which vassals owe their lords on account of the fiefs they hold from them; and we will speak in this following chapter about other kinds of services, that is to say services performed for pay [*louier*], and services performed upon authorization [*mandement*], and services performed on command [*commandement*], and services performed at will, without authorization or orders and without pay. And we will discuss those who perform greater services than are supposed to, and the danger in this, and about the accounting which employees[1] must give to their lords, so that the former know how they are to serve and their lords know how they should act towards those who perform services for them.

802. An employee should only do the job which is given to him; and if he did something else without the authorization or command of his lord and caused some loss, the lord could sue him or cancel the agreement which was made, provided he did so as soon as the knowledge of his employee's action came to him. And we mean here when the employee undertakes things which are not given him as part of his employment, for he can only take action within the bounds of the things which he is authorized to do.

803. If some lord gives power to his employee to administer justice, and while doing so the employee does something in contravention of the rights of the lord from whom his lord holds, and the lord against whom the offense was committed (or whom the employee disobeyed) wants to proceed against the lord of the employee who committed the action, he may; and the lord may not disavow the action of his employee, for then lords

could have their employees disobey on their behalf and then say that it was not done by themselves. And if the employee, who was a commoner, paid the fine, it would be sixty sous, but if the employee's lord had to pay the fine (if the offense required it) it would be sixty pounds; and the offenses which are punished by such fines are described in the chapter on offenses {Chapter 30}. And for this reason it is a good thing for lords to take care whom they have administer their jurisdiction, since they cannot disavow what their employees do when administering justice, and we have seen a judgment on this issue in the king's house.[2] Nevertheless, cases of serious crime are excepted, for if my employee, by his stupidity or his haste, commits a serious crime, you cannot call me to answer for him personally, but only the person who committed the crime, unless it is proved against me that I had him commit the crime or procured its commission, for in that case I could lose.

804. Many lords have suffered loss because of bad employees, and sometimes won ill repute [*vilenie*] along with it, for employees do many things which were not commanded by their lord, where the latter has to take the responsibility [*la ou il a a reprendre*]. And for this reason, if the employee commits any offense by which the lord suffers loss because he cannot disavow it, he has an action against the employee to recover the loss he suffered because of the employee's offense. But this refers to the offenses that the employees commit intentionally and in bad faith; for it sometimes happens that they commit an offense and they do not think they are doing so,—for example, when they arrest someone on another person's land, and they think that they are arresting him on their lord's property; or when they keep prisoners in the customary prisons for offenses and the prisoners escape somehow without the help or knowledge of the employees,—in these and similar cases they should be excused; but if they acted knowingly and without orders, then you could sue them for the loss. And we have seen this happen many times when a cowherd or a shepherd or a swineherd took his lord's animals to a place where they were seized for trespassing, for the owner of the animals must pay the fine if he likes his animals well enough to want them back, and he must pay restitution for the damage his animals did along with the fine. But he can sue for all these damages the person who was supposed to guard his animals, for that is why you hire a guard for your animals, so that they will *not* go where they should not; and if those who guard them could not be sued, that kind of employee would more easily become used to allowing the animals to trespass.

805. There are three kinds of service. The first is by agreement, for example, when someone promises to serve me well and honestly or to be my attorney until a certain time and for a fixed kind or work,—for example, when it is spelled out in the agreement what they will do, whether they will maintain justice, or look after woods or vines, or if they will do all three of these things, for example, when a lord gives his employee the administration of several things,—and in this kind of service the lord must give his employee what he needs to perform the service, unless it is part of the agreement that the employee will furnish his own supplies, out of his pay or his wages; for if an employee is to be armed in the service of his lord, and there is no agreement to the contrary, the lord must lend him arms; and if he has brought him into his house for some other employment, for example carpentry or masonry work, this kind of workman [*menestrieus*] normally brings his own tools to the place where he is hired, for that way they more easily find work. Nevertheless if they have been hired for a certain period and their tools break or are damaged, they should be repaired at the lord's expense; but this is not done when they work by the job or by the day, for then the risk of breaking their tools is borne by them; and by what we have said about furnishing to employees (but not to hired workmen) what they need to do their work, you can understand what to do about other kinds of employees we have not mentioned.

806. The second kind of employees are those who are not bound by promises or oaths or hired for a certain time, but they perform services for other people when they are asked to or appointed in writing [*par mandement*] to do so. And this kind of employment can come about in many ways, for it is sometimes by a personal request [*priere de bouche*], for example, when Pierre says to Jehan: "I ask you to buy Guillaume's land for me, and I will stand by what you do." In that case, if Jehan buys the land, Pierre must pay for it; nevertheless the said Pierre is not beholden to Guillaume, for he has not made a deal or an agreement with him, but Guillaume can sue Jehan if he does not go through with the deal, and Jehan can sue Pierre to reimburse him for what he had him do at his command or at his request; and by this you can see that Jehan is obligated by the deal he made and Pierre is obligated to Jehan because Jehan made the deal for him and at his request.

807. Sometimes the request is not made orally but by a writing, for example, when someone asks his friend in a writing to do some business for

him. And such an order can be dangerous for the person to whom the order is given, if the writing giving the order is not sealed. For if the person who gave the order or request in the writing denies it, and the person receiving it cannot prove it, he alone is obligated, even though he made the deal on behalf of another; for you can sue for a deal or an agreement only the person who made it, even though it was made for someone else, unless it concerns what attorneys do in court for their lords after depositing a valid letter of appointment with the court, for the lord is obligated by everything his attorney does which is authorized by the letter of appointment, and enough is said about this issue in the chapter on attorneys {Chapter 4}.

808. We have said that an authorization obligates the person giving the authorization to the person to whom he gave it, and we have also said that the person acting under the authorization is obligated to the person with whom he makes the deal or the agreement, even though he is acting on behalf of another; but this applies to authorizations and requests which are made according to good morals, so that if I authorize or request someone to kill a man or burn a house or commit some other evil action, I am not obligated to the person whom I authorized or requested to do it, for if he commits a crime he must be condemned for the crime, and a person who is legally condemned cannot condemn anyone else. Nevertheless this has sometimes been permitted when a great presumption is seen against the person who is said to have made the request or the authorization; but if those who commit these evil actions on the authorization of others are condemned, it is quite right, for no one should commit a crime just because he is authorized or requested to by someone else. And a person acting on someone else's authorization should be very careful not to act except as he was authorized or asked to; for if he went beyond, the person making the authorization or the request would not be obligated for the extra, for example, if I authorize or request someone to buy for me the vineyard which Pierre is trying to sell, and to give only a hundred pounds for it, and after this authorization he makes the deal for a hundred and twenty pounds without a new authorization from me, I am not obligated to pay the twenty pounds; therefore he will have to assume the deal for a hundred and twenty pounds, or let me have the vineyard for the hundred pounds, and thus he could lose twenty pounds, because he did not act according to my authorization.

809. If I ask or authorize someone to make some deal for me, and he says he is willing to do so, and later when he has made the deal, he wants to

keep it for himself, or he gave more for the deal than I told him to give on my behalf, in bad faith and so as to make me believe he could not get it for as much as I had told him to give, it should be my choice whether to have the deal for what it cost him, for as soon as he has promised me he will buy the thing for me, he cannot then buy it for himself without my permission.

810. If I make a request or give an authorization and I withdraw it before the thing has been done or promised, the authorization has ended; and if the person to whom I gave the authorization or the request acted after my withdrawal, I would not be obligated to him by the authorization since I had withdrawn it; for I can withdraw what I have requested or authorized or ordered done as long as the action has not been performed [*la chose est entiere*].

811. Everyone should know that if an authorization or request is given to someone and the person giving the authorization or making the request dies before the action has been carried out, the authorization is withdrawn, and the person who was authorized should not carry out the action. Nevertheless if he does it in good faith,—for example, if he thought the person giving the authorization was still alive, of he sees that it is the advantage of the heirs to do it,—the heir is obligated to him because of his predecessor's authorization, for it would be a bad thing if persons peforming actions for other people by their authorization or at their request were to suffer loss because of actions they performed in good faith.

812. Even though those who act on behalf of others at their request or authorization are not the employees, by oath or agreement, of those who made the request or authorization, nevetheless if they have reasonable and proper costs or expenses in carrying out the actions they were asked or authorized to perform, it should be at the cost of the person making the request or authorization; for, as we have said elsewhere,[3] no one can be made to serve another at his own cost, unless there is a reason for him to have to do so, for example, when gentlemen hold fiefs and owe services for them, or when serfs have to serve their lord at their own cost whenever their lord wants, because all they have belongs to their lord.

813. We have spoken of two kinds of service: there are those who serve through an agreement or for pay, and those who act at someone's request or authorization. There are still other kinds of service, such as is performed by those who undertake to serve others without being asked or authorized to,

and without being hired for pay or by an agreement. And this kind of service is very dangerous for those who undertake it unless they are forced to do so, for sometimes I have to serve another person against my will, without being asked or authorized to do so, or else I might suffer loss and infamy; and we mentioned in the chapter on partnerships those who have to serve their partners because the partners cannot or will not do things themselves.[4] And there is another kind of service which is undertaken without the authorization or the request of anyone else, and these services are to be rewarded because they are performed in good faith: for example, if I see my cousin or my friend or my neighbor about to suffer great loss, and I avert the loss, for example, if his house is on fire and I extinguish the fire, or if I protect him in my house from the fear of his enemies, and I have expenses in protecting him or putting out his fire, he should certainly repay me my expenses. And also if I intentionally cultivate his land, thinking it is mine, and he reaps the benefits as is his right, he should repay me for my labor. And also if I am present in some secular or ecclesiastical court and he is going to be found in default, and I make excuses for him because I know he has a legal excuse, even though he had not authorized me to do so, and I have some reasonable expenses in defending him, he should reimburse me for them; nevertheless, in this case, according to our custom, he need not unless he wants to. And when we say that service without hiring or authorization is dangerous, we mean this in two senses: the first is that, where I undertake to serve another person without being hired or authorized, the person whom I serve is not obliged to repay me for the service or the expenses, except in the cases mentioned above, or cases like them. The second is that, even with good intentions, you may undertake to serve someone and the result is that you can suffer loss and shame, for example, if you undertook to accept someone's property without authorization and without being hired to do so, for if you could be excused in such cases because of the service you were rendering, thieves who take other people's things by larceny would be excused, and for this reason this kind of action is considered not to be service but larceny. Nevertheless you sometimes take someone else's property without it being either service or larceny,—for example, when someone thinks the thing is his own, and there is a suit to find out whose it is, and the person taking it loses it in a judgment,—in such a case you sometimes take someone else's property and yet it is not larceny, for there is no larceny unless there is an intent to steal.[5]

814. The accounting which is made by the employee to the lord is sometimes done very privately, without calling in any witnesses, for the

lords sometimes do not want strangers to know how their business is doing. Now let's see what you should do if there is a dispute between the lord and the employee,—for example, if the lord says the employee has taken in more than he is reporting, or that he wants to report expenses which were not made, or which are greater than they actually were, or if the employee asks his lord to take off from the receipts some payment or other expense, and the lord does not want to.

815. If the employee denies having collected a sum due, he can sometimes prove it by the testimony of two members of his household, men or women, when there is a presumption. For example, if the employee is authorized to collect this money: for the person appointed to collect debts for someone else must say either that he has collected them or that the debtors still owe the debts; and if he says that the debts are still due, the lord can sue the debtors for them; and if they allege that they made payment to the employee, and the employee denies it, the debtors must prove it or pay the debts to the lord; and if they prove payment against the employee appointed to collect the debts, they should be acquitted and the employee must pay the lord, and also the debtors' reasonable costs for {contesting} his denial, and a fine for the denial, and he earns a bad reputation; for denying something you have collected in order to harm someone else is not something done without trickery and a desire to receive someone else's property wrongfully.

816. If the employee has charge of selling wheat, oats, or other commodities, he must report the price they were sold for or show that the goods have not yet been sold; and if the employee reports less than they were sold for, and the lord can prove by the buyers or other witnesses that the commodities were sold for more than he reported, he must hand over the extra to his lord. Nevertheless, the employee must sometimes be excused in these cases, when he shows that the extra went for the costs of selling the things, for example, for cartage or other reasonable expenses which may be made to transport commodities before they are sold, so that he only reported what he received for the things over and above the costs. But even if he were excused by this method, he did not report wisely, for those who report to their lords concerning things sold should report as received the whole price of the things they sold (and all other receipts they made) in full, and item by item [*par chascune partie en par soi*] and in writing, in identical duplicates, of which the lord gets one and the employee the other. And when all the items received have been put down and the total

added up, after that the total of all expenses, and all kinds of dues and payments which the employee paid out in order to collect the said receipts (or on the orders of his lord) should be made. And a person reporting this way is reporting wisely and honestly, for, if there is a disagreement between the lord and the employee, for example, if he says: "You did not report the receipts for this wine or that wheat which you sold," or if the employee says to the lord: "You did not take off for these expenses which I paid out at that time," you can always find out from the writing the truth about whether what is sued for was included in the accounts or not.

817. Sometimes the very content of the report given by an employee to his lord proves it to be false,—for example, if the employee reports such great expenses that the lord owes him a large sum in reimbursement, and it is clear that the employee did not have the amount of money that he says the lord owes him, and he cannot show his lord what he owes the money for,— in this kind of an accounting there is a great presumption against the employee unless he shows how he got hold of the money he lent {his lord} and why he decided to spend it, for example, if his lord was out of the district; or for example if the employee saw the threat of some great loss to his lord,—for example, that his house was about to fall down, or that he had to plow the fields which were lying fallow, or do other things to the lord's advantage,—in such a case the employee should not lose what he paid out of his own pocket, but the lord should be grateful to him for good service.

818. When the lord wants his employee to pay him what he has collected in receipts, and he will not deduct the reasonable expenses which the employee has paid out in his service, the employee should not be obliged to pay over all the receipts he is reporting until an accounting has been made between him and his lord. But what the employee admits to collecting after taking off his expenses he should pay; for example, if I admit collecting my lord's funds to a total of twenty pounds and I then say that ten pounds should be deducted for reasonable expenses which I am prepared to account for, I should only be made to pay ten pounds out of the twenty until the accounting has been made, for it would be a risky thing for all employees if they had to hand over all the receipts they had collected for their lords and afterwards sue [*pledier*] for their expenses.

819. It would not be this way for many receipts which people other than employees collect for other people; for if someone asks me to collect

twenty pounds for him from someone who owes them to him, or if he gives me twenty pounds to keep for him and I take them into my safekeeping, or someone asks me to take to him what someone owes him, and afterwards I will not hand over or give back these things (or some of these things) because I say the person owes me something and I am ready to prove it by a fair accounting, it will not save me from first having to hand over what was sent to him by my hand or which I received for him or which was given into my safekeeping; and afterwards, if he owes me something, I can sue him for it, for if I kept these things this way, I would be my own judge ordering payment to myself, which should not be permitted.

820. Everyone should know that employees must be obliged to give an accounting of the duties for which they were employed; and if the lord will not participate in an accounting because he thinks he owes some reimbursement to his employee, since it often happens that the expenses are greater than the income, the employee has a good reason to have his lord compelled by the person in whose jurisdiction he is to come to an accounting. And if the lord, when he is compelled to do the accounts, denies the expenses which his employee brings up, the employee must prove them, and in this case the employee has two ways to make his proof: the first is by {one of the methods of making} proof if he has it; and the second way, if he has no proof, is by circumstantial evidence [*l'aparence du fet*].[6] For example, if he had goods for sale transported to the town by a foreign [*estranges*] carter whose testimony he cannot obtain,[7] you can be sure the goods did not fly from one place to another: therefore it is clear from the circumstancial evidence that the cost of cartage must be taken into account according to the size of the goods and the time required. Or, for example, if the employee wants to take into account the labor required for working land or vineyards or other property and the lord denies the labor charges, the employee should be believed by the evidence of the property which has been cultivated and from which the crops have been harvested to the profit of the lord, unless the lord demonstrates clearly against the employee that the said labor costs were paid out of his own money by someone other than the employee who is trying to include them in his accounts. Or if the employee wants to give accounts for some work stopped because it was not profitable, or some new work undertaken for the profit of his lord, and the lord denies that the thing was done, and it is shown that the thing was undertaken, for example, the building of a house or a winepress or a fish-pond [*vivier*] or a mill, the employee should be believed by the circumstan-

tial evidence of the completed undertaking [*la chose fete*]. And if the lord does not want to settle accounts for any of the things mentioned above or similar things, because he says they were not done by him or at his command, this should not mean he does not have to settle accounts with his employee, for it would be a terrible thing [*griés chose*] for those in service if they had to prove that everything they did as part of their service was at the command of their lords; instead it is enough if you can see that the employee performed his work well for his lord. And a person would not be a good employee if he never did anything unless his lord gave particular orders, and employees should not wait until their lord gives them orders about every last thing, instead they should do what their position requires as long as they are employed; for as soon as someone is appointed to some position, he is given the power to do the work pertaining to it as long as he remains in the position.

821. What we have said about the service performed by employees in this chapter, and about the services which are required by reason of holding a fief, we apply in all cases of service, for women as well as for men; for if women hold a fief, they owe the same services as a man would if he held it; and if they take service under another, women must do what their position requires, except that they can be excused in many cases where men could not: for example, if the lord calls them for army service or for a mounted expedition [*de chevauchiee*] or for the defense of his house, it is enough if they send an adequate man as their substitute,—if the woman is a lady she must send a knight, and if she is an unmarried gentlewoman, she can send a squire,—for all women are excused from personal participation in all armed activity. And also if women are in the service of someone else, they can leave their masters before their time is up [*ains terme*] for a legal excuse, and they do not have to explain what their excuse is if they do not want to. And no one must give a woman work to do which is not proper [*honestes*] for a woman to do, for they must not be made to do any law enforcement [*serjanterie*] or guard duty which requires them to carry any weapons, nor be an advocate or an attorney, nor look after horses, for all this kind or work is appropriate for men and not for women. And if some lord gives some improper work to a woman and he suffers a loss because the woman does not know how to or cannot do such work, he cannot sue the woman, but has only his own folly to blame.

822. In some cases you can ask for reimbursement of what you paid, even though you were under an obligation to pay it when you did so: for

example, if I appoint an attorney and I give him money to manage my business, or as his pay up to a certain future date, and afterwards, for some reason, he stops being my employee and stops working for me, in that case I can ask him to pay back what I paid him, not all of it if he left my employment for a good reason, but in proportion to the time he had left to work for me. And if he left without a good reason before the end of the time he was hired for, I could ask for all my money back. And what we have said about attorneys applies to all other positions to which people are appointed for a certain time, when the end of the time has not come. And also if someone has agreed to serve me until a certain time, and I dismiss him from my service without a good reason, I must pay him all his pay, because it is not his fault that he is not completing the work he had agreed to do; and for this reason advocates and physicians sometimes earn large salaries with very little exertion [*a poi de peine*].

Here ends the chapter on services performed for pay or by authorization or at will, and the accounting which employees must provide.

Notes

1. I have chosen to use the neutral term "employee" to translate *serjant* in many cases, and "officer" or "agent" in others. The distinction between *serjant* and *serviteur* dates only from after Beaumanoir's time. The *serjant* could be a law-enforcement officer, or an agent (like a real-estate agent or a stockbroker today), or a domestic (sometimes an armed) servant. The word "servant" is too restricted in modern usage (although as a legal term it is sometimes still used to mean "agent"), and the term "agent" will not do for an ordinary "policeman."

2. Beaumanoir is referring to the appeals court in Paris called the *Parlement*.

3. For example, in §158.

4. See Chapter 21, §654.

5. This notion of intent is missing from the longer discussion of larceny in Chapter 31.

6. The circumstantial evidence method here described by Beaumanoir appears to be a variety of *res ipsa loquitur*.

7. Because he is from another jurisdiction, as shown by the adjective *estrange*.

30. Offenses

Here begins the thirtieth chapter of this book which speaks of offenses (crimes) and what punishment should be given for each offense, and what penalties are at the lord's discretion; and of boundary markers; and of banished persons and false witnesses, and of how long securities should be kept, and of conspiracy; and in which cases a sworn oath entails belief; and what losses must be made up to others; and how to conduct prisoners through someone else's lordship; and of those who are appealed against or imprisoned on suspicion of crime; and of those who seduce the wife or daughter of another; and of insults and fights.

823. For all those who have jurdisdiction over others, the thing they need most is to know how to distinguish offenses [*mesfès*],[1] large and small, and what punishment should be meted out for each. For just as certain offenses are not all uniform, the punishments are not all uniform. There are certain offenses which must be punished by the offender's being put to death in various ways. For example, serious crimes which are committed by criminals in various ways; and the second kind of offenses should be punished by a long prison term and loss of property, and {the penalties are} not all the same, but according to what the fact requires; and the third kind of offense must be punished by loss of property without death or maiming or prison, and the penalty is not always the same, any more than for the others we have mentioned above, but some are great and some small according to the offense, and according to who the offender is,[2] and who the person is against whom the offense was committed.[3] And so that the common people may know they are to be punished if they commit an offense, and each person separately if he commits an offense, and so that the lords know what punishment to exact for each offense, we will deal in this chapter with each offense you can commit, and what the punishment for each offense should be.

824. Whoever is arrested for a serious crime and convicted, for example for murder, or treason, or homicide, or rape, should be drawn[4] and hanged

and he forfeits all his wealth to the lord; and the forfeiture is to the lord on whose lands his possessions are situated, and each lord takes what is situated in the area under his control [*seignourie*].

825. Murder is when someone kills someone else (or has them killed) premeditatedly [*en aguet apensé*][5] between sunset and sunrise, or when he kills someone or has them killed during a truce or a guaranteed peace.[6]

826. Treachery [*traïsons*] is when you show no sign of hatred and yet you harbor a deadly hatred, so that because of the hate you kill the person you hate treacherously (or have them killed) or you beat them (or have them beaten) until they are injured [*dusques a afoleure*].[7]

827. No murder is without treachery, but there may be treachery without murder in many cases; for murder does not occur without a person's death, but treachery appears in beating or injuring someone during a truce or a guaranteed peace or in an ambush, or in giving false witness in order that someone will be put to death, or disinherited, or to have him banished, or to have him hated by his liege lord, or in many other similar cases.

828. Homicide [*Homecides*] is when someone kills someone else in a fight [*chaude mellee*], for example, it happens that a disagreement arises, and from the disagreement come harsh words, and from the harsh words the fight in which people often get killed.

829. Rape [*fame esforcier*] is when someone has carnal intercourse by force with a woman against her will and when she does what she can to defend herself.

830. These four cases of crime listed above must all be punished and avenged by the same sentence, but there are other cases of crime which are to be given a different sentence, and you will hear the cases and the punishment for each.

831. A person who knowingly burns a house must be hanged and he forfeits his possessions in the manner described above.

832. Anyone stealing another's property must be hanged and he forfeits his possessions in the manner described above.[8]

833. A person departing from the faith by disbelief so that he will not come back to the way of truth, or who commits sodomy, must be burned and he forfeits all his possessions in the manner described above.

834. Counterfeiters [*faus monoier*] must be boiled and hanged and they forfeit everything they have as is described above.

835. There are several kinds of counterfeiters. The first are those who knowingly make coinage from bad metal and they want to spend it as good; and if they were caught making the money before they had spent any of it, they would be punished for {use of metal of} improper fineness [*fausse despoise*].—The second kind of counterfeiter is those who make coins of the right fineness, but not of the proper weight.—The third kind of counterfeiter is one who coins money in secret, even though it is good and true and the right weight, but he does it without the permission of the lord who can and should make that money, for he steals the right of the lord by making coins on his lands without leave.—The fourth kind of counterfeiter is one who clips the edges of coins, for the coins lose their proper weight and the person who does the clipping steals what is not his.—The fifth kind of counterfeiter is the one who knowingly buys false coinage and spends it as good.—All these kinds of counterfeiters must be hanged, and before that, boiled, and they have forfeited their possessions in the manner described above.

836. There are still other cases of crime: for example when someone is arrested and put in prison on suspicion of some crime, and he escapes from prison and is recaptured, he is considered guilty of the thing he is being held for, and must be punished for it. And also if he is appealed against for a crime and he does not appear, but defaults until he is banished; if he is later captured he must be punished for the crime for which he was banished.

837. There are two other cases of crime: the first is poisoning and the second is suicide, for example by knowingly killing oneself.

838. We have spoken of crimes and the appropriate punishments, and now we will speak of the lesser offenses.

839. According to the Beauvais custom, if someone strikes or beats another, when it is not during a truce or a guaranteed peace, or on a market

day, and if there is no blood shed in the offense, the person doing the beating, if he is a commoner, pays a fine of five deniers, and if he is a gentleman, ten sous; and if the battery is committed during the market, or on the way to or from the market, the penalty of the commoner [*païsant*] is sixty sous and of the gentleman sixty pounds, for all those in the market, or going to or coming from the market, are under the count's protection and should come and go safely.

840. If the person beaten has a nosebleed from the beating, the penalty is not increased for this blood; but if there is blood from broken skin or if there are blows [*coups orbes*] from a fist holding a stick or some other thing, the person beating must be arrested and held without bail until it is seen that there is no danger of death from the said battery; then, when it is seen that the danger is past, the commoner's penalty is sixty sous and the gentleman's sixty pounds; and if the victim dies from the battery, the person or persons (if there are several) who did the beating should be punished in the manner described above where it talks about homicides [*occisions*].

841. A person hurting or injuring another must pay his losses, which means the cost of the physicians [*mires*] and the expenditures of the injured person and the lost work days according to his job. And if there is loss of limb, you must look to the nature of the loss [*mehaing*] and the condition of the person injured and the wealth of the person who injured him, and considering his wealth you should award it generously to the person losing the limb. And according to the old law, if a person caused loss of limb to another, the same was done to him as he had done, hand for hand and foot for foot; but things are no longer done this way according to our custom, instead you have to pay a penalty, as I said above, and serve a long prison term, and make restitution for his losses to the injured party according to his condition and what he is, and according to the wealth of the perpetrator.

842. It is annoying that our custom permits an unimportant commoner to strike a man of substance [*homme vaillant*] and only pay five sous as a penalty; and for this reason I agree he can be given a long prison term, so that for fear of prison the riffraff [*li musart*] will refrain from such insanity.

843. If a battery is committed before a judge in court, the penalty is at the discretion of the lord. And it happened that a townsman [*borjois*] of

Clermont struck a man where the provost was hearing pleas; I exacted a fine of thirty pounds; he appealed to the king,[9] and wrote a letter {requesting} to have me have the men of Clermont set the penalty in a judgment. I did not want to, and went to the Parlement and, in the presence of the townsman, I described the situation. It was ruled that it was not appropriate to ask the count's men to give a judgment on this matter because it involved contempt [*despit*] of the lord, and the townsman was told he got off lightly with a penalty of only thirty pounds. And by this you can know that in various cases which involve contempt to the lord the penalty is at the lord's discretion.

844. There are other kinds of offenses, for example offensive words [*lais dis*]. Now let's see, if a man insults another man and the latter complains, the penalty is five sous if it is a commoner, and if he is a gentleman the penalty is ten sous; and I also agree, that if a man has insulted a man of substance [*vaillant*], he should have a prison term, so that riff-raff are deterred by the prison term.

845. If an insult is made before a judge, for example where the provost or the *bailli* is hearing pleas, between commoners the penalty is sixty sous and between gentlemen the penalty is sixty pounds.

846. If a person, in court before a sitting judge, calls another wicked [*mauvès*] or a traitor[10] or he accuses him of some serious crime, he must, if the judge wishes, prove him to be so or pay a penalty at the lord's discretion.

847. If the provosts or the officers are insulted, the penalty for a commoner is sixty sous and for a gentleman sixty pounds.

848. When someone is kept in prison for offensive language, or because he will not answer in court, or for debt, or for any case which is not a {capital} crime, if he escapes from the prison the penalty is at the lord's discretion, for a man escaping from prison shows great contempt for his lord. But I never saw more than sixty sous set as a penalty.

849. The provost had a man in prison for debt; he let him out for fifteen days on the understanding that within the fifteen days he must pay {his debts} or come back to prison or else he would be treated as an escaped

prisoner. The man did not pay and he did not come back to prison. The provost had him arrested and wanted to prosecute [*suir*] him for escaping from prison; but it was considered that this was not escaping from prison, and that he would get only a penalty of five sous for disobeying an order, for many simple folk could be mistaken because they were let out of prison temporarily, without knowing the danger of escaping from prison.

850. There is yet another crime which I did not mention before, which involves larceny: it consists in pulling up boundary markers [*bonnes*] and putting them back in such a way as to bereave someone and enrich yourself. A person convicted of this would be punished as if for larceny. I mean by this boundary markers which have divided lands for a long time, for if the marker is put in next to my land without consulting me, it is not a crime if I pull it out and don't put it back. Nevertheless, if the markers had been put in by a judge, even behind my back, I would pay a penalty of sixty sous if I were a commoner, and sixty pounds if I were a gentleman; for I *should* have asked a judge to have what was done behind my back canceled and nullified, and he should do this and afterwards establish the boundaries with the parties present. If those who adjoin my property put in markers without informing me and without a judge, if I notice before the markers have been there for a year and a day, and I pull them up, I have committed no offense; or, if I wish, I can make a complaint for novel disseisin. And if I pull them up when they have been there for a year and a day, the *other* man will have an action for novel disseisin, and they will have to be put back before anything else happens; and then the suit will be on ownership, if I do not want the markers to remain where they have been put back.

851. All those who want boundaries marked should be granted this, and the parties, if they agree, can put up markers without a judge, provided it is not between different lordships where there is more than one overlord; for in marking off holdings where there are several overlords, those in possession cannot mark the boundaries without informing the overlords. Nevertheless there are several towns in the county where, even though they hold from the same lord, the holders could not fix boundaries without their overlord, and if they did the fine would be sixty sous; and for this reason you have to find out the custom in each town.

852. A person who is a sharecropper [*cil qui a le champart*] on another's land has all the jurisdiction and the lordship, according to our custom; and

a person not acting properly concerning the land he is sharecropping must pay a fine of sixty sous and surrender the property. A person carrying off his harvest sheaves before they have been divided is not acting properly as a sharecropper.

853. A person entering land confiscated by the lord, if he is a commoner pays a fine of sixty sous and must give back possession; and if he is a gentleman and the confiscated land was a fief, he must pay a fine of sixty pounds and must reseise the lord. But if the lord made the confiscation and the person who had been in possession did not know about it,—for example, if he was not there when the confiscation was made and it was reported to his household, or if it was done behind his back without his being informed,—if he entered and a fine was exacted, his oath must be accepted as proof that he knew nothing of the confiscation; but in any case he has to reseise the lord.

854. For a person disobeying the command of his lord,—for example when the lord commands a debt to be paid in time, that is to say within seven days and nights for a commoner and within fifteen days for a gentleman,—the fine of the commoner is five sous and of the gentleman ten sous; and it is the same if they fail to appear when summoned by the lord.

855. The count's sworn officers are believed without question when they testify that they served a summons. But if the officer testifies that he did not find the person summoned, and left the order with his wife or household to be given to him, the person may be excused for defaulting if he swears on the saints he knew nothing of the summons.

856. A person is sufficiently summoned who leaves the court for a recess; and if he does not reappear at the right time, or take a continuance or an adjournment, where they are permitted,[11] he is to be found in default just as if he had been summoned again.

857. A person doing what his lord has forbidden,—for example, if a lord forbids dice games on his land and someone plays dice; or the lord forbids the carrying of pointed knives, or some other sharp-edged weapon, or bows and arrows, and someone carries them; or if the lord forbids something similar,—anyone doing such a forbidden thing pays a fine, five sous for commoners and ten sous for gentlemen. But it is different if a

gentleman goes about armed anywhere in the county outside his fief, for if he is caught he pays a fine of sixty pounds.

858. On his own fief, a gentleman who does not feel secure [*qui se doute*] can bear arms, and his family can also, provided he does no harm to others, but it should really be to defend and protect himself, for example in time of open {private} war or because of threats made against him.

859. A person hiding a man banished by his lord is punished by having his house knocked down, and his fine is at the lord's discretion, whether the person concealing is a gentleman or a commoner, if he knows the person is banished; and he cannot use his ignorance as a defense if he was at the place where the banishment was made, or if it is common knowledge about the banishment in the district, or if the banished man is from his own lineage.

860. A person caught off the beaten path [*alant en faus sentier*], or cutting down timber, or reaping in the meadows, the wheat, or the small grains [*mars*], if he is a commoner, must make good the loss and pay a fine of five sous, and the gentleman ten sous.

861. A person entering land because it has been given to him, or he bought or exchanged it, without being awarded possession of it by the lord, must pay a fine of sixty sous if he is a commoner; and a gentleman who enters a fief for one of the above-mentioned reasons pays a fine of sixty pounds.

862. The commoner who owes a quit-rent [*cens*] to his lord or someone else on a certain day, as his mode of holding the land, must pay a fine of five sous if he does not pay on the due date; and a gentleman who holds land on payment of quit-rent would have the same fine. But if they owe oats or chickens or other grain as rent, penalties are not usually levied, but instead you can take the doors off their houses if the house-rents are due. And if other rents are due on land, the lord can, if he is not paid, make a seizure of the land,—as he also can of rental houses,—and keep all the crops and returns from the land until he has been paid for all the arrears; and if the lord wants to inform his tenants that they will lose the land unless he is paid all the arrears, he should order them, in front of good people, to pay up for their land by a year and a day; and if they do not, the lord can take the land for his own and do what he wants with it, unless the tenants were minor

children or the land was held in dower. But in these two cases the lord can keep the profits from the land to satisfy his back rent until the children come of age, or until the death of the dowager, unless the heir who is to take the land offers to pay {the arrears}.

863. When land is held in dower and it owes quit-rent or rent, and the lord takes possession of it because he has not been paid, the heir can have the lord from whom the land is held order the woman holding it in dower to pay the arrears within a year and a day; and if she does not pay, she is as if dead as concerns that dower property, and the heir can take it by paying what the land owes, both old and new debts; and he has an action against the woman who held the dower for the arrears, for a person holding in dower must pay what it costs to hold what she holds, or renounce her dower before there are any arrears, and as soon as she has renounced, the heir can take the land as his own real property.

864. A commoner who does not pay sales tax for villeinage property he buys within seven days and seven nights of the purchase must pay a fine of five sous along with his tax; and if a gentleman is buying a fief, the fine is ten sous; but if you let a year and a day pass without paying sales tax, the lord can take possession of the land for concealed sale [*ventes concelees*]; and if the person buying wants to get the property back, the lord can levy a sixty-sou fine for villeinages and sixty pounds for fiefs.

865. If a gentleman holds a villeinage, and he does something wrong with respect to the villeinage, the penalties are the same as if he were a commoner, that is to say he pays penalties of five sous for petty offenses and sixty sous for great ones; and if he were paying on a fief the fines would be ten sous for the small ones and sixty pounds for the great ones.

866. You should know that according to our custom if a gentleman lives on a villeinage, he can be called into court from one day to the next, and he can be ordered to pay debts, if he owes them, within seven days and nights; and in other ways he is treated as a commoner would be, except for offenses of the person, for which he would be punished according to the law for gentlemen.

867. If a commoner lives on a fief, he is treated like a gentleman with respect to summonses and orders, and can make use of the freedoms of the fief.[12]

868. A person bearing false witness must be given a long prison term, and then exposed to the people on the ladder, and his fine is at the lord's discretion; and it is the same for a person who knowingly calls a false witness.

869. A false witness is one who knowingly tells a lie in his testimony, after the oath, out of love or hatred, for pay or promise of pay, or because of intimidation. No one should say anything but the truth in his sworn testimony, even were it to save his brother from death; and a person doing otherwise is not honest.

870. Whoever denies what he is sued for in court, once it is proved against him, pays a fine of five sous and is guilty of what is proved against him; and if he is a gentleman, the fine is ten sous. And if he cannot prove {what he alleges}, he loses his suit and the fine is five sous, and for gentlemen, ten sous.

871. If someone does not obey an order to pay what is due by the due date, that is to say within fifteen days for a gentleman and seven days and nights for a commoner, if the person in whose favor the order was given complains {that the debt is not paid}, the person not obeying the order, if a gentleman, pays a fine of ten sous and the commoner five sous; and {property} should be taken from the person given the order to pay the debt, and the debt should be paid before the fine is taken out, for the fine arose from the debt. But if he has enough {property} to pay the debt and the fine, the judge can confiscate enough to pay the debt and the fine at the same time.

872. If the person owed the money makes a second complaint wrongfully,—for example, if a good security was offered him before the due date and he did not want to take it; or if he failed to ask for his money, to cause the debtor loss; or he gave an extension after the order,—he must pay the same fine as there would have been {to his opponents} if the second complaint had been a proper one.

873. Security given for a gentleman's debts should be kept forty days without selling it, unless the gentleman had offered commoners as sureties, and the sureties gave something as security for their promise to pay; for in that case you need keep the security only seven days and nights if you want.

874. When a gentleman gives commoners as sureties for his debt and the person to whom the debt is due wants a security deposit from the sureties, and the gentleman wants to pay the deposit to his creditor in order to release his sureties, the creditor need not take the security if he does not want to, for he would have to keep the security of his debtor for forty days, and he would only have to keep the security of his sureties for seven days and nights {before selling the security to satisfy his debt}. But if the sureties are gentlemen, the security must be kept forty days, as it would be for the debtor. Thus you can understand, if a gentleman gives gentlemen as sureties and he wants to give a security for his sureties, you should take it, for the securities {of gentleman debtors and gentleman sureties} are worth the same; and if a commoner gives commoners as sureties, he can give security to discharge his sureties, for the security is here also worth the same; and if the debtor is a commoner and his sureties are gentlemen and the debtor wants to give security to discharge his sureties, once again the creditors are better off taking it, for in such a case they need keep the debtor's security only seven days and nights, and they would have to keep the sureties' security for forty days.

875. When the security has been delivered to the creditor and he has kept it as long as custom requires, as was said above, he should, in front of honest folk, inform the person whose security he is holding to come and redeem the security or to the sale of it. If the latter does not want to redeem the security or go to the sale, the creditor can sell it and his account of the sale is believed on his mere oath. And if the creditor sells the security without informing the debtor, or before the time for keeping the security has expired, the person giving the security has a good action, whenever he wants, to ask to redeem his security for the money; and the creditor must be made to get the security back or make good the loss to the person who gave the security, as far as the latter is able to prove {what the security was worth}.

876. Now let's see about the resistance made to the lord who is seizing something, or having it seized, while administering justice. When a lord is arresting his commoner or his commoner's property, if the man resists arrest or resists the seizure of his property, he pays a fine of sixty sous. And his resistance might be such that that the fine would be at the lord's discretion: for example, if he raised his hand feloniously against a person with the power to make seizures while administering justice; for a man who beats his lord's officer is acting very improperly towards his lord.

877. If a man's wife or a member of his household resists arrest [*fet la rescousse*], the man answers for their offense, for he should have a wife and household who do not insult the lord in this way; that is, he answers up to the sum of sixty sous, for if the man was not in the place where the resistance was made, and his household beat or ill-treated the arresting person, there would be no reason for the man to be fined for the offense, but the lord would prosecute the perpetrators; yet if the man kept them in his service after he found out they had committed such an offense, the lord could hold him responsible [*a coupable*].

878. For gentlemen resisting their arrest at their lord's command, the fine for each resistance is sixty pounds; and if the arresting officer is beaten, the fine is at the lord's discretion; and anyone laying a hand on his lord in anger loses everything he holds from him, and it goes to the lord because of his subject's offense.

879. Animals which are caught doing damage while they are under guard,—for example in thickets, or in vines when they are off limits [*defendues*], or in pastures from the middle of March until they are mowed, or in wheat, or in small grains,—incur a fine of sixty sous and restitution for damages. And when such animals are caught not under guard, the fine is five sous. And if an animal is tied up and it gnaws through its rope and causes damage, if the person owning the animal will swear that the animal broke its rope and as soon as he realized it he went to find it, he pays no fine, but he must make good the damage done by the animal; for a person's negligence or lack of care [*mauvese garde*] does not excuse damage done to others.

880. If a knight does something for which there is a fine, and he takes a squire with him to help him, if the knight takes the responsibility, he protects the squire from paying any fine, except in the case of serious crimes; for if he committed a murder or a homicide or some other crime for which the penalty is death and loss of possessions, he could not protect him, but all those who participated in the action would be held responsible.

881. If a knight takes a knight with him, he does not save him from the law, nor does a squire save another squire, but each must pay the fine for the offense personally.

882. All the penalties mentioned in this book for five sous are, by the custom of Clermont, only ten deniers in La Neuville-en-Hez and in Sacy-le-

Grant, by long habit, although they are part of the county; and in Remy and Gournay they are seven sous and six deniers, and the same in several of the towns held by the count's vassals. But penalties for gentlemen and commoners of more than ten sous are the same everywhere in the county.

883. It is a good thing to take the initiative [*courre au devant*] against transgressors and punish and discipline them so severely according to their offenses that, for fear of justice, others take them as an example and refrain from offending. And among the other offenses of which we have spoken above, one of the greatest and which the lord should punish the most severely, is conspiracy [*aliances*] against the lord or the common good.

884. Conspiracy against the common good is when some kind of workers promise or agree or contract that they will not work for as low wages as they used to, but they increase the price on their own authority and agree that they will not work for less, and impose threats and punishments [*peine*] on their fellows who will not join their conspiracy. And if they were permitted to do this, it would be against the common law, and good deals for labor would never be struck, for those of each trade would try to obtain greater pay than reason and the common good [*li communs*] allow the work to be done for. And for this reason, as soon as the lord or other lords detect such conspiracies, they should arrest all those who have assented to such conspiracies, and keep them in strict confinement for a long term; and when they have suffered a long time in prison, each person can be fined sixty sous.

885. Another kind of conspiracy has been seen many times, by which many towns have been destroyed and many lords shamed and despoiled, for example, when the common people of some town or several towns conspire against their lord by using force against him, or by taking his property by force, or by raising their hands wickedly [*vilainement*] against their lord or his men. Therefore as soon as the lord notices that such a conspiracy has begun, he should arrest them by force; and if he arrests them soon enough that nothing has occurred except the conspiracy, he should punish all those who went along with it by long prison terms and should fine them all at his discretion according to their wealth; and when he can discover the chiefs who organized the conspiracy, if he hangs them he does them no injustice, for it was not their fault that the lord was not shamed by their handiwork [*par leur pourchas*], and therefore the lord can say that they

were traitors[13] towards him. And when the lord arrests them after the thing they conspired to do has been done, all those who went along with it and took part in the action are subject to the death penalty if their lord wishes, and have lost all their possessions, for it is clear they are traitors to their lord. Nevertheless, if there are no deaths, the lord can, if he pleases, content himself with taking their property at his discretion and keeping them in prison for a long term: and it is right for him to do enough to make the others who see refrain {from such things}.

886. As an example to lords so that they will keep themselves ready to punish and avenge such conspiracies when they see by some sign that they are beginning or about to begin, I will tell you what happened in Lombardy.[14]—It used to be that all the towns and the castles of Lombardy were held by the emperor of Rome, as his personal lands, or they were held from him, and he had his *baillis* and provosts and officers in all the towns, who administered justice and safeguarded the rights of the emperor, and up till then the Lombards had been very obedient to the emperor, as their lord. It happened that in one of the towns there were three rich Lombards to whom the *bailli* had not given everything they wanted: he had in fact ordered to be hanged one of their relatives quite lawfully for what he had done. The Lombards were motivated by evil reasons, and they wickedly procured {the services of} a clever, wicked, and smooth-talking man. On their encouragement, the latter went secretly through all the towns of Lombardy; and when he arrived in a town he sought out ten or twelve men from the richest and most powerful families, and then spoke to each of them separately, and said that the other towns were secretly agreed that they no longer wanted to be in the power of a lord, and the town which did not agree would be destroyed by the others, and each town would be its own master [*dame de soi*] and not held from someone else. This messenger did so much and accomplished so much that he spent five years and his accomplishment was that after five years, at the same day and hour, all the towns of Lombardy attacked the emperor's men and captured them, without their being aware of their danger. And when they had captured them, they cut off all their heads and established whatever laws and customs they wanted in their towns, and there was never an emperor who was later able to punish or reverse this action. And from this you can understand that it is a great danger for all lords to permit such conspiracies among their subjects, and they should instead take the initiative as soon as they can perceive them, and punish according to the offense, as I said above.

887. It is a serious offense to kill someone else; therefore the punishment should be harsh and cruel, such as drawing [*trainer*] and hanging the person who does it. However, it is possible to kill another in such a way that you do not lose life or limb, or your property, and this in two ways: the first is when there is a state of private war between gentlemen and one of them kills his enemy and it is not during a truce or a guaranteed peace; the second is when you kill someone in self-defense.

888. Killing someone in self defense occurs when a person is not expecting anyone to attack him, and he is attacked because of hatred or to rob him or at the request of someone for pay. If the person attacked in this manner sees that he is being given without mercy blows from which he might die, and he is so hard pressed that he cannot find any shelter, he is allowed to defend himself; and if he kills someone while defending himself, he should not be the subject of a complaint, for he does it to save his own life. And if he is appealed against in court for this killing, he can appear and await a trial, provided that he can prove that he did it in self-defense, as is said above.

889. When a man is attacked in a fight with fists and feet, but without a weapon that could kill him, and the person being beaten, in order to defend himself, draws some weapon and kills one of those attacking him, he has no good defense in saying it was in self-defense, because he only needed to defend himself from fists and feet, since he was not being attacked with a weapon that could have killed him. Therefore a person who kills another this way is to be punished.

890. In certain cases, if a lord is prosecuting his subjects, they need do no more than swear [*se passent par leur serement*] that they did what they were supposed to do, and you will hear the different cases where they need do no more than affirm under oath.

891. The first case is where someone who collects tolls accuses someone of not paying the toll [*il en a son travers porté*] {literally, "walking off with his toll money"}. If the accused wants to swear on oath that he did what he was supposed to do, he need do no more; but he must be careful not to admit or deny anything before his oath, for he would have waived his opportunity to take the oath, for example if he said: "I paid my toll," or "I don't owe any toll," or "I did not think I owed a toll." If he said any of these things he

could not take the oath afterwards; for if he said: "I paid my toll," and it was denied, he would have to show proof; and if he said: "I don't owe any toll," he would have to give a reason and show it was true, if it was denied. And he could give a reason which would be believed on his oath, for example: "I am a clerk" or: "These goods belong to a clerk,—*or* a gentleman, *or* a privileged person,—and they are for their use," and as to such reasons the accused would be believed on his oath. And if he said: "I did not think I owed any toll," he has waived the oath and he must pay the toll and the fine, for what he thinks does not excuse him from the offense; for anyone transporting merchandise should inquire about the customs of the country he is passing through, so that he can pay what he should without failing to pay [*en porter*] what belongs by law to the lord.

892. It is true that a clerk and a gentleman do not pay tolls for things which they buy for their own use or for things they are selling and which grew on their own land. But if they were buying for resale like other merchants, the goods would have to pay tolls and road taxes and market taxes [*s'aquitassent du travers et des chauciees et des tonlieus*] the same way merchants' goods do. And what I have said of tolls applies to all payments for passage and markets; for although the sums involved are not uniform, all kinds of payments must be made according to the above-described custom, except that a person caught not paying the toll must pay a fine of sixty sous and the toll, and for not paying a road tax or a market tax the fine is five sous.

893. The second case where the accused need do no more than swear an oath is when a lord accuses his tenant of not paying his quit-rent [*cens*] on time. In this case if the accused will swear he did what he should, that is enough. But he must be careful not to start admitting or denying, for he would waive {the possibility of} the oath, as I said above of those accused of not paying the toll.

894. The third case where the accused need do no more than swear an oath is when a lord accuses his sharecropper tenant of not paying him his share of the crop [*champart*] as he should. If the accused is willing to swear that he did what he should, he need do nothing more, as I described in the cases above, without starting into admissions and denials, and without raising any other defense than his oath. And this is true for all rents due annually, that the accused's oath that he did what he should is sufficient. But

after he has used his oath as his defense once, he cannot do so a second time for each kind of payment, for if he could do it every time, the lords could suffer much loss from tricksters who did not care about perjuring themselves in order to be discharged of their dues and their offenses.

895. Pierre gave a tenant a piece of his land as a sharecropper, and ordered him to bring in thirty sheaves as his share of the crop, for by the common law everyone must bring in his lord's share before his own; and the tenant loaded the sheaves and brought them to the said Pierre's barn. And when he counted them he found only twenty-nine; and when the tenant saw this, he said to Pierre his lord: "Sire, I am missing one sheaf of your portion. I do not know if it fell off the cart or if I miscounted, but I will go and fetch it and I will leave my horses and cart here until I bring it back." Pierre replied that he did not want this, but wanted to make him pay a fine for not paying his share as he should and as he had been ordered to do. And on this issue they requested a judgment, namely whether there was a fine in this case.

896. It was judged that there was no fine because the tenant had accused himself before he left the barn and wanted to fetch a sheaf before leading his horses and cart out of the barn. But if the tenant had led his horses and cart out of the barn, without accusing himself, and without the lord's permission, there would have been a fine. And by this you may understand that fines are established so that you will avoid doing wrong, for fear of loss; but a person who exacts fines for things not done in bad faith does not have a very good conscience, even though the custom allows you to do so in several circumstances.

897. Pierre attached Jehan's goods because he said Jehan had not paid his toll. Jehan replied that he had paid it to an officer, and he named him; and afterwards, when Pierre denied it, he wanted to affirm under oath. And on this issue they requested a judgment, namely, whether Jehan had waived {the possibility of affirming under} an oath because he had said that he had paid.

898. It was judged that Jehan could not affirm under oath, but would have to show proof of the payment. And by this judgment you can understand that a person wanting to affirm under oath, in the cases where by

custom you need only swear, should simply say: "I did what I was supposed to," and this is enough {but only} one time, as I said above.

899. On a large tract of land there were many sharecroppers, and the shares they paid were divided between Pierre and Jehan. And as long as anyone could remember, the tenants had brought the lord's shares to a barn, where Pierre and Jehan divided it as they agreed, half and half. Then Pierre no longer wanted the tenants to bring his half of the shares to the place where they had always brought it, but wanted them to bring it to a house of his out of the area, and out of the fief of which the sharecropping lands were a part. The tenants replied to this that they did not want to be made to do this, and they did not want to take anything anywhere except where they were used to taking it, and if Pierre did not want them to deliver in the accustomed place, they would deliver it anywhere Pierre wanted within the territory of the sharecropping lands.

900. It was judged that the men need not deliver the shares outside the territory and that they had made a sufficient offer.

901. The fourth case in which the accused need do no more than affirm under oath is when the lord exacts a fine for non-appearance in court and the summons was not given to him in person, but his wife or his household or his neighbor was told to tell him he was summoned to appear on such and such a day before his lord. If the person summoned wants to swear he was not told, he will not be found in default for as many times as he was thus summoned. But the lord can order such persons to have people in their houses to inform them of the summonses; and if they do not, the lord can exact a fine for disobeying an order. And if the officers who can serve summonses say under oath that they gave the summons to the man person-ally, he is in default and he cannot make use of an affirmation under oath. And this is also true for gentlemen who are summoned by their peers[15] to answer concerning their fief: if the summons is made to the person, a gentleman cannot affirm under oath that it was not; but if the summons was delivered to his house in the manner described above, he can escape the default merely by affirming under oath.

902. The fifth case where an accused need do no more than affirm under oath is when the lord accuses someone of breach of seisin, and the

seisin was made behind the back of the person breaching. If the accused wants to swear he knew nothing of the seisin, he is excused of breach of seisin, but in any case he must reseise {give up seisin of} the place.[16]

903. Pierre accused Jehan of breaching Pierre's seisin,[17] and he wanted to be reseised of the place and to exact a fine for breach of seisin. Jehan answered that he knew nothing of the seisin, for it was not reported to him nor in his presence, and he wanted to affirm this under oath; and on the issue of whether Jehan could affirm under oath they requested a judgment.

904. It was judged that Jehan could affirm under oath that he knew nothing of the seisin since it was not reported to him nor in his presence; but he had to reseise Pierre of the place, and once the reseisin was accomplished, if he breached it again he would have to pay a fine, for he could no longer use the excuse of not knowing about the seisin when he himself had reseised Pierre of the land.

905. A person doing damage to another person's sown wheat, or small grains, or woods, or pastures, should be aware that a person caught doing damage is required to make good all the observable damage, even though the person caught did not do all the damage, but it was done by other people who were not found there. For if a person only made up the damage he was doing when caught, there would be a great advantage to doing wrong [d'aler en mesfet], for any time you were not found on the site you would be free of paying damages, and in this way much wealth could be lost. And for this reason it is a good custom that the person caught pays all the damage and a fine. But the fine is small, that is five sous, and in some places seven sous and six deniers, and in some places twelve deniers, according to the custom of each place. And the damage might be done in such a manner that the fine would be sixty sous, namely if you were carrying off harvested crops, for example wheat before or after it is made into sheaves, or hay [pré fauchié], or cut timber. The way you were carrying it off could be called larceny, for example, if you were carrying it off by night on a horse or a cart or some other way up to a value of two sous.[18]

906. The customs concerning damage to vines differ so much from place to place that there is no common law on penalties, instead you have to follow the custom of each place; for a person caught among vines who is

taking only grapes to eat pays in many places only one denier, and in other places six deniers; and for this reason you should follow the custom of each town in those cases. But if a person were carrying off by night the ripe fruit to the value of two sous to make wine or grape juice, it would be larceny; and a person caught doing such things should be punished as a thief. And if he is not carrying off enough for him to be tried as a thief, the fine is sixty sous when he takes the grapes by night.

907. Anyone can arrest or have arrested a person he finds committing an offense on his land, however he holds the land, whether as fief or as villeinage. But if the arrest is made on a villeinage, the tenant must have the arrestee taken to the prison of the lord from whom he holds the land, and request the lord to make him compensate him for the loss; and the lord should ask the prisoner if what he is accused of is true, and if he admits it, the lord should have the loss made good to his tenant on the appraisal of honest men; and if he denies it, the person arresting him in his villeinage must make his proof, by his own testimony and that of another, and if he proves it, his damages should be made good and the prisoner owes two penalties to the lord: one for the offense and the second for the denial of which he is guilty. If the person arresting or having arrested had done so on what he held in villeinage, and had then placed the prisoner in his own prison, or kept the fine as a judge for the offense, and the lord to whom the cognizance belonged heard about it, everything he had done would be nullified and he would pay a fine to the lord for having acted as judge, and the fine would be sixty sous, whether he was a gentleman or a commoner.

908. If a person doing damage resists the person arresting him, although the person holding the property does arrest him, he pays a fine of sixty sous; but the money goes to the lord from whom the land is held, and if the escape is denied, the person making the arrest on his villeinage must prove it by two witnesses. And if the person resisting manages to get away in spite of the person trying to arrest him, the latter should tell his lord about it, and the lord can sue the escapee for his fine and for resisting arrest and to restore his tenant's damages. But if the lord wants to prosecute, the cognizance belongs to the lord where the prisoner has his residence. And if the lord in whose jurisdiction the arrest was made does not want to prosecute, the person who caught him in his villeinage is not prevented from going after him for his damages.

909. The officers of each lord who are appointed by their faith or their oath to keep justice, are believed concerning their arrests and resistance to their arrests, provided it involves persons whose fine for resisting does not exceed sixty sous; for if a gentleman was accused by an officer of resisting and the gentleman denied it, there would have to be two officers to prove it, or one officer and an honest witness, because the fine for a gentleman resisting arrest is sixty pounds, and it is not reasonable for a sole witness to be believed in so great a matter.

910. It often happens that an officer makes an arrest in the area under the lordship and jurisdiction of his lord, and when he has made the arrest and is taking the prisoner to his lord's prison, he has to pass through another lordship, and when the person arrested sees he is in another lordship from the one where he was arrested, he escapes and gets away by force. What can an officer do when someone escapes like that? He can follow him and have him arrested wherever he finds him, outside of holy ground. And the person in whose lordship he was arrested should hand him over to the lord in whose lordship he was first arrested, and there he should be punished for the damage for which he was arrested and pay the fine. And if the officer does not or cannot pursue him because the escapee hides in the woods or the bushes or enters holy ground, the lord in whose lordship he was arrested can still sue him before the lord where he has his residence, and he should be sent back to make good the damage and pay his fine. And the fine for escaping from custody should go to the lord in whose lands it occurred, if he wants to prosecute him.

911. A person caught in the act of an offense, whether in a fight or doing damage to someone else, is not brought back to the court of the lord where he resides; but the lord on whose land the arrest is made has cognizance. But if the offender leaves without being arrested, the cognizance belongs to the lord where he resides, except that the count has cognizance of all offenses against himself.

912. In all the cases where you can swear an exculpatory oath [*passer par loi*] according to our custom, once the oath has been taken you can no longer demand a fine of the person swearing; and if someone were accused of an offense where the exculpatory oath was not an option, and yet the person accusing accepted the oath, he would have waived his right to the fine, and by this you can see that a person swearing an exculpatory oath

must be believed on his oath; but we mean this for accusations of failure to pay tolls, market taxes, crop shares, or quit-rents, or petty fines [*menues amesures*], for which you need only swear an oath to be believed; for we see several cases where you have to swear an oath and yet you could lose a lot more than being a perjurer, and we will say how.

913. When property is divided up,[19] whatever kind of property, real or personal, each party who has any of the things which are to be divided must swear to bring everything back {to the division} and will hold back or hide nothing; and if the person swearing hides or holds back anything and it can be proved against him, he loses what was concealed or what he held back in violation of his oath, and the party takes it whom he was trying to deprive [*conchier*], and he earns ill repute. And the lord where he resides can exact a great fine for the oath he swore falsely, that is sixty pounds if he is a gentleman and if he is a commoner sixty sous. And forever after he can be prevented from testifying, for it is not right for a person to be believed on oath who has been proved a perjurer.[20] And what we have said about divisions of property is also applicable to bringing back property into the hotchpot when children come to a distribution after the death of their fathers and mothers.[21]

914. We have spoken in this very chapter of cases which make it clear that a commoner can commit an offense where the fine is more than sixty sous, even though he has not deserved the death sentence; and we will describe some other cases which we have seen judged and where fines were exacted [*esploitier*] in our time.

915. Two brothers were pleading at the assizes in Clermont before us for a division of property and one said the following against his brother: "Sire, in the past we made an agreement about the division of this property and the agreement was put in writing and sealed with the *bailli's* seal at our request, and the writing was given my brother to keep for him and for me; therefore I request that the writing be produced and that we be given our shares in the property according to what the writing says." The other brother answered: "I certainly did not bring the writing, for the content and the seal were forged [*faussement empetrees et seelees*]." And we who were presiding over the court, when we heard him say something which involved the division of property and the court, said to him: "Watch what you say!" And he said again that the content and seal of the writing had been forged.

Then we said this to him: "You have said certain words; and we order you to proceed as you should in such a case, if you admit speaking this way; if you deny it, we shall show it to be true." And he did not want to admit or deny it, and was put in prison. And the end of it was that he admitted it and wanted to have the fine set by a jury. The fine was judged by the counsels of the king of France and the count of Clermont, his brother, and it was that the count could exact any fine at his discretion, and he exacted three hundred pounds. And by this judgment you can see clearly that in several cases commoners can commit an offense for which the fine is more than sixty sous.

916. The officer managing the Forest of Hez for the count and a commoner quarreled, and the words got more heated until the commoner punched the forester, and then admitted his fault and that he owed a fine; and once he had done so, he dared not wait for a jury to set the fine, but gave us discretion, and we exacted twenty pounds. And according to the advice we took on the matter, we believe that if the affair had gone to the jury the fine would have been at the count's discretion, for a person who beats the count's officer is showing great disrespect to the count.

917. We have spoken in this very chapter about how to summon those who have been accused of a case of crime and do not appear in court as they should. Now let's consider those who are arrested and imprisoned for a case of crime when no one becomes a party and appeals against them, and the fact is not found to be common knowledge, so that they can be tried: how long must such persons be kept in prison according to our custom? We say that the time they would have, if they were appealed against according to the custom, before they were banished {for failing to appear in court}, is the same as the time they must be kept in prison before they are freed by a judgment. And by this we mean the time a gentleman has when appealed against, for we have said that the commoner is called three times to appear at fifteen-day intervals in the provost's court, and then to an assize at least forty days later, and if he does not appear at that assize he is banished. And the gentleman, along with being called to the three appearances at fifteen-day intervals in the provost's court, must be called to three assizes at no less than forty-day intervals. Thus you can see that when a man is kept in prison, whether a commoner or a gentleman, as is said above, you must announce {the following} three times in the provost's court at fifteen-day intervals and

then at three assizes at forty day intervals at least: "We are holding so and so in prison on suspicion of such and such an offense—*and you should state the offense*. If there is anyone who can make any accusation, we are prepared to give him a trial [*fere droit*]." And when all the announcements have been made, and no one wants to come forward and be a party {make an accusation}, and the judge cannot find on his own initiative that the fact is well-known, the prisoner must be released by a judgment, and once he is released he cannot be accused.

918. We kept a man in prison on suspicion for a killing as long as is said above, and made the announcements in the manner stated; and after all the announcements had been made and the periods of forty days passed, a party came forward and accused him of the fact. And the prisoner said in his defense that he had been held in prison for as long as custom required, and the announcements had been made, and in all that time no one had become a party against him, for which reason he requested to be released by a judgment since they accuser had come too late to accuse him. The accuser answered that he had come in time because he had not yet been released by a judgment. And on this issue they requested a judgment.

919. It was judged that the accuser had come in time since he found the person he was accusing in custody and before his release by a judgment; but if the judgment for his release had been given, the accuser would have been too late; but since he came before, his wager[22] was to be accepted. And by this judgment you can see the danger which there can be in being held in prison longer than custom allow; and the judge is acting wrongly [*pechié fet*] who does not make a timely judgment for release of persons held for as long as is stated above, when he does not find either the fact well-known or someone to be a party within the time stated above.

920. The provost of Clermont sued ten men saying he wanted each one to pay a fine of five sous because he had ordered them to do their duty as sureties before the due date for a debt on which they had admitted they were sureties. The men answered that they owed collectively only one five-sou fine, because the order had been made to them all in the same suit on the same debt. And on this they requested a judgment, namely whether each man would pay his share of one fine of five sous or whether each would pay a fine of five sous.

921. It was judged that each would pay five sous. And by this judgment you can see that no fine for disobeying an order can be divided, nor can any other fine. But it is true that when some suit is settled and there has been a fine during the proceedings, and the parties agree to split the fine, in that case each party owes as much of the fine as the other.

922. You do not have to make a summons in all cases because you {sometimes} find the person you want to sue in the court of the lord who has the high justice over his land, for example, when you are seeking something which has been stolen from you or when you want to accuse someone of a serious crime. Nevertheless there is a difference between these two things, for if the person is sued for something over which he has control and he is accused of having stolen it or taken it, then the person in whose court he is found guilty [*atains*] or arrested has cognizance and can punish [*vengier*] him for the offense if he is found guilty [*atains*]. But if he is accused of a case of crime, without being sued for something he has on him or in his control, the accused can say to the judge: "Sire, I shall prove myself right and honest and I am ready to justify myself [*m'espurge*] for what he is accusing me of in the court of my lord where I should be tried, that is to say the court of my lord where I have my residence or of the sovereign from which that lord holds his land." And if he says this, he should be sent back to his lord's court; and if he simply commences his defense without asking to be sent back to his lord, the lord is not acting wrongly if he continues to preside over the trial on the accusation made before him.

923. You should help people who fail to follow the proper procedure [*les negligens*], people who do not know the customs because they do not frequent the courts where pleadings and trials are taking place, should they be suddenly accused of something they were not expecting, and they depart from the custom in some way without bad faith. For example, when Pierre found Jehan in court without his having summoned him, and accused him of treason [*traïson*] and explained the case, and offered to prove it by wager of battle if it were denied. And Jehan who had not expected this answered that he would send for his family and his counsel, and was not wise enough to ask permission from the lord to leave his presence, but went to a part of the courtroom [*pourpris*] to talk to his family he had sent for and came back to answer the accusation made against him before the sitting was ended. And because he had left the judge's presence, Pierre wanted to have him

found guilty of the treason he had accused him of; and there was a judgment asked for.

924. It was judged that Jehan would not be found guilty of such a serious crime for so small a negligence, but if he had been in default without coming back that day, although he had not been summoned to answer Pierre on this case, he would have been too late for his defense. And by this judgment you can see the danger in defaulting when you are accused of a serious crime, and also that you should not condemn a person for a serious crime because of some slight negligence.

925. It often happens that men seduce other men's wives or daughters or nieces or women in their guardianship or care, and go off with them out of the area; and there are some who carry off (or have carried off by those who they run off with) whatever they can get or take from the houses which they leave. And when such cases arise and the seducers [*cil . . . qui les en menent*] are sued, you should look very carefully at the manner of the theft [*fet*] and what moved the person seducing the woman to do it,—whether love for the woman or the intention of committing a larceny,—and because we have seen many suits of this type we will mention a few.

926. If Pierre has gone off with Jehan's wife or his daughter or his niece or his female ward and he takes nothing along with the woman except what she normally wears, and Jehan wants to accuse Pierre by wager of battle of abduction [*que Pierres l'ait mautolue et traitrement*], the wager depends on the admission of the woman and her reputation, for if she admits she went off with him at her own free will and without force, there is no wager; but if she said she was forced [*force li fust fete*] and she told what force and how it was used, and that for fear of death she did what he wanted, but as soon as she could she escaped from him to be in safety, then there would be a wager because of the rape. Using force on women [*fame esforcier*] is called rape [*rat*].

927. If Pierre goes off with a female ward of Jehan's and he makes a bundle of Jehan's property and carries it off with the woman, and he is pursued by Jehan or someone sent by Jehan, Pierre should be arrested in whatever jurisdiction he is in. And if he is sued for larceny, the woman cannot protect him because she cannot say the things are hers; but she can

give him a defense against abduction [*de son cors le puet ele escuser*] if he is sued as is said above. Therefore Pierre can be tried for the theft of Jehan's things which he carried off, but not for the woman, because she willingly went off with him.

928. Now let's consider,—if Pierre goes off with Jehan's wife and also takes with the woman some of Jehan's personal property besides the woman's clothes and jewels,—whether Jehan can sue Pierre for larceny or whether the woman could defend Pierre by saying: "I took the property as my own." We say that in such a case the woman cannot defend Pierre from larceny once he has spent or disposed of [*aloués*] or sold any of the stuff as his own, for a woman has no power to do something improper with her husband's things as long as he lives; for if she lost something by making a bad bargain, her husband could call it back. Nevertheless, even though she uses the property wrongly, she should not be tried for larceny herself because of the marriage partnership and the rights given by her marriage. Therefore you can see that in such a case she will be released and Pierre who handled the things improperly will be punished as a thief.

929. A woman's complaint that she had been forced might be such that she should not be believed, for example, it could happen that Pierre had gone off with Jehan's wife or his female ward, and Jehan had worked things so that he got her back with him, and because of love for him or because he asked her to or threatened her he got her to accuse Pierre of using force (or perhaps she did it of her own will to hide her shame by claiming it was not of her free will that she went off with him). If such an accusation is made, the judge should ask many questions. First, whether she cried out when she was taken, and if she says yes, and she was near lots of people, she should not be believed unless someone testifies she was heard to cry out; and if she says no, she should be asked why she did not cry out; if she says: "For fear of death, because he said he would kill me if I cried out," this is a satisfactory response to this question. Afterwards she should be asked where he took her and how long he kept her and what sort of a life they led, and if she is caught in a lie because the opposite is proved, she should not be believed. Afterwards she should be asked if she later consented of her own free will, without force, because of a betrothal [*plevine*] or marriage. If she says yes, there is no wager. But if she says: "He used so much force and I was so afraid of death that I promised," or "He took me to a priest in a secret place who married us and I dared not say no for fear he would kill me," this is a

satisfactory answer to this question. And if it seems to the judge that she gives satisfactory answers to the questions put to her and that it could be true, the wager may be accepted. And if she contradicts herself in answering questions, so that it appears she wants to make a false wager of battle, it should not be accepted, for to refuse to accept a wager is to the benefit of both parties, and a judge who accepted wagers in a case where there should not be any is acting very wrongly [*grant pechié fet*], for he puts the parties in danger of losing life and property.

930. The forfeiture of a man and a woman who are married is not the same with respect to their possessions, for if a married woman commits an offense for which she receives punishment of death, the lord does not take her share of the personal property for the offense; but her own real property, whether she has acquired it or inherited it, is taken by the lords, and all the rest of the personal property remains with her husband. But if the *husband* receives the death penalty, he loses all his personal property along with the real property, for the wife keeps none of the personal property. And this shows that all the personal property belongs to the husband during the marriage, for after the death of the one or the other of them the heirs divide property with the woman or with the man.

931. If a woman commits an offense and subsequently hides so that she cannot be brought to trial for the offense, then once she has been banished for her defaults, the lords can take her own real property she bought or inherited, as is said above, but they should not touch the personal property or the husband's real property. But it is quite different when the husband is banished for his offense and the woman is without guilt; for although she has no guilt, she loses all her personal property, for she keeps none of it, and the lords keep all the crops from her own real property,[23] inherited or bought, as long as her husband lives, except just her house, for she must have shelter to stay alive; and thus they buy dearly the offenses of their husbands even though they have no guilt themselves. And if the husbands die in banishment or convicted of the offense, then they enjoy their own inherited or purchased real estate and their dowries; and the reason they do not enjoy these things while their husband yet lives is because the husbands own all the personal property and all the profit from their real property as long as they live, and also because if the wives received the profits, the offenders would be supported by them. Nevertheless, if the guiltless wife is thus left, and she has no family who can and will give her something to live

on [*aministrer son vivre*] it would be too great a cruelty to let her die of hunger or despair because of a poverty she had not deserved [*aprise*] and for this reason the lords who hold what would be hers if her husband were dead should give her enough, in pity, to buy food and to clothe herself; and if they will not do it, they should be obliged to by the sovereign, for even though the custom is as cruel to such women as is explained above, nevertheless the king or those who hold directly from him can give them relief out of pity.

932. Among the other offenses we have discussed, the greatest after the cases of crime is to tell someone out of malevolence that you have had sex [*geu charnelment*] with his wife, for it is the insult which makes the person to whom it is said the most distressed; and because of his great emotion many evils can come to the person who said such a thing. And as we have heard old men say, in the time of good king Philippe {Auguste} it happened that a man said to another malevolently: "You are a cuckold and I did it." And the man to whom such a great insult was said immediately became so angry that he drew his knife and killed the person who said it; and when he had killed him, he surrendered to king Philippe's prison, and admitted the fact; and he said he had killed him as an enemy, for he said he accounted him his enemy because he had boasted that he had done such a shameful thing to him, and he requested a trial. And at this point he was released by king Philippe and his counsel. And since no other case of this kind has arisen since then, as far as we know, we believe that if it did arise, a person who killed under these circumstances would lose neither life nor property.

933. Although we are in doubt concerning the above case because it has not arisen in our time, we are certain of other cases which have arisen in our time for similar offenses. For it is clear that when a man forbids another man, before a judge or good people, to stay around his wife or in his house trying to cause him this shame, and after the prohibition he finds him in the act of having sex [*gisant*] with his wife, if he kills the man and the woman, or one of them, he loses neither life nor property. And in such cases we have seen men released three times in the king's court before we wrote this book.

934. Because it is a very serious thing for two persons to be found having sex together after the above-mentioned prohibition, they may for this reason shut themselves up where you cannot come to them without making a noise, because you need to break down doors or for some other

reason, so that they realize they have been watched, and they move away from each other [*se traient l'uns en sus de l'autre*]. But this does not excuse them when they are found alone together in a secluded place, for example, if they are found putting on their clothes and shoes near the bed where they had been lying. Nevertheless, since they are not caught in the act, the presumptions must be very clear, or a person killing them would be drawn and hanged. And what we said about men not losing life or property who find their wives in the act of adultery after the above-mentioned prohibition, we apply also to those who go into another person's house after the householder's prohibition to find his daughter or his sister or his niece, except that, if the householder killed his daughter or his sister or his niece with the man, even if he caught them *in flagrante delicto,* he would not be excused as he would be were it his wife, but would be drawn and hanged. For a daughter or a sister or a niece who commits fornication after such a prohibition has not deserved death, but a married woman has if her husband wants to punish her in the above-described manner. But a husband who wants to take such a vengeance on his wife must be careful not to let the moment of the act go by, for if he killed either the man or the wife after the man had left and then offered to prove he had found them together after his prohibition, he would not save himself from being drawn and hanged, since he had let the moment of the act go by.

935. Some people believe that persons caught in the act of stealing rabbits or other big game [*grosses bestes sauvages*] in someone else's game preserve are not to be hanged; but {I say} they are if they do it by night, for it is obvious they are going there with the intention of stealing. But if they are going there by day, as carefreeness [*joliveté*] leads some people to do, they merely have to pay a fine in money: that is to say sixty pounds for a gentleman and sixty sous for a commoner. And what we have said of hunting preserves we also apply to fish in enclosed areas and fishponds [*viviers*]. And by this you can see there are many cases which are considered larceny when they occur by night, which would not be if the actions were done by day; and because some larcenies are covert and others overt, we will explain more clearly in the following chapter than we have up to now, and will make a separate chapter on larceny.

936. We have spoken in this chapter of many offenses and the punishments which are appropriate to them. However, we have not discussed them all, but the offenses we have not spoken of here are in the other

chapters of this book according to the cases; and almost all the things which result in a lawsuit are because of the offense of one of the parties, so that our whole book is based on the punishment of offenses, for if no one committed any offenses against anyone else, there would be no lawsuits.

Here ends the chapter on various offenses and the appropriate punishments.

Notes

1. The word "offense" has been chosen to translate *mesfet* since it is fairly generic. In modern American law, crimes are everywhere a matter of state law, and the common law crimes have been abolished; but "offenses" still include felonies and misdemeanors, and even gross misdemeanors, so that the word has a broad meaning. In Beaumanoir, *mesfet* also sometimes refers to acts which are not considered criminal, to be avenged, *vengié*, but wrongs to be purged by a fine or *amende* paid to the lord or some other person or both. Beaumanoir seems to reserve the word *crime* for capital offenses, that is, those offenses for which the punishment is death. I have often translated this as "serious crime."

2. The penalties mentioned by Beaumanoir are of two kinds: small (five sous for commoners and ten sous for gentlemen) or large (sixty sous for commoners and sixty pounds for gentlemen). Other amounts for fines are rare or local. See §882.

3. Crimes against the lord are much more serious, and the penalty is sometimes at the lord's discretion.

4. It is not clear what Beaumanoir means by *trainé*. It may be that the criminal is attached to something such as a hurdle and dragged around before being hanged, or that he is merely drawn in a cart like a tumbril to the gallows.

5. The expression *en aguet apensé* probably has the (figurative) meaning of "deliberately, stealthily."

6. For truces and guaranteed peace, see Chapter 60.

7. Other contexts suggest that this means the skin is broken, or there is blood. See §840.

8. For theft (larceny), see also Chapter 31.

9. Not to the king in person but to his appeals court, the *Parlement* in Paris.

10. This probably refers not to *lèse majesté* but to a kind of homicide or battery. See §826.

11. For continuances and adjournments, see Chapter 3.

12. See also Chapter 48.

13. Here the word *traître* is used to indicate persons guilty of *lèse majesté*, although there is some element of stealth involved. See §846.

14. The story concerns events which took place in 1167, when the cities of Lombardy rose up against Frederick I, Barbarossa.

15. See §58 for summoning gentlemen by their peers.

16. For a fuller explanation, see §853.

17. This was evidently a situation where Pierre had confiscated the land for some reason, and Jehan had re-entered the land, of which he thought himself to be seised because he had not received any notice of Pierre's confiscation.

18. It is not clear if the two sous refers to the value of what is being carried off or the cost of the transportation. These elements of larceny (nocturnal activity and the value of the thing stolen) and others mentioned in the following section are not mentioned in the chapter on larceny, Chapter 31.

19. I have adopted here the text of MS E, which adds the words *en partie* after *viennent*, justified by the repetition of the expression two lines below.

20. Under the Federal Rules of Evidence, when a person testifying in court has been convicted during the previous ten years of a crime which puts his truthfulness in question, this fact may be revealed to the jury in order to attack the witness's credibility.

21. For bringing back property into the hotchpot, see §479.

22. The wager (of battle) is the appeal made by a party against an accused in the case of a serious crime. The wager refers to the wager of battle, for which see Chapter 60.

23. Crops, even from her land, are personal property and therefore belong to the husband.

31. Larceny

Here begins the thirty-first chapter of this book which speaks of larcenies which are clear and open, and of those which are in doubt, and of those which are proved by presumptions.

937. There are several kinds of larcenies, for some are clear and prove themselves, and the others are not so clear and yet they are proved by presumptions and by {the suspect's} reputation, and yet others are in doubt as to whether they are larcenies or not. And we will discuss in this chapter [*partie*] the three kinds of larcenies and first we will say what larceny is.

938. Larceny is taking something belonging to another without the other's knowledge, with intent to convert [*tourner*] it to one's own profit and to the loss of the person to whom it belonged.[1]

939. An open larceny is when the person is found in possession of the stolen article, although he was not seen to steal it, for it is called larceny because the thief [*lerres*] watches for the moment and place where no one can see him, and there is no clearer larceny than that where the the person is found in possession of the stolen article; and it makes no difference whether he is found with the thing on him or is seen to throw it away from him when people are pursuing him and trying to catch him, for it is the same thing if he is seen to throw it or drop it as it would be if he were caught with it on him.

940. There are thieves who in bad faith give the stolen article to someone else to keep so that, if the larceny is investigated, they will not be found in possession, and they can avoid accusation [*se puissent destourner*] if the innocent person is arrested and denies the theft. When such a case arises, if the person who is arrested in possession can find the person [*son garant*] who gave it to him, he is released; and if he cannot, for example if he has fled or he is in a place where he cannot be brought to justice, good

reputation can come to the aid of the person arrested in possession, and he should be asked several questions, for if he has any guilt in the affair, he may be shown to be guilty by several questions. And an honest alibi [*loiaus espurge*] can be of great help to him here, for example if he explains the place where he was when the larceny was committed, and proves it, and you can see he was somewhere where he could not have committed the larceny; and if the person he names [*tret a garant*] comes forward and denies he gave him the stolen article, there can be a wager of battle;[2] and we have seen this disputed, and yet the wager was judged acceptable. But this must be restricted to suspicious persons, for if a man of bad reputation accused a man of good reputation in such a case, he should not be listened to, because there is no thief captured with the stolen article in his possession who would not willingly accuse someone else of the fact in order to escape from his offense; and for this reason you should look very carefully in such cases at the kind of persons accused and accusing.

941. A larceny which is not clear but is nevertheless proved by presumptions arises when people are caught by night in someone else's house, either by force or when someone raises the alarm [*a cri ou a hu*], {where they have entered} with a spare key [*souclave*] or on ladders or through windows, or by digging tunnels, but before they have committed the larceny; and by those who are arrested in possession of the stolen articles who are accomplices of those who go by night. And such larcenies are proved by bad reputation or by threats, for example, if the suspects threatened harm to the person in whose house they were found after curfew [*estre eure*].

942. Larcenies which are doubtful are those where no one is arrested at the scene, or with those who were found in possession of the stolen articles, but the stolen object is found at their place: for example, when someone has lost something and he has the judge look through the houses of the neighbors to see if the stolen article will be found,[3] and it is found in someone's house. In such larcenies there is grave doubt, because it may be that the master of the house did not steal the thing, but someone from his household or one of his neighbors did, and put the thing there in hatred or to escape punishment for the offense. And for this reason, when such larcenies are committed, the judge should arrest all the suspects and ask lots of questions to see if he can make clear that which was obscure; and he should keep them in a close confinement for a long time, along with all those whom he suspects because of their bad reputation.[4] And if he cannot

find out the truth of the matter in any way, he should release them if no one steps forward with an offer to be a party and accuse them of larceny.[5]

943. A person who knowingly conceals a stolen article, and knows it was stolen, and a person procuring the stealing of it, and the person by whose advice or consent it was stolen, and a person sharing in the stolen article even though he was not at the scene, all these are guilty of larceny just as if they had been at the scene, and they should be punished for the fact when they are found guilty.

944. A person is guilty of larceny who is proved to have taken money to keep for another what he knew to be stolen from someone other than the person entrusting it to him, or which he bought at less than half its worth, knowing it to belong to someone other than the seller; and for this he should be punished for the fact {larceny}.

945. It is right that a person should be guilty of larceny who has run off someone else's animals to a place where his partners can steal them; or who abets in a larceny: for example, if some member of my household opens the door to thieves, or if someone is appointed to guard my things whatever they are and he knowingly exposes them to thieves so they can steal them. And several officers, appointed to guard woods or fishponds or hunting grounds, have been caught committing this kind of larceny when they permitted thieves to cause loss there, either for pay or so as to share the proceeds with them; and such officers should be hanged higher than other thieves, because they were trusted when they promised to keep things safe.

946. He is a bold thief who sells copper for gold, or tin for silver, or glass stones for precious stones; for if this kind of larceny could continue without being punished, many people could be deceived by those who work gold and silver and by others. And for this reason the seller of such things must tell the truth about what he sells, concerning what metal and what material it is. And if he is proved to be lying, he should be punished as a thief, and for this reason it is said: "Merchant or thief."[6]

947. There are thieves who dare not commit the larceny themselves, nor have it committed by suspicious persons, but they have it done by the sons and daughters of honest folk [*preudommes*] who steal from their fathers and mothers, because if they are caught, the fathers and mothers say

nothing, so as to conceal the shame of their children; and if they speak out, the children are in any case excused because they are not of age and are in the custody [*poosté*] of their parents. But this does not protect those who made them commit the act, because although the children are cleared the receivers and those who made them steal should be tried for the offense.

948. No one should rely on family relations or any other thing in committing so wicked a crime as larceny, for those who are fifteen years or more of age and who steal from father or mother or anyone else have deserved to be punished as thieves, even though some such have been saved [*deporté*] through love of their fathers and mothers. Nevertheless, in such cases you can have mercy: for example if the fathers or mothers are rich, and out of ill-will or worry, without any fault of the children, they do not want to give them enough to live on and the children, in order to live, take their father's or mother's property; in that case you should have pity on them if they did not get a sufficient share when they were emancipated; but if they have spent their substance foolishly, they have no right to make it up [*recouvrer*] from their fathers and mothers without their consent.

949. It sometimes happens that someone takes something belonging to his relative or his neighbor or his friend, without the person's knowing, and behind his back,—for example, if I happened to go into a friend's house to borrow his horse and I found the horse in the stable but not his master, and because I trusted in him, I took the horse and the person who owned the horse was angry when he found this out and wanted to sue me for larceny, as may happen when you think someone is your friend and he is not,—if such a case arises, there should be a careful inquiry into whether there was an appearance of friendship or partnership between us, for example if he ever before lent me his help or his things, and why I trusted him so much; and if you find friendship [*familiarité*], he should not be heard to complain of larceny against me, because you should believe I took the thing without any intent to steal it. Nevertheless, to remove all suspicion of larceny, it is good for the person borrowing to do so with the knowledge or in the sight of the other person's household or his neighbors. And however the thing is taken, the person who owns it can if he wishes have the thing back and can sue for the penalty for things taken without leave, and the penalty is sixty sous, for it can be sued on as novel disseisin. And for this reason you should be careful whom you trust when you take something of his without his leave.

950. Anyone can pursue a thief who is in possession of the pursuer's thing or anyone else's, in his own jurisdiction or another's, and stop him and arrest him wherever he is except in holy ground, and hand him over to the judge of the place, for it is to the common good that everyone should be an officer and stop and arrest offenders, and the {power of the} judge in the place where the arrest was made is not harmed by this, but is enhanced [esclarcist], for he has cognizance over the prosecution [la justice] and punishment of the offense. But it is different for those who are not in possession, for if anyone wants to accuse them of larceny he must do it before the lord where the suspect has his residence, if he has one; for if he has no fixed place of residence, as many people have none, the person in whose jurisdiction he is arrested should have the cognizance of prosecuting him for a crime.

951. No one can sue another for larceny if the thing was not stolen from him, or if he has no loss if another lost it, or unless the thief is arrested in possession, as is said above. He has an interest if the thing stolen was lent to him, and thus he can sue, for if he did not sue to get it back he would have to make up the loss to the person who lent it to him. And he has an interest if he is an heir of the person who lost the object, for it could come to him; and he has an interest if the thing was given into his safekeeping, and he lost only what had been given him this way, for he is obliged to give it back to the person who gave it to him, since he lost nothing of his own; and for this reason he can sue the thief in all these cases. But if the person who lent him the thing, or gave it into his safekeeping, himself wants to sue the thief for the thing he handed over, he can; and as soon as he sues the thief, the person to whom the thing was lent or given in safekeeping is discharged, for he cannot sue one person for a thing lent or given in safekeeping and another person for larceny of the same article. Therefore he must decide at the outset which one he wants to sue: the person to whom the thing was lent or given, or the person who stole it from the person to whom it was given.

952. If a thing is rented to someone and it is stolen, the suit for recovery belongs to the person to whom the thing was rented, for he must give back the thing rented to him along with the rental fee agreed on. Nevertheless, if he does not have it to give it back, the person who rented it to him can pursue the thing wherever it is, whether because of larceny or anything else, for anyone can ask the person who has it for what is his own; and the person

who has it, if he received it from someone other than the person asking for it, should find that person; and how he should do so is explained in the chapter on warrantors {Chapter 43}.

953. If someone has a thief in prison or is escorting him under arrest, and others break into the prison or rescue the prisoner by force, so that he escapes, those who broke into the prison or carried out the rescue should be hanged, for they prevented justice from being executed; and we say the same about rescues and jailbreaks to save those who have been condemned to death, and also of those who pull down gallows and cut down the hanged.

Here ends the chapter on larceny.

Notes

1. This definition is very broad, and does not restrict larceny to acts done by night or to the taking of things above a certain value, although these elements are implied in other parts of the book. See §§905, 906, and 935.
2. For wager of battle in an accusation of crime or to challenge a witness, see Chapter 60.
3. No Fourth Amendment rights here, or at least no particularity of a warrant with probable cause.
4. No Fourth Amendment rights here, either.
5. For accusations, see Chapter 6.
6. The modern French equivalent of this proverb is "Il faut être marchand ou larron," meaning that a dishonest merchant is no more than a thief.

32. Novel Disseisin

Here begins the thirty-second chapter of this book which speaks of how you should proceed in novel disseisin and force and nuisance and of the obedience which a tenant [ostes] owes his lord.

954. After having spoken of various offenses and serious crimes and other crimes, and of the punishment [*venjance*] which is proper for each offense, it is right for us to speak in this chapter following on other kinds of offenses for which the king has established a new procedure [*voie de justicier*] and a new punishment for those who commit them. And the offenses we wish to discuss are of three kinds: that is to say force [*force*], novel disseisin [*nouvele dessaisine*], and nuisance [*nouvel tourble*].[1] And we will show what force and novel disseisin and nuisance are, and how you should make a complaint on these three issues, and on each one separately, when the need arises; and we will say how people who take the count's place {as judges} should proceed according to the king's law [*establissement*].[2]

955. Novel disseisin is when someone takes the thing which I have been in peaceful possession of for a year and a day.

956. For this reason, if I hold or try to make use of [*esploitier de*] a thing which has been in my possession peacefully for a year and a day, and someone takes the thing from my possession [*de ma main*] or from the possession of someone under my orders [*de la main a mon commandement*], or if they try to take the thing from me with the help of lots of men or by force of arms, so that I dare not stay for fear of my life, in that case I have a good action for force and novel disseisin. You can see that there is no such force without novel disseisin, but you can have novel disseisin without force, as is said above.

957. Nuisance is if I have been in peaceful possession of a thing for a year and a day and someone prevents me from making use of [*joïr*] it the

way I had before, even though the person preventing me from using it does not take the thing away from me. For example, if someone removes my harvesters or my workmen from a vineyard or a field which I had been in possession of for a year and a day, or in many other similar cases, this is nuisance and I can complain about it and I have a good action, in order to have the thing restored to me in a peaceful state.

958. How you should proceed in these three cases of novel disseisin, force, and nuisance is ordained and established in the following manner by a new law [*constitucion*] which the king has made.

959. If someone complains of novel disseisin, and the defendant is a gentleman, he should be summoned to court fifteen days later, and if he is a commoner he can be summoned to appear the next day; and the defendant must appear without taking a continuance.[3] Then the plaintiff should make his complaint in the following manner: "Sire, this is Pierre who has recently disseised me of such and such a thing,—*and he should name the thing*,— which I had been in peaceful possession of for a year and a day. If he admits it, I want possession [*resaisis*] to be given back to me. If he denies it, I offer to prove it." And if the thing was taken away from him by force, he can include the force in his complaint, along with the novel disseisin. And if no force was used and the thing was not taken away, but he was prevented from using it in the way he had before, he can make his complaint on nuisance. When the complaint has been made, the count must compel the defendant to admit or deny. But he can have a delay for an inspection day;[4] and on the inspection day the count should send an observer, and if he finds that possession of the place has been taken [*dessaisi*], he must have the plaintiff restored to full possession before listening to any of the defendant's defenses; and having restored the place to the plaintiff's possession, he should retain jurisdiction for the count and then attest to [*connoistre*] the novel disseisin on the next court date after the inspection day.

960. If the plaintiff can show by the admission of his adversary (or by making proof if it is denied) that he had previously been in peaceful possession for a year and a day of the thing of which he was deprived of possession, he should be restored to full possession and the person who took away possession must pay a fine to the count of sixty sous. And if he cannot prove it or the defendant can show good reason why there is no novel disseisin, the plaintiff must pay the same fine and lose his suit.

961. When a suit for novel disseisin is over, the person losing possession can have the person getting possession resummoned for a suit on ownership, provided this is before a year and a day has gone by since he was awarded possession; and if he lets a year and a day go by, he has waived any claim to ownership and and he can never again bring that complaint.

962. If each party says he is in the most recent peaceful possession for a year and a day, you should hear proofs from each party, and the person making the better proof should get possession.

963. My vassal or the person who holds from me cannot make a complaint against me for novel disseisin concerning anything he holds from me which I take or seize, for between lord and tenant there is no novel disseisin, because the lord can for many reasons take and seize what is held from him. Therefore a person complaining of novel disseisin by his lord from whom he holds the thing must pay a fine to the count of sixty sous and is sent back to his lord's court to have a hearing if he wants to make a complaint on some other count than novel disseisin.

964. A plaintiff in novel disseisin, force, or nuisance must make the complaint before a year and a day have passed since the removal from possession. And if the lets a year and a day pass, his action for novel disseisin is not available [*anientie*], and he can no longer make a complaint except on ownership.

965. For someone convicted of novel disseisin, the fine is the same for gentlemen and commoners, that is to say sixty sous.

966. If the thing complained about in novel disseisin or force or nuisance requires swift justice,—for example, if someone is reaping my wheat or harvesting my grapes or cutting down my wood,—as soon as it is reported to the count he should take jurisdiction and act quickly, and then proceed with the suit on novel disseisin in the way I have described above.

967. If someone whom I am not required to obey fobids me to reap benefits or harvest crops from something, I do not have an action of novel disseisin against him, for I should not refrain from reaping benefits from a thing in my possession because he forbids me to.

968. If a person holds my land for a certain length of time under an agreement that he will pay me in grain or money [*a ferme de grain ou de deniers*], if the time has passed and I re-enter my land, he has no action against me in novel disseisin. And if he has the land because he has leased it for a term of years, and the years are over, and I re-enter the property, he has no action for novel disseisin against me; for it would be a bad thing if the person holding my land for a payment in grain [*a muiage*] or on a lease could, after the time was over, acquire possession against me. But if I take the thing away from him while he is holding it for a payment [*a ferme*] or on a lease [*a engagement*], he has a good action against me for novel disseisin.

969. If I take my property away from an employee who has been cultivating it and looking after it in my name, he has no action against me for novel disseisin.

970. In some cases I can complain for novel disseisin even if I have not been in possession of the property for a year and a day: for example, if I am in possession of a horse, or another animal, or money, or any kind of personal property, or some crop from a field which I have plowed and cultivated in my own name without the authority of anyone else, and someone takes away from me any of these things and I sue to get it back, I must be given possession and the person must pay a fine. But, once I have regained possession, if the person who took it proves it to be his own, *he* must get it back. And this means that by custom you may very well regain possession of something for which you are later hanged, for example, if it is clearly proven that you had stolen or made off with the thing of which you regained possession.

971. If a woman holding in dower has her dower land taken away from her she can sue in novel disseisin, even if it is against the heir who would take the thing if the woman had died, for he takes nothing as long as she is alive.

972. A knight sued another knight saying the latter had recently accepted into his town one of his tenants [*oste*][5] who had lived under his jurisdiction because of his tenancy [*ostise*] for a year and a day, and had left without giving his house, or selling it or paying for it or leaving a tenant in it, but had left it empty and deserted, for which reason he wanted the knight

compelled to send back the tenant resident under him, or who had been, until he had done his duty towards him regarding his tenancy. The other knight answered this by saying that he was not obliged to do so, for any free person may go and live anywhere he wants, and leave his house to his lord in lieu of rent, for which reason he wanted the man to remain a resident under *him* as his tenant, for as long as he wanted. And they requested a judgment as to whether he would have to send the man back or not.

973. It was judged that he would have to send the resident back, and that he could not give him protection until he had done his duty with respect to his tenancy to his former lord, by paying what he owed [*par quitance*],⁶ or by selling or giving or exchanging {his tenancy}. But the lord could not prevent his tenant from doing one of these things, because he was a free man and not a serf. And when this judgment was given, it was said that, according to what their fathers and grandfathers had said, this agreement was made between count Raoul of Clermont and his vassals in the county of Clermont; because count Raoul had had announced in La Neuville the availability of houses free or for small rents, and he was giving them to those who wanted to live there in freedom, and with permission to cut dead wood in the Forest of Hez. And because of the free condition of the houses and the privilege of cutting wood, the tenants of his men came there without doing their duty to their lords as they should have for their former dwellings, but left them deserted. And the vassals of count Raoul complained to their lord, and then it was agreed among the lords that they could not accept each others' tenants until the latter had done their fair share for their former tenancies [*fet de leur ostises leur avenant*], as is said above.

974. Everyone should know that if I have summoned my tenant or he is engaged in a suit with me, he cannot leave my tenancy while the summons or the suit is pending, but first he must be free of the suit, or the summons to appear before us, whether the suit is against me or someone else, and then, when he is free [*en sa delivre poesté*], with no suits or summonses pending, he may go and live where he pleases, providing he has disposed of his tenancy as explained above.

975. According to our custom, you cannot force a tenant to give money or other things as security if he does not want to; but you can make him pay the quit-rent [*cens*] and the rent which he owes for his house. And in some

places you can take a blanket [*coute*] as a deposit [*pour les sourvenans*] for each house, but this is not done everywhere; and for this reason, as for taking the blanket, you can do this in places where it has been the uncontested [*pesiblement*] habit for it to be done, but not in other places.

976. A lord can in case of need mobilize [*prendre*] his tenants to protect him or his house within the fief from which the tenancies are held and not elsewhere. And if he takes them on business outside the fief at their own will, he must give each man on foot eight deniers per day, or two sous if he is on horseback. Nevertheless, they are not required to leave the fief unless they want to, unless the count summons his vassals and commands them to take their tenants to a certain place in the county; for in that case the count's tenants and his vassals' tenants cannot be excused from going there.

977. In some places in the county some people's tenants owe a certain sum of money as a tax [*taille*] along with their quit-rent [*cens*] and their rents. But we know of no place in the county where they can be taxed at will, as is done in many districts. But when they owe something because of public expenses and amenities [*aisemens*] and there is an argument about payment, the lord can assign a payment to each according to his fair share.

978. It sometimes happens that someone sues for novel disseisin and proves he has been recently removed from possession so that he must be put back in possession, and afterwards the person who took possession of the property and then restored it has an action in novel disseisin against the very person to whom he had to restore possession according to a judgment, and for the very same reason that the restoration of possession was made. And let's see how this happens, for some people might think that when there has been a complaint for novel disseisin and the plaintiff has regained possession, there could never be another complaint for novel disseisin; but there can in certain cases, and we will explain how.

979. Pierre entered a piece of land in March and had it plowed and sown without interference, and when harvest time came and he expected to reap his oats, and his workmen were there, along came Jehan and sent away Pierre's workmen, against his will, and sent in his own workmen and carried off the harvest. Then Pierre sued Jehan in novel disseisin; and when they came to court, Pierre asked to be given possession of the oats which Jehan had taken off, which he had plowed and sown and cultivated un-

challenged, after entering the property unchallenged. Jehan answered saying that he admitted that Pierre had plowed and sown and had entered the property to reap it, but according to him he had done so wrongfully, for the land was Jehan's, but Pierre had not entered with Jehan's permission, for which reason he did not want to give back possession nor give him back the oats; and especially since Pierre did not claim to have been in possession for a year and a day for which reason he could not request possession, since Jehan was ready to prove that the land was his own. And they requested a judgment on whether Pierre would be given back the oats.

980. It was judged that Pierre would regain possession, and be given back the oats which he had cultivated unchallenged, even though he had not been in possession for a year and a day. And by this judgment you can see that whatever I am in possession of, and by whatever kind of possession, valid or invalid, and for however long, a short time or a long time, if someone takes away possession from me without a judgment or a judge, I must have possession restored before anything else, if I ask for it. Therefore if it happened that a thief had stolen something and the person who owned the thing took it away from the thief without going through the courts, and the thief requested to be given back possession before anything else happened, he would regain possession and then he would have to find a good warrantor for the thing or he would be punished for the offense.

981. Now let's see how a person who has to restore something to another's possession by a judgment can sue the person to whom he has restored possession, in novel disseisin concerning the same thing of which he had to restore possession. When Jehan had restored possession of the above-mentioned oats and executed the judgment, he had Pierre, who had regained possession, summoned in novel disseisin, saying he had wrongfully and without reason taken possession of his land, and occupied it, without being given possession by a lord, and less than a year and a day before. For this reason he asked for possession to be taken away from the said Pierre and given to the said Jehan, being the person who had last held unchallenged possession for a year and a day and up to the day when Pierre entered the property to plow and sow the land. Pierre answered saying he had already brought a suit against Jehan for this same property in novel disseisin, and he had been awarded the possession in a judgment; for which reason he did not want to have to give up possession or answer except in a

suit on ownership (if he were summoned in a suit on ownership). And on this issue they requested a judgment.

982. It was judged that Pierre would have to answer Jehan's complaint against him. The fact that Pierre had been given back possession of what he had been in possession of was no obstacle to a suit in novel disseisin against Pierre (if his possession had not lasted for a year and a day), brought by Jehan, who *had* maintained his possession unchallenged for a year and a day.

983. Just as you have to sue in novel disseisin within a year and a day of the action or you will not be heard, so also a person wishing to sue because of force that was used on him, even though he is not adding a claim of novel disseisin to his complaint, must make his complaint within a year and a day of the time when force was used on him or he will not be listened to, unless it is on the ownership of the thing, with the issue of force left out.

984. If someone tries to take away some of my property by force, I can resist the taking [*rescourre*] by force, if I have the force, provided it is at the time when the person is trying to use force on me, and that it is not used against the lord who has jurisdiction over the property in question [*qui de la chose me puet justicier*]. But if I wait until the thing has been carried off by force, I cannot get it back by force, but only through the courts [*par justice*], asking for a hearing and to have my thing back.

985. It would be a bad thing, if someone took or tried to take my horse, and I had the power to resist, if I could not resist the taking without being punished by the court. But if I do not have the force {to resist}, so that the thing is taken and the person taking it has it in his possession, I should not go and take it back, but I can have it attached by a court, and make a complaint concerning the taking. And if the horse is admitted to be mine (or if I prove it to be mine), it should be given back to me, and there should be no wager of battle accepted in such a case, for if robbers and people taking things could obtain a wager of battle for their offenses, they would prefer fighting to being hanged without a battle, in the hopes of going free; and it would be a bad thing for me to have to fight for a horse which had been taken from me, and which was commonly known to be mine. Nevertheless the person I accuse of taking the thing might allege a good enough

defense and be of good enough reputation that a wager of battle could be accepted in proof of the defense he alleged: for example, if he claimed that I had sold or lent him the horse, or given it to him for his use, and I could not prove he had taken the horse and I denied his defenses of gift and loan and sale, the thing could go to a wager of battle. And what has been said about a horse can be applied to other things taken, or removed by force.

986. It used to be that when some gentleman who had jurisdiction over his lands took something belonging to another gentleman, the person whose property was taken did not only go and seek the thing which had been taken from him, with or without force, but took everything he could find belonging to the gentleman who had done this to him, both on his own land and on the land of the man who had done it to him. And because this was legally the commencement of a private war, and the cause of mortal hatred, such retaliation [*contregagemens*] is forbidden, by the power and the authority of our sovereign the king of France. And the law [*establissement*]⁷ is such that, if I am annoyed [*me dueil*] that the thing has been taken from me, whether by force or without, and I go trying to get it back by force, or to get something else belonging to the person who did this to me, I am compelled to restore the thing to his possession and to make restitution for any damages he suffers by my taking something from him. And I have to pay a fine to the king for going against his law, which is a fine of sixty pounds if I am a gentleman and sixty sous if I am a commoner. And this fine is not so firmly established that the king cannot, if he sees one of his barons⁸ or his powerful noblemen engaging in such retaliation, exact a much greater fine, for the stronger and more powerful a man is, the greater offense he gives the king by going against the laws which the king has established for the common good of the kingdom.

987. It sometimes happens that plaintifs suing in novel disseisin, when they make their complaint, join to it a claim on ownership: for example, if Pierre says that Jehan has recently removed him from possession of some land he had been in possession of for a year and a day, and then alleges that because he has held the thing for ten years or twenty years he has acquired ownership by long possession. And when such a suit is brought it should be heard under the procedure for suits on ownership; that is to say that Jehan, who was summoned to answer in novel disseisin, and who was found in peaceful possession of the property, must be given the delays permitted by custom in a suit on ownership, and Pierre will have waived use of the law

which the king made on novel disseisin, because he based his claim on ownership.

988. If it happens that someone sues only on possession, and he wins possession by a judgment, and the person losing possession sues him on ownership, and wins on a judgment, the property must be returned to him in as good and proper a state as it was in when he lost possession by a judgment. And if the person winning possession reaped any benefit from the property during the suit on ownership, he must give back all the benefits he reaped after the day he was summoned in the suit on ownership, even though he had won the judgment for possession; for you often win possession even though you have no rights in the ownership [*tresfons*] of the property. And when it appears a person had no right to hold the property, then it is clear that what was derived as a benefit [*levé*] was wrongly derived. And a judgment on possession does no harm to the person who loses, except that he must sue without possession until his rights are recognized in a judgment; and when he has regained legal possession, he can ask for a backpayment of the benefits which were wrongfully derived from the property. And what we have said about giving back the backpayments we saw approved in a judgment in the king's house.⁹

Here ends the chapter on novel disseisin and force and nuisance.

Notes

1. It is customary to translate *nouvele dessaisine* as "novel disseisin," so I have used that when the offense is mentioned by name. I have sometimes translated *saisine* as "possession." The noun *force* I have simply translated by "force," and its related verb *esforcier* by "use force," or "do something by force," etc. The definition of *nouvel tourble* makes it clear that it is what modern lawyers call "nuisance," and I have adopted this term in spite of its troublesome connotations. It should be borne in mind that the *nouvel, nouvele* part of these offenses has the meaning of "recent."

2. The law mentioned by Beaumanoir has not been found.

3. For continuances, see Chapter 3.

4. For inspection days, see Chapter 9.

5. The *oste* occupied an intermediate position between the commoner and the serf. What he holds tends to be called a *masure*, which is used in contexts suggesting

it is essentially a house or dwelling. Therefore I have translated *oste* as "tenant" and *masure* as "house." See De Lépinois, pp. 305–6.

6. This may mean, "by giving a quit-claim."

7. For this *establissement*, see §954.

8. The *barons*, such as the count of Clermont, Beaumanoir's employer, held their property directly from the king.

9. By this Beaumanoir means the appellate court in Paris also called the *Parlement*.

33. Fraud

Here begins the thirty-third chapter of this book which explains that what is done by coercion or fraud [tricherie][1] *or out of too great intimidation is not allowed to stand.*

989. All losses caused by coercion or fraud must be restored when the coercion or fraud is proved, whether in a secular or an ecclesiastical court: this means the losses suffered by reason of the act and which can be adequately proved, for the expenses of the suit itself are not reimbursed by the custom of the secular courts; but in the ecclesiastical court, the person losing the suit pays the costs, whatever the subject of the suit.

990. A fraudulent act was committed by a surety who gave security for his debtor, and afterwards compelled the person naming him a surety to give him a hundred pounds to redeem his security, and then arranged with the person to whom he had handed over the security to give it back to him for sixty pounds. And when the person naming him a surety found out about this, he wanted forty pounds back out of the hundred pounds he had given him, for it was clear he had suffered losses of only sixty pounds on his behalf, since he had redeemed his security for that much and had no other expenses or debits [*empiremens*]; and the surety tried to maintain that he should keep the hundred pounds, because he said the security would have been worth as much as forty[2] pounds to him during the time the creditor had it, and also because the security had been held so long that it was beyond the time for holding it, and the creditor could do what he liked with it; and if he had made a good deal, he did not want the profit to go to another. Nevertheless, his defense was no help to him, and he had to give back forty pounds out of the hundred he had demanded, for no surety should be enriched for standing surety to the detriment of the person naming him as surety, but should merely be reimbursed and put back in the position he was in when he became a surety.

991. Not everyone should be allowed to make a complaint of fraud. For if a son wanted to make a complaint against his father or mother accusing them of fraud; or an employee against his lord while he is still in his service; or a fief-holder against the person from whom he holds his fief, as long as he is in his homage; or a lord against a nobleman [*franc homme*]; or an excommunicated person, or one convicted of perjury; or a person convicted of a serious crime, even though he had made peace with the victim, against a person free of all such convictions; or people of bad reputation [*disfamé*] against those of good repute: all these kinds of people are not to be allowed to sue for fraud, some because they are in such a bad situation that it would seem that they themselves were trying to defraud, and the others out of the respect they owe their fathers and mothers and lords.

992. If someone is convicted of fraud, you should look at the reason why the fraud was committed, whether it was for land or personal property or to disinherit someone, or to do harm or evil to someone else, or in connection with a serious crime; and according to the seriousness of the offense, you should punish the person convicted and make him restore the losses caused by the fraud. And we agree that if the fraud was committed to disinherit someone or to give false testimony or in connection with a serious crime, the fine should be at the discretion of the lord, as to the money. And if through the fraud a serious crime is committed, for which those committing it receive the death penalty, the person whose fraud led to the crime should have the same punishment as those who committed the crime, for there is little difference betwen fraud and treachery.[3] For a defrauder tries to conceal his fraud, sometimes by fine words, and sometimes by working with such stealth [*si traitrement*] and such bad faith [*si malicieusement*] that you cannot find witnesses against him.

993. According to our custom, a person accused of fraud can defend himself against his accuser by a wager of battle if he wants; or if he wants he can have the accuser excluded because he cannot be a plaintiff in a fraud case, if it is one of the persons described above; or if he is a clerk who wants to accuse a layman, for clerks cannot enter a wager of battle; or if it is a married woman and she wants to make an accusation of fraud without her husband's permission; or an attorney for someone else, for an attorney cannot make an accusation of fraud except as a defendant; but in defending his client's [*son mestre*] case he can say that the act was committed fraudulently, which is why he does not want it to be enforced, and when he has

said this, he must have a day's adjournment to consult his client to see if he wants to pursue personally the argument of fraud brought up by his attorney; and if he wants to pursue it, the argument stands, and if not, the suit is returned to the position it was in when the attorney brought up the fraud argument; and then the attorney must pay a fine for the insult to the party made in court, and which his client does not want to pursue, but the fine is only the same as a fine for any insult.[4]

994. If I give (or promise to give) something because my enemies entered my land to come and abduct me from my house, I can sue to get it back; for I have an action for reasonable intimidation, if there were so many of my enemies that I could not defend myself against them, because my house was not solid, or because I had only a few people in my house. For if my house was strong enough to protect me, and I dared not defend myself out of cowardice [*defaute de cuer*], I do not agree that I should have back what I gave, since no one had done violence to me or the house; for a person who is attacked can and must defend himself.

995. Coercion can be exerted without physical action,—for example, when someone wants to take away by force my wheat or my wine or some other thing, and he comes armed and finds me unarmed and unable to resist, and he tells me that if I make a move he will kill me or injure me,—if I, out of fear of this, do not interfere and he takes my property, I can sue him for coercion; and if I gave him something under these conditions to save my life or my property, I could sue to get it back, and get it, for it is clear that I acted out of fear.

996. Although according to our custom gentlemen can make war on each other, and kill and maim each other, outside of times of truce or guaranteed peace,[5] they cannot steal from one another, nor burn each other's property. Instead, if they take each other's property during the war, it must be deemed robbery; and if they burn each other's property, they commit an offense against the lord from whom the things are held, for which reason they are required to make restitution for the damages to the sovereign on to whose land they came, and pay him a fine of sixty pounds. But arson or robbery committed outside of a time of war carry a greater punishment, for the penalty is death; but this penalty is removed by the state of war, and you only have to pay the damages and the fine mentioned above.

997. Fraud is defined as [*on apele tricherie*] everything knowingly done by lies which are represented as truth in order to do harm to someone, even though you do not profit by what was gained from the fraud. And in God's eyes, there is little difference between fraud and larceny; but people sometimes do things which look like fraud, although they meant no harm in doing them, but thought they were acting properly. And because it is hard to understand that fraud is committed on purpose, fraud is not considered to be larceny.

Here ends the chapter on coercion and fraud.

Notes

1. For a definition of fraud [*tricherie*] see §997. *Tricherie* has been translated "trickery" elsewhere, but since the definition given in §997 is so close to the modern definition of fraud, I have used "fraud" to translate *tricherie* in this chapter.

2. Salmon reads sixty pounds here, but many of the manuscripts say forty, and this fits better with the sense of the passage.

3. Treachery, for Beaumanoir, is an action done by stealth. Fraud appears to be an intentional crime, and therefore like stealth. *Traïson* is not to be confused with "treason," meaning "a crime against the state" or "lèse-majesté" in this context. See §§826, 885.

4. The fine is five sous for commoners and ten sous for gentlemen. See §844.

5. For truce and guaranteed peace, see Chapter 60.

34. Contracts

Here begins the thirty-fourth chapter of this book which speaks of agreements, and of which have to be kept and which do not; and of deals and leases; and of things which are enforced without any agreement, and how payment is proved without witnesses; and what coercion is; and of frauds; and of warrantees, and in what cases a warrantor can be used.

998. Many suits and disagreements arise over persons who do not want to keep their agreements,[1] or those who do not want to warrantee[2] things which they are obliged to warrantee by their agreements or by the custom of the district; and for this reason we will speak in this chapter of the above things, so that those who need to know will know which agreements are to be kept and which are not, and what you should warrantee, and which deals are enforceable and which are not, and how you should plead, and how judges should proceed when pleadings come before them.

999. All agreements must be kept (and for this reason it is said: "An agreement is better than a law"), except agreements which are made for bad reasons. For example, if a man agrees with another that he will kill, or injure or assault, a {third} man for a hundred pounds, even though he does what he agreed to do, and beats or assaults the man, the other is not obliged to pay the hundred pounds which he agreed on, for such agreements need not be kept. Therefore, if lords learn about such agreements, they should arrest the parties and punish them as if they were guilty of the act the agreement was for.

1000. There are other agreements which are not to be kept: for example, if I agree to pay debts for dice games, or for usury, or if I agree with a man that I will commit an offense against him [*li ferai lait*] or another, or something that would be more harmful than beneficial to him, such agreements are not to be kept.

1001. If I agree to give my wife or my children something which I cannot give them by the custom of the district, the agreement is not to be kept.

1002. If I agree to give some land which is not mine, or personal property which is not mine, I must do my best to obtain the thing I agreed to give, so that my agreement can be kept; and if I cannot obtain the thing itself, I must give something of my own of the same value, so that my agreement is kept.

1003. In all agreements made conditionally, if the conditions are not fulfilled, the agreement is void; for example, if I promise a man to marry his daughter if he gives me a sum of money before I marry her: if he does not give me the money I do not have to marry his daughter; or if a man agrees to give me a horse, if I perform a given service for him, and I do not perform the service, he need not give me the horse. And by the above two cases you can understand all other conditional agreements, where the condition must first be fulfilled and then the agreement kept.

1004. An agreement may be made for me or in my name by someone other than myself in person, even though I had not given instructions or even known about it: for example, if a man owes me twenty pounds and he says behind my back to my wife or my son who has reached majority, or to someone in my household, who eats at my table or is paid by me: "I owe twenty pounds to your lord and I promise [*pramet*] you I will pay them by Christmas," I can sue him once Christmas is past for what he agreed with one of those people about the payment, and he cannot say: "I have no agreement with you," for he does have an agreement with me if he has it with one of my people on my behalf; and all the above-mentioned persons could receive an agreement on my behalf and promises [*creantement*] to my advantage and not to my loss, unless I appointed one of them my attorney. But if I have appointed one of them my attorney, he can receive a promise against me as well as for me, if it is in the letter of appointment;[3] and so could an attorney who was not part of my household, so that the above-mentioned persons have no advantage over non-family attorneys in receiving agreements or promises; but if it is to my advantage they can do what is said above {even when they are not my attorneys}.

1005. Each member of my household and each of my agents [*serjans*][4] should work and have authority in the position to which I have appointed him and perform only those duties unless he has a special order from me to do something else. This means that if I have appointed someone to look after my woods and sell the lumber, and he sells my wheat out of my granaries and my wine out of my cellars without my knowledge, I need not go through with the sale unless I want to, even though the agent has already received the money for the sale. For if an agent could do this, a bad agent could reduce his master to poverty in one move. But it is true that if the agent tried to hand over the money to me or said to me: "I have sold your lumber or your wine to be paid for on such-and-such a date," and I took the sureties or had them accepted by an attorney, the sale would be enforced, for it would appear that I had assented to the deal which my agent had made.

1006. Pierre had wood to sell, and he appointed an agent to sell it. The agent sold the wood to several people, with payment to be made on the following All Saints Day; and when All Saints Day had passed, the debtors came to the agent who had sold and delivered the wood to them, and asked for an extension on the payment they owed for the sale of the wood, and he gave them a year's extension. And when Pierre, who was the owner, discovered this, he dismissed the agent and sued the debtors and asked them to pay, and they answered they had an extension from the person who had sold them the wood. And Pierre said he did not want to ratify this extension, for his agent did not have the authority or the power to extend the due date just because he had sold the wood and set the original payment day. And on this issue they requested a judgment.

1007. It was judged that the extension would not be enforced, and by this judgment you can see that the agent has no power to act except as concerns what he was appointed and given to do by his master's authority. And it would be a bad thing, when an agent had created debts owing to his master on a day certain, for him to be able to give an extension later on.

1008. Now let's see if those to whom the extension was given by the agent can sue the agent who gave the extension for the agreement he made with them. We say this, that if he simply gave the extension to them, they cannot sue him, for he gave something of someone else's, which it was not in his power to give. But if when he gave the extension he said: "I give you an extension for the debt you owe my lord and I give you an agreement to have it honored [*a fere tenir*]," if the master will not ratify the extension, they can sue the agent on *his* agreement; and the agent must persuade the lord to accept the extension, or he must lend them his own money,—so that they can pay his lord,—until the end of the extension. And thus an agent who does more on his lord's account than he should, and has an agreement to warrantee its acceptance, can incur a loss.

1009. If a person gives away something belonging to someone else and agrees to warrantee {the donee's ownership of} the gift, he cannot warrantee it against the will of the person who owns it. But he must make it up out of his own pocket to the person to whom he made the gift, according to the value of the thing by honest estimate. And he must make the same restitution to a person to whom he has sold or leased something belonging to another. And if it were not so, those who had received a third party's property from another for rent, or for a fee [*par ferme*], or for performing some service, or in an exchange, or for some other proper reason, could suffer considerable loss.

1010. An exchange agreement must be such that each party warrantees {ownership by the new owner of} what he gives for ever; and if he cannot warrantee it because the thing he gave was not his own, the person to whom he gave it must have the choice of getting back what he gave in the exchange, or forcing the person who gave what belonged to another,— which he therefore cannot warrantee to him,—to make up his loss with something as good and as valuable [*aisie*] as the thing he cannot warrantee.

1011. A person who can call a warrantor for something given him should be careful, if he is sued concerning it, to ask for a day in court to call his warrantor to defend him from whatever the complaint is about. For if he goes ahead with the suit without the person who owes him the warranty, and without informing him that he should come and be his warrantor, and he loses the the thing in a suit or an arbitration or in some other manner, the warrantor is not obliged, once the thing has been lost, to warrantee the thing for him which he has lost without warning him to come and warrantee it, unless the person who wants the warranty does something to have the thing back in his possession in the same condition it was in at the beginning of the suit; for with respect to what I should warrantee, a person to whom I owe the warranty cannot litigate to my loss without calling me; and if he litigates and loses, the loss is his own.

1012. If an exchange of property has been made, and the exchange having been made more than a year before, Pierre, who made the exchange with Jehan, is impoverished and sells what he received from Jehan, and everything else he has {to pay his debts} and afterwards someone sues Jehan for the property he received from Pierre in the exchange, and he loses it because it is found in the judgment that Pierre had no interest [*n'avoit droit*] in the property he gave Jehan: what do you do in such a case, since Pierre owns nothing with which he can warrantee Jehan? Will Jehan get back the property he gave Pierre, and which Pierre has since sold, or will the property stay with the person who bought it from Pierre?

1013. We say that the buyer will keep the property since Jehan had held it after the exchange for a year and a day. But if Pierre had sold the property he had received in exchange from Jehan within a year and a day, Jehan would have had the property rather than the buyer, since Pierre could not have warranteed the exchange, because an exchange of property is not permanent [*certainement affermés*] in that case until it has been kept a year and a day.

1014. Pierre stated that he bought a piece of land [*eritage*] and when he had been placed in possession of it by the lord and he expected to occupy [*entrer en*] the land, he found that Jehan was in possession of it and growing a crop on it. Pierre asked him to get off the land he had bought from Guillaume, and Jehan refused, saying he had leased the land [*pris l'eritage a ferme*] for a term of years before Pierre had bought it, and the term was not yet over; and because they could not agree, the said Pierre and Jehan came to the assize in Clermont and requested a judgment on the issue of whether Jehan would finish out his term of years which he had obtained from Guillaume before the latter sold the land.

1015. It was judged that Pierre who had bought the land and been placed in possession of it by the lord would have peaceful possession and would take it as it was, without any encumbrance of the rental to Jehan which Jehan had obtained, and that Jehan should sue Guillaume (who had given him the lease by an agreement) for a warranty of the deal. And by this judgment you can see there is more danger than some people think in taking a lease [*a ferme*] or a rental [*a louage*] or a prepaid lease [*engagement*] on someone else's land; and a person wanting to enter such an agreement wisely and without danger should make sure that his possession comes from the lord from whom the land is held, or else he can be evicted from the land by someone entering it after having bought it, as is said above.

1016. It is true that a person who gives his land to someone, on a lease, or for rent or for a prepaid lease, and then sells it without making a condition in the sale that the person should finish out his term of years, is required to arrange with the buyer for the person to whom he leased it to keep it in the manner agreed on. And if he cannot do this, because the buyer will not agree to it, he is required to make good the loss of the person to whom he leased it and all the profit he could have had from his deal in the estimation of honest people.

1017. When someone has leased out his land and then leases it to someone else before the first is off the land, and then goes out of the district without leaving an attorney who can be sued for a warranty, and there is a suit between the two people who leased the land, it should be given to the one who proves the first agreement, and the one who made the later agreement and who has no one to sue must wait until the first agreement is over, and he can afterwards occupy the land as proved in the second agreement. But we only mean this to apply if the suit arises before the person left the district, or if the person who left had been summoned before he left, or if one of the parties had occupied the land, for if no one had yet occupied it when he left or if there was as yet no suit against him and he had not been summoned, neither of the lessees could enforce his agreement until he came back or until he found someone holding the land as an heir or an attorney appointed by the person who left; but they could sue the latter persons in the manner described above.

1018. Some things are enforced by their nature [*d'eles meismes*] even without agreements. For example, if I rent my house, as a fief or as a villeinage, and the person who rented it has brought some of his possessions into the said house, and he does not pay the rent, by custom I can seize his things without a judge until I am paid for my rent. And if the person who rented the house makes resistance [*me fet rescousse*], if the house I rented him is a fief I can make him pay me a fine; and I get the fine of sixty sous if the person taking back his things is a commoner. And if I rented my house which is a fief to a gentleman and he resisted my taking his things when I confiscated them for non-payment of rent, I get a penalty of sixty pounds. And if the house I rented him is held in villeinage, and there is resistance when I confiscate for the rent, I should go to the lord who has jurisdiction over the place and ask him to prevent [*oste*] the use of force, and he should do so. And he receives the fine of sixty sous for the resistance made to me. And by this you can see that some things are obligations even without any agreement.

1019. There are other cases where things are required without any agreement: for example, if I lease out or rent out my land and the person taking it puts some work into it, I need not allow him to harvest the crop [*lever les issues*] until he has given me a surety to pay me what he owes, even though there was no agreement when the deal was made that he would give me a security; for by custom the work and improvement done to the land is a security to the person leasing the land, but the owner making the deal must receive adequate sureties or security for the goods that will be delivered.

1020. Again if I borrow something I am required to give it back, even though I had no agreement to give it back when I borrowed it; but I am required to by custom, and the person lending me the thing can sue me for it. And if during the time it was lent to me I have sold or lost the thing so that I cannot get it back, I must give back what it was worth when it was lent to me; and if some way or other I can get back what was lent to me, I should give back the thing itself. And if the thing has deteriorated since it was lent to me, I must make good the deterioration, but not in every instance: for if someone lends me a *muid* of wheat, and it is worth forty sous when I borrow it but only thirty when I give it back, I am not obliged to give the ten sous, because I give back as good wheat as was lent to me; for it is right that you should be all square when you give back something which is of the same kind and of as good quality as the thing you borrowed. And the deterioration which must be made up is, for example, when I borrow a horse sound in all his legs, and he goes lame before I give him back, the loss for the lameness must be given back with the horse. And by what we said about the borrowed wheat and the borrowed horse you can understand about other borrowed things.

1021. If someone leases or rents my land and he works on it and he cannot give me sureties or security, he will not lose his deal unless he agreed to give me sureties; but if it was in the agreement, and he did not do it, I could get him out of the deal. And if there was no agreement, the crops should be put in a safe place [*en sauve main*] so that first I can take what is owed me according to the agreement and then he can take the rest; and if there is not enough in all to pay me, I should take all there is and put him out of the deal for want of payment until he has made up the deficiency, and given security to keep the deal. And if he wants to profit from the deal and keep the land, he must take care to make up the deficiency in payment and give me security before I take possession of the other harvest because of his default, for I would then no longer be required to keep the deal with him because of his default.

1022. There is no due date for things lent unless it was stipulated when the loan was made. Therefore the owner can ask for it back as soon as he likes, and this is true also for things given in safekeeping [*mises en commande*]. And when the person who lent or gave something into safekeeping asks for it back and the other person does not want to give it, and he has him summoned before the judge and sues for the thing he lent him or which he gave into his safekeeping, the person being sued must be compelled to answer, and if he admits he was given the thing, he should be compelled to give it back without delay; and if he swears on the saints that he does not have it and that as soon as he can he will do what is needed to get it and give it back, he should be ordered, if he is a commoner, to give it back within seven days and seven nights, and if he is a gentleman, within fifteen days; and if they do not obey the order they must be punished without delay, until the thing lent or given in safekeeping is given back to its owner.

1023. If someone owes me a debt recorded in writing and I give back the writing to the person who gave it to me, this means that I consider myself paid or that I have forgiven the debt. Therefore I could not later sue for payment[5] unless I sued the person who has the writing for stealing or taking the writing, which counts among the serious crimes, for a person taking or stealing the writing he gave with intent to be forgiven the debt would be worth no more than a thief.

1024. A person who lends on security must consider himself repaid if he gives back the security to the borrower, unless he gives back the security on condition that payment be made, or that he be given a surety or as good a security or better. For sometimes a security is returned on one of these conditions: either out of affection, or because the security is not adequate; but it is not the custom to give back written agreements unless you are being paid or forgiving the debt.

1025. An agreement which is against the law,—for example, if I leave more than one fifth of my real property in my will, or if I give my first wife more than half my real property or my second wife more than a quarter,[6] or if I give one of my children by agreement so much that the others would be disinherited if it were permitted,—all such agreements are not to be enforced. And if it is said: "An agreement is better than a law," this means an agreement concerning your own thing which is not required to be given to another by custom; for it is true that my real property must be given to my heirs by custom unless I sell it or give it away during my lifetime for a specific good reason; I cannot encumber my real property with dower rights except those given by custom, and for this reason such agreements are not to be enforced.

1026. An agreement made against morality [*bonnes meurs*],—for example, if I agree to commit larceny or other evil deed [*lait fet*], or that I will allow myself to be excommunicated, or that I will bear false witness, or that I will assault someone, or accuse him of evil [*lui reprocherai son mal*],—all these agreements are not to be enforced, and if you swore to do them, it would be better to confess your rash oath than to do evil to keep your oath. And if you gave sureties that you would do one of the above-mentioned things, and your sureties were sued because you did not want to keep the agreement, they need not answer on such a suretyship, for all agreements to do wickedness and act against morality can be canceled.

1027. The judge acted correctly who exacted a twenty-pound fine from Pierre and ten-pound fine from Jehan because Pierre had agreed with the said Jehan to assault Guillaume whereby when he had assaulted him, Pierre would give him ten pounds. And Jehan had Pierre summoned before the judge because he would not pay, and the judge made inquiries about why the ten pounds were due until he discovered the reason. And because Jehan had made the assault at someone else's request, without the person who was assaulted having done him any harm or deserved it, he lost the ten pounds which were agreed as his fee and also paid ten pounds as a fine because he did a wicked thing out of greed. And the ten pounds that Pierre should have given him for the beating were confiscated by the judge and he exacted another ten pounds for the wicked deal he had made.[7] And by this you can understand that the *bailli* and the other judges who have the power to administer justice in their land can do much on their own authority when they see offenses wickedly committed.

1028. It is true that if the battery had not been committed for money, but in a fight [*chaude mellee*], such as when arguments arise over words, the penalty would have been only five sous according to our custom, or sixty sous if there had been blood spilled in the fight by the use of a weapon; but because this battery had been committed for an evil reason, the judge was right to exact so large a penalty.

1029. An agreement made by coercion or intimidation is not to be enforced, but there are many kinds of force and intimidation. For when you say: "I did it because I was coerced," you must say what kind of coercion and prove it if it is denied, and then it must be decided if the coercion is such that the agreement must be canceled. And also the person who said he made an agreement because of intimidation must explain the cause of his intimidation, and he must not be believed on his own evidence unless the reason for his fear is proved and that it was indeed the sort of thing you could see would cause fear. And so that you can see which kinds of coercion and intimidation are acceptable in a trial, we will describe a few.

1030. Coercion is if I keep someone in my prison locked up or in irons until he has given or sold something to me, or made some agreement to do so; and if he does so and gives me sureties or security, he has a cause of action against me where he can say that I used coercion; and once the imprisonment is proved, he can say that he made the agreement during the imprisonment; and I must be obliged to discharge his pledges and give back his security and cancel the agreement. And if he had paid me to fulfill the agreement and discharge his sureties or recover his security (or to be released from prison without giving pledges or security) I have to give him back his payment, unless I am his lord and I held him in prison (because he had obligated himself to imprisonment) for a good and honest debt; for in such a case I could use this coercion until I was paid, provided there was no loss of life or limb. And if he had nothing of his own to live on, I would have to support him out of my own pocket as long as he was in my prison. And if he had given me all he had in order to pay me, I would have to set him free, according to our custom. And either before or after, unless he has obligated himself to it, I cannot keep any person save my own serf in prison for debt (except for debts owed to the king or the count).

1031. Some people are so evil that they coerce their subjects to incur some obligation or make some agreement by putting them in prison, and when it is time {for one of them} to give a security or repeat the agreement, the lord releases him from prison before the security is given or the agreement repeated, and says to him: "Don't say you are making this agreement with me because of being in prison, for you are not in my prison, but at liberty, and I want you to admit it before making the agreement." And the man admits it and then makes the agreement.—Now let's see if he can cancel this agreement if he is deceived or suffers a loss because of the agreement. He can say he made the agreement because he was afraid he would be put back in the prison where he had been, and, if the prison had been onerous [griès], intimidation is an acceptable defense, for you might do many serious wrongs [griès meschiès] before going back to a prison you had had a taste of. But if he had never been in the prison, and had not been threatened with being put in prison, he would not be believed for saying: "I made the agreement for fear of being put in prison."

1032. A person can cancel within a year and a day of leaving prison all the sales and agreements he makes to his own disadvantage while he was in prison [griefprison]. But if he did not speak against them within a year and a day of being free, the agreements would stand, unless he demonstrated an honest reason why he was in fear of contesting them within a year and a day; or if he agreed[8] to pay for something after two or three years he need not contest it, unless he wants, until payment has been demanded; for then he can say in his defense: "I do not have to pay, since I made the agreement because I was coerced by imprisonment."

1033. No coercion is without physical contact [sans main metre], and it is not valid intimidation if I say I made some agreement because so-and-so threatened me that if I did not he would cause me shame, annoyance, or loss [feroit honte, anui ou damage], and it is obvious that the person threatening me is not my lord and not such a powerful person that I could not insist on my rights towards him; for I was afraid without reason because I could have sought a guaranteed peace[9] and thus protected myself from loss and foolish agreements.

1034. If I make peace with my enemies and give them something of mine for fear they will kill or injure me, and then I want to have back what I gave them for the peace, it should be investigated if there was some fact by which hatred or war might have arisen, and if it were seen that there could have been hatred or war, the person who gave something to have peace should not have it back because of this fear, since there was a reason for ill will; for it is of great advantage to everyone to arrange to live without hate and not to be hated. And if what was given for such reasons had to be given back, many good purchases of peace would not occur, from which many great evils could arise.

1035. If you give something to a banished person out of fear, and the man arranges to have himself recalled and his banishment lifted, you can sue him for what you sent him out of fear of him and his threats. Nevertheless, I do not recommend that those who gave or sent something should sue for it in the court of the lord who banished him, if the plaintiff is in the jurisdiction of the lord of the banished man, for he would have to pay a great penalty for having helped the banished man while he was banished. For a person helping or[10] hiding a man banished by his own lord has to pay a penalty at the lord's discretion, and he cannot use intimidation as a defense, since everyone is supposed to arrest a man banished by his lord, and, if he cannot arrest him, to raise the cry and pursue him until he is caught.

1036. If someone gives or agrees to give something to a *bailli* or a provost or an officer while they are in office, if the person giving or making the agreement is in the jurisdiction of the person to whom he gave or promised, he can ask the sovereign to make them give it back; for such people cannot and should not take anything from those over whom they have jurisdiction, unless it is owed to their lords or they are to exact it for their lords as part of their duties. For it is clear that such gifts or such agreements are only given to enlist the aid of judges, and no justice should be bought. And if it happens that they are given something by someone who is not one of their people, but who is to plead or expects to plead before them and sees that the suit will soon begin, he can ask to have back what he gave. And to speak briefly, those who hold such positions cannot and must not take gifts or promises [*pramesse*] from anyone except their blood relatives [*amis de char*] or their vassals [*sougiés*] or their comrades, for example *bailli* from *bailli*, provost from provost, officer from officer, and in such a way that they have no business to transact between them; and how you should behave in such offices is explained in the chapter on *baillis* {Chapter 1}. They can also accept gifts from their friends who are related to them by marriage, for it is certain that before they were first in office the friends accepted gifts from each other. And so that affection will not lead a judge's heart to do wrong, if someone has to plead against one of the above persons who can make gifts to judges, he can contest the judge and another judge must be given them.

1037. If a *bailli*, or provost or officer buys a piece of property from someone in their jurisdiction, we recommend they buy it at a fair price according to the local market, and that they do not pay in secret, but give a clear and open payment before the lord from whom the land is held or before good people, for otherwise the seller could contest the sale as a kind of gift or done out of fear of being harmed; and minor presumptions are sufficient to have the land returned to the seller for his price. But it is true the buyer would not be required to pay the profits on the land unless the seller proved coercion or threats against the buyer; but in the latter case, the buyer would have to give back the profits because he had not held the land in good faith. And a person seeking to get back what he sold to a person having jurisdiction over him must take care to ask for it before a year and a day after the buyer has left office, or the sale would stand, unless the seller was hindered by some reasonable cause from asking for it back within that time, for example that he had a legal excuse of illness [*essoine de cors*], or he was abroad on a pilgimage when the buyer left office.

1038. You can benefit from an agreement made with someone other than yourself: for example, if I make an agreement on behalf of my wife, or my children, or my father or mother, or my brother or sister, or for my uncle or aunt or my nephews, who were being wrongfully imprisoned. For it is natural [*resons naturele donne*] for you to be very distressed about a wrongful harm being done to so close a relative. And for this reason, if I agree to something to have them released from prison, I can get it back, unless the person who was keeping them in prison shows good reason why he was keeping them there, such that he could reasonably have exacted the same amount from them (if they had it) as I agreed to give on their behalf.

1039. Although someone may make an agreement over property for someone else, nevertheless the person for whom it was made is not obliged to deliver unless he caused the agreement to be made, or gave the power to make it. And for this reason it is a good thing to be careful how you incur debts or stand surety, or make any agreement for someone else; for a person who obligates himself must stand by it, even though no one has to reimburse him, and in this way a person binding himself could suffer a loss.

1040. If, because of duress or because of intimidation, someone swore or promised he would keep an agreement he made, and that he would never break this faith, such an oath is not to be enforced, for you can claim the oath or the promise was made under duress or intimidation, just as the agreement was. Nevertheless, in the case of an agreement sworn or promised to be kept you should look very carefully at what the coercion and the intimidation was, for without the proof of great coercion or great intimidation the agreement would not be canceled.

1041. Some people agree by their faith or under oath to give something back or pay something on a day certain, and then don't do it. Now we should ask if you can declare them perjurers or not permit them to be jurors or not let them bear witness because of such conduct. We say no, for it may well be that at the time they made the agreement by faith or under oath, they thought they would be able to keep the agreement on the day mentioned, and afterwards, when the due date came, they had such an impediment [*essoine*] they could not do it, and a person who does what he can to keep his promise is not a perjurer. But the matter is between him and God, for if he did *not* do his best, God knows him for a perjurer.

1042. Someone may happen to be arrested on suspicion of a crime, and because of his fear of a long stay in prison[11] or of being punished for the act he is accused of, even though he has no guilt, he gives or agrees to give something to be released from prison. Now let's see if he can ask to get back what he gave and if his agreement is canceled. We say he can ask for it back and cancel the agreement provided that, if he was in the sovereign's prison, he submits to a trial on the case for which he was held; and if he was in the prison of a subject, the sovereign must have restored to him what he gave or agreed to give to get out of prison. And the sovereign should retain cognizance of the offense for two reasons: the first is that vassals cannot and should not take gifts or agreements from those they are holding on suspicion of a crime, but should do justice as is explained in the chapter on offenses {Chapter 30}. The second reason is so that the vassal in whose prison he was may not harm him out of revenge [*haine*] or because he asked to have back what he had given or agreed to give.

1043. Because we speak in several places in this book of the sovereign and what he can and should do, some people might think that because we do not mention a count or a duke that this is the king; but anywhere we do not mention the king we are referring to those who hold directly from him [*tienent en baronie*], for each baron[12] is sovereign in his barony. It is true that the king is sovereign over all and lawfully has his whole kingdom in his general care; so that he can make what laws he likes for the common good, and what he legislates must be observed. And below him there is none so great that he cannot be haled into the king's court for default of judgment or false judgment, and in any other case where the king's interest is involved. And because he is the sovereign over all, we mention him when we are speaking of some sovereignty which belongs to him.

1044. When someone complains that several people together have used coercion on him, he can sue each one individually or all together; and if he sues only one, the person sued cannot say he will answer only for his part because he had accomplices [*compaignons*]. Instead, if he is found guilty, he must give back all that was stolen or taken by force. But if the plaintiff has {all} his damages from one, he can no longer sue the others. And the person found responsible for the loss can sue the others who took part in the crime to contribute to the damages, unless he was the leader; for if he was the leader and the force was used at his request, he cannot ask them to contribute to the damages, but must pay the penalty for each of those whom he led there, unless he is a knight; and if he is a knight, he will be considered the leader and will have to pay a penalty, except in cases of crime for which the penalty is death; for in such cases he cannot pretect himself or anyone else, if they are guilty, from being punished according to the crime; and also in cases which involve the sovereign, for example if they are in contempt [*font despit*], or if they go about armed on his lands when he has forbidden it, or if they join a conspiracy against him or are grossly disobedient, for in such a case the knight could not protect his accomplices, but each would have to pay the fine. And if the lord cannot arrest them when the offense is being committed, he can still sue them by having them summoned to his court, if they are living in the jurisdiction of the sovereign lord, even if it is on his sub-fief; and if they arc living outside the barony, he must sue them in the court of the lord where they have their residence.

1045. If a squire summons those who hold from him fiefs or tenancies, and leads them somewhere to apply coercion or commit an offense, he alone must make good the damage and pay the penalties for each of those who were with him, for his vassals and tenants must not refuse to come to his summons. Neverthless, if he tries to lead them anywhere to the detriment of the sovereign or to commit a serious crime, they do not have to obey; and if he wants to use coercion on them to do it, by seizing their persons or their property, as soon as the sovereign hears about it he must set them free; for if they obey their lord's command by doing something to the detriment of the sovereign or by committing a crime, they could not defend themselves by saying: "My lord made me do it by coercion," or: "I did it out of fear he would hate me or hurt me."

1046.[13] When someone sues a person to get possession of something, and the defendant says he has a warrantor,[14] he must name the warrantor and the place where he lives, and say why he should warrant his possession, so that it does not appear that he says he has a warrantor in trickery or to have a delay. Then the court should investigate and assign a day for the defendant to bring his warrantor to court, according to his condition, and according to where he is, and the importance of the dispute. Nevertheless, you should not give longer than a year and a day {for the production of the warrantor}; and a year and a day should be given only if the warrantor lives in a distant foreign land. And if it is a case of serious crime,—for example if someone is suing for a horse or something else which has been stolen from him,—the person sued should not be released because he says he has a warrantor, for all those guilty of larceny would say so in order to escape. But the judge who has him in custody should send to the lord where the warrantor is a resident,—if he lives within the kingdom,—and inform him that he has under arrest such-and-such a man who is being sued for such-and-such property, and the defendant claims as a warrantor a person residing in his district, for which reason he requests him to send him to warrant {the possession} or to say he is not a warrantor for it; and lords should do this for each other. But when the person claimed as a warrantor appears before the lord where he is sent, if it is a case of serious crime, he may say: "I will not be your warrantor in this matter, for you never had from me or at my order the thing you are being sued for." If the person who named him as a warrantor wants to prove it by valid witnesses, he should be permitted to make proof; but if he wants to prove it only by wager of battle, we do not agree that this be permitted, for all thieves could then claim someone as a warrantor in order to have a chance to get off: and many honest men might have to suffer wrongly. Nevertheless, good reputation should make a difference here, for two persons of bad reputation should be allowed a wager of battle when the case is so obscure that you will not find out the truth any other way.

1047. A person who can find his warrantor, ready to testify, and brings him to court, is released from the accusation, provided the warrantor is able to pay [*soufisans*] and resides in the jurisdiction, or gives a good security to pursue the litigation and that he warrantees the thing sued for, except in the cases of serious crime where the accused who brings forward a warrantor is said to have been at the scene of the crime, or had it done for him. For in cases of crime, for which the punishment is loss of life or limb, and in which the accusation is made directly, you cannot be released by producing a warrantor, for several persons could be accused of the same act.

1048. In order to warrantee something, a person should leave his judge and go and warrantee the thing he handed over or delivered, before the judge where the person needing the warrantee is being sued [*emplediés*]. And if he does not want to go, his lord should make him. And if he is ordered to go and he does not, and the person being sued losęs because of his default, he is held responsible for all the damages paid by the defendant because of the default of his warrantor.

1049. A good warranty is given by a person who reasonably demonstrates how the thing being sued for came to him: for example, if he bought it in the open public market, in the sight and to the knowledge of good people, for that is why markets are established, so that you can buy and sell in public. Nevertheless you should anticipate that frauds and trickery will occur in public markets as they do elsewhere, for example, when people buy things from people they do not know, and goods which the buyer does not need and at a lower price, by a third or a half, than they are worth, for in such deals there is no honesty apparent. Thus if such things are sued on by someone who can prove they are his, they should be given back or delivered to him, and the person who bought them in bad faith can go find his warrantor {and sue him}.

1050. A *bailli* or a provost or an officer who serves a person holding directly from the king, if their lord accuses them of an offense in the execution of their duties, cannot be protected by the lord under whom they reside, even if their wives and children are resident there; for if their residences are in the vassals' lands, the barons {high lords} will not sue on something involving themselves in their subjects' courts. And if they reside in a different barony, either under the king or another baron, such a defendant must be sent back to give an accounting or be acquitted [*soi espurgier*] in the court of the baron he used to serve.[15] But if the officer shows the king, in a complaint, that he is being wronged, the king should send an observer to see what sort of a trial he will get, and give him a safe conduct if he is afraid for his life, provided he submits to a trial from the men of the baron who is accusing him. And if they give him a false judgment or he is refused a trial, he can take the baron by one of these two appeals into the king's court; and if he can prove false judgment by the jurors, or default of judgment by the baron, he is discharged of what the baron accused him of.

1051. Many frauds are made in marriage agreements, but wherever they are discovered or proved they should not be permitted; and the agreements made behind people's backs by some of those who are to be married should not be observed, for they are made by deceiving others, which should not be allowed.

1052. Pierre had a son, whom he wanted to give in marriage to Jehan's daughter, and before the pledges and the betrothals were completed, they made an agreement between the father and the son such that he would place his son in homage for all his lands, on condition that he would get half the profits for life, and as to the other half the son swore that as soon as he was married he would return half of the profits for life, so that he would benefit from only one-quarter of the profits of the land and his father would get three-quarters. And when they came to the marriage agreement, the father and son concealed the quarter that the son was supposed to give back to the father, and the family of the girl assented to the marriage on the agreement that the son would do homage for the whole fief and have half the profits. After the wedding, the son delivered to his father three-quarters of the profits, as they had agreed. When the girl's family saw that the son was getting only one-quarter of the profits, and he should be getting half, they sued the father on the agreement. The father answered that he admitted to the agreements, but if his son wanted to be kind to him, he certainly could, and he had made the agreement to do this before the marriage agreement. And on this they requested a judgment, namely whether the first agreement that the father and son had made would stand.

1053. It was judged that the son could keep the first agreement or not, for you could hardly forbid him to do what he wanted and be kind to his father with his own things, if he wanted. Nevertheless, it was considered that the first agreement had clearly been fraudulently made, so that the son need not keep it unless he wanted, but he would have to have half of the profits as it had been agreed at the marriage. But even though he could, if he wanted, give his father what he had promised in the invalid agreement; nevertheless if he died, his wife would not lose any dower right, but would take as much as if the son had never had the agreement with his father, for the fraudulent agreement before the the wedding did not prevent her from having her dower according to what was agreed in the marriage agreement. And by this judgment you can see that all fraudulent agreements when they are discoverd and proved should be undone.

1054. Frauds can be perpetrated more wickedly and in more ways towards the man than towards the woman when they marry, because the man is master of himself and at liberty [*en sa franche poosté*]: and he can do what he likes with his own things as long as he lives. But a woman cannot, for what is agreed on the woman's behalf toward the husband when she marries must be kept, whatever agreement the woman had made before the marriage or after it, whether she was a widow or had never been married [*pucele*], for once she has joined another in marriage, she has no separate power to enforce her agreements without her husband's assent.

1055. When someone has incurred an obligation in writing or by oral agreement to several creditors, and he does not own enough to pay and the creditors are suing [*plaintif*], his personal and real property must be attached and sold and the creditors paid off so much on the pound according to the size of the debt; but this means when the due dates for the debts are all past, for if there is a creditor whose due date has not yet come, he cannot ask to be paid until the due date, nor have the debtor's property attached to prevent payment to those creditors whose due date *has* gone by.

1056. There was a suit at Creil concerning a man who wanted to leave the district and had debts to several people. Before he left, some of those to whom he had debts had sued him, and had received an order from the judge for him to pay them; and after the order was issued, he left the area without obeying it. And when he had left, several creditors had his property attached and requested to be paid so much on the pound according to their debts and what the property was worth; and the creditors who had obtained the order before he left argued against this that they wanted to be paid first because they had sued first and had obtained an order to be paid, and, if there were anything left over, the others could have it. And on this issue they requested a judgment, namely whether they would all get so much on the pound as far as they could prove debts past due to them, or whether the ones who had obtained the order would be paid in full.

1057. It was judged that those who had sued before he left, for whom an order had been issued, would be paid in full, and if there was anything left, the other creditors would be admitted to prove their past debts after the person who had left had been called three times for an appearance fifteen days later, and, once they had proved their debts, they would be paid out of what was left so much on the pound according to what was owed them. And by this judgment you can see that the first plaintiffs for whom an order had been obtained would be the first paid.

1058. If someone sues for something because there was an agreement to give it to him, and the agreement cannot be kept,—for example, if someone agrees to give something to his daughter Jehanne when she marries Philippe, and the daughter dies before the gift is delivered; or if someone agrees to give his white palfrey, and the horse is found dead; or if someone agrees to hand over or give or lend something to someone, thinking he has possession of the thing when he does not, because it is lost; or the person who made the agreement thought the thing was his but it belonged to someone else, so that he could not keep his agreement,—all such agreements are void. But it is true that, if a thing were to be handed over or delivered through a sale, and the seller has received some of the price, he must give back the money since he cannot deliver the thing sold. And if it is seen that he made the sale in bad faith, knowing very well that the thing was not his, he should be obliged to arrange for the sale to stand with the agreement of the owner, and if he cannot, then to pay proper damages to the buyer, and the sale is canceled.

1059. It would be different if I had sold or agreed to sell something and I offered to deliver it at a certain time, and the buyer or the person I had made the agreement with failed to take delivery, and then, after the offer had been properly made, the thing sold or agreed on died or deteriorated some other way because of the delay of the buyer or the person supposed to take delivery under the agreement, and without any fault of mine. In such a case, the person supposed to take delivery would be at risk for the loss, for I do not have to deliver the thing except as is, and he must pay me what was agreed on for the thing. And if by no fault of mine the goods he was supposed to get by the agreement are lost or deteriorate after delivery of them was offered, he should only blame his own negligence for his loss.

1060. If I agree to hand over or deliver something which is not mine, but someone else's, attention must be paid to the force of the words of the agreement. For if I say: "I say,—*or* promise,—that Jehan will give you ten pounds,—*or* that he will give you this parcel of such-and-such a property in such-and-such a place," and afterwards Jehan will not do what I said or promised, I am not thereby obliged to make him do so. But if I say: "I will arrange for Jehan to give you ten pounds,—*or* that he will give you such-and-such a piece of property, *or* such-and-such a horse, *or some other thing,*— out of affection,—*or* in exchange for your service, *or* for so much money, *or* provided that you will do such-and-such by saying such-and-such," then I am obliged to make him do so. And if Jehan will not do it, to release me, I must pay it out of my own pocket, or give the equivalent, because I agreed to arrange for Jehan to do it. But if I made the agreement at Jehan's order, or as his appointed attorney, Jehan must perform what I agreed on his account. And if I agreed to have him do something without his orders and without having the power from him to make this agreement, Jehan does not, unless he wants to, have to perform; thus I could suffer a loss because of my foolish agreement, and for this reason you should be careful how you make agreements on behalf of others.

1061. You cannot sue on an agreement made by a mute person nor a completely deaf one, nor a lunatic [*forsené*] nor a mental defective [*fol naturel*], nor a minor, nor a woman while she has husband; for a mute cannot make an agreement since he cannot speak, and an agreement cannot be made without words; nor can a deaf person, since he cannot hear the agreement (but here we speak of completely deaf persons, for a person who hears when you shout can make an agreement), nor can a lunatic or a mental defective, for they do not know what they are doing. But it is true that all those who cannot make an agreement for physical impairment [*mehaing*] or illness can be sued if they made an agreement before their indisposition. And during their impairment [*mehaing*] they must have attorneys and administrators for their business who can make agreements for them and answer on agreements they made before their sickness. But as for minors and married women, neither they themselves nor their attorneys can make agreements against their interest, because they are within the power of someone else; and children not yet of age are more especially discussed in the chapter which speaks of them {Chapter 16}.

1062. Every time a person makes a single agreement about several things, for example if Pierre said to Jehan: "I will give you ten pounds or a horse," he can fulfill the agreement by giving whichever he likes, the horse or the ten pounds, and by this you can understand all other double agreements. And if someone says: "I admit that I owe you this and this," and the things are different, for example wheat and oats, or wine and wood, the person making the agreement must fulfill both parts of the agreement. And by this you can see there is a great difference between saying: "I offer to give you ten *muis* of wheat and ten *muis* of oats," and saying: "I promise to give you ten *muis* of wheat or ten *muis* of oats." For by the first agreement you must give the wheat and the oats, but by the second you need only give ten *muis* of whichever you please, wheat or oats.

1063. If someone makes an agreement or some other deal on a condition, for example by saying: "I will give you twenty barrels of wine for a hundred pounds due on such-and-such a day, if my father agrees," and the deal depends on this condition, the father can choose to void the deal or let it stand; for if he agrees the deal must be kept, and if not then the deal is invalid.

1064. And if I said: "I will lend,—*or* rent you,—or lease you,— my horse,—*or* such-and-such a piece of land,—provided you give me security that I will have it back on such-and-such a day, in a writing from the *bailli*'s court," if the writing is not previously delivered to me, I am not required to deliver what was agreed on, and (unless I want to) I will not change the security which was promised to me for another. But if no security was specially mentioned when the agreement was made, a different adequate security is sufficient, and I must deliver the thing on the adequate security.

1065. Even though you sell or rent or lease something without putting in the agreement that security must be given, nevertheless the person taking delivery cannot take it away without giving security to pay the price of the deal on the day agreed on, or unless he pays cash; for until the delivery of the goods you are not too late to ask for a security or cash.

1066. We hold that a deal is made once fulfillment is promised by the assent of the parties, among persons who can make deals or agreements on the subject matter of the agreement, or as soon as God's denier is given,[16] or as soon as a deposit is given, for each of these three things is valid to confirm the deal. But by this we mean deals which are made without conditions; for where there is a condition, the condition must be fulfilled or the deal is invalid.

1067. If someone makes a deal or an agreement with someone on a condition he must fulfill himself,—for example if he said: "I will give you twenty barrels of Auxerre wine[17] for a hundred pounds, delivered on the Grève[18] in Paris,"—it should be understood that he must deliver it there, and the buyer need not accept it anywhere else unless he wants. And if the place was not named when the deal was made, the things sold must be delivered in the town where the deal was made, according to the measurements and customs of the said town. And if the deal or agreement is for land, it must be understood that it will be delivered where it is located, and according to the measurements of the place where it is, for it is not a thing which can be carried from place to place.

1068. If some people make a marriage agreement between their minor children and make the children pledge to each other, when the children come of age they can go back on their pledges if they wish, and the agreements are void, because the people without whom the agreements could not have been made were not of age. And if there was a penalty [*peine*] established when the agreement was made,[19]—for example if I say to someone: "I will give my daughter in marriage to your son and I agree to do so on penalty of a thousand pounds if I do not because I regret the deal or because my daughter does not want this when she comes of age,"—I am obliged to pay the penalty. But it is true that if the marriage takes place and they are married by Holy Church, I cannot be sued for the penalty because of a later suit between the married couple, because I did what I was supposed to and I delivered what I promised.

1069. It is true that if two children are married so young that it is clear they do not understand anything, for example at eight years of age or less, and as soon as one of them understands and realizes, he wants to have the marriage annulled because he was under age and subject to deception, we believe that a separation can be effected, but it must be before carnal knowledge [*compaignie charnele*] between them; for when they are old enough to have {carnal} knowledge of each other no one may agree that the marriage can be broken up because they were not of age. And for this reason Holy Church should take careful note of the age of those whose marriage it confirms, because of the dangers and the evils which can arise.

1070. You should know that a party needing to call his warrantor should ask for an appropriate day in court to do so, so that he can obtain his presence by force of law if he will not come voluntarily, and he should be given a date according to whether the named warrantor is far away or nearby. And if he cannot obtain his warrantor on the first day, because the warrantor had a legal excuse, or because he was in default or for some other reason, without the fault of the person calling him, the latter should not on that account lose his suit nor be required to answer the complaint,[20] but the suit should be delayed until the party can oblige his warrantor to appear and give him a warranty. But we apply this to those who do their best without fraud or sharp practice to bring to court those who should be their warrantors, and not just out of a wish to prolong the suit.

1071. If someone asks for a distant court date to obtain their warrantor, because they say he is in a foreign land, he should be asked the name and family name of the person they say should be their warrantor, and why he should be obliged to warrantee, for example, that he sold to them or exchanged with them what they are being sued for. And if he gives a good reason for the judge to see that a warranty is called for, and the party will swear on the saints that he is asking for a distant court date only because he does not want to make an answer on a matter where the warrantor should assume the defense, he should have a date a year and a day later. But if the warrantor comes back sooner, the date can be moved up; and if he does not come within a year and a day, he should no longer be expected, except for an absence on an overseas pilgrimage or for service in the king's army, for in this case he would be awaited until you had heard of his death or until he came back.

1072. When you are pleading with someone on a case which requires giving a court date to call a warrantor, and the warrantor appears to give his warranty, he must assume the suit in the state in which he finds it against the person for whom he is the warrantor, provided the person calling him as a warrantor has not impaired the suit by giving an improper answer or going to arbitration, for then the warrantor would be discharged from giving warranty, unless the defendant had agreed to proceed on the default of the warrantor, for then the loss would be ascribed to the warrantor.

Here ends the chapter on deals and agreements and on warranties.

Notes

1. I have used the word "agreement" here to translate *convenance*. I have avoided the translation "contract" because *convenance* is more of a promise than a contract.

2. In modern times, possession of property can generally be established by such items as deeds, bills of sale, receipts, and canceled checks. In Beaumanoir's time, where no such documents were available, ownership was often established by calling as a witness the person from whom the property had been obtained. His testimony is called a "warranty" or *garant* and the "warrantor" is the *garantissere*. The English words have been retained in modern real estate law, where a "warrantee deed" contains certain warrantees with respect to the property transferred. In this chapter, what the warrantor warrantees is that he did transfer the property and that the buyer has, as we say, good title. The warrantor then becomes the defendant in the suit, and the original defendant is discharged. This is much like impleading in modern procedure, and it explains why warrantors might be reluctant to appear in court as such.

3. For attorneys and letters of appointment, see Chapter 4.

4. The translation "agent" is preferred to "officer" for *serjans* in this chapter, because the discussion is one of agency law. Elsewhere, the term *serjans* is used by Beaumanoir to designate a minor court official or law enforcement person, and we have translated those occurrences as "officer." Note that the law of agents and principals used to be called the law of master and servant, and I have sometimes used the word "master" to translate *mestre*, which could also be translated "principal."

5. I read *la la* here in Salmon as an error for *la*. Beugnot has *le*.

6. Beaumanoir presumably means in dower.

7. It is clear that victim's rights were almost as minimal in the thirteenth century as they still are today; but the person beaten probably had a good cause of action against both Pierre and Jehan.

8. Salmon has *commença* which makes little sense; two manuscripts have *convenancha* (Salmon 2: 17 n. y.), which is what we translate here as "agreed."

9. Perhaps *asseurement* does not have its technical meaning of "guaranteed peace" here (see Chapter 60) and means rather "security, protection." But the next section does discuss something similar.

10. For *ne ne* in Salmon I read *ne*.

11. Suspects arrested for crimes could be kept in prison for weeks or months before trial if no one came forward to accuse them. See Chapter 30, §917.

12. In Beaumanoir, the word *baron* is used with two meanings: the first is the great nobles who hold their fiefs directly from the king, such as the count of Clermont, Beaumanoir's lord, who is actually the king's brother; and the second meaning of *baron* is "husband." *Baron* is not used, as it is in the English aristocracy, to mean a minor nobleman (a baronetcy is the lowest inheritable title in the United Kingdom today). Nor is *baron* used to mean a special kind of judge, as in some courts of England.

13. The material in this section is substantially repeated in §§1070-71.

14. For warrantors, see n. 2 to this chapter.

15. Beaumanoir mentions in Chapter 1, §53 that a *bailli* who has gone to serve another lord can be sent back to answer a charge against him in his old jurisdiction.

16. This refers to a small coin given to charity as a mark of a deal. Cf. *Maistre Pierre Pathelin*, ed. Albert Pauphilet, in *Jeux et sapience du moyen âge*, Bibliothèque de la Pléiade (Paris: Gallimard, 1951) 290.

17. Auxerre wine was much appreciated in the Middle Ages.

18. The Place de la Grève, today Place de l'Hôtel de Ville, was on the right bank of the Seine river.

19. For prenegotiated penalties, see Chapter 42.

20. For pleadings (complaints and answers), see Chapters 6 and 7.

35. Writings

Here begins the thirty-fifth chapter of this book which speaks of making obligations by a writing, and of which writings are valid and which are not; and of how you should enforce a writing and how you should contest a writing or the seal.

1073. After we have spoken in the previous chapter of several kinds of agreements and deals, and of warranties, it is right for us to speak in this following chapter on other kinds of agreements, for example those where you make an obligation in writing. For so that persons who have made an agreement may not deny what they agreed on without the truth of the agreement becoming known, those who accept agreements sometimes accept them in front of people who can give testimony about them later, and sometimes those who make the agreements make an undertaking in writing to keep the agreement; and we have set out to speak of this kind of obligation made in writing in this chapter, and in another chapter we will speak of another kind of proof. And because not all obligations made in writing have the same force, and because they are not all alike, we are giving them a separate chapter, for we will make plain which are the stronger and which are the weaker, and we will set out the form in which a writing should be made for personal property and for real property, and how lords should enforce the writing, and how and when you can show a writing to be false.

1074. When a person has been summoned to court to answer on his writing, you should read the writing to him in his presence and before the judge, and then the judge should ask him if he gave this writing, sealed with his seal; if he says yes, he must be ordered to fulfill the contents [*teneur*] of the writing within fifteen days. If he does not do so and the person who obtained the order complains again, the sovereign should fine the person obligated ten sous for disobeying an order, and sell without delay enough of his property (that is, personal property and chattels), and deliver the proceeds, for the debt to be paid. And if you don't find enough personal property and chattels, what should you do? If his real property is obligated in the agreement, you can treat it according to the agreement; and if it is not mentioned, the lord will take jurisdiction over it by placing guards on it and keeping it in his possession. And when there have been guards on the debtor for forty days (unless he has fulfilled his obligations in the meantime) the sovereign should command him to sell the property within forty days; and if he will not, the sovereign should sell it and discharge the debt, or give the property to the creditor at a price assessed by honest folk. And if the debtor happens to have no property except in fief, and the creditor is not a gentleman and cannot hold a fief, and no gentleman can be found who wants to buy it, the sovereign should hand over to the creditor all the fruits and benefits from the fief until the writing has been fulfilled, nevertheless safeguarding the rights of the lord from whom the land is held, for lords should not lose their rents nor their homage because of their vassals' obligations, nor the dues for the fiefs, unless the lords have agreed to renounce their rights to these things.

1075. When someone is summoned to court to answer on his writing, and he denies before the judge that he ever gave this writing, and that it is not his seal, the plaintiff must make his proof, and there are several ways of making proof.—One of the ways is by proving by two valid witnesses who were present when the writing was given and sealed with the present seal of the person denying it. The other way is when there is no witness and you prove by two good men [*preudommes*] who have had and seen writings sealed with the same seal and given by the hand of the person making the denial, or unquestionably on his orders. The third way is if the person making the denial had previously admitted before honest people, before he denied it, that the plaintiff had his writing and that he was obligated to him for what was set out in the contents of the writing.

1076. It is a very wicked thing to deny your seal, and for this reason the fine of the person convicted is large, for he gets a reputation for trickery and the fine to the sovereign is sixty pounds. And if the custom would permit it I would agree to a greater penalty, for he puts his adversary in danger of being convicted of forgery [*faussaire*]. And according to what I have heard said by learned men he should by law[1] have to suffer the same penalty as his adversary would have suffered if he were convicted. And since he only has to pay a fine, I agree that, if the plaintiff cannot prove the letter genuine by any of the above-mentioned methods, he will have a bad reputation and if he is a gentleman he must pay a fine of sixty pounds, and, if he is a commoner, the fine will be at the lord's discretion.

1077. Some people say that according to custom a commoner cannot be liable for a fine of more than sixty sous, or death, and a gentleman for more than sixty pounds, but it is not true, as you will see in several cases below.[2]

1078. If a person has assumed obligations in a writing sealed by the *bailli*, whether he is a gentleman or a commoner, there is no need for him to be summoned or given a court order to fulfill the obligations; instead, as soon as the sovereign sees the content of the writing, he can have it fulfilled without delay, and nothing the person who is obligated by it can say against it will be entertained, unless he alleges payment or extension of time. And if the person trying to use the letter denies payment or extension, because what is contained in the writing is more obvious than what is alleged against it, the writing and the sum mentioned in it are deposited with the sovereign, and then the sovereign will take cognizance of the allegation of payment or extension. And if the defendant cannot prove payment or extension, if he is a gentleman he must pay a fine of ten sous, and the deposit will be delivered to the creditor; and if he is a commoner the fine is only five sous. And if he proves payment, he will get the writing back, and the person accusing him will pay a fine for suing for payment of a debt already paid, and will be given a bad reputation. But because there is a danger that the truth will be concealed [*bestournés*] by false witnesses, the fine is only ten sous for a gentleman and five sous for a commoner, unless he already has a bad reputation. If he had already been convicted for such a case, or had a bad reputation, the fine would be at the lord's discretion, if he was a commoner, and if he was a gentleman the fine would be sixty pounds.

1079. The reason why the writing must be deposited with the judge, if the person trying to use the writing wants (whether it is a writing sealed by the sovereign or by the person assuming the obligation), even though the person who delivered the writing is alleging extension or payment, is that everyone should take back, when he pays, the writing in which he assumed the obligation.

1080. A defendant had undertaken in writing to pay a sum of money on
a day certain for a deposit made to his father, and afterwards, when the time
mentioned in the writing came, the creditor sued for his money at the assize
in Clermont, and the person assuming the obligation (who clearly did not
know the custom) answered that he was not compelled to pay because the
writing did not say that the debt was due for a deposit made to his father,
and he was ready to prove that his father had paid back the deposit, and he
had not known about that when he gave the writing. The creditor answered
this by saying that the defendant should not be permitted to allege a
payment dating from before the date of the writing in which he assumed
the obligation, and on this issue they requested a judgment.

1081. It was judged that he was too late to allege {his father's} payment
since he had assumed the obligation *after* the time he said the payment had
been made; and by this judgment you can see that an argument that alleges
payment before the time the obligation was made to make the payment is
not to be entertained, and for this reason you should take care what
obligations you assume and why.

1082. There are ways to contest a writing, in addition to those mentioned above: for example, when you see that the writing has been scraped[3]
and rewritten over the erasure, provided it represents a term of the agreement, for example, the name of the person giving the writing, or the price,
or the acknowledgment [*obligacion*], or the date. In the case of all these
terms, and others which would be dangerous depending on what the
writing said, if they are rewritten the writing could be declared invalid and
of no force.

1083. A writing torn all or part-way through is also invalid, if the tear
goes through the written part [*passe point de la letre*], for it is clear that the
writing is invalid which is not found complete and whole; and when the
agreements made in the writing have been fulfilled, and the person giving
the writing forgets to take it back, it is customary for the person having it to
tear it a bit, but not completely through, for two reasons. The first is so that
if the person who has paid the debt off wants the writing back, it can be
given back to him; for if it had been completely torn up or thrown out, and
he asked to have it, he would not have to believe it was destroyed if he did
not want to, so that he would not be satisfied until he had been given a quit-
claim writing [*letres d'aquit*]. The second reason is so that,—if the person

giving the writing forgets to take it back when he has fulfilled the obligation, and the person who received the payment dies,—the person into whose hands the writing falls, whether an heir or an executor, or some other kind of successor, cannot make use of it when they find a tear. And it is great honesty in a person who has such writings in his possession for him to tear them through in the manner described above; for if he were paid and they remained in one piece, the debt could be sued for again at a time when the payment could not be proved, and the debt would have to be paid twice.

1084. Some people think that if the seal is partly broken and the writing is brought to trial it is invalid. But when you want to exclude a writing because of a broken seal, half or more of the seal must be lost or broken; for if half or more is still whole and complete, you can prove by it what the rest of it is; but if more than half the seal is broken or lost, or so defaced that you cannot make out any letters or signs, the writing must be declared invalid.

1085. A writing may be contested in another way, for example when there is something written between the lines; for after the writing is written and sealed, you could write between the lines, and for this reason such a letter is invalid.

1086. The common practice, when you give a writing assuming an obligation for a debt or an agreement, is that you put in the writing that the person giving the writing is obligated to pay costs and expenses which the creditor may have if there is a default on the payment, or if the agreement is not adhered to, and the costs are to be declared by the holder of the writing, either sworn to or not sworn to.

1087. Now let's see,—when someone has obligated himself this way and the creditor wants costs and damages, either on his mere declaration or on his oath, according to what the writing says,—what you should do. Even though a person has obligated himself this way, you should examine the good faith. The person declaring or swearing to his damages must, before his oath, say how he incurred these damages and why, and if the judge sees that things may be as he said,—and even if he seems to have claimed a bit too much,—he should be believed on the strength of the written obligation. But if he were seen to swear or declare too exaggerated damages, so that you could see he was lying, because of greed, he would not be believed without proof; and if he had no proof, because he expected to be believed, an honest estimate of the damages should be made by the judge according his view of the dispute. And thus good faith can be preserved between the parties, for it would be a bad thing if someone, because he had not been paid ten pounds on the due date, could, on his simple declaration or oath, ask for a hundred pounds in damages.

1088. A person suing for damages because of an obligation assumed in a writing should say how he incurred the damages, as is said above; and he may have incurred damages in such a way that the person giving the writing does *not* have to pay them, for example, if he borrows at interest because of the default of the payment, without the leave of the debtor, or if he gave gifts to the judge or the officers to get paid, or if he did not ask for payment of the debt until he had incurred great damages, in order to hurt the debtor, of if he commenced a suit on things contained in the writing without calling on the debtor to be his warrantor:[4] for all these damages the debtor would not be held responsible. But the damages he *must* pay are the reasonable expenses of the creditor or his deputy in collecting the debt; and if the judge confiscates something of the debtor's on account of the debt, or puts guards on him, *these* costs have to be paid. Or if the plaintiff has brought the suit and the debtor is warned to come and defend and he does not appear, all the costs and expenses of the action must be paid by the debtor, and all the costs of seeking counsel and appointing an attorney to have the writing implemented. And when he alleges these kinds of good reasons to be paid his costs, they should be believed, unless what he says is too exaggerated, as was said above.

1089. When someone has incurred an obligation in writing to pay a debt or keep an agreement and he is sued for default, he must first be made to pay back the principal sum, and then the costs. And if there is a suit on costs after the principal has been paid back, the judge should retain the writing in his keeping, if he is asked to by the person who has paid the principal, for it would be dangerous for the writing to remain in the hands of the creditor because of the suit for costs once the principal had been paid. Nevertheless the judge should keep the writing and not give it back until the suit on costs has been tried and the judgment executed. And this applies to writings which speak of personal property or chattels, for if a writing speaks of real property or some agreement which is to last in perpetuity, we do not mean that the person who has it should have to give it into someone else's possession unless he wants to.

1090. When a writing is made on the subject of real property or some deal which concerns several people, it should be deposited in a safe place so that anyone needing it can obtain it for his purposes insofar as it involves him, by giving good security that he will bring it back, or by having it carried by the person who is keeping it for the parties, so that he always has it with him.

1091. Because several kinds of writings are made, some as warranty for real property and some for personal property and chattels, we will set out below two forms of writing, so that those who want to have a writing concerning real property or personal property or chattels can see the form in which the writing should be made; and first of all we will speak of the one which is to be used for real property.

1092. There are three kinds of writings: the first among gentlemen, sealed by their seals, for they can assume obligations by the testimony of their seals. The second kind of writing is that all gentlemen and commoners can have the lord under whom they have their residence, or the sovereign, make a record [*fere reconnoissance*] of their agreements and their deals. The third kind of writing is when you go before the ecclesiastical judge [*ordinaire*], as you should for dower, or a will, or for other suits, especially when the parties agree. Nevertheless, a writing issued by the ecclesiastical court counts as only one witness when there is a suit in the secular court; and also the writing of a secular judge counts as only one witness in an ecclesiastical court, except the king's writing, for that must be considered full and adequate testimony in both the ecclesiastical and the secular courts, and except the pope's writing, for that must count as full and adequate testimony in all ecclesiastical courts and secular courts, for no one on earth is the pope's sovereign.

1093. Just because I assume the obligation of paying costs and damages for someone on his mere declaration or oath, that does not mean that if his writing legally falls into the hands of someone else,—for example, if he dies and it passes to his heirs; or if he transfers the debt to someone else; or if he commits an offense, so that the writing passes into the hands of his lord,—I am required to believe the person who has acquired the writing. Nevertheless since I assume the obligation of paying costs and damages, they must be paid to a person proving them by honest proof.

1094. According to our custom, I cannot be sued for costs and damages for a default of payment unless I have obligated myself to pay them. So now let's set forth below the form for a writing on real property by a person who can and should own a seal:

"I, Pierre, of such-and-such a place, announce to all those who will see and hear this writing, that I, for my profit and in my great need, have sold to Jehan of such-and-such a place, and to his heirs for ever, such-and-such a real property, situated in such-and-such a place, bordering on one side such-and-such a property and on the other such-and-such a property,— and he should name all the parcels and whom they adjoin and by whom they are held, and what the dues are for each parcel, and then say:—for such a price in money and I have had and received it in good coin well counted and of the right denomination, and I have put it to my use, and I consider myself paid; and I have promised to warrantee the above deal for ever to the said Jehan and his heirs against all persons in such a way that if the said Jehan or his heirs have any labor [*peine*], costs, or damages by the failure of my warranty I would be required to reimburse to them all costs and damages they might honestly prove along with the above-mentioned warranty." And if he wants, he can make further obligations, saying: "Concerning which costs and damages the said Jehan and his heirs would be believed on their mere oath without more; and I have obligated myself and my heirs to keep this promise, and by all my property present and in the future, both real and personal, in whatever jurisdiction the said Jehan or his heirs (or whoever had possession of this letter) wanted to sue, for the costs and damages as well as for the principal, which property may be attached, sold, and the proceeds paid out with no delay until the costs and damages have been paid and I have made an honest warranty of the above said sale. And I have waived in this matter any help provided by law, by statute, by canon, or by local custom; any privilege as a crusader now and in the future; all indulgences granted or to be granted by the pope, the king, or other sovereign; {and I have waived} all delays which local custom may provide, any claim that I have not received the sum of money noted above, any claim that I have been deceived by half or more in the above-said deal, all exceptions, bars, defenses which may be raised in court or out of court by which or by any of which the above-mentioned deal may be undone, or prevented to the detriment of the said Jehan and his heirs, and {I have waived} any claim that I do not want to answer in court concerning this writing except before the lord under whom I am a resident; and {I have waived} specially the statute which declares that general waivers are invalid. And so that this may be a firm and stable matter, I, Pierre, have given to the said Jehan this writing sealed with my own seal. On such-and-such a month and year."

1095. If a writing is made concerning an exchange, it should begin this way: "I, Pierre, of such-and-such a place, announce to all those who will see and hear this writing, that I, for my profit and advantage, have made a pure exchange and transmutation [*transmutacion*] with Jehan of such-and-such a place, namely of the property which I owned lying in such-and-such a place,—and he should name the place and the neighboring properties and the dues which the property owes, and from which lord it is held; and when it is all specified he should say:—in exchange for such-and-such a property which the said Jehan has delivered to me, lying in such-and-such a place, held from such-and-such a lord, for such-and-such dues, and adjoining such-and-such properties." And when the whole exchange has been set out, the person handing over the land should obligate himself to warrantee what he gives in exchange, to him and his heirs for ever, and make waivers in the manner described above in the letter on selling real property, and then put the date.

1096. When the writing is for debt it should run as follows: "I, Pierre, of such-and-such a place, announce to all those who will see and hear this writing, that I owe Jehan of such-and-such a place twenty pounds in Paris money for the sale of a horse which he sold me, handed over and delivered, and which I have accepted." And if it is for other goods, he should name them and specify the quantity of goods, and the price and the kind of money; for a writing which says I owe money and does not mention what I owe it for bears a suspicion of bad faith; and when such a writing comes into court, the judge should find out the reason why this debt arose, before he has it paid. Therefore you should say in the writing what the debt is for, and then name the day when it is to be paid, and then obligate the person and his property and his heirs to pay, and then put down the waivers. The obligation and the renunciation are set out in the letter above, which speaks of the sale of real property. Then the date should be added, showing when the writing was made.

1097. When sales or exchanges or debts or agreements are made by persons who have no seal (or who have one but prefer to obtain a writing from the *bailli* because it is more certain and more quickly put into execution), {such persons} should come before the *bailli* and repeat the terms of the deal and their agreement, and then ask for a writing to be given them in the form in which letters from a *bailli* should be given; and then the writing should be made in the following form: "To all those who may see or hear the present writing, Philippe de Beaumanoir, *bailli* of Clermont, {sends} greetings. Let it be known that in our presence, requested for this purpose, Pierre of such-and-such a place and Jehan of such-and-such a place, legally recognized, of their own free will and for their profit, they had made such-and-such an exchange," and then the exchange must be set out and all the parcels specified. And if the agreements are for partitions, or divisions, or for settling various quarrels, or to dispose of [*ordenance*] their property, or for a marriage contract, everything they repeat and concerning which they have requested a writing should be put into the writing. And afterwards the person giving the writing must obligate himself to fulfill and warrantee the agreements; and then the waivers must be put in the writing, and the obligations and waivers are set out above in the writing which deals with the sale of real property; and then the date must be added to show the time when the writing was made.

1098. Other writings are often requested which involve only one person, and then the *bailli* should speak in the following manner: "To all those who may see or hear the present writing, so-and-so, *bailli* of Clermont, {sends} greetings. Let it be known that in our presence, requested for this purpose, Pierre of such-and-such a place admitted that he owed Jehan of such-and-such a place such-and-such a sum of money and for such-and-such a thing," and then all the agreements and the obligations should be set down, and then the waivers as they are listed above in the writing on the sale of real property. And when all this is written down the *bailli* should say: "And so that this matter will be firm and certain, I have affixed the seal of the *bailli* of Clermont to the present writing." And then the date should be added to show when this was done.

1099. We recognize a few cases where you can have a writing declared invalid even if the seal is authentic and admitted, and yet the person who sealed the writing should not be blamed: for example, when it happens that the writing attests that the parties were present in Clermont or in some other specific place and it is clear and evident that one or both of the parties was not in the district. In that case, the writing is invalid, for it is proved to be mendacious [*mençonjable*]. And the reason why the sealer should be found not responsible is that he may have been deceived, for example, when he does not know the persons in whose name the writing was made, and other persons, in bad faith, had the writing made and named themselves by the names and surnames of those mentioned in the writing, and said in bad faith that they were these persons. For example if Pierre said to Jehan: "Let's go have a writing made, saying you are Guillaume du Plessis, and let's say that Guillaume owes me a hundred pounds in Paris money, lent in cash [*sès prestés*] to be paid back at Christmas." The writing may because of such fraud be declared false and mendacious, without the fault of the sealer. But when such fraud can be discovered, all those defrauders who made the writing and those who consented to it must be punished as thieves.

1100. Speaking of fraud which may be committed in a writing, we remember another fraud which we saw at the time we were writing this book. For in Normandy there is a custom in some places that an inspection[5] of a piece of real property cannot be made among laypersons unless there are four knights there when the inspection is made, and who can testify to the manner in which it was made. And at one inspection only three knights turned up and, being favorable to the person permitting the inspection, they saw that it would be invalid if the fourth knight did not show up. And they thought up a stratagem to have the inspection accepted. They went to a highroad nearby, where a commoner was riding by on business; the knights asked him his name and he said Richard. Then the three knights said they were missing a knight for the inspection, and they would make him a knight if he would come with them to the inspection; and they told him to say he was a knight, and one of them tapped him on the shoulder and said "You are a knight." Then they went to where the inspection was to be made, and it was made. And when they went back to court after the inspection, it was declared valid, for the adverse party did not know about the fraud of the fourth knight until a long time after he had already lost his suit in a judgment. And when he found out, he went before the king and told him how he had been defrauded during the argument of his suit by the fraud of the knights, and the king had the truth discovered. And when he found out that it was true, he ordered the suit put back in the position it was in before the inspection had been made, so that the person who thought the suit was over had to permit the inspection over again; and the peasant [*paisans*] who played the knight was fined two hundred pounds, and the three knights who perpetrated the fraud were let off after much supplication with a fine of five hundred pounds; and if the person getting the inspection had been found to know about or consent to the fraud, he would have lost his suit and would not have escaped a fine. And we have put this case in our book as an example so that you will know that all agreements and all deals and all disputes in which a clear fraud or deception is discovered must be honestly redone, even if a judgment had been issued, because the jurors were not aware of the fraud or the deception when they gave the judgment; and fines which are exacted for frauds committed to disinherit others are at the discretion of the lord, as is clear from the fine the king imposed on the defrauders in the case described above.

1101. If an agreement is made, in writing of otherwise, to be paid or fulfilled within a month or within a year, you cannot compel the person making the agreement until the whole month or the whole year has passed. And if someone is supposed to do something on a day certain, you cannot find him in default nor ask a court to have him do the thing until the day has gone by, for it is not sure that he will default until the whole time has gone by, except concerning days for pleading, for there he has to announce his presence before midday or he will be in default. And except for what is promised by a certain hour, for example if you promise: "I will pay you ten pounds on Tuesday before prime,"[6] and prime passes, you can sue for the ten pounds.

1102. A certain man received good advice who recognized that his debtor was a bad payer, and because he saw that if he waited to have him summoned until the due date for the debt was past, the defendant would have to be given fifteen days before his court appearance because he was a gentleman, or because he lived on a free fief, and, before the due date for the debt arrived, had him summoned fourteen days before the due date, so that the court appearance fell on the day after the debt was due. And thus the creditor speeded up his suit, for since the due date for the debt had gone by the person summoned could not refuse to answer the complaint on it.

1103. Waivers put down in writing are valid, for if they were not you could raise many petty objections [*cavillacions*] against a writing. And when you waive making objection to a writing, or make special waivers one by one, the writing is stronger; and there are two kinds of waivers, one general and the other special. The general waiver is the one that says: "And in this matter I waive any objection that I could raise as a result of which what is said above could be undone or hindered." And the special objection says: "And I renounce in this matter any help provided by law, by statute, by canon, or by local custom; any privilege as a crusader now and in the future; all indulgences granted or to be granted by the pope, the king, or other sovereign; any claim that I have been deceived by half or more; any claim that I have not been paid what is contained in the writing; {and I waive} all delays which local custom may provide, and {I waive any claim} to the law that general waivers are invalid, and I waive the right to any claim that I was forced to do this by being kept in prison, or by intimidation; and I waive all exceptions claiming wrongs, usury, or fraud." And when each waiver that you want to make is thus specified, the general waiver is valid because it confirms what is said specially. And it could be valid for some waiver which had been forgotten, for example by saying: "And I waive any claim that I or another could raise by which the agreements mentioned above could be undone or hindered." For when there is only a general waiver in a writing, it does not waive the privilege given to crusaders, nor the defenses of coercion nor being deceived by sharp practice; but you cannot raise these defenses if you have waived them specially, except coercion, for nothing done by coercion is valid, as is said in the chapter on coercion and intimidation {Chapter 33}. It is also the king's right, notwithstanding any waiver that anyone has put into a writing, whether general or special, that the king may, if the debtor is joining the king's army or going on a crusade against the enemies of the faith, have the debt postponed [*ateminer*], according to the needs of those going with him, or who are going on some necessary business at his command, for what he wants to do should be held to be the law.[7] But this can be done by no one but him in the kingdom of France.

1104. If someone has assumed an obligation in writing, whether under his own seal or some other lord's, you should not suppose that the lord, whatever the obligation, stops enjoying and deriving benefits from what is held from him, unless he has waived it specially. For if he has permitted the agreement of his vassal, for example if he says he wants it and permits it, this means provided his own rights and those of others are safeguarded; and if he makes an agreement to warrantee it *as the lord*, he has still not waived his own right to confiscate the thing involved in the obligation, for example for his relief {inheritance tax}, if any were due, or on forfeiture, or for any of the other reasons why vassals' property can pass to their lords. But if he assumes an obligation to warrantee without more [*simplement*], then he cannot confiscate the thing whatever happens; for if he were not the lord, he could stand as a surety for the debtor if he wanted, and he is clearly doing so in this case. And for this reason lords should take care how they approve the obligations assumed by their vassals.

Here ends the chapter on writings.

Notes

1. Possibly Beaumanoir means here the Roman law taught in the universities. Louis Carolus-Barré conjectures that Beaumanoir may have studied Roman law at Orléans; Louis Carolus-Barré, "Origines, milieu familial et carrière de Philippe de Beaumanoir," *Actes du Colloque International Philippe de Beaumanoir et les Coutumes de Beauvaisis (1283—1983)*, ed. Philippe Bonnet-Laborderie (Beauvais: GEMOB, n.d. [c. 1985]) 28.

2. Beaumanoir discusses one such case in §1100.

3. A word written on parchment can be scraped or pumiced off and the parchment used over again.

4. On the obligation to call the warrantor before commencing a suit, see Chapter 34, §1072.

5. For inspections, see Chapter 9. For inspections in Normandy, see *L'ancienne coutume de Normandie*, ed. William Laurence de Gruchy (St. Helier, Jersey, British Channel Islands: Charles le Feuvre, 1881) 254.

6. Prime is at six in the morning, or earlier or later depending on the time of the year.

7. Cf. Justinian, *Institutes*, I. 2. 6: "Sed et quod principi placuit legis habet vigorem."

36. Safekeeping

Here begins the thirty-sixth chapter of this book which speaks of things deposited for safekeeping, how they should be kept and given back to those who deposited them, according to the law and custom of the district.

1105. Everything deposited for safekeeping [*baillies en garde*] must be given back to those who deposited it when they want it back, except in a few cases: for example, if a man has given into the safekeeping of another a sword or a knife, and he asks for it back when he seems to be wanting to strike someone with it, the person with whom he deposited it should not return it to him while he knows he has a wish to do someone harm; or if someone deposits something which is being sued for as taken or stolen, the deposited article should not be returned until the judge finds out who has the right to the thing.

1106. If something is deposited by several persons, the article should not be returned unless they are all present, or each sends a proper attorney with the person who wants to have the article back.

1107. If arms are deposited for safekeeping, and the person depositing them begins a war against the lord of the land, the arms should not be returned to him because of the evil that might ensue.

1108. If something is deposited with me for safekeeping and a person other than the depositor asks me for it because he says the article is his and he wants to prove this to me, I should not give him the article or accept the proof, for he must sue the person who deposited the article with me. And if I gave it to him without the order of the person who deposited it with me, the depositor would have an action against me for it, and I would be obliged to return it. But in this case there is a remedy, which is that if the depositor is out of the district and not expected to come back, the person asking for the article as being his can sue me in court, and the judge can and should listen to his arguments that the article is his; and if the judge sees that the arguments are good and compelling [*vives*] and well-proved, he must compel me to give the deposited article to him. But since I will be handing the thing over on orders from a judge, the judge must warrantee me and take good security from the person to whom he has had me hand over the article that, if the first depositor comes back, the article will be returned to the person with whom it was deposited, and in the same condition it was in when the depositor left the district.

1109. Pierre sued Jehan saying that, in the public market, he had given the said Jehan a horse to keep for him as a paid service [*par louier*], and he told him certain passwords [*enseignes*] by means of which he was to give it back to him or to someone else if he sent for it; and when he came back for his horse, he did not find it in the said Jehan's keeping, for which reason he requested the said Jehan to be compelled to return the horse which he had given him to keep. Jehan answered that he admitted that the said horse had been given to him to keep, and for money, and that Pierre, the depositor, had told him passwords by means of which he was to return the horse to the person giving him the password; and a man he did not know came to him and said to him: "Give me the horse on the authorization of these passwords," and he gave the proper passwords which Pierre had told him, for which reason he did not want to be liable for returning the horse because he had handed it over and delivered it according to the passwords which had been given him. Jehan was asked if he could prove that he had surrendered the horse according to the proper passwords which had been given him. He said no, except by his oath, and he wanted that to be enough. Pierre was asked under oath if he had sent for the horse using the passwords he had given the said Jehan; he said no. And they requested a judgment on the issue of whether the said Jehan would be allowed to clear himself by merely swearing an {exculpatory} oath, or whether he would have to make good the loss of the horse.

1110. It was judged that the said Jehan would not be allowed to clear himself by swearing an oath, but would have to pay Pierre what his horse was worth, and the jurors were persuaded to give this verdict for two reasons. The first reason was that a person's negligence does not excuse him for another's loss, and it was negligence for Jehan to agree to passwords {spoken} so loudly or so publicly that other persons besides the two of them could have heard and learned them, for it was perhaps because some thief had heard the passwords that the horse was lost. The second reason which persuaded the jurors was that a thing deposited for safekeeping, even if it is for money, must be returned to the depositor or at his indubitable [*certain*] orders. And by this judgment you can see that there is a danger in accepting things on deposit, for it could be that the depositor of the horse sent someone like a thief using the passwords he had mentioned, but with the intention of {himself} asking the person receiving the horse to give it back; and for this reason you should be careful how you accept a thing for deposit and how you return it.

IIII. Pierre sued Jehan saying that he had come to Jehan's house, where Jehan had been his landlord [*oste*]¹ before and he had stayed with him, and he asked him to put him up, along with his horse, as he had done before; and Jehan had told him he could not, since his hostelry was full of guests [*ostes*], but he would show him a good hostelry, and Pierre said to take him there. Then Jehan sent his servant [*vallet*] to take the said Pierre to Guillaume's house, who had a hostelry, and he put his horse in the stable and took some oats from the said Guillaume's house and gave them to the horse;² and when he left to go to the market, his horse was stolen from the stable; and when he returned he asked Guillaume, where his horse had been, to give him back his horse which he had lost at his hostelry; and Guillaume answered that he had not deposited the horse with him, and that he knew nothing about the horse, so that he should ask the said Jehan, who had recommended the hostelry and sent him there with his servant, to reimburse him for the loss of his horse. Jehan answered saying that he admitted to recommending the hostelry and he thought it was a good one, and he had had him taken there by his servant, but he did not want to be held liable for the loss of the horse; and on this issue they requested a judgment.

III2. It was judged that Jehan was not liable for the loss of the horse, for it is credible that, since he had formerly been Jehan's guest and been safely lodged in his hostelry, that Jehan would show him Guillaume's hostelry because he thought it was a good one and in good faith; and a judgment should lean towards the defendant's side when he alleges good faith in his defense.

III3. Now let's see, if Pierre had sued Guillaume for his horse, having left it at his hostelry in the manner described above, whether the said

Guillaume would have had to make good the loss of the horse. We say not, because it was not deposited for safekeeping, and, for landlords to be required to return things belonging to their guests and lost in their hostelries, the articles must have been deposited with them for safekeeping, and the guest had to say to the landlord: "Keep this for us"; for otherwise thieves staying in the hostelry could steal (or have members of their household or others steal) their horses or other things they took to the hostelry and then ask the landlord for them, and the landlords could be deceived, and this would not be reasonable. And even when something has been specially deposited with the landlord for safekeeping, there is a remedy for landlords so that they are not required to return things which are stolen, for example, when it is clear and well proved that the thieves stole something from the landlord as well as from the guests. But because the landlords could conceal something and say: "I have lost this article," to avoid loss and to steal things from their guests, this must be proved by signs of forced entry [*meson enfondree*], or by broken doors or chests where the things were kept, or a hue and cry after the offenders; and by such methods, when they appear to be clear and without sharp practice, landlords can defend themselves against their guests, when their things given into the landlord's safekeeping are stolen. Nevertheless the judge's duty is an important one here, for he must find out about the landlord's lifestyle and reputation; for if it is found to be a bad one, he should not be believed on the evidence of signs of forced entry or a broken chest, for he could have all that done in bad faith; and it is a good and proper thing for a judge to have a bad and suspect hostelry torn down [*despecier*], so that transients can safely go about their commerce and their business. And there is a great danger in lodging people out of a love of gain, if you do not do it honestly and unless you have a very good reputation; for it sometimes happens that those who enter a hostelry together murder each other or steal from each other, without the landlord's knowing a thing about it until the offenders have departed and he discovers the crime. In such a case you do not have anyone to disbelieve [*mescroire*] except the landlord: and many times landlords who are blameless have to suffer for this, for in such murky cases you have no one to suspect except the landlords who have lodged the guests; and nothing works as well for landlords in such a situation as finding them to be of good reputation by a thorough investigation.

Here ends the chapter on things deposited for safekeeping.

Notes

1. There is some murkiness in this paragraph because the Old French word *oste* means both "guest" and "landlord." The modern French word *hôte* still has this ambiguity.

2. It is not clear if it was the servant or the traveler who gave the oats to the horse; but this point does not seem to have been material in the decision.

37. Loans

Here begins the thirty-seventh chapter of this book which speaks of things lent and how the borrowers can make use of them.

1114. There is a great difference between things deposited for safekeeping and things lent; for a thing deposited for safekeeping may be lost in such a way that the person with whom it is deposited is not required to give it back: for example, if it is lost without the fault of the person who had it in his safekeeping, such as in a fire, or a flood, or if he lost it because of coercion, or to thieves, of because the thing perished of its own accord, for example it is a living thing which dies, or wine that goes bad, or wheat that spoils [*mesale*], or clothing that is destroyed by worms or age, or other things which can be destroyed without the fault of the person who accepted them into his safekeeping. But it is different with things lent, for however they are lost, whether by the fault of the borrower or without his fault, he must give back the thing which was lent or its value, if the thing is lost in such a way that it cannot be given back in its original condition. For if I have lent someone some wheat in good condition and he wants to give it back to me spoiled, I am not required to take it, even if it were the actual wheat I lent him which had spoiled in his granary, for something lent is something given to someone so that you get it back on the agreed-on due date; and until the due date, the borrower can do what he wants with it, and make a profit from it, but he cannot do this with something deposited in his safekeeping. And since you can do what you want with thing which is borrowed, it is right for you to give it back in as good a condition as it was when it was lent.

1115. If no due date is stated for the return of the borrowed article, the due date is whenever the lender asks for it back. Nevertheless he might ask for it back and yet the borrower would *not* be required to give it back right away, for example if someone lent me arms because I was in fear of my enemies, and he asked for them back when I was armed in a place where I could not get other arms: in such a case I would not be required to give them back to him until I was in a safe place where I could disarm myself. And it is the same with a horse, if it was lent to me to go to war, and someone asked for it back when I was riding it in a dangerous place. And by what we have said about arms and the horse you can understand about other things which are lent and the lender wants them back at a bad time. But unless there is a danger to life, or too great a danger of loss, I am supposed to give back what was lent to me without delay. Nevertheless if I do not want to give it back and the lender tries to get it back through the courts, he must have me summoned, and when I have appeared in court, he must ask for what he lent me; and if I admit that I have it, an order must be given to me to give the thing back in the way you do the debts which arise from deals or agreements, except for certain borrowed things which must be speeded up. For if I admit to a judge that I have someone's horse in my stable, or his tools which he uses for work, or some other thing which is currently in my possession,—except a debt of money,—I must be made to give it back immediately. But if I do not have the thing that was lent in my possession, then I must be given an order to return it, as was said above.

1116. A person lending must lend his own article and not someone else's; and the borrower should make sure the thing he is borrowing belongs to the lender, for if I borrow from someone something I know is not his, I cannot keep it. And if the owner sues me, it is true that I must have a day to seek my warrantor, since I received the thing from the hands of someone other than the owner. And if I cannot bring my warrantor, for example if he is dead or living in another district, a person proving the thing to be his can take it. And when Pierre has to give back to Jehan something lent to him by Guillaume, he should do it in court, for if he gave it to the said Jehan without a judge, even if he knew the thing was Jehan's, he would not be square with the said Guillaume who had lent it to him; nor would he if he gave it up in court of his own will without seeking his warrantor, for eveyone is obligated to his lender because of the loan, and he should give the thing back to the lender rather than anyone else; and when he has given the thing back, the borrower is no longer obligated [*delivres*]. And if someone else has a right to it, he should sue for it; for if someone sues me for something which another person lent me, and I give the thing back to the person who lent it to me, I should be free of obligation, and I am doing no wrong to anyone.

1117. We have said above that everyone is supposed to give back a borrowed article as whole and sound as when it was borrowed, and it is true. Nevertheless, in the case of some borrowed things the borrower is not required to give them back in as good a shape as they were in when he borrowed them: for example if someone lends me a horse to plow or to ride and I give it back thinner and more tired [*travaillié*] than it was when I borrowed it, I am not required to make any reimbursement unless I want to, since I am giving it back without its having suffered death or injury; and we also say the same thing about horses which are rented. But if the horse dies or is injured while in the possession of the person who borrowed it, he must make up the loss. And also if someone lends me some clothes for me to wear, and he leaves them in my possession so long that they wear out from old age, I am only required to give back the clothes as they are when they are asked for. For since such things wear out from being worn, or from old age, it must be supposed that the lender (who knew they would wear out) liked the person he lent them to so much that he gave him the use of the clothes for as long as he wanted; and if he took so long to ask for them back that they wore out, he can only ask for them back in their current condition. And also if someone lends a *mui* of wheat or a *mui* of rye or oats or wine which is worth forty sous on the date it is lent and then, when the lender wants it back, it is only worth twenty or thirty sous, he cannot ask the borrower for what he lost during the loan period. For if someone lends me grain or wine, I am not required to give back more grain or wine than was lent to me; and you should not take any notice of whether it goes up or down on the market, but only of the thing that was lent. Nevertheless if someone borrows [*preste*] grain or wine or clothes or horses or any other things from me, and I ask the borrower for them back and he will not or cannot give them back, and if the thing borrowed then loses value afterwards for me because it was not given back to me when I asked for it, I can rightly sue for the loss caused by the deterioration of the thing I lent from then on, for I should not have a loss because someone will not give me back what I lent, and if it were otherwise the bad payers would often benefit from their sharp practice. For example, if I lent someone my wheat when the price was high and asked for it back when the price was still high, and the borrower would not give it back, but took a delay without my giving him an extension, and against my will, and during this delay (and my suit to get back what I had lent him) wheat dropped in price because of the approaching harvest [*aoust*], or for some other reason, in that case the borrower would have to give me back my wheat to the value of what it was worth when I asked for it. But it would be different if I did not ask for my wheat back before the summer [*le bon temps*], for then I could not sue him to make me any restitution for the loss.

1118. Lenders should take care to take back something lent when the borrower offers to give it back; for if they refuse and the thing deteriorates after the offer to give it back, the borrower is not required to make any restitution for the deterioration: for example, if someone lends me a *mui* of wheat and it is worth forty sous on the day it is lent, but I have no agreement to give back forty sous for the *mui* of wheat, and afterwards I watch for a good moment to pay it back, and offer him a *mui* of wheat of as good quality as was lent to me, even though it is worth only twenty sous per *mui* when I offer to give it back, the lender cannot refuse. And if he refuses or delays taking it, because it is worth less in the market than it was when he lent it to me, and during this time wheat goes up in price until it is worth as much as or more than it was worth when I borrowed it, I am not required to give back a *mui* of wheat, but only as much as my offer was worth on the day and at the time I offered to give it back, for it would be a bad thing if I suffered loss because the borrower did not want to take my payment. But because there could be fraud or trickery in asking for what I was lent, or in offering to make payment,—for example, if I asked someone for what I lent him in an inconvenient place for him to pay, because I did not want him to pay me, for example if I said to him in passing: "Dear sir, pay me," and I did not wait for his answer, or if I asked him at a time when I saw that he would be too busy to deal with me, or in some other bad-faith manner,—a borrower could be excused for not responding to such demands, for when you ask to be paid a debt, or you ask for the thing you have lent, you should ask for it in front of good people, without seeking out an inconvenient place, or else ask for it in court. And there is no difference between a debt for an honest deal and for something borrowed, for to the borrower a thing borrowed is a debt.

1119. You should make use of borrowed articles for the purpose they were borrowed for and not otherwise; for if I borrow a horse to ride, I should not use it for plowing without the leave of the lender, or if someone lent me something for my use, I should not lend it to someone else, but should retain control of the thing borrowed so that I can give it back when the lender asks for it. And when someone does not treat a borrowed article as he should and a loss results, the borrower should make it up to the lender.

1120. If someone lends me something and it is stipulated that I will use it for a certain task, and give it back on a given day, and I do something other than what was agreed on with the thing I borrowed, the lender is not required to wait until the due date for giving the thing back, since I am using the thing for something other than what I promised when I borrowed it: for example, if someone lends me a horse to pull my plow until All Saints Day, and when I have the horse I do not use it for plowing but ride it around, in this and similar cases the lender is not required to wait until All Saints Day, because I am using the thing loaned in a different way from what I promised when I borrowed it. For it often happens that you lend your friend some article to have some particular thing done, but you would not lend it to him for him to do anything except what was agreed on when you lent it. And for this reason we have said that you should use a thing which you borrow in the manner that was explained to the lender when it was borrowed; and what we have said about things borrowed we say also about things rented out, for nothing rented should be put to any other use than what it was rented for; and if you use it for something else, and there is a loss, you must make up the loss to the person renting it to you.

1121. Not everything can be lent, for no one should lend something which would do more harm than good to the borrower: for example, if someone wanted to get into a fight and I lent him my arms or my sword to carry out his crazy wishes, I would harm him more than I helped him, for he could do something stupid with the help of what I lent him, and I would not be without liability myself if it were proved against me that I had knowingly lent him something for him to commit an offense with it [*mal fere*]. And I must also not lend or give wine to a drunken man, nor a club to a madman, and to put it briefly no one should give or lend or rent anything, or give help or comfort, to anyone against God or in contravention of good morality; and if someone knowingly does so and it turns out badly for him [*il l'en mesavient*], it serves him right.

Here ends the chapter on things lent.

38. Rentals

Here begins the thirty-eighth chapter of this book which speaks of things rented or farmed out, and things taken as security.

1122. We have spoken of things deposited for safekeeping, and then of things borrowed; now it is right for us to speak a little and briefly of things rented out for money, for there are several differences between things rented out for money and those which are deposited for safekeeping or borrowed, because of the financial gain which the person who rents the things out is supposed to derive; for a person who deposits things for safekeeping, or who lends without interest, can only ask to have back what he deposited or lent, and nothing more; but a person who rents something for money can ask for it back when the due date comes, and can also ask for the rental money along with it.

1123. Rentals are made in various ways, for some things are rented up to a certain due date and other things are rented by the day, and yet others in order to perform a given task, without naming a day or due date for the return. Yet other things are rented on a condition: and you should know that rented articles should be used according to what was agreed on when they were rented. Nevertheless, in some situations you can use what you rented in a different way than was agreed on when it was rented: for example if I rent a house intending to live in it until a certain time, and I am prevented by something from being able to live there, or from wanting to, I am not thereby prevented from giving possession of the house to someone else, and making a profit, until the due date. Nevertheless I cannot put in the house so great a lord that the rented property will be injured by his overuse [*surfet*], unless I give a damage deposit when I rent it. And also if I have rented a horse to do some plowing until All Saints Day, I may lend it or rent it to my neighbor. But with respect to all rented articles, if the renter transfers possession of them, he is still obligated to the person he rented them from, and must give back the article and pay for damages if there are any, and pay the agreed-on rent.

1124. When something is rented up to a certain due date, as soon as the day has come, the rented article must be returned along with the rent money; and if the renter [*cil qui la loua*] keeps it after the due date against the will of the owner, the owner [*cil qui la chose loua*]¹ can sue in novel disseisin,² even though the renter has had the article in his possession for more than a year or two or longer because of the rental; but the owner wanting to sue must do so within a year after the due date, and he must have asked for the article back before a judge or before good people; and then if the renter will not give the thing back, the owner can sue in the manner described above, for the renter cannot use as a defense the time during which he rented the article; and if the plaintiff wishes, he can sue him by methods other than novel disseisin, asking for the thing the renter holds to be restored to its owner.

1125. If someone rents a house or other thing up to a certain due date, and it comes about that the due date passes but the owner says nothing, and the renter continues to use the thing as he did when the rental was in force, and later the owner asks for the thing and for the rent since the due date, we believe this is not an improper demand, for since both parties said nothing, it is clear that the rental continued at the consent of both of them, especially since the renter continued to use the thing after the due date, as if it were rented and just as he had before. And it sometimes happens that the owner of a house or other things rents them out until a certain due date, and when the due date comes, he is out of the district or busy, or the renter is, so that they cannot begin a new rental agreement. Nevertheless, you should maintain good faith. And the good faith is that if the renter remains in the house after the due date, he must pay for his extra stay; and if he wants to be paid up, he should leave the house when the due date comes. And if, after each one has consented for a while since the end of the agreement (one of them to use the rented thing and the other to permit it) the owner wants the thing back, the person remaining in the house must be given a due date for being out of the house, according to his condition, either eight days or fifteen,³ according to the opinion of the judge as to what is fair, for it would be a bad thing if those who live in other people's houses were given so little time to move out that they could not get their belongings out before they had to leave.

1126. Rental of things by the day lasts only as long as both parties consent to the rental, for the owner can ask for his thing back as soon as he likes along with the rent money for the number of days the thing has been retained. And also the renter can give the thing back whenever he wants by paying for the days' rental. Nevertheless as soon as the day has begun, be it ever so little, if the renter wants to give it back he must pay the entire day's rental, whether he returns the thing at prime[4] or at vespers, for as soon as the day has begun the renter has the responsibility for the whole day. For if he has rented out my horse by the day, I cannot ask for it back at prime or terce, or until the whole day is over. If I want it back, I must ask the renter to bring it back to me when the day is over, or so early in the morning that I can use it for the whole day on the day he brings it back, such as at sunrise or before. And what we have said about the horse applies to other things which are rented by the day.

1127. If a person renting something by the day keeps it against the owner's wishes and after he has asked to have his thing back with the proper rent, with the result that the owner has to sue to get the thing back, not only is the renter required to give the rental costs for the days at the rate agreed on when he had the thing with the owner's consent, but also he is obliged to pay the damages of the owner during the time it was held against his will. For it is well known that seasons are not uniform as far as rentals are concerned: for example, a cart [*voiture*] should be rented for more money in August, or during the wine harvest, or in March than in any other season.[5] And it is not reasonable if a renter has rented someone's cart by the week or the day, and the owner wants it back to make money with it because of the approaching seed-time or harvest, if the renter who had it before keeps it during March and August against the will of the owner; and it is not right for him to pay for it at the rate at which he rented it previously, for then he would be unjustly enriched [*gaaigneroit il par fere tort*], and you should know that a person is acting wrongfully when he retains someone else's property against his will and without a good reason to retain it, such as if he had rented it up to a certain due date, or on a lease, or for payment in kind [*par ferme*], or for many other similar reasons for having someone else's possession, even though they are the owners.

1128. Certain things are rented out in a different way, such as for the accomplishment of a certain task, for example if I rent a horse to ride from Clermont to Paris. And when this kind of a rental is made, you should know that you must use the thing as agreed, for if someone rents a horse to ride to Paris, he should not ride it beyond Paris, and should not take it by some other longer or more difficult road than the one agreed on from Clermont to Paris. Nevertheless it sometimes happens that out of necessity you cannot keep such agreements, for example, if the person who intended to go to Paris heard some news after he started out which made him have to go quickly through Paris or take a different road, so that he was away for longer than he thought and went further than he expected; in such a case he should be excused because of the unexpected event, but in any case pay any damages to the owner of the horse, as a result of the longer time and the greater length of the journey. And what we have said about a horse rented to make a certain trip can be applied to other things rented to perform other specified tasks.

1129. Another kind of rental is by condition, for example if I said to someone: "I rent you my house for ten pounds until Saint John's Day," on condition I have his house for a hundred sous until the said day, if he will not give it to me for the hundred sous I am not required to rent him my house for the ten pounds. And what we say about the house we also say about all rentals and agreements and deals which are conditional, namely that you must fulfill the condition or the agreement has no force.

1130. When someone rents or bargains [*marcheande*] or agrees to something conditionally, it is the choice of the person who must peform the condition either to perform or not, so that if he wants to perform, then the deal or the agreement or the rental must be enforced; and if he does not want to fulfill the condition, he cannot be made to, unless he obligated himself or agreed to fulfill it. For example, if I rent or lend a horse to someone on condition that he lends me ten pounds until a certain due date, and makes an agrement to pay them to me, in that and similar cases he is required to perform the condition. For if he did not want to take my horse as said above, he is still obligated to lend me the ten pounds since it is not my fault he does not take the horse.

1131. However I hold my house, whether in fief or in villeinage, if someone lives in it for rent and he does not pay me my rent when it is due, I can take his belongings in my house in lieu of rent, whatever obligations he may have made on behalf of or to anyone else, except for seizure by the lord from whom I hold my house. For if the house, or the belongings of the person owing me rent, are seized by my overlord, I must ensure that the seizure is ended before I touch the stuff, or require him to pay me what he owes me because of the rental; and if the person living in my house wants to vacate the premises before the due date or after the due date, whether openly or secretly, I can attach or have attached whichever of his possessions I want, as long as they are in my house. But if they are taken out before I can have the attachment made on any other authority than my own,[6] I have no authority to attach anything and I would have to give the things back and pay a fine; instead I would have to sue for my rent before the lord of the person owing it to me, or have recourse to my sureties if I had any.

1132. Those who rent property to be held by themselves and their heirs for life or for ever [*a eritage*], are required to maintain the rented property, if they can, in as good a condition as it was in when they rented it, or at least to the point where it is worth the rental. And if they try to run it down, by demolishing houses, or cutting down fruit-bearing trees, or cutting down woods or vineyards, the lord who rented it out is not obliged to permit it, for he could suffer loss, since the renter might abandon the property when it was run down instead of paying the quit-rent [*cens*] or the rent money; but a tenant holding it without running it down can do whatever he wants with it to his own advantage. And sometimes those who take property for quit-rent [*cens*] or rental for ever give another piece of land as security [*contreacens*], so that if the persons who are taking the property for quit-rent or rent want to leave it because it seems too dear or because the property is run down, the person who transferred it to them can have recourse to the security property [*contreacens*] and the abandoned property in the condition it was in when abandoned.[7] And in this case we say that since the person is transferring the property for a quit-rent or rent on the security of the other piece of land called a *contreacens*, he cannot forbid his tenant who took the land for quit-rent or rent to benefit from the land in any manner, except by causing waste or injury; for I am not permitted to allow waste or injury even to my own property for a bad reason, since it would cause loss to the lords from whom I hold the things, and it would be against the public good.[8] And just as you should punish a person who knowingly burns another person's house, so you should if he burns his own house intending to burn his neighbor's close by; for some people have such a grudge and are so wicked that they would try to do harm to themselves in order to do harm to others; and for this reason they should not be excused just because they do harm to themselves, but should be judged according to their intent to harm others, and this intention can be known by their admission or by proven threats.[9]

1133. Concerning what we said about giving *contreacens* for property taken for quit-rent or rent, you cannot give this kind of security according to the current custom, except by permission of the lords from whom the land you want to give in security is held, because land which is given as security cannot be sold or given or left in a will, nor taken from the possession of the person who gave it as security unless the security hold on it is lifted; that is to say that if the quit-rent or rental money is not paid, the person who transferred the property held for quit-rent or rent can have recourse to what was given in security [*contreacens*] whoever has possession of it; and thus lords often lost their sales tax because the owners could not find a buyer for land encumbered as the security described above is, and for this reason there is a restraint on doing this any longer without the agreement of the lords. And if someone does it without the lord's knowledge, the lord can make a seizure of the land until this encumbrance as security is removed; and then the person who received it as security for the thing he transferred for quit-rent or rent can sue the person who cannot warrantee his security [*contreacens*], to have him compensate [*garantisse*] him or give him some other adequate security. And if the person taking the property for quit-rent or rent cannot persuade the lord to permit the use of the land as security, and he can find no other security, the person transferring to him the land for quit-rent or rent can ask to get it back, even though the person who received it says he will pay him faithfully [*mout bien*], for no one is obliged to give his property to anyone without security unless he wants to; and since the other man cannot give him the agreed-on security, the deal should not be enforced.

1134. The custom for transferring arable land or vineyards or other property which must be cultivated is that the person taking the land for rent or payment in kind [*a ferme*] must give security that he will pay the rent-money or the share of the crop before he takes for himself [*lieve*] the first of the crops, even though this condition was not discussed in the rental agreement [*ou marchié du louage*]. For I may transfer my empty fields into which the taker must put labor and expenses, without asking for security, until the crops are beginning to grow [*aparans*], for it is a security when the person taking the land puts somethinhg into it every day by improving the land until it is time to take in the crop. But before he vacates the land, he must give me security [*me doit fere seür*] if I ask for it; and if he does not want to, and he has the power to do so, I can make a seizure of the crop until I have been paid my rent money, including any arrears, and until I have security for the future, if the deal is for him to hold it for a longer time. But it would be different if he had no power to give security: for example, if he was from another district so that he could not procure any sureties, or if he is poor, so that no one wants to stand surety for him: in such a case he will be able to keep the deal, but things must be put into safe hands so that the person transferring the land for rent is first paid for his rental, and afterwards the person who made the deal has the rest for his work. And if the person transferring repents of his deal because he thinks he gave it for too low a price, and he wants to cancel the deal, and pretends that it is because the taker cannot give him any security, this argument will not help him as long as the taker puts sufficient labor into the thing and is agreeable to leaving the fruits [*issues*] in safe hands until the owner has had his full rent; for otherwise poor men and strangers would often lose the deals they took for rent, in which they earn their living by their work.

1135. Any person who takes something for rent, or accepts it into his safekeeping for money, and afterwards loses the thing by negligence or not keeping it safely, is not excused merely by paying the damages, like a person who accepts something into safekeeping for no payment; instead he is required to give the thing back along with the rental payment; for the money he took to keep the thing safe obligates him to give back the thing deposited in his safekeeping. Nevertheless, there is an exception for things seized by the lord, for however someone else's thing came into my possession, if the lord forces me to give it up or attaches it without any fault of mine, the person who deposited it with me must recover it from the lord who confiscated it or attached it, and he cannot sue me unless the attachment or confiscation was because of me. Nevertheless, it might happen that someone could in bad faith have such a thing confiscated or attached by his lord, and when the owner asked the lord for it, the lord could dishonestly say: "I do not have to answer to you for anything, because I took the thing from a person in my jurisdiction." But this reply is improper [*n'a pas lieu*], for although the lord has jurisdiction on his land and the power to confiscate things for judicial reasons [*par reson de justice*], if someone comes before him and says the confiscated article belongs to him, and wants to prove it is his, the lord should give it back to him if he proves it to be his (unless he can show that he holds it for good reason from the person asking for it) for no one should lose his belongings because of someone else's offense unless he has obligated himself as a surety or as a partner or in some other manner.

1136. The transfer of property for rent or as security cannot be permitted, as we have said elsewhere, when the lords can suffer loss because of it, and such transfers are also not permitted if they are done against God or good reputation [*bonne renomee*]. Instead, all those who enter into such rentals or security agreements should be severely punished: for example, if someone rents out or pledges as security holy objects which are consecrated or dedicated to the service of God, for if holy things are given out for rent it is simony. But if someone has chalices or vestments or other things dedicated to the service of God, he can certainly lend them or give them to a place where God is served, and nowhere else. And if a lord finds such a thing on his lands in the hands of a layman, which has been given as security or in some other improper [*leide*] manner, he should confiscate them and put them back in the holy place where they came from. And if he cannot discover where they came from, he should put them in some place belonging to Holy Church, and a person lending something on their security should lose what he lent. And we also think that he is not being dealt with unjustly if he is made to pay a fine, for no layperson should lend anything on such security. And if clerks or churches act towards each other as they should not in this matter, we do not wish to speak of that, since it is not the purview of the secular courts to speak of the punishment [*venjance*], but that of Our Lord and their ecclesiastical judges [*ordinaires*].

1137. We have heard from the jurists [*seigneurs de lois*] that a bad custom used to be current, for it used to happen that a man would hire a woman until a certain due date for a certain fee which he gave her to sin with him or with someone else, and he made the woman swear or promise to keep this agreement. And some people hired champions on the condition they had to fight for them in all their disputes, good or bad. And Jews and heretics sometimes gave money to Christians on the condition that they not enter Holy Church before a date which was agreed between them, and made them swear; and at that time they were compelled by secular judges to keep these agreements and everything they had sworn to do. But thanks be to God such bad customs are no longer current, indeed if such a hiring were made nowadays those who gave money for such things would be severely punished, both physically and by having to pay fines. And if someone makes this kind of agreement by mistake, he is not obliged to fulfill the oath, even if he has accepted the money. And it is better, if he has accepted money to do these improper things, for him to act according to the advice of Holy Church, and give the money back to the person from whom he received it. And nevertheless, if it is a woman who took money to sin, we agree that if she is poor she can keep the money for her maintenance without being forced to keep her side of the agreement; for a person hiring a woman thus should suffer this loss and more. And to speak briefly, a deal or an agreement, or a loan, or the giving of security,[10] or a rental, or a promise or an oath which is given against God or against morality is not to be enforced; and a person refraining from the evil he swore to do is not a perjurer, for the repentance for the act which he fails to do for the love of Our Lord restores him to the state he was in before he made the oath, provided he works through Holy Church concerning his rash oath; and no one should commit an act of evil to perform what he swore to do by his rash oath.

1138. Any time that lords hold something in their possession for someone else,—for example the possessions of minor children, or the possessions of someone who has gone away because he owed too much, or because of debts owed to the lord himself, or for various other reasons which necessitate the lord's selling or renting out what he holds,—the sale or rental must be made to those who want to give the most and at auction [*par renchierissemens*]; and when the things are sold or rented, time must be given for other people to redeem the deal, if they see their advantage in so doing. And the time for the auction should be according to the nature of the things, for if it is a wood which is for sale, the auction period should be longer that if it were wheat or wine or oats; and for this reason there are no set times except what is set by an honest judge according to the nature of the things. And the lord should not keep the things he needs to sell or rent for other people, for {even} if he bought them for the highest price, there would be a presumption against him that he had obtained them for less, and those who had owned the things could more easily sue him, if *their* things were sold at too low a price, or rented for too little money, and other people's things were not. For if something is sold by a judge to the person who offers the most, the judge cannot be reproached; but when the judge keeps things for himself, if he declares that higher bids will be accepted, you do not dare to offer more for the thing, as you might if you were not bidding against a judge; and for this reason no one should be able to keep things which he is supposed to sell, or which were given into his safekeeping, without the consent of the owner of the thing.

1139. You should know that there is no rental without a deal between the parties and an agreement, for one party agrees to hand the thing over for the rent money, and the other the rent money for the thing; and all rented articles must be handled according to the way they were customarily handled if they were rented before. And if they have never been rented before, they must be handled according to the customary handling of other similar things which have been rented near there in the past. For just as things are not of the same nature, but different, there are different customs in different places: for example, if someone rents a mill until a certain date or for several years, the custom is that the renter must provide pegs [*chevilles*], spindles [*fuseaux*], vanes [*aubes*], and other small items, without diminishing the rent; but if the millstones [*mueles*] or the great beams [*gros merriens*] fail, or the building collapses [*font*] by no fault of the renter, the owner of the mill must repair it, even though no mention was made of it at the making of the agreement, because that is the custom concerning mills.

1140. If someone rents a fish reservoir to fish in up to a certain date, this does not mean that he can break the banks and empty the reservoir unless this was specially agreed to in the deal, but he can fish with all sorts of other equipment [*engiens*] which is normally used to catch fish.

1141. If someone rents a winepress, the owner must furnish all the things which are needed for a working winepress. And if the renter by using excessive force breaks or shatters or loses any of the things which belong to a winepress, he must pay for the damage, whether it is the great beam [*gros fust*] or the other things. And because there could be a big argument about the great beam (since the renter could claim that it had not been shattered by his efforts, but because it was worn out or worm-eaten) you have to investigate such a case very thoroughly, for if you find the beam of the press old or wormeaten, and the renter was only using as many men as were customarily used to work the press, you should not make him pay for the damages; instead his rent should be reduced to compensate for the time he is idle. And the same is true of the miller when his mill must remain idle because of repairs which the owner of the mill should be making. But if the person who rented the mill put four or five or six men to work the press, where only two or three were normally used, or the miller carelessly let his mill grind empty, so that the beam of the winepress broke or the millstone shattered or the beam broke, in that case the people who rented the winepress or the mill must pay the damages to the owners, and their rent which they promised would not be reduced since the winepress or the mill stood idle because of their excessive force. And for this reason it is necessary for those who rent other people's things to use the rented articles as they should, for otherwise they may suffer loss as is explained above.

1142. The custom concerning the rental of houses is that the renter need not unless he wishes spend anything on the maintenance of the house; instead the owner who receives the rent should take care of it, so that the renter can make use of the house he has rented. And if the house should suddenly threaten to fall down, or it is in danger if it is not immediately repaired, or the roof fails [*ele se decuevre*] so that it rains in, and the owner is too far away to be informed of the problem with his house, the person living there should show the need to a judge, or good folk if he cannot obtain a judge, and should with their knowledge incur the costs for the good of the house. And if he acts in this manner, what he pays out should be deducted from the rent. And if he had paid the rent or did not owe as much as the repairs cost, the house owner is required to reimburse what he spent, and be grateful to him, for it sometimes happens that repairs to a house costing twenty sous would cost ten pounds if they were not attended to immediately. Nevertheless the person living in the house is not required to pay out anything unless he wants, however much damage is incurred. But he must, as soon as he can, report the danger to the house to the owner, and if he does not do so, so as to cause him loss, and secretly removes all his things from the house because of the danger, since he doesn't mind if the house falls down, because then he can say he is not obliged to pay the rent, such sharp practice should not avail him; instead if you see such bad faith, he should be made to pay all the rent, or pay for all the damage caused by his sharp practice, for no sharp practice should be to the advantage of the person knowingly doing it.

1143. Those who own houses or vineyards or pastures or other property must hand them over to the renters in such a way that the latter can make good use of them for the purpose for which they were rented. And if the owners hesitate, for example if they think better of the deal, they are not at the end of their obligation, for they must be compelled by a court to deliver the things to the renters. And if some or all of the rental period passes during the pendency of the suit, because the owner would not deliver the things on time, the renters may sue for all the profits [*pourfis*] they might have gained if the rented articles had been delivered to them according to the agreement, because it was not their fault and not because of their default that the things were not delivered to them.

1144. And we also say that if someone rents houses, vineyards, pastures, or other property until a certain date, and afterwards the person who is going to be the renter changes his mind and does not want to go through with the rental deal, the owner can, if he wants, leave the property empty and sue {the defaulter} for the rent which was agreed on. And if he wants, he can have the judge put the thing in safe hands, and take the income over and above the costs; and if there is not as much profit as the cost of the rental, he can sue the person who rented it for the extra. But if he keeps possession of the thing he rented, when he sees that the person who made the deal does not want to take it, he cannot later sue for the rent or the damages, for since he kept possession of it when someone else should have been holding it, it is clear that he consented to the breaking of the agreement, unless he did so with the consent of the person who should have gone through with the deal; for example if he had said: "Take your profit from what I rented from you and, if you make a loss, so that it is not worth as much to you as I promised to pay you in rent, I will take your word for how much you lost," in such a case he could keep the thing in his possession and then sue for the damages if there were any; and his estimate of the damages would be believed on his oath. And by the above you can see that all kinds of rentals, whether of real or personal property, should be dealt with according to what was agreed on.

Here ends the chapter on property rented or given as security.

Notes

1. The verb *louer* in Old French, like its translation "rent" in English, refers to the action of both parties to the transaction. You can rent something from someone, and he also rents the thing to you. To keep these two notions straight, I have referred to the "owner" and the "renter." The latter term always means the person who temporarily gets the article and pays money to the owner.
2. For novel disseisin, see Chapter 32.

3. Eight days is the time allowed for commoners to pay debts, and fifteen is for gentlemen.

4. Prime is about six in the morning, and vespers is in the evening. Terce is about nine in the morning. The times might vary with the time of the year.

5. August is harvesttime, and March is the time for sowing seed.

6. Beaumanoir seems to imply that the person owning the house has authority without more to attach property actually in the house.

7. Something seems to be missing from this sentence, possibly the notion that the owner of the abandoned property can use the security property to restore the losses to his own property. But the text does not say this precisely.

8. A modern formulation might be: "against public policy."

9. Threats constitute grounds for a presumption. See §1158.

10. The word *engagement*, here translated "security," could mean "lease."

39. Proofs

Here begins the thirty-ninth chapter of this book which speaks of proofs and of excluding witnesses; and of alibis and of the danger in threats, and how to speak against witnesses and which cases may be put to proof.

1145. It is true that there are several manners of proof, by which or by one of which it is enough that those who have the burden of proof can prove their allegations [*entencion*]. And for this reason, we will, in this chapter, discuss various manners of proof and the particular power which each manner has, and when the time has come to make a proof and how you can and should contest witnesses.

1146. It is our opinion, according to our custom, that there are eight manners of proof; the first is when a person who is being questioned admits [*connoist*] what is being asked, whether he admits it without {first} denying it or after he has denied it, and this is the best and clearest proof of all and the least costly.

1147. The second manner of proof is by a writing, for example, when someone has made an obligation in writing [*s'est obligés par letres*] and the person who did so denies his obligation: it is only necessary to prove it by the written contract, unless the person who denies it recites against the writing sufficient reason by which the writing is made invalid, and we speak at some length about this manner of proof in the chapter which speaks of written obligations {Chapter 35}.

1148. The third manner of proof is by wager of battle, but this manner of proof should not be accepted except in cases where wagers are acceptable; and we speak about this manner of proof and of the cases when such a proof should be accepted in the chapter on appeals {Chapter 61}. And a person who undertakes to use this manner of proof should be very wary, for it is the most dangerous of all the manners of proof.

1149. The fourth manner of proof is by witnesses, for example, when something is denied and the plaintiff offers to prove it by witnesses. And in this proof at least two honest witnesses are required, and who agree with each other [*s'entresievent*] without variation on the questions which are put to them after they have sworn the oath. And how they should be examined we shall explain below in the chapter after this one.

1150. The fifth manner of proof is by recall from memory [*recort*], for example, when there is some disagreement between the parties about what was pleaded in court before the jurors, for such kinds of disagreement must be settled by the jurors' recall from memory. And in brief no manner of proof can be accepted in any case which must be settled by memory *except* the proof of recall from memory, even if the parties want to resort to some other kind of proof. And the cases which should be settled by memory are, as we have said, concerning disagreements which arise from things which have been pleaded before the jurors. And when a judgment has been made and it is understood differently by the parties, it should be recalled from memory [*estre recordés*] by those who made the judgment.

1151. No one can recall from memory [*recorder*] concerning a dispute which was pleaded in court except those who can make the judgment {the jurors}. And when they recall something from memory, they are not subject to appeal against their memory, for if they are recalling a judgment that was made, the time for appeal lapsed when nothing was said against the judgment. And if a recall from memory is being made of proceedings in a dispute which has not yet come to judgment, there is no appeal until the judgment has been made.

1152. We have said that what is done before the men who can and should judge {the jurors} should be proved by their recall from memory and not otherwise, and that no one in such a case can say what he remembers except the jurors, and this is true. But there are various cases which can and should be proved by recourse to the memory of other honest men besides jurors, for example, when there is a disagreement about a marriage contract, for in such a case the judge should require a recall from memory of those who were at the {making of the} contract, and the contract having been recalled from memory, he should enforce it; and when people have gone to arbitration, and the arbitrators [*arbitre*] have given their report, and there is a disagreement between the parties because each one construes the report of the arbitrators differently, such kinds of disagreements can be ended by a declaration that the arbitrators make in recalling from memory; and when auditors [*auditeur*] are instructed to listen to witnesses[1] and there are various meanings in what the witnesses say, for example, when there are two meanings to a word, the true meaning must be fixed according to the declaration of the auditors, for they should know better what the witnesses meant than those who were not at the hearing.

1153. Some people believe that when a man who is presiding over his court has few vassals (jurors), for example, if he has only one, and there is a question of recalling something from memory in his court, then he can recall from memory by himself, or through other people than enfieffed men [*hommes de fief*]; but this is not so, for to undertake a recall from memory the court must consist of as many persons as for a judgment; and to proceed to a recall from memory there are required at least two men, just as we have said elsewhere that a judgment given by fewer than two men must not be held valid {Chapter 67}, and no one wins his case on the testimony of a single witness.[2]

1154. The sixth manner of proof is when some matters are alleged in court and they are not denied or contested by the other party: they then count as admitted and proved and this is quite right, for it is up to each person, when he hears said against him something which can do him harm, to contest it by making a denial, or by citing other reasons opposed to it, to destroy those things which were alleged against him. For example, if I ask a man to pay me twenty pounds which I lent him, if he will not deny or admit the loan [*nier le prest ne connoistre*], he must be forced to pay it to me, since he is obliged to answer in the court into which I have haled him.

1155. The seventh manner of proof is when the thing that you have to prove is so clear in itself that no other testimony is needed, such as when I ask one of my men to pay me five sous as a fine for a blow which he gave someone else in my jurisdiction and he admits the justice of the fine [*connoist bien l'amende*] but he denies that it is five sous. There is no need for a proof for the custom is so clear that it is proof of itself. And what we have said about this fine, we say about all similar cases which are so clear by custom that there is no need to bring any witness in to prove them; for it would be a bad thing if you had to bring in proof in cases which happen all the time [*qui sont usé communement*]. But when cases arise where there is doubt about the custom, then proofs may be required.

1156. The eighth manner of proof is by presumptions, and this manner of proof may occur in many forms, for some {presumptions} may make the facts so clear [*donner le fet si cler*] that they are proved by the presumptions, and other presumptions are so doubtful that the offense is not proved by them. And of these two kinds of presumptions we will speak a little, because they often occur, and so that you can see which ones are so clear that they are equivalent to a proof and which ones are doubtful.

1157. By means of a report made to the judge, Pierre accused Jehan of having killed one of his relatives in the sight of and to the knowledge [*a la veue et a la seue*] of honest folk, and he claimed that fact was so well known that it proved itself, as he said, for which reason he requested the judge to do his duty [*qu'il en feïst comme bons juges*]. To this Jehan replied that he certainly denied this fact and if there was anyone who wished to accuse him formally, he would defend himself. He was asked by the judge if he would or would not await the inquest into the fact: he said no. Nevertheless the judge made an inquiry on his own initiative and found through the sworn testimony [*serement*] of honest folk that the said Jehan attacked the person who was killed with a drawn knife, and immediately a great crowd of people gathered round them so that they did not see if the said Jehan struck with his knife the person who died, but they saw the said Jehan leave the crowd with his naked blade covered with blood, and they heard that the person who died said: "He has killed me." And in this inquiry you can see no well-known fact [*fet notoire*] except through a presumption: for no one saw the blow actually struck; nevertheless the said Jehan was found guilty of the fact and punished through this presumption.

1158. The second form of clear presumption, which is so clear that it is equivalent to proof, is when threats are made and after the threats the thing which was threatened is done, but the fact cannot be proved; but you prove that the person who made the threat did make it, and by the proved threat the threatener is shown to have committed the offense. And in order to make this case more easily understood, and to show the danger of threats, we will recall from memory a judgment which we saw in Clermont.

1159. A woman from La Neuville-en-Hez said to a bourgeois, with the appearance of anger, in the presence of honest folk: "You are taking away my land, and keeping in your barn what I should have, and you will never benefit from it, for I will send into your barn the red carpenters {I will set fire to it}." It was not even half a year later that fire was set in this barn, and no one knew who set it. But because of the presumption which existed against the women because of the threats recited above, she was arrested and accused of the arson; she denied both that and the threats, and, when the threats were proved, she was condemned to be burned and she was burned. You can see from this judgment the danger that there is in threats.

1160. The third presumption which is so clear that it is equivalent to proof of the fact is when someone is held in prison on suspicion of a crime and he escapes from prison; for when he has escaped from prison, the presumption is so great that he did not dare to wait for trial [*atendre droit*], that for this reason, if he is recaptured, he is punished for the thing for which he was being held on suspicion.

1161. The fourth form of clear presumption is when someone is formally appealed against on suspicion of some crime and must make an appearance in court, and he is always in default and waits so long that he is banished. If he is recaptured after the banishment, he is punished according to the crime for which he was appealed against. And by the clear presumptions which we have described, you can understand the other clear presumptions which can occur, for all those clear presumptions which occur and which are as clear as one of the four decribed above, can cause a man to be put to death.

1162. No man should punish another because of a presumption if the presumption is not very clear, as we said above, even though there are several doubtful presumptions against the person who is imprisoned: for example, it often happens that a man does not speak to another man because he hates him and then the latter is killed, and it is not known who killed him, except that the man who didn't speak to him is suspected of having done it or of having it done. If he is arrested on suspicion and he denies the fact, and the fact cannot be shown to be generally known [*notoire*] nor can it be ascertained that he threatened him, he cannot be be condemned by the presumption of his hatred. And through this presumption by which he is condemned may be understood many other presumptions which can arise, by reason of which those on whom the presumptions fall *cannot* be convicted.

1163. All the eight kinds of proof which we have described have such force that if the person who has the burden of proof proves by just one of these methods, he wins the issue which was denied. And when one of the proofs is sufficient, it is not proper for him to offer to prove by two kinds of proof, or by three, and if he were to offer to do so, it should not be accepted by the judge. Thus, if a man said: "Sire, I offer to prove this by witnesses and, if the witnesses do not suffice, I offer to prove it by wager of battle," he must not have this offer accepted. Rather he must stick to one of the kinds of proof alone. And if he fails to prove by the method he has chosen, he cannot have recourse to one of the other methods of proof, instead he loses everything he had undertaken to prove and must pay a fine to the lord in the amount that the adverse party would have had to pay if he had proved his allegations; and we have spoken about this kind of fine in the chapter on offenses {Chapter 30}.

1164. All the disagreements which arise or which can arise from something which was pleaded in front of a jury, or from a judgment which was made by a jury, must be proved by means of recall from memory, and not otherwise. But if it happened that the judge had some case before him in which there were not enough jurors to be able to give a judgment or to recall from memory, and the judge named a day to the parties to come before the jurors to submit the case to judgment, and, on the day stated, before the jurors, the judge, who had heard the case, recalled from memory what had been said before him {in the prior proceeding}, the parties, or one of the parties, would not be bound by his recall from memory if he did not wish to be. Instead, the parties would make recall from their *own* memories, and if they were not in agreement about what had been said, they could offer to prove what had happened in court [*l'errement*] by witnesses. And if they did not offer to prove by witnesses, then since the judge was alone during the proceedings what was said is invalid and they must plead again *de novo*; because since the thing cannot be either proved or recalled from memory, everything that was done improperly [*ignoranment*] must be done away with [*rapelé*] and they must begin a new trial.

1165. Those who have the burden of proof must take notice of which court they are in, and according to which custom they are proceeding; for all those who have jurisdiction in the county can run their court if they wish according to the old custom, and if they wish they can run it according to the king's statute.[3] And for this reason the person with the burden of proof must know which custom the lord wants to use in his court; for if it is run according to the old custom he will have to prove his allegation on the first day which is assigned to him for proof; and if he does not prove it on this day, he loses his case and cannot have recourse to proof afterwards. And if the court is run according to the king's statute, he has two days of proof, provided he begins his proof on the first day assigned, for if he were in default on the first day, he could not amend the situation on the other day, but instead he would lose his suit by default of proof.

1166. Now let us see how the defendant can defend himself and exclude the evidence [*preuve*] by which the plaintiff wants to make proof against him. If the proof is by a writing or a charter, he can exclude it by giving reasons why it is invalid: for example, if he tries to accuse the person who is entering it in evidence of forgery; or if he says that the writing was made more than twenty years ago, for which reason he no longer wishes to pay the debt which is contained therein; of if he claims payment or extension of time; or if it is an old charter by which the plaintiff trying to prove wishes to assert some real property right, and he says, against the writing, that he is seised of and has long had the use of that which is contained in the charter, and that he {the owner of the charter} had never acted on the charter which he has brought forward: in all such cases the writing can be contested.

1167. If someone wants to prove something by wager of battle, the appellee can defend himself for the reasons which will be set forth in the chapter which speaks of the appellee's defenses {Chapter 63}.

1168. If someone wants to prove by recall from memory in cases which should be proved by recall from memory, which are listed above, it cannot be contested. But if someone should wish to prove by recall from memory what should be proved by some other manner of proof, it can certainly be contested.

1169. That which is proved by common knowledge [*par fet notoire*] or by the admission of the party against whom it must be proved, or by the clear presumptions mentioned above, cannot be contested, for cases which prove themselves cannot be contested.

1170. If someone wishes to prove by witnesses, he must call the kind of witnesses who are true and honest, and who are certain of what they are going to say in their testimony after their oath, and they should be such that they cannot be accused or reproached for anything, so that they cannot be excluded. And because many kinds of witnesses can be prevented from testifying, we will go on to say which ones can be excluded and how and at what point they can and should be excluded.

1171. As soon as you see witnesses called against you on the first day,[4] if you wish to exclude them from testifying you must give the reasons for which they should not be admitted to do so *before they have sworn the oath*. For if they have sworn to tell the truth, unchallenged, in the sight and with the knowledge of the person against whom they have been called, or of his attorney, they cannot subsequently be excluded from testifying, but can indeed properly be heard. And the suit must be decided according to what they say in their testimony, even if the person against whom they are called could have excluded them before their oath for good reasons which he had against them.

1172. When someone sees the witnesses ready to testify against him, if he knows them, the time has come to speak against them before the oath, as we have said; and if he does *not* know them, he can ask the judge that the name of the witnesses and the place where they are from be given him in writing, and that a time be given to him to contest them, and he must reserve his right to contest them at the time that was assigned to him for doing so; and this request should be granted by the judge. Nevertheless, this should not prevent the witnesses from being heard and what they say written down; and when the time comes which is assigned for contesting the witnesses, if the person against whom they were called gives good reasons why they should not be heard, what they have said is void. And if the person against whom they were called lets pass the time which was assigned to him to contest them, he has lost his chance, and the testimony which they gave is admitted.

1173. When some people are called to testify and they have sworn the oath to speak the truth and they ask for a day to consider what has been asked them, if the court is run according to the king's statute, they should have the day, but according to the old custom they should not; for that which they have offered to prove must under the old custom be proved on the first day, as was said above.

1174. In any case where witnesses can be removed and challenged under a wager of battle, if clerks are called to testify, they can be excluded, for they cannot be either called or challenged under a wager of battle. And for this reason, they should not be permitted to testify in such a case when they are challenged.

1175. Ladies who are called to testify should not be allowed to do so if they are challenged by the person against whom they are called, whatever their estate, whether they are widows, married women, or unmarried women, except in one case alone; this is when testimony is being taken about the birth of children or to determine their age, for example, where a woman has twin male children and the elder wants to take his right of firstborn, the fact of which one is the elder could not be determined except by the testimony of women, and for this reason they should be believed in such a case.[5]

1176. Bastards and serfs must be excluded from testifying unless the suit is against a serf or a bastard, for they cannot exclude those of their own condition. But if they are called against a free person and they are challenged, they must not be heard.

1177. A leper [*meseaus*] should not be heard giving testimony, for the custom is settled that they should be excluded from intercourse [*conversacion*] with other people.

1178. My dependents [*Cil qui sont a mon pain et a mon pot*], or those under my care [*en ma mainburnie*] or in my custodianship or under my guardianship[6] or who share profits and losses with me by reason of partnership must not be admitted to testify *on my behalf* if they are challenged by the adverse party, for the presumption against them is that they might say something other than the truth for love of me even though none should perjure themselves, even on behalf of their father.

1179. Testimony should not be accepted from a person who wants to testify to his own advantage or to free him from some obligation; for example, if someone should want to give testimony that a debt for which he is a surety has been paid, he can be excluded from testifying, for if payment was proved through his testimony he would be discharged from his suretyship, and thus he would be testifying to his own advantage, which would not be right. And by this case may be understood all those in which someone might profit by his own testimony, whether for immediate or for future profit. For if I am called to testify about some piece of land [*eritage*] which someone is asking for and to which I am the legal heir, I can quite rightly be excluded from testifying.

1180. Those who are at war or in such a feud [*en haine*] that they do not speak to the person against whom they are called to testify can certainly be excluded from testifying, for it would be a cruel thing if those who are at war against me or in such great hatred that they do not speak to me should be heard to testify against me.

1181. If someone is called to testify against me, who has threatened to do harm or damage to me, I can exclude him from testifying and he should not be heard against me, for his threats prove the bias [*male volontés*] which he has against me.

1182. When someone is accused of some serious crime for which he could be put to death if he were convicted, and witnesses are to be called to ascertain the truth of the matter, no one from his immediate family or his lineage, nor his wife may be believed if they testify *for* him, for there would be a danger that they would perjure themselves to escape shame and to save him from death. And if they testify *against* him, they should be believed as much as or more than other people, for it is clear that honesty moves them to tell the truth because they do not wish to perjure themselves.

1183. No underage children or imbecile [*fous de nature*], or lunatic [*hors du sens*] may be called to testify; even if it were to happen that the person against whom they were called was so stupid [*nices*] that he did not challenge them, the judge should not permit them to testify. And if they were allowed to testify because they were not challenged or because the auditors [*auditeur*] did not know about them when testimony was taken [*ou point de l'examinacion*], if the matter afterwards came to the knowledge of the jurors, what they had said should not be part of the decision [*mis en jugement*]. But if their {the witnesses'} condition did not come to their {the jurors'} attention and they were not challenged by an adverse party and the judgment was given according to what they had said, the judgment would stand and neither party could appeal the judgment because of what the witnesses had said. And by this you may understand that everything that can be said against witnesses must be put forward at the hearing, or even before they have sworn the oath, as has been said above.

1184. However many witnesses a man has, if one of them is proved false and dishonest by wager of battle, the others may not be accepted and are worthless in the suit for which they were called; and instead the person who brought them loses what he was trying to prove. But it is not this way in cases in which an appeal by wager of battle is not made, for if a man has several witnesses to prove his contention and one or more are excluded for the reasons explained above, the others against whom nothing can be said are nevertheless admitted to testify. And the person with the burden of proof may win his suit by the testimony of two honest witnesses who cannot be excluded from testifying for any reason and who agree with each other, as you will hear later when there will be a discussion of which testimony is good and which is not.

1185. And witnesses can be excluded for reasons other than those mentioned above, for example, when I offer to prove that a person called to testify against me has been paid or promised payment to testify against me. If I can demonstrate this, he is and should be excluded quite rightly and custom is settled on this point, for there would be a danger that a person who received a gift or a promise might say something other than the truth in the expectation of gain.

1186. There are other kinds of people who can be excluded from testifying: they are those who are convicted or condemned for a serious crime they committed previously or for false testimony that they gave, or those who are perjured. All such kinds of people cannot give testimony if a party wants to challenge them at the proper time and place or at the point in the proceedings when witnesses may be challenged, as has been described above. And the reason why they should not be believed is that you should not believe a person who because of his wickedness [*mauvestié*] has been convicted of a serious crime [*vilain cas*], and it is always said that a condemned man cannot condemn another [*hons jugiés ne puet autre jugier*]. However, when judges have in prison people convicted and condemned for a crime, it is proper for them to question them about their associates, and about criminals; because malefactors [*li mauvès*] are more likely to know each other because they consort with one another in their dishonesty more than good men do with bad ones. But whatever they say, if as a result of what they say there is no other proof or clear presumption found, no one should be put to death just because of what they say; but such {denounced} persons should be arrested and kept in prison for the presumption which there is against them until it is known if something clearer can be known concerning them, either by their admission or by some manner of proof; for if you did not arrest them as a result of such a denunciation, you would give a great feeling of security to dishonest people, who would not be concerned at the arrest of their companions; and because they *are* arrested as a result of such accusations, they *are* afraid and for that reason refrain from much evil.

1187. In some cases you should be believed according to the testimony of your household by the mere presumption of good reputation. For example, in private matters which can happen inside the house, which were unexpected or which one had not hoped would happen. For example, when I am living in my house far from other people and thieves come by night and my household and I see them and attack them [*courons sus*] so as to arrest them and we capture or kill them because they turn to defend themselves: in such a case if I am of good reputation, I should be believed through the testimony of my household. But if I lived near other people, for example, in town, and neither I nor my household raised the alarm [*ne levions le cri*] so that the neighbors would hear, there would be a danger that I might be inculpated. Nevetheless if I failed to raise the alarm for some patently reasonable cause, for example, if I was at war or in a feud [*haïs*] with my neighbors, in some lawsuit or dispute, or because they were of bad reputation, in such a case I could be excused for not raising the alarm.

1188. Other private cases can occur, for example, if someone is afraid that some other certain person will come into his house by night for burglary or to fornicate with his wife, or his daughter, or a woman who is in his keeping or under his guardianship, in such a case the person who is afraid should forbid him, with honest folk as witnesses, or have him forbidden by a judge {to come into the house}; and if he who has been forbidden later comes in and harm comes to him, it is quite within the law [*a bon droit*] and the householder cannot be accused of anything. And in such cases we have seen various persons escape prosecution who had killed those who had in this fashion broken into their dwellings [*manoirs*].

1189. There is a great danger in entering the dwelling of a person by night and without the permission or knowledge of the owner of the dwelling; for it could happen that the intruder does not intend such great harm as the owner of the house and his household believe when they discover him. For example, when some young man goes there for the love of some young woman who lives in the house and he is discovered or captured, there is a presumption that he came there for theft and in such cases the honesty or reputation of the person who is found in such a manner can do much to excuse him. And if harm came to him in that place, for example, when people are afraid when they wake up and think that there are several strangers [*gens estranges*] who have come to rob them, because the dogs bark a lot or because they have heard the break-in, and they kill him because he defends himself, or because he has hidden and he is killed when they are looking for him (such as when they look with swords or lances or spears), in such a case all those in the house should be exculpated. But if he were to name himself and say why he came, or if the girl herself said it before he was killed, and then he was afterwards killed, the killers would be guilty of his death. And for this reason in such private cases you should examine very diligently the members of the household, separately, and ask everything that is pertinent to the fact and threaten that if they do not tell the absolute truth they will be held guilty, so as to find out the truth of what happened, and so that if the master of the house or various of the household all say the same thing they should be believed with the presumption which comes from it being nighttime [*le presompcion de la nuit*] and, in addition, they should not get the reputation of being thieves or murderers.

1190. Also believed are the witnesses from someone's household, whom he calls to prove the offense of one of them against his lord,—for example, if he removed something belonging to the lord without his permission; or if he {the lord} paid him his wages and his servant asked for them a second time; or if he gave him an accounting [*conta a li*] and the servant denies the accounting; or if the servant committed some offense for which he dismissed him from his service and the servant wants to serve out his term or have all his wages,—in all such cases or similar ones the lord can make proof through members of his household and on his oath, for it would be a bad thing if a lord had to call outside witnesses for all his business with members of his household.

1191. The ecclesiastics {ecclesiastical courts} say, and it is true, that you should not have to prove a negative, for a negative cannot be proved; but you should have to prove an affirmative; and so that laypersons can understand, it would be good for us to show what is an affirmative which can be proved and what is a negative that cannot.

1192. We should know that all of the complaints which are made against another party, which the plaintiff offers to prove if the defendant denies them, are affirmative, and are subject to proof when the defendant makes a simple denial or when the defendant puts forward a contrary fact and offers to prove it, which has the same effect as a denial. And we should know that all the reasons which are advanced by one party against another,—either by the plaintiff against the defendant or by the defendant to destroy the arguments of the plaintiff, which are on issues of fact,—are subject to proof; for to raise an argument and to affirm that it is true is an affirmative. And this affirmation must be proved by witnesses, or by jurors' recall from memory, or by presumptions, or by circumstantial evidence [*fet aparent*], or by the admission of the party, or by wager of battle, according to the case; and which cases are proved by one manner of proof and which by the other is explained above in this very chapter.

1193. The negative which cannot be put to proof is a simple denial, or saying: "It is not the way he declares it to be against me," or some such thing; for inasmuch as you simply deny or say: "It wasn't that way," you take yourself out of proof and the other party has to prove what he alleged. Nevertheless although a negative cannot be proved, that means when it is advanced quite simply, as is said above. But you can very well add something which *is* subject to proof, by which proof it appears that the negative that the defendant advanced is true. And the burden of proof falls on to the person who makes the denial in two ways.—The first is when the negative is derived from some affirmative, such as when a man asks me for twenty pounds and I deny that I owe it to him, because I have already paid him or he has discharged me from the debt. In such and similar cases I give a negative derived from an affirmative, for if I can demonstrate the payment, then I have proved that I did not owe anything. If I had simply made a denial without adding the affirmative, he would have had the burden of demonstrating that I owed him, and afterwards I would have been too late to put forward my negative derived from the affirmative, as shown above. And through such cases may be known the other similar cases which arise, in which those who advance a negative add some affirmative when they wish to have the burden of proof.—The second way in which a negative can be proved is by an alibi, for example, when someone accuses me of having assaulted Jehan the day after All Saints at Clermont, at the hour of prime {6:00 A.M.} or that I did something on a day certain at an hour certain and I deny that I did it, and with my denial I declare that on the day and at the hour stated when I was supposed to have done this thing, I was in Paris to plead a case or on some business I had to do, and lots of people saw me there and I offer to prove it. If I prove this alibi, the denial that I made is taken as proven, for it is clear that I did not do the thing that I am accused of. And such alibis are a good defense in many cases for those who are accused either of crimes or other offenses, for a person with an honest alibi should be acquitted of what he is charged with. Thus you can see that a negative can be proved by making it derive from an affirmative or by advancing an alibi, as is said above.

1194. Now let's see,—if I am accused of having assaulted Jehan at Clermont on the first of the year, and I deny it, and I propose the alibi that I was on that day at Boulogne on a pilgrimage or for a case, or for commercial reasons, and I offer to prove it, and the plaintiff offers to prove the aforementioned battery, and each party adduces proofs: myself for my alibi, and the plaintiff for the offense, and *each one proves his allegation,*—which witnesses are to be believed? For it can only be that one party is offering a false proof. We say in this case that you should see which are the most honest witnesses, and which would most willingly tell a lie, and which ones speak most appropriately according to the nature of the fact; and it cannot be, if the auditors [*auditeur*] examine subtly and ask subtle questions, that they would not perceive which party gives the better proof. And in all cases when each party declares he will prove what he has said and denies the contrary fact proposed against him, and it seems that each one proves his allegations, the auditors must work in the way described above.

1195. Another kind of proof can also be used by the person who declared the negative, and this is called proving by accident.[7] Proving by accident is if I can disprove what is proved against me. And since someone may say that it is impossible that I can disprove what is proved against me, I will show it by a case, so that by this one you will be able to recognize the others.

1196. If someone wants to prove by certain named persons that I did something or made a contract or some deal in such and such a town on such and such a day, and I say to the judge, "Sire, I see that the person who is accusing me of the fact, or of the contract, or of some deal, and has offered to prove it because I have denied it, is calling to prove it Pierre, Jehan, and Guillaume. And yet I can tell you that if they testify anything against me I do not wish what they say to do me harm, for I offer to prove that on the day that my adversary accuses me of doing something in a certain place, they {the witnesses} were out of town [*hors du païs*], for which reason they cannot testify from personal knowledge unless they are trying to say that I have since admitted the fact in front of them." In this case if the witnesses testify against me and they say that they were eyewitnesses and I prove that they were on that day and at that hour out of town, I destroy their testimony and my adversary has proved nothing against me. And thus my negative is proved by accident.

1197. We have said above in this chapter that women are admitted to give testimony to prove the age of children, and they are also heard according to our custom in cases which are conducted by an inquest, for it sometimes happens that they know what is being inquired into and the men do not know, and if they were not believed in such a case, certain truths could be concealed. Cases of crime, however, are an exception, for in cases where the penalty is loss of life or limb, women are not to be heard in testimony, unless it is a case of a well-known fact [*fet notoire*], something done before so many honest men [*preudhommes*] that it is clearly known, for example, in the presence of six or more persons of good reputation; and women are also heard in testimony when virginity is put to proof, as it happens in certain cases in the ecclesiastical courts, but because there is no need for it in secular courts we'll say no more about it.

1198. Although those who are underage cannot give testimony while they are still minors, nevertheless when they are of age, they can certainly give testimony about what they saw or heard when they were still underage, such as concerning what happened when they were only ten or twelve years old, for some remember very well what they saw in their childhood at the age of ten or twelve years.

1199. Attorneys and lawyers and counsel cannot give testimony in cases in which they are attorneys and lawyers and counsel.

1200. There is a custom which is no longer observed, which used to be observed as we understand it from those who know the law [*sevent de droit*], according to which no witness however much he knew about a matter was able to give valid testimony [*ne souloit riens valoir*] if he had not been specifically called by the parties to the matter in order for him to give testimony on the matter in question should the need arise. But now it is quite different, for those who were present when a thing was done or who heard it recalled from memory are heard in testimony unless they are excluded for some reason other than that they were not specifically called; and the other reasons to exclude them are explained above.

1201. When a writing which is suspect is brought to the court as a proof it must remain in the court's keeping until it is known how it will be authenticated, for if the person who brought it took it away again and he feared to commit a crime [*se doutoit du crime*], he would not bring it back, nor would he be obliged to bring it back if he did not want to, for it is better for someone to abandon his folly after it has been begun than to persevere in it.

1202. It used to be that, when someone gave a writing, there was inscribed on the writing the names of those who were called to be witnesses. But this usage is now observed in few places; and if it is observed in some place, it is dangerous, for it often happens that the witnesses die; and after their death the writing is needed but it can no longer be authenticated by the witnesses. And for this reason the writing has to be self-authenticated, and it is, for it is not for this reason shown to be false. Therefore the witnesses were inscribed in the writing for nothing, since it is authenticated by the testimony of the seal alone. But if the witnesses are alive, and they are called to give witness to what is said in the writing [*la teneur de la letre*] and they testify to the contrary, or they testify that they were not there, in such a case the writing can be voided, even though it would have been valid if there had been no witnesses mentioned in it. And to avoid this danger, the names of witnesses should not be put into a writing since the writing is the full proof by itself unless it is excluded for a false seal.

1203. If it happens that someone has a writing and he loses it, so that he cannot bring it to a court to support him, he must prove by honest witnesses or by recall from memory of the court, if it was made by a court, what was contained in the writing. But first he must swear that he has lost the writing, or that it is somewhere where he cannot get it, and that he has not arranged the loss of the writing by any bad faith, but rather that he would bring it if he could get it. And then if he proves the existence and the contents [*la teneur*] of the writing in the manner described above, it should support him such that if the writing was for a debt or for personal property that was owed to him, he must be paid; and if the writing concerned a contract for land [*convenance d'eritage*] or a lease [*engagement*] or future payment, the writing must be redone exactly as it was given by the adverse party which gave him the other writing. And if it were a charter [*chartre*] which some lord gave him, this should be given to him as well unless he has acted contrary to it for so long that he {the lord} is no longer obliged by it, as some people destroy charters because they do not act according to what was given to them in the charter. And when someone wants to have a writing in the manner described above, he must pay for the writing and the seal according to what it is customary to pay for such a seal, exactly as he would if he had never had one before; for you must know that whoever wants to have a writing must pay for it unless the contract assigns the cost to the person who is to give the writing.

1204. We said in the chapter distinguishing the cases which belong to Holy Church and those which belong to secular courts {Chapter 11} that a writing from a church official counts as valid testimony of only one witness; nevertheless this does not apply in spiritual [*espiritueus*] cases nor in cases which belong exclusively to the Church and not to secular courts, for in such cases writings from an ecclesiastic [*letres de la crestienté*] are a sufficient proof: for example, if the writing of an ecclesiastical judge testifies that a marriage is good or bad, or that a will was legally made or not, or if the person who claimed he was a clerk could not prove it or that he proved it sufficently, or that someone is a bigamist, all such cases can be testified to by the writing of the ecclesiastical judge; and there are many other cases of which they have the cognizance, as is explained in the chapter which speaks of the cognizance which belongs to Holy Church and that which belongs to the secular courts.

1205. If it happened that each party had to make a proof in a dispute against each other, as it happens often when each side proposes a contrary fact or when each party declares himself seised of the subject of the suit and offers to prove it, and each one sufficiently proves his allegation, and so equally that it cannot be decided, whether by the number of witnesses, or by the bad reputation of the witnesses, or by the testimony of the witnesses, which one has made the best proof, we say that the defendant should have the judgment; for law and custom are more inclined to find in favor of the defendant than against him; and this is shown by the fact that each person remains seised of what is demanded of him until a judgment takes it away from him.

1206. Those who are outside of the Christian faith, for example, a person who is Jewish, cannot be called to give testimony. And also those who are under ordinary or aggravated excommunication may not be allowed to testify. But speaking of Jews, if the suit is brought by Jews against each other and the case is put to proof, the Jew who has the burden of proof can make his proof by other Jews, for they are not accustomed (and we should not want them to be) to call Christians for their bad contracts or their bad deals. And when a Jew is properly heard to give testimony, he should be made to swear by his faith [*seur sa loi*] that he will tell the truth; and then he should be examined in the way we have described for Christians, according to what the matter requires.

1207. We have touched in this chapter itself on what you should do with those who knowingly bear false witness; but what we said concerns the occasions when they are called to testify concerning personal or real property. For a person called to testify in a case of crime who knowingly gave false witness in order to have someone put to death, because of hatred or for a fee, and who was convicted and proved to have done so, should die by the same death as is prescribed for the case in which he gave the false testimony; for he was a traitor[8] and a homicide in his own right when he was called to tell the truth and he tried to have someone put to death by his lies.

1208. When someone is trying to prove by recall from memory some case which may be proved that way,—for example, marriage, or the contract of marriage, or some proceedings in a court, or a judgment,—and those who should make the recall from memory are out of town [*ne sont pas ou païs*] or they have a legal excuse not to come [*essoine*], the person with the burden of proof should be given time for them to return or for their excuse to be no longer valid [*qu'il soient hors de leur essoine*]. But if the person who is asking for the recall from memory is doing so in bad faith to prolong the suit that he is defending, he should not be permitted to do so; or if there are in town [*ou païs*] some of those who were present at the matter, by whom the recall from memory can be made, for example, two or more persons, the suit may not be continued beyond two assizes, instead of the two productions [*producions*] which should be given to those with the burden of proof, to wait for the other persons who are to make the recall from memory; for various suits could be prolonged in bad faith.

1209. We have said that a serf should be prevented from giving testimony, but we mean this in all suits for crime and all disputes in which he could be subject to a wager of battle in some other court than the court of his lord; for if a serf had entered a wager of battle his lord could remove him from it in whatever court he found him [*en quel que court qu'il le truist*], and for this reason he should not be allowed to be a witness. And he is not to be a witness in any suit which touches his lord, for the lord cannot call his serf to testify on his behalf if the adverse party wishes to challenge him. But in disputes for personal or real property,—which do not touch in any way their person nor the person of the lord, in which no one intends to appeal by wager of battle because the disputes are small or because the lords run their court according to the king's ordinance by which wager of battle is forbidden,—in such disputes and in such cases they are allowed to testify, either in court or before auditors or examiners; and also they can be witnesses in disputes which arise for petty offenses in which there is no danger of losing life or limb.

1210. Attorneys and advocates cannot give testimony for their employer in the dispute in which they are attorneys or advocates, but in other disputes they could be allowed to testify.

1211. No man in religion and no women in religion, of whatever order, may be allowed to testify for their house in a secular court or against a layperson. But when they plead against each other in an ecclesiastical court—we should not speak of that since we intend to speak only of the customs of secular courts.

1212. One custom which used to be observed in the kingdom of France is no longer observed, except in the fairs of Champagne; for it used to be, that if a man bought a horse for a hundred pounds from a merchant to be paid some time in the future [*a un terme*] and the merchant asked someone if the buyer was capable of giving him the money on the due date, a person who stated that he {the buyer} was capable became a surety without further ado for the person whom he stated to be capable of paying. But this custom is no longer current except in deals which are made in the fairs of Champagne, for there it is still observed and some people who stated that some buyer was capable of paying have been hurt by this custom; and yet they would have done so {given their opinion} very unwillingly if they had expected to become a surety merely for that reason.

1213. It should be known that if the king or if some lord who holds directly from him testifies by his writing to some contract or deal which has been made between his subjects, and afterwards there is a suit about what was in the contract, the writing of the king or the writing of their lord who holds directly from the king is a full proof which cannot be contested by the subjects.

1214. If the king has made a deal or a contract with one of his subjects and it is reduced to writing and sealed with his seal, this is full testimony for him or against him even though he does not have a writing from his subject. For just as the king can legally be both judge and prosecutor [*acuseres*], and he cannot be appealed against for his judgment (which is true only for the king), also everything that he testifies to by his seal must be believed whether it is for him or against him, for it must be believed that the person who has the whole kingdom to govern would not testify to anything that was not the honest truth [*verités et loiautés*].

1215. It is different for all other gentlemen who are below the king and all the prelates and all those who can by custom have a seal; for if they testify by their writing about something which is in their favor and against their subjects, their testimony is of no avail to them; for no one's testimony {in his own favor} is believed in his dispute except that of the king. Therefore when the barons or the prelates or the others who can have a seal make some deal or some contract with their subjects they should take a writing from them, for each person is believed according to what he testifies in his own writing if it is *against* him but not if it is *for* him, except for the king, as we have said above.

1216. Even though what the king and the lords who hold directly from him testify to in their writings is believed concerning contracts and deals which were made between their subjects, nevertheless it is not necessary in any case that the seals of their lesser [*povres*] subjects should have so great an authority that they are believed with no other testimony; for it would be a bad thing if I held a fief from a lesser gentleman and he testified in his writing that I had sold the fief or given it away or pledged it or exchanged it with someone; in such a case the writing of my lord would be believed against me only as a single witness. Therefore he would need at least one honest, living witness to go with such a writing, or my seal along with my lord's seal, or some other authentic seal; and thus the thing would be proved by an honest testimony. In some cases, however, my lord's writing alone would suffice, for example, if I had ratified it by my actions: for if my lord stated in writing that I had sold my fief or given it away, or leased it or exchanged it with Pierre and the said Pierre was seen holding and benefiting from the thing and I saw it and knew about it [*a ma veue et a ma seue*] for one or two or three years without contesting it, and later I wanted to challenge it, my challenge would not avail me, for the thing would prove itself by what could be observed along with the testimony of my lord's writing; for the fact that someone is found exploiting and benefiting {from the property}, as is testified to by the writing of the lord, should confirm that testimony.

1217. If two parties have to prove something against each other, as often happens when each party claims to be seised of something or to be the owner of some piece of land and each offers to prove it, after he had denied the reason which his opponent has alleged against him, if neither party proves anything, the party who pleaded as a defendant will win the dispute, for since the person who made the complaint against him failed to prove his contention, the defendant should remain claim-free [*quites et delivres*]; and it does not hurt him that he failed to prove what he had set out to prove since the plaintiff also failed to prove his allegation. And by this you may know that custom is more likely to find in favor of the defendant in a suit than to give what is asked to those who attack others in a suit. To put if briefly, if someone attacks another person by a lawsuit and undertakes to prove the reasons why he claims what he does, and afterwards fails in his proof, he fails in his claim and the defendant receives the judgment [*est li defenderes delivres*].

1218. It is different in some cases in which it often happens that the *defendant* has the burden of proof and the plaintiff does not have to prove anything, for example, when Pierre sues Jehan for some piece of land which he is occupying, or some piece of personal property, because he says it should be his by reason of direct or lateral descent or for some other reason, and Jehan replies to this that he has a legal right to what Pierre is asking for because he bought it from someone who had the power to sell it, or because it was given to him or left in a will or exchanged by some person who had the power do so, or because he says that the thing which Pierre is asking for passed to him by reason of direct or lateral descent, and Pierre denies the reasons that Jehan gives for saying that what Pierre is asking for should remain his, in all these cases Pierre, the plaintiff, need prove nothing. But Jehan who is the defendant, has to prove the reason why he claimed the thing should still be his. Then if he fails to prove his contention, Pierre who was the plaintiff, will win the dispute; and thus the plaintiff sometimes wins when he shifts the burden of proof on to the defendant and the defendant fails to make his proof.

1219. When two parties have to make a proof in the same suit, as we said above, where each one claims that he has seisin or that he has rights to the thing, and one of the parties defaults, and does not appear on the day assigned for calling his witnesses, and the other party does appear and does bring his witnesses, the defaulter does not lose the suit for this default, but he does lose the opportunity to make his proof; instead, only his adversary's witnesses would be heard; and if the latter proves his claim, he wins the suit. And we saw a judgment on this issue at Creil, where two parties claimed to have seisin of a house and each offered to prove he was seised, and a day was assigned for them to make their proofs, and on the day one of the parties appeared and the other defaulted; and the one who came brought forward his proofs {witnesses}, and asked us to hear them; and we who were in charge of the court replied that we would not hear them, for the defaulter was supposed to see them swear their oath, but that we would willingly give him another court appearance against him, and we would give a judgment [*ferions droit*] according to what he said and the response of the defaulter; and thus we set another date and the parties appeared before us; and then the party who had appeared on the previous occasion with all his witnesses requested a judgment [*requist a avoir gaagniee*] for seisin of the house because of his adversary's default, since the day of proof had been assigned after the inspection day [*jour de veue*]; and against this the defaulter said that he should not lose seisin for this default, for that court appearance was for nothing except hearing the proofs of each party. And on this issue they requested a judgment as to what the defaulter should lose because of his default.

1220. It was judged that the defaulter would not lose seisin, but he would lose the issue he had to prove on the day that he defaulted, and that he would not be allowed to call his witnesses but only the witnesses of his opponent would be heard. And if the court date had been to hear the ultimate issue [*le principal*] of the suit after the inspection day, such as the complaint or commencing the suit [*plet entamer*] or hearing judgment [*oïr droit*], the defaulter would have lost seisin; but the day on which he defaulted was only assigned for examining the witnesses for each party. And by this judgment you can see the danger which there is in defaulting after the inspection day.

1221. According to the custom in secular courts, no one is required to give to his adversary in writing the testimony of his witnesses, but this is done in ecclesiastical courts, for in ecclesiastical courts each party can speak against the testimony of witnesses who have been called against him, and for this reason you need to know what the witnesses have said. But in secular courts you cannot speak against the testimony of witnesses once the witnesses have been admitted without being excluded from testifying; rather the judgment must be made on what the witnesses say, namely whether the contention of the person who called them is proved or not proved.

1222. Any time that witnesses are to be examined, whether in an inquest or for another reason in a secular court, they should not be heard aloud in the presence of the parties; rather, when they have been sworn in, in the presence of the parties, they should be heard without the parties knowing what they say, and what they say should be reduced to writing and judgment given [*faire droit*] according to what has been testified, except in cases where wager of battle can be made, for then the witnesses are not heard out of hearing of the parties, instead they should be asked in the presence of the parties and before they have sworn the oath, who they are going to testify for, since that is the moment when they can be challenged for false testimony. And the procedure in a case where a wager of battle is possible will be described in three chapters which will follow, God willing; and the first chapter will be called "On Appeals"; and the second chapter "Appellee's Defenses"; and the third chapter on "Procedure in cases where there can be a wager of battle, and how you should proceed to closure in disputes in suits which permit a wager of battle" {Chapters 61, 63, and 64}.

1223. We have said in general that no one should be allowed to bear witness *for* himself in a suit. We distinguish, however, three special cases in which an honest man can make a proof merely on his own oath without any other proof.—The first case concerns those who sell small quantities of necessaries, for the sellers are believed up to the value of five sous and one denier when the debtor admits that he has accepted *some* quantity of the other's goods.—The second case concerns those who have a writing from their debtor in which there is a provision that the creditor must be believed merely on oath as to costs and damages.—The third case is for example where someone who is not my lord breaks into my chest [*huches*] or my room, for because of the violence and ill will [*despit*] and for the damage which is done to me by force and contrary to law, I can sue him for my damages; and because one does not normally like to reveal what one has in one's chest or one's strongbox [*escrins*] to other people, it would be difficult to have witnesses, and for this reason I should be believed merely on my oath concerning the damages. Nevertheless, the amount of damages might well be so unreasonable [*outrageus*], for example, if my reputation was that I had a net worth of no more than one hundred pounds, and I tried to swear that my damages were five hundred or a thousand pounds, {that} I would not be believed, but instead the damages would be estimated [*avenablés*] by an honest inquest as to what was appropriate to my station and what one might think that a man of my riches could have lost by the offense which had been committed against me.

Here ends the chapter on proofs.

Notes

1. For auditors, see Chapter 40.
2. See §§1149, 1184, and Chapter 40.
3. Beaumanoir here refers to Louis IX's ordinance of 1260.
4. The "first day" refers to the first of two days assigned for the production of witnesses. See §1165.
5. Beaumanoir somewhat tempers this absolute bar against women as witnesses in §1197.
6. For custodianship and guardianship, see Chapter 15.
7. "By accident" does not here mean "fortuitously," but rather "by (dis)proving an accessory fact."
8. For the notion of treachery, see §826.

40. Auditors

Here begins the fortieth chapter of this book which speaks of examiners and auditors, and of examining witnesses, and of inquiries [aprises] and inquests [enquestes], and the difference between inquiries and inquests.

1224. After we have spoken of proofs and the way you can and should make proof, and how to challenge witnesses, we must deal with how to examine witnesses, so that by the subtlety of the examination their hearts and their opinions are known and the truth is illuminated by their testimony, so that when they are examined and all the questions pertinent to the quarrel are put to them it can be known by what they say whether their testimony will be {valid} for the person who called them or if what they say will be of no value. And in this chapter we will also speak of auditors and examiners because they are the two kinds of people who make the examination of witnesses, and for this reason we will speak of their situation [*estat*] and what they should do. And afterwards in this same chapter we will speak of the inquiries [*aprises*] which are made at the will of the lord and the difference between inquiry and inquest.

1225. Whoever hears witnesses should not be alone when he hears them, for if he heard them alone and took the witnesses' testimony to the trial, in oral or written form, and a party challenged him, everything he had done would have to be done over and the witnesses would be heard again from the beginning. Therefore you can understand that to examine witnesses there must be at least two honest and competent [*soufisans*] persons, who cannot be challenged for any reason; and if anyone wished to challenge them he would have to do so before they began to examine the witnesses. And how should you challenge them and for what reasons can you challenge them? For the reasons given in the chapter on proofs in the place where it speaks about how you can challenge witnesses {Chapter 39, §§ 1171ff.}. And the people who are appointed to hear witnesses are called auditors, because they are supposed to hear what the witnesses say and have it written down, and sealed with their seals, and to report what the witnesses say in writing under seal at the trial before the jurors who have to judge the dispute.

1226. When some dispute is put to the proof, and the court where the dispute is to be heard [*determinee*] and judged appoints auditors to hear the witnesses, the court should supply to the auditors the issues on which the witnesses are to be examined, so that the auditors know what to ask. And these lists of issues supplied to the auditors are called rubrics [*rebriches*]; and these rubrics should be agreed on by the parties who are pleading, according to what they pleaded. And if they cannot agree on making the rubric, those who are to judge the dispute {the jurors} and before whom the pleadings were made should settle [*acorder*] the rubric by their recall from memory of the pleadings which were made before them and supply the rubric all settled to the auditors.

1227. In speaking of auditors and their power, we affirm that they can be appointed in all cases, except in the cases where you can or you are trying to exclude [*lever*] a witness; for in such a case you cannot appoint auditors, and the witnesses must come into the full court to give testimony at the hearing [*en audience*] and there you can try to exclude them in the way which was explained in the chapter on proofs.[1] But in the case of any other challenge which can be made to a witness brought before the auditors, the latter should not fail to hear what the witnesses say individually; but they should also hear all the things said against the witnesses by those trying to have their testimony excluded, and the auditors should have these written down in the following form: "Pierre called Jehan to prove his claim against Guillaume, and the said Guillaume said he did not want the said witness's testimony to be held valid [*vausist*]; and he asked for him to be excluded from testifying for this reason and that reason." And they should have all the reasons written down, so that when Jehan's testimony has been written down, and also the reasons raised against him as to why his testimony should not be valid, the auditors can report the whole thing at the trial in the court where the dispute is to be decided. Then if the jurors see by what Jehan says that it is worthless in itself and will not help Pierre who called him as a witness, there is no reason for the jurors to look at the reasons which were given for excluding Jehan's testimony, since his testimony did not help the person who called him. But if he has clearly testified in favor of

Pierre who had called him, then the jurors should look at the reasons given for excluding his testimony, and if one or more of the reasons are valid, and well proved, the testimony is invalid.

1228. When the auditors have come to the place where the witnesses are to be heard, they should take the oath of the witnesses and charge them [*escharir*] in the following manner: "You swear, so help you God, and the saints, and the holy words which are in this book, and the earthly and heavenly power of God, that you will tell the truth about what you are asked concerning the dispute for which you are called to testify, according to what you know and without adding any falsehood, that you will not lie because of love or hatred, for money or for promises you have received or expect to receive, or out of fear or dread of anyone." And the witnesses should reply: "As you have said so do we swear." And then they should all withdraw except one, and each should be listened to separately, attentively, and diligently.

1229. In all disputes for personal property, chattels, real property and offenses,—except cases of serious crimes, and except the cases which can go to a wager of battle,—the principal parties must swear to tell the truth in their dispute, for if {their stories} under oath agree, there is no need to call witnesses on one side or the other; instead they should be given a judgment [*leur doit on faire droit*] according to what they have sworn. And if they disagree, then the party with the burden of proof must produce his witnesses on the day assigned to him for making his proof. But in a case where there is a wager of battle, the principal parties do not swear the oath until the battle has been approved [*jugiee*] and they are to begin to fight [*aler ensemble*], but then they should swear the oath in the manner set forth in the chapter on the formalities for wagers of battle {Chapter 64}. And in cases of serious crime, no one is obliged to swear an oath against himself, as is said above.

1230. When the auditors have taken the oaths of the witnesses they are to hear, they should examine them: for example, if the dispute is for a debt that Pierre claims against Jehan for money lent [*deniers prestés*], or for specified goods sold [*denrees nommees vendues*],—for whoever claims a debt must say why there is a debt and why the debt is payable,—and Jehan denied it in the manner claimed against him, and Pierre undertook to prove it,[2] the witnesses should be asked if this debt was incurred, and why, and for what goods, and when it was, and the place and day and time, and who was present at the agreement of terms [*as convenances*], and at what time, and the auditor should put the reply to each question in writing, so that when all the witnesses have responded to these questions, it can be seen if there are two valid witnesses who agree with the claim Pierre made against Jehan. And if they agree, Pierre has made his proof; and if they do not agree, they may disagree on the answer to a certain question, in such a way that Pierre has not made his proof, or {alternatively} in such a way that Pierre will *not* lose even though he has failed to make his proof; for if the witnesses disagree about the price that Pierre is asking,—such as if one says more and the other less,—Pierre has proved nothing; and if all the witnesses report a larger price than Pierre is asking, Pierre has made his proof, for it could be that he was already paid the rest of his price. But in that case Pierre must be asked under oath if the debt was ever greater than he is asking; and if he says yes but that he was paid the extra, his witnesses are good and Pierre should be awarded only what he is asking. And if he says that the debt was never greater than he is asking, the testimony of his witnesses is not valid, for each of his witnesses should be believed according to what he testifies against him, but not for him. And if the witnesses agree at a lower price than he is asking, and agree on their anwers to the other questions, Pierre should have the price they testified to. Nevertheless Pierre will pay a penalty to the lord, because he has not proved his claim, even though he has proved it in part; but the part he has proved he does not lose.

1231. The second question put to witnesses, which makes their testimony worthless if they do not agree, is the reason for the debt, for if Pierre says in his complaint that it was for money lent, and the witnesses say in testimony that it was for wine or other goods sold, their testimony is invalid, for on this question they are in direct opposition to the party who called them to testify. Or if Pierre says that the money he lent was in Paris money, and the witnesses say it was in Tours money,[3] or some other kind, their testimony would be invalid. But if the witnesses said they did not know what kind of money it was, since it was already counted when they arrived, but they heard the agreement repeated, their testimony would be valid.

1232. The third question on which the witnesses should agree is when they are asked when the debt was made, for they could diverge so much on this question that their testimony would be invalid: for example if one said:

"A year ago and it was in May," and the other said: "Two years ago and in August," their testimony would be invalid. But if one of the witnesses agreed well with Pierre's claim on the time and the hour that the debt was made, and the second witness said under oath: "I am not sure of the time and the hour, so that I cannot say for certain, but it seems to me it was on such-and-such a day and time"; for even though he did not state the correct time in his opinion, but came close, such as in the right week or month, his testimony would not be invalid for this reason, provided he was in agreement {with the complaint and the other witness} on several other pertinent questions.

1233. On the other questions which are appropriately asked, such as the place where the deal was struck and who was present at the deal, if one of the witnesses says: "In Paris," and the other says another town, the testimony is invalid, unless one of the witnesses says plainly that a given deal was made in Paris and he was present thereat, and the other says: "I heard Pierre and Jehan recall from memory[4] in Senlis that they had made a given deal together"; in that case the testimony would be good, for if often happens that deals and agreements are made in one town, and because there is doubt that there are enough witnesses should the need arise, the deal that was made and how the deal was made is recalled from memory in another town; and a party wishing to prove the agreement can make use of those who were present at the making of the deal and those who were present at the recall from memory of the deal, even though they are not testifying about the same time and the same place, for some of them are testifying about the agreement and the others are testifying about the recall from memory of the agreement; and you can see that in such cases witnesses can be valid, even though they do not testify about the same place and time, for one is testifying about the agreement itself and the other is testifying about the recall from memory of the agreement, which was made later. But if one of the witnesses says: "I saw the agreement made in Paris and the goods delivered right there so that the person receiving them was satisfied," and the other said: "I saw this agreement made in Senlis and those goods delivered," the testimony would be worthless, for it cannot be that the same thing which creates a debt is delivered in two places, and for this reason the testimony should not be considered good in such cases.

1234. Those who are appointed auditors or examiners or judges, who can and should hear witnesses, should carefully watch and listen to how the witnesses reply to the quesions put to them: either by personal knowledge [*savoir*], or by conclusion [*par croire*], or by belief [*par cuidier*]. For if a witness says : "I know it," the auditor should ask: "How do you know?" and if the witness replies: "I heard it from this and that person," this testimony is invalid, for it is self-contadictory, when he says he knows for certain what he knows only by hearsay [*par oïr dire*]. Thus a person who wants to say: "I know it for certain," cannot say so unless he says: "I was present and I saw it." And thus you can testify to knowing for certain what you are testifying. And when the witness says: "I believe the agreement was this way," the auditors should ask him why he believes this; and if the witness replies: "I believe it because of this and that presumption," if the presumptions are clear, as is explained in the chapter on proofs {Chapter 39, §§1156 ff.}, the testimony is valid if it agrees with that of a witness testifying from knowledge, but by itself it would be invalid. As for those who testify only from belief and from hearsay, it is certain that their testimony is invalid, however numerous they are. Therefore you can know that no testimony is worth anything unless the witness is speaking for certain, such as from knowledge or from conclusions drawn from sure bases [*croire par certaine cause*], and the basis on which the conclusion is founded must be so clear that the conclusion [*creance*] is seen to be certain.

1235. When examiners hear witnesses they must examine them and listen to them separately after their oath and put their testimony in writing as is said above of auditors. But because there are some cases which require an *inquest* [*enqueste*] and some which require an *inquiry* [*aprise*], we will speak of several cases where there is an inquest and of others where there should be an inquiry, so that, by the example of the cases we shall discuss, you will be able to see the other similar cases in which there should be an inquest or an inquiry.

1236. When someone is arrested on suspicion of having committed a serious crime, for which he could lose his life if found guilty [*atains*], and the fact is not so clear or so well-known that he can be condemned [*que justice i apartiegne*], the person arrested should be asked if he wants to wait for the inquest on the fact for which he was arrested; and if he says yes, he should be told the names of all the witnesses in the inquest so that if he is suspicious of any of these witnesses he can have them prevented from testifying for the reasons given in the chapter on proofs, in the place where it talks about the reasons for excluding witnesses {Chapter 39, §§1171 ff.}.

1237. If the suspect does not want to await the inquest on the fact, then an inquiry is appropriate: that is to say that the judge may *sua sponte* learn and seek out whatever he can get to know about the fact, and if he finds out from the inquiry that the fact is well-known to a good number of people, he can seek a judgment on the result of the inquiry [*metre l'aprise en jugement*]: and the jurors might find the fact so clear from the inquiry that the person arrested would be judged. But for him to be condemned to death on an inquiry, the fact must be clearly known to more than three or four witnesses, so that the judgment is not made on the inquiry alone but because the fact is well-known [*notoire*].

1238. The difference between inquiry and inquest is that an inquest brings an end to the dispute, and an inquiry does not, for an inquiry serves only to make the judge more informed about the matter he inquired about: for example it happens that, when the lord thinks he has some right over his vassals, it is good for him to make an inquiry as to whether he has the right or not, so that when the inquiry is over, if he sees he is not right about the thing, he can desist, for it is a sin to plead against his vassal over something where he is not in the right; and if he sees after his inquiry that he is right, then he could begin a regular procedure on the matter.

1239. Many inquests have been made which were invalid because they were not conducted as they should have been; now let's see how you should conduct inquests. No one should hold an inquest alone, without calling good men [*bonnes gens*] to conduct the inquest with him, men who can give testimony about the inquest, if need be; for an inquest made by dubious [*soupeçoneus*] or incompetent [*mal soufisans*] persons can be challenged as witnesses can be challenged, for the reasons given in the chapter on proofs {Chapter 39}.

1240. At an inquest, the parties for whom it is made should be present so that they can see the witnesses called to the inquest swear their oath, and they can challenge the witnesses if they want; and what they say against the witnesses must be put in writing at the inquest and taken to court, as is said above where it speaks of auditors in this very chapter.

1241. The examiners [*enquesteur*] should examine the witnesses and ask all the questions which are appropriate in the inquest, as is said above in this very chapter.

1242. We saw a man judged for a murder which was committed, and it was not found in the inquest that anyone had seen the fact, for murder is so called because the fact is done by such stealth [*si traitrement*] that no one sees it, and we will say how this happened.

1243. A man was murdered on the road that goes from Clermont to La Neuville-en-Hez, and because we saw that he had been killed by a single blow from a hammer or a club, we arrested a butcher who had supped with him the night before; we asked him where he had been on the morning the other man was killed, between first light and sunrise, for he had been killed at that time; he replied he had left Clermont at first light and had taken the main road from Clermont to St. Just on business [*pour sa marcheandise*]. He was asked who he had been with; he replied Pierre, Jehan, Gautier, and Guillaume, who were butchers traveling on business. He was also asked if he would await the inquest on the fact on the the following conditions: that if he were found to be lying in what he said he would be found guilty, and if he were found to be telling the truth, he would be acquitted. He said yes. Then we sent for the four men in whose company he said he had been, and asked each man separately under oath if he had told the truth, and they all said no. And afterwards we found out that someone had met him that morning on another road than the one where he said he had been, and the road where he had been seen was between where the fact had occurred and St. Just, in which town he was seen by many people coming so late that he could have arrived since the time of the fact. And we requested a judgment on the results of the inquest, and there was a great debate over the verdict; for some {of the jurors} wanted to condemn him and give him sentence of death as a result of the inquest, and the others said that, since the fact was not proved by the inquest he should not lose his life, and the others said he should, for there was no way to prove murder in an inquest except by finding the suspect in an open lie and in a clear presumption {of guilt}. And the upshot was that he was condemned for the fact by the result of the inquest, and was drawn and hanged; and before he died he admitted that he had done it. And by this judgment you can see that you can be found guilty of a serious crime when you are caught in a lie concerning what is asked you about the fact and there is also a clear presumption, and this is especially true of a person who agrees to an inquest.

1244. Certain complaints can be made which can be proved merely by swearing an oath, with no other proof, even though the party against whom the claim is made denies the claim as made; but it is when he admits a part of the claim, such as when a man who sells goods from a stall or in a tavern claims five sous from a man for his goods, and the defendant admits to two, or six, or twelve deniers; if he admits anything at all [*riens*], the person asking payment for his goods is believed on oath up to the value of five sous and one denier.[5] But if the person against whom the claim is made admitted nothing at all, the person complaining would not be believed without witnesses; but if he can prove anything at all, however small, against the person who denied the whole debt, he is believed on oath for the rest of the claim up to five sous and one denier. And this is a good custom, for it would be a bad thing for those who live from small sales [*de menues denrees*] to have to take two witnesses with them each time they give credit [*creance*] for their wares; and against the witnesses called in such cases there is no wager of battle, but you can challenge them by other challenges than a wager, that is to say in the ways you can exclude witnesses, as is explained in the chapter which speaks of proofs {Chapter 39}.

1245. The examiners, and the auditors and the judges and arbitrators, who lean more to one side than the other in performing their duties are not honest; for you sometimes see a kind of person who, when they have to examine witnesses, behaves more leniently [*legierement*] and by asking fewer questions of the witnesses of one party than of those of the other, so that when they see a witness who is testifying for the party they prefer, they quickly write their testimony down, and do not ask various questions which make his answers invalid. And when they are examining one of the witnesses of the other party which they like less, and he is testifying to something which could be of value to the party who has called him, they ask him so many different questions that they make his testimony worthless, and this is sharp practice and trickery and dishonesty. For a person who is trying to be honest should not be more favorable to one party than to another, and should ask each party the questions which are appropriate, with neither love nor hate, with neither payment nor promise, without fear or dread, and with no evil greed, which has thrust [*osté*] many a man from the straight path of honesty, for in a heart full of great greed honesty cannot find a place; and we will give you the example of a case of *Pierre vs. Jehan*.

1246. An ecclesiastical judge had before him a dispute, and the trial was so far advanced that all the arguments of one and the other party were put forward, and the parties were only waiting for the final verdict to be announced. And the official thought diligently about which party should have the verdict, Pierre or Jehan, and when he had thought for a long time he found that for many reasons of law [*resons de droit*] Pierre had won the suit, and he decided in his heart that on the next day he would find in his favor. And the night before he was to give this verdict, Jehan sent the said official a golden cup; the official accepted it and that night he thought much about the courtesy of the said Jehan, and he thought he would very much like to find a legal reason [*voies de droit*] by which he could find for Jehan, and he studied his books more carefully than he had before; and when he found something that favored Jehan, he remembered it in his heart for Jehan's sake, and decided [*afermoit*] that he could indeed announce a verdict in favor of the said Jehan; and when he found something for Pierre, the good will [*la volentés*] he had towards Jehan did not allow him to remember it, and he made up his mind that he could easily find for Jehan. And next day when he was on the bench and was supposed to give the verdict, his conscience pricked him and reminded him that before the cup had come to him he had decided that for many legal reasons he was going to find for Pierre, and that since he had taken the cup he had found no reason in favor of Pierre that stayed in his heart, and for this reason he remanded the parties for the verdict on the next day. And as soon as he reached his house, he took the cup and sent it back to Jehan who had presented it to him, and then studied his books and found that the law agreed that he should give a verdict for Pierre, and he did so. And by this example you can see and understand that greed which is harbored in a judge's heart can work much evil; for a person who accepts a gift from a party who is in a suit before him is in danger of leaning more towards one party than the other, and for this reason we recommend all kinds of judges to refrain from accepting gifts which might corrupt them.[6]

1247. It sometimes happens that when auditors have met to conduct some inquest they have to ask questions about several claims [*articles*]; and to do this, they should have one of the parties state all the claims he wants to state against the other party, each claim separately without mixing them up, and then have him swear by the saints that he believes that all the claims he is stating are good and honest, and that if he must call witnesses, he will call proper ones, and that he will not seek any art or artifice [*art ne engien*] with the intention of delaying the inquest. And then when he has sworn this oath, the auditors should have the other party respond to the first party on each claim separately, and take the oath that he will admit any true claim

made against him and, if he responds by any contrary fact and witnesses on
the rival claims [*sur la contrariété*] are appropriate, that he will call good and
honest ones as far as he knows, and that he will not seek any art or artifice
with the intention of delaying the inquest. And then, when the responses
are made on each claim and put in writing, the auditors should look at what
is admitted under oath, for there is no need of proof for these things, and as
for what is denied, they should instruct the party against whom denial is
made to call his witnesses without delay; and he should be careful to have
his witnesses there if the auditors were sent to conduct the inquest by
hearing the witnesses needed in the dispute. For if they were thus charged
and the party with the burden of proof does not have his witnesses there
before the auditors leave the inquest, he is found in default, unless he can
give sufficient reason to the auditors why he cannot obtain them; and if the
auditors think the reason valid, they can give him a second opportunity to
produce witnesses [*seconde producion*].

1248. When someone cannot obtain his witnesses and he asks the
auditors to require them to come, the auditors must do so, for the auditors
who are sent by the court to make an inquest have the power of the court
which sent them to require attendance by [*faire venir*] all those who are
necessary to the conduct of their inquest.

1249. Each auditor can have his clerk [*clerc*] to write down what is said
at the inquest, and when each one has finished writing, what they have
written should be read to the auditors so that they know that one text is the
same as the other. And the clerks must swear to write only what the
auditors say to them, and that they will not reveal to any of the parties what
is written by them or by anyone else. And if the auditors wish, they can use
just one clerk under oath.

1250. Each time the auditors leave the place where they have assembled
for the inquest, they should close up the completed part of the {record of
the} inquest and seal it with their seals, until it is all finished; and then, when
it is finished, they should arrange the record in the same order as the issues
were ordered in the complaint, as is said above, and then close it up and seal
it with their seals, and then take it to the court where it is to be judged.

1251. In challenging witnesses by wager of battle, there is a custom
which is not used before auditors who are hearing witnesses on cases of

personal or real property or chattels. For in a case where there is a wager, or a case of crime or even other cases, when the witnesses are heard in court, they must be challenged before they have taken the oath or else the challenge is not valid. But before auditors, you can make a reservation to object to the witnesses called against you, and then ask the auditors for their names and family names and the towns they are from, and a day to consider challenging them. But if you do not object before the oath, they are considered valid witnesses as to what they testify in this dispute; and if you preserve the right to speak against them and a day is assigned for speaking against the witnesses, and you default on that day, you cannot later say anything, but you lose by your default what you might have said against the witnesses.[7]

1252. When you want to challenge witnesses for some reason in order to have them excluded from testifying, the reason must be stated openly in front of the party who called the witness; for if he admits the reason, the jurors at the inquest should decide if the reason is such that the witness should be excluded; and if he denies the reason, the person challenging the witness must prove it. And the ways of challenging witnesses and for what causes can be clearly seen in the chapter which speaks of proofs and challenging witnesses {Chapter 39}.

1253. Those who are summoned by the auditors to appear at a certain place for the inquest they have been ordered to make lose as easily by making a default as they would by defaulting at a hearing before those who are to judge the inquest on the main dispute that necessitated the inquest; for otherwise if you did not lose by a default, a person who feared losing would not appear, and the inquests could never end.

1254. If the {record of the} inquest (or some other record of the proceedings [*errement de plet*] which does not include an inquest but which has been put in writing by the parties and declared ready for trial) is brought to the trial, and the jurors take a recess [*prenent respit*] because they are not ready to proceed [*ne sont pas sage de jugier*], the writings should be closed up again and sealed and given for safe keeping to the judge or the jurors, and brought back to court still closed and sealed until the trial is held. And if something else is done, so that a party sees the writings come into court unsealed, he can object to having a trial on this record, for something for or against him might have been added or removed. And we saw this happen at Creil, where a {record of an} inquest had been brought sealed to court for trial, and the jurors recessed [*pristrent respit*] and the record was not resealed, and when the next session came on, one of the parties objected. It was judged that the record of the inquest was not valid, and the inquest had to be done over; and thus all that had been done was lost, and the dispute was in the same posture as it had been when the inquest had begun.

1255. If I am an attorney [*procureres*] appearing for a party before auditors or judges, and I have to swear to reply truthfully about the issues on which I am questioned, and my replies are written down, and then another time, a great while later, they try to make me swear to reply truthfully again concerning this same dispute about which I had replied the other time, I am not obliged to do so unless I am assured the writing has been lost or I see it burned. For it could well be, because of the time elapsed, that I would not remember the matter as well as I had the other time, so that if I answered differently from the other time and thought I was telling the truth, I could impeach myself [*cheoir en vilenie*] if the two writings were seen to be in contradiction [*li uns de bout a l'autre*]. But it is also true that if the auditors did not ask me enough of the questions which they were supposed to ask the witnesses, I have to reply to these questions since they were not asked me the other time.

1256. When two auditors are sent to hear witnesses and one is unwise [*mal avisés*] in asking his questions, or he asks too much for one party and not enough for the other, he must be set right [*avisés*] by his fellow; and if they cannot agree, so that there is a dispute between them, they should follow one of the following two procedures. The first procedure is to write down their disagreement in the {record of the} inquest itself: such as if Pierre and Jehan are auditors and Pierre says to Jehan: "The questions you are asking are not proper in this inquest, and you will not allow me to ask certain proper questions," and Jehan responds that his questions are proper, but the ones Pierre wants to ask are not. Then they should write in the record: "Pierre wanted these questions asked of the witnesses and these not asked, and Jehan wanted the opposite," so that, when the record comes into the trial it can be seen in the {record of the} auditors' disagreement whether Pierre was right or not. And if it is considered at the trial that few questions were asked, the disagreement at the inquest should not be decided but the part of the inquest where too little was asked should be redone. The second procedure to be followed when there is a disagreement between auditors is that they should not proceed with the inquest until they have reached agreement, and if they cannot agree by themselves or with the aid of counsel, they should go and request a ruling [*querre leur acort*] from the court that appointed them auditors, and there they should be given the certain form of conducting the inquest.

1257. When each side has to make proof on the same issue, it often happens that one of the parties wants to call more witnesses than the other; but by the custom that is now in force, if a party or an auditor wants to object to this, they can call only ten witnesses on any one issue; but if they are not challenged, any more than ten count according to what they testify. And when the proof is on both sides on some issue, a party should take great care to bring to court as many witnesses as his adverse party will, if he can obtain them; for if he proved his contention by three witnesses and his adverse party proved his contention by four or more witnesses, the party that proved his contention by more witnesses would win the suit, even though it says in the chapter on proofs {Chapter 39} that two witnesses are enough to prove the contention of the party who calls them; but this means that two witnesses are enough in suits where there is proof by only one party, and even in the kind of suit where both parties make proof, unless the adverse party makes proof by *more* than two witnesses.

1258. When both parties produce witnesses on the same issue, and both parties make their proof by their witnesses, and neither one has more witnesses than the other in the dispute, and the issue comes to trial, you consider which witnesses are more credible and of better reputation, and the verdict should be given to the person who has called these; for since the parties have an equal number of witnesses it is reasonable for the better and more credible witnesses to win the dispute.

1259. We said in the chapter on proofs that bastards and serfs and women should not testify {Chapter 39, §§1174, 1175, 1197, and 1209}, and it is true in cases of crime or in cases where there can be a wager of battle; but when an inquest is held on personal property, or chattels, or for defamation, or for real property, they can be called as witnesses, unless they are excluded for some other good reason, always excepting that a serf cannot testify in favor of his master in a suit.

1260. When witnesses are called before judges or arbitrators or auditors, and they have replied to the questions put to them, and their replies have been put in writing, what they have said should be read back to them [*recorder*] for two reasons: one so that the clerk [*clers*] should not have made a mistake in writing down his reply [*sa verité*]; the other is that if the witness has said two different things or made a mistake on anything, he can make corrections on some point while he is still before the auditors, without leaving. But after his testimony had been written down and his answers had been read to him, if he came back, he would not be permitted to change anything in his testimony. And if he had left without his answers having been read to him, and then he thought about it while the auditors were still sitting and came back and asked for his replies to be read back to him, he should have them read back. And if something had to be corrected because of a mistake by the scribe [*escrivain*], it would be corrected by the decision of the auditors according to what he had actually said. But if a witness wanted to say the opposite of what he said before he would not be allowed to, for he would have the appearance of being suborned, and he would prove himself to be a perjurer.

Here ends the chapter on examiners and auditors and on examining witnesses.

Notes

1. Chapter 39, §1222. This is not just a case of excluding [*debouter*] witnesses for bias, for that can be done before the auditors; when witnesses were challenged by wager of battle it was for false testimony. See §1762.

2. This is a case where only one party, Pierre, is calling witnesses, so that if he produces enough unexcluded testimony he will win. His opponent Jehan is not calling witnesses, but denying, and perhaps trying to discredit Pierre's witnesses. Another kind of case calls for both sides to produce witnesses to prove their version of a disputed set of facts.

3. The money minted in different mints, although of the same face value, had different actual values in the thirteenth century.

4. For recall from memory, or *recort*, see Chapter 39, §§1150–53, 1208.

5. See also §1223.

6. Beaumanoir permits judges to accept gifts of food. See §29.

7. This section repeats the information that was contained in §1172.

41. Arbitrators

Here begins the forty-first chapter of this book which speaks of arbitrators and the power they have, and which arbitrators are valid and which are not, and how an arbitration fails, and the kind of cases which can go to arbitration.

1261. Since we have spoken in the chapter before this of examiners and auditors, and how you should examine witnesses, it is right for us to speak in this following chapter of a kind of judge called an arbitrator. And we will explain which arbitrators are valid and which are not, and how they should carry out their duties, and how protocols[1] should be drafted, and who can perform arbitration and who cannot, and in what case they can resign from their arbitration, and how they should make their report.

1262. The custom of arbitrators is that they should proceed according to the authorization which is given to them; and if they go beyond and a party challenges it, the arbitration is invalid.

1263. Again according to custom, parties who go to arbitration must bind themselves in the protocol by a promise [*foi*], by sureties or by a penalty [*peine*], and if they do not bind themselves by one of these three things [*liens*], the arbitration is invalid.

1264. There is another custom which says that if there is a certain day stated before which the agreement must be pronounced, and the day passes without any extension by the agreement of the parties, the protocol is invalid.

1265. Again if the parties have chosen two or four or six or more arbitrators, but an even number, and half of them do not agree with the other half on the report, the report is invalid. And for this reason, if you choose arbitrators, you should choose an uneven number, for the opinion of the majority should prevail.

1266. When an arbitration has been begun without giving a date for the making of the report, and a party complains of the delay, the judge at the request of the party should compel the other party and the arbitrators to proceed according to the protocol and give their report according to what the matter requires.

1267. Some people believe that when they have taken on an arbitration, they can resign when they want; but they cannot unless it is with the consent of the parties. But if the parties agree to abandon the arbitration, they can do so and come back before their judge, even if this is against the will of the arbitrators; for an arbitrator is a kind of judge without jurisdiction, except what the parties give him by the power of the protocol.

1268. If one of the arbitrators chosen for a case dies, or is so sick that it is not expected that he will be able to work for a long time, or he is so busy with his sovereign's affairs that he cannot attend to other matters, or he has a legal excuse [*essoine*] or is out of the country without expectation of his speedy return, the arbitration is invalid.

1269. Jehan sued Pierre saying that the said Pierre was wrongfully holding personal and real property, for he said that they had belonged to his father; and he asked to be placed in possession [*saisine*] before answering any defense Pierre might raise, because the dead place the living in possession [*li mors saisist le vif*]. And if this argument was not valid, he said that a married child is out of the care of his father, and he had come back to live with his father and brought back all his belongings and his wife's, and his belongings and his father's were mingled together for six years before the father died, so that if he were not to take a half as an heir, he asked for half because of the partnership.[2] Pierre answered this by saying that this suit had been brought before, and they had agreed on a protocol before a judge, and the protocol was sealed with the *bailli*'s seal, and the report was given. And he was agreeable to keeping the agreement, and he did not want to answer on any other issue unless forced to by a judgment. And on this issue they requested a judgment.—It was judged that because Jehan had previously joined in a protocol, he would take only what was in the arbitrators' report.

1270. Not everyone can take on the task of being an arbitrator, even though he was selected by the parties. For a serf, or a deaf person, or a mute, or a minor child, or a man subjected to another in religion without the permission of his superior, cannot take on the job of arbitration. And if the parties have gone to arbitration, they can have the arbitration cancelled, provided it is before the report is given, for then it would be too late. And the reasons for exclusion are good ones, for a serf is not believed as a witness or in making a recall from memory, against a free person; therefore if there were a disagreement about the arbitration, he could not testify or give a recall from memory, and for this reason he should be excluded from being an arbitrator. Nevertheless if free persons chose him as an arbitrator and did not challenge him until after the arbitration report was given, the report should stand, for the parties would be too late to cancel the arbitration, as we have said above.

1271. There is a good reason why a mute should not be an arbitrator, for you cannot arrange an arbitration by signs, but it must be made and determined by words, and a person who cannot speak cannot do this; and for this reason he should be excluded from being an arbitrator. And if he could speak well at the time when the arbitration was begun, and afterwards he lost his power of speech before the report was made, we agree that for the sake of honesty, if no set date was given for the arbitration to be finished, you can wait for a year and a day to see if his power of speech returns. And we also say that those who go off for good reasons to distant lands, or who are in prison, or who lose their memory, should be awaited a year and a day; and if they do not return within a year and a day to a condition in which they can proceed with the arbitration, the arbitration should be invalid and the parties should come back into court with the suit in the position it was in when they went to arbitration.

1272. When we say that deaf persons should not be arbitrators, we mean those who are so deaf that they hear nothing at all; those who, in spite of being deaf, hear quite well when you shout, should not be excluded, but can be arbitrators. And if someone could hear when the arbitration began, but afterwards became too deaf to hear anything at all, you should wait a year and a day to see if his hearing has come back. And if he does not recover from his deafness, the parties come back into court as was explained above.

1273. There is a good reason why those who are minors cannot be accepted as arbitrators, for while they are below the age of fifteen years they are children; and they cannot have the wisdom [*sapience*] to be a judge, nor to examine witnesses, nor do what is needed in arbitration; and for this reason they can be challenged.

1274. Now let's see,—if the parties choose [*se metent seur*] a child of fourteen and before the report is given, he turns fifteen,—if a challenge from one of the parties will be entertained. We say that if he proceeded with the case before turning fifteen, such as by examining witnesses, the party can {successfully} challenge him so that he cannot give his report, because his judgment would be based on what was done while he was a minor. But if the parties had waited long enough to call their witnesses for him to be of age, they could not contest his report on grounds he was a minor, because he had taken care of the dispute after coming of age.

1275. Those who choose minors to be arbitrators should take great care, for if one of the parties requests it, you can wait until a minor comes of age, and then it is his choice whether to accept the task of arbitration or not; and if he had agreed to be an arbitrator while he was a minor, he can still refuse when he comes of age if he wants; for as long as he is a minor, he cannot take on any tasks or obligations that he cannot cancel when he comes of age.

1276. When a case of arbitration is given unconditionally [*simplement*] to two or three or more persons, and one of the parties can for good cause exclude one of the arbitrators, the arbitration is invalid, for the party is not required to take a substitute unless he wants. And all the arbitrators unconditionally appointed must be present to hear the truth from the parties, and examine the witnesses, and make the report. If one is missing, the parties are not required to proceed unless they want; and if one of them fails in bad faith to bring along his arbitrator, because he wants to stretch out the proceedings, or he wants the due date for the end of the arbitration to pass, he should be compelled to have the arbitrator there on a day certain or pay a penalty which the judge thinks appropriate.

1277. If there are three arbitrators who are to decide a dispute, and the third person will not agree, the report of the two others must be enforced [*tenir*]. Nevertheless the third arbitrator must attend court on the day assigned for the business and to give the report. And if he is not there, everything the two others do is invalid, but this means when the three are unconditionally chosen.

1278. An arbitrator has good reason to withdraw from the arbitration if he is insulted and vilified [*disfamés et despisiés*] by either of the parties who accepted him. Nevertheless it could be that one party insulted him on purpose to exclude him from the dispute or to prolong the dispute; and for this reason we agree that the arbitrator should not be excluded, but should be compelled to proceed with the arbitration, and the party who insulted and vilified him should, unless he had a good reason, be compelled to pay a fine for the insult. But if there was a good reason,—such as because of a war or hatred which had arisen between them personally or between their families, or any other good reason why you can challenge your arbitrator, as is explained in this chapter in several places,—if he wants to exclude him for a good reason he should be listened to.

1279. If an arbitration is assigned to two persons, and the protocol says that if they cannot agree the two of them should find a third, and then afterwards they disagreee and cannot agree on a third person to join them, they must be compelled by the judge having jurisdiction, or by the parties, to take a third; and if they cannot in any way agree to take someone, they should be made to swear on the saints that they are not doing this to cancel the arbitration or prolong it, except in all honesty according to their understanding; and once this oath has been sworn, the arbitration should be cancelled, unless the parties agree to try again.

1280. Once the arbitrators have given their report, they are finished with the arbitration, unless their report has to be clarified or repeated [*recorder*]; for each time there is a need for it, they must be made to repeat [*recorder*] their finding [*sentence*], unless they gave it in writing and sealed to the parties, for in that case they would be finished with it. And if there is anything in their report which needs to be clarified, for example if there is an ambiguous word in it, the meaning of the arbitrators must be inquired about under oath. And if the arbitrators are in disagreement about their meaning, their report must be judged according to the construction of the majority and the wisest of the jurors, in the court where their report is to be executed. And we say the same about all words which are submitted in a trial or said in court, that you should take the clearest meaning in accordance with the dispute.

1281. Once they have given their report, the arbitrators cannot add or take away or change anything except any part of the business they have reserved for completion: for example, if they were arbitrators for two disputes and they only gave a report on one, they have not waived their proceeding with the other; or if they heard witnesses on some issues, and they gave their report on some of the issues, they have not waived proceeding on the other issues. But this means when the issues are in different disputes, for however many issues there are, if they all come down to the same end, they should give only one report on all of them together, and not give partial reports; and if they were to give several reports, only the first should be enforced, according to what was said before: that they have no power as soon as they have given a·report on the dispute, and the parties are no longer required to heed them.

1282. When arbitrators or auditors[3] announce a hearing date [*donnent jour*] to the parties who have to appear before them, they should announce a place certain, appropriate and safe, at the convenience, as far as they can, of both parties, and in a place where they can consult their counsel according to how great the dispute is. And the hearing might be assigned to a place where a party would have a good reason not to want to appear, for example if the place was among his enemies, or a place where he would not dare take his witnesses, or where he could not have his counsel; nevertheless if someone wants to contest the venue assigned, he should let the arbitrators know before the hearing date, if he has enough time before the day to be able to inform them; and if there is not enough time, he can take an adjournment [*essonier*] for that day, and he has a reasonable excuse [*resnable cause d'essoignement*][4] for doing so.

1283. Any time it is necessary to assemble arbitrators or auditors to proceed with their official duties, they can recover their expenses from the persons on whose behalf they attend; and there is no estimate made of their expenses, for if they are arbitrators, they were vouched for as being honest when they were chosen, so that their word should be believed as to their expenses; and if they are auditors sent by the court where the dispute is to be heard, you should believe that the court will select honest men to carry out these duties. Nevertheless, since you sometimes believe men to be honest who are not, if they asked for such great sums of money that it could be clearly seen that they could not have expended that amount by the life they led and in so short a time, the extra should be brought back into line by the sovereign; for otherwise, if they were dishonest, they could bring shame to their parties.

1284. When arbitrators or auditors have written down and sealed their official report, and they need only deliver it to the court, they need not deliver it unless they want to until their request for reimbursement for the business expenses has been honored. And if the parties, to avoid the expense, wanted to drop the suit, the arbitrators and the auditors should not suffer loss on that account; instead, they must have their expenses for the work they did up to the day when the parties decided to drop the suit, for it would be no gain to them if they kept the report and paid their own expenses.

1285. If the arbitrators' report says that someone must pay a hundred pounds by a certain day, and a late fee was agreed on in the protocol, and the party to pay the hundred pounds does not do so by the due date, the person who was to receive them can demand the penalty; but he must make sure to have the penalty paid before the hundred pounds, for if he takes the hundred pounds first he waives the penalty. And it is the same way for those who want a penalty because their quit-rent [cens] was not paid on the due date, and after the due date they took the quit-rent and then wanted the penalty; but there is no penalty since the quit-rent was paid first. Therefore if you want to be paid a fine, you must take it first, as we have said about penalties. And it is a good custom, for it is clear that once the principal is paid you should say no more.

1286. So that serious crimes are not concealed from the sovereign who should mete out the punishments for offenses, no compromise must be permitted, and no making of peace between subjects over a serious crime, without the knowledge and permission of the count, for two reasons: the first is that various serious crimes would not be punished; and the second is that the rights of the lords might be diminished.

1287. It is certain that women subordinated to others, such as in marriage or in religion, cannot and should not agree to be arbitrators. But those who are independent [en delivre poesté] certainly can, and give the report, even though the law says that women cannot give a judgment; but this means judgments given in court in a judicial proceeding [plet ordené]; for judgments given by arbitrators are given by the will and consent of the parties, and by their consent parties can make judges out of those who are not judges [pueent fere de leur non juges leur juges].

1288. Although we have said that women should not give judgments in court trials [ples ordenés], nevertheless if a woman holds in fief and in homage and she is unmarried, she can be compelled to go to judgments or send a man on her behalf to do the service owed by the fief. But it is a courteous and kind thing to excuse women, since there are plenty of men to be jurors. Nevertheless if the lord wishes, she must come or send a substitute; and if the lord wanted to excuse her, and her peers wanted her to come or send a substitute, the lord must comply with their request.

1289. In some cases the son inherits the arbitration agreement his father made: for example, if the report was given during the father's lifetime, even though it was not executed nor the penalty paid, nevertheless the son is bound, or the custodian of the son, if the son is a minor, since the custodian must pay the son's debts. But if the report had not been given at the time of the father's death, even though the suit had been brought and witnesses examined and nothing remained but to make the report and {yet} the report was not made during his lifetime, the son is not bound to proceed to hear the report unless he wants to; instead the suit is void, since the father died before the report was given, unless the father agreed to something else in the protocol; for if there was an agreement in the father's protocol that the son would be bound if the father died, or if he obligated his heirs to be bound by the arbitration, the heir would have to proceed as the father had obligated him to.

1290. If someone goes to arbitration and he obligates his heirs and then dies before the report is given, and the heirs are minors so that they are in custodianship, if the arbitration was on real property, it remains in the position it was in when the father died until the heir comes of age. But if the arbitration was for debt or for personal property, the custodian must proceed according to the protocol, for he is the heir of the deceased in this regard, since he takes all the personal property and the fruits of the real property, to pay the debts with. But it would be otherwise if the minor was in his mother's guardianship and the father had gone to arbitration; for if the arbitration concerned an agreement or personal property, the mother would proceed with the arbitration representing the person of the minor, and the minor would receive the gain or the loss. But if the arbitration was for real property which the father was in possession of and occupying when he died, the arbitration would remain in the same state until the child came of age, except in cases of force or novel disseisin,[5] or redemption;[6] for in such cases you would have to proceed with the arbitration whatever the situation of the minor children, for such cases brook no delay, but they should all be brought to a conclusion.

1291. A party may have to pay the penalty promised in the protocol, even though a report was not given, for example if one of the parties defaults, by not appearing and not sending an attorney, and without taking an honest adjournment, so that the date on which the report should have been given passes by: in that case the other party can demand the penalty agreed on in the protocol, and then come back into court on the substantive issue before the judge in the court where the dispute is to be heard.

1292. All the honest legal excuses [*essoine*] which are valid in court can be used before arbitrators. But in arbitration there are no continuances such as are permitted in secular courts, for arbitration should be used to shorten disputes, not prolong them. Therefore a person who merely takes a continuance for the appearance scheduled before the arbitrators, and not an adjournment, is in default for that appearance, and must pay the penalty for default agreed on in the protocol. The legal excuses which permit an adjournment are explained in the chapter on adjournments and continuances {Chapter 3}.

1293. Lords are strictly bound to enforce arbitrated agreements and to enforce payment of what a party is awarded by the arbitration report; and they should not permit issues which were sent to arbitration to come back into court, unless it is by consent of the parties, or because the arbitration has been canceled for good reasons, which are mentioned earlier in this chapter. And when we say they should enforce arbitration awards, we mean in cases where an arbitration is appropriate, for all cases of serious crime are excepted; and anything done by arbitration in a case of serious crime without the consent of the lord holding directly from the king can be canceled by the said lord; for sovereigns should know how the serious crimes committed in the jurisdictions of their subjects are punished, and should not permit an arbitrated settlement or a peace without their consent; and they themselves should not agree except out of mercy [*pitié*].

1294. When arbitration is commenced on certain issues and the parties agree to appoint different arbitrators than those first appointed for those same issues, or they plead before a judge and commence the suit [*entamerent plet*] on the issues which went to arbitration, the first arbitrators are released from their arbitration, as soon as the parties have chosen other arbitrators or pleaded or answered on the issues before a judge. And if the parties agreed to go back to arbitration, the first arbitrators would no longer undertake the new arbitration unless they wanted to, because they were de facto [*par fet*] refused when the parties went to other judges.

1295. There are two ways of going to arbitration: the first way is when you undertake to proceed on the issues according to the form of a trial, for example, taking the oaths of the parties, then taking evidence under oath on the issues in dispute, and then giving a verdict according to the findings; this kind of arbitration is in the form of a trial. The second way to proceed is when you place yourself completely in the discretion of those chosen to be the arbitrators. And there is a great difference between the two kinds of arbitration, for those who are arbitrators in a trial-type procedure cannot make peace or issue orders without the consent of the parties, nor proceed except in the form described above; but those into whose discretion the dispute is placed *can* do so, for if they want they can proceed in the form of a trial and then carve out [*taillier*] a peace agreement however they wish, or arrange a concordance or an order, and the parties must comply with all orders concerning the disagreement. Nevertheless such settlements must be moderate, and they could issue such an outrageous order that a party could contest it and have the order reduced to an honest judgment; and the truth of this will be demonstrated by a case which we saw.

1296. A bourgeois committed an offense against another by attacking him in such a way that he killed his horse under him, and beat him, without killing or injuring him, because of a dispute that had arisen among their relatives [*amis*]. And after doing this, he repented and tried to arrange a peace with the person he had assaulted; and the peace was made on condition that the offender would be penalized according to the report and order of three of the relatives of the person assaulted, and they were named. And the arbitrators accepted by the assaulter did not take any notice of the form of the offense, and did not make the report in conformity with law or pity, but were so outrageous as to make their report and issue an order that the assaulter would have to go to Notre Dame of Boulogne, barefooted, and would set out the day after the report was made; and when he came home, he could stay only eight days, and on the ninth must set out for Santiago de Compostella, and when he came home he would leave on the ninth day to go on foot to St. Gilles in Provence; and when he came home, on the fifteenth day he would leave for overseas, and must stay away three years, and bring back valid writings to show he had stayed there for three years. And along with this he was to give the person he assaulted three hundred pounds, and swear on the saints that if the assaulted man ever needed his help, he would help him if requested to do so as readily as he would his own first cousin. And when the person against whom this order was issued heard this, he said he would never observe such a report and order, because it was exaggerated for such a small offense. And the person on whose behalf the order was pronounced sued the sureties named by the assaulter to guarantee his observance of the report of the three arbitrators. And the person naming the sureties, in order to release them, said that he was not bound by such an outrageous order, for if he agreed to their arbitration of his order, it was in good faith, in the belief they would give an order in good faith appropriate to the offense, and that they had abandoned mercy and good faith and had proceeded like persons full of cruelty and bearing a grudge [*haineus*], which two things should be absent from arbitrators and those issuing orders. And the other party answered saying that he must observe their report, because he had obligated himself to do so and given sureties. And they requested a judgment on whether such an order had to be observed.

1297. It was judged that the order would not be enforced, and that what the arbitrators had said would be invalid because they had gone outrageously beyond moderation. And the dispute was reduced by an estimate to an honest judgment, that is to say that the person committing the assault paid a fine to the victim and paid his damages for killing his horse; and he paid a fine to the lord of sixty pounds, and a guaranteed peace was made between the parties. And by this judgment you can see that too-outrageous orders are not to be observed, nor are orders from arbitrators when they depart from what is contained in the protocol, such as if they give a report on what they were not charged with, or on more than they were charged with.

Here ends the chapter on arbitrators.

Notes

1. By *compromis* Beaumanoir means "the agreement to go to arbitration, as opposed to going to trial." Since this agreement is not yet the binding decision of the arbitrators, but contains some other kinds of agreements, such as a date on which the attempt to arbitrate must end and a promise to observe the arbitrated

settlement or pay a penalty for not doing so, I have used the word "protocol" to translate *compromis*. Ordinarily a protocol is the first draft of a treaty.

2. See Chapter 21 on partnerships.

3. For auditors, see Chapter 40.

4. For *essoines* 'legal excuses,' see Chapter 3.

5. For force and novel disseisin, see Chapter 32.

6. For redemption, see Chapter 44.

42. Liquidated Damages

Here begins the forty-second chapter of this book which speaks of prenegotiated penalties, in which cases they are to be paid and which not; and of the difference between physical penalties and money penalties.

1298. It is right that after we have spoken of arbitrators and those who go to arbitration we should speak of assurances [*seurtés*] which are given that the arbitration will be observed, and these are called penalties [*peines*]. And we will discuss when penalties can be promised, and when they cannot be asked for.

1299. Our custom permits certain penalties to be paid, but not others; for when a penalty is promised in the protocol[1] if an arbitrated settlement is not observed, a party who will not observe the terms of the settlement is certainly bound to pay the penalty. And if I have an agreement with a man to do a certain job, and he would suffer loss if I did not do it, and I obligate myself to do the job on pain of a ten-pound penalty, and then I do not do the job, I must pay the penalty, for he may be caused a loss because he relied on me, so that the penalty can be considered a restitution of his damages.

1300. If a penalty is promised for breaking the peace in some dispute, and the peace is broken, the person promising to pay the penalty must pay it. And the person breaching the peace is not free of all obligation when he has paid the penalty, but should be punished according to the offense; for if you were only obligated to pay the penalty, it would seem that the person who improved his position merely by paying the penalty had made a deal to assault the person, which is not to be countenanced.

1301. When a penalty is assigned for some good reason, it is a good thing for the lord of the district, who has jurisdiction over the parties, to get some of the penalty, at least a third or a half, so that the party who agreed to the penalty will be more prepared to keep his agreement for fear of the lord's justice. Nevertheless, even if the lord has no part of the penalty, he must enforce all honest agreements.

1302. I cannot agree with a case I saw, whereas some other people agreed with it. And the case was like this, that Pierre and Jehan, who had had a dispute, went to arbitration on the condition that the person who did not observe the arbitrated agreement would pay a penalty of a hundred pounds, fifty to the observing party and fifty to the arbitrators. And after the report was given, Pierre and the arbitrators sued Jehan saying he had not properly observed the terms of the agreement, for which reason they reqested to be awarded the hundred pounds, and they offered to prove it. And Jehan contested, saying the arbitrators were partners in the dispute inasmuch as they were asking for a share of the penalty. And the case was settled. But I think that if that matter had come to trial, the arbitrators would not have been taken at their word [*creu*], because they would have been witnesses in their own dispute, which should not be permitted.

1303. *Baillis*, provosts and officers are not allowed to take any penalty for a deal or an agreement or an arbitration which is completed under their jurisdiction or between their subjects, nor for anything which pertains to their duties or their work [*serjanterie*]; for if they could receive penalties in the arbitrations and agreements made under their jurisdiction, those with business to do would promise them things more readily than to their lords, because offenders [*rebelle*] must be punished by their hand. Nevertheless, if a *bailli* or a provost or an officer has business in his own dispute and concerning something other than his official duties, and someone obligates himself to pay him a penalty, if the person does not perform he must pay the penalty, for one should not be in a worse position in one's own dispute than a stranger would be.

1304. When there is a penalty promised for the non-payment of a debt, for example, if I promise in a writing or otherwise that I will pay a hundred-pound debt, this penalty is not to be enforced, for it is a kind of usury. But if I obligate myself to pay costs and damages incurred by the person on my default, or to give a sum of money for each day for the expenses of collection, or the expenses of his messenger who is awaiting the payment, I am bound to pay such a penalty, for it is a good reason, because of the expenses you can have in suing for your debt.

1305. It sometimes happens that someone obligates himself to pay on a day certain some rent for real property, on condition that, if the due date passes without payment, he must give for each day of default a certain sum of money as a penalty, because of the loss that can arise from the default on the payment. And afterwards the person to whom the rent is due lets a long time pass before asking for his rent, in bad faith, so that he can ask for a large sum of money for the default. When such a case arises, you should look very carefully at whether the default is to be charged to the person owing the rent or not, for if he is found liable, it is clear that he must pay the penalty, and if it is not his fault,—for example, if the person to whom the rent should be paid did not go and ask for it, and did not send anyone on the day it was due, to the place where it was supposed to be paid, or if the person owing the rent sent it on the right day to the place where he was supposed to pay it and could not find the person supposed to accept it, nor a message undoubtedly from the person to whom he was supposed to pay it,—in that and similar cases he is not required to pay the penalty except starting from the day he was asked to pay the rent; for according to our custom I must ask the person who owes me for what I am owed before I can have him found in default, unless he makes an agreement that he will bring the payment to my house or another place certain on a given day, for then I am not obliged to go and ask for it, except in the place which was named in the agreement.

1306. There is a great difference between a money penalty [*peine d'argent*] and a physical penalty [*peine de cors*], for physical penalties are established so that you refrain from doing evil, and, if you do not refrain, you get a penalty according to the offense; and these penalties are adequately dealt with in the chapter on offenses {Chapter 30}. And the other penalty is agreed on, as is explained above in this chapter, or is such as custom permits without a promise or an agreement, for example fines for certain offenses, larger or smaller according to the offense; and such fines are discussed in the chapter on offenses and in various other places in this book, as they come up in the cases.

1307. Although custom requires you to go and ask for payment of your debts, if you ask properly one time after the due date, it is enough; and afterwards you can ask for the penalty promised for default of payment, on account of the damages and expenses thus caused.

Here ends the chapter on penalties.

Note

    1. For protocols, *compromis*, see Chapter 41, §1263.

43. Sureties

Here begins the forty-third chapter of this book which speaks of sureties, and how they should be discharged, and on the payment of damages to be enforced in secular courts.

1308. We have seen many times great disputes commenced by those who were caused a loss by being sureties[1] for others or in some other way,[2] and wanted to be reimbursed by those who had occasioned the loss; and because there are many cases where the loss must be made good, and many where it should not, according to the custom of the secular courts, we will speak in this chapter of those cases where the loss should, and those where it should not, be made good, and how you should discharge [*delivrer*] those who have become sureties or suffered some other harm on your behalf, so that those who have loss because of others may know how their loss should be reimbursed.

1309. Because it used to happen often that a man who owned property would obtain sureties and then leave them to pay, and, because he was not subject to jurisdiction, he would go away and his sureties were only reimbursed out of the profits from his real property, so that the sureties very often had to sell their own land to pay the debts of their principal, and {yet} he would keep his land, we assembled the count's men, at an assize in Clermont and at another in Creil, at the request of many people who had lost in such cases, and a judgment was agreed on as follows:

1310. If a man goes out of the district and lets his sureties pay his debts, the sureties can summon him before the lord where he was a resident, or in the count's court, unless someone wants the case sent down to his court, three times on fifteen days' notice; and if he does not appear, his property will be sold or conveyed to his sureties at a price set by honest men [*preudommes*], and the lord from whom the land is held will warrantee the said sale[3] in writing.

1311. If a surety is summoned for his obligation so that an order is issued before he dies, his heir must take on the obligation; for as soon as he has received an order to meet his obligation, he is the debtor for the thing. But if he dies before he has been taken to court and an order issued, the heirs are not in any way obligated, for they need not meet the obligation of their father if the father did not assume the debt or receive an order to pay.

1312. A person who obtains a surety must reimburse his surety for his costs and expenses so that he is in as good a position as he was before he stood surety.⁴

1313. If someone is called on to meet his obligation and he denies in court that he was a surety, and then he is proved to be so, he must meet the obligation and pay a fine for his denial; and the fine is ten sous if he is a gentleman and five sous if he is a commoner. And the person for whom he stood surety is not obligated to reimburse him for the fine unless he wishes, for he should suffer this loss because he denied the truth out of fear of loss.

1314. Pierre sued Jehan as his surety for a hundred pounds according to the usage and custom of the district. And he requested him to meet the obligation if he admitted it; and if he denied it, Pierre was ready to prove it. Jehan answered saying that he admitted to being a surety as had been said, but that he had co-sureties so that there were ten of them, and they were all able to pay [*soufisant*], so that he requested that he should only be required to meet the obligation for ten pounds as his share, and that Pierre should sue his co-sureties for their shares, and if there were any of them who was unable to pay, then he could be asked again: he would make up the default along with the others who were solvent. And Pierre answered that he could sue any surety he wished for the whole sum; and the one sued could track down [*queïst*] his co-sureties. And on this issue they requested a judgment.

1315. It was judged that Pierre could sue whichever of the sureties he wanted for the whole sum, and the person sued had an action against the above-mentioned sureties for their contribution; for if the creditor had to go to each of the sureties, the more sureties he accepted the more costs there would be to sue them, and he accepts a surety so that, if his debtor does not keep his agreement, he can get what is his.

1316. No one has to pay his opponent's costs in a case in the secular courts according to our custom, except in a few cases, for example if he has assumed the costs in writing or before honest people; otherwise, without any special agreement, you should reimburse your surety for any costs or losses he may have had because of the debt as well as for the debt itself.

1317. If men in the county become sureties for the count and they die, their heirs incur the same obligation; and there is no difference between being a surety and being a debtor to the count if you are his subject.

1318. No surety should plead in a suit or go to arbitration as a surety without the authorization of the principal, for if he were to lose by inadequate pleading, the debtor would not be obligated to reimburse him for such a loss. Nevertheless, if the debtor cannot be summoned to come forward to reimburse his sureties, or he is out of the district and the sureties allege that the debtor made payment, so that they are discharged from obligation, they should be permitted to plead.

1319. If a man has obtained sureties and he makes a new agreement with his creditor,—for example, if they were sureties for grain he owed and it is agreed after the giving of sureties between the debtor and the creditor that this grain is liquidated into money,—the sureties are discharged, for they were sureties only for grain and the debtor {now} owes only money by the latest agreement. And you can understand by this that if they were sureties for money and it was converted into grain, or wine, or something else, or a new agreement was made by which the agreement when the sureties were given was changed, in all such cases the sureties have been discharged.

1320. A surety for me cannot force the creditor to give me an extension, or as long as he likes to pay, and he cannot prevent him from doing so, provided that the debt on which he has an obligation is not changed or altered.

1321. A clerk cannot be sued as a surety except before his ecclesiastical judge, unless he gives his real property as security to the lord from whom he holds it, for he can give his real property as security in the secular courts. But his person and his personal property are in the jurisdiction of his ecclesiastical judge in this and any other case.

1322. Widows and crusaders can contract debts or obligations as sureties, or in any case they want, before the secular courts; but if they wish they need answer only before the ecclesiastical judge.

1323. In the county of Clermont, no one can take things from his surety directly [*par abandon*] without bringing a complaint to the court (unless the surety gives the thing up of his own free will) except in the castellany of Creil and in the town and the locality [*terroir*] of Sacy and La Neuville-en-Hez. But in these places anyone can take things from his pledges without a judge; but the person taking must be careful, for if he takes wrongfully,—for example if the person from whom he takes is not his surety, or he takes before the due date, or he takes after the sureties have been discharged by payment or alteration of the debt,—he makes good all the losses and pays a fine of sixty pounds to the lord in whose land he has done the taking, unless there is a complaint to the count for novel disseisin, in which case the fine goes to the count.

1324. A person preventing something being wrongfully taken from him [*resqueut la prise*] commits no offense, unless it is the judge who is taking the thing, for when a judge takes something, whether rightfully or wrongfully, if there is resistance, the person resisting pays a fine of sixty sous, or sixty pounds if he is a gentleman, as is said in the chapter on offenses {Chapter 30}.

1325. If resistance is made to the person who can take the thing, in the above-mentioned places where you can take from your surety, and it is rightfully taken, the person taking must be reseised of the thing and the person resisting pays a fine of sixty sous, or sixty pounds if he is a gentleman.

1326. When the surety has no personal property or chattels to meet his obligation, if he has real property he must be ordered to sell it within forty days. And if he will not, the judge must sell it for him and meet his obligation or pay his debt. But if he has nothing, he is not taken into custody for his obligation or his debt, unless the debt is to the king or the count.

1327. If someone claims to be a surety and he is not, and he pays the debt or incurs costs or expenses, he need not be reimbursed, for it is obvious that he did it to harm someone.

1328. No one should hasten to meet an obligation or pay a debt for someone else until he is asked to by the creditor, for it would appear that he wanted to harm the person for whom he is a surety; and people should become sureties in good faith to help the people for whom they stand as surety.

1329. As soon as a surety is asked, summoned, or forced to meet his obligation, he should sue the principal to reimburse him, and should not wait until he has incurred great expenses, for it would look as if he were doing it to harm his principal; and he could wait so long and incur so many expenses that when he wanted to be reimbursed his principal would have good defenses for being discharged from reimbursing the expenses. For if he could say that he was residing in the district, and available for an appearance and with sufficient assets to pay the debt, and the other person, without letting him know, has incurred expenses, I think that in such a case he would not be liable for the expenses, but he should reimburse him for the main debt.

1330. A married woman cannot be a surety or incur debts, and if she does, her husband is not obligated to meet them.

1331. If a serf stands surety for people of the same condition and in the same lordship, the suretyship stands. But if he stands surety for a free person or in another lordship, his lord can cancel the obligation because everything belongs to him; and how could a serf be liable in an obligation outside his lordship, when he can leave nothing but five sous for the good of his soul? Nevertheless, the lords permit it in some places, and enforce their obligation at their own will, although by law they can cancel the suretyship. And they do this because it is to their own advantage, because their serfs buy and sell and trade merchandise, for as soon as it was known that the lord would not enforce their suretyships, they could not continue to trade.

1332. A surety cannot lose his life because of some obligation he has taken on, even if he is a personal surety [*cors pour sors*] for someone held for a serious crime, that he will appear in court and go on trial, and the person runs away. In such a case, the surety may have to pay the lord everything he owns, and he has lost all he had.

1333. If a man has obtained sureties in a case of serious crime,—which the lords should not permit except when there is a wager of battle,—and then flees so that the surety has lost everything: if the surety can manage, by force or by some arrangement [*par son pourchas*], to hand over the fugitive to the lord, the surety should get back his property and the fugitive should be punished as guilty of the offense for which he was being held; for whoever does not dare await trial for what he is accused of, in the court where he should be tried, is considered guilty and convicted of the offense of which he was accused.

1334. If a widow stands surety or incurs a debt during her widowhood and then remarries, you can sue her husband in the secular courts and he must answer, for she returns to the secular jurisdiction.

1335. If a woman stands surety while her husband is alive without his permission, and he dies, and she is sued on the suretyship, she must answer; for as soon as her husband dies, she becomes independent [*revient en sa pleine pooesté*] and she must answer for her actions, even though she was not obliged to answer during her husband's lifetime.

1336. In some cases a woman will have to answer on her debts or as a surety in her husband's lifetime: for example if her husband is mad or insane, so that it is obvious that he takes no part in things and that the wife does and takes care of everything that concerns them; or if she is a merchant in some business that the husband cannot take part in, which the husband allows her to carry on for their mutual advantage; or if the husband is in a foreign country, a fugitive, or banished, or imprisoned with no hope of returning; for otherwise many good people, who give their things to such women, would be badly treated [*honnies*], and the women themselves would lose their subsistence.

1337. Here is another case where you must reimburse for expenses in the secular courts, even though I said before that the general custom is that you are not reimbursed for court costs [*damages de plet*] in the secular courts.

1338. Pierre sued Jehan for ten pounds he said he owed him, and Jehan alleged payment, which Pierre denied, and Jehan offered to prove it. The said Jehan brought forward his proof, and proved adequately that he had paid the debt to the very person asking for payment, and it was declared that he had proved payment. The Jehan asked for costs and expenses he had incurred, because his security [*nans*] had been taken for the debt, and for the lost workdays of his witnesses. Pierre raised defenses, saying that he did not want to be made to pay these damages, according to the custom of the secular courts.

1339. It was judged that Jehan should have his expenses because of the obvious trickery of Pierre who wanted to be paid twice for the same debt; and Pierre had to pay a sixty-sou fine for bringing such a complaint. And most of the jurors agreed that the fine was at the lord's discretion, for there was a great presumption of larceny in trying to get other people's property with evil intent [*par mauvese cause*].

1340. If someone brings a suit wrongfully in the secular court, and the defendant wins, he has a good action in the ecclesiastical court for his expenses, and he should not be prevented from bringing suit; for since the secular court does not award expenses, it should permit the person who incurred the expenses without fault to sue for them in the ecclesiastical court.

1341. Several sureties were held in prison for their obligation, for they had agreed to this when the suretyship was established. When they had met their obligation, they sued for their expenses. The principal said that they had incurred outrageous expenses; he requested that an estimate be given by a judgment as to what expenses and how many days' wages they should get.

1342. It was found by a judgment that a commoner would receive eight deniers a day, and a squire on horseback two sous per day, and a knight with one shield [*d'un escu*] five sous per day; and if the knight were a knight banneret[5] the daily cost would be augmented according to his condition— for every knight in his household residing with him, and to whom he was entitled by his rank, five sous apiece and for the banneret himself ten sous.

1343. When someone brings a suit in the court of a lord, and he is not the lord's man or his tenant [*ostes*], he should furnish sureties {and promise} that he will press his claim, and not harass his opponent in an ecclesiastical court; and the sureties must be such that the the lord who has the suit in his court can summon them. And if the person who should give sureties swears that he cannot obtain sureties in this jurisdiction, but he will give adequate sureties from the castellany from which the lord holds his land, the lord should not refuse them. And if he wants to swear he cannot obtain any sureties, he will not be refused a hearing, but he must swear that he will pursue his claim in the dispute and that he cannot obtain any sureties, for otherwise poor people who cannot obtain sureties would lose their {right to a} hearing.

1344. When the lord accepts sureties for the litigant's pressing his claim, he should accept sureties who are laymen and whom he can summon.

1345. If someone gives sureties that he will press his claim, and afterwards he becomes a clerk, so that he cannot be summoned for the dispute on which he furnished sureties, the surety is liable for whatever is proved against the person whose surety he was; even though he does not want to maintain the suit because he is a clerk, the court will proceed and register the defaults.

1346. There is a great difference between a suretyship which is given for pressing the claim and that which is only for appearing in court; for a person who is a surety for pressing the claim is a surety for the whole dispute, and {he promises} that the judgment against his principal will be observed or paid in the case in which he was a surety. But a surety only for someone's reappearance in court is discharged once he has brought him back to court in the same state he was in when he obtained the surety.

1347. A surety who promises someone will reappear in court must bring him back in the same condition he was in when he left it. Nevertheless, some accidents can discharge the surety: for example, if the principal dies in the meantime; or if he has a legal excuse of sickness which is obviously without fraud or trickery; or if he is arrested and put in prison because of a war, for if he were arrested on suspicion of a crime, you would nevertheless proceed against the surety; or if his sovereign detains him for some business; for all these legal excuses the surety can be excused from bringing his principal back to court. And the surety who warrantees that his principal will press the claim can also be excused for these same legal excuses. But as soon as the excuses are no longer valid, the principals must have themselves summoned again, or the sureties can be made to meet their obligation.

1348. A person who is in the jurisdiction of a secular court and who has obtained sureties ({to warrant} that he will press the claim or that he will reappear in court) takes the cross, if he comes back as a crusader to his appearance, discharges his sureties if he wants to proceed in the dispute for which the sureties were obtained, for a crusader can make agreements [*se puet bien obligier*]. And if he wants to proceed only before his ecclesiastical judge, the sureties can be sued by the other party on their suretyship.

1349. Now let's see,—if a man sues another for twenty pounds and the defendant answers by a denial, and a day is assigned for making proof, and the person making the denial obtains a surety to pursue the claim and then does not reappear, because he becomes a clerk or because he goes off to be a resident in another jurisdiction, or because he went out of the district,— what is the position of the surety: can he use the defenses the principal could have used, or not? In our opinion, he could not plead or contest witnesses unless he was appointed an attorney by his principal; instead the court should hear the witnesses, and according to what is proved, recourse can be had to the sureties. But it would be different if the principal had not made a denial, but alleged payment, or that the due date had not arrived, or that he had an extension, for if he had alleged one of these things and did not reappear in court to prove it, and the surety was sued on his suretyship, the latter should be permitted to prove one of these things in order to be discharged; and when it is said that a surety cannot plead, it means that he should endeavor to be discharged: you cannot ask more of a surety than that he should be in the same condition as his principal, and for this reason the surety should be heard if he tries to prove payment, or that the due date has not come, or discharge, or a new agreement by which he can be discharged from his suretyship.

1350. When it is commonly said that you do not get costs and expenses in the secular courts, it means the costs and expenses incurred by a party in suing another party. And yet there are a few cases where you can ask for costs and expenses, as we mentioned above concerning those who stand surety. And we also say that if a man brings a suit wrongfully against his attorney or his agent [*serjans*], he must pay their expenses if he loses the suit; and also those who beat or injure others must pay their expenses. And how you should proceed is explained in the chapter on offenses and their punishment {Chapter 30}. And also if someone causes damage to my wheat or my vines or in my pastures, or my gardens, I can legally make a request for those damages in the secular court, for all such damage must be paid by those who are the cause of it.[6]

1351. If I lease or rent my house and it catches fire because of the carelessness [*outrage*] of the occupant, he must repay me for the damage; and also if I have lent it to him, for things which are lent must be given back in the condition they were in when lent. But if fire broke out without the fault of the person leasing, renting or borrowing, for example by accident, as when lightning strikes a house and it burns; or fire starts at a neighbor's house, so that this one cannot be saved; or someone sets fire to it because he hates the person who owns it: in all such cases, the person living there is not obliged to pay for the damage. The cases when he is obliged to pay, then, are when the house is burned by him or his wife or by those in his guardianship or his care; and he cannot use as a defense that he had damage himself, for example, that his wheat or clothes or other things were burned; for his own loss and his negligence and his lack or care do not excuse him {from his responsibility} for other people's loss.

1352. There are even other losses which can be sued for in the secular courts, for example when people cause loss to a whole community, by blocking roads or other public thoroughfares [*aisement*]; or when they fight in a cemetery or a church and blood is spilt, so that no masses are sung until a fine has been paid to the bishop and the place reconsecrated [*reconciliés*]: in all such cases and similar ones, if the community of the town is caused a loss, it can sue the person causing the loss for damages.

1353. Again, if someone spoils [*essile*] my wheat, or damages [*estrepe*] or pulls up my vines, or cuts my timber or my trees, or spoils my trees bearing fruit,⁷ in all such cases I can sue for damages. But a person suing over spoiled wheat or trees bearing fruit or uprooted or spoiled vines should be careful, for all these are serious crimes and those accused of them can defend themselves by a wager of battle, unless the fact is found to be so clear and obvious that justice can be done without a full trial [*plet ordené*]. For if someone threatens in the hearing of a quantity of people that he will spoil my vines, or my wheat, or cause any other damage, and afterwards the damage occurs, the person who threatened me is found guilty of the offense because of the threats, even if you cannot tell for certain if he did the thing. And for this reason it is very dangerous to make threats, for you could not even get a wager of battle if the threats are clearly proved. And if someone does me harm so openly that he does not conceal himself from those who could see, and I accuse him of the offense as a well-known fact [*fet notoire*], he must await the trial of the fact without obtaining a wager of battle; for it would be a bad thing if someone set fire to my house in the presence of the neighbors and I had to fight the offender to get vengeance and damages for his offense.

1354. There is yet another kind of damages that should be paid according to the custom of the secular courts, and where the plaintiff's word is taken as to the damages on his oath: for example, if someone wrongfully and using force breaks into someone's room or his chest and steals something of his, and not as you would on a court order [*en justiçant*] but as you would in a war or out of anger: in such a case, if someone causes me these damages and I sue him before the lord who has jurisdiction over him, I should have the damages I declare under oath I have suffered; for no one knows what I had in my chest, and it would be bad if I could not get back my belongings which had been thus wrongfully taken from me. Nevertheless, in such a case you should look carefully at the defendant and the reputation of the person who wants to swear his damages, and adjust them to his condition, if it were perceived that he might be perjuring himself out of greed.[8]

1355. If someone has a piece of land where there had never been any access road, and the holder of the land wants to make a road, he should be allowed to have one by making good the damages, kept at a minimum to him and those bordering his land, for otherwise the land would have to remain fallow for lack of a road, which should not be permitted.[9]

Here ends the chapter on suretyships.

Notes

1. A surety is a person who promises to be liable for a debt or some other payment if the person incurring the debt fails to pay. The person obtaining a surety is called the *replegiés* which I have translated as "principal." The pledging itself is called *plegerie*, which I have translated "suretyship." Note that the English word *pledge* tends to refer to objects, whereas the Old French *pleges* is clearly a person. For this reason I chose the word "surety," which generally refers to people and not things. A person co-signing on a note or a check is today called a surety, and has precisely the obligations and rights of the person Beaumanoir describes in this chapter.

2. The second part of the chapter is concerned with collecting *damages* for loss caused by other people, and does not necessarily have anything to do with sureties.

3. For warranty of sales, see Chapter 34.

4. This is the general rule for suretyship.

5. A knight banneret was a rank of knighthood held by a knight who could raise and bring a company of followers to service or war.

6. Beaumanoir appears to switch between the two meaning of damages in this section: the kind I have translated as "costs and expenses" and the kind I have translated "damage." On the one hand, the "costs and expenses" are incidental to a suit where nothing is technically "damaged" or spoiled or trampled; and on the other, the "damage" is the subject of the suit itself, because something has been spoiled or destroyed.

7. The Old French seems to specify "trees bearing fruit" not "fruit-bearing trees."

8. Similar material is found in Chapter 39, §1223.

9. This rule permits the establishment of prescriptive easements at the lowest cost to all concerned. It also illustrates the fact that Beaumanoir and those who "make" the customs would rather not permit waste.

44. Redemption

Here begins the forty-fourth chapter of this book which speaks of redemption of real property, and exchanges, and of how no fraud is permitted.

1356. It is a good thing that, after we have spoken of sureties and the damages which should be paid in secular courts, we should speak in this chapter following after of the way that custom permits the redemption of real property, and how long you have in order to make the redemption, and who can redeem and who cannot. And we will speak of the danger to those wishing to redeem if they do not make full payment; and how the fraud, deception, and trickery that buyers try to use to keep relatives from making redemptions should not be permitted. And we will speak of those who make exchanges, and add some money to the exchange. And we will speak of all the cases which we can remember which can arise from redemption.

1357. Jehan sued Pierre saying that the said Pierre had bought some real property from Guillaume, Jehan's first cousin,—which property passed by descent to Guillaume from Thomas, his father and Jehan's uncle,—and because the property came from his lineage, and a year and a day had not passed by, he requested to have permission to buy it as the closest relative. And Pierre answered saying that Thomas, who was Guillaume's father, had bought the said land and could give it, leave it to charity, or sell it without redemption, and there was no redemption when the father had bought the property. And on this issue they requested a judgment.

1358. It was judged that there was no redemption if a person who had bought land resold it; but if he died, the land passed to the heirs as inherited real property, and if the heirs sold it, the relatives of the heirs could redeem it from the buyer, and for that reason Jehan was able to buy it back for money.

1359. All frauds are forbidden: so let's see what fraud is.—Pierre came to Jehan and asked him to buy his land. Jehan said he would not, for he expected it would be redeemed, but he would exchange it for a different piece of land; and when Pierre had been placed in seisin by the lord of the property he received in the exchange, he could sell it, and if he made less than a hundred pounds he would make up the difference. Pierre acted in the manner described, and as soon as he was placed in seisin he sold the piece of property he received, for a hundred pounds. Then Pierre's brother took Jehan to court and requested to redeem the property which had been his brother Pierre's for a hundred pounds. Pierre[1] said he had not bought it, but had made an exchange, and said that there was no redemption in an exchange of property. Pierre's brother responded that it was not a fair [drois] exchange, for it had been done by fraud, to take away the right of redemption from Pierre's property. And they requested a judgment on the issue of whether Pierre's brother could redeem his brother's property for the hundred pounds which Pierre had received for the exchange property which he sold.

1360. It was judged that Pierre's brother *could* redeem the property for the money, for it appeared that the exchange had been made in bad faith, in order to keep Pierre's lineage from making a redemption. The jurors added more, for they said it was not a fair exchange unless each person held his land for a year and a day without selling it.

1361. If you give in exchange for a property another property and some cash, or other personal property which is worth cash, there is a redemption right and you can redeem for cash and a piece of property of the same value.

1362. Those who wish to make an honest exchange in which there is no redemption should give land for land, with no personal property involved, and each one must keep what he received in the exchange for a year and a day; and the exchange must be such that you can see the advantage to each party without sharp practice, and then the exchange is good.

1363. I have the same redemption rights in what my relative acquires by a fair exchange of property as I had in the property which was given away in the exchange; that is, if my relative sells the land he received in a fair exchange, I can redeem it, as I could have {redeemed} the first piece of land he gave in the exchange, as if no exchange had ever taken place.

1364. If you want to redeem some property, you must prove two things if the buyer requests it: the first thing is that you must prove you are from the lineage of the person who sold it; the second thing is that the property descended on the side of the seller's family to which you belong. For if I had a brother who was my half-brother through my father, and he had property from his mother, if he sold it, I could not redeem it for money, for the property is not held through the side of the family of my father, through whom I am related to my half-brother; but yet my brother's relative through his mother could redeem it, even if he was related only in the fourth degree: indeed, you can redeem property even up to the seventh degree of kinship on your own side of the family if you can prove it.[2]

1365. I saw a case where the person redeeming did not have to prove the property was from the side of the family by which he was related to the seller, and the case was one where the buyer insisted that the person wanting to redeem prove his lineage and that the property had descended on the side of the family by which he was related to the seller. The person wanting to redeem answered this by saying that he would prove his lineage, but that he could not prove that the land came from his side of the family, since the seller had held the land so long, and his father before him, from whom the land had passed, that there was no one living who could know what stock [*estoc*] the property had originally come from. And as it was clear that he was a relative of the seller, and the latter had held the property so long, he requested to be able to redeem it for money, unless the buyer proved that the land had come from another side of the family. And on this issue they requested a judgment.

1366. It was judged that if the person wanting to redeem proved his lineage, and the buyer could not prove that the property came down from another side of the family than the one by which the person redeeming was related to the seller, the person wanting to could redeem it; and what persuaded the jurors to make this decision was the long tenure of the property.

1367. If you want to redeem property, you must do so within a year and a day from when the buyer is given seisin by the lord; and once a year and a day has gone by, you can no longer redeem, and the property remains the purchased property of the buyer.[3]

1368. If a man buys some property from a relative, property which he could have redeemed if a stranger had bought it, a closer relative to the seller than the buyer can redeem it, but a more distant relative cannot. And if he is of the same degree of lineage as the person redeeming, can he get partition? I say no, for you do not have to be a broker [*marcheans*]⁴ for someone else unless he can say: "I am more closely related."

1369. If someone buys property from his relative and then sells it to a stranger, there is a right of redemption, for that is when the property first goes out of the lineage. Therefore you can see that, in that case, what I have bought within my family and on my side of the family is not in the same position as if I had bought it from a stranger; for if I sold what I had bought from a stranger, there could be no redemption after I had been in seisin for a year and a day. But if I resold my purchase, which I had not held for a year and a day, the relatives of the first seller would not thereby lose their right to redeem within a year and a day of the first transfer of seisin.

1370. The reason why you can redeem property sold by your relative up to the seventh degree of kinship is that formerly marriage was prohibited up to the seventh degree. But since the pope saw that many marriages were being made between people of the same family, because no one remembered who was in the lineage, and especially because the lineages were so great that the nobility had difficulty finding someone to marry, the pope, by the counsel of Holy Church, made a new law [*constitucion*] that marriages may be contracted after the fourth degree of kinship.⁵ But secular rulers did not repeal the law as it was at that time that you can sue to redeem property.

1371. Advice was sought by a party from the wise men of the county in a case where there were four brothers, all of age and holding their portions of land: one brother sold his portion to one of his brothers, and the buyer was placed in seisin by the lord; within a year and a day of his brother being placed in seisin, the third brother made a court appearance and asked to have half of the property for money. The buyer answered saying that he did not want this for several reasons: the first reason was because the third brother had not asked to become a partner in the deal before he was placed in seisin by the lord; the second reason was because his brother could not claim he was of closer kinship, and therefore able to redeem; and the third reason was because he was not required to be his broker [*marcheans*]. It was considered that for these reasons the third brother could not legally make the requested redemption, for an equally distant relative cannot redeem, but a closer one can.

1372. If it happens that someone buys some property and pays for it before he is placed in seisin by the lord, and afterwards the seller will not appear to place the buyer in seisin, and the buyer summons him before the lord from whom the property is held, and the seller defaults three times, the lord should entertain the proofs of the buyer, and when he has made proof of the purchase, he should place him in seisin of the property. And as soon as he has seisin from the lord, the year and a day for the redemption begins, and the relatives of the seller can make a redemption, even though seisin was not transferred by the seller.

1373. If one man sues another over a purchase and the suit proceeds to the point where seller has an inspection day[6] of the thing, and after the inspection, he defaults even a single time, the buyer gets seisin and you can redeem as soon as he is placed in seisin by the lord.

1374. When someone loses seisin of property in any kind of a suit whatsoever, unless he summons the person obtaining seisin in a suit on ownership within a year and a day, his complaint must not be entertained.

1375. Pierre sued Jehan before the lord from whom he held some property and claimed that Jehan had sold him this property and that he had paid for it, for which reason he requested that Jehan be made to surrender seisin and have Pierre placed in seisin by the lord. Jehan answered saying that the suit was on an agreement and that he demanded to be sued before the lord where he was a resident, so that he did not want to answer in the first court, unless legally compelled to [*se par droit ne le fesoit*]. They requested a judgment as to whether Jehan would answer in the court of the lord from whom the property was held, or if Jehan would have to be sued on the agreement in the court of the lord where he was a resident.[7]

1376. It was judged that Jehan would answer in the court of the lord from whom the property was held, because the agreement was dependent on the property; and by this you can understand that the cognizance of all suits on property belongs to the lord from whom the property is held.

1377. Bastards cannot make redemptions, because they do not belong to the lineage, as I have said elsewhere.

1378. A married woman cannot make a redemption without the authorization of her husband, and no one is required to answer any complaint she may make in court without the authorization of her husband, unless her husband is out of his senses or an imbecile, or out of the district without hope of his return, for in that case you would have to answer a woman's complaint or otherwise women could suffer severe loss.

1379. There are buyers who, in order to drive up the price for those redeeming, buy on condition that the seller takes wheat or oats or wine at a higher price than they are worth, and then the buyer is placed in seisin by the lord and pays the sales tax according to the price of the goods as agreed in the deal. But such trickery is not valid if the person wishing to redeem can contest it, for the goods which were given for the deal must be appraised at an honest price according to what they were worth at the time the deal was concluded, and the person redeeming has to pay {only} this amount of money.

1380. When someone buys by giving goods without naming a sum of money,—for example if he gave ten *muis* of wheat or twenty barrels of wine for a piece of property,—and the goods happen to go up in price at the time when the person wants to redeem, the person redeeming is not required to give the same goods that the buyer gave, instead he need pay only what the goods were worth on the day they were appraised and promised to the seller. And also if the goods have gone down in price, and the person redeeming wants to redeem by giving the same goods, he should not be able to get the property except at the price explained above; for the buyer should rightfully be protected from loss just like the person redeeming. And what I have said about wheat, oats, and wine I apply to all other personal property which can be given instead of money.

1381. A person wishing to make a redemption must be careful to make the payment on the day he offers, if he is acknowledged to be a successor[8] by the buyer, and the buyer wants to receive his money without delay, for if full payment is not made at that time, the person redeeming and who offered the payment can never redeem or offer to again; but other persons from his lineage and from the side of the family on which the property came down do not thereby lose their opportunity to offer to redeem.

1382. Pierre sued Jehan saying he should be able to redeem the property his father had sold, and offered full payment. Jehan answered saying he should not be able to redeem because he was in his father's custodianship [*bail*]⁹ on the day the property was sold, and because he was an heir of his father who sold the property, who {as heir} should warrantee the father's sale. Pierre admitted these things, but he said that he had received money as a gift from someone other than his father. And they requested a judgment on these arguments, as to whether Pierre could redeem the property.

1383. It was held in the judgment that Pierre could redeem the property for money, even if he paid the price with money that had come from his father; for it would be a bad thing if minor children lost their rights by being in custodianship or the guardianship of their fathers.

1384. I do not see how anyone selling property can ever again come back into the property, except in one kind of redemption: if I sell my property to a relative, on the same side of the family on which the property comes down, and he resells it to a stranger out of our lineage, I can redeem it, and in this situation there is no one closer to him in kinship than I am.

1385. If several persons of the same degree of kinship go to court to redeem a piece of property all at the same time, each should pay his share of the sale price, in equal shares, and then take equal shares in the property.

1386. When I want to redeem some property on behalf of my wife, and my wife has a reason [*essoine*] why she cannot appear in court,—for example lying in at childbirth, or sickness, or pregnancy near to term,—and there is a danger that the year and a day might pass if I waited for her recovery, I should ask the judge to come or send someone to be assured of the authority my wife was giving me to redeem the property, and after she had given me the authority in the presence of the judge with the jurisdiction (or before his deputy sent to ascertain this by the judge, and able to testify in a sealed writing if the judge cannot come), the buyer cannot prevent me from being heard just as if my wife were present, for otherwise my wife might lose her rights to redeem the property because of her impediment [*essoine*], which would not be right.

1387. There are some towns in the county where they want to uphold as a custom that when someone buys property, there is an announcement in the parish that such-and-such a property has been sold, and that if someone wants to redeem it he must do so within fifteen days or his plea in a redemption suit will no longer be heard. But such an announcement and order is not valid, for it is against the general custom of the castellany [*chastel*] of Clermont; and subjects of the count cannot and must not make customs which are contrary to the custom of the castellany which is their chief town [*chiés*]. And I have no doubt that if someone in the above-mentioned towns, where such an order was given, tries to redeem a property by the end of the year, he will be able to, if he pursues the suit to a judgment. If the opposite were judged, he would have a good appeal.

1388. There are some people who buy property, and when they have made the purchase, they have the deal offered by a judge to persons they are afraid may redeem the property. And the judge says to each person individually: "Jehan has bought such-and-such a property from Pierre, your cousin, for such-and-such a sum of money. And we order you to redeem it within fifteen days or give a quit-claim [*quitiés*]." But such an order is invalid if anyone wants to or knows how to contest it, for it is against the general custom of the castellany, and an order issued against the common law [*droit commun*] should not be enforced. Therefore a person receiving such an order should tell the judge who gives it to him that he should withdraw it, and that he will not give a quit-claim [*quitance*], but that he wants the time that law and custom afford him; and he should ask for a hearing [*que drois li soit fes*]. And if a good judgment is given I do not doubt that it will be in his favor; and if it is against him he has a good appeal. But if it happens that he obeys the order and gives the quit-claim, he can never sue for redemption, even though the order was invalid.

1389. When a buyer has been placed in seisin of his purchase, it sometimes happens that he goes out of the district and stays away until after the year and a day has passed; what must a person do who wants to redeem? If the absent person has left a competent attorney, who has the power by an adequate letter of appointment[10] to win or lose suits on real property, the person wanting to redeem should sue him; but if he has not left an attorney, you should have him summoned by the lord from whom the land is held in the place where he used to live, provided it is in the castellany where the property is situated, for you need not summon him if it is farther away. And he should be summoned but one time on the redemption; and if he does not appear or there is no place to summon him in the castellany, and he has left no attorney, then the lord from whom the property is held should hear the proofs of the person wanting to redeem, concerning his lineage, and the side the property comes down on. And when he has made a good proof, the lord should take the money into his charge and place the person redeeming in seisin of the property. And when the buyer comes back into the district, the lord should give him his money; and if he stays away with no hope of his return,—for example if he had taken up residence outside the district, or he is imprisoned by unbelievers, or undoubted news has come of his death,—the lord should give the money to his closest heir (taking sureties, so that if the buyer returns he can get his money without dispute); and if he never comes back or if no heir makes an appearance, the money goes to the lord.

1390. There should be no doubt that if someone buys a property on which there are buildings or fruit-bearing trees, he should leave the property in the same condition, without demolishing the buildings or impairing the trees, until a year and a day have passed; and if he does otherwise, he must pay the damages to the person redeeming; and also if there is timber of under seven years' growth, he cannot cut it. And he can cut and haul away mature timber, and he may by law reap any benefits in the way of wheat or oats or wine or hay, or quit-rents or rents, or fish, or other fruits of the land; it is all his by law without making any restitution to the person redeeming. But as soon as the money for the redemption is offered to him, and he will not take it without a suit, the judge of the place, at the request of the person redeeming, should take charge of everything, so that if the person redeems the property for money, he can enjoy all the fruits derived from the property while the suit was pending.

1391. If someone wants to redeem and he has the buyer summoned[11] so that the summons is served on the last day of the year given for redemption, and the suit itself begins after the year and a day have passed, it may be asked whether the buyer can say, when he appears before the lord, that the year and a day has passed, and that for that reason he does not want to answer. I say that my opinion is that since the offer of money was not made to the buyer within a year and a day, whether before a judge or not, that a summons which does not include an offer of the money is not of such great effectiveness [*vertu*] that the year and a day does not pass to the advantage

of the buyer, so that the buyer does not have to answer. And I am persuaded of this for two reasons: the first is because then the person redeeming would have the power to redeem after the year and a day have passed,
which should not be, according to the common law. The second reason is
that the time between the summons and the appearance in court belongs by
law to the person summoned, for example, a gentleman who is summoned
must have fifteen days and a commoner can be summoned for the next day,
and time which you have by law should not be to your detriment.

1392. If someone has a summons served in a suit on redemption, and
the first court appearance falls within the year and a day time period, and
the buyer takes an adjournment or the judge continues this appearance to
another day, and during the delay the year and a day passes, it is not to the
detriment of the person redeeming, because the delay does not come from
him. But if the delay did come from him, and the year and a day passed, he
would lose the opportunity to redeem. And however the delay occurs,
during the pleadings or in waiting for the judgment, providing the suit has
begun within a year and a day, the time spent during the suit [*li debas du
plet*] is not to the prejudice of the person wanting to redeem.

1393. A person maintaining a suit for redemption should be careful to
bring enough to pay the price, if he should need to, every day he comes to
court; for if there is a judgment in his favor, or the buyer wants to stop
fighting the suit, if the person redeeming does not make full payment on
the same day, his suit is dismissed and he should not be entertained any
more; for since he has what he asked for, that is the property for the money,
and he does not pay, he is in default. And a single default after the inspection day would lose him his suit, so he should certainly lose it for a default
of payment.

1394. Again, a buyer who for fear of redemption harvests his wheat or
small grains or wine on a property he bought, before the regular time of
maturity, so that it is clear that the crops have been harvested too soon, and
the person redeeming comes into the property before it would have been
time for the harvest, the buyer must pay for his damages, for it is better for
him to have to pay for his spitefulness [*malice*] than others.

1395. There is another custom in redemptions which is that if I offer
money as a successor and the buyer acknowledges me as a successor and

offers to accept my payment, and I make a partial payment, so that I do not pay it all on that day, the buyer takes what I paid him along with the property. But when I say that the payment must be made on that day, if the payment was so large that the day passed while it was being counted, the person redeeming would not lose it for that reason, unless the failure to pay was because of a lack of money; for it could be such a great sum of money that you would take two or three days or more to count it, and this would not be a reason for the person redeeming to lose because of the delay.

1396. If the person redeeming accepts the word of the seller and buyer under oath as to how much the sale was for, without question, he cannot later adduce proofs against what they swore, but they must be believed. Therefore if the person redeeming suspects or believes there was fraud or trickery in the deal, he should speak in this manner: "Sire, I say that the deal was this way, and by such-and-such an agreement, and I require the seller and the buyer to swear an oath, and if they say under oath it was otherwise, I am ready to prove by good people who were there my contention that the deal went that way." And if the person redeeming proceeds in this manner, his proofs should be listened to, and he should have the testimony under oath of the seller and buyer first of all.

1397. When someone buys on condition that he will pay the price in installments, if a person wanting to redeem appears, he should have the same payment schedule as the buyer had and must give good security to the buyer that he will take over his payments to the seller on the terms which were agreed to when the deal was made. And he must give this security to the buyer, because the seller need not change his sureties or his debts unless he wants. But if the buyer has costs and damages, the person redeeming must pay him back; and if the person redeeming cannot or will not give security to indemnify the buyer towards the seller, and to repay him his costs and damages, if he has any because of a failure to make his payment [par defaute de son aquit], the buyer need not sell in a redemption unless he is·given the whole price, or a good surety, so that by recourse to the surety he can pay off the seller.

1398. When someone buys a property, and it is held from several lords, and a price is put on each parcel so as to pay the sales tax to the lord, even though the deal was made between the seller and the buyer for a single sum of money and with a single handshake [paumee], some people think that a person wanting to redeem may redeem what is held from just one of the lords; but it is not true. The person redeeming must redeem the whole deal however many lords there are, since it was made with a single handshake and since one parcel came down through his side of the lineage as much as the others did. But if one parcel of the property came down through his lineage but the other did not, he could only redeem what came from his side of the family. And even if the buyer wanted to acknowledge him as being the successor to all of the property, he could not enter the part of which he was not the successor, unless he gained seisin from the lord by paying sales tax. And if he entered the property without being given seisin by the lord, the lord could seize the land until the first buyer came and surrendered seisin, and the person redeeming had paid a fine for entering the land without a lord and with no right to do so; and the fine would be sixty sous if the property were held in villeinage, and if the land was held in fief the fine would be sixty pounds.

1399. In a regular redemption of property, when it is certain that the person redeeming is the successor [*heritiers*], there is no need for the lord to remove or give seisin, nor for sales tax to be paid, since the person redeeming takes all the rights the buyer had by law; and when the buyer has been placed in seisin by the lord, this seisin passes to the person redeeming as soon as he has paid the price; and if he is acknowledged by the buyer to be the successor, he has no need to go before the lord to make the redemption. But if the buyer contests the redemption, then the suit must come before the lord.

1400. Now some people could say: "Fair sir, you say that you have to redeem the whole of the property which was sold in a single deal, even though the property was held from several lords. And how can this be, for if he wants, the person redeeming need only summon the buyer before *one* of these lords, and the lord can take cognizance only of the property which is held from him? And therefore when the person redeeming had redeemed what was held from this lord, it seems that he could stop there if he wanted." But the buyer can raise good reasons and reasonable arguments to all this, by saying to the lord before whom he is summoned: "Sire, even though you cannot take cognizance of anything but the land which is held from you, the person redeeming need not, unless he wishes, appear before you or any other lord, for I acknowledge him to be the successor of the whole deal I made with such-and-such a person who was from his lineage.

And since I acknowledge him as successor without any dispute, and he does not have to appear before a lord unless *I* am raising some objection, and I made the deal with a single handshake, I say that my deal is so much of one piece that no person redeeming should take it apart or split it up, since he is a successor to the whole deal. For which reason I request that you do not make me split up my deal, which was all put together by a single handshake." And if he gets a hearing on this issue, I have no doubt that the person redeeming will have to redeem the whole thing or nothing, if the judgment is sound.

1401. When someone redeems a property and there are crops to be harvested, for example grains or wine, he should be sure to make the redemption before the buyer has had the wheat reaped or the grapes picked, even though the wheat or grapes are still in the place where they grew, for the buyer could cart them away as soon as their stem was cut, once it is time to reap or to pick grapes. For if the buyer took them away in bad faith before they were ripe, he would have to pay the damages to the person redeeming if he redeemed before the time of maturity, even though the buyer tried to claim he had reaped the wheat green in order to feed his horses or his other animals, or picked the unripe grapes, for it is not the custom in the county to reap wheat green in order to feed animals, nor to pick unripe grapes to make juice [*verjus*]. Therefore if anyone did this, it would be clear he was doing so to the prejudice of the person redeeming. And that the buyer takes the wheat and grapes as soon as their stem is cut, even though they are still in the place where they grew, is approved by the judgment which follows.

1402. Pierre sued Jehan saying that the said Jehan had bought a parcel of property which he had the right to redeem [*en son eritage*] and on which there was wheat growing, and just as Jehan was reaping his wheat, Pierre offered him the money and because he did not want to take it Pierre had the wheat (both what was reaped and what remained to be reaped) attached *in situ* by the judge, requesting that the said Jehan be made to take his money, and that he be given all the wheat, both what was reaped and remaining on the land, and what was still to be reaped. Jehan answered that he acknowledged him as a successor, and he was willing to take his money, but he wanted to take the wheat which had been reaped before Jehan offered him the money; and he requested to be paid for his loss by reason of the workmen he had hired to reap the wheat, who had not completed their days of work. And on this issue they requested a judgment.

1403. It was judged that the buyer would take the wheat which had been reaped before the offer, and the person redeeming would take the rest, and the buyer would pay the workmen for what they had done before the offer, and the person redeeming would pay for the rest. And by this judgment you can see that things are as was said above.

1404. We have said above that a buyer must not reap green wheat, not pick unripe grapes, nor cut down timber of less than seven years' growth. But if he has meadows on the land he purchased, he can cut the hay any time he likes, or reap the green fallow fields [*reces*] to feed his animals or to sell, and he is not bound to give any restitution to the person making redemption, for it is the custom to take advantage of this crop as soon as it can be put to use.

1405. Some people who have bought property and are afraid it will be redeemed leave the land fallow until a year and a day have passed, to depreciate and devalue the property for those who have the right to redeem. And because this is premeditated sharp practice and to another's detriment, if the person making redemption were to complain, it is our opinion that the buyer would have to make restitution for the damages; for it would have been better if the person redeeming had paid more for it according to the advancing season than that the buyer should have left the field waste, for the money is to the advantage of the buyer and a property left fallow does no good to anyone. And although we have not seen such a case reach trial, I agree that if such a case *did* reach a judgment, the person making the redemption should be given in damages the fair price the property would have brought in during the year it was left fallow by the above-mentioned sharp practice.

1406. A person wanting to redeem must give the buyer an inspection day if he wants it.[12] And if he wants an inspection, and the person making the redemption shows him some property other than the property he is trying to redeem, and the year and a day since the buyer bought goes by during the suit, the person trying to redeem has lost his opportunity; for if he offered the money within a year and a day and the inspection day was assigned, and he did not show in the inspection the parcel on which he had made the offer, the suit would be dismissed as if no offer had ever been made. But if the person wanting to redeem noticed he had made an inadequate inspection within the year and a day within which his redemption rights last, he could dismiss the suit he was prosecuting futilely [*folement*] and make a new offer, and thus he might be able to make a redemption. But if a year and a day have passed before he gives notice of his erroneous inspection by making a new offer, he cannot redeem his land, as is said above.

1407. Pierre made a redemption on behalf of his wife because she was at the *third* degree of kinship from the seller, and having made this redemption, Pierre was sued by Jehan who said he was of the lineage of the seller and he wanted to redeem the property; and Pierre answered: "If you can prove you are from her lineage I am willing for you to redeem the property." And the Jehan proved he was at the *fourth* degree of kinship to the seller; and when Pierre saw that he was of a more distant degree of kinship than Pierre's wife, he said he could not redeem the property, for his wife was closer in kinship; and Jehan said that he could, since Pierre had told him unconditionally [*tout simplement*] that if he could prove his kinship he could redeem. Pierre replied that this concession could not and should not disinherit his wife, especially since she had not been there when he made the concession, and had not consented to it. And Jehan said yes it did, and that Pierre could dispose of the property by his agreement or his concession without his wife's consent. And on this issue they requested a judgment.

1408. It was judged that the consent that Pierre had given Jehan gave him no right to redeem the property.

1409. Now let's see what should be done if Jehan sues Pierre on this agreement; for since the property which has passed to the wife from her side of the family cannot be transferred without the wife's consent, it seems to us that you should make an honest estimate of the value of the property and what it cost and Pierre should have to pay the said Jehan the value over and above the price paid, because he gave his consent to the redemption, which he cannot deliver or warrantee; and he foolishly left himself open to a suit, for if he had said: "I consent to your redeeming the property if you can prove you are closer in kinship than my wife," he would have been free of this suit because Jehan could prove only the fourth degree of kinship, and

Pierre's wife was at the third degree. And Pierre may well have meant that by what he said, but you judge by what is said, and not by what people intended to say.

1410. It sometimes happens that while a man and a woman are living together in marriage and have children, they purchase some property which descends on the father's side and afterwards the mother dies, and the minor children remain in their father's guardianship. Now let's see how the father can redeem from the children their mother's portion of the purchased property. We say that according to our custom, as long as the children are still minors, the father is not obliged to offer the money to his children, for he holds everything because of his guardianship. But as soon as one of the children comes of age, he must offer him the money within a year and a day; and if he lets the year and a day pass, he has no recourse, but the children take half of the purchased property as heirs of their mother. And what we have said about a father redeeming property bought on his side of the family applies also to property on the mother's side which is bought, and the father dies and the mother wants to redeem half of the property.

1411. If a father and mother redeem a piece of property on the father's side and the father dies, the children can redeem their mother's portion within a year and a day of the father's death. And if they are minors when the father dies, the year and a day redemption period begins to run as soon as the oldest child comes of age. And if the oldest child does not want to or cannot redeem, the other children are not prevented from redeeming within a year and a day after they come of age. And in the same way, if the property was redeemed on their mother's side and the mother died, the children can redeem the property from their father. And in all these purchases that father and mother can make from their children, and children from their fathers and mothers, as is described above, when the fief is redeemed for money there are only as many homages due for it as there were when it was bought. But if there was no redemption and each person takes his or her portion, each person must pay homage for his or her portion, and in this way lords may receive two or more homages where there was only one before.

1412. If someone wants to challenge someone else's ownership of something, he should do so in court before the lord who has cognizance of the suit and on the day assigned; for a dispute made outside the presence of the judge with jurisdiction is worth very little, and it cannot hurt the person in seisin. Therefore if I want to redeem some property and the buyer does not want to take the money or he delays, I should not wait before offering the money in the presence of the lord; for the offer I made to him out of the presence of the lord would not avail me, and he would remain in possession of the property; and we have seen things dealt with this way. And also if you hold land belonging to me, or you collect the rents which should go to me, or you cut my timber and I challenge this and demand that you leave, all these disputes are worth nothing until they are brought to court before the judge having jurisdiction; and no such disputes would disturb my defense of peaceful possession [*teneure paisible*] for peaceful possession is that which is enjoyed with no hindrance from the lord.

1413. No one must be deprived of seisin of something as long as he claims to be in proper seisin of it until he is legally removed from seisin according to the complaint of the other party. And the request of the plaintiff is not enough for the lord to remove seisin at the beginning of the case, for each person should carry on his suit in seisin of the thing he was in seisin of at the beginning of the suit, unless the suit is for force or novel disseisin,[13] confiscation, robbery,[14] or larceny.[15] For in these cases the lord can, at the beginning of the suit, take charge of the thing which is in dispute. Nevertheless, if the person found in seisin gives sureties, the thing can be give back to him, on his request,[16] and in the other cases he is not required to give sureties; instead he should be restored to full seisin before he answers any complaint made against him. And it is right for him to defend himself only while in seisin of what was in his seisin when the suit began.

1414. We have spoken of much sharp practice [*baras*] between buyers and sellers to avoid redemption; and those who have to sell go along willingly with any agreements the buyer wants; for the sellers don't care much provided they get what they want for the land they are selling. And along with what we have said, we have subsequently heard tell of a piece of chicanery [*malice*] which was used to exclude parents from a redemption. For Pierre offered to sell his property to Jehan, and Jehan said he would not buy the property, but would buy the fruits for six years. And a deal was made for the said fruits and, under a lease, Jehan was placed in seisin by the lord from whom the land was held. And within the first or second year, the said Pierre and the said Jehan renegotiated the deal on ownership, and the deal was that Jehan (who was holding under a lease) bought the property, and they paid the proper sales tax to the lord for the price of the property; and if the lease had not been made at the lord's consent, he would also have had some sales tax for the difference between the price and what it would have brought without the lease as encumbrance. And afterwards within a year and a day of the sale of the property, one of Pierre's relatives appeared in court and offered to redeem; and Jehan replied that he would willingly take the price he paid for the property, maintaining his right to the years he should hold the land because of the previous lease; and the person wishing to redeem said that since he saw his relative's property leaving his possession for ever, he wanted to regain it, whatever the deal was by which his relative left it. And they requested a judgment on the issue of whether the buyer would enjoy the remaining years of the lease or whether the person redeeming would get possession right away. The jurors giving the ruling discussed it for a long time, looking at the danger for the successors if Jehan continued to enjoy the remaining years of his lease, for all those wanting to exclude in bad faith successors and persons redeeming property would then first lease it for six or ten or twelve years, or more, for a small sum of money, and afterwards they would buy the property for a great sum of money; and thus if such leases were upheld in a redemption, few or none would want to redeem because they would only get possession after the lease was over. And for this reason the jurors gave a judgment[17] that if someone holds property on a lease, and within the years of his lease he buys the property and someone wants to redeem it, the person redeeming must pay the price for the ownership of the property, and the price of the lease, according to the time the lease still had to run under the lease agreement, not according to the value of the fruits, but according to what had actually been paid for their enjoyment. And thus the person redeeming entered into possession of the property by giving the price of the property and four-sixths of what the six-year lease had cost; and he only gave back four-sixths of the lease money because the buyer had already harvested crops for two of the six years of the lease when he bought the property, so that he had only four more years to hold it under the lease. And by this judgment you can see that a deal for the lease of property is canceled when the person taking the lease buys the property within the term of his lease.

1415. When we said in the above judgment that Jehan was only paid for four of the six years of his lease because he had already taken a harvest for two years when he bought the property, it was because the property being sued on bore a crop each year. For if it had been immature timber which he had leased to cut when it matured, or fallow land from which he had not yet taken a crop, or a fish reservoir from which he had not yet taken any fish, or some other property from which he could not have taken any profit, he could have had the price of the lease for all six years, and the reasonable costs for cultivating and labor along with the price of the property, so that the person redeeming would not benefit from his not having taken any crop up till then. And anyone can see that this is reasonable.

1416. It would have been different in the above-described judgment if Jehan had held Pierre's property under a lease and then did not want to buy the property during his lease, and Pierre sold it to someone else, for in that case Jehan *would* enjoy his lease in which he had been placed by the lord, and no buyer or person redeeming could enter until he had finished his lease time; but provided this was not done in bad faith, for example, if someone took a lease and then had the property bought by someone else once the year and a day had passed, or during the time of the lease, and afterwards he obtained ownership of the property from the person who had gained seisin. Wherever such frauds are discovered, the property must go back to its original condition, so that no one loses by sharp practices knowingly engaged in.

1417. If someone leaves a fifth of his inherited real property to be sold by his executors and the executors sell it outside the lineage of the deceased, the deceased's relatives can redeem it just as if the deceased had sold it during his lifetime; for the fact that property is sold because of a will should not make the relatives lose their right which is vested in them because of their lineage. But it would be different if the deceased had bought the property, for then there could be no redemption if the executors sold the property.

Here ends the chapter on redemptions.

Notes

1. Since Pierre's brother had sued Jehan, it would make more sense if this response were made by Jehan and not Pierre; but Pierre would have to be the

warrantor of Jehan for the land, and would be involved in the suit. Beugnot has Jehans here.

2. For degrees of kinship, see Chapter 19.

3. Purchased property has a different status from inherited property, because it can be sold by the original buyer, or left in a will, and does not descend automatically to the heirs. Once purchased property has been inherited one time, however, it becomes inherited real property. Beaumanoir uses the word *eritage* for "inherited real property," and *aquès* or *conquès* for "purchased property." When the difference is not critical, both have been translated simply "property" or even sometimes "land."

4. It is the first buyer who makes the deal and therefore sets the price at which the redeeming buyer can buy back the property. In that sense he is the other's broker.

5. The reform was introduced at the Fourth Lateran Council in 1215.

6. For inspection days, see Chapter 9.

7. This suit is essentially a repetition of the one described in §§770–71.

8. Here the successor means a person closely enough related to the seller to have a right of redemption.

9. For custodianship and guardianship, see Chapter 15.

10. For attorneys and letters of appointment, see Chapter 4.

11. Beaumanoir seems to mean that no offer has been made to redeem and that the summons does not mention a redemption, but merely calls the defendant buyer into court without saying why.

12. For inspection days, see Chapter 9.

13. For force and novel disseisin, see Chapter 32.

14. For robbery, see Chapter 30.

15. For larceny, see Chapter 31.

16. For this kind of recovery of seized property, called "reclamation," see Chapter 53.

17. Here is a clear case of jurors making law, not merely remembering it. Their decision is clearly based on public policy grounds.

45. Avowals

Here begins the forty-fifth chapter of this book which speaks of avowals and disavowals, serfdom and freedom, and the danger in disavowing and how you should sue those who disavow.

1418. A person who disavows[1] his true lord and avows holding his land from another lord is not keeping his faith towards his lord; and there is a danger of disastrous loss [*de perdre vilainement*] by the improper avowals which are made to the detriment of lords. And so that you can avoid making improper avowals, in this chapter [*partie*] we will speak of making avowals and disavowals, and the losses which can arise from such things, and of serfdom and freedom.

1419. If a gentleman holds or should hold a fief from Pierre, and he claims to hold it from Jehan, and Pierre confiscates the fief, and makes a seizure of it because of the disavowal, Jehan from whom he claims to hold it, should request Pierre to release possession, since the fief has been claimed to be held from Jehan. And if Pierre wants to say that the fief should not be held from Jehan but from him, and that because it was claimed not to be from him he took possession of it, this does not mean that he should not relinquish possession and reseise the holder, if he has confiscated any profits; and then he should summon the holder before Jehan, from whom the holder has claimed to hold it. And the suit on the disavowal should be brought in the court of the said Jehan. And if Pierre does not want to act in this manner, but tries to hold the fief and reap the profits because of the disavowal, he should be obliged by the count, at the request of Jehan and the holder, to relinquish possession and reseise the holder, and then sue the holder in Jehan's court if he wishes, in the manner described above; for he cannot get a judgment against the holder who made the disavowal any other way. Thus you can see that a person wishing to sue because there has been a disavowal of what should be held from him must sue for his rights in the court of the person from whom it is claimed the fief is held.

1420. A disavowal can be made in several ways. The first way is if I have summoned a man I believe to be, or who should be, my vassal, and he is in default every time, and because he has defaulted I make a seizure of property on the fief, and he comes to me to ask why I have made the seizure, and I say: "For these defaults," and he replies: "I did not have to appear when summoned, for I hold nothing from you, nor should I, but I hold my property from this other person." If he speaks in this manner, it is a legal disavowal, and the person who has made the seizure of property for the defaults should give it back, and then he should sue him in the court of the person from whom he claims to hold the fief. But if he says: "I hold nothing from you," and he will not name the person he holds from, the first lord should not give back what he seized for the defaults, and should continue to reap the profits of the fief (as if for lack of a vassal) until the other has named the lord from whom he claims he should hold, for a disavowal has not been made until he has named the person he holds from. And the profits taken during the period when he would not name his lord should be given back to the holder, once he has named his lord, but on his giving security [*par recreance*] that if the first lord can (in the court of the lord he has named as his lord) find him guilty of an improper disavowal, the first lord can get back what he rightfully confiscated. And the profits reaped during the suit should be given to the holder, not at his reclamation² but freely, for it would be a bad thing for him to be giving security for things for which he had a lord whom he wanted to acknowledge in his hearing; for he could otherwise hardly fight the suit if he had no other possessions but what was in dispute.

1421. The second way in which a disavowal is made is when the person claiming to be the lord confiscates the property for some reason and the holder does not go to him, but to some other lord to ask him to warrantee what he holds from him; and the lord to whom this request is made goes to the lord who made the confiscation and says to him: "I have a vassal who holds the fief which you have seized and he declares he holds it from me; and I request you to relinquish possesson. And if you want to sue him, appear in my court: I will give you a fair hearing." In that case, the person who made the seizure should relinquish possession and unconditionally give back to the holder anything he has taken in the way of profits and summon him to appear before the lord who claimed the fief was held from him. And there the holder must declare that he holds from him the fief the first lord had seized, for until he has said this, there is no disavowal. At this point if he realizes or believes he has made a mistake in not obeying the lord who made the seizure for his defaults or disobedience, he can make amends to his rightful lord by paying the fines for the defaults or the disobedience. But if he waits until he names another lord, he cannot make amends to the first lord who is suing him; if the latter can show him guilty of a false disavowal, the holder loses the fief and the lord who sued him in the court of the lord he falsely claimed to hold it from wins the fief. And by this you can see the danger and the loss which can come of avowing the wrong lord, and disavowing your rightful lord.

1422. The third way of disavowing is when the holder will not obey or pay the dues owed on the fief, but renounces all rights to the fief by saying to the lord that he does not want to hold anything from him, and that he renounces everything he holds, or by saying nothing for so long that the lord can win by long tenure against him; but this tenure must be a peaceful one of ten years, in the sight and knowledge of the person who could ask for his fief. And even ten years would not suffice, unless he had made seizure and reaped the profits pursuant to a judgment of his peers, to prevent the vassal coming back by paying the fines for his defaults and disobedience.

1423. Everyone should know who he holds from, and ask his lord to protect what he holds from him if someone is using force on him or preventing his enjoyment of it; and the lords have to warrantee what their vassals hold from them. And when it happens that the lords do not know who he should be holding from, and Pierre says to the holder: "You should be holding this from me," and Jehan says: "No, from me," and there is a suit because they both want the homage to be theirs, the holder in such cases is not obliged to avow one and disavow the other, for he could lose because of the lords' dispute. Therefore in such a case the lords should plead in the sovereign's court over who should receive the homage, and when one of them has been given the judgment, the holder should be obliged by the sovereign to do homage to the person winning the judgment. And in such cases the holders are better off not to make an avowal, for they could lose as is described above.

1424. The fourth way of disavowing is when a serf [hons de cors] disavows his lord because he says he is free and should be free, or because he says he is the serf of another lord. Therefore when a man makes such a disavowal, if he says he is free, the lord wishing to claim he is a serf should sue him before the lord under whom he is a resident; and if he says he is the serf of another lord, he should be sued in the court of the lord he avows.

1425. Although custom permits, and reason supports it, that you should sue those who disavow {being the serf of some lord} or disavow their fiefs, in the court of those whom they avow, nevertheless if the lords to whom the avowals are made are honest, they should not accept the avowal if they do not know or believe it is their right. Instead, if they want the right and honest thing, as soon as they see someone trying to make an avowal to them to which they have no right, they should say: "My friend [*beaus amis*] you are trying to make an avowal to me for holding this fief;" or: "You say you are my serf; do not make the avowal, for I have no right to accept it." And if he acts in this manner, he creates three great benefits: the first benefit is his own, for not wanting to claim [*aheritier*] someone else's rights; and the second benefit accrues to the person who wanted to make the avowal, for he can make amends to his true lord, without losing what he was about to disavow, because he has not yet made the disavowal; and the third benefit is to the lord who wanted to sue for his rights, for he saves him great costs and expenses.

1426. As we have said there are several kinds of disavowals and as we have spoken of several, it is right for us to say how you can and should get a judgment against [*ataindre*] those who falsely disavow themselves or their fiefs to their true lord, and there are several ways of doing this as you will hear.

1427. When someone disavows holding his fief from Pierre and says he holds from Jehan, and Pierre sues him in Jehan's court, he can if he wishes sue the holder by a wager of battle, saying that the holder of the property has falsely and dishonestly disavowed what he should hold from him. And to this {charge of} disloyalty the holder must answer and defend himself, or else the court will consider him as guilty and as having lost the fief concerning which he was being sued, and in such a case there can be a wager of battle.

1428. If Pierre prefers to sue the person who has disavowed the fief he holds from him by a procedure other than a wager of battle, if he wants to prove by live witnesses that the person disavowing did indeed become his vassal, or his father's vassal, or some other person's, from whom the right passed to Pierre, this is certainly enough to prove his contention. Nevertheless, the person disavowing can contest the witnesses, if he has a reason why they should be kept from testifying; and if he prefers, he can go by way of challenging the testimony by wager of battle, and how he can and should proceed is explained in the chapter on proofs {Chapter 39, §§1171 and ff. and see also Chapter 61, §1762}.

1429. The third way for Pierre to get a judgment against the holder who has disavowed him is by a writing, if he has one sealed by the seal of the person disavowing. And in this method there is no wager of battle, for if the holder acknowledges his seal, the writing is enforced; and if he denies it, it should be proved {genuine} in the way described in the chapter on agreements in writing {Chapter 35, §§1074–76}.

1430. There are other arguments to defeat your vassal who has disavowed, if you have them: for example if the holder had disavowed previously, and claimed to hold from another lord, before whom he was sued and found guilty of false disavowal, for the suits of dealers in sharp practice would never be over if they could make good their losses by pleading in a new court on the same issue they had already lost by a judgment in another court.[3]

1431. The serf who claims to be free should be sued on his birth [*orine*] by his true lord in the court of the lord where he is a resident, and if he claims to be the serf of someone else, then in that man's court. And he has no defense against the proof of his birth if it is made by his own lineage {family}. But if the lord suing him wants to prove his birth by some other witnesses not of his lineage, the defendant can challenge the witnesses if he has a reason why he can and should have them excluded, or by a wager of battle.

1432. A person sued on the charge that he is a serf can defend his freedom in the following ways, if he has any of them available. The first is if he and his mother have been in freedom all their lives without ever paying dues by reason of serfdom, in the sight and knowledge of the lord who is suing them or of his predecessors. Neverthless they might have used their free state in such a way that it would not avail them if the lord suing them proved that the mother of the mother[4] was his serf, for example, if they had been living for a long time outside the jurisdiction of the lord suing them, for it would appear that they had gone away to escape from servitude. But if the lord could not in this case prove their birth, they would remain free, and the lord would not be allowed to make any other proof than birth; for no one may say to a person who has always been free: "You are my serf," and try to prove it. If he does not claim the servitude by birth, or that they once paid him fees as serfs, his suit should not be entertained, and they should remain free.

1433. The second defense a person who is sued by someone claiming that he is a serf can raise, is if he admits his mother, or his grandmother, or his great-grandmother was a serf, but that she was freed by a person having the power to do so. And this must be proved by a writing or by live witnesses; and this proof having been adequately made, he should remain free.

1434. It is true that servitude passes through the mother, for all children of a servile mother are serfs, even if the father is free. Even if the father was a knight and married a serf, all the children he had by her would be serfs. And the children would be refused the rank of gentlemen in that they could not be knights, for a serf cannot be a knight, even though the gentle blood[5] which allows you to be a knight passes from the father; for it is a custom in the kingdom of France that those who are gentlemen through their fathers, even if their mother is a commoner [*vilaine*], can be knights, provided she be not a serf, for then it could not be, as is said above. When the mother is a gentlewoman, and the father is not a gentleman, the children cannot be knights; nevertheless, the children do not lose all their condition of gentlemen, but are treated as gentlemen personally, and they can hold fiefs, which commoners cannot do. And in this case you can see that the fullest condition of being gentle passes from the father, and servitude comes from mothers who are serfs. And it also follows that when a man who is a serf takes a wife who is free, all the children are free; and by this you can understand what is said above.

1435. The third defense which a person sued by someone claiming that he is a serf can raise is a reason which is not complimentary [*courtoise*]; nevertheless we have heard it raised several times in his defense by a person being sued as a serf: it is when he claims and wants to prove he is a bastard, and, having made this proof, he is free of the servitude. And the way to prove bastardy is when he proves he was born before his mother married her husband; or, although his mother had a husband, when he proves that his mother's husband, when he was born and for ten months before, had been in lands over the sea, or in a distant foreign country, without coming back, for by this proof it is obvious that he was not the son of the said husband. But in that case, if he wanted to prove the husband was a fugitive [*eschis*] for the above-mentioned ten months or longer, because of a fight, or debts, or banishment, this proof would not avail him, for it often happens that those who are on the run for such things occasionally come and go where their wives are, secretly and covertly, and he could have been conceived on such visits, which is more credible than the opposite. The third way he can prove bastardy is when he proves he was born ten months after the death of his mother's husband and during her widowhood. And when he has proved he is a bastard, he is discharged from servitude and is under the law of bastards. And because some people might think he would not gain from being born out of wedlock, the reason is that a bastard does not follow the condition of his father or of his mother, in lineage, in real property, or in anything they have;[6] and just as he would not share in any of their possessions or their good {gentle} condition, he should not share their bad {servile} condition or in the dues they owe their lords.

1436. The fourth defense a person sued by someone saying that he is a serf can raise is when he is a clerk and has been a clerk for ten years in the sight and knowledge of the person suing, and that person has never challenged his tonsure; for the lord who sees his serf becoming a clerk may go to the bishop and ask him not to tonsure the man, and if he has done so, to cancel it, and the bishop must do so; but the bishop must be asked before the man is of higher rank than a simple clerk, for if he waits until he has reached a higher rank, the clerk must remain free and he cannot be sued for servitude. And if the bishop makes my serf a clerk against my wishes, I have an action against him to get my damages for what he is worth and for his *personal* property which comes under the bishop's jurisdiction; but as for the *real* property of a clerk there is no doubt that I can take it and consider it mine.[7]

1437. For those trying to be freed from their servitude it is a good thing to have their freedom confirmed by the sovereign from whom their lord holds; for if I have serfs, which I hold from my lord, and I free them without the lord's authorization, I lose them; for I must maintain the freedom I have promised them as far as I can; but my lord would acquire them, for they would become his serfs, and thus he would get a benefit. And if I took some money to give them their freedom, I must give it back to them since I cannot ensure their freedom; for it is right that because I did what I could not and should not have done, they should pass into the possession of my lord as rich as when they were in my possession. And I must also pay a fine to my lord for having reduced {the value of} his fief, and the fine would be sixty pounds.

1438. Personal servitude arose in many manners, one of which was that formerly, when a person summoned his subjects for army service or for the defense of the crown, the penalty attached to the summons was that those who did not come, unless they had a good reason, were to remain forever serfs, they and their heirs; and many became serfs for this reason. The second reason many became serfs is that in past times, many devoted themselves to the saints, in great piety, along with their property and their heirs, and paid what they had promised in their hearts. And the financial officers [*receveur des biens*] of the churches wrote down what they could force them to admit, and thus they took profit from them and have always subsequently taken profit from them, more and more because of the wickedness which has grown in them more than it should have, so that what was originally done in good faith and piety has turned into the loss and ruin [*vilenie*] of the heirs. The third way in which some have become serfs is by sale, for example, when someone lapsed into poverty and he said to some lord: "You will give me so much and I will become your serf." And sometimes they gave themselves to be protected from other lords or from people who hated them. In all these ways people became serfs, for according to natural law everyone is free; but this natural freedom is ended by the acquisitions mentioned above. And there are other ways of entering servitude, for there are certain lands where, if free persons who are not of gentle birth go to live there and reside there a year and a day, whether man or woman, they become the serfs of the lord under whom they want to be resident; but this custom is not legal anywhere in the county of Clermont. Here, if a free man wants to stay, whether he lives among serfs or not, he does not lose his freedom, and if a serf comes to live here from another area and his lord comes after him and he admits he is his serf, he must be delivered to the lord and he can be taken away; and if he disavows him, and says he is not his serf, his lord must show him guilty by a proof of birth, as is said above; and when he is proved to be a serf, he must be given up along with all he owns.

1439. When a serf holds tenancies [*ostises*] from some lord other than the lord whose serf he is, and they pass to his lord because of the serfdom,[8] the latter cannot take possession of them unless the lord from whom they are held wishes it; instead he must sell them, or give them away, or exchange them with people who can and should do what the holding of tenancies requires. But the inheriting lord can keep and call his own other land held for quit-rent or for rent or for a share of the crop, by paying the rents and other dues to the lord from whom the lands were held, except that religious houses cannot do this: for because they hold in mortmain,[9] they can be forced to relinquish possession, within a year and a day, of the real property which passes to them, and which is held from some other lord than themselves, however it passes to them.

1440. By the present custom, serfs, male or female, may procure their freedom and that of their children, if they can obtain it from their lord and by the authority of his sovereign. But if a serf obtains freedom for himself and his children, and he becomes a serf again, his children are not thereby made serfs, for he may free his children but cannot make them serfs.

1441. A female serf who procures only her own personal freedom does not make free her heirs born when she was a serf; but those born after the freedom was given are free, and this is quite right, for the first children were born to a woman serf [*feme serve*], and the later children were born to a free woman [*fame franche*].

1442. If a pregnant woman who is a serf procures her freedom during her pregnancy, and then, before the child is born, she becomes a serf again, it might be asked whether the child is a serf or free. We say that the child is free for if it was free for however short a time in its mother's womb, the mother cannot make it a serf again.[10]

1443. We have spoken of disavowals and the danger which stems from them, and because some people might think that you can disavow *any* real property held from a lord, and that you have to sue over it as described above, we will show that this is not so; for land held in villeinage, for example, tenancies [*ostises*] or land held through a lease or for rent or for a share of the crop, cannot be disavowed. Now let's consider,—if someone holds land from me for a quit-rent and he pays someone else the quit-rent money and says he should hold the land from him,—what I should do. I should confiscate personal property[11] on the land for the non-payment of the quit-rent and until the fine is paid off. And if the lord to whom the quit-rent was paid says the land is held from him, I should not plead in his court because of what he or the tenant says; but he can sue in the sovereign's court and say that I took property wrongfully, where I cannot and should not take it, and then the lord can take charge of the dispute and find out who can make the best proof that the disputed land should be held from him, and give seisin to the person who obtains the favorable ruling. And what we said about land held for quit-rent [*censives*] we also say about all land held in villeinage.

1444. Now let's see, in a suit such as we have just described, which lord should get the seisin: the one who has recently received the quit-rent, or the person who confiscated property on the land because of non-payment of quit-rent? We say it is the one who received the quit-rent, if he received it a year and a day before the other made a confiscation on the land for non-payment of quit-rent; but if it is less than a year and a day, then he should not; in that case, the one who has made the confiscation for non-payment of quit-rent should keep what he has confiscated, until the ownership is determined by a judgment, for otherwise the lords from whom such lands are held could have lots of problems, if they lost possession of what they had confiscated each time their tenants said it should be held from someone else.

1445. Just as you cannot alienate your fief or sell parts of it without the consent of your lord from whom you hold it, you cannot free your serf without the approval of the person from whom you hold the serf, for the rights I have over my serf come from my fief. Therefore if I give him his freedom, I reduce the value of my fief by as much as it was greater when he was a serf than now when he is a free man. And a person who thus frees a serf loses him as for himself, for he is released from his servitude to that person; but the lord from whom he was held can sue him as his serf, so that he becomes the serf of the lord from whom he was held; but a serf can be freed by his former master in such a way that he can sue him before the sovereign and ask him to guarantee his freedom as he agreed to do for his work or his payment, or if he gave him a writing in which he bound himself to guarantee his freedom. When the lords lose a suit brought against them by those they have freed concerning such agreements, they must be required to guarantee their freedom by making it right with the lords, from level to level, that he should be freed. And if he cannot do so, because the lords do not wish to agree to his remaining free, the person who freed the serf must recompense him for his loss in remaining a serf, and this can scarcely be evaluated. And when an estimate is made for the the value of a woman, it should be greater than for a man, because the children of the man can win freedom if the father marries a free woman, but no matter whom a serf woman marries all her children remain serfs; and for this reason it would be hard to overestimate the value to a woman of her loss in remaining a serf. And if those who have serfs are wary of giving freedom they will be acting wisely, and if they want to give freedom they should do so only in respect to their own rights, with the rights of their lords remaining intact; then they will only be able to be sued for guaranteeing freedom as far as they are concerned personally.

1446. Just as we have said above that no one can free his serf without the authorization of his sovereign, so no one can reduce the services required for a fief [*donner abriegement de services de fief*], or make a villeinage into a fief [*franchise d'eritage*], without the authorization of his overlord [*pardessus*]. And if someone does reduce the services required for a fief held from him, or frees some piece of land {converts it from villeinage to fief}, the lord from whom the land is held takes over the homage; and full service is owed, both for the land he finds thus freed and for the fief which is given in villeinage [*fief. . . donné a vilenage*]. And if those who are the owners of the property want to sue the lord who reduced the services for the fief, or who gave them a fief in villeinage, or who freed the villeinage which depended on the fief, they can sue the lord who gave this to them, and he must guarantee what he gave them in the manner described above for those who free their serfs without the consent of their lords.[12]

1447. Now let's see, if the serfs whose freedom cannot be guaranteed by those who freed them are recompensed for the loss of their freedom, whether the money they receive as recompense is like the money they had before;[13] for in this case they would gain but little, if what they received instead of their freedom remained servile {could be seized by their masters}. And for this reason we are of the opinion that if the {new} lords of the serfs want the recompense money, they should grant the serfs freedom to get it. And if they will not grant freedom to the serfs, we believe that the serfs should be free to do what they want with the recompense money, either leaving it in a will or anything else, for they should be able to make free use of what they receive instead of their freedom.

1448. There is a recent [*de nouvel*] law that no serf should be so bold as to make his or her son a clerk, nor put his or her daughter into a convent.

And all the other serfs who know that someone is doing this are ordered to inform their lord as soon as they can. And if they do not inform him, they will be punished in the same way as those who do such a thing, that is to say prison with hard labor [*grief prison*] and forfeiture of their possessions to the lord; for by such concealed actions various lords have lost some of their serfs, those who became priests, deacons, or subdeacons, for they remained free by reason of the freedom of the condition they entered. But now you can sue as serfs those who are tonsured, provided it is before they have become deacons or subdeacons, and they are brought back to the servile condition and lose the tonsure, because they cannot be serfs and clerks, since freedom and serfdom are two different things.

1449. We heard someone tell a tale that not long ago a gentleman married a serf thinking she was free. They had children. One of the children, when he came of age, became a knight because he was a gentleman through his father. After he was a knight he was accused of being a serf, and when he learned the truth from his mother, he saw that he could not claim to be free by birth. He chose another argument, for he said he should remain free because his mother was a serf of the lord who had made him a knight: and he could not accuse him of being a serf since he had made him a knight. And the lord replied that when he made him a knight he did not know that he was a serf. And on this they requested a judgment, namely whether he would remain free or a serf.

1450. It was judged in the king's court that the knight would remain free because the person who had the right to make him free had made him a knight, for by giving him the freedom of knighthood he took away his serfdom. But it would have been different if someone other than his lord had made him a knight; for his lord could sue him as a serf who had become free without his permission, and could have taken him back, and he would have had his knighthood taken away from him, for he could not be a knight and a serf at the same time, since they are two opposite conditions, one of freedom and the other of serfdom. And when it is said that gentlemen whose fathers were gentlemen can become knights, although they are not of gentle blood by their mother, this is when the mother is of free birth, for example a daughter of townsmen or commoners, free and not servile.

1451. You should know that there are three conditions of laypeople. The first is being of gentle condition [*gentillece*]. The second is the condition of those who are free by nature, such as those born of free mothers, and this freedom is possessed by all those who can and should be called gentle-men. But not all free persons are gentlemen; instead there is a great difference between gentlemen and free commoners, for we call gentlemen those who come from a free lineage, such as kings or dukes or counts or knights; and this gentle blood comes down through the fathers, and not through the mothers; and this is obvious, because no one, however gentle he is through his mother, can be a knight if he is not gentle through his father, unless the king grants him special permission. But it is different with commoners, for their freedom comes from their mothers,—and whoever is born of a free mother is free,—and they are free to do what they want, except commit crimes and offenses, which are forbidden among Christians for the public welfare.

1452. We have spoken of two conditions, that of gentlemen and that of free commoners, and the third condition is that of serfs. And all these people are not the same, but there are several kinds of serfdom. For some serfs are so subjected to their lord that he can take all they have, when they die or when they are still alive, and he can keep them in prison any time he wants, rightly or wrongly, for he is answerable for them only to God. And the others are treated more leniently, for unless they commit some offense their lord cannot ask them for anything for as long as they live except their quit-rents and their rents and their dues they pay as serfs. And when they die or marry free women, whatever they own passes to the lord, both real and personal property; for those who marry outside[14] must pay a penalty to the lord and he sets it at his discretion. And when a serf dies, he has no heir but his lord, and the children of a serf take nothing unless they pay the lord for it as an outsider would. And this last custom we have described is the one current in the customs of Beauvais for both successions [*mortes mains*][15] and marriages outside; and for the other conditions of serfs in other lands we can be silent, because our book is about the customs of the Beauvais region.

1453. Although there are several conditions of men now, it is true that in the beginning they were all free and with the same freedom, for everyone knows we are all descended from one father and mother. But when the people began to grow in numbers, and wars and ill will began to arise through pride and envy, which was greater then than it should be and still is, the community of people, those who wanted to live in peace, saw that they could not live in peace if each one thought he was as great a lord as everyone else, and they chose a king and made him lord over them and gave him the power to punish them for their offenses, to give them orders and make laws; and so that he could protect the people from their enemies, and bad administrators, they sought out among themselves those who were the most beautiful, the strongest, and the wisest, and gave them lordship over themselves to help them to remain in peace and to help the king, and they would be his vassals to help him protect them. And from these people have descended those who are called gentlemen, and from the others who chose them those who are called free but not gentle. And serfs have acquired their servility in many ways. For some have become so by being captured in a war; and they accepted serfdom for themselves and their heirs as ransom or in order to be let out of prison; and others have become serfs by selling themselves, out of either poverty or desire for gain; and other serfs were made when the king had affairs of state and he went to fight foreign people, and he ordered all those who could bear arms to go and help him, and if anyone remained behind, he and his heirs would be of servile condition; and some have been made serfs because they fled from battles; and some have become serfs because they gave themselves to the saints out of devotion when the Christian religion began to grow; and others became serfs because they could not defend themselves against lords who wrongfully and by force placed them in servitude. And however they became serfs, it is a great act of charity for the lord to remove them from servility and to give them freedom, for it is a great evil when any Christian is in the condition of a serf.

1454. It often happens that the property which passes to lords by reason of the death of their serfs is held from lords other than the serf's lord; and for this reason, as long as they hold the land, the lords must pay the dues owed by the land to the lords from whom they are held, just as the serfs had done. And when such a piece of property passes to a religious house, the house must relinquish possession of the property to a layperson, by sale or gift; for even though the land came from the house's serf, what the serf of a religious house acquires does not pass to the house unless it is permitted by the sovereign. But the houses can sell the property without paying sales tax [*ventes*], for sales tax should not be paid for property sold by a religious house on the order of the sovereign; because the house is not selling of its own free will, it can put to its own use the price of the sale.

1455. There is no doubt that if someone marries a woman who was his serf, whether he knew it or not, he gives her her freedom, even though there was no mention of it, nor a charter nor a declaration [*otrois*]; for it would be a bad thing if the children which were to be born remained in servitude after he had married their mother. And although we have said above that you cannot free your serfs without the consent of the lord you hold them from, in this case the lord must permit {her to be freed} provided that the person who married his serf makes up the value of the fief, or repays his lord in some other way.

1456. If freedom is granted to a serf without any mention of other persons, you should know that all the heirs of the freed man who are born after the grant of freedom are free; but those who were born before the grant remain in servitude, because they were not named specially in the grant of freedom. And if the man who is freed has a wife who is a serf, or marries a woman who is a serf after his freedom has been granted, the grant of freedom is good only for him personally; for all children born of a woman serf, whoever the father is, are serfs, except the children born to her out of wedlock; for a bastard is not considered a serf, because he has no lineage and he cannot inherit by descent or laterally.[16] Therefore if a bastard happens to acquire some property, real or personal, and when he dies not everything has been left in his will, what remains after his testamentary gifts have been paid passes to the lord in whose land his possessions are found, like lost property, although he may have had a father and mother, or sisters and brothers, or other relatives a bastard can have by natural relationships, for according to our custom a bastard has no lineage; for which reason we have seen pleadings by persons trying to prove themselves bastards in order to escape a suit claiming they were serfs through their mothers.[17]

1457. Our custom is more lenient toward serfs than it is in many places, for in many other districts the lords can confiscate property from their serfs when they die or while they are still alive, any time they want and as much as they want. And they can force them to live always on their land [*dessous aus*]; but they are treated more leniently in Beauvais, for as long as they pay their lords the customary rents and poll tax [*chevages*] they can go and work or live outside their lords' jurisdiction,—provided they do not disavow the right their lord has over them to confiscate their property if they marry outside,—except in the places where they could acquire their freedom by taking residence, for example, in certain towns where all the inhabitants are free by privilege, or by custom. For as soon as a lord knows his serf is setting up residence in such a place, if he sues to have him returned within a year and a day,—or within whatever length of time is established by the custom of the place where he has gone to live,—he must get him back, and several serfs have by this method acquired their freedom, who secretly left their lords and went to live in such places.

1458. By our custom also the serf can win and lose by trading, and can live more or less independently on what he has, for his lord cannot and must not prevent him from doing so. And they can have this control over the things they acquire by hard and painful work, and the lords only gain by it; for the serfs enrich themselves more willingly and then the property that passes to the lord when a serf dies or marries outside is that much greater. And it is said in a proverb that you can only skin a cat once [*cil qui une fois escorche ne .II. ne .III. ne tout*]; and it is obvious in the districts where the property of serfs is confiscated every day, that they only want to earn enough to support themselves and their household.

1459. Everyone should know by what we have said in this chapter the danger in disavowing what you should hold from some lord, and we have said that you have to sue a person who disavows in the court of the lord who *is* avowed. Nevertheless, you cannot disavow everything; for although a serf can disavow his true lord and claim to be the serf of another lord, and the lord whose serf he is may lose seisin of him because of the disavowal, and must sue him in the court of the lord he claims as his, if he wants to get him back as his serf, nevertheless this is not true of land held as villeinages, which I have described above, for according to our custom these lands cannot be avowed or disavowed whatever the tenant says or does. Therefore if Pierre asks for jurisdiction over one of these villeinages because he say it is held from him, for quit-rent or for a share of the crop, and the person occupying the land says he holds nothing from Pierre, but he holds from Jehan, Jehan will not get seisin because of the tenant's words; instead, if the said Jehan believes he is entitled to anything on the land because he has jurisdiction over it or because quit-rents or rents are due to him, he can confiscate some property if Pierre will let him; and if Pierre will not let him because he claims the judisdiction and the dues are his, and Jehan says they are his, in that case there should be a full hearing between Pierre and Jehan in the count's court, to find out who has the jurisdiction and seisin; and by this you can see that a villeinage can be neither avowed nor disavowed. And if Pierre and Jehan plead on seisin, and each one claims to be properly seised, in that case proof must be made by both parties, and the person best proving his most recent peaceful seisin for a year and a day will win the ruling, and then the other party can sue on ownership if he wants.

1460. We have said that you cannot avow or disavow a villeinage, and likewise not everyone can make an avowal or disavowal, for those who hold other people's fief in custodianship or guardianship, or in dower, or for a lease, or for a term of years, or for a payment [*a ferme*] cannot avow or disavow when they are not the owners of the property. And for this reason they cannot put the land in danger of being lost; for a person disavowing who is legally able to do so because he is the true heir, loses everything he disavowed if he loses the suit on false avowal, as we have said elsewhere in this very chapter.

1461. Although villeinages may not be avowed or disavowed, as we have said, nevertheless the tenants of land can suffer loss if they avow holding the land from a different lord than they should, and the loss is not losing the land, but a fine. For example if I hold a piece of land from Pierre for quit-rent or for a share of the crop, and I do not give him his quit-rent or his share of the crop, but I pay it to Jehan saying that I hold the land from him, Pierre can in that case come on to the land and confiscate some property because I am not paying him his share of the crop or his rent as I should; and what such fines should be is explained in the chapter on offenses {Chapter 30, §§852, 862 and 865}.

1462. There is a great difference between disavowing a guardianship and disavowing real property, for disavowing land which can be disavowed puts you in danger of losing the land, but {wrongfully} disavowing guardianship is punished by a fine. For certain lords have the guardianship of certain religious houses, but do not for that reason have the lordship or jurisdiction over them: therefore when the houses disavow the guardianship of the person in whose guardianship they should be, and claim to be in the guardianship of some other person, and they are proved to have disavowed falsely, they must pay a fine of sixty pounds and remain in the guardianship of the person they disavowed.[18]

1463. Religious houses, if they make a disavowal concerning the property left to them and exempted from taxes [*amortis*] or concerning guardianship, cannot lose the ownership of the land given to them and exempted from dues; for the property which was given to them and exempted from taxes, for the service of God, by lords who could lawfuly do so, cannot come back into the hands of laymen because of the offenses committed by the administrators [*gouverneur*] of the houses. For if they could come back into lay hands because of the improper conduct of those who hold them for the houses, the houses would lose often, and could thereby be destroyed or diminished; and for this reason, the administrators [*mainburnisseur*] of religious houses pay money fines for any offenses they commit, according to the offense and what is said in the chapter on offenses {Chapter 30}.

1464. Those who can make avowals and disavowals can also do this through an attorney, provided that the power to do so is contained in the attorney's letter of appointment; for the chapters [*couvent*] attached to religious houses do not need to go to court to proceed with their hearings, and neither do great lords nor persons who can appoint attorneys for themselves. Nevertheless, those who cannot appoint attorneys, such as commoners, or the mass of gentlemen who do not hold directly from the king, cannot make disavowals by attorney, but must appear in person and disavow. Therefore what we have said about disavowing by attorney applies only to religious houses and the great lords who hold directly from the king, and to those who have received special permission from the king to plead through an attorney both as plaintiffs and as defendants.

Here ends the chapter on avowals and disavowals, and on servitude and freedom.

Notes

1. *Aveus* and *desaveus* have been translated here as "avowals" and "disavowals." The former might have been better translated as "acknowledgment [of lordship]," but there would have been no good parallel term for the negative, although "denial" might have done. Therefore I have kept words which look a bit like the Old French equivalents; and the reader should remember that it is the lower of the two persons involved who avows or disavows, meaning that he acknowledges someone as his lord or denies that someone is his lord, respectively. The penalty is for *false* avowal or disavowal only, of course.

2. For reclamations, see Chapter 53.

3. Lawyers will recognize here the venerable principle of *res judicata*.

4. Some manuscripts omit the words "of the mother."

5. Beaumanoir does not mention blood, but this is a common way to express the inheritance of rank in English.

6. I have followed the lesson of MSS A, B, C, and G, which have the plural *qu'il aient*, even though Salmon has chosen to follow the manuscripts with the singular *qu'il ait*.

7. Beaumanoir does not explain at this point how it is that a serf who became a clerk would have been a holder of real property. Normally a serf has no possessions of his own, for anything he has or acquires belongs to his lord.

8. Beaumanoir probably means the lands passing to the lord when his serf dies, for a serf can leave only five sous by will. See Chapter 12, §365.

9. Land held by the church never changed ownership, and hence never paid inheritance taxes. This was referred to as mortmain.

10. This paragraph is clearly identical to a passage of Justinian, *Institutes*, 1, 4, *De Ingenuis*.

11. The profits from real property, such as harvested crops and cut timber, are considered personal property and can be transported after confiscation.

12. This somewhat confusing section suggests that it is difficult (but not impossible) to make a freehold fief, owing services of homage to the overlord, into a servile fief, owing money rents or a share of the crops, and vice versa. For either of these operations the overlord's permission is required.

13. A serf's possessions belong to his lord, in other words they are servile like the serf himself. Beaumanoir here addresses the problem by saying that the money the serf is awarded because the promise of freedom could not be kept should not go to his new master.

14. *Formariage* includes marriage of a serf with another serf belonging to a different lord, or with a free person.

15. In some places serfs could leave these possessions to their children who were still in their household, but not to those who were emancipated. This was true for men called *hommes de main morte*. But in the Beauvaisis, it appears that even children living at home took nothing by action of law.

16. For inheritance by direct descent or laterally, see Chapter 15.

17. See §1435.

18. The pronouns and grammatical constructions in this last sentence are somewhat confused, but there are no variant readings. I have given what I take to be the sense of the passage, in the light of the next paragraph.

46. Religious Houses

Here begins the forty-sixth chapter of this book which speaks of the guardianship of religious houses [eglises],[1] *and how they should be protected from offenders and those who ill-treat them.*

1465. There is a difference between guardianship[2] [*garde*] and jurisdiction [*justice*], for a man may have jurisdiction over a place where he does not have guardianship, and another man have the guardianship without jurisdiction; and it is true that the king has the general[3] guardianship of all the religious houses in his kingdom, but each baron[4] has the guardianship specially in his barony, unless he has waived it. But if the baron makes a special renunciation of the guardianship of some religious house, then it comes specially to the king.

1466. By saying that the king has the general guardianship of religious houses under the barons, we do not mean that he should intervene in their guardianship as long as the baron carries out his guardianship properly. But if the baron does harm to these houses by his guardianship or will not protect them from those who do them harm, then they may appear before the king as their sovereign and, if they prove their contention against the baron who was supposed to protect them, the king retains them in his special guardianship.

1467. Some houses have a privilege from the king of France, which shows that they are under the king's guardianship, both the mother house and the daughter houses.[5] Nevertheless if such houses or daughter houses are on the lands of any of the barons and were there when the privilege was given to them, the privilege does not remove the special guardianship of the baron; for when the king gives, confirms, or delivers something, it is understood that the rights of others are preserved. Nevertheless if the baron permitted the king to exercise his guardianship after the privilege for thirty years, peacefully and without protest, the king should retain the special guardianship according to the privilege, for a person who remains silent and does not protest for so long certainly agrees to what his sovereign is doing. And if the house, when the privilege was given, was in the king's lands and afterwards came to be under some baron, the king retains the guardianship according to the privilege. But if the king has not taken it under his special guardianship in the privilege, the guardianship goes to the baron into whose lands the house moves. For this reason, if the king has the general and special guardianship over the mother house which was founded in his own lands, it does not follow that he has guardianship of the daughter houses of the said foundation, the daughter houses which are in the lands of his barons; instead each baron has the guardianship of the daughter houses in his barony.

1468. When a person holding less directly than a baron gives some property to the church and has it declared mortmain[6] by the baron, he can no longer demand to be the guardian of what he gave to the church, but he can demand jurisdiction, if he retained it when he made the gift. And if he gave all he had without retaining anything, he no longer has the guardianship or the jurisdiction over it.

1469. It is true that no one has the guardianship of religious houses except the king or a baron holding directly from the king; and for this reason when the religious house makes a complaint to a person in whose guardianship it is, because of some injury done to it, the case should not be sent down[7] to anyone else; instead the cognizance belongs to the person who has the guardianship of the religious house, unless it is a suit on real property and the religious house admits that it is a villeinage held from the person wanting the suit sent back down to his court; for in that case the suit goes down, unless the lord had renounced his rights in the privilege.

1470. When some baron has the guardianship of religious houses on his lands and they complain that a wrong has been done them by someone over whom the baron has no jurisdiction, and whom he cannot summon, the baron can complain to the lord under whom these persons who committed the offense are resident, even though the house itself does not want to lodge a complaint; and a fine must be paid. But if the men from the house were not plaintiffs, they will receive no fines and their damages will not be paid, because they did not want to lodge a complaint, for no one can make a complaint on another's behalf unless he is an appointed attorney,[8] or unless those who have a right to the complaint are present. But everyone can make a complaint to the extent of his interest[9] in the matter, and for this reason a baron can lodge a complaint against those who committed an offense in a place under his guardianship.

1471. When a religious house makes a disavowal[10] of the guardianship of the person in whose guardianship it should be and avows itself to be under the guardianship of another,—for example if it should be under the guardianship of the count of Clermont and it claims to be under the guardianship of another baron,—the count of Clermont must sue in the court of the person under whose guardianship the house claims to be, in a full procedure without a wager of battle;[11] and if he wins his suit, he has not won the religious house's lands, but only the guardianship and a fine, and the fine should be to pay the costs and expenses incurred in pursuing the suit for guardianship, and some extra in money, at his discretion, except that the sum of money should not be so great that the house [*couvens*] must be abandoned [*departis*] out of poverty and the service of God no longer said, for this would be impermissible; instead the king should take counsel and abate the fine as the sovereign having general guardianship of religious houses.

1472. If two barons are in a suit concerning who has guardianship of a religious house, the religious house is wise to stay out of the suit, saying it will obey whoever wins the guardianship rights as the religious house's temporal guardian. And if during the suit the religious house must say in whose guardianship they think they are, they can and should give their true testimony. Nevertheless since they are not parties to the suit, they cannot be made to give testimony except by their ecclesiastical judge; and whether or not they are a party, they must not be forced to bring their privilege[12] to court unless they want to; but they (or their attorney for them) should be obliged to give testimony, for otherwise the proceeding would not be wisely conducted, since what is admitted by a party need not be proved, but only what is in dispute.

1473. Although all religious houses hold their property in mortmain, this does not mean that the temporal jurisdiction and the temporal guardianship are not in the cognizance of the secular baron, because persons in religion have little power to enforce judgments. And if the religious house has jurisdiction which is exercised by its men, its *baillis*, or its officers, and someone wants to complain that the house has done too much or too little, the cognizance belongs to the baron who has the special guardianship because their ecclesiastical judge could not be the judge.

1474. There are two swords by which all the people should be governed spiritually and temporally, for one of these swords should be spiritual and the other temporal: the spiritual sword should be given to Holy Church and the temporal sword to the princes of the Earth; and the one given to Holy Church is called sprritual because the person struck by it perishes spiritually in his soul, for example those who die in mortal sin or excommunicated, or who have acted against the faith: and cognizance of all such things belongs to Holy Church. And because the spiritual sword is more severe [*crueus*] than the temporal, since the soul is in danger from it, those who have it in their power must take care not to strike with it without reason, for example by excommunications too lightly declared. Nevertheless, however an excommunication is imposed, it is to be feared, and the person excommunicated should be at great pains to seek absolution; for if he took no notice of the excommunication and disobeyed the orders of Holy Church, then he would be excommunicated by God *and* this world, and he would be making things worse for himself [*feroit de bonne cause mauvese*]. And children who disobey their mother are not good children, and Holy Church is our spiritual mother: and we should obey the church and its teachings and orders, which it gives us for the salvation of our souls.

1475. The temporal sword has a different temper, for justice must be done with it without delay, and offenders punished in their bodies. And when one sword has need of the other, they should give each other aid, except that the spiritual sword should not be involved in any temporal justice in which anyone might lose life or limb; but especially the temporal sword should always be ready to protect and defend Holy Church any time there is a need. And we would find much to say on the power [*vertu*] of these two swords, but other material awaits our attention [*nous queurt sus*], and we will stop there: and we will come back to what we set out to do.

1476. If some religious house makes an avowal that it is under the king's guardianship and disavows the guardianship of some baron, and loses the suit, so that it remains in the baron's guardianship, if the baron wants to exact too great a fine the king should not permit it, but should abate it according to the condition of the house and whether the avowal was made in bad faith, even though in the case of disavowals there can be no fixed estimate [*certaine estimacion*] of the fine, except for losing the thing disavowed (in the case of laypersons), or a discretionary sum of money (for religious houses).

Here ends the chapter on the guardianship of religious houses.

Notes

1. The context of this chapter suggests that *eglise* should be translated "religious house" rather than "church." The normal word for "church" in Beaumanoir is *moustier*.

2. For guardianship, see Chapter 15.

3. In this chapter "general" and "special" are used to translate *general* and *especial* in their normal legal sense. In non-legal language, the more normal translation of *especial* would be "particular."

4. The baron is a person holding directly from the king. The count of Clermont was a baron in this sense.

5. Beaumanoir is referring here to monastic orders, having a central foundation of which other foundations are the satellites. An example would be the Cistercian order, whose mother house was at Cîteaux, with daughter houses in many provinces and in other countries.

6. Mortmain property, held by the church, does not owe homage as it would if held by a layperson. Similar tax-free status is enjoyed by church property in the United States today (1992).

7. For sending cases down, see Chapter 10.

8. For attorneys, see Chapter 4.

9. Interest here means a legal interest, not just a casual interest as in something interesting.

10. For disavowals, see Chapter 45.

11. For wager of battle, see Chapter 61.

12. That is, the charter given them when the house was founded.

47. Subinfeudation

Here begins the forty-seventh chapter of this book which speaks of how fiefs can be held more or less directly from their lords according to the custom of Beauvais, and on how the holders of fiefs should refrain from dividing them in contravention of the custom.

1477. By custom the lord must permit what is held from him in fief to be held partly as a sub-fief. And we will explain how, and also how what was a sub-fief can come back to being held directly from him.

1478. When a fief is distributed among brothers and sisters by descent[1] and the younger siblings take a third, and pay homage to their older brother for that third, the third which they hold must become a sub-fief of the lord, for if the fief could not be removed further from the lord, they would have to pay homage to the lord, and this is not required of a fief which passes by descent; instead the younger brothers and sisters must pay homage to their oldest brother as is said above.

1479. When sisters take shares of a fief by descent and the oldest receives the homage of her younger sisters, even though each takes as much as the oldest sister (except that the oldest sister takes the principal residence before the division is made), the lord must permit all the younger sisters' portions (which had been held directly from him) to be held as sub-fiefs, because custom awards the homage to the oldest sister; and because of such distributions which are made of fiefs which are taken by descent, the fiefs which are held directly from lords are considerably reduced.

1480. A brother making distribution to his younger siblings should be very careful to give them only a third of each fief, for if he gives them more than a third he loses his brothers' homage; and in this way the brothers can come to pay homage directly to the lord. Therefore if the oldest brother wants to make a proper [*sainement*] distribution so that the homages remain his, he should have the whole fief appraised by honest men and according to the appraised value he should give a third to his brothers. And also the portions distributed among sisters should be equal; and if the oldest sister wanted to give one of the younger sisters more than her portion, that sister would have to pay homage to the lord.

1481. It is a good thing, and approved by custom, that all property which is to be divided,—whether among brothers and sisters, or among other people, whether it is in fief or in villeinage,—should be divided as profitably as possible, with the least cutting up and the least impairment of the property.

1482. In personal property and chattels there is no right of firstborn; instead all personal property and chattels which are distributed, whether through direct or lateral descent, must be divided equally among the siblings, with as much going to the oldest as to the youngest.

1483. I see no way that a fief can become a sub-fief of a lord without his consent, except by reason of the distribution because of a direct descent of the property, as I said above; but a sub-fief can come back to being held directly from the lord in several ways, and we will see how.

1484. If the fief-holder buys from his vassal what the latter held from him in fief, the sub-fief becomes a fief held directly from the lord, for the buyer must now hold directly from his own lord what his own vassal formerly held as a sub-fief; and he does not owe any more homages for that reason, for since he held everything for one homage, both his own property and the homage [*l'homage*] of the seller, the homage of the seller now becomes void and the property held directly by the buyer increases and he owes homage for it all in one parcel.[2]

1485. The second way in which sub-fiefs can go back to being held directly from a lord is by exchange, for example, if Pierre holds from the count and Jehan holds from Pierre and Pierre exchanges for Jehan's land some other land which is not held from the count, what Jehan held from Pierre comes back to being held directly from the count by Pierre: thus what had been held in sub-fief before the exchange comes back to being held directly as a fief.[3]

1486. The third way is when someone forfeits because of some offense[4] the fief he held from a lord, for then the property which was held as a sub-fief comes back to being held directly.

1487. Vassals can increase the fiefs which they hold from their lords directly by adding property which is held from them in villeinage: for example, if I hold a fief from the count in which there are villeinage lands which are held as sharecrop lands [*champars*] or as lands owing quit-rent [*cens*] or rents, and I procure the ownership of these lands held from me, however I acquire them they take on the condition of the fief I held as my own property.

1488. Pierre had bought a piece of land which was held from him for twelve deniers in quit-rent [*cens*], and held the parcel as part of the fief he held as his own property [*demaine*]. When Pierre had held the parcel thus for a while, he voluntarily gave it out again for twelve deniers of quit-rent. The lord from whom Pierre held the twelve-denier parcel in fief with the rest of his property saw that Pierre had acted in such a way that his fief was increased by this parcel of land, and that afterwards Pierre had on his own authority reduced it again by giving away possession of the parcel by which his fief had increased, and the lord proceeded to confiscate [*saisi le tresfons*] the parcel for the offense, saying that Pierre could not do this. Pierre answered saying that he could, for if he bought the twelve-denier parcel and then gave it out again for twelve deniers, he had neither increased nor decreased the fief he held from his lord. And on this issue they requested a judgment.

1489. It was judged that since Pierre had joined with his fief the parcel held in villeinage, he could not separate it or make it into a sub-fief without the permission of his lord; and the lord could confiscate the parcel as the subject of an offense and an illegal subinfeudation [*fief esbranchié*]. And by this judgment you can clearly see that anyone can increase and enlarge the fief he holds from his lord, but he cannot, even though he has increased it for good reason, reduce or impair his fief by splitting it up or creating a sub-fief. But if a man had increased his fief by confiscation or by force, without a good reason, and in order to right the wrong he restored the parcel to those from whom he had taken it, his lord could not sue him, for anyone can give back what he took for a bad reason.

1490. Sub-fiefs can also come back to the status of fief in another way: for example if a distribution is made among children, where the oldest takes two-thirds and the younger children the other third,[5] and the younger children die without heirs so that their portions come back to the oldest brother laterally. For then the whole fief is reunited, as if it had never been split up. And also among sisters, if the younger ones in the homage of the oldest die, the property comes back laterally into her possession, and she holds if from the lord directly, as if no distribution had ever been made.

1491. According to our custom, fiefs can also become more remote from a lord in another way from what is described above, for if someone holds in fief and he has children, he can give one or more of his children up to a third of his fief and retain the homage, but when he dies no more than that third which was given by the father may be separated from the fief; for if the father gave away a third and kept the homage, and afterwards he died and the oldest son wanted to split off a *different* third and give it to his younger siblings, two-thirds of the fief would have been split off from the fief and held in sub-fief from the lord, and the lord need not permit this unless he wants to. Therefore the third that the father and mother give as a gift must be shared among the {younger} children, or it must be brought back into the whole at distribution, and then a distribution made so that the oldest takes two-thirds and the others a third among them; and they must hold this third by paying faith and homage to the oldest; and thus no more than a third may be split off during the lifetime of the father and mother to give to the children.

1492. If it happens that a fief passes to me by descent from my father or mother and my younger siblings take a third, which they hold from me, and I have children and I die, the oldest of my children takes two-thirds of my fief and the other children a third, and this happens notwithstanding the fact that the fief was once before divided in thirds. Thus you can see that however many times the fief passes by descent where there are several children, it is divided in thirds that many times, and fiefs which used to be large are thus divided up into many small parcels.

1493. If the oldest son has several fiefs in the same castellany and he has younger brothers who should take a third of each fief, it may be asked whether each younger brother will pay him homage for the share he should take in the third of each fief. We say that if the fiefs are all in the same castellany, and held from a single lord, each of the younger brothers will pay only one homage; but if the fiefs are in several castellanies, they will pay one homage for what they hold in each castellany, even though the two castellanies are held by the same lord, since the oldest son is a vassal twice because of the two castellanies. And if the oldest holds from several lords in the same castellany, the younger brothers must pay for what they hold in each fief as many homages as there are lords from whom the oldest holds.

1494. The lords from whom fiefs are held must take care that they do not permit the fiefs to be reduced and divided more than custom permits, for they lose three times by allowing subinfeudation: in sales taxes, in relief, and in forfeiture. For what was their fief becomes their sub-fief, and if it is sold, a fifth {of the price} goes to the lord from whom it is held, and also the relief when it is due, and also the forfeiture; but when there is a forfeiture, the lord gains by having the former sub-fief held from him directly again, as it was before it was split off according to custom.

1495. If the lord permitted the oldest son to give a greater portion to his younger brothers than they should take in each fief, and yet keep their homage, or if he permitted the fief to be reduced, or given to the church [amortir], or any other thing by which the fief was lessened, the overlord is not required to permit it, and can confiscate the land as the forfeiture of his vassal who permitted it. And however many lords there were one above the other up to the count, if they all permitted it, the count need not permit it unless he wants to; instead, he can confiscate, if his vassals have not done what they should.

Here ends the chapter on how fiefs can be held more or less directly from the lord, according to the custom of Beauvais.

Notes

1. For direct and lateral inheritance, see Chapter 14.

2. This paragraph is somewhat confusing. There are three lords involved, an overlord and a second lord, who himself has a vassal holding some of the land as a sub-fief; the lowest lord owes homage to the middle one, who owes homage to the

overlord. The question is: what becomes of the homage of the lowest when the middle one buys up the sub-fief and incorporates it back into his personal holdings? The answer is that it is simply nullified.

3. This exchange is like the purchase described in §1484. The middle lord now controls the land formerly held as a sub-fief by the lowest lord, who now owes homage to some fourth lord for the property he got in exchange for what he held from the middle lord.

4. For forfeiture of property for an offense, see Chapter 30.

5. The younger children would owe homage to the oldest brother, so that their holdings would become a sub-fief. See §469.

48. Freehold

Here begins the forty-eighth chapter of this book which speaks of how commoners can hold freehold fiefs in faith and homage, and how they should fulfill the obligations of holding them.

1496. According to the king's law [*establissement*],[1] commoners cannot and should not hold freehold fiefs or acquire freehold fiefs. Nevertheless we see a way in which they can have fiefs, without the law being broken; for the intention of the law is not to take away others' rights, but so that things are done according to reason, and to terminate bad customs and favor the good ones.

1497. The first reason for commoners to have fiefs is that they had them before the law was made and they have since passed from person to person by descent; and these fiefs are not taken away from them, for the law did not take away what was already in place; instead it was made so that they should no longer do it {acquire fiefs}, for townsmen [*bourjois*] and commoners were acquiring many fiefs, so that in the end the rulers [*princes*] might have had less service from gentlemen.

1498. If the townsman or commoner who has held a fief since before the law wants to sell it, he must do so to a gentleman, unless he has special permission [*grace*] from the king or the count from whom it is held; and as long as he holds it, he must fulfill the obligations [*le deserve*] according to what the fief requires and would require if it were in the hands of a gentleman.

1499. No gentleman lower than the king can any longer permit a townsman to buy a fief, for it would be against the king's law made by the king for the advantage of gentlemen in general throughout the kingdom. But when the king makes a special law for his own domain, the barons who hold from him need not on that account stop acting according to the old customs in their lands. But when the law is general, it is applicable in the whole kingdom, and we should believe that such laws are made after much consultation [*par tres grant conseil*] and for the common good.

1500. The second reason why a commoner can hold a fief is that he has married a gentlewoman, who holds a fief as real property, whether in custodianship,[2] or which passed to her from her father or mother by descent, or which passed to her laterally, since there is no reason for a gentlewoman to lose her rights to real property because she marries a person of a lower class. And in such a case the commoner does not hold the fief as his own but as his wife's. And yet if he has children by the gentlewoman, they can inherit it, even though they are not of so gentle blood that they can become knights, for the quality of being gentle [*gentillece*][3] so that you can become a knight comes from the father, whether the mother is a gentlewoman or commoner. Nevertheless, if the mother was a serf, and the father a gentleman and a knight, we do not agree that the sons could be knights, because they are serfs through their mother.

1501. Now let's see,—if a knight has married a serf and the gentleman owns a fief,—if the children who are serfs can become the heirs and hold the freehold fief. We say this, that if the fief is held from the lord whose serfs they are, they can hold it by an oath of fidelity [*par feuté*] without doing homage, because after them the fief will come back to the lord. But if the fief is held from another lord, he need not accept them on an oath of fidelity nor in homage unless he wants to; instead he will or can order them to sell the fief within a year and a day. And if they do not, the lord can take possession of the fief for lack of a vassal, for a male or female serf may not hold a fief, unless it is from the lord whose they are, in the manner described above.

1502. Although fiefs [*li serf*][4] should belong to gentlemen by ancient custom and new law, that is no reason why gentlemen cannot hold villeinages. For according to our custom they can purchase [*aus acroistre en*] villeinages, provided they do what they should for the villeinages, just as if commoners held them, for the freedom of the holder does not free the villeinage. But the freehold fief frees the commoner inasmuch as he enjoys the freedom of the fief, if he has his residence on it.

1503. The third reason why commoners can hold a freehold fief is special permission obtained from the king or a lord holding directly from the king.

1504. The fourth reason is that he has married a gentlewoman and someone in the woman's lineage has sold a freehold fief on the woman's side: the commoner who has married her can redeem it,[5] for otherwise he would lose her right to the property. But if they have children and after the mother's death the children do not take back from their father the half of this[6] redeemed property, in this case the commoner will retain the half of the freehold fief.[7] But the lord from whom the fief is held should not accept him as a vassal, but order him to alienate it within a year and a day; and if he does not, the lord can take the half of the fief, which he is holding, for lack of a vassal, until the commoner obeys his order.

1505. However a commoner holds a fief, and for whatever reason, the lord from whom he holds it need not accept him as a vassal except as a favor [*grace*], but he should take from him an oath of fidelity. And the oath of fidelity is that he should swear on the saints that he will serve his lord and do everything the fief requires him to do, and that because of the fief he will keep his faith and loyalty as one should do for one's lord.

1506. When the commoner has sworn fidelity to his lord from whom he holds, he must be careful not to offend against his lord or to disobey in ways you should obey your lord because of the freehold fief, for he would have to pay the same penalty and the same damages to his lord as if he were a gentleman and had done homage; for he owes all the obligations and obedience to his lord that he would as a gentleman. And just as gentlemen must ask their lord to be accepted as vassals,—that is within forty days of taking the fief, however they take it,—so a commoner must ask in the same manner that his oath of fidelity be accepted. And if he does not do so, the lord can take the crops from the fief for lack of an oath of fidelity, and harvest and appropriate them, as he would in the case of a gentleman {if he confiscated} for lack of a vassal.

1507. No one should be in doubt that if a commoner rightfully holds a fief and someone sues him for something that concerns the fief, whether it his lord or someone else, he is to be dealt with [*demenés*] by his peers, as if he were a gentleman, except that if he appealed, he would not fight as a gentleman but as a commoner.[8] But in all other suits which arose by reason of the fief he should be treated as a gentleman.

1508. The fifth reason why a commoner can hold a fief is that it passed to him laterally, as the next of kin, whether the person it passed from was a gentleman or a commoner, for the intention of the law is not that anyone should lose his rights to property which should come to him for family reasons; but the law is so that commoners not be allowed to obtain fiefs by buying or exchanging them.

1509. The sixth reason why a commoner can hold a fief is in custodianship or guardianship, for example, if a minor child comes under his guardianship or custodianship as next of kin,[9] and the fief rightfully belongs to the child.

Here ends the chapter which speaks of how commoners can hold fiefs in homage.

Notes

1. Beaumanoir most likely means the *establissement* of King Philippe III, the Bold, promulgated on All Saints Day or Christmas Day, 1275. See *Ord.* 1, 303.

2. For custodianship, see Chapter 15.

3. "Gentility" will obviously not do here for *gentillece*, so "gentle" in this context must do. If I had chosen to translate *gentius homme* throughout as "nobleman," I could have used "nobility" here.

4. It is reasonable to suppose that *serf* here in Salmon is a typographical error for *fief*, which is what appears in Beugnot. In neither edition is there a notice of any variants for this word.

5. For redemption, see Chapter 44.

6. Salmon has *eel*, which I have taken as a misprint for *cel*, which is what appears in Beugnot.

7. For the redemption by the children of their dead mother's property, see §1411.

8. For fights between gentlemen and commoners, see Chapter 64, §§1828–31.

9. For custodianship and guardianship, see Chapter 15.

49. Necessity

Here begins the forty-ninth chapter of this book which speaks of laws [establissemens] *and the times when a custom should not be observed for reasons of necessity.*

1510. There are exceptional times when you cannot and should not do what has been lawful [*pour droit*] by long custom and practice, for example anyone can know there are two kinds of times: war and peace. And it is reasonable for peace time to be dealt with according to the usage and custom which has been habitual and developed [*usees et acoustumees*] over a long period for life in peacetime; for instance, in such a time anyone can do what he wants with his own things,—for example give or sell or spend them,—as several chapters of this book explain. But in times of war or fear of war, kings and princes, lords who hold directly from the king [*barons*] and lower ones, have to do many things which, if they were done in times of peace, would be wrongs towards their subjects; but the emergency [*tans de necessité*] excuses them, so that the king can make new laws for the common good of his kingdom: for example, when he thinks he will have to defend his land or attack someone who has wronged him, he is accustomed to order that gentlemen who are squires be all made knights, and that rich men and poor should be furnished with armor, each according to his position, and that the towns should repair their fortifications [*services*] and their fortresses, and that everyone will be ready to move when the king gives the order. The king can give all such laws and others which seem right to him and his counsel in time of war, or fear of war to come; and the barons can do the same in their lands, provided it is not in order to take arms [*emprendre*] against the king.

1511. And there are other times when you have to do things other than what custom allows even in times of peace, for example, in times of famine when some things needed to feed the common people are in short supply, for example when there is a shortage of wheat and wine. In such times you can restrict people from doing what they like with things in short supply; for if the rich were permitted to buy up these things to store them in granaries, and then keep them without selling them so that they would increase in price, it would be insufferable [*ce ne seroit pas a soufrir*]. Therefore, when such a time arrives, the lords of the land can order their subjects to store up only enough of the scarce things to get them and their household through the year, and to put the rest on sale at the fair price which things are worth on the open market, for it is better to do things for the common good than according to the wish of those who want to profit from bad times [*le tans enchierir*].

1512. No one can make a new law [*establissement*] which will be enforced as such [*pour droit*], or a new market, or new customs, except the king in the kingdom of France, save in times of emergency [*necessité*], for in those times every baron can force the sale of his subjects' goods, as we have said above; but they cannot make new markets, nor new customs [*coustumes*][1] without the king's permission. But the king can do this when he likes, and when he sees it is for the common good, for example, we see the king giving new customs every day to certain towns which are his own or to certain lords among his subjects, for example to repair bridges, or roads, or churches, or various other public works [*aaisemens communs*]; in such cases the king can act, but not others.

1513. You should know that if the king makes some new law for the common good, it does not affect things done in the past, nor things which will happen in the future, until observance of the law has been ordered. But as soon as it is promulgated [*peupliés*], it should be strictly enforced in the manner ordered, either for ever or for a set time. And whoever goes against the law is to pay the penalty established by the king or his counsel; for when he gives laws, he also sets the penalty for those who go against the law. And all the barons and those who have jurisdictional power [*la justice*] in their lands receive the fines paid by their subjects who break the laws, according to what was fixed by the king; but this presupposes that they enforce the king's law in their lands, for if they are disobedient [*rebelle*] or negligent {in enforcing it} and the king, because of their failure, takes a hand, he can collect the penalties.

1514. What we have said about emergencies that arise because of famine we extend to other times of necessity: for example, if you happen to need to undertake public projects [*communs ouvrages*], for example churches, or roads, or wells, or fortifications because of the fear of war; in all such cases and others like them no one should be exempted from contributing according to his position, for no one should have to be the only one to pay for what is to the common advantage of all his neighbors as well as himself. And because we have seen various gentlemen who resisted and said they should not pay the city tax [*estre taillié*] along with commoners, it is right for the lord who has them in his jurisdiction to warn them to make a sufficient voluntary contribution; and if they will not, he can forbid them to use or take advantage of anything done when they would not contribute. And they can also be put under reasonable pressure to contribute, for they cannot do without public facilities. And if it is clerks who do not want to contribute, and they make use of the public facilities, they must be obliged by their ecclesiastical judge to contribute sufficiently, for no one should be exempted.

1515. Although the king can make new laws, he must take great care to make them for reasonable causes and for the common good, and after much consultation [*par grant conseil*], and especially they must not be made against God or against morality [*bonnes meurs*]; for if he did (which will never happen, with God's help), his subjects should not permit it, for each person should above all things love and fear God with all his heart and for the honor of Holy Church, and after that his earthly lord. And everyone should obey the commandments of Our Lord in the hope of the reward of heavenly treasures [*des biens celestiaus*], and after that obey his earthly lord according to what you should do for your temporal goods [*les possessions temporeus*].

Here ends the chapter on laws and times of emergency.

Note

1. Note that customs, which normally come about over time and from the bottom up as it were, can be created from the top down by the king, or so it appears from this section.

50. Communes

Here begins the fiftieth chapter of this book which speaks of people in towns [bonnes villes] *and of their rights, and how they should be protected and disciplined.*

1516. Towns which have a charter as a commune, those where there is no charter, and the common people, need to be protected so that no one does them harm and they do no harm to anyone else; and especially the charters of communes should be protected according to the terms [*teneures*] of their privileges, unless they have allowed things to be done without heed to their privileges for so long that the latter have come to an end [*corrompu*], for an oven that does not cook is worth as much as a charter which is not observed, once things have been done the opposite way.

1517. In the kingdom of France no one except the king can make a town into a commune for the first time, because all innovations are forbidden. And if the king wants to make some {communes}, or has made some, it must be contained in the charter of freedoms [*franchises*] that he gives them, that the rights of religious houses and lords [*chevaliers*] are preserved, for he cannot and should not {create communes} by doing harm to religious houses or reducing the rights of lords.

1518. When we say that all innovations are forbidden, this means the innovations which are made against the rights of others, for no one is forbidden to build a bakehouse or a mill, or a winepress or a house, or a fish reservoir [*vivier*] or some other thing in a place where there never had been any. But this means it may not be against the rights of others. And in some cases it can come about that the people nearby [*li marchissant*] suffer a loss without the innovation being forbidden [*ostee*] for that reason: for example if I construct a mill on my land where I can and should, and my neighbor's mill diminishes in value because fewer people go there than before, or since I give a better price for milling than he does; because of such losses my mill will not be torn down, since it is for the good of all [*li communs pourfis*] that each person may better himself [*fere son preu*] and improve his property without doing harm to anyone else.

1519. Any lord who has on his lands towns in which there is a commune, must find out each year the state of the town, and how it is administered and governed by the mayors and by those who are appointed to protect and govern [*mainburnir*] the town, so that the rich should fear that if they behave improperly they will be severely punished and so that the poor in the said towns can earn their bread in peace.

1520. In free towns we have seen lots of quarrels of one group of people against others, for example, poor against rich, or the rich themselves one against another, for example, when when they cannot agree among themselves to appoint a mayor or an attorney[1] or an advocate; or, for example, when some of them accuse the others of not doing what they should with the town income, or of accounting for too great expenses; or, for example, when the affairs of the town are going badly because of arguments and grudges between one lineage and another. In all such cases as soon as the lord of the town hears about it, he should take immediate counsel so that, if the dispute is over appointing a mayor or other proper persons to protect the town, the lord should on his own initiative appoint such people as he knows to be appropriate for the office in which he places them. And if those who are appointed by the lord in this way to offices in towns (because the townspeople cannot agree) do their duty in office, they should remain there at least a year; and at the end of the year if the town has calmed down so that they can agree to appoint other people, they can do it as they have been accustomed to do; and if they still cannot agree, those whom the lord appointed remain (unless the lord removes them to appoint others). And the lord should have them paid by the town according to their office.

1521. If the disagreement in the town is over the accounts of the town, the lord should send for all those who have made the receipts and the outlays of the town since the time they began to receive and disburse, and he should discover if they are giving good and honest accounts, so that the town is not hurt by their desire to retain the commune funds improperly. And if those who should give accounts use as a defense that they made an accounting once before, in the presence of the common people, and the latter were satisfied because they did not dispute them, in such cases they are not required to make another accounting; for it is enough if you have accounted once to those to whom you have to give accounts, once you have left the {place of} accounting without challenge, and unless it happens that those who received the accounting point out some miscalculation [*mes-conte*] or deception, for then it would be proper for the former accounting to be recalled from memory [*recordés*].[2]

1522. We see several towns where the poor and average citizens have none of the administrative positions of the towns, instead the rich have them all, because they are feared by the common people because of their riches or their lineage. And it happens that some of them are mayor or assessor [*juré*] or treasurer [*receveur*] one year, and the next year they have their brothers or their nephews or their near relatives appointed, so that for ten or twelve years all the rich have the administrative positions of the towns and afterwards when the common people want to have an accounting they defend themselves by saying they have given an accounting to each other. But they should not be permitted to do this, because the accounting for the commune affairs should not be made to those very people who give the accounts. Therefore such accounts should be given in the presence of the lord of the town (or other people sent by the lord) and in the presence of various representatives of the common people, to hear this accounting and to challenge it if there is any need. And when such an accounting is given, the first people to be made to render an account are those who received the income, and afterwards you should know what has happened to this income; and by the seizure of their persons and their funds they should be compelled to restore without delay everything which they cannot account for.

1523. When there is a disagreement among people of a town because of a fight or because of hatred, the lord should not permit it, even if none of the parties makes a complaint; instead, by his own authority, he should arrest the parties and keep them in prison until a sure peace [*certaine pes*] is made between them, or a guaranteed peace [*asseuremens*] if a simple peace [*pes*] cannot be made, for otherwise towns could be destroyed through the enmity of lineages one for another.

1524. It is sometimes very necessary to help communes in some situation just as you would a minor child: for example if the mayor or the assessor, who have to take care of the business, committed fraud or acted in bad faith [*malice*] by reason of which the town was impoverished or indebted, and they had profited from this in bad faith; for in such a case they would be obliged to make up the loss to the town. And if they did not own enough to do so, the thing which was done improperly and in bad faith should not be allowed to stand. But because acts in bad faith [*li malice*] are sometimes done by those who have control over the affairs of the town and those who deal with [*reçoivent*] them sometimes do not suspect any trickery, but believe instead that they are acting for the good of the town, it is rightful that they should be allowed to keep their property[3] [*chatel*] since they knew nothing about the trickery, for otherwise no one would dare to make deals or contracts with those who take care of the business of towns. But if it can be known that they were partners in the deception, they should be partners in making good the loss.

1525. Many disagreements arise in communes because of their communal tax assessments [*tailles*],[4] for it often happens that the rich who are administrators of the business of the town estimate the taxes of themselves and their relatives lower than they should, and reduce the taxes [*deportent*] of other rich men so that they in their turn will have theirs reduced, and thus all of the expense falls on to the mass [*communeté*] of the poor people. And for this reason many crimes have been committed, because the poor did not want to put up with it but they did not know the proper way to pursue their rights except by attacking them {the rich}. And some of these have been killed by the others and the towns damaged [*mal menees*] by these dishonest tax assessors. Therefore when the lord of the town sees such a disagreement begin, he should intervene and tell the common people that he will set their taxes properly, and for the rich also. And then he should assess the tax in his town by an honest inquiry, the rich as well as the poor, each person according to his estate, and according to the need of the town for the tax to be great or small; and then he should force each person to pay what he has been assessed; and afterwards he should have what was collected by the assessment paid where there is the greatest need, for the benefit of the town; and by doing this the disagreement and the town can be quieted {Beamanoir's syntax}.

1526. Those whose tax is assessed according to their worth in real and personal property should be very careful to tell the truth when they have to swear what they are worth; for if they swore to less than they had and they were found out, they would have lost all the undeclared amount [*le seur-plus*], which would go to the lord making the assessment, except what would have gone into the taxes proportionally: this means that if he should have paid ten pounds per hundred [*de .c.lb .x.l.*], and a hundred pounds more than what he swore to were found, ten pounds would go into the tax and the ninety pounds would go to the lord. But if the town were making the assessment without the lord, the undeclared amount found for those who swear falsely goes to the town and not to the lord; and this is true for towns which have the power to assess taxes as items of their privileges.

1527. If a commune owes more than it is worth because it has been badly administered for a long time, so that it will have difficulties in paying all that is due [*ele soit a meschief pour paier ce qui a esté acreu*],[5] and it cannot pay everything, it should be decided which debts should be paid first; for if money had been lent them without interest [*sans usure*] the creditors should be paid before those who lent at interest [*les usuriers*]; and if they had been given money for safekeeping, it should be given back in full and without discount [*sans deport*], before the annuities on which security had been received [*les rentes a vie desqueles li chatéus a esté levés*].Thus when a town has reached the point where it cannot pay, first of all it must cancel orders [*rendre les commandes*], then {pay back} what was lent without interest, and then what was lent at interest, and afterwards the property [*chatel*] they received from persons to whom they owe annuities, according to their assets; and for the rest they can be given a discount [*deport*] by the sovereign lord so that the town is not completely destroyed and dismantled; nevertheless if they have enough assets to pay all their enforceable contracts, without the complete devastation [*degastee*] of the town, they must be forced to do so.

1528. If someone owns an annuity from a commune[6] and he sells the annuity to someone else, the town can purchase it instead if it does so before making any payment to the buyer; for once the commune has made a payment it could not have the thing at that price, for it would have agreed by its conduct [*acordee de fait*] to the wishes of the seller and the buyer. And for that reason the annuity would be paid to the buyer during the life of the seller, for the contract of the town is not changed except that the buyer will henceforth receive the payments as the seller had been doing, during the lifetime of the seller, for the life in question could not be changed without the consent of the town.[7]

1529. Not all those staying and living in communes are required to be on their tax rolls [*a leur tailles*]. Indeed certain persons are excepted, for example those who do not belong to the commune, or gentlemen who do not engage in trade but live off their land which they hold as fief [*franc fief*] from the lord; or clerks who do not engage in trade but live off the fiefs [*frans fiés*] which they have inherited or the benefices which they have in Holy Church; or those who are on the king's service, for their services, as long as they last, free them from paying exactions [*toutes*] or communal taxes [*tailles*]. Nevertheless if any of the persons mentioned above has a villeinage[8] within the boundaries of the commune, devolving from [*mouvans*] and under the jurisdiction of said town, these parcels are not free from the communal tax whatever person holds them, unless some of these parcels are exempt through a privilege: for example we see that certain religious houses have in towns some villeinages for which the quit-rent [*cens*] and the rent is paid to the commune, and they cannot be taxed [*taillié*] because this {freedom} was given to them of old, or they have held them for so long without paying tax [*taille*] that by their long tenure they have acquired the freedom of being exempted from this tax [*taille*]. But if it had never been necessary to assess a communal tax [*taillier*] on the real estate of some commune and the need arose to commence this tax, long tenure could not be used as a defense. Therefore if a person is trying to say that his land should not be taxed [*taillieé*] because it never had been, this is a good argument when the other pieces of real property *were* formerly taxed and this one, at a time when the others had been taxed several times, remained free.

1530. We have seen some lords who did not want to permit people from the commune to acquire property in their lands in fief or villeinage; and as to the fiefs they are right because it is forbidden by the king's law [*establissement*] for a bourgeois or a commoner to buy a fief.[9] But those who do not want to allow the buying of villeinages are wrong, because any person from a commune can increase his assets in villeinages both in the town where he is and in another; for if he does not do what he should in respect to the land, the lord from whom the land is held has jurisdiction over his tenant for legal complaints against him because of the land. And if the person from the commune does not want to appear nor have a hearing before him, the lord can have recourse to the land to pay the penalties for the defaults and to give a ruling on the demands and complaints with respect to the land, for each person should defend his land before the lord from whom it is held.

1531. Although we have said that each person from a commune can increase his own personal assets in villeinages, if the community wanted to increase its assets this would not be permitted; for a minor lord would find it difficult to exert jurisdiction over the land which belonged to a commune; and in the same way sales tax could not come to the lord unless it was sold by a common agreement, which would not be an easy thing to achieve; and any lord is allowed not to take so powerful a tenant that he cannot exert jurisdiction over him if it becomes necessary. Therefore if any such land is sold to a commune the lord can refuse to grant seisin;[10] and if the land was left to the commune by a will, the lord from whom the land is held can command the commune to give up possession within a year and a day, as is done for land which is left to religious houses.

1532. Each person in the commune which has the power to hold court hearings should seek justice before those who are appointed [*establi*] to maintain the court. And if he is refused a hearing, he can certainly appeal against them for default of judgment or for false judgment, as indeed would a stranger who was not part of the commune. And the appeal must be made before the lord who has superior jurisdiction [*li resort*] over the commune, and not by a wager of battle but on the record of the arguments [*les erremens du plet*]. And how you should proceed in such a case we will explain in the chapter on appeals {Chapters 61, 62}.

Here ends the chapter on communes and their rights.

Notes

1. See Chapter 4, §169.
2. For the *recort*, or recall from memory, see §§1150–53, 1208, 1226, 1233, and 1818. It is clear that what is meant here is not a written record, as the modern version of the word would seem to indicate.
3. That is, not be called on to contribute in making good the losses.
4. There are various taxes called *taille*, but the one described in this paragraph is clearly a kind of city tax, which is assessed, collected, and spent by the members of a commune.
5. This situation appears to be a kind of default or corporate bankruptcy.
6. This might occur if the commune has contracted to pay him at fixed intervals until he died for some interest, such as a piece of land or an easement or some piece of personal property.

7. Modern legal terminology keeps the Old French term of a life interest *per* (or *pur*) *autre vie* when a person's interest is terminated by the death of *another* person.

8. For villeinages, see Chapter 14, §467.

9. This law is most likely the one given by Philippe III on All Saints Day or Christmas Day, 1275 (see *Ord.* 1, 303). See also Chapter 48, §1496.

10. That is, the lord can prevent the buyer from taking possession of the land.

51. Seizures

Here begins the fifty-first chapter of this book which speaks of the reasons why lords may make seizures and take possession of property, and how they should act for the good of their subjects while maintaining their rights.

1533. It is a good thing for lords to know how and for what reasons they may make seizures of other people's property and for what reasons they may keep in their possession property (owned or leased) of which their subjects have given up possession. And we will speak briefly of this in this chapter.

1534. You should know that the reasons why lords can make seizures of their subjects' property include suspicion for all cases of serious crimes; and the lord also has the suspect himself arrested, and held along with the confiscated property until he has been cleared [*espurgiés*] of the crime, or punished if he is convicted. And what the cases of crime are, and how you should proceed, is explained in the chapter on crimes {Chapter 30}.

1535. Although the lords attach the person and the possessions of the person held on suspicion in cases of serious crime, or who has been accused of such, nevertheless as long as the suit lasts, or as long as the person is in prison, the lord should not fail to give him (and also his wife and household) enough to live on, out of his own money, for until he is convicted of the offense he should not fail to have his maintenance provided out of his own things; but at all events this should be done by the lord who has jurisdiction over him. And if the accused holds from several lords, and each lord holds attached what is held in his jurisdiction, if the accused or suspected man can give sureties to the value of the attached property, he should be allowed a reclamation[1] of the attached property. And if he cannot or will not, each lord can in his own jurisdiction keep the property attached until he is acquitted [*assous*] of the offense except that each one should contribute to the maintenance of the man and his family, according to what he holds under each lord. And if the accused proceeds to a wager of battle for the crime he is accused of, then he can freely have and control all his belongings while the suit is pending, and can take what he wants for his maintenance and his household's and to spend on his defense in the suit, for otherwise he could hardly mantain so costly a suit.

1536. If anyone is accused of a serious crime in the court of the lord in whose jurisdiction he is, and he has property under several lords, he does not have to defend in the court of each one to get back his property free and clear; it is enough if he is acquitted in the court where he was accused of the offense; but he must be acquitted by a judgment, for if he left the court by giving a gift or a promise to the lord or to his adverse party, we believe that in such a case he would not get back the property that was in the jurisdiction of other lords unless he has been acquitted [s'espurjoit] in such a way that the lords knew he was not guilty. But this is when the accused's property is in such different jurisdictions that one of the lords does not hold his jurisdiction from the other. For it is true that if the king recalls some banished person, even though he had been banished from the kingdom on pain of death [sur la hart], or the king permits peace to be made in some serious accusation, all the lords from whom the banished or accused man held property must give him back whatever property of his they held attached because of the banishment or the accusation, except that they do not have to give back the fruits they have reaped from the real property nor the personal property they gained during the banishment. And we also say that when some banished or accused person makes peace with the baron who holds directly from the king, that lord's subjects must return property as is explained above concerning the king's subjects, for whoever has the peace of the sovereign should have the peace of the subject. And everyone should know that the king can recall anyone {from banishment}, or make peace with anyone he wishes, as of right, and the barons also in their baronies, concerning anyone who is banished merely from their own bar- onies; for they may not do so concerning those who have been banished from the kingdom without the king's consent; the king can do this without them, and none of those below him can. And after {this level} the lords have no power to recall persons banished for serious crimes or to take any money or promises for any serious case where the trial is in their court; and if they do, the lords from whom they hold can confiscate their jurisdiction for im- proper use thereof. And should they have taken something for the peace or the recall, if the lords do not make a seizure, from level to level as they hold from each other, their lord who holds directly from the king can make the seizure, and arrest the banished person and punish him as a banished man, or undo the peace which was made in the court of the subject, and have the case tried before him; for a person holding his jurisdiction from another should administer proper justice, and not sell it or take money for leniency [*deport*]. But where mercy or pity are appropriate, they may be kind and permissive without taking money; and what these cases are is explained in the chapter which speaks of misadventure [*aventure*] {Chapter 69}.

1537. We have spoken of confiscations which lords may make in cases of serious crimes. There are other cases in which you should take stern measures by attaching persons and property: these are cases where you are going to compel someone to make a guaranteed peace, or where someone will not extend a truce under the same conditions which he formerly gave, but wants to fight, against the will of the king or the baron holding from the king. In all such cases and for all such disobedience the lords should make harsh seizures and cause expenses with a large number of guards, until peace is made or a truce given;[2] and the way to do this is adequately described in the chapter on truces and guaranteed peace {Chapter 60}.

1538. There are other kinds of seizures, which should be more kindly than those described above, for example, when the lord makes a seizure for debts owed to him or for fines owed to him, or for debts owed to someone else. And yet there is a difference between a debt owed to the lord and a debt owed to someone else, for the king or the baron may, for debts or fines owed to him, keep his subject in prison, but he cannot do this for debts owed to someone else, unless the debtor has agreed to it in writing or before the judge or before good people.

1539. When someone has obligated himself to go to prison for his debt or someone else's, if he can give a deposit up to the value of the debt, he should be released from prison. And if he is so poor that he cannot give a deposit or even live on what he has, the creditor should give him enough to eat; and not the kind of food given to those held in prison for serious crimes, but better food; for those imprisoned for serious crimes have their ration established at water and one pennyworth of bread a day and it would be a bad thing for those held in prison for debt to be so harmed. And for this reason if they have any money, it can be spent for them as they choose;

and if they have nothing, the person having them imprisoned must give them bread and wine and as much soup as they can eat at least once a day. And even then, once the prisoner has been held forty days in prison, if the lord holding him sees he can do nothing about the debt for which he is held, and he abandons his property, he should be released from prison; for it would be inhumane to leave a man in prison for ever for a debt once you can see that the creditor will not be paid by keeping him in prison.

1540. We have explained some of the reasons why lords can attach the persons and property of their subjects. Now we will explain the reasons why they can seize and take possession of their subjects' belongings for safekeeping [*comme en main sauve*].

1541. When a suit is brought between two parties before some lord and each of the parties claims to be in possession of some property, the lord should take possession of the thing until he finds out from the suit who is entitled to possession, and then give the thing back the person who should have it.

1542. Any time someone makes a complaint concerning force or novel disseisin, the lord should take possession and then make inquiries about the most recent possession [*la nouveleté*], as is explained in the chapter on novel disseisin {Chapter 32}.

1543. If there is a suit between executors (or between the executors on the one hand and other people on the other hand) concerning possessions left in a will, the lord should take possession of the property in dispute, so that it is not destroyed during the suit. And we say the same thing {should be done} on behalf of orphans and minor children, for the deceased and orphans and minor children have great need of the lord's intervention when there is a suit concerning their property.

1544. It sometimes happens that someone threatens another person with harm to his property, and the threatened person appears before the lord asking him for help [*qu'il i met conseil*]: the help should be that if the threats are proved, he should have the security of the things guaranteed [*face les choses asseurer*]; and if the threats are not proved, but there are presumptions, for example rancor and anonymous messages [*paroles couvertes*], the lord can by virtue of his office take the things into his protection [*en sa main*], and his safekeeping, and forbid the person he suspects of making the threats to do anything to the other person, on pain of losing everything [*seur quanque il puet mesfere*]. And if the person suspected commits an offense after this warning, he must pay for the damages and pay a fine at the discretion of the lord.

1545. When there is a dispute between parties, whether gentlemen or commoners, for example a fight or threats, and neither party is willing to lodge a complaint, the lord can by virtue of his office take the dispute under his jurisdiction, and take the thing that the dispute was about into his possession, and forbid them to do harm to each other, and offer to give a hearing if they complain about each other. And if neither party wants to obey the lord's orders, or if one party does and the other does not, then the lord should arrest them and seize their property for disobedience. And if he cannot because they have withdrawn [*tret arriere*], he must summon them to his court and have a guard placed on them, so that to avoid loss and for fear of being banished they appear in court. And if they will not appear in court whatever he does, they must be banished, and all their property and its fruits and revenues taken by the lord; and how you banish someone is explained in the chapter which speaks of cases of crime {Chapter 30}.

1546. It sometimes happens that two parties have made war or threats or been in an argument, and one of the parties is in the jurisdiction of one lord, and the other of another, and the lords are not vassals of each other, for example, if one of the parties was a resident under the count of Clermont and the other lived under the count of Dammartin.[3] And sometimes it happens that one of the lords is willing to take cognizance of the dispute on behalf of the party in his jurisdiction, and the other lord is not willing to because neither of the parties wants to request it. And it would be a bad thing if one of the parties was in prison on his lord's orders and the other was at liberty; and for this reason we are of the opinion that if the two lords are not willing to act in the same way as each other in taking jurisdiction, then the first should not take action since the other is not involved and neither party is requesting him to be. But if the party in the count of Dammartin's jurisdiction asks the count of Clermont to obtain a truce or a guaranteed peace from the party in his jurisdiction, the count of Clermont should do so on condition that the party requesting it be also bound in the truce or the guaranteed peace in the same way. And if the truce is later broken or the guaranteed peace is breached, each of the lords should take jurisdiction over the party in his jurisdiction, and not the other party, unless he is arrested on the scene of the offense. And when truces are to be extended, each of the lords should have them extended individually if the party requests it; and if no party requests it, because they want to go back to war, the lords can take cognizance of the dispute and bring it to an end.

1547. Now let's discuss why the lord can seize and take possession of his subject's land as his own when the latter gives up possession of it, and how he can sometimes take it for himself, even though the subject does *not* formally abandon possession.—One of the reasons is when the lord has asked his subject to pay him the quit-rent or the rent he owes, and the back-payments, within a year and a day; and if the subject does not do so, the lord can seize the ownership of the land as his own and can still demand the back-payments for the time when he held the land without paying, except in the case of sharecropped lands, for they are not lost to the person who has them because they have been left fallow for a year or two; but if they are plowed afterwards, the lord can have the crops attached until he is satisfied as to the share he could have taken if the land had been managed as he would have wished. And if the land is left fallow for more than three years, the lord can have it plowed at his cost if he wishes, on condition that if the owner comes back, the lord will first take the cost of his labor and his share of the crop for the current year and the past years when the land should have borne a crop. And if someone has left his sharecropped land fallow for ten years, the lord can from then on take it as his own, for it is clear that the person who has left it that long without plowing it has abandoned it as sharecrop land; except the land of orphans and minor children, and those held in custodianship or guardianship, or in dower, and land held by those who are overseas or in foreign lands, which remains fallow because there is no one to take care of it for them, for all these people can return to their land by paying the back-payments to the lord.

1548. The lord can also take his subjects' land as his own in other cases, even though the subject does not formally give up possession: for example in a forfeiture, when the forfeiture means that the real and personal property go to the lord of the place where they are situated. And the crimes which are so great that the property of the offender goes to the lords are explained in the chapter which speaks of crimes {Chapter 30}.

1549. And the lord can also confiscate his subject's land without the latter's giving up possession when a debt is owed to the lord or to someone else, admitted or proved before the lord, or where the debtor has obligated himself, or because he leased the land without the permission of the lord, or because he has disposed of the land by gift, or by will, or by exchange. But when the lord confiscates in such cases, the land held in villeinage is not lost to the owner; he can pay a fine according to the offense and the custom of the place; and what the fine is for each offense is explained in the chapter on offenses {Chapter 30}.

1550. When the lord sees that someone is holding land for an orphan or a minor child or an imbecile who needs a guardian, or holding it in custodianship or guardianship or in dower, and that such persons are not managing the land as they should,—for example, if they are trying to sell or give or alienate or spoil the land, or cut down fruit-bearing trees or trees more than sixty years old, or cut immature timber less than seven years old,—the lord can and should take possession of the land on his own initiative as soon as he learns of the situation, in order to look after it and safeguard the rights of the above-mentioned persons, even though no one sues any of those who are trying to deal improperly [*mauvesement*] with the land which should belong to one of the above-mentioned persons, for they are all in the guardianship of the lord, when the administrators do not do their duty in respect to their property.

1551. If someone gives up possession of property he believes to be his, or which he knows very well is not his, when making a sale, or a gift, or a charitable gift, or an exchange, or a lease, and someone contests this at the moment of giving up possession, saying that the person trying to give up possession has no rights in the property, and that he himself has the rights in the property, the lord should take cognizance of the giving up of possession; and then, before he bestows possession on anyone, he should inquire into the rights of the person who protested against having possession speedily given to someone else. And if he sees that the person who contested did so because of ownership, while admitting that the other person (who was giving up possession) really had possession, in that case the lord should place in possession the person in whose favor possession was given up, under the conditions the land was held by when the previous person gave up his possession; and after that the person contesting can sue over the ownership. But if the person contesting said to the lord: "Sire, Pierre, who is trying to give up possession of this land and have you give possession to Jehan, is not in possession if it, but I am," in that case the lord should retain cognizance over the giving up of possession until he finds out who *should* be put in possession, and act in accordance with what he discovers.

1552. In respect to what we have just said, namely that property is not forfeited when the lord takes possession of it because he finds it alienated without his permission, or in some other improper way, we did say that that meant property held in villeinage. For it is quite possible for property held in fief to be alienated or subinfeudated in such a way that it forfeits to the lord; and we explained the cases where it forfeits in the chapter which speaks of how fiefs can be held more or less directly from their lords {Chapter 47}.

1553. Everyone should know that when a property is sold, whether it is in fief or in villeinage, and the seller gives up possession to the lord from whom he held it, asking him to bestow possession on the buyer, if the buyer is from the seller's lineage or from the side of the family on which the property comes down, the lord cannot retain possession and redeem the property for money. But if the buyer is a stranger,[4] or he belongs to the other side of the seller's family than the side on which the property comes down, the lord can retain possession by paying the purchase price to the seller, for the lord is closer for the purposes of redeeming property held from himself than is any stranger.

1554. A lord wanting to redeem a property held from himself must take care to retain possession when the seller has given up possession, and not to give possession to a stranger who bought the property; for once he has given possession, he cannot afterwards say that he should be able to redeem, since he had as lord of the property given possession to the stranger. Therefore when a lord wants to redeem, he must retain possession and not give it to someone else. And if the lord says: "My employee gave possession to the buyer out of my presence and without my orders," it will not avail him, if the employee had the power from his lord to act as his agent [*serjanter*] in such cases, for example if you see that the employee has the job of accepting and giving possession on his lord's behalf; for every lord should be careful whom he employs to do his business in his jurisdiction; for he cannot undo what his employee has done while administering justice, instead he must enforce it, except in cases of serious crime for which you may lose life or limb, for in such cases the lord can disavow the action of his employee unless he is convicted of soliciting the act.

1555. When the lord retains possession of some property which is held from him and which has been sold, the relatives of the seller, who could make a redemption against strangers, have not lost their right to the redemption because the lord has kept possession by paying the selling price, indeed they can make a redemption from the lord as they could from any stranger; and they have a year and a day to make the redemption from the lord as they would against a stranger; and the year and a day redemption period begins to run on the day the lord kept possession. And the lord contesting this, or who causes problems for the person redeeming because of this, is not acting honestly; for you should have no ill will towards a person who requests his rights in a gentle and courteous manner [*debonaire-ment et courtoisement*].

Here ends the chapter on how lords can take and seize property, and for what reasons, and how they should proceed.

Notes

    1. For reclamations, see Chapter 53.

    2. The use of guards on property to create expense is dealt with in Chapter 54.

    3. Dammartin en Goële, near the Charles de Gaulle Airport, northeast of Paris.

    4. "Stranger" here means only a person from outside the seller's lineage.

52. Trespass

Here begins the fifty-second chapter of this book which speaks of prohibited actions and arrests made for offenses or damages, and how you should deal with them, and of sales taxes.

1556. All those who have lands and jurisdiction over them should know how they can and should make arrests[1] as part of their administration, so that they do not commit offenses towards others. And although we speak of seizures in various places in this book, such as in the chapter on offenses and elsewhere, we will still make here a separate chapter on seizures to show which are properly and which improperly made.

1557. Those who in their own jurisdiction and their own lands (or in those which they hold in guardianship for someone else) arrest persons or seize animals at the scene of the offense [*en present mesfet*] (for example, people fighting or causing damage in prohibited areas or cutting wood, or animals under guard in prohibited places) are making proper arrests and seizures. And what the fines are, according to the offenses, is explained in the chapter on offenses {Chapter 30}.

1558. No arrests should be made in land not under crops when entry is not prohibited, for example in fields where the wheat or three-month wheat [*tremois*][2] has been gathered in; for you can go through these fields until they are made ready to bear crops again. For as soon as the earth has been plowed to the last furrow to sow wheat, according to our custom entry is prohibited. And entry is prohibited into the fields where small grains [*mars*] are to be sown as soon as they are plowed for sowing, and into pastures from the middle of March until they are mown, and into enclosed places at all times, and into woods at all seasons, and into vineyards according to the custom of the place where they are situated; for there are some towns where animals may go into vineyards from the grape harvest until they are pruned in the spring, and in some towns animals may not go into vineyards at all;

and the customs for vineyards must be observed. But for the other land which we have discussed the custom is general in all the Beauvais district: and you should know that in land where entry is prohibited at all times you can make arrests at any time, if you find someone trespassing [*forfesant*], and in the other lands you can make arrests when entry is prohibited by custom.

1559. People can go into fields sown in the spring to gather grass and greens, and cross them providing they do not make a path, until this is prohibited because of the growth of the wheat; for when the wheat is small, people only help by picking grass, and the land is improved. But as soon as the wheat has grown up and is sending up stems, it would be impaired; and for this reason people can then be prohibited from entering. And if anyone tries to prohibit people from going on to his lands at all times, it should not be permitted, if anyone complains, because this would be against the public good.

1560. Pigs should not be permitted in pastures at any time, because they spoil the fields by rooting, nor cows, sheep, horses, or goats in thickets, because they do damage in all seasons of the year, and for this reason they can be seized in all seasons.

1561. If a person confiscating another person's animals which are causing damage kills them while making the seizure, he must pay the damages to the owner and he loses his fine and the damages he could have claimed from the owner if he had wanted to get them back. And if he does not kill them during the seizure, but he locks them up [*les en mene en prison*] and holds them so confined that they die from being locked up [*par destrece de prison*], or because they have nothing to eat, once again he must pay the damages and loses his fine. But if some of the animals die without the intervention of the person making the seizure, he does not lose his fine, and pays no damages for the dead animals. And also if the owner does not want to have the animals back, by a reclamation[3] or in any other way, the person properly making the seizure may enjoy the benefits of the animals as long as they with him, as if they were his own, without making any restitution when they are requested back, except that he may not sell them or give anyone else possession of them until he has made an official inquiry [*sommé*] of the owner as to whether he wants to get them back by paying the fine and for the damages they caused, or if he wants to renounce any claim to them;

and this inquiry must be made before the lord where he is a resident. And if the owner of the animals will neither renounce his claim to the animals nor take them back, the lord must order him to do so within seven days and seven nights; and if he lets this time pass, the person confiscating can treat them as his own, for it is clear that they have been abandoned because of the offense.

1562. Any time someone seizes another's animals, and they remain in the possession of the person confiscating because of some dispute,—for example, when the owner says they were not rightfully seized, or when he requests a day for an inspection of the place where they were seized, which should not be denied,—in that case the person confiscating should put the animals in a place on his land where the owner can give some of his own feed to the animals; for the person confiscating need not feed them unless he wants, since the seizure suit is being delayed by the challenge of the owner; for the animals might starve to death before the suit was over, so that if the person confiscating won the suit, he would have nothing by which to get his damages or his fine.[4] But when the person confiscating does not want to feed the animals, he must let the owner know, so that he can take care of them and give them what they need, so that the owner, if harm comes to his animals, cannot say that he depended on the person confiscating to feed his animals.

1563. When property is seized for an offense, and the property is hard to keep so that it does not perish or spoil (for example if someone seizes the animals of a foreign[5] merchant, or his wine or wheat or oats or other merchandise, and the merchant cannot come before the seized merchandise spoils or loses its sales value; or for example if someone seizes the property of a person accused of a serious crime, for which he is not yet condemned; or if the lord seizes something in his jurisdiction as unclaimed lost property, whose owner is not known), in all these and similar cases the seized property should be sold to the highest bidder, in such a way that if the finding is that the property should be given back to the owners, they must be satisfied to get the price, since the property was sold in good faith.

1564. Everyone should be very careful not to arrest his lord's officers in his jurisdiction, because it would be a grave offense to his lord and he would have to pay a great fine to his lord, except in the following cases: namely, if my lord's officer, in my jurisdiction and on my land, begins a fight by his bad conduct [*outrage*] and not as part of his duties as an officer, I can arrest him, and having done so, I should take him before my lord and explain the reason for the arrest, and my lord should let me receive the fine or punish him for the fight. There are other cases in which I can arrest my lord's officer in my jurisdiction: namely, for all offenses he commits in my jurisdiction, except what he is permitted to do as part of his duties, for example if he causes damage to property or commits arson, or any other serious offense for which he should be punished; and I should not believe him if he says he did it as part of his official duties, for he cannot use this as a defense in so serious a crime.

1565. If someone tries to make an improper seizure [*prendre vileine-ment*] in my house and says he is my lord's officer and that he has come to make the seizure as his official duty, and I suspect he is lying and I have a presumption he is a thief because I never before saw him performing duties and because he gives me no true information [*nouveles*] and no certain signs by which I can know whether he is telling the truth or lying, it is no great wonder if I will not permit the seizure, for in that case all thieves could pretend to be officers. But if he shows he is an officer by a writing, or by true information or by true signs or by witnesses, I must allow him to make the seizures he wants to as an officer. And if I resist or commit any offense against him, I have to pay a fine to the lord; and what such fines are is explained in the chapter on offenses {Chapter 30}.

1566. The testimony of all officers properly appointed in the jurisdiction to make seizures is to be believed on their oath where it concerns their seizures; and so it is concerning any resistance to their authority, if there is any made, up to a fine of sixty sous; and the count's officers are believed up to a fine of sixty pounds. Nevertheless you can make an argument against officers of a grudge [*haine*] or threats, and if you prove it they are not to be believed.

1567. The officer who knowingly makes a wrongful arrest, or makes one where he should not, in order to cause loss without a good reason, must on conviction pay for all the damages to the person whose property was seized, and must lose his job as an officer, for he performed it dishonestly. And if the person suing an officer on this count cannot get him convicted by the circumstantial evidence or by witnesses, he must pay a fine to he lord of sixty sous, if he is a commoner, and sixty pounds if he is a gentleman.

1568. Some people say that an arrest has not been made unless the person arresting places his hand on the arrestee when he does so, but it *is* in all the cases where you cannot place your hand on the person because of some obstacle, for example if the arresting person sees offenders in the water, and he cannot reach them because of the danger, if he arrests them by speaking to them and looking at them, and by ordering them to come out of the water, the arrest is properly made. Therefore if they do not submit to the arrest, but go away so that they person arresting cannot place his hand on them, they must also pay a fine for resisting arrest along with the fine for the offense, as if they had resisted and he *had* put his hand on them. And what we have said about the obstacle of the water applies to other obstacles which may hinder the person arresting, so that he cannot place his hand on the prisoners when making the arrest.

1569. You can pursue someone on to someone else's land in order to make an arrest: for example if an officer sees animals in his lord's wheat, and when is he going to seize them the shepherd removes the animals from the wheat on to someone else's land, neverthless if the officer is willing to swear he saw them doing damage to the place he was responsible for, and that they were removed as he was going to seize them, he can seize them wherever they are by following up the crime, for no bad faith should be to the advantage of a person who knowingly acts in bad faith.[6]

1570. If those with the power to arrest are in need of help in carrying our their duties,—for example in arresting banished men or thieves or offenders; or for example if resistance is made to them when they are making an arrest,—if they ask for the help of their lord's subjects and the latter do not obey the order, they must pay a fine to the lord; and the fines for these offenses are not all alike, but according to the situation in which the help was asked for; for a person disobeying my order to help arrest a thief, or a murderer or a banished man, or a homicide who escapes me because I lack help, should be more severely punished than a person who disobeyed my order to help me drive a flock of animals which I have seized for causing damage. And for this reason we agree that serious disobediences should be fined at the lord's discretion, and the little ones where there was not much at stake should be fined as disobedience to an order.

1571. We have announced several times in the assize that everyone has the power to arrest all kinds of offenders or persons suspected of serious crimes, and all those who are fleeing and behind whom there is a hue and cry, until you know what the hue and cry was about, and also all those seen actually fighting; and anyone who does not assist [*met conseil*] in making such arrests and who could have done so must be fined for disobedience, according to what we said above.

1572. Sometimes you cannot administer justice immediately because of some impediment: for example when there is a jurisdictional dispute among several lords, to see who has jurisdicton, for in that case justice must be delayed until you know who is to administer it; or for example when someone is convicted of murder, or homicide, or treason, or poisoning, or rape, for which reasons his house should be burned or demolished, and some lady has dower rights in the house for her lifetime, in such a case the house must be spared while the woman is alive. But if the offender had a share in the house as his property and other people also have a share in it, so that you could hardly burn down the offender's share without also causing injury to the other person's portion, or to a neighbor's, in that case you should not execute the sentence by fire, but just knock down the offender's portion with mauls and hammers, so that justice is done without loss to those who have no guilt.

1573. We have said in this chapter that a person convicted of a serious crime is condemned to death and all his property is forfeit. Nevertheless if the offender has children and a father or mother, or grandfather or grandmother, the property which passes by descent from them, and which had not passed when the offender committed the offense, passes to the offender's children; for the offender could not forfeit what was not yet his, and it does not pass to his heirs through him, but passes to them by descent through their lineage, to the nearest heirs; but it is true that they take nothing from the offender himself.

1574. A person who is arrested, whether for an offense or for debt, is not required, as long as he is in prison, to answer any complaint against him, except for the case for which he was arrested. And if he is made to answer anything against his will and alleging that he does not want to answer as long as he is in prison, everything done against him is invalid, for he can have it all canceled when he leaves prison. But we make an exception in such cases for bad faith which could be used, for example, if someone had himself put in prison for debt because he did not want to answer other creditors [*deteurs*] to whom he owed money, or if he remained in prison at his own wish and had the power to be released: in such cases prisoners should have to answer other people's complaints, for they should not be able to profit from their own bad faith.

1575. Those who have gone insane [*forsené*] should be bound by those who must guard them and everyone must help do this to avoid the damage they might do, for they could easily kill themselves and others. And if they are not bound, and because of their insanity they commit a homicide or some other serious crime, they are not punished like other people because they do not know what they are doing, and their heirs do not for this reason lose what the insane person had, unless the heirs had them in their care and the offense was committed because of their lack of proper care [*mauvese garde*]. But in any case the insane person must be placed in perpetual confinement, and maintained from his own property as long as he is crazy. And if he comes back to his senses, he should be released from prison, and his property returned to him. But in this case you should examine very carefully if this was not done in bad faith, for example some people, when they had committed offenses, might pretend to be insane in order to escape punishment: and you should look very carefully at what moved the person to commit the offense, and by this you will know if there was sharp practice [*barat*] involved.

1576. When a lord attaches or seizes something belonging to a person in his jurisdiction *at the request of someone else*, he should examine whether the case requires him to make the seizure before the parties have commenced a suit before him, for no lord should, because of an *ex parte* request, remove possession from a person in his jurisdiction until he has heard his defense or the person has failed to make an appearance in his court, except for certain special cases: for example, if Jehan complains that Pierre has threatened him and has him summoned to establish a guaranteed peace, the lord can forbid Pierre to do harm to Jehan while the appearance is pending; or if he complains of force or novel disseisin, the lord should, on the inspection day, take possession of the property and then deal with it in the way we explained in the chapter on force and novel disseisin {Chapter 32}; or if he complains of some situation from which great harm or great injury [*vilenie*] could come to him if the appearance is delayed, for example if someone had forcibly abducted [*ravie a force*] his wife or daughter, or another woman in his care, or robbed him of his palfrey or his horse or some of his property: in all these and similar cases the lord should take possession of the things said to be stolen or taken or abducted, in order to remove the risks which could occur; and also in other cases, for example interference with dower or a will, the lord can take possession as soon as the complaint reaches him, for these are two cases where the lords should be anxious to give a speedy hearing [*de fere droit hastif*]. And also in all cases where things can perish while waiting for trial, the lord can take possession and if the person he finds in possession does not give good security to give back the value of the property, should he lose it in a trial and by the judgment: for example if Jehan has in his possession ten barrels of wine, and Pierre is suing for them and says they should be his, and, while the suit is pending, they are in danger of spoiling or missing a good market, Jehan should give security to the value of the ten barrels of wine, and then he can drink them or sell them; and if he will not give security, the lord should take them and sell them and afterwards give the price to the winner of the suit. And what we have said about wine applies to the other things which can perish or deteriorate because of delay.

1577. Every time a lord seizes property at the request of someone else (in whatever kind of a case it is) and the person at whose request the seizure was made fails to appear in court on the day assigned by the lord, the lord should surrender possession of the thing he seized; and if he took some property, he should give it back without obligation to the person he took it from, without the person having to obtain a reclamation.[7] But the person at whose request the seizure was made does not on that account lose his right to sue some other time on the *ownership* of the property; for by his default he only loses the chance to sue while in possession, if he still wants to sue. And if he takes a continuance on the day when he should have appeared to tell the lord why he asked him to make the seizure, he should not be permitted to take the continuance, but the lord should surrender possession just as if the person had defaulted. But it would be different if he had a legal excuse [*essoine*] not to appear and he adjourned [*essoinoit*] the appearance,[8] for in that case the lord should not surrender possession until he is sure that the person at whose request he made the seizure no longer has a legal excuse. But if he adjourned without having a legal excuse, or if he has recovered from his indisposition [*essoine*] to the point where he is seen publicly carrying on his business as he used to, and he does not have the person whose property was seized summoned, then the lord should surrender possession; and when he thinks it is right, he can summon the person to a suit on the ownership of the thing, and the lord can give a hearing.

1578. Any lord can attach and seize real property held from him any time the holder is not doing what he should with respect to the property. And among other reasons for making such a seizure, he is right to seize when his sales taxes were concealed from him or when they were not paid by the time established by custom for paying sales taxes, for example seven days and seven nights after the seller has surrendered possession. But there are some sales for which no sales taxes are due, however the property was held, whether in fief or in villeinage; for if some real property passes to the lord or a religious house because of the death of his serf, and the property should be held from some other lord than the one to whom it passes because of his serf's death, in such cases the lord from whom the land is held can compel the religious house to surrender possession of the land within a year and a day, but he cannot order laypersons to do this, if they are willing to pay the proper dues to him for the property. And if he makes such an order to a religious house and it sells the property because it cannot hold possession of it, the religious house owes no sales tax; and this is true of all the property which is left to religious housees in charity, or which can pass to them for any other reason, if they have to surrender possession at the compulsion of the lord [*par force de seigneur*], they owe neither sales tax nor relief.

1579. Because we say that religious houses which sell under compulsion owe neither sales tax nor relief, some people might think that all those who sell under compulsion would owe no sales taxes. But it is not so, for if a lord compels someone to sell property in order to pay debts, the lord nevertheless receives his sales taxes.

1580. Those who enter property by purchase should be careful that the lords from whom the land is held are satisfied, with respect to the sales tax; for although it is our custom that the seller owes the sales tax, if the lord is not paid by the seller, he can have recourse to the property until he is paid for his sales tax and for the fine for not paying the tax on time, which is a small [*simple*] fine; but if the sales tax was concealed in bad faith, there is a fine of sixty sous. And for this reason the buyer may retain the value of the sales tax out of the price he paid, in order to pay the lord to clear the seller and guard himself from risk. And if he retains the sales tax, as we said, in order to pay the lord, and he does not pay it as he should, so that the lord wants a fine, the damages should be paid by him and not by the seller. And if he gave security for the price he paid for the property, and the seller will not pay the sales tax, but wants to be paid the whole price, the buyer can have the lord forbid his sureties to pay anything until the property which is encumbered [*empeechiés*] because of {nonpayment of} the sales tax (or for any other action of the seller) has been delivered to the buyer, for a person who sells should deliver and warrantee {the property}.

1581. Some sales are concluded under an agreement that the buyer will pay the sales tax. And you should know that when such an agreement is made, if the tax is not paid, all the loss should be suffered by the buyer and not by the seller. And in such cases you should know that both sales tax and sales surtax [*ventes et reventes*] are due.[9] For example if the property sold is real property held in villeinage, and the deal is for sixty pounds net to the seller [*quites au vendeur*], the buyer owes in sales tax a hundred sous, being every twelfth denier, and for sales surtax every twelfth denier of the hundred sous, which is a hundred deniers.[10] And if the property sold to the buyer for sixty pounds net was in fief, he would have to pay twelve pounds, being every fifth denier on sixty pounds, and afterwards for sales surtax every fifth denier of the twelve pounds, which is forty-eight sous. And by what we have said about the sales taxes and surtaxes for a sixty-pound sale, you can understand that you should take proportionately more for deals of more than sixty pounds, and less for those under sixty pounds. And any time the deal is concluded without conditions, without agreement that the price is net to the seller, the seller owes the sales tax, that is to say every twelfth denier for villeinages, and every fifth denier for fiefs; but he does not owe any sales surtax; and you should know that in many of the towns in our district a levy of one denier is exacted for all sales of villeinages, but we do not know how this custom arose or why.

Here ends the chapter on seizures and sales taxes.

Notes

1. *Prendre* and *prise* can be translated as "arrest" and "seize," "seizure" according to whether the action is taken against a person or a thing. In some of the later

sections of the chapter, Beaumanoir uses two verbs together, *prendre et saisir* (e.g., §§1576–78), with a direct object which is a thing, not a person. I have therefore translated *prendre* and *prise* sometimes as "arrest," sometimes as "seize," "seizure," as the context seems to require. I have used "seize" to refer to a temporary or preemptive taking of things, as opposed to "confiscate," which I reserve for the permanent taking of things, with change of ownership.

2. *Tremois* is defined as three-month-old wheat which is sown in spring, sometimes called "spring wheat." In Beauvais, wheat sown in the autumn survives the winter.

3. For reclamations, see Chapter 53.

4. That is, he would have no security, for the owner could abandon the dead animals.

5. Foreign here means from outside the jurisdiction.

6. This is the modern doctrine of "hot pursuit."

7. That is, without having to deposit security for it.

8. For continuances and adjournments, see Chapter 3.

9. In what follows it is helpful to remember there are twenty sous to the pound, and twelve deniers to the sou.

10. If the seller had paid the sales tax, he would have charged the buyer more. Thus by charging a sales surtax the lord is only recouping the tax the seller would have paid on the larger price. In Beaumanoir's figures, the seller could have charged £65 (£60 for himself and £5 to pay the sales tax), paying £5 8s. 4d. (one-twelfth of £65) as the sales tax. If he sells for less and has the buyer pay the sales tax, the buyer pays one-twelfth of the buying price of £60, namely £5 in tax, and an additional twelfth of this £5 in sales surtax. It is the extra 8s. 4d. which is recouped by charging a sales surtax of one-twelfth on the £5 (one-twelfth of $5 \times 20 \times 12$ deniers, namely 1200 deniers, is 100 deniers, or 8s. 4d.).

53. Reclamation

Here begins the fifty-third chapter of this book which speaks of reclamations,[1] *and in which cases you may permit reclamations, and in which not; and how a reclamation may be requested and how it may be made in those cases where it is appropriate.*

1582. In the preceding chapter we spoke of seizures; and it is right for us to speak in this one following of reclamations [*recreances*], for it is from the seizures which are made that arise the requests which should be made for reclamation.

1583. A reclamation is {temporarily} getting back what was confiscated, by giving security to give the thing back to the person confiscating on a day certain which is named, or sometimes on the summons of the lord who made the seizure.

1584. A reclamation should be requested from the lord (or his deputy) in whose jurisdiction the seizure was made, for the officers who are appointed just to make seizures cannot and should not allow reclamations of what they confiscate; for when they have made the seizure, they must present the things to their lord and say why the seizure was made; and if the lord sees that they have no good reason for the seizure, he should give the things back freely; and if he sees that the seizure was made for a good reason, he is not required to give the things back, except if security is given, and this is called reclamation.

1585. In all seizures of whatever property (except in cases or crime, or suspicion of a crime, for which the penalty is loss of life or limb) if the {criminal} action is not admitted or proved, reclamation should be permitted if the person from whom the seizure was made requests it. But in cases of crime this reclamation should not be permitted except in one case, which is where a wager of battle between one party and the other is allowed in a case of serious crime. In this case if the parties can pledge themselves by good sureties that they will reappear in court, they should be allowed a reclamation so that they can prepare themselves to proceed with what the case requires.

1586. If someone requests a reclamation from somebody and a reclamation should be permitted, and the lord who has the confiscated property refuses to permit the reclamation, the person from whom the seizure was made should appear before the sovereign of the lord who is holding the confiscated property, or the count who is the sovereign of those who hold directly from him and of all the sub-fiefs, and should show him in his complaint the seizure made of his property, and should say he believes the seizure was not made for a good reason, and that he has tried to obtain a properly secured reclamation of the property, and it has been refused him. Then the count should send a provost or an officer with orders to the lord that if the seizure was made without good reason [*sans reson resnable*] he must give the property back and appear at the first assize to pay a fine for making an improper seizure. And if he says that the seizure was properly made and that he is willing to allow a reclamation, if the person whose property was confiscated wants to continue to maintain and prove that he asked for a reclamation previously and it was refused, he is not required to accept a reclamation except from the possession of the count; and the person refusing to allow a reclamation cannot have the case sent back down, and he cannot have cognizance of the seizure, but he must show cause in the count's court why the seizure was made, and in that case he loses his jurisdiction because he refused to allow a reclamation when it should have been permitted. And if the lord who made the seizure answers the provost or the officer carrying out the count's orders that the seizure was made for a good reason and admits that a reclamation was requested of him and that he denied it because it was inappropriate, and that he will explain this in the count's court, in that case the person carrying out the count's orders should find out what the things were that were confiscated; for if it is personal property which can be injured, such as horses or other animals, he should order a reclamation into the count's possession and assign a court date to the person refusing the reclamation to show cause why the reclamation was inappropriate. And if the arrest[2] was that of a man who is being kept in prison, and he names the crime for which he is being held, the count's envoy should not permit a reclamation, for the person allowed bail might consider himself so guilty that he would not appear in court whatever security he had given;[3] but he should assign a date for a speedy appearance to the lord holding the man, for him to state in the count's court the reason why he is holding the man, and also assign an appearance to those who are asking bail for the prisoner, and a hearing should be given there, as to whether bail is appropriate or not.

1587. When the count personally hears a reclamation request because his vassal refused to allow it, and the vassal can show good cause why it is inappropriate to give a reclamation, the count should restore the relaimed property to the vassal as it was when he took it away to hear the reclamation request. And for this reason, each time a *bailli,* provost, or officer permits a reclamation in the name of their lord, they should keep the property so securely that they can restore it to the person they took it from and then order a hearing to be held in the court of the person who first made the seizure, according to the offense that led to the first seizure.

1588. When someone states in the count's court the reason for making the seizure, in order to have the case sent back down to his own court, if the reason is such that the seizure was proper, and the person whose property was confiscated admits it, the case should be sent down. And if the party denies it, the person who wants the case sent down must prove his contention; and once he has proved it, the case can be sent down and he can permit a reclamation until he has given a hearing, if a reclamation is appropriate in the case.

1589. When a reclamation has been permitted of some confiscated property because the party contests that the seizure was properly made, the reclamation should last until it is proved that the seizure was proper, in the way that proper seizures must be proved; for they are sometimes proved by circumstantial evidence [*l'aparence du mesfet*] and sometimes by witnesses, for example, when there is a dispute over the jurisdiction of the person making the seizure, for if he is trying to take advantage of [*joïr de*] the seizure, he must show it was made in his jurisdiction.

1590. If a person obtains a reclamation of what was confiscated from him, and defaults on his court appearances concerning the seizure, the person making the seizure can sue the sureties until the confiscated property is back in his possession and then reap the profits from the property [*esploitier les choses*] until he has recovered the fine and the damages from the original offense, for inasmuch as the person obtaining the reclamation is in default, he loses his opportunity to allege that the seizure was improperly made, since he is in default.

1591. Any time grazing animals are confiscated for some offense because of which the person confiscating wants a fine and compensation for the damage they caused, and the owner offers to give adequate sureties, or adequate security in the form of property [*gages gisans*], for the damage and the fine demanded by the person confiscating, the latter should give back the animals in exchange for the property or the sureties; and if he refuses, he must pay for the loss incurred by the owner of the animals. But if the lord had good cause to say that the animals were forfeit and that he had acquired ownership of them because of the forfeiture,—for example when an animal kills a child, or when a person must lose his horse or donkey {when he is caught} transporting his wheat to a different mill than the one where he is obliged to go [*ou il est baniers*], or for any other reason why animals can be forfeited according to custom,—in all these cases the person confiscating is not required to give them back nor to take any other property in exchange for them, since he can dispose of the animals as his own property. And if there is an argument over whether the animals are forfeit, and the person confiscating loses the suit, he must give the animals back to the person from whom they were confiscated, along with any profit he made from the animals while the suit was pending. And what we have said here about animals we apply to all other things wrongfully confiscated.

1592. If the lord has made a seizure or has something belonging to his vassal in his own possession, without the judgment of the man's peers, if the man requests reclamation, he should not refuse him; and if he does refuse, the reclamation should be permitted by the sovereign; and if the lord offers to give him a hearing on the issue of whether a reclamation is appropriate, the man need not go to trial [*ne se couchera pas en cel jugement*] unless he wants to, for he is not required to go to trial when he is not in possession, except in the cases which we have set out in the chapter on summonses {Chapter 2}. Nevertheless, if the lord is holding in his possession something belonging to his man, and there is a doubt whether a reclamation is appropriate or not, and he offers to give his man a hearing by his peers on the issue of whether a reclamation is appropriate, the man must accept the court appearance and the hearing on the reclamation; and how you should proceed in an appearance before your lord, and how you must petition [*sommer*] your lord before you can complain about his default, will be explained in the chapter which speaks of how you can sue your lord for default of judgment {Chapter 62}.

Here ends the chapter on reclamations.

Notes

1. I have chosen to use the word "reclamation" to translate the French *recreance*. There is no convenient term in English. The person whose property has been taken by another can get it back by giving security that he will bring it to court and hand it over to the seizor when the case comes on. This security is referred to in early English law as "gage and pledge"; see Frederick Pollock and Frederic William Maitland, *The History of English Law Before the Time of Edward I*, 2d. ed. (Cambridge, Eng.: Cambridge University Press, 1923) 2: 576. It is tempting to use the words "replevy," "replevin," but they refer to actions for permanent recovery of property the plaintiff claims was improperly seized. "Reclamation" is the equivalent for property of our "bail" for persons.

2. Beaumanoir uses the same noun, *prise,* for seizures of property (here translated "seizure") and of persons (here translated "arrest"). Likewise Beaumanoir uses *recreance* to mean the release (on the giving of security) of property (here translated "reclamation") and of persons (here translated "bail").

3. The modern idiom is "jumping bail."

54. Creditors' Remedies I

Here begins the fifty-fourth chapter of this book which says how creditors should be paid and kept from loss, and how you should attach things in a house; and it also says how you put a guard on someone.

1593. When someone owes a debt and must be taken to court to pay, his personal property must be taken before his real property is cut into, for if the personal property is enough, the land should be left alone; and if it is not enough, then he can be forced to sell some real property within forty days; and then if he has not sold it, the lord should sell it and warrantee the sale either to the creditors or to someone else. And if there happen to be more personal property than the total debts, it is not the choice of the person who must deliver them as to which personal property he will deliver, for if he wants to give vats, or chests, or large pieces of timber [*gros merriens*], or things like that which are hard to handle, the creditor need not take them unless he wants if there are wheat, or oats, or wine, or other things and which are lighter and easier to sell quickly. But it should not be entirely the choice of the person taking delivery for his debt to have whichever personal property he wants, if there is other property from which he can easily be paid: for example if the debtor is a smith, and the creditor wants to be given his anvil or his hammers, and the smith has other personal property he wants to give him for what the debt is worth, in such a case you cannot give the creditor the above-mentioned tools, for the smith needs them to earn his bread,[1] and there could be a public loss. And what we have said about the smith can be extended to all kinds of people who have a trade. Therefore every time that personal property is seized by the court for debt, and there is more personal property than debts, you should take what harms the debtor least and through which the debt can be most quickly paid.

1594. Any time personal property is attached for debt, the costs of attaching it, moving it, taking it to market, and securing it, if it consists of things which must be kept secure, and all other reasonable costs which can arise because of the attached property, must be paid out of the proceeds, so that the creditor receives his money free and complete. And this loss should go to those who wait so long to pay their debts that their property has to be attached by the court, for it would be a bad thing if creditors had such a loss because their debtors did not pay.

1595. When you have to attach someone's {personal} property for debt, it is not surprising if you take the things you see under his control, such as what is in his house or at his command. Nevertheless, if someone else comes along and proves that the thing seized was his, he should have it back; but he should say and demonstrate the reason why it was in the possession of the debtor when it was attached: for example if it had been lent or rented or given in safekeeping, for this is how you come to have in your possession someone else's property, and it is good to know this to prevent frauds.

1596. There are people so wicked that when they think their property is going to be attached for debt, they go to their lord and make some deal whereby they owe him something, and then they tell him they cannot give him a surety except by using what they have in his jurisdiction as a security, and they ask him to take possession of all of it in lieu of a security; and the lord, who probably knows nothing of their trickery (or perhaps he knows all about it and permits it to help them and harm their creditors) takes possession of everything; and when the creditors sue for payment, the lord says everything is in his possession because of what is owed him as debts or fines; and thus, if there were no remedy, the creditors could lose without good reason. But there is a remedy, which is that the lord can be sued before his overlord, and he must say what his subject owes him, and swear the debt is valid and honest, and that he made it without fraud or sharp practice; and when he has sworn this, he will not necessarily keep possession of all his subject's property, but only of as much as the total of the debt, so that the creditors can obtain payment from the rest, for it would be a bad thing if I could protect a hundred pounds' worth of my vassal's property that he held in my jurisdiction as security for ten or twenty pounds that he owed me. And for this reason, I must take what is due me and then have his creditors paid out of what is left.

1597. There are other kinds or dealers in sharp practice who dare not make such deals with their lords because they fear their lords will not permit their sharp practice; so they go to a relative or a neighbor and make some fake agreement, or a fake deal, or a fake gift, and then come before their lord from whom the person who is afraid of his creditors holds his land and the subject says: "Sire, here is a relative of mine,—or a neighbor of mine,—for the service he has done me, I have given him all I have and I want you to place him in seisin of it," or he says to him: "Sire, I have sold him everything I have and I consider myself paid up," and the lord, who is not on the watch for sharp practice, accepts the disseisin of his subject and gives seisin to the other; and later the creditors appear before the lord and ask to be paid by the man who has been disseised of everything he had. What can you do in such a case? If the lord does not act wisely, the creditors are in danger of losing what is owed them because of the trickery of the debtor. Then the lord should look at the reason for the disseisin, for if the seller was disseised in an alleged sale, he should look at who is holding the things and treating them as his own, the buyer or the seller, and if he finds that the seller has them and is using them to his own benefit, as he might use his own things, the lord should seize possession for two reasons: the first, because the person could not enter the property except by permission of the lord once he had left,[2] and the second to have the creditors paid. And if the lord sees the buyer holding the thing he bought as his own, he should inquire what happened to the money from the sale and when payment was made; and if he finds the money has not been paid, he should take possession of it and have the creditors paid; and thus he can neutralize their sharp practice. And if the money was paid to the seller and he went out of this lord's jurisdiction, in that case the creditors must sue him where he is a resident, unless what he sold or gave away or pledged [*engaja*] had been specially pledged as security to the creditors: for in that case the creditors should sue only on the things that were given as security for the debts. And if they prove against those who are currently holding the things that the things were pledged as security, then a sale or gift or pledge made later is invalid. And if the disseisin was made because of a gift, the lord should look at what was the reason for the gift, for you do not often see a man give away what he has in order to remain poor; and in the same way, when a man has debts and he makes a gift, it may be believed that he did it to harm his creditors in the hopes that the person receiving the gift will do him some kindness for the things given. And for this reason, we agree that to give away every-thing, and keep nothing with which to pay the creditors what was due them when the gift was made in sharp practice, is invalid. And if the lord finds fraud or sharp practice, he should undo the pledge of security in such a way that the person pledging simply gets his chattels back and the creditors are paid. And if the pledge of security had been made without sharp practice and without a fake agreement, that is not a reason for the creditors to lose what is theirs; but since they did not contest the giving of security, and it was administered by a lord, they must wait to be paid until the time of the pledge of security is completed, unless the things given in security had been pledged to them already by the lord; for the lord who has agreed to a giving of security by his subject cannot permit giving the same thing as security to another person until the first agreement is terminated.

1598. It sometimes happens that someone owes more than all his assets and yet he wants to pay what he can, so that he comes to court and gives up all he owns in payment. In this case, the judge should look at the value of his assets, and pay the creditors as far as the money will stretch, according to the assets and the total of the debts, so much to the pound; for it would be a bad thing for a person who was owed ten pounds to take as much as a person to whom twenty pounds were owed. And for this reason, if the person owed ten pounds takes forty sous, the person owed twenty pounds should take four pounds. And by what we have said about ten pounds and twenty pounds you can understand the calculation [*du plus et du meins*] according to the size of the assets and the size of the debts. And if it happens that all the assets are insufficient to pay all the debts, and the creditors have no security, they must take their losses for giving credit unwisely. Nevertheless if it should happen that the person owing, who gave up all his assets in order to pay, acquires some property because some assets passed to him on the death of someone else, or he earns something by working or some other way, he is not paid up to the creditors to whom he gave up his possessions; but he must pay them what they are lacking because they were not paid in full. And in such a case the creditors can recover what was owed them.

1599. When someone abandons all his assets to pay his debts, the assets should not be reduced by the cost of guards and live-in enforcers [*manjans*], but delivered to the creditors with minimal costs deducted; for the more there is lost, the less there is given in repayment. And the person giving up his assets should not be imprisoned unless he is suspected of concealing or keeping back something of what he gave up. And he should not be stripped of the clothing [*robe*] he wears every day, for it is a wicked thing, and against humanity, to strip a man or woman for debt.

1600. It is forbidden to go and attach things in the room of a lady or young lady or of a woman in confinement for childbirth. And it is forbidden to take the beds or bedclothes of those who are sick or ill, for there could be great danger to those from whom they were removed. If ladies or young ladies in bad faith put all their things in the room so they could not be taken, however, we would not want this bad faith to avail them; instead we want them to be asked in such cases for an adequate security [*nans*] for the debt for which they can and should be sued, and if they will not give security willingly, people should go boldly into the room and take possession of things. Nevertheless we forbid the taking of ladies' beds and their everyday dresses in any way for debt, but everything else may be taken.

1601. Any time someone goes to make a seizure of things because of a court order for debt, and the persons whose things are to be seized do not want to show their things quietly [*debonairement*] but keep their doors and their trunks closed, against the will of the court, the "king's keys" should be used, which means that the officer who is going to make the seizure on the order of the lord can and should break into what is closed against him, and take what he finds, and arrest the person who disobeyed his order, both for the debt and for the penalty. But those who have such business to do, when they have to break down doors or force open chests or other things because they have been disobeyed, should in any case take with them honest folk to see what they take, and who can testify about it afterwards before the lord if there is a need. And if they do not act in this manner and the lord whose things were taken can prove by good folk that the officer took more than he will admit, the officer must be made to give back what he denied and be dimissed from the service, and he will be of bad repute, for it seems that he hid the thing with intent to commit larceny. But the witnesses who appear against officers should be very carefully examined, and you should make sure they are without suspicion, and hear what the officer says against them, for the duty of seizing people's property to pay debts is an ungrateful one [*office haineus*]: and the lords should not lightly believe in the offenses of which their officers are accused until they know the pure truth. And a person who accuses his lord's officer of such a serious crime and then cannot prove it should have a great loss, as great as or greater than he wanted to cause the officer.

1602. It used to be that as soon as a debt was admitted or proved, guards or live-in enforcers [*nans manjans*] were assigned to the debtor. But because we have seen many losses where the property was used up and the debts were not necessarily paid, we have ordered that, as soon as something is found that can be confiscated, it should be taken without such losses; and if the thing is personal property that needs to be harvested, for example wheat or oats to be reaped or threshed, or wine to be harvested, one single man should be set to guard them until they have been worked on; and thus the creditors can be paid without great loss to the debtors. And if there is no personal property to confiscate, but there is real property, an order should be issued to sell within forty days; and if the debtor will not sell, the lord should sell the land or give it to the creditors as is said above. And if the land is such that it cannot be sold,—for example if it is held in custodianship or in dower, or a lease; or if it is so great a fief that the whole thing should not be sold for such a small debt and it cannot be split up,[3]—then let the guards be assigned to the person who holds land for those reasons, so that he will find a way to pay his creditors and avoid loss.

1603. The custom concerning guards assigned to a house is that when they live in the house where they are assigned and they are given adequate bread and soup and a bed, they can only ask for an additional four deniers a day. And if they are outside the house, such as if the lord prefers them outside rather than inside, or there is no one in the house to feed them, then each guard gets eight deniers per day. Nevertheless, it is not the choice of the person being assigned guards whether they will live in the house or not, but the choice of the person assigning guards, according to the condition of the house and the reasons why guards are assigned. For if the lord is assigning guards to his subjects to guard the property or to pay debts or because of forfeiture, the guards are better off inside than out; for otherwise they could not take care of what is under their guard. But when they are assigned to run up costs,[4] for example, to oblige someone to appear in court to make a guaranteed peace or to do something else, the lord who assigned them can permit them to be outside the house, in as close a lodging as possible, if that is what the person to whom they were assigned wants; for if the assigning lord wanted to put them outside in spite of the householder, and the latter offered to put them up and feed them adequately, it would be unfair to him; and for this reason if guards are assigned to someone and they lodge outside the house, of their own will and without blame to the person to whom they were assigned, we agree they should be paid not eight deniers a day but only four, just as if they had lodged in the house itself.

1604. There used to be an evil custom of assigning guards to people which we have abolished in our time. For the officers appointed to assign

guards to other people came to the house of such people and said to those
in the house, for example to the lord or the lady, or the members of
household when they did not find the lord or the lady: "I am assigning four
foot guards here,"—or four horse guards, or whatever number they were
told,—and then he left without leaving any guards in residence; and after a
month or two, when the person assigned these guards had settled up with
the lord, he came to the officer and settled up with him as cheaply as he
could, sometimes for a third or a quarter of what it would have cost if the
guards had actually been in residence. And sometimes, when the lord had
ordered the officer to assign four guards, he only assigned two for a
kickback [*pour déport*] or for the kindness shown him by the person to
whom they should have been assigned, and the officer pretended he had
assigned as many as the lord had ordered him to; and sometimes the officer
assigned the right number, but he privately told the guards, when they had
been there two or three days, to go off and do their other business and turn
up once or twice every day where they had been assigned, and then the lord
settled up with them for less than for their full time; and sometimes they did
not settle up for less, and the officers split the proceeds with the guards; and
sometimes the officers said they did not find an adequate place for the
guards to sleep in the house, and that they had been lodged in some house
as close as possible, and lied for the kindness they expected to have for this
or for a kickback. And what did we see happen because of these things? We
saw that when we wanted to have someone forced to appear by the guards,
he would not come because of a small sum he gave the officer, and when
guards were assigned because of debt, the creditors always sued again
because they could not get paid; and we saw that the officers were becoming rich through their conduct against the lord's orders. And for all these
reasons, and for quite a few other dangers that could arise from a weak
administration of justice [*foiblement justicier*], we ordered in full session [*en
pleine assize*] that no officer was to be so bold as to assign guards except as he
was ordered, neither more nor less; and if he did it otherwise, he would be
dismissed from his duties and would pay a fine at the lord's will. And we
ordered that all guards assigned to people to control [*justicier*] them must
stay in the place where they were assigned, sleeping and living there day and
night, without doing any other work or business, if the house was such that
they could stay there; and if they could not, they should be in the closest
place to it; and if bad behavior or sharp practice were found between the
guards and those to whom they were assigned, each party would be fined.
And we ordered that every time guards were sent somewhere, they would

receive a writing from the *bailli* or the provost showing the day they were assigned, because there had been several arguments because the guards said they had been on assignment more days that were admitted. And we ordered that no empty seisin [*vuide saisine*] was to be paid and that the officers were to take no pay except the established rates, that is: officers on horseback, two sous per day, and officers on foot, twelve deniers; but they could charge their expenses as well, if they were not given, without using force or duress. And we ordered that no guards were to be assigned to a person for debt if personal property and chattels were found ready to be seized up to the value of the debt, except by special instructions of our lords or our masters or ourself; and if the provosts or the officers went against this, they would pay the guards out of their own pocket. We had all these orders obeyed, if anyone complained to us while we had the office of the *bailli* of Clermont in our safekeeping, with the result that the district was for this reason more peaceful and with less loss, and justice was better administered, and the creditors more quickly paid what was owed them.

1605. Any time guards are assigned to some good house, or any other kind of house, you should not assign riff-raff and dishonest people, but honest folk [*preudommes*] and those who need to earn their bread. And preferably you should assign those who willingly earned a living while they could, and have become incapable through old age or illness; for when someone has to suffer a loss, it is in any case better that good people should gain from it than bad ones. Yet we do not permit to be assigned to such duties madmen or quarrelsome people, nor blind men, nor completely deaf ones, nor perjurers, nor those who allow themselves to be under ordinary or aggravated excommunication [*renforcié*]. And anyone can see why we forbid such people to be assigned as guards or to seize other people's property; for the madman would soon do something from which loss and ill will [*vilenie*] could arise; and the quarrelsome person would fight the residents if they did not do his will; and the blind man would see nothing, so that he could not give testimony; and the deaf man would not hear what was said, although he could testify to what he saw; but you cannot ask a deaf man questions, and for this reason he should not be given these duties; and the perjurer would soon give false witness, and is not to be believed; and the person under ordinary or aggravated excommunication causes all those who speak to him to sin. And what we have said about such people not having these duties, we extend to all other duties in which honest and sound [*bien entendant*] men are needed.[5]

Here ends the chapter on having creditors paid and assigning guards to other persons.

Notes

1. For Salmon *en a gaaignier*, I read *en a a gaaignier* as in Beugnot 2: 307.

2. The mention here of "entering the property" implies that the property is real estate; but the analysis is the same for other property described later in this section as chattels. The *engagement* described in this section must therefore refer to any kind of property given as a security, as in a modern mortgage or pawnage.

3. This part of Beaumanoir's sentence is obscure, and I have had to guess somewhat at the translation. He says: "ou il est de si grant fief qu'il ne doit pas estre vendus pour si petite dete pour ce qu'il ne se puet vendre par parties, s'il ne se vend tous ensemble."

4. Presumably the costs referred to here are the costs to the property owner of paying the guards.

5. Beaumanoir adds at the end of this chapter "exceptés ceus qui sont escommenié pour leur service," which makes no sense. I have therefore omitted it from the translation.

55. Creditors' Remedies II

Here begins the fifty-fifth chapter of this book which speaks of follow-up suits {for debt}, and shows which ones are rightfully brought and which are not.

1606. When an order is given to someone to give satisfaction to his creditor "within the nights," that is to say within seven days and seven nights for a commoner, and fifteen days for a gentleman or a gentlewoman who lives on a freehold fief, the order must be obeyed and the person not obeying must pay a penalty to the lord for disobeying an order; and the penalty is simple {small}, according to the custom of the place. But a person bringing a follow-up suit {for non-payment} must take care not to bring the suit wrongfully; for if he does so, he must pay the same penalty the debtor would have had to pay if the suit had been proper; and so that creditors can know what suits are wrongfully brought, we will describe several.

1607. A creditor to whom good security [*nant*] worth the value of the debt has been offered, before the due date of the order, brings a follow-up suit wrongfully.

1608. The creditor brings a follow-up suit wrongfully if he gives an extension [*respit*] or postponement [*soufrance*] to his debtor after the order has been issued but before he brings his suit; for since the date of the order thus passes at the will of the creditor, the debtor has fulfilled the order, because the words of the order are these. "We command you to do his will before 'the nights'." Since "the nights" have passed at the creditor's will, the debtor has fulfilled the order.

1609. A creditor brings a follow-up suit wrongfuly who waits forty days after the day when the "the nights" are over to bring it, unless he had an honest impediment [*empeechement*] whereby he could not bring his suit sooner, such as that he had been out of the district, or in prison, or busy at so great tasks that he could not pay attention to this matter; for if he has let forty days go by when he was not so busy [*jours bien aasiés*], and could have brought his suit if he wanted, it appears that the debtor must have failed to act by his postponement or his extension; thus, in such a case, if the creditor can only obtain payment by suing, he will have to have a new order issued.

1610. The creditor brings his follow-up suit wrongfully who does not say or have said to his debtor that he will bring another suit if he is not paid, for it is sufficient for a debtor to pay when his creditor demands payment; and it is not right for debtors to summon their creditors in order to pay them. Instead, debtors should be summoned by their creditors unless they have made an agreement to the contrary: such as if someone makes an agreement to repay a debt in some place certain, for in such a case the debtor must keep his agreement. And if the debtors hide so that the creditor cannot ask them for their payment, the creditor can rightfully bring a suit if the due date in the order has passed, for he does not have to go and seek them out, unless he wants, outside the place where they are residents. Nevertheless, if he comes across his debtor by chance, wherever that may be, he should tell him to pay or else he will bring suit; and if he does not give him notice thus, and brings a suit, it is wrongful since he saw him in a place where he could have given him notice {that he was going to bring a follow-up suit}.

1611. If someone has taken security [*nans*] from his debtor, and thought the security was worth as much as the debt, and, when he sold the security because the debtor did not want to redeem it, he could not cover the debt and yet sold the security for as much as he could, and afterwards, without speaking to the debtor, he has brought a follow-up suit, in that case he has done so wrongfully. But if he had asked the debtor to pay him the unpaid portion of the debt, or give him sufficient security, and the debtor would not, in that case he would have brought a follow-up suit rightfully. Nevertheless, you should look carefully at the words spoken when the security is given. For if the debtor gave the creditor a security for a debt of a hundred pounds and said that he would add enough for it to be worth a hundred pounds within the time you should keep the security {before selling it}, and afterwards he did not keep his agreement, and, because he did not make the security up to a hundred pounds, the creditor brought a follow-up suit, it would be brought wrongfully, for since the creditor had believed the debtor to the point where he took insufficient security, and had believed him when he said he would make it up, the due date would have passed at the will of the creditor. Therefore if the debtor did not make up the rest beyond the value of the security, the creditor would have to sue him on the agreement, and, once the agreement was admitted or proved, the debtor would have to be given a new order to make the security up to a hundred pounds. And for this reason everyone should know that no one is required to take security for his debt, unless he wants, if the security is not equal in value to the debt.

1612. A creditor wrongfully brings a follow-up suit if he has an agreement with the debtor that he will postpone doing so until a day certain, and he does so before the due date. But in that case, if the day passes, he can bring a follow-up suit, for it is one thing to say: "I will postpone a follow-up suit until such and such a day is past," and another thing to say: "I give you an extension until such and such a day." And for this reason he can bring a follow-up suit after the postponement, but not after an extension. And any such postponement must not go beyond forty days, as is said above.

1613. When the order is issued, the parties can agree if they wish that the lord should give a longer time to pay; for if the parties assent, the lord can order a debt to be paid, or an agreement fulfilled, at the end of a month, or two months, or longer, as the parties agree. And if the due date of the order passes, the creditor can bring a follow-up suit just as if the order were given for the local customary period.

1614. When we say that the creditor cannot bring a follow-up suit when the due date passes because he gives an extension, we mean when he gives an unconditional extension; for if he gives an extension on the condition that if the end of the extension passes and he is not paid, he can bring a follow-up suit, then he can do so on the day after the extension is past, just as he could have on the day after the end of the original order. Such an agreement is quite possible between the debtor and the creditor, and the creditor can certainly in that case bring a follow-up suit the day after the end of the extension.

1615. As soon as a follow-up suit has been brought for non-compliance with the order, the penalty is due to the lord who gave the order, either from the party who brought the suit wrongfully or from the party who did not fulfill the order. But when there is a suit between the debtor and the creditor to see if the suit was brought rightfully or not, the lord must do without his fine until the suit is concluded, and then exact it from the party losing the suit. And because it often happens that the party suing holds nothing from the lord who is presiding over the suit, the lord can attach the debt as soon as the debtor claims the suit was wrongfully brought, up to the value of the penalty, unless the plaintiff gives a surety for the penalty if {it turns out that} he is bringing the suit wrongfully, and, once the surety is given, he should not fail to have his debt paid because there is a suit about the penalty. And if it happens that the debtor has paid him before hearing about the new suit, or before the lord had made the attachment, and the creditor owns nothing in the jurisdiction, and will not appear in the follow-up suit which he brought wrongfully, according to the debtor, then in that case, if the debtor wants to be released from the penalty, he must sue the creditor before the lord who has jurisdiction over him; and there he must complain about the wrongful follow-up suit which the creditor brought, and if the creditor's lord sees that his subject did bring the suit wrongfully, he should force him to go and discharge the debtor from the penalty.

Here ends the chapter on follow-up suits.

56. Incompetents

Here begins the fifty-sixth chapter of this book which speaks of those who should not hold property, and of leper-houses and poor houses.

1616. Those who have been in a religious order [*en religion*] long enough to take their vows, according to the custom in the order for taking vows, cannot come back to the secular world. And if they some back and their order [*religions*] is seeking them, the secular courts, at the request of the religious house [*l'Eglise*], should arrest them and send them back to their abbots. And if it happens that the religious house does not seek their return, because they are considered wild [*fous*] and quarrelsome [*mellis*], so that they remain in the secular world, they have no rights to hold property which may pass from someone in their lineage, whether by descent or laterally;[1] for as soon as they had made their vows in the order [*l'eglise*] and dedicated themselves to the service of Our Lord, they had *de facto* renounced all temporal things outside their order; and a cousin of the third or fourth degree of kinship to the clerk's [*au religieux*] father should take the property before his son if the latter left his abbey in order to inherit property.

1617. When someone becomes a leper, so that he has to leave the society of people, he no longer has any rights to own any real property, either his own or what may pass in his lineage. But it is true that if he has personal property or purchased property when the illness strikes him, he can dispose of it as he wishes, and also a fifth of his real property, as you can in a will, for as soon as he is stricken with this sickness he is dead to the secular world. But if he leaves a fifth of his inherited real property, or some property he has purchased, to the leper-house where he is to go, or to some other religious house, he may; but the lord from whom the land is held can order the religious house to surrender possession within a year and a day; and the year and a day period begins to run when he gives the order.

1618. Leper-houses are established by the towns to accept the men and women stricken with this sickness, who are born in the town, or who have married there or settled down there with no expectation of their departing, for example if they have bought houses or inherited them [*prises a eritage*] there, or for quit-rent or rent; the leper-houses are not for transients. For if a stranger stays in a town for a year or two without showing any appearance of settling there and he becomes a leper, the town leper-house is not required to accept him; instead he should go to the town where he has his own house, and if he does not own a house or anything else anywhere, he should be accepted in the town where his father lived, if he was born or raised there.

1619. We have seen an argument over whether those who were bastards and became lepers should be accepted into the leper-houses of the towns where they had been born or brought up, because the guardians [*gardes*] of the leper-houses said that bastards had no lineage and inherited no rights, so that they could not take refuge in the leper-house any more than could a stranger who showed up there [*qui venist d'espave*]. But we, who presided over this dispute, considered that leper-houses were founded for a charitable purpose and for the public good, to keep the healthy from the hell of leprosy, and we considered that in any case the bastards were Christians, and born and raised in the town; and we were persuaded by pity, and by the advice we received that it was right for them to be accepted, and we had the person accepted. And we have spoken of this case so that if it happened again people would be persuaded to act in the same manner.

1620. It is true that according to the common law the guardianship of leper-houses belongs to the bishop in the diocese where they are situated, because Holy Church has the guardianship of things given in charity and in mortmain. Nevertheless we know of several leper-houses which are specially in the guardianship of secular lords, and they can admit and exclude whatever people they want for the good of the the establishment. And the guardianship of each foundation should be maintained as it has been for a long time.

1621. Because all leper-houses were constructed and founded for the public good of the towns where they are situated, the guardianship must be exercised by the bishop or the secular ruler. The guardian must choose a citizen [*preudomme*] of the town, or two or three according to what the leper-house requires, who will undertake to watch over the condition of the house and supply and administer the needs of the house. And those who undertake this overseeing must perform it diligently and render accounts once a year to the lord, or to the guardian of the leper-house, at his command. And what we have said about the guardianship of leper-houses applies also to the poor houses which have been established to house the poor.

1622. If it happens that some leper or some inmate of a leper-house or a poor house behaves badly and will not reform upon the warning [*amoneste-ment*] of his superior, he should be put out of the place like a stranger; and if he is convicted of a serious crime, the hospital or the leper-house cannot protect him from being punished according to the offense. And if he is a clerk, the jurisdiction belongs to his ecclesiastical judge, according to the custom of Holy Church; and the secular courts should hand him over if he is held by them.

1623. You can prohibit lepers from entering towns without thereby treating them wrongfully, giving them a place well outside, where they can be found by those who want to give them charity. For it would be a dangerous thing to mix lepers with healthy people, because the healthy might become lepers, and for this reason leper-houses were built outside the towns.

1624. Those who are completely insane [*fol de nature*], so insane that they have no judgment [*discrecion*] which allows them to look after themselves, should not hold property if they have brothers or sisters, even though they are the oldest. Therefore if the oldest is completely insane, the right of firstborn should pass to the oldest after him, for it would be a bad thing to leave anything in the possession of such a man; but he should be properly [*honestement*] supported out of what would have been his if he had been a person who could hold land. But we mean this to apply to those who are so insane that they would not know how to behave if they were married or not; for if a person had enough intelligence to be married, without more, so that he could have heirs, he and his property should be under guardianship until the heir came of age.

1625. The lords from whom property can be held need to know that those persons described above cannot hold property; for if they had no relative, it would be better for the property to pass to the lord, like unclaimed lost property, than for it to pass to those who have made their vows of religion, or to lepers, or to those who have forefeited all rights to property because of serious crimes, or to bastards, or to those who concealed their lord's rights, thereby deserving to lose their rights to the property.

Here ends the chapter on leper-houses and poor houses and on those who should not be permitted to hold property [estre eritié].

Note

1. For direct and lateral inheritance of property, see Chapter 14.

57. Marital Maintenance

Here begins the fifty-seventh chapter of this book which speaks of incompatibility between married persons, how their lords should deal with it, and the reasons why one can leave the other.

1626. We often see that bad feeling arises between a man and woman who are together in marriage, so that they cannot remain or live together, and yet they have no reasons to have the marriage dissolved and to marry someone else. And yet they hate each other so much that they do not want to live together, and sometimes it is one person's fault, and sometimes both are at fault. And when such a thing happens, Holy Church has cognizance of the incompatibility, if there is a suit. Nevertheless the women have sometimes come to us to ask to be given some of the common property for their living expenses and their maintenance; and sometimes the husbands do not agree because they say they are masters of the property and it is not their fault that their wives are not living with them; and because such complaints come to the secular courts every day, we will discuss in this chapter what you should do about such requests according to our custom.

1627. If a woman requests a division of her husband's property during his lifetime, her request should not be honored, for by the common law the husband is the manager of his own property and his wife's property. Nevertheless the judge should look at the reason why she is no longer with her husband, and according to the causes he sees he should act; for if he sees that the husband, arbitrarily and without reason, has thrown her out, he should order the husband to take her back and support her as an honest woman according to her station; and if the husband will not and the judge sees that it is not the woman's fault, and that she wants to live as an honest woman, he should take enough of the husband's property for her to be properly provided according to her station. And if he also puts the husband in fear of damages or a prison term if he does not take her back, he is quite right to do so; for it is the duty of judges to punish and correct the cruel for their cruelty, so that each person in their care does what reason dictates.

1628. If a woman leaves her husband without the husband's fault,—such as when some wives go off to commit adultery [*pour fere folie de leur cors*]; or they have no such intention, but they hate their husband's society [*conversacion*];[1] or they leave because their husbands have a private war or an argument with their fathers or their mothers or their relatives, and they prefer these to their husbands; or a wife left because her husband beat her for some offense or some foolishness she said, although he was not in the habit of beating her and he was sorry she left; or if she left because he would not give her some clothes or some jewels she was asking for for herself or her children,—in all such cases, if she wants to have some of her husband's property for her maintenance, she should be given nothing; instead she should be reprehended for leaving her husband so foolishly and for so little reason, and she should be ordered back to her husband; and if she will not go, and she is poor or in need, it serves her right; and she should get little pity.

1629. No one should be surprised when some wives leave their husbands when the reasons are reasonable [*les resons sont resnables*]; but an honest woman should put up with and endure a great deal before leaving her husband's company.[2] But in some cases it is no good for them to stay, and they should be excused for leaving if they do so; for when their husbands threaten to kill or wound them, or when they will not give them, through no fault of their own, anything to eat or drink or wear, so as to kill them; or when the husband wants to sell a woman's real property or her dower, by force, and because she will not agree he leads her such an awful life that she cannot endure it; or when he willfully throws her out without her having committed any offense; or when she leaves because he keeps another woman with him in the house, and the neighbors see and know about it; or when she leaves because her husband leads such a life that she could be condemned to death if she remained in the {marriage} partnership, such as if the husband is a thief or keeps on committing some other kind of crime for which the punishment is death, or if she knows he is planning [*pourchace*] some other great crime or some great treachery[3] and he will not abandon it for her sake: in all these cases a woman may be excused if she leaves her husband. And she can ask the judge for some of the common property for her maintenance; and the judge should provide her with enough. Nevertheless, there is no division, in halves or quarters, she does not even take the profits from her own real property, according to our custom: therefore such women have to be provided for by the judges' order and according to their[4] honest estimate {of their needs}. And if the husband will take her back and make an agreement not to do anything which would make her leave, and she will not go back, then the judge should not let her have any maintenance. But if she goes back and her husband lied about everything, and leads her a worse life than before, so that she leaves him again, it is no wonder if she does not believe him when he calls her back again, for she may presume that he is lying as he did the other time. Therefore in such cases she should have her maintenance, as we have said above.

1630. Although a woman leaves her husband for one of the above reasons and the judge gives her some of the common property for her maintenance, if she leads a bad life when she is away from her husband,—such as if she commits adultery [*fet folie de son cors*], or keeps a disorderly house [*tient mauvès ostel*], or keeps bad company, or if she is convicted of a crime,—she should lose what the judge ordered to be given her for her maintenance. And thus some wives are destroyed through the incompatibilities which arise in marriages, which is a pity and a loss.

1631. In various cases men can be excused for the suffering they cause their wives, and the judge should not meddle in them: for a man may beat his wife (although without loss of life or limb), when she offends against him, such as when she is committing adultery, or when she contradicts her husband or curses him, or when she will not obey his reasonable orders as an honest woman should: in such and similar cases a man should punish his wife moderately. But if they are chaste, wives must be excused many other vices; and nevertheless, the husband should punish and correct his wife according to the vice, in any way he sees fit (excepting where it causes loss of life or limb) to rid her of this vice.

1632. Sometimes the disagreements in a marriage arise from the hatred which stepfathers and stepmothers have towards their stepchildren. And when a woman wants to leave her husband out of hatred for his children, the man should look carefully at which party is wrong, the children or the stepmother; and if he sees it is the fault of the children, he ought rather to send away the children than permit his wife to go away. And if he sees that the stepmother has behaved badly towards the children without their fault, if he is an honest man his love for his children should only increase, for he should remember the love they lost when they lost their mother. In such cases, then, he should politely [*courtoisement*] require his wife to love and honor his children, and if she will not, he should give her a fair share of the property [*l'en face a l'avenant*] and keep his children near him until they are emancipated [*pourveus*] as an honest man should look after his children, and he should not fail to do so on account of the stepmother.

1633. What we have said of stepmothers who hate their stepchildren we cannot say of stepfathers who hate their stepchildren, for women have no power to deal with their children against the will of their husbands who are the stepfathers, in the way the father can deal with *his* own children in spite of the stepmother. Therefore when a woman ses that her husband hates her children, if she sees that this is the fault of the children, she must correct them and punish them and order them to obey; and if they will not, it is better for the woman to send them away than for her husband to continue to dislike them. And if the hatred of the stepfather is not the children's fault, he is acting badly, but in any case if he wants they must leave the household [*compaignie*],[5] for the mother cannot keep them against his will. And if the mother leaves her husband because she hates her stepchildren or because her husband hates her own children, this is no reason to give her maintenance, because the husband would like her to remain with him and to support her as his wife. And to put it briefly, married persons must put up with a good deal from each other, for when contention arises between them because of the fault of one of them, it is not easy to settle.

1634. A woman has good cause to separate from her husband and dissolve the marriage entirely or leave him when the husband tries to make her have sex [*la veut fere pechier de son cors*] with someone else, either for money or for some other reason. Therefore if any woman leaves for such a reason, and a bad reputation argues against the husband in the case, and the woman shows the judge some presumption, she should not be permitted to live in discomfort for leaving her husband in this way, as long as he has any possessions; indeed she should be given a generous award from him for her maintenance.

1635. Foolish husbands should be warned not to allow other men to sin with their wives [*pechier en leur fames*] against their will, by force or intimidation, or by threats they make to them; for just as those who had sex [*compaigneront*] with them by force would be tried for rape, there is even more reason why the husbands should be punished for allowing them or forcing them to do this, for they are treacherous, wicked, and dishonest; and it is to be wondered at when such a wicked intention enters the heart of a man, for generally it is one of the things that men are most angered by in all the world, when they discover that their wives are giving themselves to another man. Therefore a man who arranges such a thing for his own wife is very wicked.

1636. It used to be that when husbands went away out of the district and stayed away seven years or more the wives could remarry. But because of the dangers that arose, this was stopped and it was confirmed by Holy Church that no married woman, however long her husband stayed away, could remarry unless certain news of his death had been received. And if a woman remarries because she deceives the court by false witnesses or in some other manner, she is nonetheless in concubinage with her second husband, and all her children born of this marriage are bastards born in adultery, even though the first husband never returns or he dies after his wife has remarried; for since the marriage was bad from the start, it can never be made good, unless all the truth about the offense is confessed to Holy Church and the pope gives a dispensation, which it is hard to believe he would want to do for people who had made an adulterous marriage.

1637. If a man sees a presumption that another man is coming to his house to see his wife,—such as if there is a rumor about this, or he has found them alone together in a secluded place,—he can forbid the man, in front of good people, to come into his house any more, or he can have it forbidden by a judge; and if he comes in after being forbidden to do so by the husband, and the husband can catch him in the act with his wife, such as if they are lying together, if he kills him and calls in witnesses [*lieve le cri*] so that the truth can be known, he loses neither life nor limb, according to our custom; and we have seen three men acquitted in such cases in our time in the Ile de France [*en France*].⁶

1638. Any time there is a suit between husband and woman to dissolve the marriage, they do not live together during the suit. If the husband will not give maintenance to his wife, the judge should make him do so, even if she is the plaintiff. Nevertheless she should not be given the costs of the lawsuit, unless it is seen that she has a very good reason [*grant droit*] to seek the dissolution, such as for the serious crimes mentioned above.

1639. When a marriage between man and woman is dissolved for a reasonable cause confirmed by Holy Church, you should know that if they purchased land while they were married, each one should take a half; and if they have personal property, each should take a half; and each one takes his or her own real property. And if they have children over seven years old, the father should have guardianship of half the children; and if there is only one, he can take the child if he wants, and the mother must supply half of the child support [*au nourir*]; and if the children are under seven, the mother should get custody, and the father must pay half their reasonable support. And all such cases {of support} when they arise must be provided for by the estimation of honest judges.

1640. Everyone should know that a man should not obey his wife, nor a wife her husband, nor a vassal or an officer his lord, nor should any other persons obey each other in any case or with respect to any order, which is contrary to God, or to morality [*bonnes meurs*] so that it is a good reason for a woman to leave her husband when he wants her to sin [*quant il li vuet fere fere*],[7] and good reason for others not to obey [*partir de l'obeïssance*] those who give them such orders.

Here ends the chapter on those who are discontented in their marriage.

Notes

1. *Conversacion* may have a more specifically sexual connotation than "society."
2. "Company" here translates *compaignie*, which has resonances of the marriage "partnership."
3. *Traïson*, here translated as "treachery," is itself a crime. See Chapter 30, §826.
4. It is not clear if this means the judges' estimate or the estranged wives' estimate, but it is more likely the former; cf. §1639.
5. "Household" here translates *compaignie*, but again there is a resonance of partnership, since the children are also part of the partnership formed by the family. See Chapter 21.
6. Substantially the same material as that recounted in this section is found in Chapter 30, §933.
7. This part of the sentence presumably refers to the reasons for leaving a husband discussed in §1635.

58. Jurisdiction

Here begins the fifty-eighth chapter of this book which speak of high and low justice, and the cases which fall into one or the other, and how each man should administer his own justice.

1641. We said in the chapter which speaks of the superior jurisdiction [*resors*] which the count of Clermont has over his men {Chapter 10} that all the men in the county of Clermont who hold fiefs have high and low justice on their fiefs; and so do religious houses which hold freehold fiefs and have long done so without owing anything to anyone for them. Nevertheless, because there are many districts where one person holds the high justice and another the low, and such a thing could happen even in Beauvais by reason of a sale or exchange, or by the delegation of a lord, that one person might have high justice in a certain place while another had the low, it is right for us to say briefly what high justice is, and what low justice is, so that each person can administer the justice that is appropriate for him.

1642. You should know that all cases of serious crime, whatever they are (for which the sentence is and should be death for those found guilty and convicted), belong to high justice, except larceny; for even though the thief loses his life for his larceny, nevertheless larceny is not a case in high justice. But all other serious cases [*cas vilain*] are, such as murder, treason, homicide, forcing women, damage to property by fire or destruction [*est-reper*] by night, and all cases which can lead to a wager of battle, and counterfeiting, and consenting to or procuring {such crimes}; and all these offenses are cases in high justice. Thus when one of such crimes is perpetrated, the cognizance and the trial goes to the person who holds the high justice; and the cognizance of larceny and all other offenses for which there is no risk of the death sentence goes to the person holding low justice. And what should be done concerning the crimes mentioned above and many others which we do not bring up here, is made clear in the chapter which speaks of offenses {Chapter 30}, so that there is no reason for us to speak more of them.

1643. We have said which cases of crime should be handled by those who have the high justice, and there is also some income which should be theirs by reason of the high justice, such as all the property of those found guilty of any of the above-named cases. But this means the property which is in the person's jurisdiction [*en sa haute justice*], for each person who has high justice in his own domain takes the offenders' property which is found on his own land.

1644. Unclaimed found objects and lost property not being actively sought [*Les choses trouvees et les espaves lesqueles n'ont point de suite*], and what passes to the lord from bastards because they have no lineage, and property passing from strangers when no one from their lineage comes forward to claim it, all these things should go to the lord who has high justice and never to the one who has the low, unless he has had it for a long tenure or because it was given to him as a privilege, for example in several places the lords give to religious houses all such acquisitions [*esploits*], even though they retain the high justice in any real property they give.

1645. The person who has the high justice cannot forbid the person with the low justice or his officers from going about in arms to administer the low justice, and the person with low justice cannot forbid the person with the high justice or his officers from administering the high justice, for each one may see to his duties without doing harm to anyone else.

1646. It sometimes happens that some cases arise which are so obscure that you cannot know right away whether it is a case pertaining to high justice or to low; for example when a fight [*chaude mellee*] breaks out between persons, and wounds are inflicted, but it is not known right away if the wounded will recover from their wounds or die of them; and because there is doubt, if the offenders who caused the wounds are caught, they should be kept for forty days in the prison of the person having the high justice, for within that time those who are going to die of their wounds will do so. And if the wounded recover, the person with the high justice should transfer the prisoners to the person with the low justice, so that he can receive the penalty according to the offense; and if the wounded man dies of the wounds inflicted on him, the punishment of the offense belongs to the person with the high justice.

1647. Broken truces or guaranteed peaces[1] are certainly cases of high justice, and for this reason they must be given when they are asked for, and the guarantees made, by those who have the high justice and not by those with the low justice. And since those who have only low justice cannot compel the giving of truces or guaranteed peaces, they should not have the cognizance of infractions against them.

1648. We do not praise {approve of} those who gave a truce or guaranteed peace to each other before some lord who had no power of jurisdiction in such cases, and then boldly broke the truce or guaranteed peace; for if they had given to each other the truce or the guaranteed peace of their own will and without appearing before a lord, and then one of them broke the agreement later, he would have as great a penalty as if the truce or guaranteed peace had been given by the king, for a truce or a guaranteed peace can be made between parties by words completely without a judge; and how you should deal with such things, and what punishment is given to those who break them, and what difference there is between truce and guaranteed peace, is explained in the chapter on truce and guaranteed peace {Chapter 60}.

1649. When someone is suspected of a case of serious crime as described above, such as through a presumption, or because someone sues him, or because he flees and will not come when summoned, everything which should be done towards his condemnation or acquittal falls to the person having the high justice and should be judged in his court; and the person with the low justice cannot forbid him to seize the man's property, or confiscate it, or call him to appear in court, or to banish him when he has called him as many times as custom requires. But if the accused or suspected person can demonstrate his innocence [*s'en puet espurgier*], he should be released and put in the condition he was in before. Nevertheless, if he suffered a loss because of the seizure of his property because he was suspected of the offense, or because he was put in prison, the lord who has the high justice over him is not required to give him damages for his actions in administering justice.

1650. If the person having the low justice in some place holds it in fief and in homage from the lord with the high justice, and he encroaches on the jurisdiction of his lord by taking income [*esploite*]² from cases in high justice, he must pay a penalty to the lord of sixty pounds; and he must reseise his lord of all the income he took; and if he claimed it was rightfully his [*l'avoua a son droit*], he should remain seised of the income until it is taken away by a judgment; but if he loses it by a judgment, then because of the false claim of right he made respecting his lord he loses all the low justice he held from his lord and anything dependent on his holding it [*cel fief*].³

1651. In some cases a person with the low justice could encroach on the person with high justice, and yet he could be excused without a penalty to the person with high justice, such as if he held the low justice from another lord than the one with the high justice, for in such a case, unless he were caught in the act [*en present mesfet*] and he was a resident in the jurisdiction of the person with the high justice, he would have to be sued before the lord where he was a resident. And even if he were convicted of having encroached on the high justice, he would give back possession of the place and give back the income he had derived and would pay a penalty to the lord before whom he had been convicted.⁴

1652. In some cases the person with the low justice can be excused if he takes jurisdiction of something belonging to the high justice, provided that, as soon as he realizes that high justice is involved, he hands it over to the appropriate person: for example if he arrests people in a fight to exact the penalty for fights, which comes to him, that is permitted; but if it is shown that there has been a death or danger of death, he should surrender the prisoners to the person with the high justice until the danger of death is past, as we said above in this very chapter.

1653. The jurisdictions of various lords are interwoven and form enclaves in each other, so that those whose duty it is to keep the peace [*garder les justices*] can sometimes not go to perform their duties without passing through another jurisdiction: and we have seen several disagreements, for example, when some lords wanted to make it difficult for [*destourber*] the officers of other lords by not letting them go through their jurisdiction bearing arms, or bows and arrows, or sword, or axe, or guisarme,⁵ or other forbidden weapons. And since it is proper for those who keep the peace to

be armed so that they can arrest those who commit offenses in the jurisdiction, and they cannot easily get there without passing through other
people's land, we made an ordinance and had it kept as a custom in
Clermont in our administration, namely that if someone needs to pass
through another's jurisdiction armed in order to keep the peace, he can bear
arms in the following manner. If he wants to carry a bow and arrows, the
bow must be unstrung, and the arrows in his hand or in a quiver; and if he
wants to bear a sword, he must wear it on his belt [*ceinte*] or under his
overcoat [*surcot*] and not in a sling [*en escherpe*]; if he wants to carry an axe
or guisarme, he should carry it under his arm or resting on the ground until
he leaves the other jurisdiction; if he wants to bear arms openly to protect
and arm his whole body, he must carry the arms sheathed, and if the group
trying to go through consists of several persons with quite a few men in
arms, such as wearing hauberks and carrying the weapons that go with
them, for instance in order to escort prisoners or for any other reason
someone might want to go in force into the jurisdiction, he should be sure
to obtain the permission of the lord who has the jurisdiction, for someone
might pretend that he was going to his jurisdiction when he was really on
his way to commit some offense. And if someone does not want to or
cannot obtain leave {to cross the land}, he can take his armor across on
horses or on carts until he has passed through the jurisdiction where he
cannot obtain permission to cross under arms, and is back in his own
jurisdiction; and there he can put on his armor in order to keep the peace
and defend himself if he is attacked. And if he tries to cross another person's
jurisdiction by force and under arms [*a force et a armes*][6] without asking for
permission or because he cannot obtain it, the penalty for this use of force is
paid to the lord who holds the land directly from the king, not to the lord in
whose jurisdiction the force of bearing arms was used without asking
permission from the person who could give it; for all the lords who are
subjects of the barons should know that they may not give permission for
people to bear drawn weapons in their jurisdictions, because the king's law
[*establissement*] forbids such expeditions [*chevauchiees*] in force and under
arms, by which you can see that a person giving permission would be
colluding [*consentans*] with those who went armed against the law; and the
penalties for bearing arms go only to the king and to the barons in their
baronies.

1654. If some persons go about in someone else's jurisdiction in force
and bearing arms, and they commit an offense in that jurisdiction and they

are caught and arrested by the person to whom the jurisdiction belongs, he should receive the penalty and jurisdiction over the offense; and the king, or the baron, if it was committed in his barony, should receive the penalty exacted for bearing arms; for if they passed through without doing offense, they would still be subject to the penalty for bearing arms, so that they owe a penalty for the offense *and* for bearing arms against the king's law; and the penalty for bearing arms is sixty pounds for a gentleman and sixty sous for a commoner.[7]

1655. In some cases permission should be given to someone to go armed where he needs to for his business,—such as when he is in a private war and not during a truce or a guaranteed peace, or when he requests a truce or a guaranteed peace and cannot obtain it because his adversaries will not come forward or obey the lord's orders; or when a truce or a guaranteed peace is given and those giving them excluded from them banished men from their lineage or bastards or those who were in distant lands with no expectation of their return,—in all these cases permission should be given, when it is requested, for men to be armed.[8] But in such circumstances, if the permission is *not* asked for or given (although the lord should give permission when he is asked to) there is no defense to the penalty by saying you were going about under arms for one of the above reasons.

1656. Those who have high and low justice in their lands may mete out punishment for offenses of which they have cognizance, but they should be careful to maintain their high justice with rigor, for if they are holding someone in prison who has been found guilty of a serious crime by common knowledge, or by witnesses, or by wager of battle, and they make peace with him, or they allow peace to be made without the permission of the baron from whom they hold, they lose their power to administer justice. And this does not prevent the lord of the land, such as the king or the baron, from arresting those who escaped from the prisons of their subjects as a result of this peace, nor will the lords from whose prison they escaped have a lesser loss because the escapees are recaptured.

1657. It is true,—if any of the vassals in the county holds prisoners for serious crimes and the prisoners break out of prison so that the count takes away and confiscates the vassal's power of jurisdiction,—if the vassal can manage to recapture the escapees, he should be all square [*delivres*] with the count. And if the count recaptures them, he does not give back cognizance to the person who lost them by insufficient watchfulness, but he should try them for the offense and for escaping from custody. The vassal should be less likely to suffer the loss of his power to administer justice if the count sees that the prisoner escaped against the vassal's will; but nevertheless, it is in the count's power to give him back his power to administer justice, or withhold it, for if the vassals were not in danger of losing their power in such cases, some of them would purposely put offenders in insecure prisons, out of affection, or because they were asked to, or for money, and for this reason it is good for all their sharp practice to be worthless to them.

1658. Just as we have said that the vassals who are judges in their lands should not make or allow peace to be made with those who are convicted or accused of crimes, they must also not release on bail those who are held for serious crimes, unless the trial has begun, and it has moved to a wager of battle; for in that case bail should be allowed for those who have given good pledges, man for man, to appear on the appointed day and go to trial; and others should not be allowed bail. And if the vassals allow bail in cases of crime where it should not be permitted, there are two risks to them. And one risk is greater than the other, for if the person out on bail goes off and does not appear when he should, like a person who dares not go to trial, the person releasing him loses his power of jurisdiction, and he is not protected by the fact that he took pledges, for the pledges cannot be put to death because of their being pledges, but the offender might have been, had he not been released on bail. The second risk to the vassals when they allow bail in cases where it is not appropriate is that if the count sees that the persons released on bail have too great a freedom [*trop large prison*] because of their bail, or that they go where they want, he can arrest them and not give back the costs [*coust*]⁹ or the cognizance to the person allowing the bail. Nevertheless, in this case the man does not lose his power to administer justice, but he loses the cognizance and the punishment of the offense; and he could give bail in such a way that he *would* lose his power to administer justice, such as if he were accustomed to giving such releases on bail or if he allowed bail after the lord had forbidden it, for disobedience along with unwise release on bail could occasion the loss of the power to administer justice.

1659. It could also happen that a man who permitted peace to be made in a case of serious crime, or who knowingly permitted his prisoners to escape, would not merely lose his power to administer justice, for certain people could have a person in prison yet they would rather lose their power to administer justice than prosecute him: for example if their prisoner was from their lineage, so that they did not want to bring him to trial; or if the prisoners were such great lords that they refrained from doing justice out of fear, and let them go; in such cases they would pay a penalty at the lord's will, to the sovereign of their jurisdiction and their other property, unless they recaptured [*rendoient*] those who departed with their consent.

1660. We have seen several cases where vassals held prisoners for serious crimes, and they were held because of public knowledge and were *prima facie* guilty [*ataint du fet*] yet nevertheless the vassals did not want to try them, either out of fear or for money, but they did not dare to free them or let them out of prison for fear of losing their power to administer justice, and thus the prisoners were kept too long in prison. And we gave them some help in this matter, for we gave them an order in the count's name that all those who had prisoners accused and convicted of serious crimes must proceed against them within forty days or lose their power to administer justice; and the count, and all those who are barons, can do this to their vassals. And if the men do not obey the order, they can take the prisoners from their men's prisons and administer justice according to the offense, and take away the power to administer justice of those who disobeyed.

1661. When we said the count can give an order to his men to proceed within forty days, we said it was in cases which are clear or proved. And we also say, that if there has to be an inquiry or an inquest,[10] the count can order them to proceed to the trial and the judgment of the case within forty days. Nevertheless, when the cases are doubtful and full of risk, he should not make them hurry so much they cannot have good advice; and if they need such advice, they should obtain it from their peers at the assizes and take it back to the judgments made in their own courts. And also if the delay goes beyond forty days because their jurors take the permitted postponements before making their judgment, or because of a suit between the accusers and the accused, they should not be so hurried along that they cannot take the customary postponements, and what the delays are which are sanctioned by custom is explained in the chapter which speaks of the delays given by custom {Chapter 65}.

1662. The count and all those holding directly from the king have, as sovereigns, right to appropriate their men's fortresses if they need them for war, or to house their prisoners or their troops [*garnisons*], or to protect themselves, or for the public good of the district. Nevertheless this might be done in such a way as to be wrongful towards the vassals, such as if they pretended they were doing so for one of the above reasons, and it was not true; for if the count said: "I took it to help me in my war," and there was no war, then it would appear that he was only doing it to harass his vassal. And also if he took {the fortress} to house his prisoners, and he left them living there a long time, and he could have helped it, for example, if he could easily have removed them from there and put them in his own prison: in such a case he would be doing something wrongful towards his vassal. And also if he pretended he needed the fortress and he had shown hatred or made threats towards the person holding it, or if he requested it because he wanted to plan wickedness towards his wife or daughter, or some other woman in his safekeeping; in all these cases it would be wrongful. And as soon as he does something improper and will not desist at his vassal's request, unless the vassal makes a report to the king, the king should not allow a regular suit between the lord and his vassal in such a case; but instead, he should immediately find out why the lord has seized his man's fortress, and if he sees he has seized it for a good reason or an honest need, it should be permitted, and if not, it should be taken away {from the lord} and given back to his vassal, and he should be forbidden, on pain of confiscation of all his possessions [*seur quanqu'il puet mesfere*], to take it again, except for his clear and patent need.

1663. If a lord who holds directly from the king appropriates his vassal's fortress for his need, it should not be at the expense of the vassal; for if he places troops there, it should be out of his own pocket, and if he has prisoners, he must have them guarded out of his own pocket. And if he causes any damage to the fortress, he must pay for the repair; if he improves it, to make it stronger or more attractive for his needs, the vassal is not required to reimburse him for it, since it was not done by him, even though it is his gain.

1664. It could happen that my lord had need of my fortress, and I too at that moment had need of it, being at war: it would be dangerous if people other than my family entered or lived in it, for even though my lord did not wish it, I could be harmed by those who were in it on his business. Therefore in such a case I am not required to hand over my tower at the order of my lord if he is not there in person, and unless he undertakes to help me and protect me in my war as long as he lives in it; for when we said that lords could take the fortresses of their men for their own needs, it meant that the men must be protected from loss and danger.

1665. Although lords can take the fortresses of their men in the manner we have described above, nevertheless the men cannot take or ask to be given the fortresses of their lord, for their wars or to guard their prisoners; for if the lords were obliged to hand over their fortresses for their wars or to keep prisoners in, it would seem that lord and man were equal, which should not be; in fact the lord has several rights over his vassal which the man does not have over his lord, for the lord can summon him and make him answer for what he holds from him, and take his fortress if he needs it, as we have said above; but the man cannot do this to his lord, and when it is said to be true that the lord owes the same faith and loyalty to his man as the man to the lord, this should be understood as meaning in the way that each is obligated to the other, for in this regard, if a lord punishes [*justice*] his man for good cause against his will, he is not breaking faith towards him.

1666. There are yet other ways in which a man who holds directly from the king has rights [*seignouries*] over his man which the man does not have toward him, for if the count of Clermont has a man who holds a piece of land, which is very detrimental to his house or his fortress, or to the public good, the man cannot refuse to take an adequate exchange for it if the count wants; it is true that he may not be compelled to sell it, unless he wants, but he cannot refuse an adequate exchange.

Here ends the chapter on high and low justice.

Notes

1. For truces and guaranteed peaces, see Chapter 60.
2. The income might be real property seized from executed offenders, so that the lord can be reseised of it as the next part of the sentence suggests.
3. The power to administer justice is considered real property by the customs of Beauvais, so Beaumanoir refers to it as a fief, although it is obviously not land. See §§656, 664–67.
4. In other words, as Beaumanoir predicted, he would pay no penalty to the lord whose high justice he had actually encroached on.

5. The *guisarme* was a weapon a bit like an axe or halberd, consisting of a metal blade on a long pole. The blade had a curved cutting edge, and the shape of the blade somewhat resembled a crescent moon about five days old.

6. The regular words for this in the older English law were *vi et armis*. The expression is often left this way in the beginning of descriptions of trespass to land: "Quare clausum fregit vi et armis . . ." (a clause which many lawyers still recognize from having seen it in law school).

7. Note that in §§1654 and 1655 the king's law is not referred to by Beaumanoir as *droit commun*. See the Introduction, "Beaumanoir and the Common Law."

8. These situations are discussed in §§1695, 1697.

9. The costs would be the income that the vassal could get from the accused man both during the wager of battle (when he confiscates the horses and armor of the combatants) or on conviction of the accused, for then the vassal would be entitled to all his possessions.

10. For inquiries and inquests, see §§1237–38.

59. Private War

*Here begins the fifty-ninth chapter of this book, which speaks of
{private} wars, how wars come about, and how wars are ended.*

1667. Since we have spoken in various places of wars, we want everyone to know that war cannot be made between two full brothers, born of
one father and one mother, for any dispute which there is between them,
even if one had struck or injured the other, for neither has a lineage which is
not as close to the other brother as to himself. And anyone who is as close in
lineage to the one party as to the other who are principal combatants of this
war should not get involved in this war. Thus if two brothers have a dispute
and one commits an offense against the other, the offender cannot use as a
defense the right of war, nor can anyone of his lineage who wants to aid him
against his brother, as might happen to those who prefer one to the other;
thus when such a dispute arises the lord should punish the one who
commits an offense against the other and do justice in the dispute.

1668. If it happens that various of my relatives are at war and I am as
close in lineage to the one as to the other, and I do not join in the war on the
one side or the other, and one of the parties does harm to me because he
believes that I prefer the other party, he cannot use as a defense the right of
war. Instead he should be dealt with according to the offense. But it would
be otherwise if I went to the aid of, or in the company of, one of the armed
parties, or if I lent him my arms or my horses or my house, to assist him and
to do harm to the other. For in such a case I would join the war by my act,
so that if harm came to me afterwards from the adverse party, even if that
party was as close to me in lineage as the other party, he could raise as a
defense the right of war. And by this you can see that people can join a war
who lend aid to those who are making war, even if they did not belong from
the point of view of lineage.

1669. Although we have said that war cannot be made between two full
brothers of one father and one mother, if they were not brothers except by

the mother or by the father, then war could very well be made between them according to custom, for each would have a lineage which did *not* belong to the other; so that if they were brothers by their father but not by their mother, the lineage that each one had through his mother would not belong to the other brother and for this reason they would be able to engage in war with each other. However, although custom allows these wars in the Beauvais region, between gentlemen, for a *casus belli*,[1] the count (or the king if the count will not) can require the parties to make peace with each other or to make a truce; but they must do without a guaranteed peace [*asseurement*][2] unless one of the parties requests it. And likewise when there is a war between those who are of the same lineage, the lord should make great efforts to end the war, for otherwise the lineage might be destroyed, since each one in the war would be opposing his closest relative, whereby sometimes one cousin kills another.

1670. War can arise in various ways, for example by deeds or by words. War arises by words when one party threatens the other with insults[3] or bodily harm [*a fere vilenie ou anui de son cors*], or when he defies him or his people; and it arises by deeds when a mutual combat in anger [*chaude mellee*] arises between gentlemen. And it must be understood that when war arises through fact, those who are present at the fact are at war as soon as the fact is completed; but the lineages of the one party and the other do not enter the war until forty days after the fact. If war begins by threats or by defiance, those who have defied each other or threatened each other begin to be at war from then on. But it is true that because very sharp practice could occur in such a case, for example, if someone had made ready to act before he had threatened or defied another person, and then, at the time of the fact, he threatened or defied the other person, he could not use that threat or that defiance as a defense. Therefore the gentleman who threatens or defies must abstain from fighting until the person who has been defied can put himself in a position of defense, or otherwise he has no excuse for the offense, and must be punished if he commits an offense.

1671. According to our custom war cannot begin between commoners [*gens de poosté*] or between townsmen. Therefore if threats or defiance or fights begin between them, they must be dealt with according to the offense, and they cannot claim a right of war. And if it should happen that someone had killed another person's father, and the son, after the first act, killed the person who had killed his father, he would be tried for homicide, unless it should happen that the person who had killed his father was under banishment, because of offenses for which he did not dare come to court to await a hearing [*atendre droit*]; for in such case leave is given to the family to arrest those who have committed an offense toward them, after they have been banished, either dead or alive. And if they take them alive, they must surrender them to the lord for him to deal with them according to the crime and according to the banishment. And they may not kill them at the time of arrest unless they defend themselves. And if they defend themselves, so that they cannot take them alive, but must kill them, they must immediately go to the judge and make a report, and once the truth is known they should not be accused of anything.

1672. Now let's see whether, if a threat or defiance or a fight commences between a gentleman on the one side and a commoner or a townsman on the other, there can be war between them; for no one but gentlemen can make war, as we have said. Therefore we say that war cannot be made between commoners and gentlemen, for if the gentleman made war on the townsman or commoners, and townsmen or commoners could not make war on gentlemen, they would soon be dead or in terrible trouble [*mal bailli*]. Therefore when such a case arises when the townsmen or commoners request a guaranteed peace, they should have it; and if they do not want it or deign to ask for it and they have committed an offense towards the gentlemen and the gentlemen take vengeance on them, the gentlemen cannot be accused of anything; and if it is the gentlemen who have committed an offense towards the townsmen or the commoners, and afterwards they do not deign to ask for peace or guaranteed peace, the townsmen or the commoners cannot for this reason take vengeance for the offense, for then it would seem as if they could make war, which they cannot do. For this reason when a gentleman commits an offense towards a townsman or a commoner, the latter must seek justice through the courts, not by war.

1673. Although gentlemen can make war according to our customs, the judge should not for that reason refrain from taking steps on his own initiative [*de son office*] to set right the first offense, for if a gentleman kills or does bodily harm to another gentleman, without open war between them, and the families on both sides want to turn this into a war without having resort to a judge, the judge should not for this reason refrain from doing everything in his power to arrest the offenders and to try them according to the offense. For those who commit such offenses do not offend only against their adverse party or their adverse party's family, but also against the lord, who has to protect them and discipline [*justicier*] them. For we see nevertheless that when some crime of homicide or bodily harm or other serious crime is committed and peace is made between the families of both parties, nevertheless it is appropriate that the party be pursued by the lord such as the king or the baron in whose jurisdiction the parties are. For another lord cannot make or permit such a peace, and for this reason it is clear that those who commit these serious crimes are not only committing offenses against their adverse party or his family but against the lord as we have said above.

1674. The gentleman who has committed a *casus belli* against another gentleman, or who has threatened or defied him, must know that as soon as he has done one of these things he is at war; for the person who threatens or defies another one with death in war must know that he himself is at war even though the person whom he defied did not send back any defiance. And for this reason it is said that "Whoever threatens another or defies him should be on his guard," for a person who wants to commit an offense against another should not feel entirely secure in his person. And this is what we also say about an act which is a *casus belli*.

1675. If someone wants to make war on another through his words, he must not make them ambiguous or secret, but so clear and so evident that the person to whom the words are spoken or sent knows that he must be on his guard, and if a person acted otherwise it would be treachery [*traïsons*].[4] And if defiance is announced to someone, it must be announced by people who can testify to it {to having done so} if there is a need, as to the place and time. And the same thing is true when someone wants to accuse another of doing some harm [*fere vilenie*] with premeditation and without defiance, for in such a case there is a need to prove the defiance as a defense to an accusation of treachery.

1676. We have explained above in this chapter how war is made according to our custom. Now let us say how war ends, for it may end in various ways.

1677. The first of the ways in which war ends is when peace is made by the agreement of the parties, for after the keeping of the peace is promised [*creantee*] or covenanted, all those who were at war (in the war in which the peace was made) must be at peace with each other; and if anyone breaks this peace and is convicted, he is to be hanged.

1678. If peace is made between the parties who are at war, it is not necessary for the whole family of each party to be there when peace is made or promised. Rather it is sufficient if peace is made or agreed between those who were the leaders of the war [*chief de la guerre*], and if there are people in the family who do not want to consent to the peace which is made and agreed between the principal combatants of the war [*chevetaigne de la guerre*], they must make it known that people must be on their guard against them, because they do not want to be a part of that peace. And if they do not make this announcement, and they harm the adversaries who thought they were at peace with them, they can be sued for breaching the peace and they cannot use as a defense that they did not know about the peace, or say that they did not agree with the peace; for when peace is made between the chief parties [*chevetaignes*] in the war, it must exist between all the lineages of the one party and the other, except those who say or send word that they do not want to be part of that peace.

1679. When peace is made between those who are chiefs of some war [*chevetaigne d'aucune guerre*] and some people of one family or the other do not want to be in that peace and instead say or send word that people must be on their guard against them, none of those who agree to the peace and none of those who did not make the announcement that people had to be on their guard against them may give aid or comfort to those that remain at war, for they could be accused of breaching the peace [*pes brisiee*]. And after they have {once} assented to the peace by act or by word they cannot go back on this but they must keep the peace. And since we have said that those who have assented to the peace in word or by deed cannot renounce this, nor announce that others should be on their guard against them, it is right that we should declare how a person consents to the peace by both deed and word, or by deed without word, or by word without deed.

1680. It should be known that a person consents to the peace both by deed and by word who drinks and eats and speaks and keeps company [*tient compaignie*] with a person who used to be among his enemies. Therefore after he has done this, if he does or procures shame or annoyance [*honte ou anui*] to that person, he can be accused of treachery and breaching the peace. And those who are in the peace by their words without deed are those who at the peacemaking, and in front of good people or a judge said that they are bound by the peace and that they want peace. Those who are in the peace by deed without words are those who are in the family of the principal combatant and have made no announcement of defiance but rather go around without arms among those who used to be their enemies, for they show by their deeds that no one should be afraid of them. And I explain these three manners of {making} peace so that people may know who is breaking them, for such persons can be accused of treachery and breaching the peace.

1681. The second way in which a private war ends is by giving of a guaranteed peace [*asseurement*], for example when the lord obliges the principal parties [*les parties chevetaignes*] to give guarantees to each other [*asseurer li uns l'autre*]. And although the peace which is made by the families and the peace which is made by a judge is a good and strong and binding peace, nevertheless the binding of peace by guarantees [*asseurement*] is stronger; and we will speak of this in a chapter which comes after this one which discusses truces and the giving of a guaranteed peace {Chapter 60}.

1682. The third way in which war ends is when the parties plead in court by wager of battle concerning the action because of which they were, or could have been, at war. For you must not seek vengeance on your enemy by war and by going to court at the same time. Therefore when there is a suit in court on the dispute because of which the war occurred, the lord should take the war into his hands and prevent the parties from doing harm to each other and then give judgment on what is pleaded in his court.

1683. The fourth manner in which war ends is when punishment is meted out by the judge for the offense which caused the war, for example, when a man is killed and those who killed him and were guilty of his death are arrested by the judge and drawn and hanged. In such a case, the family of the dead man must not maintain a war against the relatives of those who committed the offense; for when the crime is punished [*vengiés*], the family of the dead person should count themselves as properly satisfied [*bien paié*] and they should not keep up a war against those who had no guilt in the offense.

1684. By what is said about war in this chapter it can be seen that gentlemen are at war because of the actions of their family even if they were not present at the action, but only when forty days have elapsed after the fact. However, if anyone wants to take himself out of the war, he can do so in one way, which is to summon his enemies before the judge and force them to appear and after, when they have appeared, in their presence and in front of the judge, he must ask that he should not be considered at war, inasmuch as he is a person who is prepared to reject those who committed the offense. When the rejection has been made of those who were guilty of the offense, the lord should give him a guaranteed peace individually, and the oath that he must make must be to swear that he has no guilt in the offense which was the reason for the war, and that he will give neither aid nor help to those that he may know to have been guilty, nor to any of those of his lineage who want to continue the war to the detriment of the family of the person against whom the offense was committed. And after he has made this oath, if the adverse party does not wish to make a formal accusation against him as guilty of this offense, he must be left and must remain in peace as an individual [*en sa persone*], as is said above.

1685. If any one has taken himself out of the war in the manner stated above, he must be careful not to go against his oath; for if he gives aid or companionship in arms [*compaignie a armes*] or lends horses or armor or houses, or he causes them to be lent, he puts himself back in the war by his act, and if harm comes to him then it is right and proper, for at the very least he is a perjurer. And if the adverse party wants, he can consider him at war like the others, and if he prefers he can accuse him in front of the judge of having broken his oath; and if he is proved or found guilty, he has deserved a long prison term and his lord can impose any fine he wants. But it would be different if he had, after the announcement, beaten or struck or wounded any of those whom he had requested to consider him out of the war, and for whom he rejected his relatives who were keeping up the war and those who were guilty of the offense, for in this case, he would be as liable to be hanged as those who break a guaranteed peace.

1686. It used to be that you could take vengeance by right of war as far as the seventh degree of kinship, and that was not surprising at that time because marriage could not be made up to the seventh degree; but now that marriage can be made up to the fourth degree of kinship, war cannot be made on a person who is more distant than the fourth degree of kinship, for in all these cases kinship ends as soon as it is so distant that a marriage can be made, except for redeeming land [*rescousse d'eritage*],[5] for you can still buy back land up to the seventh degree by reason of kinship. So, according to what is said above, it can be known that those who attack because of their private war persons beyond the fourth degree of kinship from those who were guilty of the action by which the war began cannot use as a defense that they did so because of the right of war. But instead they must be brought to justice according to the offense as if there were no war at all.

1687. It would be different if a person, who was distant in kinship up to the fifth or sixth or seventh degree, entered the war either by deed or by word along with those of whose family he was, for then he could be counted at war just like the others, and that would be true also for a person who was completely a stranger who, on either side, had never belonged nor did belong {to the family}; for a person who loves one of the parties who are at war, to the point where he gives him his aid and his company against his enemies, puts himself into the war even though he does not belong to that family, excepting the mercenaries which people pay to be on their side in a war: for these mercenaries, as long as they are of assistance to one of the parties, are in the war, but when they have left, because their term of service has ended, or because they wish to, or because they are no longer wanted, they are out of the war. Therefore if harm were done to them after they had left, no excuse could be found in the right of war. And what we have said about mercenaries, we also say about those who have to give aid by reason of suzerainty, as it is proper that vassals who hold fiefs or tenants holding tenancies from them [*li ost qui tienent d'aus ostises*] and serfs give aid to their lords when they are at war, even though they do not belong to their family. Therefore as long as they are supporting their lords they can be counted as at war, and as soon as they have left they are out of the war and you should not make war on them for having done their duty towards their lords.

1688. Certain persons are exempt from wars, even though they are part of the natural family of those who are at war, such as clerks, and those who have entered religion, and women and minor children and bastards— unless they join the war by their acts—and those who have been placed in or sent to leper-houses or hospitals. All such persons must be out of danger of war carried on by their families. And if anyone attacks them, his action cannot be excused by right of war.

1689. And there are even other persons who must not be accounted at war because of the war of their relatives, such as those who, when the quarrel began, were on a journey overseas or some distant pilgrimage, or sent to foreign countries by the king or for the common good. For if such people were at war for the quarrels which arose when they were out of the country, then they could be killed wherever they were, or on the way out or back, without their knowing anything about the war, which would be a terrible thing and a great danger for those who go on journeys to distant lands; and it would be a poor and dishonest vengeance on the part of those who took their vengeance in this manner, and it would not be vengeance, but treachery.

Here ends the chapter on war.

Notes

1. I have translated the expression *fet aparent* as "*casus belli.*" The *fet aparent* was the equivalent of what is called elsewhere a "serious crime," namely a crime against the person for which the punishment might be death (see §824). The private war may thus be seen as a kind of self-help, where the mover tries to kill or injure a person who might otherwise, if convicted in a judicial procedure, suffer this fate at the hands of the law. Some clarification of the words *fet aparent* may be found in *L'ancienne coutume de Normandie*, ed. William Laurence de Gruchy (Jersey, British Channel Islands: Charles le Feuvre, 1881) 162.

2. For the *asseurement*, here translated "guaranteed peace," see Chapter 60.

3. *Fere vilenie* usually means "insult, libel." It is hard to see how anyone can threaten to insult somebody (*menace l'autre a fere vilenie*), but this is what Beaumanoir seems to be saying; unless *vilenie* can refer to physical acts as well as verbal ones, in which case it is a synonym for *anui*, with which it is coupled. The notion of physical harm seems justified by the last sentence of §1675 below.

4. *Traïson* or "treachery" is an act which is unexpected or stealthy, rather than *lèse-majesté*. See §826.

5. For redemption, *rescousse d'eritage*, see Chapter 44.

60. Truces

Here begins the sixtieth chapter of this book, which speaks of truces and guaranteed peace [asseurement], and of who can be excluded from them, and of the danger of breaking truces and guaranteed peace.

1690. It is true that we have spoken in the chapter before this one of wars which can occur according to the custom of our district [*païs*]. And it is right that in this chapter following after we should speak of truces and guaranteed peace because a truce is a thing which gives protection from private war for the time that it lasts and a guaranteed peace creates a confirmed peace for ever by the force of law. And we will speak of the difference that there is between truces and guaranteed peace, and how they should be made, and what sort of people can be excluded from them, and how those who break truces and guaranteed peace are to be punished.

1691. It is the custom in the county of Clermont that if commoners have harmed each other as it were by a serious crime [*de fet aparent*][1] and one of the parties asks the other in court for a truce, he does not get it, but rather the judge will make a full guarantee of peace if the parties do not make peace between them; for commoners cannot, according to custom, carry on a war, and between people who cannot make war on each other there is no possibility of a truce.

1692. Jehan, who was a gentlemen, sued Pierre, who was a gentleman, saying that he and Pierre had had a fight and blows had been struck, for which reason he requested his sovereign's truce [*trives par souverain*], as a person who was in fear. To this Pierre replied, that he did not want to give a truce, since in respect of the act in question he was in a state of friends' armistice [*astenance . . . par amis*],[2] and he was willing to prolong this friends' armistice any time it should be asked. And upon this they requested a judgment on the question of whether Jehan would have his sovereign's truce.

1693. It was found in the opinion that, according to the custom, Jehan would not have his truce, but that the sovereign would oblige Pierre to extend his friends' armistice any time that he showed signs of not keeping it. And it was also said that, when a war has begun between gentlemen, the party who wants to be safe may seek this by one of three different methods, whichever he pleases: either by friends' armistice, or a truce (through family or through the court), or a guaranteed peace. And once he had chosen one of these methods, he could not abandon it to pursue one of the other methods.

1694. There is a great difference between truce and guaranteed peace, for a truce lasts for a specified time, and a guaranteed peace lasts for ever. And again, when someone breaks a truce, only those who break the truce are accused, and when a guaranteed peace is broken, both those who break it and also the person who made the guarantee are accused, even though it is openly known that the person who made the guarantee was not part of the act of breaking it; for a guaranteed peace has such force that the person who gives a guarantee takes responsibility thereby for his whole lineage, except for those that he can properly exclude, for there are certain persons he can exclude when he gives the guarantee, and if they are not excepted, then they are all included.

1695. Those who can be excluded by custom are those who are living in distant lands outside the kingdom, concerning whom there is no hope of their speedy return. But if it happens that they are excluded and they do come back, the person who gave the guarantee must warn the person to whom he gave it to be on his guard that people have come back to the district who were out of the guarantee; and if he does not so inform him, and they remain forty days in the district, and then after the forty days they break the guaranteed peace, then the person who gave the guarantee is held responsible; and if he does make it known, the person to whom the guarantee was given must force them through the sovereign to be in the guarantee, and if he does not force them they are in the guarantee by custom when they have been in the district for forty days. But if the person who gave the guarantee can do nothing to make them want to abstain from harming the person to whom the guarantee was made, he must so inform the person to whom he gave the guarantee, and also the sovereign, and swear on the saints that he cannot make them do it; and then the judge must arrest them if they can be found, and keep them in prison until they have joined the guarantee. And if they are not found, if they are commoners, they must be summoned three times to come fifteen days later to the provost's court; and if they do not come in that time, at the end of the third period it must be announced that they must come to the next judge's assize on a guaranteed peace matter, and if they do not come to the assize they must be banished. If they are gentlemen, and have come back from outside the country in the manner described above, they must be arrested without delay, if they can be found; and if they run away so that they cannot be found, then a great many guards must be placed on their property, if they have any, and they must be called three times to appear fifteen days later in the provost's court on the sovereign's business [*au droit du souverain*]; and if they do not appear, they must be called at three subsequent assizes when there are at least forty days between assizes; and if they do not come by that last assize, they must be banished. Truces between gentlemen, whether friends' truces or those given by a judge, must be handled in the same way as described above.

1696. The second kind of persons who can be excluded from truces or guaranteed peace are those who were banished before the guaranteed peace was made; but if they are recalled and absolved from banishment by the will of the sovereign, so that they come back into the district, they must be treated in the manner described above concerning guaranteed peace.

1697. The third kind of persons who can be excluded from truces and guaranteed peace are bastards, for by our custom a bastard has no lineage; and this is clear, for my relatives at the fourth degree would inherit my estate if I had no closer relative than my bastard son. But nevertheless, since bastards are moved by natural love to give aid to their relatives, those who give truces or guarantee peace must name them at the time of giving the truce or guaranteeing the peace, so that those to whom the truce or the guaranteed peace is given know whom they should beware of; and if he does not exclude them from the guarantee, the person who gives the guarantee is to blame; but in the case of truces, as I said before, only the person who actually commits the offense is accused.

1698. If these three kinds of people described above are summoned to court to give a guaranteed peace or a truce, and they let the time run until they are banished, and then they are arrested after the banishment, they have deserved a long prison term and their fine is at the sovereign's discretion, whether they are gentlemen or commoners. And when they have paid the fine to the lord and they are out of prison, they are to give their word on the guaranteed peace (or the truce, if they were summoned for a truce). But it is different for those who are summoned on suspicion of serious crime, of which they have been accused, for example murder, or treachery, or homicide, or rape, or arson or willful damage to property, or escaping from prison,—in other words whenever someone is arrested for any crime for which the punishment is death if he were found guilty,—or larceny, for if anyone is summoned for one of the cases described above and waits so long that he is banished by the custom of the area and he is caught after the banishment, in that case he has lost his life and his property and he is dealt with as if he had committed to the common knowledge the crime for which he was summoned.

1699. When any *casus belli* occurs between gentlemen who can make war, if there is a death, the truce or guaranteed peace must be requested from the closest relative of the deceased, provided he is fifteen or more years old; and if he refuses because he does not want to give a truce or guaranteed peace, the count must summon him to court at fifteen-day intervals. And nevertheless, because of the danger that there is in delay, the count should send guards to the person from whom the truce or guaranteed peace is requested, and double them each day, so that the person appears in court to avoid loss; if he does not want to come, whether to avoid loss or for anything else, and he has been summoned three times to appear fifteen days later in the provost's court and then to three assizes, if he does not appear, he must be banished; and after he is banished, the truce or guaranteed peace can be requested of the nearest relative after him. But because of the danger of delay, when they refuse, the count can and should take the quarrel into his own hands and forbid them on pain of life and property to do harm to each other. And if they do harm to each other in spite of the count's prohibition, if there is a death, all those who were present at the offense fall into the count's discretion as to life and property; and if there is an action without death, such as an injury or a battery, the fine of each person who is guilty of the offense is sixty pounds to the count.

1700. If there is a fight between gentlemen in which no one is killed, but there is injury or battery, and someone wants to request a truce or guaranteed peace, the person must ask it of those to whom the action was done, and he cannot ask it of anyone else in the family until the person to whom the action was done has been banished in the manner stated above.

1701. It often happens that there is a fight or a quarrel or a threat, between gentlemen or between commoners, and then each party is so proud that he will not condescend to ask for a truce or guaranteed peace; but because of the statute of good King Louis,[3] that does not mean that there should be nothing done; rather each person who holds directly from the king, such as the count of Clermont, and the other barons, when they know that there is some action or threat between parties, and the latter do not condescend to request truce or guaranteed peace, they should have the parties arrested and force them to give a truce if they are gentlemen; and if they are commoners, they must be compelled to give a formal guaranteed peace; and if they flee, so that they cannot be arrested, the escapees must be forced by guards {scil. placed on their property} and summoned and even eventually banished, in the manner stated above.

1702. There used to be a very bad custom concerning private wars in the kingdom of France, for when some case of death arose, or of injury or battery, the person to whom this harm had been done looked for one of the relatives of those who had done the wrong to them, and who lived far away from the place where the injury had been done, so that they know nothing about the injury, and then they went there, riding night and day, and as soon as they found him, they killed him or injured him, or beat him, or did whatever they wanted to him, as it was possible for them to do to a person who was not on his guard and did not know that anyone who belonged to his lineage had done them any wrong. And because of the great danger which arose because of this, good King Philippe made a law[4] which says that, when some harm has been done, those who are present at the action must be on their guard directly after the action and they have no truce until it has been made by a judge or by their family; but all those in the lineage of either party who were not present at the action have by the king's law forty days of truce, and then after the forty days they are in the war; and because of these forty days people in the family have time to know what is happening to their lineage, so that they can make ready either to make war or to seek a guaranteed peace, a truce, or {simply to make} peace.

1703. If some action occurs by reason of which it is appropriate for those who were present at the action to be at war, and there are some men of their lineage who join with them to help them, for example if they consort with them in arms, or they protect them in their houses, such people are in the war as soon as the begin to help them in their war, and they have no benefit of the forty-days' truce described above, for it is clearly evident that they know very well about the action when they undertake to make war along with those who were present at the action.

1704. When someone who has been the victim of an offense takes revenge on some of those who were not present at the action within the forty days that they have a truce according to the above-mentioned law, it should not be called vengeance but treachery; and for this reason, those who in this way do harm to those who are under a truce must be dealt with: if there is a death they must be drawn and hanged and lose all their property; if there is only a battery, they should receive a long prison term and the fine is at the discretion of the lord who holds directly from the king, for it is not right that any lord below the one who holds directly from the king should receive the fine for a broken truce which is confirmed by the sovereign; rather, the fine and cognizance of the offense belong to the count.

1705. It often happens that some families are in a state of truce or guaranteed peace with each other, and yet it happens that some new dispute arises among some of the those in the family so that by this new action there is a fight or some *casus belli* [*fet aparant*]. Now let's see if a truce or guaranteed peace is broken in such a case. And we say no, for to accuse someone of a broken truce or guaranteed peace, the offense by which the truce or guaranteed peace is broken must derive from the first offense by reason of which the truce or guaranteed peace was given, so that those who are defendants cannot claim that there is some new action. And in this case the judge must take great care to discover what was the first action for which the truce or guaranteed peace was given and what was the later action by which they hoped to have a defense to the accusation of having broken the truce or guaranteed peace. And if the judge sees that the latest incident took place because of the first, he should proceed in such a case as if it were a broken truce or guaranteed peace. But if the action is so new that it cannot be shown that it derived from the first action, but rather it is clear that the quarrel arose between the parties because of a new action, then there should be no punishment of this action for a broken truce or guaranteed peace; instead, punishment should be made according to the action as if there never had been any truce or guaranteed peace.

1706. What we have said about a new action which arises between those who were under a truce or guaranteed peace, we mean to apply {only} to those persons of a lineage on either side who did not swear to the truce or guaranteed peace; for as for those who formally [*droitement*] gave a truce or guaranteed peace, if they fight again afterwards, they cannot have the defense of a new incident. So that if there is any contention between them, they must seek justice through law or custom; and if they fight or if there is some other *casus belli*, the person who began the action must be tried for broken truce or broken guaranteed peace, but the person who defends himself should not be accused of anything, since any person who is attacked is permitted to defend himself to avoid danger of death or bodily harm.

1707. Pierre and Jehan had fought each other and there was a *casus belli* and each was so proud that the did not condescend to request truce or guaranteed peace or to make a complaint about the action. We learned of the action: we arrested them and wanted them to make a formal [*droit*] guaranteed peace, and each party declared that he was not obliged to make peace when neither party requested it, and they asked us to hold a hearing. And at their request we called for a judgment on the question of whether there should be a guaranteed peace between them.

1708. And it was judged that when we learned of the *casus belli* we could and should keep the parties imprisoned until a guaranteed peace was given, or a good and certain peace {established} by the assent of the parties, for much harm can be avoided in this manner and all princes and barons should, by exercising judicial control [*en justiçant*], prevent such evils as might otherwise occur.

Here ends the chapter on truce and guaranteed peace.

Notes

1. For the *fet aparent*, see note to §1669.
2. De Laurière comments on this very usage in Beaumanoir under the word *Atenanche*: "C'étoit, ce semble, un retardement d'hostilitez, ou une suspension d'armes pour quelque-temps, que les amis communs obtenoient de Gentilhommes qui étoient en guerre, pour tâcher de les accommoder ensemble, et de négocier la paix entr'eux." ("It appears that this was a halt in hostilities, or a suspension of arms for a period, which common friends obtained of Gentlemen at war, to try to affect a reconciliation or to negotiate peace between them.") François Ragueau and Eusèbe

De Laurière, *Glossaire du droit françois* (Niort: Favre, 1882) 43. The word *amis* is often used to mean "family," so that although I have chosen to use the term "friends' armistice" it should be borne in mind that the friends in question may be family members.

3. This statute may be from 1245. See *Est.*, 1: 182 and 4: 322.

4. This statute has not been preserved.

61. Appeals

Here begins the sixty-first chapter of this book, which speaks of appeals and how one should appeal, and how to word your appeal, and about banishment.

1709. It often happens in secular courts that the cases result in a wager of battle[1] or that someone deliberately accuses someone else before the judge of a serious offense: and it is a good thing for us to make a special chapter on this subject which will show which cases can be appealed, and which persons can appeal and be appealed against and which cannot, and how the appeal should be worded and the danger present in such appeals, and which appeals the lord should not permit, so that those who want to appeal will know how they should behave in a wager of battle, and what can happen to them if they lose their appeal [*enchieent du plet*].

1710. In any case of serious crime there can be an appeal, or a wager of battle, if the accuser makes a formal [*droite*] accusation in an appealable matter, for it is right that an appellee should defend himself or be convicted of the act for which the appeal is made. But there are other ways of proceeding besides a formal appeal, for before the appeal has been made, if the person who is going to be the accuser wants to, he can state to the judge that a certain offense has been committed in the sight and knowledge of so many honest men that it cannot be concealed, and that he must do his duty as a judge. Then the sovereign should investigate [*en enquerre*], even though the party does not want to submit to an inquest [*se couchier en enqueste*]; and if the finds the offense well-known and public knowledge, he can deal with it [*justicier*] according to the offense; for it would be a bad thing if, when my close relative had been killed in the middle of a celebration or in front of a quantity of honest men, I had to go to battle to obtain vengeance; and for this reason in such cases which are open knowledge, one can proceed by means of a statement of denunciation.

1711. And if someone wants to make a formal appeal, he should say the following, if it is for a murder: "Sire, I declare concerning so-and-so—and he should name the person—that he, unlawfully and treacherously,[2] has murdered so-and-so—and he should name the murdered person—who was my relative, by his act [*tret*] and by his deed and by his procurement. If he admits it, I request you to treat him as a murderer; and if he denies it, I wish to prove the fact in personal combat against him, or by means of a man who can and should do it for me, because I am a person who has a legal excuse,[3] which I will make known in the proper time and place." And if he makes an appeal without retaining a person to act for him, he will have to fight in person and cannot have anyone to act for him. If he appeals for something other than murder, for example for homicide, or for any of the cases named above for which an appeal can be made, he should name the reason why he is appealing and describe the kind of action and offer to prove it if it is denied by the adverse party, either fighting himself or by having another fight for him, as has been said above.

1712. The person who has been accused should not go away from the judge's presence until he has answered the appeal.[4] And if there are any reasons why he wants to claim that the appeal should not lie, he must mention them all and request a ruling on each argument as it has been advanced, going from one thing to another; and he must say, that if the ruling is that his claims are not good for saying that the wager does not lie, then he will set aside all less important matters [*si met il jus toute vilaine euvre*] and deny the fact brought forward against him and offer to defend himself in person or by means of some man who can and should do it for him as for a man who has a legal excuse and will make it known in the proper place and time. And then the judge should accept the wagers[5] of the appellant and appellee, pending a decision on the claims of the appellee that an appeal does not lie.

1713. If the appellant or the appellee wants to have someone to fight for him, he must put forward his legal excuse when the judgment for the battle is given. There are various legal excuses for any one of which someone can be substituted for a party. One of the legal excuses is if the person who wants to have a substitute shows that he has lost one of his limbs, which makes it clear that his body is weaker for that reason; the second legal excuse is that you have reached the age of sixty years; the third legal excuse is that you have an illness which comes on suddenly, for example gout; the fourth legal excuse is that you are sick of quartain, or tertian fever, or some other sickness which is openly known and not fraudulent; the fifth legal excuse is if a woman is appellant or appellee, for a woman does not fight, as is said above.

1714. If a gentleman appeals against a gentleman, and each one is a knight, they fight on horseback, armed with any armor they wish, except a pointed knife [*coutel a pointe*] or a mace. In the way of sharpened weapons [*arme moulue*] each may carry only two swords and his spear [*glaive*]; and if they are squires, also two swords and a spear.

1715. If a knight or a squire appeals against a commoner, he fights on foot, armed like a champion,[6] just like the commoner, for since he is stooping to appeal against such a lowly person, his dignity is reduced in such cases to the same kind of armor as the appellee has a right to; and it would be a very cruel if the gentleman appealed against a commoner and he had the advantage of a horse and armor.

1716. If the commoner appeals against a gentleman, he fights on foot like a champion, and the gentleman on horseback in full armor, for it is right that they {gentlemen} should use all their advantages when they are defending themselves.

1717. If a commoner appeals against another commoner, they fight on foot. And the champion of a gentlewoman, whether she is appellant or appellee, fights under the same conditions as would a gentleman, as was said above.

1718. The horses and armor of those who come into the sovereign's court to fight go to the sovereign whether a peace is made or not; and there can be no peace made, nor can one combatant yield the victory to the other, without the sovereign's assent. But if they fight and the horses are killed and the armor damaged, the lord receives no recompense, but the person who is beaten loses his life and all his property, from whatever lord he holds it; and he forfeits to each lord from whom he held his land, and loses also his personal property and goods to the lords in whose domains they are. And in this way if someone is condemned for an offense for which he must lose his life, his personal property and land are dealt with in such a way that the lords who come into possession of his property because of forfeiture are not required to pay anything that was owed as a debt by the person who was condemned for the offense.

1719. On each day that a gentleman appears in court for an appeal, or to take a continuance, for those appearances which can be continued, on the first appearance he owes ten sous and the second appearance twenty sous and the third appearance forty sous; and for each of the appearances fixed by the judge or put off by agreement of a party, each day the fine doubles. And if the battle is between commoners, the first day's fine is five sous, the second day's ten sous and the third day's twenty sous; and it doubles each day.

1720. If the battle, for personal property or land, is in the court of any of the count's men, between commoners the loser loses the suit for which the wager was given and also pays a fine to the lord in whose court the battle was, and the fine is sixty sous. And if the battle is between gentlemen, the loser loses the suit and pays a fine of sixty pounds to the lord.

1721. According to the custom of Clermont, anyone in a wager for personal property or chattels can have a representative in the fight if he wants one, whether he has a legal excuse or not; and the champion who is defeated has his hand cut off; for if it were not for the injury that he risks, someone might deceitfully take a bribe, and use pretense, and declare himself defeated, for which his principal would bear the cost and the loss of reputation, and he would go off with the money; and for this reason the imposition of an injury is a good one.

1722. The count may at will reestablish [*remetre*] in his court whenever he wishes the use of wagers of battle for personal and real property, for when King Louis excluded them from his court, he did not exclude them from the courts of his great vassals [*barons*]; and if the count could not bring them back into use [*rapeler*] in his court, then he would have less jurisdiction in his court over these cases than *his* vassals in their courts.

1723. The count's vassals in the county of Clermont have the discretion to proceed in any case in their court according to the old custom or according to the king's ordinance {regarding procedure};[7] but if the suit is brought according to the king's ordinance, by permission of the lord, the vassal cannot then permit a wager of battle, if a party wishes to elect that choice; and also, if the suit is begun on a wager of battle according to the old custom, the vassal cannot make it conform to the king's ordinance, except by the agreement of both parties, for all disputes on a wager and all other disputes must be conducted according to the way that the suit was begun.

1724. If the wager is for some bar, and not on the main issue, the winner wins only the bar for which the wager was given; and in this regard, it must be understood that if the bar was dilatory,[8]—for example if one man sued another for a hundred pounds, and the latter said that the due date would not come until some time he stated in the future, or if he alleged {he had been given} an extension of time, and either the due date or the extension was denied by the plaintiff and the defendant offered to prove what he said and the plaintiff challenged by wager of battle one of the witnesses,—then if he were the winner, he would win that the due date for the debt had come; and if he were defeated, the defendant would have the extension; and because the other had required payment of the debt before the due date, the defendant would be awarded the complete term and {in addition} a period after the due date equal to the time before the due date when the suit was brought.

1725. We have spoken of these two dilatory bars because through these two you can understand the others; and to speak briefly, all bars and all exceptions[9] are dilatory by reason of which the matter which is being contested is merely prolonged, and those which are called peremptory are the claims which are advanced by which or by one of which, if it is proved, the suit is won; for example, if someone is demanding a hundred pounds of me and I claim that he gave them to me for my services, or I allege payment, if I prove one of these things, the plaintiff's suit is lost; or if someone claims my land and I say that it descended to me from my father or my mother, or that I bought it, or that it passed to me laterally, all these reasons are peremptory, for if I can prove one of them I have won the suit.

1726. If it happens that one of the count's vassals has caused a truce or a guaranteed peace to be given to one of his subjects, and the truce or the guaranteed peace is broken, the lord should summon him three times to appear in court fifteen days later, if he is a commoner, and then at a forty-day interval instead of an assize {regular sitting} (which he would have if he were summoned to the sovereign's court), and if he does not make an appearance he should be banished and punished for that offense if he is later arrested.[10]

1727. Now we should discuss this: if someone is banished by the court of one of the count's vassals, for whatever crime, what should the count do? He should summon him to the court where he normally lives at the next assize, provided there are yet forty days before it. And if he does not appear, and honest men give witness that he is banished by the court of one of his vassals, he should be banished from the whole county. And if he appears, or if he is arrested before he is banished from the county, in the count's territory or on the land of any of the count's vassals by whom he was not banished, he is entitled to a trial as to the fact, if he will submit to it, and he will be given judgment according to the trial. And if he does not want to submit to the trial, the count will make an inquiry *sua sponte*; and if he finds the fact is publicly known, he will be be punished for the offense; and if the fact is not clearly proved,[11] then because of the suspicion inherent in the fact that he waited until he was banished, and did not want to await the trial about the fact, he should be imprisoned for life, so that others may be deterred from such offenses.

1728. When a man is banished by the court of one of the count's vassals, none of the count's other vassals can or may give him asylum, but should arrest him if he finds him on his lands, and must send a message to the count that he has arrested such-and-such a fugitive [*bani*], and should treat him as has been said above that the count should treat him when he has him in prison.

1729. If any are banished by the court of any of the count's vassals, the banishment only reaches to the edge of the lands held by the lord in whose court he was banished; but he must be arrested if he is found in the county, and treated as was said above.

1730. Things should be different if he is banished by the count's court; for a banishment which is made in the count's court is good in the whole county, both in his lands and in the lands of all his subjects; and if anyone gives him asylum, knowing about the banishment, that person's house should be demolished and the fine is at the count's discretion, up to everything he owns, and in addition a prison term, for a person who gives asylum to a fugitive who has been banished by the lord acts wrongly toward his lord.

1731. If the count recalls some banished person out of mercy,—for example if he has heard that the person who was banished, at the time when he was summoned and banished, was in a foreign country or on a pilgrimage, and it is obvious that he knew nothing about the appeals or the banishment, nor was there anyone who at the time of the banishment or the appeals took his part, or if the count has subsequently found out for certain that he was not guilty of the offense for which he was banished,—he is performing an act of mercy to repeal such a banishment.

1732. If a banished person is recalled by the sovereign for some such merciful reason as I mentioned above, he ought to have back all of his goods that were seized because he was suspected of having committed an offense, whether the count or some other person has them in his keeping; for a person who is absolved in the court of the sovereign cannot be held guilty in the court of his subject. But it would be different if the count recalled the banished person because of a payment, or at his request, or at the count's own will without reason to be merciful, for in such repeals the subjects of the lower vassals would not give him back those possessions of his which they had in their keeping because of the offense, unless he had himself declared innocent [*se fesoit purgier*] by a judgment of the offense for which he was banished, for example if he were appealed against and he won the appeal, or if he submitted to a trial and he was cleared by the trial, for then it would be proper for him to have back his own things, whoever had them in their keeping.

1733. Vassals who have banished someone in their court for a crime cannot repeal the banishment for any reason without the agreement of the count, but the count can certainly do this, as I have said above.

1734. Again, according to our custom, no one can appeal against the lord whose vassal he is, in body and hands [*de cors et de mains*], until he has abandoned the homage and what he holds from him. Therefore if anyone wants to appeal against his lord for any serious offense for which an appeal lies, he should, before the appeal, come to his lord in the presence of his peers, and speak in this manner: "Sire, I have been for a while in your faith and your homage, and I have held from you such-and-such a piece of land as a fief. I renounce the fief and the homage and the faith, because you have committed an offense toward me, for which offense I intend to seek vengeance through an appeal." And after this renunciation, he should cause him to be summoned into the court of his sovereign and proceed with his appeal; and if he appeals against him before he has renounced his fief and the homage, then there is no wager, and instead he must recompense his lord for the insulting thing he said in court and must also pay a fine to the court, and each fine will be sixty pounds.

1735. We say, and it is true according to our custom, that just as the man owes his lord faith and loyalty by reason of his homage, the lord owes just as much to his man; and for this reason we can see that, since the man cannot appeal against his lord while he is in his homage, the lord cannot appeal against his man until he has renounced the homage. Therefore, if the lord wishes to appeal against his man, he must end the homage in the presence of the sovereign before whom he is making the appeal and then he can proceed with his appeal.

1736. Some people think that I can abandon the fief that I hold from my lord, and the faith and the homage, any time that I want, but I cannot unless there is a good reason; nevertheless when you want to abandon them the lords are eager to take them back because of their greed. But if it should happen that my lord called on me in his great need or to join the army of the count or the king, and I should at that time want to abandon my fief, I would not be keeping my faith or my loyalty toward my lord, for faith and loyalty is of such a noble [*franche*] nature that it must be kept and especially to the person to which it is promised. For when you make your homage you promise to your lord faith and loyalty; and once it is promised, it would not be loyalty to renounce it at the moment when the lord had need of it.

1737. Now let's see, if I renounce my fief because I do not want to give aid to my lord in his time of need, what my lord could do about it, for he can only confiscate what I hold from him, and I have given this back to him. What should he do then? I say, that if he wishes, he can hale me into the sovereign's court on an appeal, and can accuse me of acting falsely, unlawfully, and disloyally toward him, and he would have a good appeal suit.

1738. Because I now say that the lord owes as much faith and loyalty to his man as the man does to his lord, this is not to be understood as meaning that the man is not obligated to many kinds of obedience and to many services, to which the lord is not obligated with respect to his man, for the man must appear at the bidding of his lord, and he is obliged to execute his judgments and to obey his reasonable orders, and to serve him as I have said before. And in all these things the lord is not obligated to his man, but the faith and loyalty that the lord owes his man must be understood as meaning that the lord must avoid doing harm to his man, and he must treat him equitably and lawfully [*debonairement et par droit*]; and he must keep for him and protect for him that which he holds from him, in such a way that no one does harm to it; and in this way the lord can keep his faith toward his man and the man toward his lord.

1739. A lord would not be doing his duty toward his man if he required of him four packhorses [*roncis*]¹² which he owed him for four fiefs and he summoned him to appear in fifteen days for one, and on the next day to appear in fifteen days for the second, and on the third day to appear in fifteen days for the third one, and on the fourth day to appear in fifteen days for the fourth one, and on the fifth day he had him summoned to reply to any and all complaints; it is clear that the lord was making such summonses to his man only to harass him, for the lord can ask his man on a single day everything he had him summoned for on five different days. Now let's see what the men can do who are summoned in that manner. They can appear on the first day and require their lord to repeal the summonses for the other days and ask them on that first day everything that he wants; and if the lord will not do it the man should ask him for a hearing. And if the lord refuses to give a hearing, he has a good appeal to his overlord for default of judgment when he has requested and demanded it three times at fifteen-day intervals, in the presence of his peers; and if his lord gives a judgment and the judgment is against the man, the man has a good appeal for false judgment.

1740. If someone wants to appeal against his lord for a default of judgment he must first of all, in the presence of his peers, request his lord to give him a hearing. And if his lord refuses, he has a good appeal for default of judgment. And if he appeals before he has made a request to his lord in this manner, he is sent back to the court of his lord and he must pay a fine for having taken him to court in the sovereign's court on such a serious matter; and the fine is at the will of the lord up to all of what the appellant holds from him.¹³

1741. In the same way, if a commoner wants to appeal for default of judgment, he must make his request, to the lord from whom he holds, three times at fifteen-day intervals, as was said before; and if he goes too fast or if he loses his appeal [*enchiet de son apel*] he is sent back to the court of the person against whom he appealed and the fine is at the will of the lord up to all that is held from him.

1742. If you appeal for default of judgment against someone other than your lord, for example if I plead in the court of some lord and I am not his man, nor do I hold land from him, nor am I his tenant, I must, in the presence of his men, make my request of him three times at fifteen-day intervals that he give me a hearing; and if I cannot obtain the presence of his men, I must make my request in the presence of other good men who can testify to it for me; and when I have made my request in this manner, if he does not give me a hearing or if he refuses to do so, I have a good appeal. And if I hurry too much or if I lose my appeal, the lord in whose court I made the appeal must force me to pay damages to the appellee, and the fine if I am a gentleman is sixty pounds and if I am a commoner, sixty sous. And the reason why the fine is not at the will of the appellee, as it would be for his vassals or his tenants, is that everyone owes more obedience and reverence to his lord or to the person of whom he is a tenant, than to a stranger.

1743. All those who appeal for default of judgment and who lose their appeal have not come to closure merely by paying a fine to the appellee, but they pay a fine to the lord in whose court they made the appeal. And if the appellant is a gentleman the fine is sixty pounds and if he is a commoner the fine is sixty sous; and by this it can be seen that in this case there are two fines for a single offense, and there are also in many other cases.

1744. It is not proper for the appellant for false judgment to delay his appeal; indeed he must appeal as soon as the judgment is given, for if he does not appeal immediately, the judgment should be held as good, whether it be good or bad.

1745. If the appellee for default of judgment or for false judgment is defeated in the appeal and found guilty, he loses his judicial power and his jurisdiction over his land and the fine is sixty pounds. If the appeal is for a case of crime and he loses the appeal, he loses his life and all his possessions, as I have said elsewhere.

1746. We have spoken above of several cases of serious crime for which an appeal lies, and now we will speak of two other cases which can be proved on appeal. The first case is when someone breaks a truce or a guaranteed peace, and the offense cannot be shown to be a well-known fact; the suspects can be appealed against, for it is a case of crime and great treachery to do harm to a man who is confident because he thinks himself in a state of truce or guaranteed peace. The second case is to appeal against procurement, as when the appellant does not accuse the appellee of being present when the act was done, but that he had it done for a payment, or a promise, or on request, or by his orders; and I saw an appeal of this kind which occurred in the following manner.

1747. Pierre accused Jehan saying that the said Jehan by his procurement had had an uncle of his murdered; and he did not say in his claim that the said Jehan had been there in person; but he said that he had had it done, and that he had procured the doing of it; and to bolster his claim he gave a motive, for he said that the said Jehan had threatened that personal harm would come to him. To this Jehan replied that he was not obliged to answer, because the appellant had not stated in his claim that the appellee had been there in person when the act was done, and an appeal for having something done is not to be accepted; and if the judgment was that an appeal was proper, he offered to defend himself. And upon this they requested a judgment. At this judgment there was a big argument and some wanted to say that there was no wager; but at all events the upshot was that there *was* a wager, for a person who has something done has done enough {to support an appeal}, and he should have as great a punishment for having some serious offense committed as if he had committed it himself.

1748. A person who wants to appeal against someone else or several other persons for some case of serious crime must be careful how he makes the appeal; for if he wants to appeal against two or three or more, and he wants to wager battle against them all, he must appeal against only one in person and must have present in court some of his family to appeal against the others, so that each person appeals one on one; for if he appealed in person against all of them and they all offered to defend themselves, he would have to fight alone against all those he had appealed against; and we saw the following in the king's court with respect to this situation.

1749. A knight appealed against three other knights for a homicide done wickedly and treacherously: if they admitted it, he requested that they should be treated as guilty, and if they denied it, he offered to prove it by himself and others by wager of battle. To this the three appellees replied that they denied the fact and offered to defend themselves against the person who had challenged them in person in court; but as for his saying that he would prove it by others along with him, and that these others were not named in the appeal, they did not want him to be able to include in his wager any help other than himself, indeed they required,—since he was alone in making the appeal and had appealed against all three in the same serious case in which they had offered to defend themselves,—that he fight against them all three by himself without the help of anyone else. And upon this they requested a judgment.

1750. It was judged that the knight who was making the appeal would fight alone against the three, for no one can make an appeal on behalf of a person who is not present in court. And the day of battle was fixed, and before the day one of the three died, and the two others came to the court in armor and the appellant did so also; and after all the oaths and when there was nothing left but to join battle, peace was made. And by this judgment it can be seen that when you want to accuse and make a wager of battle against several persons for a crime, then each one should appeal his own adversary because of the above-mentioned danger.

1751. If it happened that someone had appealed against another for a serious crime, and before the battle someone from the lineage of the appellant, or several of them, appealed against others for this same case, the wager should be received, for several people can be guilty of one crime: and the law and custom should allow vengeance to be sought against all the guilty. It would be different if the last appellant waited so long to appeal that the first appeal was ended either by a battle or by peace, for then the last wager could not be accepted. And if it were otherwise, then the wagers for a single case could last for ever and this would not be reasonable.

1752. In appealing for a false judgment in the court where enfieffed men are the jurors, there is a certain way of appealing prudently. For it would be possible to appeal in such a way that the appellant would have to fight by himself all the men who had made the judgment, or in such a way that he would have to fight two or three but not all the men. And if you appeal wisely, you only need to fight one person; and an appeal can be made wrongly so that it is no good, and so that the appellant has to pay a fine for the insult made to the jury and the judgment; and you can see all these kinds of appeals in the following paragraphs.

1753. When someone appeals for false judgment and he waits until the judgment is pronounced and all the men have agreed with the judgment and the appellant says afterwards: "This judgment is false and wrong and I will prove it in this court or another wherever the law takes me," in such an appeal he would have to fight alone against all the jurors, if all the jurors offered to defend the judgment.

1754. If it happened that the person wishing to make the appeal for false judgment made such haste to appeal that there had as yet concurred in the judgment only two or three or more but not all the jurors, and he appealed in the manner described above, he would have to fight against all those who had concurred in the judgment but not with those who had not yet concurred in the judgment.

1755. A person who wants to appeal and to manage his appeal wisely, so that he has only to fight against one person, should, when he sees the jurors ready to give judgment (but before they say anything), speak in this manner to the lord who is presiding over the court: "Sire, I am to have a judgment today at the hearing. And I request that you have it pronounced by one of the jurors, and whatever judgment he prounounces, I request that you ask each man separately and in due time [*par loisir*], if he concurs with the judgment, so that I can see, if the judgment is against me and I wish to make an appeal, which one concurs with the judgment." And the court should grant this request. And then, when the judgment is pronounced by one of the jurors, and the second concurs, the appellant should not wait to make his appeal, but he should appeal against the person who concurs with the judgment, and he should speak in this way to the judge: "Sire, I say that this judgment which is pronounced against me, and in which Pierre has concurred, is false and wrong and dishonest; and I will prove it so against the said Pierre who has concurred in the judgment, either I myself or my man who can and should do so for me, as a person who had a legal excuse, which I will make known in the proper place in this court or another, wherever the law takes me because of this appeal." And when he has spoken thus, the vassal who is the appellee must say that the judgment is right and honest, and offer to confirm it, either he himself or by another who can and should do it because of his legal excuse, in this court or in another, wherever the law should take him. He should request that all the men should be asked if they concur in the judgment because his defense is better when they have all agreed. And then the judge should receive the wager and take a good surety from the appellant that he will pursue his appeal. But there is no need to take a surety from the person who defends the judgment, because he is his lord's man and, if he did not uphold the judgment, he would lose his right to judge and would have to pay a fine of sixty pounds to the lord. And also if the appellant does not prove the judgment to be wrong, he pays a fine of sixty pounds to the lord, and sixty pounds to the person against whom he appealed; and if he appealed against several of the jurors, he pays a fine to each one and each fine is sixty pounds, and for this reason it is right that he should give good security to the judge that he will pursue his appeal.

1756. When the wagers have been received, whether for a case of crime or for false judgment, the parties may not make peace without the consent of the lord.

1757. If someone appeals against the men who are the jurors in the court of one of the count's men, the wager should not be removed from that same court, and the lord should request the count to lend him some of his peers to help to continue the operations of his court, and the count should certainly grant this request to his man.

1758. When someone makes an appeal for false judgment in a suit for personal property or for chattels or for land, and the lord sees that the case in which the judgment was made has arisen many times and the custom is established and well-approved in the county, according to which custom it is clear that the judgment is right, he should not allow a wager of battle, but should make the appellant pay a fine for his insult to the court,—but this fine is only ten sous,—for it is not appropriate to make an appeal for {false} judgment in a suit for personal property or chattels or land, when the custom is well-approved. And if the lord allows the wager, and the men defend, then the count should stop the appeal because he should uphold customs and have them kept among his subjects. For if someone appealed a judgment that appears correct by the clear custom, there would be a danger, if the wager were allowed, that the custom would be ended [*corrompue*], for example if the appellant won the battle, and for this reason, such wagers should not be permitted.

1759. When someone appeals rashly, for example if he said: "This judgment is false and wrong," and he does not offer to prove it, the appeal is worthless, and he must pay a fine for the insult to the court and the fine is ten sous to the lord for an insult, if he is a gentleman, and if he is a commoner, five sous. But if a man is in the habit of speaking insultingly [*vilainement*], and he did so in our court, he would not get off without a prison term, for there are many who for so small a sum of money would not refrain from speaking calumny [*dire vilenie*] in court, and for this reason a prison term is properly employed in these cases.

1760. It is true that one man by himself cannot make a judgment anywhere in the county of Clermont, but two men can do it; and for this reason an appeal against the second is sufficient, as soon as he concurs with the judgment. Therefore if it should happen that any man in the county should wish to make a judgment all alone, the person against whom such a judgment is made should say: "Sire, I do not consider what you have said to be a judgment, when I see no one who can or should judge in this court who concurs with you, and I request that you give me a hearing by a group of jurors." And if the lord will do no more, the person should petition him correctly three times to appear fifteen days later in the presence of good men; and if the lord will do no more for him or he says he will do no more, and wants to execute his judgment, the person who has properly summoned him in the manner explained above will have a good appeal in the count's court for default of judgment.

1761. The appeals which are made for default of judgment are not and should not be pursued through a wager of battle, but by showing the reasons through which the default of judgment is clear; and these reasons must be affirmed by honest witnesses, if they are denied by the person who is appealed against for default of judgment. But when the witnesses appear in court to testify in such a case, by whichever party they are called, either by the appellant or by the appellee, those against whom they wish to give evidence can, if they wish, challenge the second witness and accuse him of being false and perjured. And in this way a wager can come about in an appeal which is made for default of judgment, in the manner we have described above, whereby whoever wants to appeal for false judgment must appeal against the first juror who agrees after the first juror who renders the judgment. And in the same way, a person who wants to challenge testimony should let past the first witness and challenge the second by wager, for the quarrel is not lost or won through one witness, but by two it would be, so that if he let pass the two witnesses and he appealed against the third or the fourth, the appeal would be worthless, if the first two witnesses had testified clearly against him, for to win a quarrel two good witnesses are worth as much as twenty.[14]

1762. A person who wants to appeal against testimony as false and perjured must be careful not to allow a witness to be sworn before the appeal, for if the oath were made and there had been no appeal, it would be proper for the witness to be believed about what he said in the case under oath. Therefore a person who wants to appeal against someone for false testimony, must say to the judge: "Sire, such-and-such a party has called witnesses against me; I request you to let me see each one swear the oath separately, so that I know who wants to give testimony and so that I can speak out against them or against one of them." And the lord should grant this request; and when the first has sworn the oath he should give his testimony before everyone, in cases where a witness can be challenged by a wager, for witnesses cannot be challenged in all cases, as you can see in the chapter on proofs {Chapter 39}. And when the first witness has sworn and given his testimony, if the testimony is against the person who wants to appeal, he should say, "Who is it that wants to swear an oath, and concur in the testimony by that oath?"[15] And as soon as the second man kneels down and puts his hand on the saints to swear the oath, the appellant should say to the judge, "This witness whom I see ready and prepared to give witness against me, I challenge his testimony as false and perjured, and if he admits it, I request you to treat him as he deserves, and to prevent him from testifying." And if the witness offers to defend himself, the wager should be received and treated according to what is said in the chapter on presentations {Chapter 64}.

1763. When wagers of battle are given and received by the judge in suits for real or personal property, the dispute for which the wager is given should remain in the state where it is at the point when the wager is given. And whatever the wager is for, good sureties should be taken to maintain the wager hand to hand [cors pour cors], and a person who cannot or will not give a surety must be kept in prison until the end of the dispute.

1764. If it happens that a witness who is challenged by a wager for false testimony (or his champion if he has a champion) is defeated, whether the battle is for personal or real property, he must have his hand cut off, the one who fights.[16] If the champion fights and is defeated, the person who was accused as a false witness is found guilty of false testimony, and he is at the will of the lord who may impose any fine he wants. And if the case for which he was challenged was a crime, he would lose his life along with the suit; and the same penalties that we have spoken of for the appellee should be suffered by the appellant, if he does not prove his contention.

1765. If someone's witness is proved false by a wager of battle, so that he is not allowed to give testimony, the person who called him as a witness cannot call another witness in that case, and has failed in his proof, and he must suffer this loss because he called a false witness, in addition to his fine which is at the lord's will.

1766. No one is obliged to give testimony for another in a case where there can be an appeal, and no one should be compelled to do so by any judge if he does not want to; and if he wishes to give testimony, he must have a good security, if he requests it, from the person who has called him as a witness, that the latter will indemnify him for all costs and all losses he has or might have because of his testimony. And by this surety, if he is appealed against, all the costs and damages of the appeal are paid by the person who has called him as a witness, and he must justify his witness. And if he does not want to step forward to justify his witness, then the person who is appealed against can be defended at the cost of the person who called him, by means of the security named above. But if he gave testimony *without having a security or a promise* from the person who called him, to recover costs and damages, and the person who called him then backed down, like a person who would rather lose the dispute than enter a wager of battle and justify his witness, the witness could well receive loss and damage, since he would have to demonstrate his own honesty, or else appear in his lord's eyes as a bad witness, and he would not recover his costs or damages from the person who called him; and for this reason everyone should be careful about becoming a witness in the case where a wager of battle lies.

1767. If any of the witnesses of a person who has to make proof by some means other than wager of battle are excluded, those who are excluded for good reason are not permitted to testify. But this does not mean that the person who called them cannot call others, unless he has elected not to use witnesses and the time has passed when he should have brought forward his proofs; and the reasons for which witnesses can be excluded by means other than a wager of battle can be seen in the chapter on proofs {Chapter 39 §§1170–1187}.

1768. Everyone, willing or not, must be forced by his judge, on a request to the judge, to bear witness in a case where there is no danger of a wager of battle, so that by the facts becoming known, quarrels come to an end, and everyone can receive a judgment. But in a case where there can be a wager of battle, a person who does not want to does not give testimony, as is said above; and for this reason it is good for a person who wants to give testimony for someone else to know in which cases there can be an appeal and in which there cannot, so that he can defend himself against a wager if someone should want to appeal against him, and you can see the cases in which there is no wager in the chapter which speaks of appellee's defenses {Chapter 63}.

1769. A person who is arrested as a suspect for a crime, and who is tried to see whether he has deserved death for the case for which he is held prisoner, if he is condemned by a judgment, cannot appeal against this judgment; for there are few or none who, if they were condemned to death, would not seek to appeal in order to save or prolong their lives, or to be out of jeopardy for their offense, and if it were allowed, many criminal acts would be poorly avenged.

1770. And that it is true that when he fights a squire can have an iron helmet with a visor, and the other arms which we have spoken of, appears from the battle which took place when we were writing this book, between my lord Renaut de Beaurein, and Gilot de la Houssoye in the Bois de Vincennes; for the knight claimed that the squire should not have such a helmet, nor a spear nor a shield, for he said that a squire who was fighting a knight did not rate such arms, especially when the squire had made the appeal. And the squire said in answer to this that indeed he did {rate such arms}, and that as the knight had a helmet that was covered with studs [*broches*] on the back, he requested that such a helmet be taken away from him; and he also said that the knight had appeared {only} at midday, and for that reason he wanted to have his appeal declared won; and Sir Renaut said against this that he had appeared within the time and in good time, and said that he *was* permitted to have such a helmet. And then they requested a judgment on the issue each party had moved.

1771. It was judged that the knight could have the helmet with *broches* and that he had appeared before midday had passed, meaning that he had come in time, and that the squire would fight in such armor as he had brought with him. And in this way they fought for about as long as it takes a man to walk a league, until the king[17] permitted peace to be made. And by this judgment it can be seen that what we said above about a squire's arms is true and that a person might well lose by default if he did not turn up before the hour of noon.

1772. We have seen an appeal for broken faith, of that faith which belongs to homage, in the following way, that the appellant said of his man that he owed him his faith because of his homage and that he had become his fellow-godfather [*compere*],[18] and afterwards he gave him into his safe-keeping [*baillie a garder*] his land and his wife, and he had treacherously seduced [*fortrete*] his wife, and had lain with her like a traitor, and he offered to prove it by a wager of battle if it were denied. And the appellee said in his defense that for such accusations he was not obliged to enter into a wager of battle because he was not accused of larceny, or robbery, or murder, and that it was not a case where treachery [*traïsons*] could be an element,[19] and he offered to defend himself if it was found that a wager was appropriate. And upon this they requested a judgment as to whether a wager of battle was appropriate or not.

1773. The judgment was that there was a wager. But now it might be asked which of these issues gave rise to the wager: whether for broken faith in the homage, which he was accused of, or because of the wife or the land which had been given into his safekeeping, or for the relationship [*comperage*] which there was between them. And we make a decision by saying in our opinion that if the appellant had complained only that the faith in the homage had been broken by doing so shameful a thing as seducing his wife, then there would be a wager; and if there had been no question of homage and he had given him his wife and his land into his safekeeping and the appellee had made such a poor job of the safekeeping, then he could have been accused of treachery [*traïson*]; but if the appellee had done no homage to the appellant, and if the latter had not given into his safekeeping his wife or his possessions, we do not agree there that the wager of battle would have been appropriate just because of the relationship [*comperage*]; and for this we believe that the wager was found appropriate because of the faith in the homage and for the safekeeping.

1774. A person who appeals for default of judgment or for false judgment should appeal before the lord from whom was held the court where the false judgment was given; for if he passed over him and appealed before the count or the king, the case would be remanded to the court of the person from whom the jurisdiction where the judgment was given was directly held, for appeals must be made from stage to stage, that is to say in the same way as the homage passes down, from the lowest to the next higher lord after, for example from the provost to the *bailli* to the king, in courts where provost and *bailli* give judgments [*jugent*]: just as the homages go down, the appeals must be made going up from stage to stage, omitting no lord. But it is not that way in the ecclesiastical courts if you do not want it to be, for from any judge you can appeal to the pope, and if you want you can appeal from stage to stage, for example from the dean to the bishop and from the bishop to the archbishop and from the archbishop to the pope.

1775. When someone has made an appeal for default of judgment or for false judgment, he must not be slow in pursuing his appeal, so as not to lose it through his default; for when an appellant does not pursue his appeal as he should, the judgment remains good, and the appellant is guilty of false appeal. And the time for pursuing appeals is this, that if you are appealing against the king's *bailli* for false judgment, you must pursue it at the first sitting of the *parlement* after the appeal, but it is not necessary to serve notice on the *bailli* if you do not want to, because they are under notice to appear at the *parlement* every day on which cases from their jurisdiction are discussed [*as jours de leur baillie*][20] to respond to all those who wish to complain about them; and if you want to appeal in the count of Clermont's court against the count's subjects, you must serve notice or summon the person or persons you want to appeal against at the first assize which falls, but there must be enough time for those served to have fifteen days or more after the notice has been served. And if the assize comes on so soon that they cannot have fifteen days, then you would have to wait for the following assize. And if the appellant does not proceed in this way, he can lose his appeal by default. And if he appeals in some court other than the count's court, for example in the court of one of his subjects,—for example, if it happens that the appellee holds from some lord below the count,[21]— because there is no assize {regular sitting} in their courts, the appellant must go to the lord before whom he is appealing and have notice served on the appellee; and he must require that the notice be given for an appearance within forty days of his apppeal or he will lose his appeal by default. And notwithstanding that notice has been served of the appeal, if the appellant has a legal excuse for ill health, he can be excused, and after that he can come back to pursue his appeal in a timely way.

1776. If it comes about that someone who should have appealed before one of the count's subjects passes him by and appeals before the count, or if he should have appealed before the count and he passes him by and appeals before the king, and the matter is sent back down to the count's court [*li cuens en ra sa court*] or to the count's subject's court, and the suit comes on, if the appellee wants to use as a defense that the appellant is too late to pursue his appeal in this court, this defense motion will not avail him, because the appellant came in time to pursue his appeal in the sovereign's court if he had been allowed to; for if the lower court had not requested that the matter be remanded, the appeal would have remained before the sovereign, and if the suit had been actually begun before the sovereign's court, the matter would not have been remanded. And each time a lower court has a matter remanded on request, the count must give the parties a hearing exactly as the matter stood before the sovereign. And no one can fine his subject or find him in default if he wants to plead his suit before his sovereign against someone other than his own lord. For if I bring suit against my lord in the sovereign's court for some crime, and I cannot get him convicted, I must be sent down to his court, and I have to pay him a fine according to the gravity of the case; and the nature of the fine is laid out in the chapter on offenses {Chapter 30}.

1777. If several persons have a suit on the same issue and the judgment goes against them and one of them wants to appeal and the others do not, if he has the judgment reversed the appellant has not because of this won everything that was at issue in the suit, but only his own share, had the judgment included both him and his fellow-litigants. And his fellow-litigants have not for this reason won what *they* had at issue, because they did not appeal, so that they lose,—even if the judgment was wrong,—because they failed to appeal.[22] For if the appellant had lost his appeal, his fellow-litigants would not have had to participate in the costs or damages, and the appellant could not have won more than what he had at stake in the dispute.

1778. Default of judgment is to refuse to give a hearing to a person who requests it. And it can come about in another way, for example, when the lords postpone the suits in their courts more than they may or should in contravention of the custom of the region. And the postponements that they, and also the vassals who give judgment, can claim are explained in the chapter which speaks about the postponements permitted by custom {Chapter 65}.

1779. We saw a suit by the citizens of Ghent against the count of Flanders in which the citizens of Ghent complained to the king against the count of Flanders for default of judgment; and the arguments having been put forward by each party, the judgment was that they had come too soon to appeal for default of judgment, for the count had offered to give them a hearing, and had not taken all the postponements he was entitled to (according to the custom of the region) before his subjects could appeal against him for default of judgment; and for this reason they were sent back to the count's court and the count was ordered to give them a hearing. And when they came into his court, he obliged them to pay a fine for having complained about him for default of judgment. And for the fine he seized and confiscated their property up to a value of forty thousand pounds [.XL^m. lb], and because of this the said citizens came back to complain to the king, asking for a judgment on this fine. And although the count could have had the matter remanded to his court if he wished, he agreed to have a judgment from the king's council as to whether he could and should levy such a fine. And upon this it was judged that he could and indeed should fine them that much and more if he wished; for if he had been found guilty of a default of judgment for which they had appealed against him, he would have lost the jurisdiction which he had over them and the power which he had to regulate them, and along with that they would have made him have to pay a great fine to the king. And if a person puts his lord in such jeopardy and cannot get him convicted, it is no wonder that the subject's fine is at the lord's discretion, according to the temporal goods he holds from him. And we have brought up this case so that those who want to appeal against their lord for default of judgment may see the danger that they risk if they cannot get their lord convicted.

1780. Everyone should know that in appellate suits, whether for default of judgment or for false judgment, whatever procedure is used, whether wager of battle or the regular procedure, the court where the appeal is being heard should proceed according to the custom of the place where the appeal was made and according to the custom which was current when the appeal was made: for example you see every day that if people from Arras or

Vermandois, or Beauvais, or other regions, plead before the king in Paris in various appeals which are made to him because of his sovereignty, or in other cases which are before him rather than the lower courts because of superior jurisdiction [*resort*]²³ the causes are not judged according to the custom of the Ile-de-France, which is current in Paris, but according to the custom of the district where the suit originated, or which *was* current in the district when the suit began; for {in that way} if the custom changed during the suit because of some new law, the parties would not be harmed by it. And what we have said about the king's court, we also say about all other courts to which you can come because of superior jurisdiction, just as jurisdictions and suzerainties are held one from another, from level to level.

Here ends the chapter on appeals, both for crimes and for other cases, and appeals for false judgment.

Notes

1. "Wager of battle" translates *gages de bataille*, which is a challenge made by one party to another to fight a judicial duel, in which the winner is supposed to be helped to victory by God. Louis IX had made an effort to prohibit the use of the wager of battle as a judicial procedure, but he was not completely successful; and Beaumanoir devotes a good deal of discussion to the wager as a means of appealing decisions in lower courts and of accusing persons who had committed crimes against the accuser's family. An appeal by wager of battle might thus be a first-level complaint brought against a defendant, with no preceding trial; despite this appearance of being a trial stage procedure, it is called an appeal because the commencement of the proceeding is made in the form of an appeal by one person against another. The parties are called *apeleres/apeleur* and *apelé(s)*, which I shall translate as "appellant" and "appellee" as in modern American appellate court usage.

2. Treachery or *traïson* does not imply some crime against the state but rather that the act was committed without forewarning (such as when two men are in a private war) and perhaps even in an ambush. The word is similar in meaning to *stealth*, which contains the notions of furtiveness and surprise. See §826.

3. Legal excuses or *essoines* included age, sickness, etc. See §1713 below.

4. Cf. §§923–24.

5. *Gages* means "deposit, security, caution money" and the *wager* accepted by the judge may have been a token, such as a glove or some other small object.

6. This probably means with shield and staff, *escu et baston*. Cf. Conon de Béthune's poem "Si voirement con cele don je chant":

Si va de moi con fait del champion
Qui de lon tens aprent a escremir,
Et kant il vient ou champ as cous ferir,
Si ne seit rien d'escu ne de baston.

(Ed. Axel Wallensköld [Paris: Champion, 1921] 4.)

7. King Louis' ordinance permitted a formal court proceeding instead of wager of battle when it was requested. See *Est.* 1: 487ff.

8. Defenses to a complaint are divided into two kinds, dilatory and peremptory. Dilatory issues tend only to prolong a suit, not to decide it. See §1725 below and Chapter 7.

9. For exceptions, see Chapter 7.

10. Cf. §917.

11. I have read Salmon as if there were a comma after the word *clerement* 'clearly.' Beugnot does have a comma at this point (Beugnot Chapter 61, §20).

12. For the *ronci de service*, see Chapter 28.

13. See §§1783-85.

14. This is true only if the proof is being made by only one party. Where both sides are making proof, the number of witnesses may be decisive. See §1257.

15. I have not followed here the punctuation of Salmon, which places the end quotation marks after the word *jurer* 'oath.' Beugnot does not use quotation marks to show a direct speech in this sentence.

16. This is the only place where Beaumanoir seems to say that a person *not* a champion might have his hand cut off. See §1721. It may be that the wording of this paragraph implies such a punishment only through inadvertence on Beaumanoir's part.

17. Beaumanoir identifies the time of the incident as about the time the book was being written (c.1280-83), so that the king must have been Philippe III, le Hardi. Although this king allegedly no longer allowed wagers of battle in his court, he evidently attended judicial battles fought in other courts, as this story testifies.

18. A kind of family relationship was established between those who were godfathers to the same child, and a man could not marry a woman who was godmother to a child of which he was the godfather. See §585. As shown in §1773, this relationship is not considered by Beaumanoir to have the same legal effect as homage or a bestowal of trust.

19. The defendant is relying on the kind of definition of *traïson* and *traitre* which is given in §826. However, the meaning of breaker of a solemn promise (such as to safeguard a person or a kingdom placed in one's care) was also current for *traïson* in Beaumanoir's time. See *La Mort le roi Artu*, ed. Jean Frappier, 3d ed., (Geneva: Droz, 1964), §§134, 165.

20. *As jours de leur baillie* could mean "when they are in office" but then the *bailli* would have to be in Paris every day, which is absurd. I have taken the word *jours* here to mean the court appearance, indicating that when cases from Clermont were discussed in the *Parlement* or appellate court in Paris, the local *bailli* would have to be present. This meaning is consistent with the rest of the section.

21. I have not followed Salmon's punctuation here, but preferred to end the parenthesis after *conte*.

22. Since the appeal has to be made immediately after the judgment, the others are too late to appeal and cannot use an offensive *res judicata*.

23. In §1776 Beaumanoir says that no one pays a penalty for going to a higher court to plead unless it is against his own lord. I have chosen to use the words "superior jurisdicton" to indicate that courts above the lowest one available to a plaintiff may also have jurisdiction over his suit. The Old French word for the superior jurisdiction of a higher court is *resort*.

62. Default of Judgment

Here begins the sixty-second chapter of this book which speaks of appeals for default of judgment and the way to petition your lord.

1781. We have spoken in the chapter before this one of three kinds of appeals, that is to say appeals made through a wager of battle, and appeals for false judgment which use standard procedure [*erremens de plet*] and appeals for default of judgment, for example when a hearing is refused or when you have petitioned [*sommé*] the person against whom you wish to appeal often enough for the appeal to lie. And we shall speak here some more about this last kind of appeal, namely default of judgment, for we have seen some lords use such bad faith toward those to whom they do not wish to give a hearing that you can hardly get them convicted of default of judgment. And those who need to appeal must be skillful [*soutil*] enough to petition adequately, so that they can get a hearing in the court where they are trying to obtain it, or else have a sure appeal for default of judgment. And because not all people are of the same condition, and some must petition differently from others those against whom they wish to appeal, we will speak briefly of the three kinds of people who must use different methods to petition those against whom they want to appeal, and what kind of a petition is appropriate for each.

1782. The first kind of persons are those who hold in fief and homage from others, and their lords do not want to give them a hearing, or they delay their hearings too long. These people, if their lord has taken possession of their land, or seized or confiscated it, or is preventing them from enjoying it, should ask their lord to give it back or permit a reclamation[1] and schedule a court appearance in their court, and give them a hearing by their peers; and anyone can make this request to his lord, in whatever jurisdiction he finds him. And when he makes this request, he should take with him at least two of his peers; and if they will not come at his request, he must ask the king or the baron holding directly from the king to command his peers to go with him, at his cost, each time he needs them, every fifteen days, to observe how he petitions his lord. And then if the request is made outside the lord's jurisdiction, and the lord answers in bad faith: "Come to my court and make whatever request you want to me there, and I will give you a hearing," then his man should ask him to assign a day, and should say he will gladly go to his court and ask for his release or his reclamation, and that he wants a hearing [*et drois li soit fes*]. Then if the lord wants to schedule an appearance more than fifteen days later, and he is holding something in his possession, or he has seized something, so that the petitioner could incur expenses and damages, the latter need not accept this scheduled court appearance unless he wants to; and if he does not want to accept that day, he must petition for an earlier [*avenant*] {lit. "convenient"} date (because he might be caused damages by the delay), and if the lord will not agree, the current appearance must be counted as one of the lord's defaults.

1783. We have said elsewhere in this chapter[2] that every time that vassals holding from some lord in fief want to appeal against them for default of judgment, they must petition them three times at different appearances [*journees*], and along with this we say that there must be at least fifteen-day intervals between the appearances, and we have said above how the lord can be in default for one of those appearances.

1784. The second way is if the man makes the above petition and the lord says nothing, not wanting to answer whether he will comply with his request {give him his hearing} or not, or he fraudulently claims to be busy, pretending he cannot deal with him. If this can be testified to by the peers, it should also be counted as a default day, for a lord is in default of judgment who does not condescend to answer his man when he is asking for a hearing.

1785. The third way in which the lord can be in default of judgment toward his vassal is if he bargains with [*convenance*] him or assaults him [*fet vilenie de son cors*] for asking for a hearing. And for this kind of default, it is not necessary for the vassals to petition their lord on three different days, for if they were assaulted or struck on their first appearance, it would be hard for them to go to another; and for this reason once such a thing is made known to the sovereign he should take possession of the property and have the lord summoned to appear and answer his man, without sending the case back down or giving back cognizance, and then give a hearing according to the pleadings, and first of all give safeguards to the person who was threatened. And we have adequately discussed in this chapter the other ways in which lords can be found in default of judgment toward their vassals in fief in matters involving their fief.

1786. Now we will discuss the second kind of people who need to petition their lords until they can sue them for default of judgment because they are not given a hearing: these are people who are their tenants [*oste*], residing in their jurisdiction, or who hold villeinages the cognizance of which belongs to the lords. Such persons can appeal against their lords for default of judgment more quickly than can holders of fiefs, for they are not required to petition in the presence of their peers (since they have none) and they are not required to petition at fifteen-day intervals; it is enough if they can show that their lords have defaulted three times on three different days, before good people who can testify to the default in the right time and place. And all the avenues by which vassals holding in fief can have their lords found in default are open to those holding in villeinage, for they are supposed to give them hearings as well as the others; and the reason why the petition process is longer for gentlemen than for those holding in villeinage is because of the promise given by the one to pay homage to the other; for in order to keep your promises [*foi garder*] to your lord, you must make it very plain that you are suing him for default of judgment. And in addition to the problem of the promises, there is a great danger of loss, for if the lord is convicted of default of judgment, he loses his man's homage and must pay a great fine, such as we have explained elsewhere in this chapter;[3] and if the vassal cannot get his lord convicted, he loses his fief and it reverts to the lord.

1787. If it happens that a lord has confiscated or taken some of his vassal's property, and afterwards,—before the man has asked him to give it back or permit a reclamation or give him a hearing,—the lord leaves the district to reside in another castellany, what can the man do, since it would be hard for him to have to sue his lord in a foreign land or a castellany other than the one from which the fief is held? Therefore if such a case arises, the man should find out if the lord has left in his place someone who has as great a right to give a hearing as the lord would have if he were there; and he should make his request to the person, and petition him in the presence of his peers in the manner described above, as you should petition your lord. And if he is refused a hearing by the person left in his place by the lord, and if he defaults often enough for an appeal to lie, the man can appeal against him for default of judgment as if the lord were present; and for this and other dangers lords should be very careful what persons they leave in their place to take care of their jurisdictions.

1788. When a lord has confiscated or seized some property belonging to his vassal and then gone away to live in another castellany, or he goes out of the district, or if he already lived in another castellany before he confiscated the man's property, and he leaves no one in his place whom the man can ask to give him back his property and give him a hearing, in such a case the man should make an appearance before the lord from whom his own lord holds the jurisdiction which allows him to make confiscations, and should explain to the overlord in his complaint that his lord has confiscated his property, so that he dares not take the profits from it [*esploitier*], and that he does not know whom to ask for a hearing, for his lord is not in the district, and has left no one in his place, so that he is incurring losses every day, for which reason he asks for his lord to be compelled to give him a hearing. In such cases the overlord should summon the lord of the plaintiff to a hearing in fifteen days, and if he appears, his man can make his request to him there in the presence of the overlord from whom he holds, for him to give back his property, or permit him to make a reclamation of it and proceed to a hearing; and if he will not, he should ask him to stay in the place, or appoint someone to take his place, so that he can petition that person in a proper place; and if he will not, but goes away without appointing a man in his place to give a hearing (or he promises to and then does not), in that case he can be found in default of judgment, and his vassal or his subject has a good appeal against him.

1789. If someone has his lord summoned before his overlord, because some of his property has been taken or seized and so that he can ask him to give it back or permit a reclamation and give him a hearing, and the lord defaults or takes a continuance, then the overlord should take the property into his possession so that if the man's property was seized and not forfeited, he should permit a reclamation until his man (the plaintiff's lord) appears; and when he appears, his lord's sureties will answer concerning the things which were seized if he has been awarded them in a judgment, or otherwise not, for a reclamation which is permitted by the sovereign because of the lord's default should last until it is known if the seizure was made for a good reason. And if the lord has taken as forfeit his man's property, and afterwards defaults or takes a continuance as was said above, in that case the overlord cannot permit a reclamation since the property is forfeit; but he should proceed more strictly in another way, for it might seem that it was in bad faith that the person did not want to appear concerning the property he had taken as forfeit [*levé*]; and for this reason the overlord should distrain him by putting guards on his property, and by seizing and confiscating [*lever*] what he holds from him until he appears and permits his man to make a reclamation of what he confiscated [*leva*] from him, or until he gives a good reason why he is not obliged to permit a reclamation. And he should take care, for if he is in default three times in a suit against his man in the sovereign's court, the things he took or seized from his man must be given back to the man unconditionally, for a lord can lose against his man by defaulting when he is summoned to the overlord's court just as the man can in a suit against his lord.[4]

1790. Every time someone needs to petition his lord so that he can later sue him for default of judgment, if there are no peers he can take with him,—for example if there is only one (and he needs at least two); or there are none; or there are several but they are out of the district or they have a legal excuse [*essoine*] for not accompanying him,—in all these situations the man should ask the overlord to send him some men at the petitioner's expense; and in the presence of those sent he can petition his lord, for this is the way to petition your lord for those who have no peers available.

1791. We have spoken of two kinds of persons who need to petition some lord so that they can later sue him for default of judgment, that is to say those who hold fiefs and those who do not (but who do hold tenancies [*ostises*] or villeinages, for which they have to answer to their lord from whom they hold). Now we will speak of a third kind of person who sometimes needs to appeal against some lord for default of judgment: those who are neither vassals nor tenants, and who hold nothing from those they want to sue for default of judgment, but who are plaintiffs in their courts against some of their subjects for the payment of debts, or for real property, or on some agreement. And we can say that this kind of person can much more easily sue for default of judgment, if a proper and speedy hearing is not given to them, than can those who hold in fief or villeinage from the lord against whom they want to appeal, for those who hold from a lord owe him respect and obedience for what they hold from him, but those who hold nothing owe no such thing. Therefore we say that if they can obtain a speedy hearing according to the custom of the district they should do so;

and if it is refused them a single time, or the lord delays the hearing for longer than custom allows, or the lord has threatened them or says he will do no more for them, in all these cases those who were requesting a hearing against the lord's subject can hale their adverse party before the overlord; and then if the {lower} lord who refused to give a hearing or who did not do what custom requires, wants to have the case sent down, then the plaintiffs, to prevent the case from going down, should show that they have applied to his court to the point where because of default of judgment they have appeared before the overlord; and they should explain the default and prove it if it is denied by the lord who wants the case sent back down. And because we have said that everyone who wants to sue somebody for default of judgment must allow to pass the delays permitted by custom, we will make a special chapter so that those who need to appeal for default of judgment or false judgment know how long they must wait before they can have a good [*resnable*] appeal {Chapter 65}.

1792. Some lords find it difficult to give judgments in their courts because they have no vassals, or because they have too few. Nevertheless they should not lose their jurisdiction for this reason, but there is a sure way {to keep it} which we have seen approved in a judgment. For they can request their own lord to lend them some men, at their expense, to give them advice [*conseiller*] in making a judgment, and the lord should do this; and then the lord can give a judgment in his court in the presence of the men the overlord has lent him.[5] But he should be careful because if there is an appeal for default of judgment or false judgment, the danger of the appeal falls on him and not on the men the lord lent him. Even though the overlord's men were lent to him to advise him, they are not required to give the judgment, unless they rashly undertake to do so, for if they voluntarily gave a judgment, they could be appealed against for false judgment, and they would have to defend it; and if they do not want to give a judgment, it is the responsibility of the lord to whom they were lent, as we have said above.

1793. When there is some poor lord who has no men who can act as jurors in his court, and who does not borrow some of his peers either because he is too poor, or too lazy, or because his lord will not lend him any (even though he should not refuse him), he cannot give a judgment all by himself; and for this reason the suits should go up to the court of the overlord who has vassals able to give judgments, for no one is obliged to plead in a court where a judgment cannot be made in the dispute in which he is pleading.

Here ends the chapter which shows how you should petition your lord before you can appeal against him for default of judgment.

Notes

1. For reclamations, see Chapter 53.
2. Actually in the previous chapter, §§1739, 1741.
3. Again, actually in the previous chapter, §1745.
4. The words *lever, prendre,* and *saisir* are used apparently interchangeably in this paragraph, although at one point *saisir* and *lever* are contrasted.
5. This rule seems to contradict the rule given elsewhere by Beaumanoir that vassals do not give judgments alone in their courts (§24).

63. Defenses

Here begins the sixty-third chapter of this book, which discusses what defenses are valid for those who are appealed against to avoid the battle and the cases where the wager of battle should not be accepted.

1794. For a person who is appealed against there are several defenses [*resons*] available such that if he can demonstrate one of them, there is no appeal.

1795. The first defense is if a woman has appealed against him, and she has not named a substitute in her appeal. The appeal is invalid, for a woman may not fight.

1796. The second defense is where a married woman makes the appeal without the authorization of her husband: the appeal is invalid, for without the permission of her husband a woman cannot go to court to appeal in such a case; but she may be appealed against, whether her husband wishes it or not.

1797. The third defense is if the appellant does not belong to the lineage of the person concerning whom he is making the appeal; for it is not allowed to appeal for any person except oneself or one's lineage or one's liege lord.

1798. The fourth defense is when the appellee has already been appealed against in the same case, and the judgment was in his favor; for otherwise the appeals would never end if those of the same lineage could appeal one after another for the same action after the appellee had won the first appeal on a judgment.

1799. The fifth defense is if the appellant is a male or female serf, and for two reasons: the first is that a serf is not allowed to fight a free person; the second reason is that the serf's lord could remove him from the court at whatever stage of the case he found him in, and this would be true even if he had already taken up the shield and the staff to fight.

1800. The sixth defense is if the appellant is a clerk, for he cannot assume obligations in a secular court except concerning his temporal possessions. A bigamous clerk[1] we do not consider to be a clerk, for he has returned in all things to the secular jurisdiction, and for this reason he can be an appellant or an appellee; but a clerk cannot appeal; for he cannot assume obligations in a secular jurisdiction nor renounce his privilege.

1801. The seventh defense is if the appellee is a clerk, for he does not have to respond in a secular court,—even if he should wish to pursue the wager of battle,—for the judge should not allow him into the suit after he knows that he is a clerk, for the honor of Holy Church, and because his ecclesiastical judge [*ordinaire*] would take him out of the secular court at whatever stage of the case he found him in that court.

1802. The eighth defense is if the appellee has been appealed against in the court of the sovereign for suspicion of having committed the action on which the {second} appeal is made, and he came to court to get a judgment [*pour prendre droit*] and was kept in prison and the sovereign caused it to be generally known and announced at the assizes that he was keeping this man in prison on suspicion of such-and-such a crime, and that if anyone was prepared to step forward {and make an accusation} he was ready to give a hearing; and then he was released from prison by a judgment since no one came forward to accuse him of anything and because the fact was not well-known enough for him to be convicted by a judgment: for it would be a bad thing if he could be haled back into court for a case from which he had been released by a judgment of the sovereign.

1803. The ninth defense is where the offense for which the appeal is made has not occurred; for example, if the appellant said that someone had killed his relative Pierre and it was shown that the said Pierre was still alive, for an appeal which is not truthful is not to be accepted, and this kind of appeal is called frivolous [*auvoire*], and frivolous appeals are like jokes which are brought to trial.

1804. The tenth defense is if the appellant says that the appellee did something on such-and-such a day, and in such-and-such a place and at such-and-such a time, and it is proved that the appellee was at that moment so far from the place that it is certain that he could not have been present at the occurrence; for the appeal is considered frivolous [*en bourde*], as was said above.

1805. The eleventh defense is where the appellant is a bastard, and the appellee is a free man, for a free man does not have to do battle with a bastard; but if both appellant and appellee are bastards, the appeal is good.

1806. The twelfth defense is if peace has been made concerning the occurrence for which the appeal is made and the appellant assented to the peace; and if he did not assent to the peace and he made peace with several of the relatives closest to the dead person, and the peace was confirmed by the sovereign's court [*justice souveraine*], the peace is good. And if it is not made by sovereign justice the appeal is good, for if the sovereign knows that peace has been made for a serious offense where someone has undertaken to give money or money's worth, or perform a task, for example going on a pilgrimage, or some other task, a sovereign can consider that person as *prima facie* guilty.

1807. The thirteenth defense is when someone is appealed against for homicide and the dead person, before he died, named those who had killed him, and declared innocent the appellee; and to make this case clear, we will tell what we saw on this issue in the court of Compiègne.

1808. Pierre appealed against Jehan saying that the said Jehan by his action or his deed or by his procurement had murdered an uncle of his. And Jehan replied that he did not want to be obliged to defend himself on this appeal by battle unless a ruling said he had to; for he said that the person because of whom he was appealed against, before he died, some of his relatives, and other people, came to him and asked him who had done this thing {syntax imitated from Beaumanoir}, and he said that Guillaume and Thomas and Robert had done it to him; he was asked if Jehan had any guilt in the matter, and he said no; and whereas he had been declared innocent by the very person about whom the appeal was made, and who had accused others by their names, Jehan requested that the appeal should be annulled. And on this issue they requested a judgment.

1809. It was judged that after Jehan had been declared innocent [*descoupés*] by the person for whose sake the appeal had been made, and others accused, there was no wager of battle against the said Jehan. But if it had happened that the person on whose behalf the appeal was made had *not* named those who had done it to him, or had not declared anyone innocent, the appeal was good; and if he had declared Jehan innocent, and had not wanted to say who had done it to him, as when it happens that someone forgives the person causing his own death for the sake of God, this would not have prevented the appeal from being good, for the pardon of the person who is killed[2] for such a bad reason does not remove from his relatives the possibility of seeking vengeance for the action by an appeal, nor of engaging in a private war if the action [*li fes*] is against gentlemen who can wage war.

1810. The fourteenth defense is when the appellant or appellee is under the age of fifteen years, for it would be a bad thing to allow children into a wager of battle before they reach an age where they should know the danger which there is in a wager of battle. And in many districts they have to be older still; and by our custom I believe they should have a substitute until they are twenty years old.

1811. It is true that when there is a private war between gentlemen for some action, and someone in the lineage makes a wager of battle on this action, then the private war stops, for it is clear that vengeance [*venjance*] for the offense is being sought through the courts, and for this reason the war must stop. And should anyone during the pendency of this suit do harm to someone, he would be punished according to his act as if there had been no war; and when the wager of battle is over, either because the appellee is discharged by a judgment or because the wager is carried out in a battle, the lineages cannot and must not subsequently make war; and if they make war over the action about which the wager was made and they harm each other, they should be tried according to the offense as if there had never been any private war.

1812. The fifteenth defense of the appellee is when the appellant himself is convicted by public knowledge of the matter on which he is appealing: for example if Pierre appealed against Jehan for the homicide of one of his relatives or for a larceny, and it was a well-known thing that the said Pierre himself had committed or procured the committing of the homicide or the larceny, it would not be law or reason that he should be able to displace the offense on to someone else; for everyone who is accused and convicted by public knowledge of a crime would be glad to make a wager of battle to avoid being punished for the offense. But we mean in this case that the facts [*li fes*] must be quite clearly against the appellant, for where there was a *presumption* against him, if the thing was not clear and obvious, he could get a wager of battle; and you can understand this clearly by what follows, which is what we saw in the court of Compiègne.

1813. A woman was required by the *bailli* to tell him what she had done with a child of hers, for it was common knowledge that she had been pregnant and she had been heard in labor, and it was not known what had happened to the child. The woman answered that her mother had taken the child when it was born. The mother was summoned into court, and the judge asked what she had done with this child. And the mother answered that it was true that she had received the child from her daughter, and she said she had given it to a young man who was the father; and she stated against this young man in court that he had contracted with her that he would take the child to a wet nurse in a good and sure place, for which (according to him) he had already made the arrangements. And, if he admitted this, she demanded that he should produce the child; and if he denied that she had given him the child, she offered to prove it by a wager of battle, either herself or by a substitute which she was permitted, being a woman. The young man replied that he was not obliged to make a response to the woman on the accusation because she admitted that she had received the child; and as she did not show or identify [*ne moustroit ne enseignoit*] the child, according to him it appeared that she was guilty of the child's death; and she could not, nor should she, make a wager of battle against some one else for something of which she was herself guilty; and if the ruling were to say that this defense was not available to him, he offered to defend himself, and denied that she had ever given him the child. And on this issue they requested a judgment.

1814. It was judged that the defense of the young man against the wager of battle was not a good one; for although there was against the woman a strong presumption of the death of the child, nevertheless the facts were not so clear or so apparent that the woman could be punished especially when she said that she had given the child to the young man as the father of the child. And by this judgment it can be seen that an appellee who advances the defense that the appellant is guilty of the offense for which the appellee is being appealed against, the thing must be very clear or well-proved, and then the defense would be valid {syntax copied from Beaumanoir}.

1815. It can happen that a thief commits a larceny and he gives the thing that he stole to someone else to carry through bad faith for a fee or at his request. Afterwards the stolen object is tracked down and the person who is carrying it and has it in his possession is arrested. When this person finds himself under arrest he says that a certain person gave the thing to him and this other person denies it. Now we need to know whether the person who is arrested with the stolen object in his possession can obtain a wager of battle against the person whom he accuses of giving it to him to carry, for the person who is appealed against for handing the object over says to the judge that the person who was arrested in full possession of the stolen object is convicted of the offense by common knowledge; and when he is guilty he cannot and should not accuse someone else but he should get the punishment for the offense. And now we say that when such a case occurs, or a case like this one, that the reputation of the parties should carry great weight, which means that if the person who is arrested in possession is of good reputation and is willing to wait for the inquest, and the person who is supposed to have given him the stolen object to carry is of bad reputation, or he does *not* want to wait for the trial, the wager should be accepted. And also if the person who is arrested in possession is of bad reputation, and the other person who he says gave him the stolen object to carry is of good reputation, the wager should not be accepted but instead the person who has been arrested in possession should be punished for the larceny. And if they are both of bad reputation, or neither one wants to wait for the trial, the wager may be allowed, for it does not matter which one loses. And if they are strangers, so that their reputation cannot be known, the wager is to be accepted, for it happens every day that strangers wandering through the area have their burdens carried by someone else, so that if the stranger committed a larceny and he had the booty carried by a stranger, if the wager were not accepted, it could happen that the person who was innocent of the larceny might be hanged. And if each one is of good reputation, and is willing to wait for the trial, once again the wager is to be accepted; for it often happens that certain people are considered good who are not good, and one of them *must* have committed the larceny. And if it should happen that the person who is arrested in possession of the stolen object cannot find or have arrested the person who gave him the stolen object to carry, and along with this the arrestee is of good reputation, the stolen objects should be restored to their owner and the person who has been arrested should be discharged. But if he cannot find the person who gave him the object and he has not been able to exclude any witnesses, he must be punished for larceny, and for this reason everyone should be careful about receiving something belonging to someone else.

1816. Now we need to know,—if the person who is arrested in possession and has had arrested the person who is supposed to have given the thing to him, and this person denies giving him the object, and the person who is arrested in possession wants to prove by good witnesses that the other person gave it to him, and the person who is accused of this wants to challenge one of the witnesses for perjury,—whether the wager {against a witness} is to be accepted in such a case. We say no, and that there should be no wager accepted against the witnesses in such a case; and for this reason: the person who is arrested has two ways of making his proof: either by a wager or by witnesses. But if he has chosen one of these methods of proof, he cannot use the other. It would be as if he said: "I want to make a proof through witnesses and if I cannot prove it that way I offer to prove by wager of battle." If he did not prove his case through witnesses, he could not go back to the use of a wager but instead would be punished for larceny.³

1817. The sixteenth defense is when a leper appeals against a healthy man, or when the healthy man appeals against a leper: the leper can say in his defense that he is outside of earthly law [*la loi mondaine*] and that he is not obliged to answer in a wager of battle; and if the leper appeals against a healthy man, then the more so can the healthy man defend himself by saying he is not obliged to answer a leper in such a matter.

1818. The seventeenth defense is when someone appeals in a matter where no appeal lies: for example, when someone wants to appeal against the judgment of arbitrators, for there is no appeal against such judgments; or when jurors are making a recall from memory of a judgment because of the disagreement of the parties, for in recall from memory there is no appeal; or in a dower case, for there is no appeal in dower; or in the case of an ecclesiastical suit [*plet d'eglise*], or a personal suit against a privileged person [*persone privilegiee*], for there is no appeal against them on a personal {non-property} matter (although if the suit concerns real or personal property there can be a wager if you want to challenge the witnesses). And in minor matters wagers are not to be accepted, that is for matters of twelve deniers or less; or in suits on the real property of underage orphans, whether they are plaintiff or defendant, there can be no wager, because their rights must be preserved without any loss through wager of battle. Thus in all these kinds of suits you must use the regular procedure [*plet ordené*] with no wager of battle.

1819. You cannot appeal in all cases or have a wager of battle, but there is no case which you cannot appeal on grounds of false judgment or default of judgment, when you have been refused a hearing, or when you have sufficiently petitioned the lord who should give the hearing or have it given by his men, and he is in default more often than the usage and custom of the place allow. And how you can appeal for default of judgment is explained in the chapter which talks about the delays permitted by custom {Chapter 65} and in the chapter which speaks about this {i.e., default of judgment, Chapter 62}. And the cases which should be exempt from wagers are those which are listed in what follows.

1820. The cases already mentioned, and those which arise from re-demption,[4] should be exempt from wagers of battle, for if you could exclude witnesses who are called to prove the lineage and the side of the family [*eritage*] of the person who wants to redeem, a poor man would scarcely be able to redeem property which is sold out of his lineage, for fear that the buyer would make a wager of battle against him.

1821. The second case where a wager of battle should not be accepted is concerning things left by a will, things which are to be paid by the execu-tors; for it would be a bad thing if the executors spent on the appeal the things which should be devoted to the good of the soul of the person who made the will. Therefore, if someone wishes to challenge a will or any part of a will, he must use a different procedure than wager of battle, for example by showing that the will was not legally made, or that the thing that was left did not belong to the person who made the will. And if the executors were so crazy that they wanted to accept the wager of battle, or if they had already done so, the judge should not allow it, for everyone is supposed to assist in the accomplishment of the wishes of those who make their will, as we would wish our own wills to be executed after our death. And it is a great sin to obstruct the execution of wills which are legally made. And how you should make a will is explained in the chapter which speaks about wills {Chapter 12}.

1822. The third case in which a wager should not be accepted is in cases of dower, for the privilege of women who hold in dower is so precious [*est si frans*] that their dower should be reserved and guaranteed to them without delay. And how you can begin a suit which is for or against dower is explained in the chapter which speaks of dower {Chapter 13}. However, although we have said that in suits for dower or redemption there should be no wager of battle, this means when the appellees wish to avoid the wager, for if they wish they can certainly renounce this right and proceed to the wager of battle; and if they wish, they can use a defense and avoid the wager by custom, provided it is before the wager has been accepted. Yet in suits on wills a wager is not to be accepted either before or after.

1823. The fourth case in which a wager of battle should not be accepted is when a suit arises from real estate belonging to the church, for the rights of Holy Church should be peacefully preserved without wager of battle, so that those who are particularly expected to serve God should not be obstructed by such a troublesome suit as a wager of battle. Nevertheless we have in a few cases seen a wager against the church, for example when some prelate who has jurisdiction over what he holds from Holy Church wants to accuse of being a serf a person who claims to be free, and in proving whether he is a serf or free we have seen wagers arise from a challenge to witnesses. Nevertheless if the prelate had wanted to prove merely by the lineage and nothing more, and had wanted to refuse the wager of battle, we believe that there would have been no wager; but the prelate proceeded into the wager without making use of any defense which could prevent the wager; and we believe that it was for this reason that the wager stood.

1824. The fifth case in which wagers should not be accepted when a party wishes to offer a defense against them is in a suit for novel disseisin, for the rule of novel disseisin is that the person who is found to be seised in unchallenged possession a year and a day should be maintained in possession; but when the case of ownership comes on, then wagers are possible. Nevertheless when it happens that each party says that he is the person in most recent peaceful possession for a year and a day, and each party brings witnesses to prove this and one of the parties wants to challenge a witness and the other party does not contest this but agrees to have a wager of battle, the count, to whom the cognizance of novel disseisin belongs, may allow the wager or not allow it, at his discretion.

1825. The sixth case in which a wager of battle is not to be accepted is when someone who has been appointed a guardian or a trustee of minor children is in a suit to maintain the rights of the minor child, because all minor children are by law and custom in the guardianship of the sovereign and everything which is in the guardianship of the sovereign must be safely maintained without involving such great costs as are necessary for an appeal by wager of battle. Nevertheless a person who is holding property in custodianship for a minor child can if he wishes wager (and lose) in the suit the gain which should come to him because of his custodianship; but when the child comes of age he does not fail to come into his inheritance because of the suit of the person who held it in custodianship. And if the person holding in custodianship wishes, he can avoid a wager of battle even though the other party wants to have it. And if those who hold in guardianship or custodianship or in dower or as trustees or on a lease for a term of years wanted to have a wager of battle in some suit which arose from any of these things, the persons against whom they are in the suit can avoid the wager of battle if they wish to, because, since those who hold for the reasons mentioned above can avoid a wager of battle, it is reasonable that those against whom they are in the suit should have the same advantage, for otherwise the law would favor one side over the other.

1826. The seventh case in which there is no appeal is a case which can be proved by recall from memory, and the cases which can be proved by recall from memory are enumerated in the chapter on proofs;[5] and the reason why a wager of battle cannot and should not arise is because each person could relitigate what he had lost in a judgment made against him; for if a person appeals for false judgment he must appeal as soon as the judgment has been made, and if he leaves the court without appealing the judgment he loses his {chance to} appeal and the judgment is good. And if he could appeal for a false recall from memory, he could make good this loss: since a long time after the judgment he could have it said that the judgment was made differently, and thus there would be a recall from memory and when the recall was being made he would challenge one of those recalling and thus he would have recovered by the use of sharp practice what he had lost by allowing the judgment against him to pass unchallenged; and for this reason we believe that in a matter which can be proved by recall from memory there should be no wager of battle.

1827. The eighth case in which a wager of battle should not be accepted (if a party wants to challenge it) is when someone requests something according to an obligation made in writing, when all defenses to the writing have been stipulated away in the writing, except in a single case; for if a person challenging the writing said that it had been falsely and improperly obtained without him and without his assent, or by forgery of the seal, in this case there could be a wager of battle, for the person who wanted to use the writing would have to remove this challenge to his good faith; and there still could be several reasons why there might be no wager of battle, for example if the writing was sealed with the court's seal, or the seal of the sovereign lord of the person obligating himself, for the authentic seals would show the writing to be genuine, so that there would be no wager but instead the challenger would have to pay a fine to the lord and the other party for the slander which he had said against the writing; and if he still wanted to appeal, he could not, as we have said, against the party; but he could appeal by wager of battle against the lord who sealed it by saying that he had sealed it falsely and dishonestly for money or for some {other} bad reason. And if the writing has been sealed with the seal of the person who wants it declared false, he cannot appeal,—if he has made the stipulation mentioned above,—unless he accuses him {the other party} of forging his seal. And if he accuses him of forging it, and the other party can prove by two honest witnesses that they were present at the sealing or that they heard him admit that he had sealed it, or that they were present at the making of the contract which the writing deals with, there is no wager, but instead the challenger pays a fine for his slander. And between gentlemen these fines are sixty pounds and damages to the party, and between commoners the fines are at the lord's discretion.

Here ends the chapter on appellees' defenses and of the cases in which a wager of battle should not be accepted.

Notes

1. The *clercs bigames* were clerks who had remarried or who had married a widow. Pope Gregory X (1271–76) took away their privileges as clerks.
2. For *qui l'en ocist* I read *que l'en ocist*. Beugnot has *qui* also.
3. This paragraph is somewhat confusing, for there are two accuseds, and the one challenging the witness has not chosen to make a proof through witnesses. But perhaps it is enough that he has not made a wager of battle when first accused himself.
4. For redemption, see Chapter 44.
5. See §§1150–53, 1208, 1226, 1233, and 1818.

64. Judicial Battles

Here begins the sixty-fourth chapter of this book which speaks of presentations, how wagers should be handled, and the things that follow up to the end of the battle.

1828. There is great danger in a suit which is carried on by wager of battle, and both appellant and appellee have to proceed very carefully in such a case. And for this reason we will discuss in this chapter the presentations which should be made after the wagers have been accepted[1] and how the participants should behave up to the end of the battle.

1829. When wagers have been accepted by the judge and the judge has assigned them a day on which to appear as they should, the appellee and appellant should pay attention to their estate, so that the appellant, if he is a gentleman and is appealing against a commoner, must take care not to appear on horseback and armed like a gentleman, for he should appear on foot in a champion's dress. And if he appears on horseback and armed as a gentleman, and the commoner [*païsans*] against whom he is appealing appears on foot like a champion, the gentleman is the worse off: for since he loses his arms in which he appeared, once he is disarmed he stands there just in his shirt, and he must fight this way, without armor, shield, or staff. And the truth of this is approved by a judgment which was made in Crépy,[2] and because this book speaks particularly of the customs in Beauvais, it does not mean that a case from a neighboring castellany does not confirm a rule, if there is no memory of such a case in Beauvais itself. For if a case came to judgment in Clermont for which no custom could be found because such a case had never arisen, the judgment would be made according to the customs of the neighboring castellanies where the case *had* been judged.

1830. Pierre, who was a gentleman, appealed against Jehan, who was a commoner. On the day for the presentations, after the wager had been accepted, and on the day which had been assigned to them to appear as they should {for the battle}, both parties presented themselves witlessly, for the squire came forward, on horseback, armed like a gentleman, and the commoner appeared on foot, in his tunic with no arms but shield and staff.[3] Jehan, who was on foot, said that Pierre who had appealed against him had come forward in armor in which he could not fight; and he requested that the armor be taken away from him and that he should fight on foot without weapons, as a person who had come forward without proper arms to fight against him according to the appeal. To this Pierre answered that he had come forward properly {armed}, for he was a gentleman and should fight with a gentleman's weapons, and he demanded that the battle begin. And in addition he requested that Jehan should have no other arms than the ones in which he had come forward, that is to say his tunic, his shield, and his stick and nothing more. And on this they requested a judgment.

1831. It was judged that Pierre would lose the arms and the horse as penalties to the lord and would fight in the condition he was in when the arms were removed, that is to say in his shirt, without shield or staff, and likewise Jehan would fight the said Pierre in his coat of mail as he had appeared, as was said before, and he would have the shield and the staff. And by this judgment you can know the danger in presentations and how you should pay attention to what sort of person you are and who is the appellee and the appellant; for if Jehan who was a commoner had appealed against the said Pierre, Pierre would have been properly armed, for when defending himself he would have fought armed and on horseback and the commoner {would have fought} as he came, or armed as a champion if he had come that way.

1832. When commoners appeal against each other, they should appear on the assigned day after the wager has been accepted, on foot and armed as champions; and if they are gentlemen, they should come on horseback, in full armor; and a person who comes less fully armed than he might cannot make any correction later.

1833. Just as it is important to take care how you should be armed according to your station, it is also important to speak correctly when you present yourself, and you can do this properly in two ways, the first generally and the second specially.[4]

1834. The general presentation which should be made is such that the person speaking for the person who is presenting himself should say: "*Sire, this is Pierre who is coming before you as he should today against Jehan of such-*

and-such a place; and if he had been otherwise appealed against, Pierre would not want to lose on that account,—and if he has a substitute he should introduce the party and his substitute,—*and he presents himself reserving the right to change arms and counsel, and all such changes as law and custom entitles him to up to the point of battle, as to all that should be done on this day or another, if a different day were assigned to him by the will of the court or the consent of the parties or in any other manner whatever."*

1835. The second presentation procedure, which is made specially, should be made such that the person speaking for the person presenting himself should say: *"Sire, this is Pierre who is appearing before you, he and his substitute, as he should today, against Jehan of such-and-such a place; and if he had been appealed against differently, Pierre would not want to lose on that account. And he reserves the right to change arms and counsel, to tighten and loosen his armor* [d'estraindre et d'alaschier]; *to put on ointment and have his hair cut* [de oindre et de rooignier]; *to a needle and thread; to change arms, taking off what is too much, taking up what was lacking; to change shield and staff, if necessary; to take a substitute other than the one who appears with him, if he wants; and all other things which he can and should reserve the right to do by the customs of this court, up to the beginning of the battle. And if today's appearance is continued* [alongiés] *by the will of the court or the agreement of the parties, he reserves the right to have all the above-mentioned things at the other appearance, and all the kinds of changes."* Of the two manners of presentation described above, the second one which speaks specially is the better and more beautiful, and there are fewer defenses to it; nevertheless, the other is also proper.

1836. When the parties have presented themselves, the appellant should repeat his appeal and ask for the battle, and the appellee, if he has any reasons why he wants to say there is no wager and he brought them up on the day the wager was accepted, should remind {the court} of them by repeating them and ask for a judgment on each defense and offer to prove it if it is denied; and after repeating his defenses, he should not forget to say that if his defenses are not good, he offers to defend himself and proceed with the battle, according to what the judgment says. Then the judge should take counsel on the appellee's defenses and if there is any good defense admitted or proved, as to why the wager should be quashed, the court should announce this judgment; and the kinds of defenses the appelleee can raise can be seen in the chapter which speaks of appellee's defenses {Chapter 63}.

1837. When some defense is raised by the appellee, by which he says there is no wager, and the appellant denies it in the way it is raised, and the appellee calls witnesses to prove it, the appellant cannot challenge the witnesses by a wager of battle, for a wager on a wager is not to be accepted. And if you allowed a wager in such a case, there could be ten or more duels [*peres*], one after another, and thus the appellee would be better not to raise his good defenses, if he had any, and go ahead with the {main} wager; and this would not be reasonable. Therefore the appellant, if he wants to say something against the appellee's witnesses, can contest them {only} if they are the kind of people who cannot testify; and a person wanting to contest witnesses can see how to contest them, in this case and others, in the chapter which speaks of proofs {Chapter 39}.

1838. If the appellee cannot raise or prove defenses which would make the wager be quashed, the battle should be ordered [*jugiee*]; and when it is ordered the time has come for those who want to raise legal excuses for having a substitute {to fight for them} to bring them up, and the legal excuses are explained in the chapter on appeals {Chapter 61}. And when the legal excuses have been accepted, they must appoint the persons who will undertake the battle for them. And then they should proceed to the oaths in the following manner.

1839. The appellant must swear first on the Holy Gospels, saying: "*So help me God and all the saints, and these holy words,*—and he should place his hand on the book,—{*I swear*} *that Jehan whom I have appealed against did the thing,*—or *had it done* if he is accusing him of having it done,—*in the manner I claimed against him and I will prove this by my right* [a l'aide de mon droit]." And when he has said this, the appellee should say: "*I challenge you* [je vous en lieve] *as a perjurer.*" And then he should kneel and put his hand on the book and say: "*So help me God and all the saints and these holy words, {I swear} that I had no fault in the thing for which Pierre appealed against me. And what he said against me was a lie and he is a perjurer, and I will prove him such with the help of God and my right* [mon bon droit]." And when they have sworn these first oaths, and they are approaching the battle, they must swear a second oath in the following manner.

1840. The appellant and appellee must make the following last statement under oath: "*So help me God and all the saints, {I swear} that I have not sought or procured any art, trickery, nor artifice, nor sorcery, nor magic by which the person I am to fight will be wounded in the fight, except by myself* [mon cors] *and my weapons only, as I have shown them to you openly today in this court.*"

1841. When all the oaths are finished, the judge should ascertain if the battle is by substitutes and what the case is. And if it is a case where the losing party is to be put to death, and the battle is by substitutes, he should have the appellant and the appellee put in prison where they cannot see the battle, and the rope round their necks with which the one whose substitute is defeated will be executed; and if it is a woman, she should be given the shovel which will bury her.

1842. When all the above-mentioned things have been done, those who are going to fight should be placed in the field of combat, and then the lord should have announced three prohibitions: the first, that if there is any member of the lineage of either party present, he must leave the field and go away, on pain of death and forfeiture [*seur cors et sur avoir*]. The second prohibition is that no one should be so bold as to say a word, and that everyone should be still and silent. The third prohibition is that no one, on pain of death and forfeiture, may give aid to a party or hinder the other party, by any act or by procuring any act, nor by speaking or making signs or in any other manner. And if anyone should break any of these three prohibitions, he is at the mercy of the lord who can exact what penalty he likes and give a long prison term; and you could break the prohibition in such a way as to lose your life, if it is clearly seen that one of the parties was defeated with the help of the person breaking the prohibition.

1843. When the prohibitions have been announced and the lineages have left the field, the judge's men should guard the battleground so that no one interferes; and then the judge should order those who are to fight to do what they are supposed to do. And then the appellant should make the first move, and as soon as the defendant sees him move, he can move to defend himself. Nevertheless, if the defendant made the first move, the appellant cannot be blamed, for each party is allowed to do his utmost once they have leave from the judge to engage.

1844. If it happens meanwhile that while those who are fighting are engaged there is talk of making peace, the judge should look carefully at the position of each party and make them stay still in the same position so that, if there can be no peace made, neither of the parties gains by the stoppage when they have orders to re-engage. And on the issue of keeping still we saw the following case.

1845. A knight and a squire were fighting in the king's court in Paris, on horseback and in full armor. When they had fought for a while, one of the reins of the squire's horse twined round the knight's foot, and at that moment they were told to keep still to discuss making peace. And during the stoppage for the discussion, the knight took his foot right out of the stirrup and untwisted the said rein, and then put his foot back in the stirrup. But he was told by those guarding the battleground to be ready to make peace, for if they re-engaged, then the squire's horse's rein would be twisted round his foot again in the same position as before; for which reason the knight was more ready to make peace, and peace was made. And by this you can know that each party should be put back into the battle in the position he was in when the call came to keep still.

1846. No peace may be made in a wager of battle without the agreement of the lord in whose court the wagers are deposited. But any lord who has a wager in his court may allow peace to be made if he wants, provided it is before one of the parties is defeated, for if you waited any longer, peace could not be made without the assent of the count; for when the thing has progressed that far, it only remains for justice to be done; and concerning anyone proved worthy of punishment and found guilty of crime no peace should be made without the count's assent.

1847. If any of the count's subjects, as a result of a payment, made peace or allowed a peace to be made for any of their subjects who had deserved death, they would lose their jursidiction over the court and would pay a penalty of sixty pounds, and the count could still punish the offender.

1848. The count's subjects should be careful that if they are holding prisoners for crimes they do not let them escape from an insecure prison or because of poor guarding, nor that they take money to make peace, for they would lose jurisdiction over their court and pay a penalty of sixty pounds. And the count could cancel the peace and punish the offender, for the justice held from the count must not be sold to those who have deserved to be punished. And if the count's subjects could make or permit peace between their subjects, many serious crimes could occur which would not be punished.

1849. When someone is fighting as a substitute for someone else, and there is talk of peace, he cannot make peace in the absence of the person for whom he is fighting; but the person he is fighting for can make peace with the agreement of the lord and the adverse party, whether the substitute wants it or not. But the substitute, after the first skirmish [*estour*] of the battle, will still be paid if he wishes.

1850. A person receiving an appointment as a substitute should be careful, for he may not think again about his appointment once he has accepted it on the day when he receives it. But if the appearance was postponed and he had not contracted to fight the battle on whatever day it occurred, he would not be required to accept the appointment on the other day unless he wanted to; and {even} if he wanted it, he would not receive it if the person with the battle wanted another substitute, provided he had reserved in his presentation the right to change his substitute, as is said above.

Here ends the chapter on presentations which are to be made in wagers of battle and what follows up to the end of the battle.

Notes

1. This means accepted by the judge. The *gages* 'wagers' are objects, such as a glove, which are accepted by the judge when he decides that a judicial battle is a proper way to settle a disputed question. See Chapter 60.

2. Crépy-en-Valois, near Senlis, southeast of Clermont.

3. In what follows, it appears that a champion was armed with more than a tunic (*cote*). See the last sentence of §1831.

4. Beaumanoir used the terms *general* and *especial* in the sense in which they are still used in the law, where "special" means "particular."

65. Jurors' Delays

Here begins the sixty-fifth chapter of this book which speaks of the delays permitted by custom and the delays permitted to jurors before giving judgment.

1851. There are many delays permitted by custom to lords and the vassals who are jurors in their courts, so that those who want to appeal for default of judgment must take care that those against whom they are appealing cannot use these delays as their defense, and take care that before they appeal they have waited for all the delays given by custom to the person they are appealing against. Now let's see what kinds of delays custom obliges you to permit.

1852. If they wish, lords can on their own authority continue[1] [*continuer*] cases before them for three fifteen-day periods in the same state; but if they do it to harm one or both of the parties, it is not honest; nevertheless they can do it if they want to. And a person appealing for default of judgment for these three continuances would not have a good appeal.

1853. The men responsible for giving the judgment can if they wish take three delays [*respit*] before giving a judgment, where each delay can last at least fifteen days, and afterwards they can take a delay of forty days; and then, if they want, a delay of seven days and seven nights, and then if they want a delay of three days and three nights. After that, when they have taken all these delays, the lord should keep them in prison until they have given a judgment; and anyone appealing during these delays would not have a good appeal, for lords cannot compel their men to make a judgment except according to the custom of the county.

1854. When there is a suit in the count's court and the jurors take their delays before giving a judgment, they can take delays for three assizes,[2] and after the three assizes, for forty days, and then seven days and seven nights, and then three days and three nights. But if the count wants to speed up the judgment, he can hold assizes every fifteen days, until the first three delays pass, but he cannot shorten the other delays (forty days, then seven days and seven nights, then three days and three nights) which the jurors can take after the first three assizes. However, the count may give them longer if he wants.

1855. The suit which is begun in the assize should be pleaded and decided in the assize, unless the count sends it down to the provost's court with the agreement of the parties. And if the count sent it to the provost's court after the complaint had been answered in the assize, without the consent of the parties, he would be acting wrongfully.

1856. If a suit is begun in the provost's court, the provosts cannot on their own authority send it to the assize, unless it is by consent of the parties. But when the pleadings are to go to trial, and the jurors say they are too few to make a judgment, and that they cannot make up their minds, they can send the trial to the assize because there are normally more men at the assize than there are at the provost's court. And when the judgment is given, if it is on some bar so that the dispute is not all won or lost,[3] the suit should be sent back to the provost's court, unless it remains in the assize by the consent of the parties.

1857. If the jurors have taken a delay during some trial, and the lord, on his own authority, continues or extends the next appearance of the jurors in court, this extension is not counted as one of the jurors' delays. And the jurors cannot be deprived of all the delays which are mentioned above by any continuance or extension made by the lord.

1858. If the parties who are pleading request by joint consent a delay of the suit to another appearance, in the status it is currently in, the lord should not refuse their request, unless the dispute involves the lord and his rights would be delayed [arrieragiés] because of the parties' delay: for example, if the suit is on some matter where the lord cannot fail to receive a fine or some other benefit from the party losing the dispute. Nevertheless he should, if they request it during the suit, grant a delay of three fifteen-day periods, if the parties request them in hopes of reaching a settlement. And if there is a settlement, it should be reported to the lord so that his rights are not extinguished and he knows which party to fine [aerdre]. And by such delays, which the lord should give, many cases and contentions are settled.

1859. When the jurors are to make a judgment and they are ordered by the lord to pronounce it, if the men have considered the evidence on the judgment, they should not seek a delay, for delays are only so that jurors who have not sought advice and who have not considered the evidence concerning the judgment can have a space of time to seek advice and consider the evidence. Therefore you can see that jurors who do not pronounce a judgment when they have sought advice and considered the evidence are acting improperly. But the count cannot sue them for this offense, for they are believed if they say: "I have not considered the evidence," and if they commit an offense it is hidden and lies on their conscience.[4]

1860. If often happens that when the jurors are together to make a judgment one group of them have made up their minds and the others have not. When this happens, those who have made up their minds are committing no offense if they request a delay along with those who have not made up their minds, so that by the delay those who have not made up their minds can do so, so that the judgment can be given all together, and with agreement, for it is a bad thing when the jurors who are peers disagree about the judgment; and for this reason, when there is a disagreement, delays are good to take.

1861. The jurors who form the jury should use great care and attention in giving a proper and honest judgment, for whoever agrees in a bad judgment is required to pay the damages of a person who loses by a false judgment, if he wants to be pardoned by God for the offense; and for this reason it was said to judges: "Be careful how you judge, for you will be judged."[5] And those against whom false judgments are made often fail to appeal out of fear of rancor and the expenses which arise, and thus by these two kinds of fear many people lose their rights.

1862. As I said before, the jurors can take long delays in considering their judgments. Now let's see what the lord should do when the jurors have taken all their delays and some of them come to court to pronounce judgment and the others default. If those who come do not give the judgment, he should keep them in prison;[6] and if they say they will not give the judgment until the other jurors appear, the lord should compel the attendance of those in default by putting a great number of guards on them until they appear without delay to give a judgment along with the men who came first.[7] And if the firstcomers swear by the faith they owe their lord that they refrained from giving a judgment only in order to wait for the defaulters, the latter are required to help pay the reasonable costs and damages of those held in prison; and if they are in disagreement about the judgment, so that one group wants to give a judgment in favor of Pierre who was a party and the others want to rule in favor of Jehan who pleaded against the said Pierre, you should take the judgment of the wisest and the majority.[8] And if one group wants to give a judgment and does so, and the others do not want to give a judgment and will not agree with the judgment that is made, the lord should liberate those who have given their judgment and keep in prison those who do not want to give a judgment or agree with the one given, until they have either agreed with the judgment or given a different one. And if they give a different one, you should take notice of the most competent group, as I said before.

1863. If it happens that the jurors have met to give a judgment and they are in disagreement, so that you cannot tell which side has more adherents, the lord, when they cannot agree, can on his own authority take two men (or three or four according to the importance of the matter) from each group, and put in writing the arguments on which a judgment is to be given, and give the writing to the men he has chosen from each group and send them to seek advice in the superior court; that is to say, if the disagreement is in the court of one of the count's subjects, they should go and get advice in the court of Clermont; and if the disagreement is in the court of Clermont, they should go to the *parlement* to get the advice of the king's court. And whatever advice they bring back to the court where the disagreement arose should be upheld by the lord and pronounced as a judgment, for if there were an appeal, the appeal would go to the court from which the advice had been brought back, and it would be good security that the jurors would be able to have their judgment upheld if they had given it on the advice of those who would have to uphold or reject the judgment, for those who had given the advice would be unwilling to overturn what they themselves had advised doing.

1864. When the jurors are charged with giving some judgment, and some of the men are not there when a delay is requested, this does not mean that the delay is not running for those who defaulted, for otherwise they would gain some advantage by their default. And those who attended the appearance before the lord would be the losers, for when they had taken all their delays they would have to give a judgment without the contribution

of those who had defaulted. Therefore when they see that there are defaulters, they should ask the lord to compel the defaulters to come to the
judgment with them; and then the lord should compel them and punish
them by seizing their fiefs and placing guards on them until they come and
give the judgment with the others; for if the lord merely fined them (and
the fine is only ten sous for each default), there are quite a few of those men
who would not come on pain of such a fine. And for that reason the lord
should punish them in the manner described above.

1865. All the continuances and the adjournments that each person can
take according to the custom of the area, as I described them in the chapter
on adjournments {Chapter 3}, do not and should not reduce the continuations which the lord can take nor the delays that the jurors can take, for if a
party takes a continuance or an adjournment, the suit remains in the same
status as it was in until the day when they reappear in court.

1866. If the jurors have to report for army service or go out of the
district on orders from the king or the count, the disputes which are in
progress must remain in that same status until they return, and delays
caused by the orders of the sovereign do not deprive the jurors of their
delays.

1867. If a married woman needs to bring a suit concerning her real
property, and her husband does not want to bring the suit, and a long time
later he dies, the woman can bring the suit over again, and the time which
has elapsed during her husband's lifetime does her no harm,[9] for she had no
power to make the complaint if her husband did not want her to. But she
must bring such suits within a year and a day of becoming completely
independent as a result of her husband's death. And if she lets pass the year
and a day, the whole time will have elapsed against her[10]: that is to say that
the adverse party in the suit can make use of long tenure if it is so long that
he should thereby win his suit, that is to say ten years in a suit on real
property, and twenty years in a suit on personal property and chattels, as I
said in the chapter on being too late to bring a suit {Chapter 8}.

1868. When a lord wants to continue the appearance he has scheduled
for a man who holds property from him, if he waits to make the continuance until the day the man appears in court, or so close to the day that the
man cannot cancel the appearance of his counsel, he should not continue

for one or two or three days, but for at least fifteen, for it might be very hard for the man to obtain the services of his counsel so soon after, so that he might lose through lack of counsel. And if the lord is the plaintiff against his man, he can give longer than fifteen days, for he cannot make it so far off that the man would not wish it were even further. But if the man is the plaintiff against his lord, and the lord assigns an appearance more than fifteen days thence, without a good reason, he is acting wrongfully. Nevertheless he should give him at least fifteen days, whether the man is the plaintiff, or the lord; for the proper continuance of an appearance is after a fifteen day interval, and the lord cannot assign less time, as you will hear in a judgment that follows.

1869. The count was suing one of his men and he assigned him a date for an appearance. The count's vassal appeared, and his counsel with him; the count and the person representing him did not appear, but he sent the *bailli* and had the appearance continued. On the next day the *bailli* appeared and made his complaint against the man, and the man anwered: "Sire, I was summoned for yesterday against the count and I came, with my counsel, and I was on time. Sire, I admit that you continued the hearing until today, and my counsel left. I cannot obtain his services today, for which reason I do not wish to be obliged to answer today, unless it is ruled that I must. Instead, I request you to assign me an appearance in fifteen days' time." The *bailli* said he *could* continue the hearing thus {to the very next day} without doing anything wrong; nevertheless he did not want to, if the other lords in the county could not do it for their subjects. And on this issue they requested a judgment.

1870. It was judged that the count's man was not required to answer unless the new appearance was scheduled for fifteen or more days later; for since a gentleman is entitled to at least fifteen days before a scheduled appearance, and he is not required to answer before then unless he wants to (especially in cases which can stand a delay) the continuation should be for not less than fifteen days later, in whatever manner the count continues the appearance on his own authority. But there is a difference if the lord has a suit with his commoner, for he can have him summoned by his officer, from one day to the next, three times before making his complaint. But if he has made a complaint and it concerns real property, once the complaint has been made all the appearances which are continued or assigned should be scheduled for fifteen days later. And if the complaint is on personal property, chattels, or some other forfeiture, the lord can schedule appearances at eight-day intervals, and prosecute his case until the end by such scheduled appearances.

Here ends the chapter on the delays permitted by custom.

Notes

1. "Continue" is here used in the legal sense of "postpone."

2. The assize is the count's court, often presided over by a *bailli* such as Beaumanoir himself, which he recommends should sit at intervals of about every six or seven weeks. See §32.

3. For bars, or dilatory exceptions, see Chapter 7.

4. I have translated *s'aviser* as "consider the evidence" in this section, because the procedure seems like that used in modern French courts where a *juge d'instruction* considers and gathers evidence until he or she thinks it is probative, and then declares an end to this part of the trial (*clôture de l'instruction*). Beaumanoir also uses the expression *sage de juger* (§§1254, 1886), which corresponds to the Modern French *instruit*. In Beauvais, the jurors might have read the report on the inquest, for example. However, *s'aviser* may mean more simply "form an opinion," based on the word *avis* 'opinion.'

5. Matthew 7:2. "In quo enim judicio judicaveritis, judicabimini." I have translated Beaumanoir's words, rather than giving a standard translation from the Bible.

6. In some circumstances, the jurors who were present when the judgment was announced could be challenged by the losing party to a wager of battle; those who were not present could not be thus challenged and escaped the risk of having to fight. This explains the reluctance of the jurors who *were* present to take all the risk on themselves.

7. The use of guards as a means of judicial coercion is discussed in §1603.

8. It appears from this sentence that unanimity is not required.

9. That is, it does not count as peaceful possession by the person against whom she wants to claim possession (seisin).

10. That is, the time since she could have first brought the suit if her husband had been willing.

66. Recusal

Here begins the sixty-sixth chapter of this book which speaks of recusing judges and having judgments executed.

1871. Now we must speak of those who want to recuse judges,[1] for if those wanting to recuse judges do not do so before the judgment is given, after judgment they cannot recuse them except in an appeal; but before judgment you can recuse them for various reasons. And we will mention some.

1872. One of the reasons why judges can be recused is if the person going to judge is my enemy, so that he refuses to speak to me, or there is a *casus belli* [*fet aparent*][2] between us or people from our lineages so that a war has begun, or we are in a truce; for in those cases there is a danger that I may be given an unfavorable judgment out of hatred. But if a settlement has been made in the dispute, I cannot recuse him, for it must be supposed that once a settlement has been reached passions [*les cuers*] are quieted. And if we are in a guaranteed peace, those who are in the peace with me can make a judgment, provided there are other men; for our understanding is that if all the men who are to judge me in my lord's court are in a guaranteed peace with me, I can refuse to be judged by them because there is a suspicion of hatred. And if someone has a good reason to exclude *all* his peers who should judge him in his lord's court, the case should go to the court of the overlord, and the suit should be fought there, except if it is the count's court; for if anyone could for good reason exclude all the count's men from judging, the count would keep the case and would have it judged by the men of his personal counsel [*le conseil de son ostel*]. If the men of his personal counsel were appealed against for false judgment, the appeal procedure would be heard in the king's court with no wager of battle, for when the judges are the members of a counsel there can be no wager; but when vassals judge, wagers can arise, as is explained in the chapter which speaks of appeals {Chapter 62}.

1873. There are other reasons for recusing judges, for example if they have threatened to do me harm, or if they have said before good people that I am going to lose my case, or if they have been attorneys or advocates or counsel to my opponent, or if they have or could have an interest[3] in the subject of the suit, or if they are parties against me in any part of the dispute, or if the case may involve them [*est en aus alligant*], for example if they are sureties or in debt to my opponent, or if they have received money or promises to be favorable to the other party, of if one of them is father or son to my opponent; and if the case concerns a crime which involves death or dismemberment, I can exclude all those of the victim's lineage from the judgment. All those mentioned above can be recused as judges for the above-mentioned reasons.

1874. Others who may be recused are those who cannot be challenged in a wager of battle, such as clerks or minor children whom the lord has graciously accepted as vassals, and idiots, whose memory is clearly defective either because of age or natural insanity or some other sickness which has taken away their former memory: all these persons can be excluded from giving judgment, for the reasons are good.

1875. A baron who holds directly from the king should be zealously firm [*durement riguereus*] in enforcing judgments which were made in his court, and should not permit the matter to be relitigated which was already judged against the person trying to make a complaint (or against his predecessor). And if the person losing the decision himself makes the complaint again, he cannot escape a fine for going against the judgment. But if another person makes the complaint, he should be warned that he is going against the judgment because the case was previously decided against his predecessor, or against the person he is complaining about. And when he is warned, if he abandons the suit, he should not have to pay any fine for speaking against a thing already judged, for perhaps he knew nothing about it. But if he maintains the suit after the warning, he must pay a fine to the lord for going against the judgment, and his complaint should not be accepted. And the fine for knowingly going against what has already been judged is sixty sous for commoners and sixty pounds for a gentleman.

1876. Not all judgments are made in the courts of the barons who hold directly from the king; indeed many of them are made in the courts of their subjects, who have vassals and jurisdiction and lordship over their lands.

Therefore if a suit is brought in the baron's court and a party wants to use as a defense that a judgment has been given on that dispute in another court, the other party should be warned not to go against the judgment; and if he will not desist, the party wanting to use the other decision will be allowed to prove that he won the judgment in the suit in the other court; and he should make the proof by invoking a recall from memory by the jurors who made the judgment. And if he cannot obtain the appearance of the jurors, because they have a legal excuse [*essoine*] or they live too far away, for example if the judgment was given in another region [*contree*], he can make his proof by witnesses. And having proved the judgment, he should be free and clear of the complaint, for every court should uphold the judgment of other courts, or otherwise suits could be begun all over again.

1877. There are many disputes which cannot be proved by live witnesses in attendance, or by the recall from memory of a jury, for example if my relative, whose heir I should be, has died abroad. Now let's see how I obtain my inheritance in that case. I say that if there is testimony in a writing sealed with an authentic seal, and the content of the writing is that the writer has heard honest testimony under oath concerning the death of the relative, this proof should be valid. And if the lord of the land where he died holds as a sovereign, such as a duke or a count or a prince or a king, in those cases the seal should be authentic.

1878. If the ecclesiastical court undertakes to judge a case the cognizance of which belongs to the secular court, the judgment should be upheld because the parties consented to it and commenced the suit. And if one of the parties wants to use the judgment as a defense and the other party denies it, so that a proof is required, a writing from the ecclesiastical judge is worth only one witness, according to our custom; but a party who has a valid witness along with the writing from the ecclesiastical judge has made an adequate proof.[4]

1879. If the subjects of some baron go and plead in the ecclesiastical court some case of which he has the cognizance, he can compel his subjects to stop the suit by confiscating their property, for otherwise he could lose his cognizance. But if they are pleading cases which belong to Holy Church, he should not forbid them or compel them to desist, for he would be acting against the rights of Holy Church. And which cases belong to Holy Church and which do not, and which belong to the secular court, is explained in the chapter which speaks of which cases belong to which of the two courts {Chapter 11}.

1880. A judge can also be recused if he is litigating, in the court where the judgment is to be made (or in another court in the same castellany), a suit similar to the one in which he would be making the judgment, because of the suspicion that he might help to give a decision against the party, so that when his own suit came to judgment the first decision would be taken into account, for you would not willingly make two different decisions in similar cases in the same castellany, and it would not be right to do so. And for this reason the judge who is litigating a similar case should be excluded from participating in the judgment. And we mean this to apply to *baillis* in the courts where they can give a judgment, and to the jurors in the courts where the jurors give the judgment.

1881. There are yet other reasons for excluding the judge or any of the jurors from making a judgment, for example when one of the parties needs his testimony, for in that case he must according to the rule [*selonc droit*] refrain from being a judge in order to be a witness. But this rule has been badly observed for a long time in the castellany of Clermont; for the vassals say they can be witnesses in disputes or counsel to one of the parties, provided it is not for pay or he is not of the closest degree of kinship to the party (and provided he is not his heir), and they will not on that account refrain from being part of the jury and giving their opinion. Nevertheless we have not permitted it while we have been the *bailli*, if a party challenged them; but when a party did not challenge, we have had to permit it.

Here ends the chapter on recusing judges.

Notes

1. By *juges*, Beaumanoir mostly means "jurors" in courts where the judgment is given by a jury. However, there were some courts or cases where a judge could give a judgment from the bench, and the reasons given in this chapter for recusing a juror would also apply there (see the last sentence in §1880 and the first sentence of §1881).

In this chapter, therefore, I translate *juge* as "judge," meaning "the person giving the judgment, whether judge or juror."

2. On the *casus belli* see note to §1669.

3. "Interest" here is, for example, a financial interest, not merely intellectual curiosity.

4. Two witnesses are needed because the secular court could have heard the case. For cases where the ecclesiastical court has exclusive jurisdiction, only the writing of the one ecclesiastical judge is needed as full proof. See §1204.

67. Judgment

Here begins the sixty-seventh chapter of this book which speaks of judgments and the way to make judgments and how you should judge.

1882. It is right and timely that after we have spoken in the preceding chapter on how you can refuse judges, we should in this following chapter say what kind of people can and should judge and how you should make a judgment, and how you can appeal for false judgment, and how the lords can send to find out what hearings their subjects are giving; and we will also touch on the manner of vacating judgments and on which judgments are valid and which are not.

1883. By our custom no one can give a judgment in his own court or in his own dispute for two reasons: the first is because a single man by himself cannot judge, but two or three or four or more are needed, apart from the lord; the second reason is that the custom of Beauvais is such that the lords do not judge in their courts, but their men give the judgment.[1]

1884. If someone has too few vassals to give judgments in his court, he should ask the lord from whom he holds to lend him some men who are his peers, and the lord should do this. But now let's see,—if someone borrows some of his lord's men to give judgments in his court and someone appeals for false judgment,—if they will have to uphold the judgment as if they had given the decision in their lord's court. We say yes, for since they are supposed to give judgments at the command of their lord, in the court of their peer who lacks jurors, they must uphold their judgment, and the appeal must be brought in the court of their lord who sent them there, if he has enough other men to hold court; and if he does not have enough, the appeal should come up to the count's court.

1885. The count is not obliged to lend his men to go and give judgments in his subjects' courts, unless he wants, as the other lords below him have to lend men to their vassals, for his court should be maintained at full strength by his men; and those who lack jurors so that they cannot give judgments in the courts can send suits up to the count's court and the count's men can give the judgments there.

1886. We have sometimes seen that the count's men did not want to give a judgment because all of the count's men were not there. But this is not to be permitted, for if you waited until they were all there, with so many judgments to be given the men would be too burdened [*grevé*] and the disputes would be too long delayed; and no one should fail to do his duty because his fellows do not do theirs. Therefore those who appear in court at the order of their lords should not wait for those who are not there, if they are in a position to give a judgment [*sage de jugier*], unless the dispute is so great that they fear an appeal, for in such a case the count can oblige all his men to be there, those he can get or the most capable [*soufisans*].

1887. When a lord pleads against his man in his own court before his men in a formal procedure, he can take as many continuances and adjournments² and other delays as custom permits to a man pleading against his lord, that is to say regarding summonses, continuances, and adjournments.³ And the lord must show, as his vassal would have to do, that his adjournment was for a valid legal reason. And if he took an adjournment, and the man requested him to justify it, he would {have to} do so.

1888. When the lord pleads in his court against his own man, he is not a juror and should not be part of the jurors' deliberation in his court. And when the men announce the judgment, if they give it against him, he can appeal against it for false judgment, and the appeal must be conducted in the court of the lord from whom the lord holds the homages of those against whom he is appealing for false judgment. And if he makes a simple appeal, saying: "This judgment is false and invalid, and I require it to be reversed in my lord's court," this kind of appeal is not by wager of battle of the lord against his men. But if he says to the person against whom he wants to appeal for false judgment: "You have given a false and wicked [*mauvès*] judgment, like the wicked person you are, for pay or for a promise,"—or for some other bad reason which he states,—the appeal is by wager of battle, for a man may defend himself against his lord when he is accused by him of wickedness; and he will not by reason of having to defend himself against his lord's charge of wickedness have to give up the fief he holds from him; but if the man accused his lord of wickedness, he would first have to abjure his homage. And when the lord appeals simply, as is said above, the record of the pleadings [*errement*] on which the judgment was made must be taken to the court where the appeal is brought, and the jurors in the court should examine whether the judgment was right or wrong according to the proceedings in the court from which the appeal was made. And if it is found to be wrong, each of the men who concurred in the judgment must pay a fine of sixty pounds to the lord, and may no longer be jurors. And if the appeal is such that there is a wager of battle, the person who loses, whether it is the lord or the man, loses his life and his possessions; but the other men who concurred in the judgment lose only their power to be jurors, and they must each pay a fine of sixty pounds.

1889. By what was said before you can see that there are two ways to appeal for false judgment, one of which is by wager of battle: it is when you add an accusation of wickedness [*vilain cas*] to the appeal. The other procedure is to look at the record of the proceedings on which the judgment was made. Nevertheless, if you are appealing for false judgment against the jurors in the count's court, and the appellant does not put in his appeal an accusation of bad faith, the person appealed against for false judgment can choose to proceed by a wager of battle before the count and his counsel; for the count can take jurisdiction of appeals against his men for false judgment, and give them a hearing by the other men who did not concur in the judgment.

1890. A person appealing for false judgment who does not win his appeal must pay a fine to the lord of sixty pounds, and must pay sixty pounds to each of the men who concurred in the judgment and was present when it was announced. But those who concurred in the judgments but were not present at the announcment should receive nothing, since they were in no personal danger of being appealed against.[4]

1891. A person who fights or is represented by a champion, if it is in a case other than serious crime (for example for false judgment without adding an accusation of bad faith to the appeal, or for preventing witnesses from testifying, or for land), if he is defeated loses only his suit, and his horse and armor which go to the lord,[5] and pays a fine to the jurors, if the appeal was for false judgment; but if the battle was fought by a champion, the latter has his hand cut off.[6]

1892. Pierre did homage to Jehan for a fief which he had inherited, and when he had done homage, he went to a foreign country. And before he came back, Jehan alienated the right to Pierre's homage to Robert, and Robert confiscated the fief because Pierre did not do homage to him. Pierre's attorney came to the said Robert and asked him to release the fief, saying that Pierre had left the district in Jehan's homage, and if Jehan had abandoned his right to the homage and alienated it to another, Pierre should not on that account be the loser, since he knew nothing about it and was not in a place where he could easily hear about it. And Robert replied that because the homage belonged to him, he could take all the profits from the land until Pierre did him homage. And on this issue the said Robert and Pierre's attorney requested a judgment.

1893. It was judged that Robert had no right to take the profits because Pierre had left in the homage of his lord, for Robert represented the person of Jehan and Pierre was in Jehan's homage; but if the said Pierre had been in the district he could have ordered him to do him homage within forty days. And even if he were there and Robert ordered him to do him homage, Pierre would not have been obliged to obey the order until Jehan had ordered him to do so, for no one should leave the homage of his lord to do homage to another lord without the order of his lord, unless the lord is dead or in a place where he cannot give orders, and the man knows for certain that his homage should go to the person requesting it, for in such a case a man can do homage without the orders of his lord. And the above-described judgment is very good, for it would be a bad thing if those who go out of the district for good reasons, and who are in the faith and homage of their lords, lost because the lordship changed hands. Nevertheless, although an absent holder cannot do homage to the new lord, the latter should not on that account be deprived of the other rights of the fief, for example, the service owed by the fief or a fifth of the sale price or the relief if they are appropriate.[7]

1894. Just as we have said that there are two ways to appeal for false judgment, there are two ways to sue for default of judgment. The first is when you accuse the lord forthrightly for default of judgment as a party; and the other is when you plead against someone in the the count's court and some lord asks for the suit to be sent down to him, and the party says he should not have it because he is in default of judgment, just so that the case will not be sent down. And there is a great difference between these two suits, for if the lord is sued forthrightly as a party and he loses, he loses his jurisdiction over his court and pays a fine to the count of sixty pounds; and if you sue him the other way so that a suit will not be sent down and the judgment goes against him and he is shown to have failed or refused to give a hearing, or to have given up the case to the person he is now asking to send it down, he loses only insofar as the suit will not be sent down from where it was brought. For he can lose only what was in his dispute, and the dispute was only over his request to have the suit sent down; and for this reason, in this kind of suit for default of judgment, there is no wager of battle. But in the other kind of suit, with a direct accusation, there can be a wager, for this is the nature of your complaint if you add an accusation of bad faith to your appeal for default of judgment. But if the claim is simple, for example if you say: "He failed to give me a hearing, and I wish to prove it, if he denies it, by the recall from memory [*recort*] of those whom you sent to find out what kind of a hearing he would give me, or by that of other adequate witnesses who saw and took note of the defaults." In such a complaint there is no wager of battle, except to prevent from testifying witnesses called to bear false witness, for a wager can arise from that, although not concerning those whom the lord sent, for these cannot be challenged by wager of battle because of what they say when repeating what they saw, and their recall must be accepted [*veus*] and believed.

1895. A lord to whose court his own lord sends observers to see what sort of a hearing he gives should take careful note of who it is that is sent, for if he does not challenge them for a good and adequate reason before they give their report, he cannot contest what they say. And there are several reasons to challenge them, for example that they were part of the counsel of the party on whose behalf they came, or if they threatened loss to the other party or the lord; if this is discovered to be true, their recall from memory {of the proceedings of which they were observers} should not be believed, instead the lord must send the case back down and send other and unimpeachable observers to see what kind of a trial is given.

1896. Every time a party asks the count to send observers to his subject's court to see what kind of a hearing he is giving, he should do so; and any time someone does not dare appear at a trial for fear of his enemies, he should give him an escort. But the cost of the escort and the observers he sends to someone else's court must be paid by the person who requested them.

1897. For a party appealing against a judgment it is important not to accept a judgment {in some other case} by those against whom they appealed while the appeal is pending, for they would have waived their appeal by accepting the judgment of those against whom they had appealed. Therefore if the person who has appealed has other business in the court where he appealed for false judgment, in the case he appealed from or any other, and his lord asks: "Are you ready for judgment?" he should answer: "Yes, by those who can and should judge me. And I raise the objection that those who concurred with the judgment I appealed should not judge me. But if you have other jurors, I agree to have them give a judgment." And if all the lord's men concurred in the judgment, he should not go to trial in that court while the appeal is pending, but should plead his other cases in the sovereign's court where the appeal will be heard.

1898. A party wishing to contest jurors must do so before they announce the judgment, for if he waits until they have given the judgment, he can only challenge them by appealing for false judgment. But this means when the jurors are men of the court; for if his lord gave the judgment personally, or by men from a castellany other than the one where he has jurisdiction, or by townsmen, the party could challenge the judgment without an appeal, unless he had agreed specially to accept them as jurors, for you can make an agreement to have as your juror a person who has no right to be. But if there had been no agreement, and the party said nothing at the time of the judgment, and went away without comment, the judgment can stand, for he could have contested it when it was given. In such cases the challenge, if the lord gives the judgment personally, should be as follows: "Sire, I do not accept what you are doing as a judgment, for in Beauvais lords do not judge in their courts, but their men do, and what you are trying to do contrary to the custom cannot and should not be valid." And if the judgment was by men from another castellany or by townsmen, he should say: "I do not accept this as a judgment, for it was given by those who cannot and should not judge me." And thus he can escape such judgments without an appeal.

1899. There are several ways of preventing from being jurors those men concerning whom you have suspicions, even though they are men of the court and peers of the person who wants to have them excluded. And one of the ways is if the juror has been counsel to the other party, for it is to be feared that he will not willingly give a judgment against the person he has counseled. Nevertheless, our men of Clermont claim they can be in the counsel of a party and afterwards in the jury, but we do not believe this should be permitted if a party contests it; and whatever the men say, we have not permitted it in our time when a party wanted to contest it.

1900. The second way you can challenge jurors is when they are heirs or could share in anything which is part of the dispute; for they would be jurors in their own case, and no law or custom permits this. And for this reason, when some case arises between my lord the count and his subjects, and the case involves all the men, we will not allow them to give judgment because they are all parties. But when some case involves the count, for example, the clarification of a custom which could go against the men in their own courts just as it would go against the count, we allow them to give judgment in such cases.

1901. The third way to challenge a juror is when he has been convicted [*atains*] of a serious crime, even though the kindness of the lord has permitted him to escape punishment for the offense, for anyone convicted of a serious crime should not be participating in a judgment. But let's see if there is a wager of battle when someone wants to challenge a juror for such a reason. We say no, for the crime is only mentioned so that the person will be prevented from giving a judgment, when he has made peace in the case he is accused of. But if he accused the man directly saying: "You are the sort of person who should not give judgments, for you are a thief,—*or* a robber; *or* a traitor; *or* you took this woman by force in such-and-such a place; *or* you burned this house in such-and-such a place; *or* you were convicted of false judgment; *or* you wickedly killed this person,—and if you deny it I want to prove it before this court," upon all such accusations the accused would have to defend himself by a wager of battle. But another way he can challenge him without a wager is by denunciation, for example by saying: "Sire, I am reporting to you that Jehan committed such-and-such an offense and was found guilty [*atains*] of it in such-and-such a court, and, by the will of the sovereign, he was not punished [*delessiés a justicier*]. And since he was in any case found guilty of the offense, I request that he should not be part of the jury. And if you do not know that this is true, I will demonstrate it by the recall from memory of the the court where this was done." And by this method there is no wager of battle, for there can be no wager if you are not a party. And when such a thing is reported, the lord should ask the person thus accused if he wants to step down from the jury;

and if he will not, but says the accusation was never true, the judgment should be delayed until the court finds out if the declaration made against him is true. And when the court needs to know the truth of the reasons why you are trying to exclude jurors, only one day for proof is to be given the person denouncing or accusing, unless he has a legal excuse so that he is given a second day for proof, for the judgment could be too long delayed.

1902. The fourth way to challenge jurors is concerning a payment or promise, for example if the person challenging says: "I request that Jean not participate in the judgment, because he has accepted money,—or received a promise,—from the party against whom I am pleading, to help him in this dispute." If this thing is proved, he should be excluded, for a person who is to give a judgment is not honest if he accepts money or a promise to be more on the side of one party than of the other. And in such a case the court should take the testimony under oath of the party, concerning whether he has given or promised anything, and Jehan's testimony under oath as to whether he has accepted anything or expects to. And if the court cannot discover the truth from them, it should be found out through the witnesses called by the person making the denunciation. And if Jehan is found guilty, he must be excluded; and we agree that the lord should make him pay a fine of sixty pounds because he accepted money or promises in contravention of morality [*bonnes meurs*].

1903. The fifth way you can challenge a juror is concerning threats and mortal hatred. For it would be a dangerous thing if the person who has threatened to do me harm, or who hates me so much that he refuses to speak to me, or is at war so that he would like to kill me, should be a juror in my case.

1904. It is a good judgment and current custom in Beauvais that everyone can and should arrest offenders, both with and without the help of the authorities, and especially thieves and banished men and homicides, and all those who are running away for whatever reason when there is a cry[8] after them; and everyone is permitted to catch them alive if they can and hand them over to the authorities. And if the offenders turn and defend themselves and they are killed while being arrested, the arresting persons should not be accused of anything, for it is better for the offenders to be killed than to escape. And we have several times announced in our assizes that when there is a cry everyone must get up [*saillent*] and make an effort to arrest the aforesaid offenders, and this makes for the commission of fewer crimes [*malice*] and the swift punishment of those which are committed.

1905. Now let's see what you should do if there has somehow or other been a wager of battle, and the appellee[9] gives his reasons why there is no wager, and they go to a judgment, and the judgment is that the wager is permissible, and the appellee wants to appeal for false judgment. The first wager on which the judgment was given must remain in the same state until the wager of battle on the issue of false judgment has been resolved; and if the appellant for false judgment can demonstrate that it is wrong, he is released from the other battle that had been judged permissible, because that judgment has been shown to be wrong. And if the judgment is proved right {by the result of the second wager battle}, by the defeat of the appellant, he is not released from the first wager of battle, but he must fight it against the person who appealed against him in the first instance; and thus you can have a wager of battle over a wager of battle [*gage seur gages*]; and when we have said elsewhere that wagers on wagers are not to be accepted, this means in procedures [*erremens*] which can arise from the suit between appellant and appellee.

1906. Those who serve others and then go away without their master's leave to live in another district should be sent back to their masters to give an accounting when they have been responsible for their things. And if the employee[10] is afraid he will be caused bodily harm, the lord who wants to have him sent back for the accounting must give him assurances that he will be able to come and go in safety. And the first lord must give the security to the lord he is asking to send the employee back, and if there is a disagreement over the accounting between the lord and his employee, jurisdiction over the disagreement goes to the lord under whom the employee has become a resident.

1907. There are various people, for example merchants or people passing through the district, who have no residence [*mansions*], or their residence is outside the kingdom: such people can be tried for their offenses in whatever jurisdiction they enter, and their property can be attached for debts when the the person having them attached gives a security that he will repay costs and other loss to the merchant if he does not prove his contention; for it would be a bad thing if you had to go outside the kingdom, to where they have their residences, to sue such people. And it would also be a bad thing if they could be wrongfully arrested without being awarded damages.

1908. There can be several judgments given in the same dispute before you reach the principal issue of the dispute, for example, when a party raises exceptions to delay the suit by asking for a counsel day or an inspection day or any other of the dilatory issues which are explained in the chapter which speaks of exceptions {Chapter 3}, and the other party argues he should not have the delay he is asking for, and they request a judgment on this issue: these judgments are not on the main issue in the dispute. And for this reason the ecclesiastical courts differentiate between these judgments and the one which is on the main issue, for they call all these judgments that are collateral *interlocutory sentences*, and the judgment on the principal issue they call the *definitive sentence*. But we do not give them different names, but call them all judgments; and you can appeal both those which arise from collateral issues and the one on the principal issue.

1909. In the king's court, the custom when the judgments are announced is that the parties are not called to hear them: if they want, they can be there, and if they do not want, they need not. And this is because there is no appeal, for you cannot appeal their judgments; but you cannot and should not do this in courts from which an appeal can be made. Instead, when the jurors or the *bailli* is going to announce a judgment, he should call the parties and make sure they are present, and if they are, he can announce the judgment; and if one of the parties is in default, it should be inquired if the party had been summoned to hear the verdict on that day. And if the party had been summoned and defaulted without taking an adjournment, the judgment should not be announced on that day, but the party must pay a fine for the default and be resummoned to hear the judgment on another day certain which must be communicated to him; and he should be told in the summons that whether he comes or not the judgment will be announced on that day. And then if he does not appear, the judgment can be announced, unless he takes an adjournment because of a genuine physical excuse, for then you would have to wait until his excuse was no longer valid. But if he had announced his presence on the day when the judgment was to be announced, and afterwards, when the moment came for the announcement, he defaulted and went out of the court without leave in bad faith because he did not want to be present at the judgment, he should be called into court, and then whether he came or not the judgment could be given out since he had announced his presence for the day; for otherwise you could profit from your bad faith default after you had announced your presence in the court. But it is true that if someone went out into town with the intention of returning and he heard that the judgment had been announced against him, he could request the judgment to be announced a second time, and he would be in time to appeal, for otherwise, when judges were afraid of an appeal, they could announce the judgment at the moment when they knew the party losing the decision was not there; and the losers would lose their opportunity to appeal because in 'the secular courts by custom you have to appeal as soon as the judgment is given, except that you can take counsel whether to appeal or not.

1910. Each time judgment is announced in the absence of a party without calling him in to hear the judgment announced, the judgment must be repeated in the presence of the party who is dissatisfied, so that he can appeal if he is advised to do so.

1911. Judgments differ in many ways between the secular courts and the ecclesiastical courts, for when an ecclesiastical judge has given a sentence against a party on a collateral issue, not the principal issue,—and these sentences are called *interlocutory*,—if he sees that he has made an error or been deceived he can cancel the sentence and give a different one. But you cannot do this in the secular courts, for once the jurors (or the *bailli* in courts where the *bailli* decides the cases) have announced the judgment, either on the main issue or on collateral issues or bars, they cannot cancel it, or change or alter what they have announced as a judgment. Instead it must be accepted by the parties or found false on appeal, for if they wanted to cancel or change or alter it, the party who had won the judgment would not allow it unless he wanted, and there cannot be two opposite judgments in the same suit; and for this reason the first judgment must be maintained.

1912. A judgment made in the presence of an unauthorized [*faus*] attorney is invalid; this means that, if a party accepts as valid an invalid letter of appointment for the other party's attorney, and a judgment is given on the pleadings against the attorney, the attorney's principal is not obliged to be bound by the judgment, but he can say that he had not given such a power to his attorney, and thus the whole suit which was argued against the attorney will be canceled and the judgment declared null, and the parties will begin the pleadings again. And for this reason you should be very careful what attorneys are accepted in court, so that the court and the other party do not labor in vain; and in the chapter which speaks of attorneys {Chapter 4} it is explained which attorneys are valid [*convenable*].

1913. Those who are to give the judgment should make sure before they do so that it is their responsibility to do so. For otherwise they would labor in vain, for example, if an ecclesiastical court gave a judgment on land held from the count of Clermont, or if the men of Clermont gave a judgment on a case of which the secular courts do not have cognizance, the cognizance of which belongs to Holy Church; or if the men of one castellany give a judgment on a case which should be tried by men of a different castellany, or the vassals of a gentleman gave a judgment in his court on a case over which their lord has no cognizance: all such judgments are invalid, for they cannot execute their judgments. Nevertheless, if the parties agreed of their own free will and without coercion to seek a judgment in a court where they need not seek it unless they wanted, it is valid, and the party who won the judgment can make use of the decision in the court of the lord who had cognizance of the suit, by saying his opponent assented to seeking a judgment in a court on the same issue without challenging the jurors or the judgment itself; and for this reason it is said that you can make your judge of a person who is not your judge. But *baillis* and those who give judgments are not required to give judgments unless they want to in cases the cognizance of which does not belong to them, and if they tried to and a party challenged it, the judgment would be invalid.

1914. Just as we have said that a judgment made in the absence of a party who has been insufficiently called into court is worthless, it is also worthless if it is given against a minor, with the idea that a minor cannot have it canceled when he comes of age, unless it is one of the cases mentioned in the chapter on minors {Chapter 16}, for there are some cases in which a person having a minor child in his custodianship or guardianship must plead, and uphold what is judged for or against the children, and what those cases are is explained in the chapter on minors.

1915. When we said that a judgment should be immediately executed,[11] we meant in cases where this can be done without danger and without too great a loss to the party losing the decision, for there are cases in which the judgment cannot be executed immediately, for example when a judgment is given for debt and the due date is in the future, for in such a case you must wait for the due date; or when a judgment is given on land, it is executed by giving peaceful seisin to the person winning the decision; or when a judgment is given concerning some thing that is not in the possession or control of the losing party, but he must procure it or give the equivalent: in such a case he must be given time to procure the article (or to give the equivalent, if he claims under oath that he has done his best to get the thing back, and he cannot).

1916. When you give a judgment, there is no need to repeat [*recorder*] the arguments of the two parties on which they requested a judgment, indeed it is dangerous to repeat it all, for when the person giving the judgment repeats the substance [*procès*] of the trial, we have seen the party who was afraid of losing the decision say that the pleadings were not as stated, but were different, and he said what they were; and because of this disagreement the judgment had to be delayed until the recall from memory of the trial had been made: and some judgments have been delayed this way. Therefore, you should not repeat everything; instead, it is enough for the person announcing the judgment to speak in this manner: "Pierre and Jehan pleaded against each other on the seisin of such-and-such a piece of real property,—*or* concerning such-and-such a thing, *and he should say what the thing is that is the subject of the suit.*—Each party has raised arguments in support of his position; their arguments having been heard and declared ready for judgment, we find by law [*par droit*] that Jehan will take the seisin,—*or* the ownership,—of the subject of this suit." In the ecclesiastical courts, when the sentence is given they always repeat all the pleadings; but there is no danger because the pleadings are written down and sealed by the court, so that the parties cannot say they were different, and for this reason the judge can repeat the pleadings without danger when the sentence is given.

1917. There was a dispute between a lord and his man because the lord wanted him to pay relief [*relever*] for a fief which had passed to him laterally, on which fief there was a principal holding [*demaine*] and sub-fiefs [*homages*]¹² : and he wanted him to pay relief [*rachat*] on the principal holding of the value of a year's profits, and also sixty sous for each sub-fief. And the man answered that he had agreed to pay relief for the principal holding, but not for the sub-fiefs. And on this issue they requested a judgment, namely whether the man would pay relief for the sub-fiefs.

1918. It was judged that the main holding would pay relief but not the sub-fiefs, because there was a principal holding; but if there had been no principal holding and there had been sub-fiefs, for each twenty pounds' worth of land twenty sous would have been paid in relief. And by this judgment you can know that the principal holding dispenses the sub-fiefs [*arrierefiés*] from payment of relief.

1919. All the men who have to be jurors in the court of some lord should know that they are not required to give judgments except on matters in the jurisdiction of the castellany to which they owe their homage, for if the lord has several castellanies or men from several castellanies, he cannot take jurors from one castellany to give judgments in another.

1920. Everyone should know that no one is excused, for any reason [*pour service qu'il ait*], from giving a judgment in the court where he should do so as part of his homage; but if he has a genuine legal excuse, he can send a man to be his personal representative according to his rank [*selonc son estat*].

Here ends the chapter on judgments.

Notes

1. Beaumanoir has already mentioned that all trials in the Beauvaisis are conducted under a jury system, where the jurymen or *jugeurs* give the judgment and the judge, *juge* or *bailli*, merely presides (Chapter 1, §24). The terminology is a trifle unclear, however, for sometimes he says *juge* when speaking of a juror. I have tried to interpret what he means. It appears that when the judge is not a party, he can join the jurymen in their deliberation and opinion (see §1888 below). In addition, a lord can be a party in his own court, but on those occasions he does not join in the opinion.

2. For continuances and adjournments, see Chapter 3.

3. Beaumanoir's sentence seems overburdened here.

4. For an explanation of the appeal against a judgment, and the danger to the jurors, see Chapter 61, §1755.

5. The lord in whose court the appeal by wager was conducted confiscated the horses and armor of both combatants. See Chapter 61, §1718.

6. This cruel custom is justified by Beaumanoir in Chapter 61, §1721.

7. For sales tax (a fifth of the sale price) and relief (one year's average income), see §§1581 and 762.

8. One supposes that the cry is something like "Stop, thief!"

9. In this section, the same person is appellee (in the first appeal leading to the wager of battle) and appellant (in his appeal against the juryman who judged the first wager permissible).

10. Beaumanoir's word *serjans* is often used for an officer in the legal system (a sort of policeman) and for an agent. Here, the neutral term "employee" fits the context.

11. See §246.

12. The homages came from sub-fiefs, as will be seen at the end of the next section, where the word *arrierefiés* is actually used.

68. Usury

Here begins the sixty-eighth chapter of this book which speaks of usury and mark-ups [termoiemens][1] *and of what usury is, and how you can avoid paying usurious charges.*

1921. We said in the chapter on agreements that agreements against morality are not to be enforced, and we have also said that it is against morality when the agreement includes usury and grasping [*rapine*]. And it is right for us to say briefly in this little chapter what usury and grasping is, and how it can be proved.

1922. Usury is when someone lends money for other money to be paid either weekly or some time in the future. For example, if someone lends twenty pounds for three sous per week, or four, or whatever the agreement requires; in that case all the money which comes to the lender over and above the twenty pounds is clearly usury. Or if someone lends twenty pounds at Christmas, to be repaid twenty-five pounds on St. John's Day or St. Remi's Day: in this case the hundred sous[2] are usury.

1923. There are other kinds of usury, for example when it is summer some people lend the needy some rye, to be paid back in wheat after the harvest; in that case there is usury by the amount that the wheat was worth more than the rye when the wheat was delivered, for it sometimes happens that rye is worth as much money before the harvest as wheat is afterwards; and when this happens the person borrowing the rye cannot sue for anything from the lender as usury, for the lender merely gets his capital [*chatel*] back, and if he lent with the intent of obtaining interest, it is between him and God and his conscience.

1924. Usurers and those selling with a mark-up who fear the shame of this world more than the sin of usury are wickedly clever at figuring out how they can lend in such a way that the borrowers cannot raise usury as a defense against them. There are those who sell a horse or other goods, and the horse and the goods are worth no more than twenty pounds in the public market, and they sell it for thirty pounds, to be paid on a future due date which is named; or sometimes they lend money and give goods along with the money, for example wheat, or wine or horses or other personal property, and make a single charge for the goods and the money, to be paid on a future due date. In all these cases, whatever is above the value of the money and goods should be held to be usurious.

1925. It is true that if someone wants to sue for usury, the cognizance of the case goes to Holy Church. Nevertheless, if a usurer was suing for his debt in the secular court, and his opponent raised usury as a defense, the secular court could take cognizance of the usury issue. Therefore it is the defendant's choice to go to the ecclesiastical court or to stay in the secular court. But once he has begun the suit in one of the courts, he cannot abandon that suit to get a hearing in the other, but the dispute must be decided in the court where the suit began.

1926. If someone has obligated himself in writing or by sureties in the secular court to give back a certain sum of money, and he acknowledged when the agreement was made that he owed this debt for money borrowed, for a horse, or for other goods which were delivered to him, then afterwards when the creditor sues to be paid and the debtor summons the creditor on usury in the ecclesiastical court and has the ecclesiastical court forbid the secular court to have recourse to his property or his sureties until the dispute over usury has been decided, the secular judge is not obliged to obey this order unless he wants to; instead he should punish [*justicier*] the debtor at the request of the creditor until he is paid. But this does not mean that the debtor cannot pursue his claim in the ecclesiastical court, for if he wins his case against the usurer, Holy Church can declare the usurer excommunicated unless he gives back to the debtor what he exacted as usury, and then each court will have done its official duty.

1927. You cannot sue for usury in all cases where things are sold with a future due date, for some things are sold with a future due date by custom and necessity, for example timber, farms, rented property, for you could not find someone to buy them for cash without losing money on the price, and the future due date must be set so that the person buying can take and sell the goods and make a profit that way. Neverthless if someone who buys [*achate*] someone's timber or takes someone else's farm gives two prices for the same commodity at the same value, one price for cash and the other on credit [*a creances*], for example if he offers a *moulle* of logs for eighteen deniers cash and he sells [*vent*] it for two sous on credit with a future due date, in that case we believe that for each *moulle* sold on credit there are six deniers of usury;[3] but this is with respect to God, for as far as this world is concerned we never saw this usurious money returned, since the usurers protect themselves by saying they are discounting [*font meschief*] their goods, and giving some of them for less than they are worth because they need the cash.

1928. When someone is married and his conscience reminds him that he acquired something improperly by usury, by a mark-up, or otherwise, his wife cannot prevent him while he is alive from making complete restitution. But if he commands in his will for it to be repaid by his executors, his wife can take a half of the wrong on herself, unless those who are to receive the restitution sue her for it, because of usury or some other reason, until she makes restitution, either *inter vivos* or in her will; for the deceased's estate should not pay the whole restitution while the wife keeps her part without paying anything. Therefore, if you want to sue the wife, you have good cause to sue her for a wrong. And if those who can sue in this way care to do so, the woman will have to make restitution to them, for she keeps the money at the peril of her soul.

1929. Christians are prohibited from lending at usury. And if it is prohibited for Christians, that does not mean that it is permitted for Jews, for usury must be prohibited to all people at all times, and no judge should enforce payment of it once it is proved.

1930. When someone lends money on security [*seur gage*] and the person depositing the security wants to get it back by paying the money he borrowed on it, and the lender denies taking the security he is being asked for, if it is proved against him, he must give back the security to the person depositing it and also lose his money he lent on the security, and pay a fine to the lord; and he should suffer this loss because he wickedly tried to keep the security for himself. Nevertheless if there was an agreement that the security had to be redeemed by a certain time, or else it would belong to the lender as beyond the time [*forgagiés*], in that case the lender would keep it if he wanted to use as a defense the above-mentioned agreement.

1931. There is yet another kind of usury, which we have not spoken of, which is called a mortgage [*mort gage*], for example, when someone lends a sum of money on the security of a piece of real property which is named, on the condition that as long as the borrower holds the money, the lender will hold the property and take all the profits [*despueilles*] until he recovers the money he lent, without any deduction for the profits taken from the property. In that case we say that there can be no clearer usury than for the lender to carry off the profits from the property. Therefore if the borrower[4] in mortgage wants to sue for usury, all the profits taken by the lender are deducted from the debt.

1932. You can raise the issue of usury in the secular court as a defense to having to pay a debt to a usurer. But if the debt has been paid, and the borrower has the usurer summoned in the secular court to make a direct charge of usury against him, the usurer need not answer unless he wants to except in the ecclesiastical court.

1933. If he hears about an obvious usurer somewhere in his lands lending money for money by the week or on a mark-up, a baron holding directly from the king can arrest the usurer and attach all his property and make him give back all the usurious gains. But this means when he has prohibited lending in his lands, for since the usurer who is his subject is acting in disobedience to his command, the lord can take him into custody until he has given back all the usurious payments made since the prohibition, and he can exact a fine for disobedience to an order.

1934. A person lending at usury can be personally sued for the usury, as we said above. But if he dies without commanding that his usurious gains be paid back, you cannot sue his heirs for them after the debt is repaid; but if I owed money to the deceased in usury, and the heir sued for it, I could plead usury as a defense against him as I could have done against the father. Therefore you can see that I should be able to plead the usury as a defendant, but not as a plaintiff against the heir.

1935. So that those who live by such grasping as usury, or theft [*toute*] or larceny, or mark-ups, or other wicked modes of acquiring property, may know what danger they are in if they do not give back ill-gotten gains, we will describe for them the fall which is in store for them if they die undivested. They should all know, then, that their souls are given to the devils in hell [*as enemis d'enfer*] and their bodies to the worms and their property to their relatives. And none of these three groups would exchange their share for the other two, for the devils would not give the soul for the body and the possessions, and the worms would not exchange the body for the soul and the possessions, and the relatives would not give the property for the soul and the body. And each is satisfied with what he has, and the deceased [*chetis*] is lost for ever.

1936. Although you cannot directly sue the usurer's heir for usury, the heir should not suppose that this means that in God's eyes it is all right for him to keep the money; for if money derived from usury passed down from heir to heir until the tenth generation, the heir holding it would be supposed to give it back to those it was taken from; and if he does not, he has the same punishment as the person who acquired it wickedly: that is to say that if he dies in possession of it his soul is damned.

1937. Some things are usurious in your conscience which are not visible to the world, for all agreements and all deals which are made in such a way that the creditor cannot lose but can gain according to the agreement are usurious in God's eyes; and such usury can be concealed in many ways from the world, and usurers customarily protect themselves in these ways; and what their defenses are and can be we will not discuss, so that usurers cannot learn from these bad examples and continue their usury.

1938. There are usurers who rent out their animals on terms whereby, if the animals die, those who rented them must give back the animals and the rent. And such dealings can be sometimes usurious and sometimes not. For if I rent my horse to someone and it dies while in the renter's posession, it is not usury if I want my horse back along with the money; and it is the same with my cow or my sheep, since the renter used the profits to his own advantage, by paying the rent. But if I rented out my cow or my sheep on condition that I received all the profits in exchange for a loan of money or other things, and the animals died without the fault of the person into whose care I had given them, and I wanted to get them back according to the agreement, it would be usury, and this kind of usury is called "iron stock" [*bestes de fer*] for as far as their lords are concerned these animals can never die.

Here ends the chapter on usury and mark-ups.

Notes

1. I use the invented term "mark-ups" for this financial manuever, which is explained in the last sentence of §1922.

2. At twenty sous to the pound, a hundred sous are five pounds.

3. Seller and buyer seem to be mixed up in Beaumanoir's sentence here, but the sense of two prices for the same goods remains clear.

4. The verb *preste* found in the manuscripts can only be supposed to be an error for *emprunte*.

69. Misadventure

Here begins the sixty-ninth chapter of this book which speaks of cases of misadventure which arise out of ill-luck, in which pity and mercy should temper justice.

1939. Various situations often occur in which lords have great need to be merciful and have pity and not always apply the law strictly. Nevertheless the law permits mercy in some of the cases we are going to discuss, and they are called cases of misadventure. And we will discuss some but not all of these, for no one knows all the situations which can arise by misadventure. But those we describe you can use as examples for others which can arise, and which we will not mention.

1940. If I go with my father or my son or my brother or one of my cousins to help him in his {private} war and our enemies attack us, and while defending myself I think I am killing one of our enemies and I kill one of my relatives, no one should doubt that this is misadventure, for no one is more distressed that I am. And for this reason I should not be prosecuted in this case, except that in order to avoid the frauds and sharp practice which can arise through the evil cupidity of the world, I should agree that if I am the heir of the deceased I should inherit nothing, but lose any right to take from him. Nevertheless we have never seen a judgment given on this, but I think that it is right so that people will protect more carefully [*curieusement*] those whose heirs they are.

1941. It sometimes happens that a man is at target practice with others, and as he looses his shot someone walks in front so that he is struck by the arrow and as a result he dies or is injured. In that case, if he dies, the person firing the arrow should not be prosecuted nor should you make {private} war on him. But if the victim were only wounded, so that he had expenses in caring for his wound, the person firing the arrow must pay the expenses. And because of the misadventures which can arise it is good to avoid shooting in places where there are people passing. And what we have said about people shooting at targets also applies to a person shooting at wild birds and animals in a place where he did not expect people to be around. For if someone shot an arrow at a bird on a tree where there were people around the tree, and the person shooting saw them and knew they were there, and the arrow fell down on one of the people and killed or wounded or injured him, the person shooting would not be without obligation for the offense, but would be punished for his stupidity [*sotie*] according to the offense.

1942. A person cutting down a tree near a public highway where people ordinarily pass by and who sees people coming when the tree is about to fall must shout to them from afar to take care; and if he does not shout and the tree falls, killing or injuring or wounding someone passing on the highway, it seems to me he should be guilty of the offense, for anyone obstructing the public highway to the detriment of others is held liable for the damages. But I think it would be otherwise if the person killed or wounded was with the person cutting the tree, for no one should remain in a place where there is danger without taking care, once he is of age; but if he was still a minor, he would be in the care of the person cutting down the tree. And also if the tree was so far off the road that it could not fall on the road, the person cutting down the tree would not be in danger {of liability}, for those who work in places where people do not ordinarily go do not want to pay attention to anything except their work; but those who are working in public places where people pass by should not pay so much attention to their work that they do not pay attention to avoiding danger to the public [*as trespassans*]. And what we have said about trees applies to all kind of dangerous work in public places or so close to the public highway that those on the highway are in danger.

1943. When someone has killed his child, for example by fire or water, or because he was smothered in his sleep, or because he was not watched [*mauvese garde*], the father and mother should not be prosecuted, for their great distress should exempt them from civil prosecution [*du damage temporel*]; and a child's nurse should also not be prosecuted, for if they were punished for such accidents no woman would be stupid enough to be a nurse. But a father and mother should be very careful whom they use as a nurse for their child, for careless nurses have caused the death of many children.

1944. Some people with jurisdiction on their lands punish animals when they kill someone: for example if a sow or other animal kills a child, they hang it and draw it. But this should not be done, for dumb animals have no discrimination of good and evil, and for this reason the punishment is lost on them, for punishment should be executed to avenge the offense, and so that the offender will know and understand that he has a certain penalty for a certain crime; but dumb animals do not have this understanding, and for this reason a person who puts to death a dumb beast as a kind of punishment for an offense is doing something to no effect; but the lord should take charge of the animal as his own, for it is his by right; and in any case if it is a bull or a pig or a sheep or an animal of whatever kind that has gone wild [*enragie*], it is better for him to kill it and take his profit from it, so that it will not do the same thing again; and if it is a horse or a mule or a donkey, the lord can keep it and use it without killing it.

1945. For this reason, if my horse or any other kind of animal belonging to me kills someone, I cannot be prosecuted for the offense. But if it only wounds or causes injury to the person, I am compelled to pay the damages, and once the fine is paid I get my animal back. And if the animal causes loss of life or limb, it is forfeit to the lord and I cannot be prosecuted. Nevertheless, my animal could cause loss of life or limb for which I would be liable, for example if I had caused the animal to do what it did. I would be the cause if I was riding my horse and I spurred the horse in a crowd of children or adults and my horse killed someone by its impetuosity: in that case I would be responsible. But if it was obvious that my horse had got away from me by its hard mouth or restiveness, I could use that as a defense.

1946. If someone causes injury or loss of life or limb in a fight, this is not a misadventure which can excuse the person who started the fight or those on his side who get into the fight; instead they must be punished according to the offense. But if the person attacked kills someone while protecting his own life he cannot be prosecuted.

1947. Now let's see,—supposing a fight had started and someone got between two combatants to stop the fight and a blow fell on him by accident, causing loss of life or limb,—whether the person striking the blow can be prosecuted. We say this, that if the injured or dead person was a relative from the lineage of the person striking the blow, mercy is appropriate, for no one is more unhappy than the person striking the blow. But if the person killed or injured was a stranger or a relative of the other party in the fight, the person striking the blow would be punished for the offense.

1948. A person killing himself by misadventure,—for example if he falls in a well or a river and drowns; or if he falls off a tree or a house; or kills himself by any other accident,—does not forfeit his property,[1] and it must be distributed to the heirs. But if it can be clearly known that he did it on purpose to kill himself, for example if he is found hanged, or he had said: "I am going to drown myself,—or kill myself,—because of this thing that someone did to me,—of for that thing that happened to me,"—he must be punished, and his property is forfeit to the lord in whose lands the property is situated.

1949. It sometimes happens that someone is found dead and it cannot be discovered if he killed himself or was killed by someone else, or if he killed himself by accident. And when such a case arises, which is so obscure that you cannot discover the truth, the judge must pay great attention to the way the action occurred and the manner of death. For if he is found hanged in a private place, you should incline to believe he did it to himself rather than otherwise, and on purpose, for this is not death by misadventure. And if he is found drowned in a well, you should look at where the well is, and the reason he had to go to the well, and the habits [*maniere*] of the deceased when he was alive. For if the well is in a secluded place, where not many people go, you should inquire whether he was hated or threatened by anyone, or if he was mad or drunk so that he went there, or if he was in the habit of going to the well to get water; and if you find he was threatened or hated by people of ill repute, there should be a strong presumption that they did it or had it done, rather than thinking he did it to himself on purpose, or accidentally, especially if he was not in the habit of going to the well to get water, and if he was not insane or a drunkard. And if you cannot find any hatred or threats, but you find that the well is dangerous and that he often went there for his convenience, you should rather believe that he fell in by accident than otherwise. And if you cannot progress by any of these two methods, but you find he was insane or delirious [*frenetique*] or a drunkard, you had better believe he did it on purpose than otherwise. But if you think it probable that he killed himself because of some illness which disturbed the balance of his mind [*il ne fust pas bien a soi*], his heirs should not lose what passes from him; because for the heirs to lose in the case of persons found dead where it is not known who caused the death, you need many clear presumptions. And to illustrate this better, we will recount a case which we saw.

1950. A woman was found drowned in a well; the lord wanted to take her land and possessions, because he said she had killed herself on purpose, and he tried to prove it by saying she had threatened herself and because it was not easy to fall into that well accidentally, and because it was in a secluded place where not many people went, and it was not dangerous, and because she had no reason to go to that well, as it was not the closest one. And the heir answered these arguments saying that if all the things the lord said were demonstrated [*trouvees*] (and he did not admit any of these things but denied them all), it was not a clear proof that he should lose the inheritance; and after the lord had proved all his presumptions, they requested a judgment on the issue of who should take the property, the lord or the deceased woman's heir.

1951. It was judged that the property was forfeit to the lord. And what persuaded the jurors the most to give this judgment was that it was proved that she had said she would do something to bring shame on her family, and they were persuaded by this along with the other presumptions mentioned above. And by this judgment you can see that all the obscure cases which arise in such a way that you cannot discover the truth can only be proved by presumptions.

1952. It is true that when someone is found dead, by whatever death, and you cannot find out the truth of the matter, or clear presumptions that the deceased committed suicide, the property should be distributed to the heirs, for you should not believe that anyone committed suicide on purpose unless it it is proved clearly or by clear presumptions.

1953. Since we have said above that the judge should pay great attention to the manner of death and the surrounding circumstances, and we have already spoken about those found hanged and those found drowned in a well, we will speak of some other kinds of death. Now let us consider people found drowned in a river, in a fish reservoir or a pond: if they are found drowned there in a place where they were in the habit of going,—for example to bathe, or to fetch water, or to fish,—you should incline to believe that the death was accidental rather than otherwise. But if a person is found drowned in a sack or bound or wounded, it is clear that this was done to him, rather than that he did it to himself or that it came about by accident.

1954. When someone is found dead and there is no sign on the body of how death occurred, it is better to believe that the death was accidental, for it is difficult to kill someone or to commit suicide in such a way that no marks appear on the body; and for this reason, where you cannot discover the truth, you should adhere to the clearest idea of what can happen.

1955. It sometimes happens that a husband is found dead next to his wife, or a wife next to her husband. And when it happens, you should examine the deceased to see if there is evidence that this was done to him, and if there is, there is a great presumption against the survivor unless he cried out or tells who did this thing; and a deceased might be found where the survivor's reputation and the life they led together should be examined very carefully. And if it is found that the survivor treated the deceased badly, that is a sufficient presumption against people for them to be put in prison for life, unless their innocence was proved by what was discovered later. And as an example of how you should investigate all murders, we will give an account of a case which we saw.

1956. A woman had made an arrangement with two ruffians [*ribaus*] that they would kill her husband, and she would provide them with an opportunity to do so easily. And she told them to come to her house at dusk, and they would find her washing his hair: "And at that time you can club him to death [*assommer*]." And the ruffians murdered him this way, and when they had murdered him, they took a stick of medlar[2] wood and made nicks in it with a sword to give the impression that the man had defended himself; and when they had done this, they left the house, and the woman stayed behind and put away all the things that could have shown she was washing him, and then raised the cry: "Haloo, haloo, they're killing my husband!" The neighbors ran in and found the deceased in the house and the stick next to him, and reported the crime to the judge. The judge came and interrogated the woman, asking how her husband had been killed; she replied that armed men she did not know had come in and attacked him, and he had defended himself as well as he could with a stick, and that this was apparent from the nicks in the stick made by the swords. She was asked what weapon he was killed with, and she said: "Swords," and it was true that after they had clubbed him they had struck his head with swords to hide the mark of the club. And the judge, who was clever, took the stick and made as if to defend himself with it against a person holding a sword, and saw that the nicks in the stick could not have been made as they were by a person defending himself. And afterwards he had the head of the dead man examined, and found it split in a way that could not have been done with a sword. Then he confronted the woman with the two lies she had told, and accused her of having had this done; and as soon as he was going to put her to the torture [*metre en gehine*], she admitted the whole truth and was burned, and the ruffians were summoned so many times that they were banished on pain of death. And we have described this case so that judges can use it as an example for investigating obscure cases which arise, so that by their cleverness offenses can be punished.

1957. Sometimes people begin a game, for example jousting or *fouler*[3] or *barres* or some other game, and someone happens to be killed or injured in the game, because he is struck near the heart, or the lance kills him, or for some other reason. And when such a thing happens, the person responsible should not be prosecuted, for when a game is begun in sport, without ill-feeling, and there is an accident during the game, no judicial action is appropriate. But it would be different if the players got angry during the game, so that the action came about because of the anger, for in such a case the person responsible would be punished: for as soon as there is anger, the game is over.

1958. If someone is driving a cart and he kills or maims someone when his cart turns over, it is misadventure, and you should have mercy on the carter, unless it is clear that he overturned his cart on purpose to injure the person out of hatred, for in that case he should not be excused, but punished for the offense.

1959. In all cases of misadventure where a person injures himself and someone else at the same time, the injury or danger to himself should excuse what happened to the others: for example I am demolishing a house or cutting down a tree or something else, and it falls down sooner than I or the people with me thought, and I am injured and some of the others killed or hurt, in that case my injury is my excuse. And also if I am next to my cart and it overturns and injures both me and someone else, I should not be accused of doing it on purpose, for it is hard to believe I would have put myself in such danger in order to do harm to someone else.

1960. For this reason, if I take someone with me without expectation that harm will come to him, for example to bathe in a river or a fish reservoir, or to climb up to pick fruit on a tree, or to catch birds, or for some other reason why you take people with you to do something together, or to help you in some task which is not improper [*malicieuse*],—and some harm comes to the person I took along,—for example if he falls off the place where he climbed up, or he drowns, or he has a fall from his horse,—I cannot and should not be prosecuted for any of these reasons. But it would be different if I were taking him along to commit some offense, and during the commission of the offense he was hurt, for the offense (for example it might be a case of crime) might be such that I could be accused of deliberate injury [*mauvestié*], even though the injury had happened to the person whom I had procured to commit the offense, for it has long been said that a person knowingly receiving stolen goods is as guilty of larceny as the person doing the stealing, for if there were no receivers, there would be fewer people committing offenses.

1961. It sometimes happens that a person intending to commit an offense takes a companion with him, for example one of his relatives or his friends, and he does not tell them what he is intending to do for fear they may advise against it, or not want to go with him, and he thinks that once the thing has been begun they will not fail him in this task. It is a very evil thing to act this way, and many have been tricked this way, for such a subterfuge does not excuse them if they are present at the scene and give help or aid or encouragement. And if they wish to dissociate themselves from the offense, then as soon as they realize what the person they are with wants to do, they must stop him from doing what he is trying to do, or they must leave immediately, without giving aid or comfort to the person they went with, and in this way they can be excused of the offense.

1962. It is a great misadventure when an honest man [*preudons*] is arrested along with dishonest people; and everyone should be very careful whose company he keeps, for many people have been made to suffer [*destruit*] who had no part in the offense, and the truth of this will be demonstrated by an example.

1963. A pilgrim came to a town, and one evening, as he was going outside the town to amuse himself, he heard a group of people singing and playing various instruments in a tavern. He wanted to hear their songs and see what kind of people they were. He went to the door of the tavern, and saw that it was six young men and some women with them, sitting all together at a table. When they saw him looking at them from the door, they asked him in such polite terms to come and drink with them, that he went and sat with them; and while he was in their company, those with whom he was sitting were accused of being murderers and thieves, and it was said that many of them were in this tavern. The judge took plenty of armed men and came to the tavern and found them and arrested them, and the pilgrim along with them. And soon afterwards they were hanged and drawn for various crimes and the pilgrim along with them, for no one would believe he was not their associate, and {they thought he was} all the worse for pretending to be a pilgrim: and thus a person without guilt was put to death because he fell in with bad company. And in this story you can find two morals: one, that a judge who arrests a lot of people on suspicion of an offense should inquire into each person's guilt before punishing him; and the other that you should refrain from keeping bad company, even if you have no bad intentions, because of the dangers that may arise.

1964. It is a dangerous thing to hit someone, for it has long been said: "What you thought was hitting was killing [*teus cuide batre qui tue*]." And when a person who has been beaten dies of the battery within forty days after the battery, or even later than forty days if it is clear he died as a result of the battery,—for example if he never got up with the appearance of being cured,—his death is blamed on those who committed the battery; and if there was someone present at the battery who did not raise his hand, but nevertheless gave aid and comfort to those committing the battery, he is not excused from the action, for it may be that the others would not have started to commit the battery unless they were expecting help from those who came with them.

1965. If I am in a place where there are plenty of my relatives, and relying on their help (even though I said nothing to them) I attack someone and kill or wound him, I alone should be punished for the offense, for since the others did not come there with me on purpose to commit this act, and did not participate, they should be excused.

1966. Just as there are accidents which can cause injury to people, as we have described above, there are also other cases which are called misadventure, for example unclaimed lost property [*choses espaves*], for it sometimes happens that someone has his animals enclosed and they escape so that the owner does not know where to find them, and this unclaimed lost property belongs to the lord of the place where it is found.

1967. A thing is not unclaimed lost property which is sought by the owner or on his orders, and he proves that it is his. And if he was not looking for it, but he heard later where it was, he should get it back if he proves it is his; but this means things that you can prove certain ownership of, for there are some things you cannot easily prove are yours, for example, a swarm of bees when it goes so far that the person pursuing it loses sight of it; or wild animals that escape from hunting preserves; or fish which go from one reservoir to another or from one pond to another: you cannot prove that these things and others like them are yours, even though you can prove that you have lost such things.

Here ends the chapter on misadventures in which pity and mercy are appropriate.

Notes

1. Suicide is a serious crime, for which the offender's property is forfeit to the lord. See §837.
2. The medlar tree resembles the crab apple.
3. A ball game resembling rugby.

70. Unenforceable Gifts

Here begins the seventieth chapter of this book, which speaks of gifts which should not be enforced, and those which can be enforced and which you cannot contest.

1968. We have mentioned in various chapters various kinds of gifts, for example in the chapter on direct and lateral inheritance {Chapter 14}, and in other places where it was appropriate according to what the case we were discussing required, but this will not prevent us from speaking briefly about some kinds of gifts which we have not mentioned elsewhere; and we will make this chapter which we have begun, which will explain which gifts are to be enforced and which are not.

1969. Everyone should know that gifts which are made against God, or against Holy Church, or against the public interest, or against morality, or which disinherit someone, are not to be enforced; instead they must be undone and nullified as being invalid; and we also say that anything promised for any of the above reasons should not be paid.

1970. It sometimes happens that someone gives something he thinks belongs to him and it does not, for example, if someone gives me a parcel of land which he thinks is his and afterwards, after he has had me placed in possession, someone hales me in front of a judge and says he has the rights to that land: in that case I can use all the defenses that the donor could have used. But I cannot make the donor come and be my warrantor unless he obligated himself to do so when the gift was made; for if someone gives something unconditionally, without assuming an obligation or warranteeing, he gives only the interest he had in the thing given. And from this you can understand that a person who gives away someone else's property without assuming an obligation of giving a warranty gives nothing. But it would be otherwise if the thing were sold, for whoever makes a sale, whether of his own property or someone else's, is required to warrantee the property or pay the loss to the buyer if it is a thing which cannot be warranteed.

1971. The great lords who hold directly from the king can give their real property to their vassals or their employees or other people, when they think it will be well-used, and retain the homage from the land, even though by making this gift they make part of their lands which they hold in fief into a sub-fief. Nevertheless, they could be such rash givers, and give away so much, that the king would not have to permit it; and we believe they cannot go beyond a fifth of their lands. And if a baron gave away parcels that make up a fifth during his lifetime, and afterwards died and left a fifth of his real property in a will, the king or his heirs could contest it for good cause, for he would thus have separated off two-fifths of his real property and subinfeudated it, which he cannot do. Nevertheless, according to our custom, all *inter vivos* gifts made in good faith are to be enforced, always preserving the rights of the lords from whom the property is held. But you should know that gifts given against God and against the local custom, or in order to disinherit your heirs because of hatred (unless there is a good reason for the hatred), are not given in good faith.

1972. As we have said in several chapters that all frauds should be destroyed where they are admitted or proved, we also say in this chapter that if a person fraudulently gives to one person in order to take away from another, the gift is invalid; and especially, no one can give his children any of his real or personal property or his purchased property (except what they can take by the custom of the area) without the other brothers and sisters being able to demand a partition after the death of the father who gave the gift, with respect to over-generous gifts. Nevertheless, a father or mother can give to whichever of their children they like some of their personal property and purchased property, and warrantee the gift as long as they live. But after their death if the gift was so unfairly given that the others are disinherited, the gift is not to be enforced, for it is not fair that one brother or sister should have everything and the others nothing. And what share each should have according to our custom is explained in the chapter which speaks of direct and lateral inheritance {Chapter 14}; and when it is said that children who were married off by the father and mother have the choice of bringing the gift back into the hotchpot and making a partition, or else of staying silent without bringing the gift back and without making partition when they consider themselves satisfied with what was given to them when they married, this means when the gifts were not so unfair that the other children are disinherited, and gifts which are that unfair should be reduced by the estimation of an honest judge.

1973. It sometimes happens that a stepfather or stepmother, because of the love between them in the marriage, give their stepsons their real property or their purchased or personal property, in whole or in part, and bypass their children; and when such a case arises you should look very carefully at what motivated the stepfather or stepmother to do this. And if they were not persuaded by a good reason, the gift should not be enforced as far as the real property is concerned, for they can certainly bypass their children and give their personal and purchased property to their step-children, as they could give them to strangers if they wanted.

1974. It is true that no gift made during her marriage by a married woman, whether of real or personal or purchased property, is to be enforced so that her husband or her heirs cannot cancel it, unless she made the gift on the authority and with the consent of her husband. Nevertheless, if she gives something and the husband says nothing because he does not know about it, or because he is happy for the gift to be given, even though he gave no leave, and afterwards he dies and the woman wants to cancel the gift, her plea should not be entertained in this case; instead the gift should be enforced so that she cannot cancel it, for although the husband could have canceled it during his lifetime, since she is now in charge of her own affairs [*en son franc pouoir*] she must honor the gift.

1975. We have seen some people who had children who themselves had children, and the grandfather or the grandmother wanted to bypass the children and give to the grandchildren; but according to our custom, this cannot be done by devise or by will, for my father, unless I commit an offense against him, cannot bypass me to give to my children after his death; but as long as he lives, he can marry off my children with his personal property or his purchased property if he likes. And if grandparents could do this after their deaths, they would sometimes do it fraudulently to block a current custom. And the custom is that if I have brothers or sisters, my father or mother can give me only what my brothers and sisters cannot partition with me after our parents' death, except gifts to children that the parents marry off, as is said above in this chapter. And because my father saw that he could not make me a gift separate from the distribution because of the above-mentioned custom, he might give to my children. And a gift to my children who are in my care and my guardianship is very much to my advantage, and to the detriment of my brothers and sisters; and for this reason such gifts should not be permitted.

1976. If it happens that Guillaume and Pierre sue Jehan at the same time, one for an overdue debt owed him, and the other for a promise and agreement he made to give him something, and the debt is admitted or proved and the promise of a gift also, and Jehan does not have enough money to pay the debt and the gift, the debt should be paid first in its entirety. And afterwards if there is anything left, an agreement for a gift which was made for a good reason should be enforced out of what is left when the debt is paid, and it is right that debts should be paid before promises.

1977. We saw in the king's court a suit against the count of Guines who had made a general obligation in security [*avoit obligié generaument*] of himself and all his possessions, real and personal, to his creditors, and when he saw the due date of several of his creditors approaching, and some due dates already past, and considered that if he sold all his land it would be hard to pay all his debts, he made great gifts of real property to some of his near relatives, keeping a life interest in the fruits of some, but not of others. And when the creditors saw that he had surrendered possession in a gift of real property that was pledged to them as security, and he was defaulting on the payments, they haled the said count and those to whom he had made the gifts into court. And once the truth about his gifts after pledging the property as security was known, it was found in a judgment that the gifts could not be enforced, and that the property would be sold to pay the creditors, and once the debts were paid the gifts would be validly paid out of what was left. And by this judgment you can understand that gifts given after property has been generally pledged in security cannot be to the detriment of the creditors.

1978. It would be different if I *sold* my property after I had generally pledged it in security, for I am not prevented from selling my property and warranteeing it to the buyer because of a general pledge of security. But if I had pledged it specially, then I could not sell it or give it or alienate it in any way to the detriment of those to whom it was specially pledged in security.

1979. Because we have spoken above of a difference between a general and a special pledge of security, we will define what is a general and a special pledge of security.

1980. You should know that a general pledge of security [*obligacions generale*] is when you pledge all your property without naming anything separately. For example if someone says in their writing, after they have set out their agreement: "And to confirm this agreement, I have obligated myself and my property, real and personal, present and to be acquired," a general pledge of security is created by these words. And a special pledge is made in a different way, for example if someone says in his writing: "And to confirm this agreement, I have obligated this wood,—or that vineyard or these pastures,—lying in such-and-such a place." Such a pledge is special, and once it is made, the obligor cannot alienate the property without the permission of the obligee, until he has fulfilled the agreement for which the security was pledged. But when he has fulfilled the agreement, the security property returns to its original state free and clear.

1981. When a person gives something to someone according to an agreement that the donee must provide some service or owe some duty to the donor, if the donee will not provide the service or perform the duty that was agreed on, the donor cannot sue to get back his gift, but he can have the donee compelled by a court to perform what he agreed to do in exchange for the gift. Nevertheless if the gift was in the form of real property, and some service or duty was agreed on for giving the gift, and the donee cannot be compelled by the court to perform the service or duty he promised, because he is too poor, or because he resides out of the district, or for some other reason, in such cases the donor should summon him before the lord from whom the property he gave him is held, and if he defaults three times, the gifted land should be given back to the donor on the condition that if the donee appears before a year and a day from when the lord took the gift away from him, and he will honor his obligations for the past time, he must get the property back; but after a year and a day his plea must not be entertained, unless he can demonstrate an honest legal excuse, for example that he was in prison, or on a crusade, or prevented by the king's command on the king's business or the public good, or because he was sick for so long that he could not appear because of his sickness. In such cases he can come back after a year and a day by fulfilling his obligations with respect to the land and also paying arrears.

Here ends the chapter on the gifts which are to be enforced and those which are not.

Conclusion

Here begins the conclusion of this book. DEO GRATIAS.

1982. You, king of kings, lord of lords, true God, true man, Father and Son and Holy Spirit, and you, very glorious Virgin Queen, mother and handmaiden of Him who made all and can do all, I thank and praise and adore you, because you have given me the time and the will to think, to the point where I have arrived at the end of what I undertook in my heart to do, that is to write a book on the customs of Beauvais. And I know for certain that I am not so capable or knowledgeable or worthy that I could have persevered with this work unless it had been by your tender mercy, so that it may be to the profit of some of those who wish to study it in the times to come. And since the truth is that customs come to an end because of young jurors who do not know the old customs, so that in the future the opposite of what we have put into this book will be observed to happen, we pray to all to excuse us, for when we wrote the book, we wrote as far as we could what was enforced or should have been done ordinarily in Beauvais; and the corruption of the time to come should not bring us into ill repute, or be blamed on our book. And after we had set out the customs and written them down, we observed the world, and the movement of those who are eager to plead and accustomed to pleading; and the more we observed, the less we esteemed them, and the more we despised them, and thought of things they would be better to do in this world. And when we had thought much about this matter, it seemed to us that there is nothing that anyone should desire as much as a firm peace [*ferme pes*], for a person who has set his heart on a firm peace is rightfully lord of this world and a companion of God. For he is lord of this world inasfar as he has good thoughts, and his heart at peace, so that he does not immoderately desire any earthly thing; and he is a companion of God because he is in a state of grace and without sin; and except in these two ways no one can have in his heart a firm peace, for if he is desirous of earthly things in any improper manner, his heart is warring and full of care for gain, and then he does not have a firm peace in his heart; and if he is not in a state of grace, for example he is in mortal sin, his own conscience makes war on him; for we do not believe there is any man so bad that his own heart is not attacked by his own conscience. Therefore those who want to have a firm peace must above all things love and esteem God and despise earthly things, and whoever can do this possesses God and this world, as we said above. And although some people say that not every one who wants peace can have it, they do not speak the truth; for if someone is attacked in a private war, or by lawsuits, or he loses friends or property, and he loves God and desires a firm peace, he will bear his tribulations so patiently that they will hurt him little or not at all, and he will seek with all his strength the way for complete peace to dwell in his heart. And since we have said that a firm peace is the best thing to seek, we pray Him who is the fountain of peace, namely Jesus Christ, the son of Saint Mary, and Her who takes peace from that fountain when she pleases for her friends, that is to say his blessed Mother, that they may give and send us peace according to what they know we need for the salvation of the souls belonging to Our Lord, according to his power and his mercy, which power is omnipotent and which mercy is to be compared to no other; and may he grant us this at the prayer of his tender Mother. *Amen.*

Here Philippe de Beaumanoir ends his book which he wrote on the customs of Beauvais, in the year of Our Lord's incarnation 1283.

May God give him a good end,
Who reigns and will reign without end.
AMEN.

Glossary of Selected Terms Used in the Translation, with Their Old French Equivalent(s).

In each entry, the alphabetically arranged term is that used in the translation. There follows the Old French word or words which the term translates, and an explanation. Finally, the reference to a paragraph number shows where the term is used, in a definition, a discussion, or a typical context. References are not given for all the occurrences of the term in the translation.

ABBREVIATIONS IN THE GLOSSARY

adj.   adjective
adv.   adverb
def.   definition
f.   feminine
i.   intransitive
m.   masculine
n.   noun
pl.   plural
r.   reflexive
sbdy.   somebody
sthg.   something
t.   transitive
v.   verb

Adjournment sine die. *Essoine* n. f. Good legal excuse for not coming to court when summoned, and with no date fixed for new court appearance (Chapter 3). See Continuance.

Advisory day. *Jour d'avisement* n. m. Time to seek advice (275). Same as Counsel day, q. v.

Advocate. *Avocat* n. m. Advocate, speaker, barrister (Chapter 5).

Agent. *Serjant* n. m. The person who acts on behalf of another, called the principal (Chapter 29). See Principal.

Agreement. *Convenance* n. m. Similar to modern contract (Chapter 34).

Answer. *Defense* n. f. The response given to a complaint when the allegation is not admitted (Chapter 7).

Appeal. *Appel* n. m. Protest against (lack of) action in a lower court (1739, Chapter 62) or accusation of the perpetrator of a serious crime (Chapter 61).

Arrest. *Prise* n. f. Seizure of persons by some authority (Chapters 51, 52). See Attachment.

Attachment. *Prise* n. f. Seizure or property by some authority (Chapters 51, 52). See Arrest.

Attorney. *Procureeur* n. m. Person representing party in a lawsuit (Chapter 4).

Auditor. *Auditeur* n. m. Person appointed to examine witnesses (Chapter 40).

Avowal. *Aveu* n. m. Acknowledgment, claim (to hold land from sbdy, be a serf of sbdy) (1418). See Disavowal.

Banish. *Banir* v. tr. Declare a person a fugitive for not appearing in court after several summonses (Chapter 30).

Bar. *Barre* n. f. Side issue, collateral issue (249), dilatory exception (1724, 1911).

Baron. *Baron* n. m. Great lord, baron, holding directly from the king (314), husband (430).

Bastardy. *Bastardie* n. f. Condition of a person born out of wedlock, illegitimacy (Chapter 18).

Believe (a witness). *Croire* v. tr. Give credence to (a witness) (129, 131, 1396). Some witnesses were believed on oath, and no further proof of their claims was required. See Hear.

Casus belli. *Fet aparent* n. m. Legal reason for a gentleman to start a private war, such as a serious crime (1669).

Challenge. *Debouter* v. tr. (Try to) have a witness excluded (1175–90). See Exclude.

Champion. *Champion* n. m. Substitute fighter (212, 1137, 1832, 1891, Chapter 61).

Chattels. *Chateus* n. m. Personal property (not distinguished from *mueble*) (18). See Personal property, Real property.

Church. *Sainte Eglise*, n. f. The Church as an institution (50). *Moustier*, n. m. A church building, wherein services are read (332).

Clear (proof). *Cler* adj. (208), *apert* adj. (208). Clear, obvious, well-known, patent, apparent.

Clerk. *Clerc* n. m. Person in holy orders, generally under ecclesiastical jurisdiction (1436).

Coercion. *Force* n. f. Making a person do something by force or threats of force (258, 315).

Cognizance. *Conoissance* n. f. Jurisdiction, being able to summon and deal with a person or issue in court (39, 72).

Commoner. *Homme de poosté* n. m. Free person not a nobleman, but not a serf (def. 1451).

Commune. *Commune* n. f. Chartered town (Chapter 50).

Complaint. *Demande* n. f. (Chapter 6), *claim* n. m. (923). The accusation made by a plaintiff against the defendant.

Confiscate. *Seisir* v. tr. Take away something permanently from sbdy (Chapter 51). See Seize.

Continuance. *Contremand* n. m. Temporary postponement, with fixed date for new court appearance (Chapter 3). See Adjournment sine die.

Contract. *Convenance*, n. f. Agreement, promise to do something (201). See Agreement.

Council. *Conseil* n. m. Group of advisers (3).

Counsel. *Conseil* n. m. Adviser (1, 8, 174), advice (195).

Counsel day. *Jour de conseil*. Time to seek advice or advisers (218).

Creditor. *Creancier* n. m. (90, 1597), *deteur* n. m. (225, 521). Person to whom something is due or owing. See Debtor.

Crime (serious). *Crime* n. m. Offense for which penalty is death and confiscation of property (Chapter 30).

Custodianship. *Bail* n. m. Custody of a fief on behalf of a minor child (197, Chapter 15).

Custom. *Coustume* n. f. Unwritten law, enforceable in the district (Chapter 24). See Privilege.

Damage(s). *Damage* n. m. Damage caused to property (1557). Costs (841). See Loss.

Default. *Defaute* n. f. Failure, without excuse, to come to court in response to a summons (60).

Default of judgment. *Defaute de droit* n. f. Failure to give a hearing to a person requesting it (Chapter 62, def. 1778).

Defense. *Defense* n. f. Answer raised against an accusation (Chapter 7).

Denial. *Niance*, n. f. Rejection of allegation (157).

Dilatory exception, see Exception.

Direct descent. *Descente* n. f. Way property passes in a direct line, e.g., father to son (Chapter 14). See Lateral descent.

Disavowal. *Desaveu* n. m. Claim not to hold property from sbdy, or not to be the serf of sbdy (Chapter 45). See Avowal.

Discretion. *Volonté* n. f. The lord's right to set a punishment for a serious offense (1779).

Disseise. *Dessaisir* v. tr. and r. Take away possession of, give up one's own possession of, property (Chapter 32).

Dower. *Douaire* n. m. Widow's rights in (half of) deceased husband's property (Chapter 13).

Ecclesiastical court. *Cour de crestienté*, n. f. Court under control of church authorities, with jurisdiction over certain parties and subject matters (Chapter 11). See Secular court.

Exception. *Exception* n. f. Defense or answer to accusation. Either dilatory (serving to prolong the suit) or peremptory (bringing suit to conclusion) (Chapter 7).

Exclude. *Debouter* v. tr. Prevent (a witness) from testifying because of possible bias (1170, 1175–90). *Lever* v. tr. Challenge veracity of witness, by offer of wager of battle (1765).

Farm horse. *Ronci de service* n. m. Horse given as part of homage owed for fief (Chapter 28).

Fief. *Fief* n. m. Land or other income-producing property held from an overlord by giving homage (def. 672).

Fine. *Amende* n. f. Payment to lord as penalty for an offense (882).

Force. *Force* n. f. Use of force or coercion (def. 956).

Forfeit. *Forfet* n. m. Loss of all property by a person convicted of a serious crime (824).

Fraud. *Fraude* n. f. (1099), *tricherie* n. f. "Dishonest" behavior, leading to another's loss (def. 997).

Free. *Franc* adj. Freedom as applied to both persons and real property. Freehold (property) (48), (person) not a serf (1424). See Serf.

Fruits. *Despueilles* n. f. pl. (679), *fruits* n. m. (687), *levees* n. f. (64, 988). Personal property in goods or money derived from real property.

General. *General* adj. Universal, not particular (140). See Special.

Gentleman. *Gentius homme* n. m. Nobleman, aristocrat, lord, permitted to hold a free fief (1453).

Guaranteed peace. *Asseurement* n. m. End of feud or private war sworn to by the hostile parties, and providing safety from attack (299, 347, Chapter 60).

Guardianship. *Garde* n. f. Holding of non-fief property for minor child (Chapter 15) or of fief property if for own child on death of spouse (517).

Harvest. *Lever* v. tr. Gather (even non-agricultural) personal property, such as rents, etc. (78, 612).

Hatred. *Haine* n. f. Feud, hostility, ill-will, grudge (826).

Hear (a witness). *Oïr* v. tr. Admit to testify, not necessarily believe the testimony (1225). See Believe.

Hearing. *Droit* n. m. (795) *Plet ordené*, n. m. (46) A court proceeding, trial.

High justice. *Haute justice* n. f. Jurisdiction over personal crimes (Chapter 58). See Low justice.

Homage. *Homage* n. m. What a lord owes his overlord for his fief, sworn to within forty days of inheritance (483).

Homicide. *Homicide* n. m. Manslaughter, killing (def. 828).

Honest. *Loial* adj. (21). Could be same as loyal, but has a wider connotation, e.g., honest or valid (truthful) witnesses (226).

Honest folk. *Bonnes gens* n. f. pl. Persons able to testify in court, and who therefore make good witnesses to transactions, etc. (1786).

Honest man. *Preudhomme* n. m. Reliable person, able to witness transactions, etc. (1075).

Income. *Fruits* n. m. (687) *Levees* n. f. pl. (64). Personal property in goods or money derived from real property. See Fruits.

Inquest. *Enqueste* n. f. Examination of witnesses, proof through witnesses (def. 1235–38).

Inquiry. *Apprise* n. f. Preliminary inquiry by judge (def. 1235–38).

Inspection day. *Jour de veue* n. m. Showing and identification of property under dispute (Chapter 9).

Intimidation. *Paour* n. f. Great fear is the result of intimidation. (956).

Judge. *Juge* n. m. *Jugeor* n. m. The *juge* hears pleadings, supervises the cases, while the *jugeor*, like jurors, or a panel of judges, participates in the verdict (23–24).

Judgment. *Jugement* n. m. Verdict rendered by the *jugeors* based on the pleadings and the inquest (Chapter 67).

Jurisdiction. *Justice* n. f. Power to summon and give trial to sbdy (Chapters 10, 11, 58).

Juror. *Jugeor* n. m. Person giving vedict on a case (23–24). See Judge.

King's law. *Establissement* n. m. Ordinance of king, having legal force (1513).

Kinship. *Lignage* n. m. Relation between blood relatives (Chapter 19), the group formed by such (1671).

Lateral descent. *Escheoite de costé* n. f. Inheritance out of the direct line (Chapter 14). See Direct descent.

Lease. *Engagement* n. m. Prepaid lease; resembles a mortgage, but lender gets use of the property (1414).

Loss. *Damage* (60). Harm that must be made up by person causing it (1561).

Low justice. *Basse justice* n. f. Jurisdiction over crimes against property (not crimes against the person) (Chapter 58). See High justice.

Murder. *Murtre* n. m. Premeditated homicide (def. 825).

Novel disseisin. *Nouvele dissaisine* n. f. Ouster from real property, conversion of personal property (Chapter 32, def. 955).

Nuisance. *Novel tourble* n. m. Prevention of enjoyment of property (Chapter 32, def. 957).

Oath. *Serment* n. m. Declaration under oath may be sufficient proof of certain issues (890–912).

Offense. *Mesfet* n. m. Crime or misdemeanor (Chapters 30, 31).

Officer. *Serjant* n. m. Low-level arresting officer, process-server, etc. (909).

Ownership. *Proprieté* n. f. More than mere possession, can be proved even if possession has been lost (988).

Partition. *Partie* n. f. Dividing of property, especially after a decease (482).

Partnership. *Compaignie* n. f. Alliance formed for business, in marriage, etc. (Chapter 21).

Peremptory exception. See Exception.

Personal. *Personel* adj. Touching the person (not property) (def. 229).

Personal property. *Mueble* n. m. Anything movable (Chapter 23, def. 673). Often coupled with *chatel* but not distinguished from it. Also called personalty.

Personalty. See Personal property.

Pleadings. *Paroles* n. f. pl. (211), *posicions* n. f. pl. (140), *errements de plet* n. m. pl. (1781). The claims of the plaintiff and defendant relative to the issues. Given orally before the judge (211).

Presumption. *Presompcion* n. f. Some presumptions are stronger than others (1156–62).

Principal. *Mestre* n. m. (Chapter 29). The person for whom an agent acts. See Agent.

Privilege. *Usage* n. m. Like a custom, but observed for an individual, not enforceable for all, similar to a modern easement (Chapter 24).

Proceedings. *Errements* n. m. pl. Where an appeal is not by wager of battle, it must be on the (record of the) proceedings (24, 1781).

Protocol. *Compromis* n. m. An agreement to go to arbitration, and specifying the terms (Chapter 41).

Provost. *Prevost* n. m. (27, 42). A judge of lower rank than the *bailli*.

Punishment. *Vanjance* n. f. This word used by Beaumanoir for punishment by the authorities implies retribution (823).

Purchased real property. *Aques* n. m. pl. (1367), *conquès* n. m. pl. (17, 254, 362, 931). Purchased (not inherited) real property. Can be left in a will or sold by purchaser. Once inherited, it becomes inherited real property (*eritage*) (505).

Quit-rent. *Cens* n. m. Kind of rent, perhaps originally paid in lieu of labor (467).

Real. *Reel* adj. Concerning property (def. 230). See Personal.

Real property. *Eritage* n. m. Income-producing property of all kinds (Chapter 23, def. 672).

Recall from memory. *Recort* n. m. Recall of something (e. g., of pleadings) not recorded in writing, repetition (1150–53).

Reclamation. *Recreance* n. f. Recovery of persons or property seized, arrested, or attached by authorities (Chapter 53).

Redemption. *Rescousse* n. f. Right of family members to buy back any property sold to buyer outside the family (Chapter 44).

Relief. *Rachat* n. m. Tax paid to lord by inheritor of a fief by lateral descent (def. 762).

Religious house. *Eglise* n. f. Monasteries, etc. (Chapter 46).

Reputation. *Renommee* n. f. Can be good or bad, may be taken into account in criminal trials, etc. (940).

Reseise. *Ressaisir* v. tr. Give back possession (237, 980).

Safe passage. *Travers* n. m. Protected road, for which a toll, also called *travers*, is exacted (891, in both senses).

Seal. *Seel* n. m. Impression in wax attached by a ribbon to a writing (1075).

Secular court. *Laie juridicion*, n. f. Non-religious court (Chapter 11). See Ecclesiastical court.

Security. *Seurté* n. f. Property deposited with court or party to ensure payment, compliance, etc. Could sometimes be a mere promise (1583).

Seisin. *Saisine* n. f. Possession granted by a lord, or acquired by peaceful occupation of a year and a day (955).

Seize. *Seisir* v. tr. (Chapter 51), *prendre en sa main* v. tr. (1546). Take temporary possession of sthg in dispute or which constitutes an offense.

Serf. *Serf, serve* adj. and n. Servile person, serf (1451). See Free.

Share-cropping. *Champart* n. m. Right to farm a piece of land by promising a share of the crop to the owner (895).

Sharp practice. *Barat* n. m. A kind of trickery or fraud, often in a legal context (3, 123)

Special. *Especial* adj. Particular, detailed, specified, not universal (140). See general.

Sovereign. *Souverain* n. m. The King, or great lords holding directly from him (1043).

Sub-fief. *Arrierefief* n. m. Fief held from a person who holds his own fief from an overlord (Chapter 47).

Summons. *Semonse* n. f. Order to appear in court on a certain day (Chapter 2).

Surety. *Plege* n. m. A person who undertakes to ensure compliance, payment, etc. (1585).

Tax. *Taille* n. f. City tax (1525). *Ventes* n. f. Sales tax (1580. 1581). *Rachat* n. m. Relief, inheritance tax (def. 762).

Tenant. *Oste* n. m. A tenant usually held a house and small area of land, or *masure*, for rent (972–73).

Treachery. *Traïson* n. f. Stealth, unexpected action, especially homicide (def. 826).

Trickery. *Tricherie* n. f. Fraud (Chapter 33, def. 997).

Unencumbered. *(Quite et) delivre* adj. Not subject to debts, liens, security deposits, etc. (509).

Valid. *Loial* adj. (Witnesses) not excludable for bias (1149).

Villeinage. *Vilenage* n. m. Land held for rent, quit-rent, a share of the crop, etc., not a fief (def. 467).

Wager of battle. *Gages de bataille.* Duel, or judicial battle (Chapters 61, 65).

War. *Guerre* n. f. Private war, between gentlemen (Chapter 59).

Warrantor. *Garant* n. m. Person who can confirm one's possession, etc. (1011).

Writing. *Letre* n. f. A written document with a seal, enforceable in many cases (Chapter 35).

Wrong. *Torfet* n. m. Refers to wrongs to be righted in a will (426).

Index

Note: Numbers following each entry refer to section numbers in the text. Numbers in italics indicate occurrences of particular significance.

Account, accounting, 20, 53, 164, 358, 395, 424, 459, 504, 513, 516, 549, 564, 566, 571, 650, 801, 814, 816–20, 1050, 1190, 1520–22, 1621, 1906

Adjournment sine die (Chapter 3), 57, 59, 63–64, 98–99, 101, *106–10*, 112, 119–21, 123–28, 132–34, 136, 237, 239, 288, 297, 856, 1282, 1291–92, 1392, 1865, 1887, 1909. *See also* Continuance

Admit, admission, 81, 201, 226, 242, 245, 247, 252, 256–57, 259, 274, 280, 286, 303–4, 309, 314, 355, 358, 364, 382, 397, 426, 580, 593–94, 596, 701, 745, 771, 798, 818, 891, 893–94, 907, 915–16, 920, 926, 932, 959–60, 979, 985, 1022, 1031, 1052, 1062, 1075, 1098–99, 1109, 1111, 1115, 1132, *1146*, 1154–55, 1169, 1186, 1192, 1196, 1223, 1243–44, 1247, 1252, 1314, 1382, 1433, 1438, 1469, 1472, 1549, 1551, 1585–86, 1588, 1601–2, 1604, 1611, 1711, 1749, 1762, 1813, 1827, 1836, 1869, 1950, 1956, 1972, 1976

Advocate (Chapter 5), 34, *174–95*, 258, 399, 821–22, 1210, 1520, 1873

Agent, 252, *1005–8*, 1350, 1554. *See also* Officer; Principal

Agreement (Chapters 34, 35), 42, 154, 169, 171, 176–77, 179, 252, 261, 286, 297–98, 318, 342, 359, 377, 400, 449, 541, 544, 562, 569, 624, 628, 645, 649, 653–55, 658, 662, 669, 695, 697, 754, 768–72, 792, 799, 802, 805–8, 812–13, 915, 968, 973, *998–1004*, 1008, 1010, 1015, 1017–19, 1020–21, 1024–26, 1029–33, 1036, 1038–42, 1051–55, 1058–68, 1073–74, 1082–83, 1086, 1089, 1092, 1097–98, 1100–1101, 1103–4, 1115, 1118, 1125, 1128–30, 1133–34, 1136–37, 1139, 1143–44, 1164, 1230–34, 1256, 1264, 1269, 1289, 1290, 1293, 1295, 1299, 1301–3, 1305–6, 1315, 1316, 1319, 1348–49, 1375–76, 1396, 1407, 1409, 1414, 1429, 1445,

1531, 1581, 1597, 1610–14, 1629, 1648, 1653, 1677, 1719, 1723, 1733, 1791, 1835, 1846, 1849, 1855, 1860, 1898, 1921–22, 1926, 1930, 1937–38, 1976, 1980–81. *See also* Contract

Answer (a complaint) (Chapter 7), 53, 91–92, 173, 196, 198, 212–13, 215, 217, 222, 224–25, 233, *237–39*, 551–53, 576, 619, 667, 674, 688–89, 739, 744, 770–71, 795, 803, 848, 877, 901, 903, 915, 918, 920, 923–24, 972, 979, 981–82, 987, 1006, 1022, 1026, 1044, 1052, 1061, 1070–72, 1074–75, 1080, 1094, 1102, 1109, 1111, 1135, 1154, 1269, 1294, 1296, 1314, 1322, 1334–36, 1349, 1357, 1365, 1371, 1375–76, 1378, 1382, 1391, 1402, 1407, 1413, 1427, 1488, 1574, 1586, 1665, 1712, 1747, 1770, 1789, 1791, 1813, 1817, 1830, 1855, 1869, 1870, 1897, 1917, 1932, 1950

Appeal (Chapter 61), 23–24, 36, 44, 122, 592, 663, 836, 843, 888, 917, 1050, 1148, 1151, 1161, 1183–84, 1209, 1214, 1222, 1387–88, 1507, 1532, *1709–12*, 1714–17, 1719, 1731–32, 1734–35, 1737, 1739, 55, 1757–62, 1766, 1768–70, 1772, 1774–77, 1779–81, 1783, 1786–88, 1791–92, 1794–98, 1800, 1802–9, 1812, 1814–15, 1817–19, 1821, 1825–27, 1829–32, 1834–36, 1838–39, 1851–53, 1861, 1863, 1871–72, 1882, 1884, 1886, 1888–91, 1894, 1897–98, 1905, 1908–11

Arbitration, arbitrator (Chapter 41), 140, 569, 1011, 1072, 1152, 1245, *1260–63*, 1265–73, 1275–85, 1287, 1289, 1290, 1292–99, 1302–3, 1318, 1818

Argument, 15, 23, 33, 43, 83, 111, 134, 156, 180–82, 184, 235–41, 243–44, 248–50, 254, 260, 280, 454, 501, 683, 690, 993, 1081, 1108, 1134, 1192, 1246, 1269, 1382, 1400, 1430, 1449, 1529, 1532, 1566, 1712, 1779, 1863, 1916, 1950

Arrest, 16, 41, 50, 55, 302–3, 325, 326–28, 334, 350–56, 640, 668, 696, 742, 758, 804, 824, 836, 840, 849, 876, 877–78, 884–85, 907–11, 917, 922, 927, 940–42, 950–51, 953, 999, 1035, 1042, 1044, 1046, 1159, 1162, 1186–87, 1236–37, 1243, 1347, 1523, 1534, 1536, 1545–46, 1556–58, 1564, 1567–71, 1574, 1586, 1601, 1616, 1652–54, 1656, 1658, 1671, 1673, 1683, 1695, 1698, 1701, 1707, 1726–29, 1769, 1815–16, 1904, 1907, 1933, 1962–63. *See also* Attach

Arson, 207, *831*, 996, 1159, 1564, 1698. *See also* Burn; Fire

Attach, attachment, 41, 90, 206, 210, 214, 277–78, 379, 442, 538, 696, 897, 985, 1055–56, 1094, 1131, 1135, 1402, 1535–37, 1540, 1547, 1576, 1578, 1594–96, 1600, 1615, 1907, 1933. *See also* Arrest

Attorney (Chapter 41), 72, 91, 117, 128, 132–34, *136–43*, 145–46, 148–56, 158–73, 237, 351, 567, 574, 665, 667, 805, 807, 821–22, 993, 1004–5, 1017, 1060–61, 1088, 1106, 1171, 1199, 1210, 1255, 1291, 1349, 1389, 1464, 1470, 1472, 1520, 1873, 1892, 1912

Auditor (Chapter 40), 140, 211, 293, 1152, 1183, 1194, 1209, *1224–28*, 1230, 1234–35, 1240, 1245, 1247–51, 1253, 1255–57, 1260–61, 1282–84

Avow (Chapter 45), *1418–19*, 1421, 1423–25, 1459–61, 1464, 1471, 1476. *See also* Disavow

Bad faith, 52, 93, 224, 398, 558, 562, 584, 594, 613, 640, 652, 708, 756, 759, 804, 809, 896, 923, 940, 992, 1049, 1058, 1096, 1099, 1113, 1135, 1142, 1203, 1208, 1276, 1305, 1360, 1401, 1414, 1416, 1476, 1524, 1569, 1574–75, 1580, 1600, 1781–82, 1789, 1815, 1889, 1891, 1894, 1909. *See also* Good faith

Bailli (Chapter 1), *11–35*, 37–38, 40–56, 92, 140, 145, 170, 184, 189, 193, 211, 251, 298, 322, 426, 518, 845, 886, 915, 1027, 1036–37, 1050, 1064, 1078, 1097–98, 1269, 1303, 1473, 1587, 1604, 1672, 1774–75, 1813, 1869, 1880–81, 1909, 1911, 1913. *See also* Ecclesiastical judge; Provost; Secular judge

Banish, banishment, 411, 590, 700, 827, 836, 859, 917, 931, 1035, 1161, 1336, 1435, 1536, 1545, 1570, 1649, 1655, 1671, 1695–96, 1698–1701, 1726–33, 1904, 1956

Baron, 314, 322, 332, 379–80, 387, 445, 986, *1043–44*, 1050, 1215, 1465–73, 1476, 1499,

1510, 1512–13, 1536–38, 1653–54, 1656, 1660, 1673, 1701, 1708, 1782, 1875–76, 1879, 1933, 1971. *See also* Directly

Bastard, bastardy (Chapter 18), 187, 333, *578–83*, 585–87, 589–91, 594, 596–97, 599, 600–601, 1176, 1259, 1377, 1435, 1456, 1619, 1625, 1636, 1644, 1655, 1688, 1697, 1805

Battle, wager of. *See* Wager of Battle

Believe (a witness, testimony), 42, 52, 68, 129, 131, 144, 162–63, 242, 251, 382, 402, 418, 514, 580, 586, 588–90, 593, 820, 855, 875, 891, 909, 912–13, 929, 1029, 1031, 1083, 1087–88, 1093–94, 1113, 1144, 1175, 1182, 1186–87, 1189–90, 1194, 1197, 1214–16, 1223, 1230, 1234, 1244, 1247, 1267, 1270, 1283, 1396, 1564, 1566, 1605, 1762, 1859, 1894–95

Benefits (reaped from land, etc.), 78, 376–78, 448, 483–84, 486, 491–92, 564, 566, 571, 576, 612, 617, 622, 630, 638, 642, 660, 687, 788, 813, 967, 988, 1074, 1104, 1132, 1159, 1216, 1390, 1415, 1561, 1597, 1858. *See also* Fruits; Income

Bishop, 93, 145, 313, 322, 326, 351, 353, 379, 387, 392–93, 395, 518, 589, 700, 1352, 1436, 1620–21, 1774

Bourgeois, 1159, 1296, 1530

Burden of proof, 1145, 1163, 1165, 1184, 1193, 1206, 1208, 1218, 1229, 1247

Burn, 328, 331, 808, 831, 996, 1132, 1901. *See also* Arson; Fire

Challenge (a witness), 34, 40, 111, 112, 130, 139, 148, 156, 175, 177–78, 206, 210, 212, 233, 237–39, 242, 244, 249, 271, 439, 538, 1174–76, 1178, 1183, 1186, 1209, 1222, 1224–25, 1227, 1239–40, 1244, *1251–52*, 1257, 1428, 1431, 1724, 1761–62, 1764, 1816, 1818, 1823–24, 1837. *See also* Exclude (a witness)

Champion, 212, 1137, *1715–17*, *1721*, 1764, 1829, 1831–32, 1891. *See also* Substitute

Chattels, 18, 36, 72, 140, 197–98, 214, 264, 277–80, 297, 317–18, 379, 382, 576, 770, 1074, 1089, 1091, 1229, 1251, 1259, 1326, 1482, 1597, 1604, 1721, 1758, 1867, 1870. *See also* Personal property; Personalty

Church: building, 116, 396, 618, 647, 733, 737, 1352, 1512, 1514; institution, 332, 411, 578, 700, 1468, 1495; Holy Church, 13, 39, 50, 55, 188, 192, 262, 311–15, 317–31, 333–34, 337–41, 343–44, 346, 348–50, 354–56, 361, 367, 386, 427, 579, 581, 583–88, 593–95, 598–600, 698,

1068–69, 1136–37, 1204, 1211, 1370, 1438, 1474–75, 1515, 1529, 1620, 1622, 1626, 1636, 1639, 1801, 1823, 1879, 1913, 1925–26, 1969

Clerk, 39, 168, 188, 196, 228, 316–17, 325, 336, 338, 340, 345–47, 350–56, 358–59, 599, 734, 891–92, 993, 1136, 1174, 1204, 1249, 1260, 1321, 1345, 1349, 1436, 1448, 1514, 1529, 1616, 1622, 1688, 1800–1801, 1874

Coercion, 220, 989, 995, 1029–30, 1033, 1037, 1040, 1044–45, 1103, 1114, 1913. *See also* Force

Cognizance, 39, 44, 72, 214, 233–34, 277, 294, 297, 299, 302–3, 312–14, 317–22, 332–33, 342, 379, 428, 578, 585–88, 637, 669, 770, 907–8, 911, 922, 950, 1042, 1078, 1204, 1376, 1400, 1412, 1469, 1473–74, 1546, 1551, 1586, 1626, 1642, 1647, 1656–58, 1704, 1785–86, 1824, 1878–79, 1913, 1925. *See also* Jurisdiction

Common good, 51, 87, 97, 168, 354, 356, 648, 663, 720, 724, 726, 734, 883–84, 950, 986, 1043, 1499, 1510–13, 1515, 1689. *See also* Public good

Common law, 214, 330, 348, 533, 552, 571, 703, 718, 721, 724, 884, 895, 906, 1388, 1391, 1620, 1627

Commoner, 97, 145, 168, 241, 305, 365, 456, 536–37, 628–30, 644, 683, 698, 732, 747, 756, 803, 839, 842, 844–45, 847, 850, 853–54, 857, 859–62, 864–67, 871, 873–74, 876, 882, 907, 913–17, 935, 959, 965, 986, 1018, 1022, 1076–78, 1092, 1100, 1313, 1342, 1391, 1434, *1450–52*, 1464, 1496–98, 1500, 1502–9, 1514, 1530, 1545, 1567, 1606, 1654, 1671–72, 1691, 1695, 1698, 1701, 1715–17, 1719–20, 1726, 1741–43, 1759, 1827, 1829–32, 1870, 1875

Commune (Chapter 50), 154, 157, 171, 620, 646–47, *1516–17*, 1519, 1521–22, 1524–25, 1527–32

Complaint (Chapter 5), 25, 53, 57, 59, 61–62, 97, 109, *196–97*, 199–207, 209–11, 213–20, 222, 224–25, 227–39, 241, 243, 248, 250–51, 256–58, 262–63, 265–66, 270–71, 275, 280, 300, 303, 315, 354, 357, 359, 360, 554, 558, 562, 667, 704, 795, 850, 872, 888, 929, 954, 959, 961, 963–64, 978, 982–83, 985, 987, 991, 1011, 1050, 1070, 1102, 1192, 1217, 1220, 1231–32, 1244, 1250, 1323, 1339, 1374, 1378, 1413, 1469–70, 1523, 1530, 1542, 1545, 1574, 1576, 1586, 1626, 1707, 1739, 1788, 1855, 1867, 1869–70, 1875, 1894. *See also* Answer

Confiscate, confiscation, 53, 59, 77, 80, 376, 530, 612, 640, 697, 758, 853, 871, 1018, 1027, 1088, 1104, 1135–36, 1413, 1419–21, 1443, 1444, 1457–58, 1461, 1488–89, 1495, 1506, 1534, 1536–37, 1549, 1561–62, 1583–84, 1586, 1588–91, 1602, 1649, 1657, 1662, 1737, 1779, 1782, 1787–89, 1879, 1892. *See also* Seize

Continuance (Chapter 3), 57, 59–60, 62–65, 71–72, 74, 98, *106–12*, 119, 121–22, 127, 130–31, 134–36, 147, 237, 239, 297, 310, 793, 856, 959, 1292, 1577, 1719, 1789, 1852, 1857, 1865, 1868, 1887. *See also* Adjournment

Contract (Chapters 34, 35), 52, 92, 140, 197, 201, 213, 221, 229, 237–38, 242, 245, 514, 522, 539, 1097, 1147, 1152, 1196, 1203, 1206, 1208, 1213–16, 1524, 1527–28, 1813, 1827, 1850. *See also* Agreement

Council, 19, 25, 44, 523–24, 680–81, 1779

Counsel, 32, 34, 115, 174, 177, 179–81, 193–95, 258, 374, 399, 425, 915, 923, 932, 1088, 1199, 1256, 1282, 1370, 1471, 1510, 1513, 1520, 1834–36, 1868–69, 1873, 1881, 1899, 1909

Counsel day, *217–18*, 237, 239, 249, 276, 309–10, 431, 1908

Counterclaim, 91, *357*, 359–60

Creditor (Chapters 54, 55), 90, 223, 225, 442, 521, 527–30, 538–40, 576, 649, 792, 874–75, 990, 1055–57, 1074, 1078, 1080, 1086–89, 1102, 1223, 1315, 1319–20, 1328, 1527, 1539, 1574, 1593–94, 1596–99, 1602, 1604, 1606–15, 1926, 1937, 1977

Crime (Chapter 30), 48–49, 97, 129, 152, 197, 207–8, 212, 215, 225, 242, 262, 318, 332, 350–51, 355–56, 560, 619, 634, 640, 701, 759, 803, 808, *823–24, 830*, 836–38, 846, 848, 850, 880, 917, 922, 924, 932, 948, 950, 954, 991, 992, 1023, 1042, 1044–47, 1113, 1160–61, 1193, 1197, 1201, 1207, 1209, 1251, 1259, 1347, 1451, 1525, 1535, 1545, 1548, 1564, 1569, 1585–86, 1630, 1642–43, 1658, 1671, 1673, 1683, 1727, 1733, 1745, 1750, 1756, 1769, 1776, 1802, 1812, 1846, 1848, 1904, 1944, 1956, 1963. *See also* Serious crime; Offense

Crusade, crusader, 39, 265, 318–19, 1094, 1103, 1322, 1348, 1981

Custodian, custodianship (Chapter 15), 197, 203, 240, 374, 411, 484, 504, *506–16*, 518–33, 535, 537–48, 550, 556–57, 564–66, 568, 570–71, 621, 630, 632–35, 638–40, 660, 677, 1178, 1289–90, 1382–83, 1460, 1500, 1509, 1547, 1550, 1602, 1825, 1914. *See also* Guardian

Custom (Chapter 24), 23, 26, 28, 31, 45, 54, 57, 64, 72, 77, 82, 92, 96–97, 123, 130, 133, 136–37, 144, 147, 160–61, 168, 174, 176, 194, 199, 210–11, 214, 227, 232, 237, 246, 249, 255, 262, 271, 280, 283, 293, 314, 321, 342, 346, 357, 365–66, 373–74, 378–79, 381–82, 387, 403, 405–6, 422, 429–30, 432–33, 439, 445, 450, 452–53, 455, 457, 459, 461, 482, 490, 495, 497, 500, 518, 520, 522, 536, 544, 546–47, 551, 554, 571, 600–602, 621, 625, 629, 631, 639, 647, 659, 670–71, 674–75, 682–84, 688, 692–93, 695–97, 703–4, 715, 717–18, 721–23, 731, 734, 741, 743, 745, 748–49, 751, 753, 755, 757, 760–61, 766, 770, 773, 778–79, 788, 790, 792–93, 804, 813, 839, 841–42, 851–52, 866, 875, 882, 886, 891–92, 896, 898–99, 905–6, 912, 917–19, 923, 931, 970, 975, 987, 989, 993, 996, 998, 1001, 1018, 1020, 1024–25, 1028, 1030, 1067, 1076–77, 1080, 1083, 1094, 1100, 1103, 1133–34, 1137, 1139, 1141–42, 1146, 1155, 1165, 1173, 1177, 1185, 1197, 1200, 1203, 1205, 1211–12, 1215, 1217, 1221, 1244, 1251, 1257, 1262–64, 1285, 1299, 1305–8, 1314, 1316, 1337–38, 1354, 1356, 1387–88, 1395, 1401, 1404, 1410, 1425, 1434, 1438, 1440, 1452, 1456–58, 1459, 1477, 1479, 1481, 1491, 1494, 1496, 1499, 1502, 1510–12, 1549, 1558, 1578, 1580–81, 1591, 1603–4, 1606, 1613, 1616, 1622, 1626, 1629, 1637, 1649, 1653, 1661, 1669, 1671, 1673, 1676, 1690–91, 1693, 1695, 1697, 1702, 1706, 1721, 1723, 1734–35, 1751, 1758, 1778–80, 1791, 1810, 1819, 1822, 1825, 1829, 1834–35, 1851, 1853, 1865, 1878, 1883, 1887, 1898, 1900, 1904, 1909, 1927, 1971–72, 1975, 1982

Damage, damages, 15, 52, 86, 259, 328, 398, 449, 550, 691, 700, 710, 716–17, 719, 727, 729, 735, 758, 804–5, 879, 905–11, 986, 996, 1044–45, 1048, 1058, 1087–88, 1093–94, 1123, 1127–28, 1135, 1141–42, 1144, 1181, 1223, 1297, 1299, 1304, 1307, 1338, 1350–56, 1390, 1394, 1397, 1401, 1405, 1436, 1470, 1506, 1544, 1557, 1560–62, 1564, 1567, 1569–70, 1575, 1580, 1590–91, 1627, 1642, 1649, 1663, 1698, 1718, 1742, 1766, 1777, 1782, 1827, 1861–62, 1907, 1942, 1945. See also Loss

Deal, 52, 221, 449, 490, 539, 558, 561, 563, 649, 674, 677, 746, 750, 754, 769, 772, 806–9, 884, 990, 998, 1005, 1015–16, 1019, 1021, 1027, 1049, 1063, 1065–68, 1073, 1090, 1092, 1094, 1097, 1100, 1115, 1118, 1129–30, 1133–34, 1137–40, 1143–44, 1196, 1206, 1212–16, 1233, 1300, 1303, 1371, 1379, 1388, 1396–98, 1400, 1414, 1524, 1581, 1596–97, 1937–38

Debt, 28, 83–84, 90, 214, 220, 223, 237, 242, 262, 264, 266–67, 269, 274–75, 281–82, 310, 357–59, 368, 377, 382, 396, 397–98, 408, 412, 419, 426, 440–42, 444, 456, 509, 512, 521, 527–28, 531–32, 538–40, 550, 564–66, 574, 576, 629, 649, 658, 669, 674, 677, 683, 696–97, 703, 776, 792, 815, 848–49, 854, 863, 866, 871–75, 920, 990, 1000, 1006–8, 1012, 1023–24, 1030, 1039, 1055–57, 1074, 1078, 1080, 1083, 1086, 1088–89, 1093, 1096–97, 1102–4, 1115, 1118, 1138, 1166, 1179, 1193, 1203, 1223, 1230–33, 1244, 1289–90, 1304, 1307, 1309, 1310–11, 1315–20, 1322–23, 1326–30, 1334, 1336, 1338–39, 1397, 1435, 1524, 1527, 1538–39, 1549, 1574, 1579, 1593–1604, 1606–15, 1718, 1724, 1791, 1873, 1907, 1915, 1925–26, 1931–32, 1934, 1976–77

Defamation, 212, 229, 1259

Default, 60, 62–64, 69, 71, 74, 83–86, 94–96, 107, 110–11, 114–16, 121–22, 127, 130–32, 134–35, 139, 147, 159, 161, 170, 194, 224, 258, 284, 287–88, 376, 657, 665, 793, 795, 813, 836, 855–56, 901, 924, 931, 1021, 1048, 1070, 1072, 1086, 1088–89, 1094, 1101, 1143, 1161, 1165, 1219–20, 1247, 1251, 1253, 1291–92, 1304–5, 1307, 1314, 1345, 1372–73, 1393, 1420–22, 1530, 1577, 1590, 1771, 1775–76, 1782–87, 1789, 1819, 1862, 1909, 1981

Default of judgment (Chapter 62), 219, 237, 295, 320, 322, 1043, 1050, 1532, 1592, 1739–43, 1745, 1760–61, 1774–75, 1778–81, 1783–88, 1790–92, 1819, 1851–52, 1894

Defense (Chapters 7, 63), 61, 65, 83, 119, 121, 149, 196, 215, 221, 226–27, 235, 237–38, 242, 248, 257, 280, 282, 306, 314, 357, 360, 398, 400, 442, 569, 584, 594, 658, 687, 711, 859, 889, 894, 918, 922, 924, 927, 959, 985, 990, 1031–32, 1035, 1071, 1094, 1103, 1112, 1124, 1167, 1193, 1222, 1269, 1329, 1338, 1349, 1351, 1412, 1431, 1433, 1435–36, 1521, 1529, 1535, 1564, 1576, 1655, 1667–68, 1670, 1675, 1678, 1686, 1705–6, 1755, 1768, 1772, 1776, 1794–1807, 1810, 1812–14, 1817–18, 1822–24, 1827, 1835–38, 1851, 1876, 1878, 1924–25, 1930, 1932, 1934, 1937, 1945, 1970

Deny, denial (of accusation), 200, 202, 204–7, 209, 238–39, 243–45, 247, 256–57, 261,

281–82, 304, 309, 678, 697, 701, 807, 815, 820, 870, 891, 893–94, 897, 907–9, 915, 923, 940, 959–60, 985, 1029, 1073, 1075–76, 1078, 1146–47, 1149, 1154–55, 1157, 1159, 1162–63, 1190, 1192–94, 1196, 1217–18, 1230, 1244, 1247, 1252, 1313–14, 1338, 1349, 1429, 1586, 1588, 1601, 1711–12, 1724, 1749, 1761, 1772, 1791, 1813, 1815–16, 1836–37, 1878, 1894, 1901, 1930, 1950. *See also* Answer; Complaint

Descent (direct) (Chapter 14), 62, 198–99, 202, 238, 250, 379, 447, 452, *461–62*, 464–66, 468–69, 470–72, 474, 476, 483, 490, 495–96, 500, 505, 507, 509–10, 514, 517, 557, 579, 595–96, 599, 604, 609–10, 614, 618, 686, 697, 764, 1218, 1357, 1456, 1478–79, 1482–83, 1492, 1497, 1500, 1573, 1616, 1968, 1972. *See also* Lateral inheritance

Dilatory exception (Chapter 3), *236–37*, 248–49, 281, 239–40, 1724–25, 1908. *See also* Peremptory exception

Directly (holding from king), 97, 168–69, 262, 289, 294, 322, 428, 664, 721, 731, 800, 931, 1043, 1050, 1213, 1216, 1293, 1464, 1468–69, 1503, 1510, 1536, 1653, 1662–63, 1666, 1701, 1704, 1782, 1875–76, 1933, 1971. *See also* Baron

Disavow, *1418, 1419–30*, 1438, 1443, 1457, 1459–64, 1471, 1476, 1554. *See also* Avow

Discretionary fines, 26, 756, 843, 846, 848, 859, 868, 876, 878, 885, 915–16, 986, 992, 1035, 1076, 1078, 1100, 1339, 1452, 1471, 1476, 1544, 1570, 1685, 1698–99, 1704, 1730, 1740, 1742, 1779, 1827. *See also* Will, discretion

Disseise, disseisin, 73, 80, 237, 274, 536, 1579

Distribute, distribution, 254–55, 261, 320, 390, 426, 450, 452, 456, 458–59, 461, 475, 478–79, 481–82, 490, 498, 500–502, 518, 557, 564, 595, 614–16, 619, 628, 644, 670, 683, 697, 776, 913, 1479–80, 1483, 1490–91, 1975

Dower (Chapter 13), 44, 71, 197, 202, 297, 306, 376, 378, 429–34, 436–40, *444–55*, 458–60, 491–92, 503, 601–2, 612, 622, 660, 669, 674–75, 677, 687, 862–63, 971, 1025, 1053, 1092, 1460, 1547, 1550, 1572, 1576, 1602, 1629, 1818, 1822, 1825

Duel (judicial). *See* Wager of battle

Ecclesiastical court (Chapter 11), 91, 93, 96, 140, 161, 196, 211, 248, 306, *311*, 314–16, 320, 342, 347, 357, 397, 426, 428, 442, 592–94, 813, 989, 1092, 1191, 1197, 1211, 1221, 1340, 1343, 1774, *1878–79*, 1908, 1911, 1913, 1916, 1925–26, 1932

Ecclesiastical judge, 140, 188, 321, 333, 347, 350, 352–53, 356, 359, 588–89, 734, 1092, 1136, 1204, 1246, 1321–22, 1348, 1472, 1514, 1622, 1801, 1878, 1911

Encumber, encumbrance, 96, 368, 376, 452, *508*, 538, 540, 542, 564–65, 629, 704, 1015, 1025, 1133, 1414, 1580

Estate, 255, 392, 394, 396–98, 402, 406, 423, 473, 477–79, 614–18, 644, 1697, 1928

Exception, 196, 215, *235*, 250, 256–57, 259, 1094, 1103 1725, 1908. *See also* Peremptory exception; Dilatory exception

Exclude (a witness), 187, 212, 234, 913, *1170–71, 1174, 1176, 1179–81, 1184, 1185–86*, 1200, 1221, 1227, 1236, 1244, 1252, 1259, 1270, 1431, 1767, 1815, 1820. *See also* Challenge (a witness)

Excommunicate, excommunication, 50, 91, 191, 314, 316, 321, 323, 342, 354, 588, 698, 991, 1026, 1206, 1474, 1605, 1926

Excuse (legal) (Chapter 3), 32, 37, 40, 63, 65, 71, 99, *107–12*, 117, 121–23, 126–29, 135, 152, 288, 297, 426, 793, 813, 821, 1037, 1070, 1208, 1268, 1282, 1292, 1347, 1577, 1711–13, 1721, 1755, 1775, 1790, 1838, 1876, 1901, 1909, 1920, 1981

Execute (a will), executor, 199, 210, 320–21, 361–64, 379, 381, *391–99*, 403, 406, 408–9, 414, 419, 422–24, 426–27, 449, 456–57, 459, 474, 676, 680–81, 776–77, 1083, 1100, 1417, 1543, 1821, 1928

False judgment, 36, 93, 219, 237, 296, 322, 1043, 1050, 1532, 1739, 1744–45, *1752–54*, 1756, 1758, 1761, 1774–75, 1780–81, 1791–92, 1819, 1826, 1861, 1872, 1882, 1884, 1888–91, 1894, 1897–98, 1901, 1905

Fief, 19, 21, 23, 44, 58–60, 62, 65, 67, 77–78, 80–82, 87, 199, 203, 241, 295, 317, 322, 343, 348–49, 373, 376–77, 386, 434–35, 452, 454, 461, 464–65, 467–72, 475–76, 483–84, 486–87, 489–92, 497–99, 501, 507–8, 510–18, 521–25, 531–33, 537, 542–46, 556–57, 564, 566, 578, 602, 643, 646, 688, 722, 761–68, 788, 792, 794, 798–99, 801, 812, 821, 853, 857–58, 861, 864–65, 867, 899, 901, 907, 976, 991, 1018, 1045, 1052, 1074, 1102, 1131, 1153, 1216, 1288, 1398, 1411, 1419, 1420–22, 1425–28, 1434, 1437, 1445–46, 1455, 1460,

Fief (*cont.*)
  1477–81, 1483–95, *1497–1509*, 1529–30, 1552–
  53, 1578, 1581, 1602, 1606, 1641, 1650, 1687,
  1734, 1736–37, 1739, 1782–83, 1785–87, 1791,
  1864, 1888, 1892–93, 1917–18, 1971
Fine, 26, 38, 51, 53, 85–86, 121, 180, 188, 212,
  225, 295, 303, 326, 344, 376, 640, 666, 668–
  69, 693–94, 700, 703–4, 721, 726–29, 738,
  747, 756–59, 798, 803–4, 815, 839, 843, 851–
  54, 857, 859–62, 864–65, 868, 870–72, 876–
  81, 884–85, 891–92, 895–96, 901, 903–10,
  912–16, 920–921, 935, 960, 963, 965, 970,
  986, 992–93, 996, 1018, 1027, 1044, 1074,
  1076–78, 1100, 1131, 1136–37, 1155, 1163, 1278,
  1285, 1297, 1306, 1313, 1323–25, 1339, 1352,
  1398, 1421–22, 1437, 1443, 1461–63, 1470–
  71, 1476, 1513, 1538, 1544, 1549, 1557, 1561–62,
  1564–68, 1570–71, 1580, 1586, 1590–91, 1596,
  1604, 1615, 1685, 1698–99, 1704, 1719–20,
  1730, 1734, 1740–43, 1745, 1752, 1755, 1758–
  59, 1764–65, 1776, 1779, 1786, 1827, 1858,
  1864, 1875, 1888, 1890–91, 1894, 1902, 1909,
  1930, 1933, 1945
Fire, 1159, 1351, 1353, 1642. *See also* Arson;
  Burn
Firstborn, 434–45, 452, 466, 469, 472–73,
  476–78, 601–2, 1175, 1482, 1624
Force (Chapter 32), 41, 49, 55, 85, 197, 204,
  206, 210, 214, 220, 239, 258, 307, 551, 612,
  829, 885, 910, 926, 929, 941, 953–54, *956*,
  958–59, 964, 966, 975, 983–86, 995, 1018,
  1029, 1044, 1103, 1223, 1290, 1354, 1413, 1423,
  1453, 1489, 1542, 1576, 1604, 1629, 1635, 1653–
  54, 1901. *See also* Coercion
Forfeit, forfeiture, 45, 77, 411, 515, 531, 824,
  831–35, 930, 1104, 1448, 1486, 1494–95,
  1548, 1552, 1573, 1591, 1603, 1718, 1789, 1842,
  1870, 1945, 1948, 1951. *See also* Seize
Fraud (Chapter 33), 30, 60, 123, 129, 397, 449,
  514, 522, 524, 541, 558, 592, 640, 739, 989–93,
  997, 1049, 1051, 1053–54, 1070, 1099–1100,
  1103, 1118, 1347, 1356, 1359, 1396, 1416, 1524,
  1595–97, 1713, 1784, 1940, 1972, 1975. *See also*
  Trick; Sharp practice
Free (not a serf) (Chapter 45), 158, 365, 456,
  552, 631, 972–74, 1176, 1270, 1331, 1418, 1424,
  1431–38, *1440–42*, *1445–53*, 1455–57, 1502,
  1799, 1805, 1823
Fruits, 79, 367, 449, 685, 687, 1074, 1134, 1290,
  1390, 1414, 1536, 1545, 1977. *See also* Benefits;
  Income

Gentleman, gentlewoman, 57–58, 65, 121,
  144, 168, 241, 295, 297, 299, 304–5, 365, 371,
  434, 456, 472, 490, 536–37, 571, 629–30,
  643, 683, 698, 700, 732, 734, 747, 792–93,
  812, 821, 839–40, 844–45, 847, 850, 853–54,
  857–62, 864–67, 870–71, 873–74, 878, 882,
  887, 89–92, 901, 907, 909, 913, 917, 935, 959,
  965, 986, 996, 1018, 1022, 1074, 1076–78,
  1092, 1102, 1215–16, 1313, 1324–25, 1391, 1419,
  1434–35, 1438, 1449–53, 1464, 1497–1502,
  1504, 1506–8, 1510, 1514, 1529, 1545, 1567,
  1606, 1654, 1669–70, 1672–74, 1684, 1692–
  93, 1695, 1698–1701, 1714–17, 1719, 1720,
  1742–43, 1759, 1786, 1809, 1811, 1827, 1829,
  1830, 1832, 1870, 1875, 1913
Gentlewoman. *See* gentleman
Good faith, 99, 102–4, 119–20, 124, 126, 129,
  312, 321, 329, 419, 449, 559, 611–13, 617, 625,
  637, 811, 813, 1037, 1087, 1112, 1125, 1296, 1328,
  1438, 1563, 1827, 1971
Good folk, good men, good persons, 17, 131,
  247, 680, 732, 734, 862, 933, 1037, 1049,
  1075, 1118, 1124, 1142, 1239, 1396, 1538, 1601,
  1605, 1637, 1680, 1742, 1760, 1786, 1873. *See
  also* Honest folk
Guaranteed peace (Chapter 60), 44, 297,
  299, 300, 303, 347, 825, 827, 839, 887, 996,
  1033, 1297, 1523, 1537, 1546, 1576, 1603, 1647–
  48, 1655, 1669, 1672, 1681, 1684–85, *1690*,
  1693–1702, 1705–8, 1726, 1746, 1872
Guardian (Chapter 15), 118, 197, 203, 314, 411,
  447, 504, 506, 509, 511, *513*, *516–18*, 520, 522,
  524, 533–34, 537, 545, 547–50, 552, 564, 566–
  68, 570–71, 617, 629–35, 638–40, 643, 925,
  1178, 1188, 1290, 1351, 1383, 1410, 1460, 1462–
  63, 1465–73, 1476, 1509, 1547, 1550, 1557,
  1619–21, 1624, 1639, 1825, 1914, 1975. *See also*
  Custodian

Harvest, 73, 78, 96, 198, 444, 449, 457, 484,
  541, 673, 676–77, 704, 820, 852, 905, 966–
  67, 979, 1019, 1021, 1117, 1127, 1394, 1401,
  1414–15, 1506, 1558, 1602, 1923
Hatred, 42, 159, 193, 381, 400, 580, 590, 593,
  826, 869, 888, 942, 986, 1034, 1162, 1180,
  1207, 1228, 1278, 1523, 1632–33, 1662, 1872,
  1903, 1949, 1958, 1971
Hear (witnesses), 23, 25–26, 42–46, 52–54,
  57, 61–62, 70, 87, 91, 94, 96–97, 102, 111,
  129–31, 137, 139–40, 178, 184, 189, 209–12,
  219, 237, 239, 241, 260, 280, 293, 311, 315,

342–43, 354, 949, 962, 983, 987, 1171–72,
1176–77, 1180–81, 1197, 1200, 1206, 1219–20,
1222, 1225–28, 1230, 1234–35, 1247, 1251, 1256,
1276, 1281, 1283, 1289, 1291, 1349, 1386–87,
1389, 1522, 1576, 1587, 1601
Hearing, 44, 219, 315, 718, 795, 963, 984, 1152,
1183, 1227, 1253, 1282, 1343, 1388, 1400, 1420–
21, 1459, 1464, 1530, 1532, 1545, 1576–77,
1586–88, 1592, 1671, 1707, 1739–40, 1742,
1755, 1760, 1776, 1778–79, 1781–82, 1784–89,
1791, 1802, 1819, 1869, 1882, 1889, 1894–96,
1925
Heir, 164, 210, 216, 223, 225, 238, 241–42, 255,
273, 310, 333, 363–64, 366, 368–69, 375–76,
378, 381–86, 389–91, 395, 398, 400–402,
422–24, 435, 440–42, 444, 447, 449–51,
454–57, 459, 461, 465, 469–70, 474–76,
482–85, 491, 493–96, 498, 501–3, 505, 509,
515, 518–22, 524–32, 536, 538–41, 543, 551–52,
559, 572, 574, 576, 578–79, 583–84, 586–87,
590–91, 593–97, 600–601, 612, 614–20,
634, 676, 680–81, 683, 687, 702, 704, 762–
64, 776, 777, 811, 862–63, 930, 951, 971, 1017,
1025, 1083, 1093–96, 1132, 1179, 1269, 1289–
90, 1311, 1317, 1358, 1382, 1389, 1410, 1438,
1441, 1452–53, 1456, 1460, 1490, 1501, 1573,
1575, 1624, 1877, 1881, 1900, 1934, 1936, 1940,
1948–50, 1952, 1971, 1974
High justice (Chapter 58), 233, 295, 322, 332,
737, 922, 1641–47, 1649–52, 1656
Homage, 65, 199, 343, 373, 375–76, 434–35,
461, 464–65, 469, 472–73, 478, 483–86,
487–92, 497–99, 507–8, 514, 521, 526, 531,
541–42, 544, 546, 564–66, 672, 688, 722,
788, 792, 794, 798–99, 991, 1052, 1074, 1288,
1411, 1423, 1446, 1478–80, 1484, 1490–91,
1493, 1495, 1501, 1506, 1650, 1734–36, 1772–
74, 1782, 1786, 1888, 1892–93, 1919–20, 1971
Homicide (Chapter 30), 207, 214, 824, 828,
840, 880, 1207, 1570, 1572, 1575, 1642, 1671,
1673, 1698, 1711, 1749, 1807, 1812, 1904
Honest folk, honest man, honest person,
honest woman, 94, 399, 427, 548, 568, 875,
907, 947, 1016, 1046, 1074–75, 1152, 1157,
1159, 1188, 1197, 1223, 1225, 1283, 1310, 1316,
1480, 1601, 1605, 1627, 1629, 1631–32, 1710,
1727, 1962. See also Good folk
Hotchpot, 254–55, 480, 619, 913, 1972

Income, 64, 71, 242, 622, 656–57, 659, 661,
762–63, 765, 780–82, 787, 790–91, 820,

1144, 1520, 1522, 1643, 1650–51. See also Benefits, Fruits
Indemnify, 528–29, 540, 611, 1397, 1766
Inheritance tax, 471, 491, 508, 514, 517, 523,
542, 544, 1104. See also Relief
Inquest, 47, 250, 293, 556, 1157, 1197, 1222–24,
1235–43, 1247, 1249, 1250, 1252–54, 1256, 1259,
1661, 1710, 1815
Inquire, inquiry, 304, 412, 418, 428, 593, 637,
720, 949, 1027, 1157, 1197, 1224, 1235, 1237–38,
1280, 1525, 1542, 1551, 1561, 1597, 1661, 1727,
1909, 1949, 1963
Inspection (of property), 74–75, 148–49,
283–84, 288–90, 292, 309, 593, 1373, 1406;
inspection day (Chapter 9), 74, 110, 148–
49, 218, 237, 239, 248, 276, 278–79, 283–84,
288–89, 291–92, 309–10, 431, 959, 1219–20,
1373, 1393, 1406, 1562, 1576, 1908
Insult, 204, 212, 344, 844–45, 847, 877, 932,
993, 1278, 1670, 1734, 1752, 1758–59
Intimidation, 220, 239, 869, 994, 1029, 1031,
1033, 1035, 1040, 1103, 1635
Issue, 81, 93, 98, 111, 148, 197, 199, 209, 211,
233, 239, 242, 248–49, 257, 281, 286, 292,
295, 390, 414, 426, 450, 477, 487, 490–91,
501–511, 523–24, 542, 544, 551, 578, 593–94,
674, 680, 689, 758, 770, 776, 803, 807, 895,
897, 903, 918, 954, 981, 983, 1006, 1014,
1056, 1080, 1109, 1111, 1163, 1192, 1219–20,
1226, 1250, 1255, 1257–58, 1269, 1281, 1291,
1293–95, 1314, 1357, 1359, 1365, 1400, 1402,
1407, 1414, 1430, 1488, 1592, 1724, 1770,
1773, 1777, 1807–8, 1813, 1844, 1869, 1892,
1905, 1908, 1911, 1913, 1917, 1925, 1932, 1950

Judge, 12, 15, 19, 21, 24, 34–35, 38, 40–41, 46,
52, 91, 93, 101, 111, 118, 121, 139–40, 145, 151,
153, 161, 163, 175–76, 181, 184, 188, 191, 195,
197, 201, 208–9, 210–11, 216, 227, 237, 239,
272–73, 280, 282, 306, 311, 315–16, 320–21,
333–34, 347, 350, 352–54, 356, 358–59, 369,
379, 392, 397, 426, 431, 442, 482, 547, 557,
567, 570, 578, 615–16, 619, 631–32, 637–38,
640–41, 649, 654, 657, 697, 718, 737, 740,
843, 845–46, 850–51, 871, 907, 917, 919,
922–23, 929, 933, 942, 950, 954, 980, 998,
1018, 1022, 1027–28, 1036, 1046, 1048, 1056,
1071, 1074–75, 1079, 1087–89, 1096, 1105,
1108, 1113, 1115–16, 1124–25, 1138, 1142, 1144,
1152, 1157, 1163–64, 1172, 1183, 1186, 1188,
1196, 1214, 1234, 1237–38, 1245, 1254–55,

Judge (*cont.*)

1260–61, 1266–67, 1269, 1273, 1276, 1279, 1287, 1291, 1294, 1323–24, 1326, 1386, 1388, 1390–92, 1402, 1412, 1538, 1598, 1627, 1629–31, 1634, 1637, 1638–39, 1648, 1658, 1671, 1673, 1680–81, 1683–85, 1691, 1695, 1702, 1705, 1709–10, 1712, 1719, 1755, 1762–63, 1766, 1768, 1774, 1801, 1813, 1815, 1821, 1829, 1836, 1841, 1843–44, 1861, 1871–73, 1880–82, 1909, 1913, 1916, 1929, 1949, 1953, 1956, 1963, 1970, 1972. *See also* Ecclesiastical judge; Provost; Secular judge

Judgment (Chapter 67), 23–26, 30–34, 36, 42–43, 44–46, 61, 64, 76, 81, 93, 111, 118, 122, 133, 140, 148, 150–51, 156, 195, 211, 216, 240–41, 244, 246, 248–49, 260, 274, 279, 281, 286–87, 290, 334, 342, 354, 369, 380, 414–15, 434, 439, 450, 454, 472, 476, 477–78, 487, 489, 490–91, 501–2, 511–12, 542–45, 553, 586–87, 592, 594–95, 612, 625, 666, 673–75, 677, 683–84, 689–91, 693, 703, 745, 758–59, 770–71, 775–77, 792–93, 795, 803, 813, 843, 895, 897–98, 903, 915, 917–21, 923–24, 972–73, 978–81, 988, 1006–7, 1012, 1014–15, 1052–53, 1056–57, 1080–81, 1089, 1100, 1109–12, 1150–51, 1153, 1158–59, 1164, 1183, 1205, 1208, 1214, 1217, 1219–22, 1229, 1237, 1243, 1269, 1274, 1287–88, 1295–97, 1309, 1314, 1341–42, 1346, 1357, 1359, 1365, 1375, 1382, 1383, 1387–88, 1392–93, 1400–1403, 1405, 1407, 1414–16, 1419, 1422–23, 1426, 1429–30, 1444, 1449, 1473, 1488–89, 1536, 1576, 1592, 1650, 1661, 1682, 1692, 1707, 1713, 1727, 1732, 1738, 1744, 1747, 1749, 1753–55, 1758–61, 1768–75, 1777–79, 1789, 1792–93, 1798, 1802, 1808, 1811, 1813–14, 1818, 1826, 1829–31, 1836, 1853–54, 1856, 1859–64, 1868–69, 1871–76, 1878, 1880–86, 1888–90, 1892–94, 1897–1902, 1904–5, 1908–20, 1940, 1950–51, 1977

Judicial duel. *See* Wager of battle

Jurisdiction (Chapters 10, 11), 4, 34, 36, 44–55, 70, 72, 90–93, 154, 156, 169, 188, 214, 219, 230, 233, 262, 295–96, 299, 311, 313–14, 317, 319, 322–24, 326, 330, 332, 339–40, 344–45, 348, 353, 360–61, 378–80, 443, 552, 573, 615, 646, 651, 656, 658–59, 661, 663–69, 689, 721–23, 729, 732, 756, 769–70, 788, 803, 820, 852, 908, 910, 927, 950, 959, 966, 972, 984, 986, 1018, 1035, 1036–37, 1044, 1047, 1074, 1094, 1135, 1155, 1165, 1267, 1279, 1293, 1301,

1303, 1309, 1321, 1334, 1343, 1348–49, 1354, 1386, 1412, 1432, 1436, 1457, 1459, 1462, 1465, 1468, 1470, 1473, 1513–14, 1529–32, 1535–36, 1545–46, 1554, 1556–57, 1563–64, 1566, 1572, 1576, 1584, 1586, 1589, 1596–97, 1615, 1622, 1641, 1643, 1648, 1650–54, 1657–59, 1673, 1722, 1745, 1774–75, 1779–80, 1782, 1786–88, 1792, 1800, 1823, 1848, 1876, 1889, 1894, 1898, 1906–7, 1919, 1944. *See also* Cognizance

Juror (Chapters 65, 67), *23–24*, 26, 31, 36, 42–46, 93, 184, 186, 189, 195, 211, 240, 260, 410, 677, 792, 1041, 1050, 1100, 1110, 1150–53, 1164, 1183, 1192, 1225–27, 1237, 1243, 1252, 1254, 1280, 1288, 1339, 1360, 1366, 1414, 1661, 1752–55, 1757, 1760–61, 1793, 1818, 1851, 1854, 1856–57, 1859–66, 1876, 1880–81, 1884–85, 1888–89, 1891, 1897–1903, 1909, 1911, 1913, 1919, 1951, 1982

King, 35–36, 44, 51–52, 65–66, 93, 97, 124, 137, 145, 168–69, 176, 227, 237, 262, 277, 289, 293–94, 298, 314, 322, 374, 387, 428, 445, 454, 663–64, 683, 696, 721, 724, 731, 753, 800, 843, 915, 931–32, 954, 958, 986–87, 1030, 1043, 1050, 1094, 1100, 1103, 1213–16, 1293, 1326, 1451, 1453, 1464–67, 1469, 1471, 1476, 1498–99, 1503, 1510, 1512–13, 1515, 1517, 1536–38, 1648, 1653–54, 1656, 1662, 1669, 1673, 1689, 1701–2, 1722, 1736, 1771, 1774, 1776, 1779–80, 1782, 1866, 1877, 1971; king's court, 36, 803, 933, 988, 1043, 1050, 1748, 1780, 1845, 1863, 1872, 1909, 1977; king's law, 227, 293, 445, 954, 986–87, 1043, 1103, 1165, 1173, 1209, 1450, 1496, 1499, 1512–13, 1515, 1530, 1653–54, 1701–2, 1723

Kinship (degrees of) (Chapter 19), 62, 463, 494–96, 501–2, *603*, *605–11*, 1364, 1370–71, 1384–85, 1407, 1409, 1616, 1686, 1881

Knight, 132, 133, 227, 373, 375, 450, 477, 487, 1342, 1434, 1449–51, 1500, 1501, 1510, 1714–15, 1749–50, 1770–71, 1845

Land, 20, 25–26, 28, 44, 54, 62–64, 67, 72, 77, 87, 90, 92, 109, 118, 140, 169, 202, 210, 224, 230, 233–34, 240–41, 250, 273–74, 277, 279, 280, 285–89, 291, 301–3, 306, 314, 322, 332, 343, 345, 349, 373, 379, 392, 412, 414, 416, 421, 436, 437–38, 446, 448–49, 452, 454, 458–59, 482, 485–86, 491, 499, 506, 541, 544, 546, 559, 564, 568–69, 613, 646, 662,

666, 672–73, 677, 685–88, 694, 695, 703–6,
710, 719–24, 728, 730, 734, 749, 752–56,
760–63, 770–71, 773–74, 776, 779–80, 782,
788–89, 792, 804, 806, 813, 820, 824, 835,
850, 852–53, 857, 861–64, 886, 892, 895, 899,
904, 907–11, 922, 968, 971, 979, 981, 986–
87, 992, 994, 996, 1002, 1014–17, 1019, 1021,
1027, 1037, 1044, 1046, 1050, 1052, 1064,
1067, 1071, 1074, 1095, 1107, 1132, 1134–36,
1159, 1179, 1203, 1217–18, 1271, 1309–10, 1323,
1343, 1355, 1357–60, 1362, 1363, 1365, 1371,
1389–90, 1398, 1400, 1402, 1404–6, 1412,
1414–15, 1418, 1435, 1438–39, 1443–44,
1446, 1452, 1454, 1456–57, 1459–63, 1467,
1470–71, 1485, 1487–88, 1495, 1499, 1510–11,
1513, 1518–19, 1529–31, 1547–51, 1556–59, 1562,
1564, 1569, 1578, 1580, 1593, 1597, 1602, 1617,
1624, 1639, 1643, 1653, 1655–56, 1658, 1666,
1686, 1689, 1695, 1718, 1720, 1725, 1727–30,
1734, 1742, 1745, 1758, 1772–73, 1782, 1787,
1876–77, 1891–92, 1913, 1915, 1918, 1933,
1944, 1948, 1950, 1970, 1971, 1977, 1981

Larceny (Chapter 31), 326, 560, 701, 711, 736,
813, *850*, 905–6, 925, 927–28, 935, 937–52,
997, 1026, 1046, 1339, 1413, 1601, 1642, 1698,
1772, 1812, 1815–16, 1935, 1960. *See also*
Theft; Thief; Steal

Lateral inheritance (Chapter 14), 62, 198–
199, 216, 240, 379, 446–47, 450–52, 461,
463, 466, 468–71, 474–75, 483, 485, 490–
91, 493–95, 500–502, 505, 509–10, 517, 557,
579, 603, 609, 617, 686, 697, 762–64, 1218,
1456, 1482, 1490, 1500, 1508, 1616, 1725, 1917,
1968, 1972. *See also* Descent

Law, 18, 51, 52, 176, 199, 205, 233, 248–49, 293,
330, 350, 381–82, 405, 445, 495–96, 520, 536,
546, 647, 688, 718, 821, 841, 866, 881, 891, 954,
958, 986, 999, 1025, 1070, 1076, 1094, 1103,
1188, 1200, 1205, 1223, 1246, 1287, 1296, 1331,
1370, 1388, 1390, 1391, 1399, 1435, 1438, 1448,
1496–99, 1502, 1508, 1512–13, 1530, 1653–54,
1690, 1702, 1704, 1706, 1751, 1753, 1755, 1780,
1812, 1817, 1825, 1834, 1900, 1916, 1939. *See also*
Custom; Common law; King's law

Lease, 54, 286, 612, 660, 687, 968, 1009, 1014–
17, 1019, 1021, 1064–65, 1127, 1203, 1216, 1351,
1414–16, 1443, 1460, 1533, 1549, 1551, 1602,
1825

Letter of appointment, attorney's, 137, *139–51*,
153, 156, 161–67, 170, 173, 237, 807, 1004,
1389, 1464, 1912

Lineage, 16, 103, 105, 178, 188, 190, 216, 374,
382, 474, 505, 548, 1182, 1357, 1360, 1364–66,
1368–70, 1377, 1381, 1384, 1389, 1398, 1400,
1407, 1417, 1431, 1435, 1451, 1456, 1504, 1520,
1522–23, 1553, 1573, 1616–17, 1619, 1644, 1655,
1659, 1667–70, 1678, 1684, 1686–87, 1694,
1697, 1702–3, 1706, 1751, 1797–98, 1811, 1820,
1823, 1842–43, 1872–73, 1947

Lordship, 67, 230, 322, 349, 485, 637, 689, 721,
723, 756, 851–52, 910, 1331, 1453, 1462, 1876,
1893

Loss, 16, 19–20, 25–26, 30, 32–33, 41, 57, 86,
118, 123, 159, 167, 170, 204, 210, 258, 419, 421,
426, 431, 449, 493, 499, 512, 520, 525–26, 532,
543, 550, 567–68, 572, 574, 587, 611, 613–14,
620–23, 640, 644, 647, 650, 653–55, 660,
663, 690, 701, 705, 711–12, 716, 719, 735, 737,
742, 759, 763, 786, 793, 799, 802, 804, 811,
813, 817, 821, 823, 841, 860, 872, 875, 880, 894,
896, 907, 938, 945, 951, 989–90, 992, 1004,
1008–11, 1016, 1020, 1031, 1033, 1039, 1044,
1059, 1060, 1072, 1109–13, 1115, 1117–20, 1132,
1136–37, 1141–42, 1144, 1178, 1203, 1284,
1290, 1299, 1305, 1308, 1313, 1316, 1318, 1323,
1351–52, 1378, 1380, 1402, 1418, 1421, 1430,
1438, 1445, 1447, 1461, 1518, 1524, 1545, 1567,
1572, 1581, 1591, 1593–94, 1598, 1601–2, 1604–
5, 1630–31, 1649, 1656–57, 1664, 1699, 1721,
1765–66, 1786, 1788, 1818, 1826, 1895, 1907,
1915, 1930, 1945–47, 1970. *See also* Damage

Low justice (Chapter 58), 233–34, 295, 322,
332, *1641–42*, 1644–47, 1649–52, 1656. *See
also* High justice

Make good, 41, 159, 520, 587, 710, 860, 875,
879, 905, 907, 910, 1016, 1020, 1045, 1308,
1109, 1113, 1430, 1826. *See also* Reimburse;
Repay

Market tax, 346, 659, 661, 892, 912

Marriage (Chapter 57), 103, 193, 202, 254–55,
313, 333, 335, 373, 382, 429–30, 434, 445,
448, 460, 487, 489, 499, 503, 544–45, 548,
578–79, 582–86, 588, 590–91, 593–95, 598–
603, 609–10, 622, 628–29, 632, 644, 674,
677, 928–30, 1036, 1051–54, 1068–69, 1097,
1152, 1204, 1208, 1287, 1370, 1410, 1452, 1626,
1629–30, 1632, 1634, 1636, 1638–39, 1686,
1973–74

Marry, married, remarry, unmarried, 71, 90,
103, 202, 373, 422, 429–30, 443, 446–48,
477–78, 482, 490, 497–99, 503, 544, 546,

Marry (*cont.*)
579, 581, 584–85, 594–95, 599–601, 624, 628,
632, 635, 640, 643–44, 674, 821, 929–30,
934, 993, 1003, 1051–52, 1054, 1058, 1061,
1068–69, 1175, 1269, 1288, 1330, 1334, 1378,
1434–35, 1445, 1449, 1452, 1455–58, 1500–
1501, 1504

Measure (Chapter 26), 726, 743–61, 773, 780,
790, 1067

Minor (Chapter 16), 118, 197, 203, 237, 266,
269, 271, 504, 506–8, 510, 513, 518, 520, 522,
533–34, 544–46, 549–62, 564, 566–68, 570–
74, 576–77, 617, 626, 637, 660, 862, 1061,
1068, 1138, 1198, 1270, 1273–75, 1289–90,
1383, 1410–11, 1509, 1524, 1543, 1547, 1550,
1688, 1825, 1874, 1914, 1942

Misadventure, 246, 1536, *1939–41*, 1946, 1948–
49, 1958–59, 1962, 1966

Murder, 36, 207, 560, *824–25*, 827, 880, 1113,
1242–43, 1572, 1642, 1698, 1711, 1747, 1772,
1808, 1955, 1956

Murderer, 355, 741, 1189, 1570, 1711, 1963

Novel disseisin (Chapter 32), 85, 197, 205–6,
214, 289, 297, 307, 612, 669, 850, 949, *954–
56*, 958–61, 963–71, 978–79, 981–83, 987,
1124, 1290, 1323, 1413, 1542, 1576, 1824

Nuisance (Chapter 32), 197, 206, 297, 307,
954, *957–59*, 964, 966

Oath, 29, 51, 53, 68, 88, 101, 108, 129, 140, 175,
178, 185–86, 188, 226–27, 251, 283, 405, 558,
563, 568, 619–20, 714, 732, 734, 806, 812, 853,
869, 875, 890–91, 893–94, 897–98, 901–3,
904, 909, 912–13, 1026, 1040–41, 1087,
1093–94, 1109–10, 1137, 1144, 1149, 1170,
1171–73, 1183, 1190, 1219, 1222–23, 1228–30,
1232, 1235, 1240, 1243–44, 1247, 1249, 1251,
1279–80, 1295, 1354, 1396, 1501, 1505–6, 1566,
1684–85, 1750, 1762, 1838–41, 1877, 1902, 1915

Obligate, obligation, 167, 193, 201, 229, 285,
342, 347, 376, 442, 515, 688, 692, 695, 698,
746, 787, 796–97, 799, 806–8, 810–11, 822,
1018, 1030–31, 1039, 1054, 1073–75, 1078–81,
1083, 1086–89, 1092–98, 1104, 1116, 1123,
1130–31, 1135, 1143, 1147, 1179, 1275, 1289–90,
1296, 1299–1300, 1303–5, 1311, 1313–14, 1317–
18, 1320, 1322, 1326, 1328–32, 1341, 1347,
1498, 1506, 1539, 1549, 1577, 1665, 1738, 1800,
1827, 1926, 1941, 1970, 1977, 1980, 1981

Offense (Chapter 30), 14, 19, 26, 77, 208, 225,

262, 300–304, 325–26, 328–29, 332, 341,
354, 376, 411, 497, 530, 547, 549, 640, 663,
665, 668, 693, 700, 718–19, 721, 729, 739,
741, 758, 760, 803–4, 823, 838–39, 844, 850,
865–66, 877–78, 881, 883, 886–87, 891, 894,
907, 911–12, 914–15, 917, 922, 930–33, 936,
940, 942, 947, 950, 954, 980, 985–86, 992,
996, 1000, 1027, 1042, 1044–45, 1050, 1093,
1121, 1135, 1156, 1158, 1163, 1190, 1193–94,
1209, 1223, 1229, 1286, 1296, 1300, 1306,
1324, 1333, 1350, 1353, 1451–53, 1461, 1463,
1470, 1486, 1488–89, 1535, 1536, 1544, 1546,
1549, 1556–57, 1561, 1563–65, 1568, 1570, 1573–
75, 1587, 1590–91, 1601, 1622, 1628–29, 1636,
1642, 1646, 1649, 1653–54, 1656–57, 1660,
1667–68, 1670–74, 1683–86, 1697, 1699,
1704–5, 1709–10, 1718, 1726, 1731–32, 1734,
1743, 1746–47, 1769, 1776, 1803, 1806, 1811–
12, 1814–15, 1859–61, 1901, 1907, 1941–42,
1944–45, 1947, 1956, 1960–63, 1965, 1975.
See also Crime; Serious crime

Officer, 19, 26, 48, 53, 68, 131, 140, 283, 305,
308, 322, 356, 847, 855, 876, 878, 886, 897,
901, 909–10, 916, 945, 950, 1036–37, 1050,
1088, 1303, 1438, 1473, 1564, 1565–67, 1569,
1584, 1586–87, 1601, 1604, 1640, 1645, 1653,
1870. *See also* Agent

Orphan, 482, 567, 571, 573, 660, 1543, 1547,
1550, 1818

Ownership, 63–64, 197, 199–200, 237, 276,
280, 291, 375–76, 551, 553–54, 587, 660, 685–
87, 699–700, 704, 850, 961, 964, 981, 983,
987–88, 1009–10, 1374, 1412, 1414, 1416,
1444, 1459, 1463, 1487, 1547, 1551, 1577, 1591,
1824, 1916, 1967. *See also* Seisin

Parlement, 843, 1775, 1863. *See also* King's
court

Partition, 62, 291, 379, 396, 472–73, 475, 490,
568–69, 622, 625, 644, 661–62, 714, 1097,
1368, 1972, 1975

Partner, partnership (Chapter 21, 22), 193,
503, 547, 557, 583, 593, *621–31*, 639, 641–47,
649–69, 813, 928, 945, 949, 1135, 1178, 1269,
1302, 1371, 1524, 1629

Peremptory exception (Chapter 3), 236, *238*,
248, 281, 240, 1725. *See also* Dilatory exception

Perjure, perjuror, perjury, 29, 122, 212, 620,
894, 912–13, 991, 1041, 1137, 1178, 1182, 1186,
1260, 1354, 1605, 1685, 1761–62, 1816, 1839

Personal (suits), *228–29*, 231–32, 234, 317, 338, 649, 1818, 1934

Personal property (Chapter 23), 18, 26, 36, 57, 62, 72, 90, 92, 118, 140, 156, 197–98, 213–14, 225, 227, 242, 254, 264, 277–80, 297, 314, 317–18, 362, 365, 368, 373–74, 379, 382–84, 387, 402, 414, 422, 426, 440–42, 449, 456–57, 459, 518, 534, 557, 564, 574, 576, 597, 614, 618, 622, 625, 628–29, 641–42, 671, 697, 703, 713, 770, 775–76, 913, 928, 930–31, 970, 992, 1002, 1055, 1073–74, 1089, 1091, 1094 1144, 1203, 1207, 1209, 1218, 1229, 1251, 1259, 1269, 1290, 1321, 1326, 1361–62, 1380, 1436, 1443, 1452, 1456, 1482, 1526, 1536, 1548, 1586, 1593–94, 1602, 1604, 1617, 1639, 1718, 1720–22, 1758, 1763–64, 1818, 1867, 1870, 1924, 1972–75, 1977, 1980. *See also* Personalty

Personalty (Chapter 23), 474, 479, 493–96, 502–4, 670–71, *673*–77, 679, 680–81. *See also* Personal property

Plead, 23, 26, 31, 33, 35, 41, 72, 90–91, 96, 115–17, 130–32, 136, 140, 156, 165, 169, 172, 174–76, 178, 180–81, 184, 188–89, 193–94, 196, 206, 210–12, 216–17, 219, 224, 227, 240, *248–50*, 280, 290–91, 301, 303, 306, 315–16, 321, 342, 379, 389, 397, 399, 546, 551, 575, 667, 669, 915, 998, 1036, 1072, 1150–51, 1164, 1193, 1211, 1217, 1226, 1238, 1294, 1318, 1349, 1423, 1430, 1443, 1459, 1464, 1682, 1742, 1776, 1780, 1793, 1855, 1858, 1862, 1879, 1887–88, 1894, 1897, 1902, 1914, 1916, 1934, 1982

Pleading, 33, 42, 43, 93, 666, 923, 998, 1101, 1226, 1392, 1456, 1785, 1856, 1888, 1912, 1916

Presumption, 304, 418, 581, 739–40, 758–59, 808, 815, 817, 934, 937, 941, 1037, 1138, *1156–62*, 1169, 1178, 1186–87, 1189, 1192, 1234, 1243, 1339, 1544, 1565, 1634, 1637, 1649, 1812, 1814, 1949–52, 1955

Principal, 127, 131, 135, 137, 147, 149, 156, 158–59, 161, 163, 170, 740, 1089, 1094, 1309, 1318, 1329, 1341, 1346–47, 1349, 1721, 1912. *See also* Agent

Principal dwelling, 434–35, 439, 464–65, 472

Privilege, 128, 137, 262, 325, 332, 340, 346, 353, 682, *684–92*, 698–700, 702, 710, 715, 717, 742, 751, 891, 973, 1094, 1103, 1457, 1467, 1472, 1516, 1526, 1529, 1644, 1800, 1818, 1822. *See also* Custom

Proceeding, 34, 342, 921, 1151, 1164, 1186, 1208, 1254, 1276, 1287, 1472, 1888–89, 1895

Provost, 19, 26, 37–38, 40–42, 48, 53, 140, 301, 322, 718, 843, 845, 847, 849, 886, 917, 920, 1036–37, 1050, 1303, 1586–87, 1604, 1695, 1699, 1774, 1855–56. See also *Bailli*; Ecclesiastical judge; Judge; Secular judge

Public good, 265, 289, 1132, 1559, 1619, 1621, 1662, 1666, 1981. *See also* Common good

Punish, punishment, 15–16, 19, 21, 37, 39, 48, 52, 85, 188, 300, 304, 329, 340, 354–55, 560, 619, 640, 665–66, 701, 759–60, 803, 823, 830, 835–36, 838, 840, 850, 859, 866, 883–87, 889, 906, 910, 922, 928, 930, 934, 936, 942–44, 946, 948, 950, 954, 980, 985, 992, 996, 999, 1022, 1042, 1044, 1047, 1099, 1132, 1136–37, 1157, 1160–62, 1286, 1293, 1300, 1303, 1333, 1350, 1448, 1453, 1462, 1475, 1519, 1534, 1536, 1564, 1570, 1575, 1864, 1901, 1904, 1926, 1936, 1941, 1943, 1944, 1946–48, 1956–58, 1963, 1965

Purchased real property (Chapters 14, 23), 362, 365, 367–68, 373–74, 378, 382, 384, 387, 402, 406, 414, 421–22, 426, 433, 488–90, 493–95, 503, 505, 555, 597, 612, 614, 618, 628, 645, 931, 1367, 1404, 1410, 1617, 1639, 1972–75

Quit-rent, 230, 317, 467, 672, 688–90, 692–94, 703–5, 755, 782, 862–63, 893, 912, 975, 977, 1132, 1285, 1390, 1439, 1443–44, 1452, 1459, 1461, 1487–88, 1529, 1547, 1618

Real (suits), *228, 230–34*, 771

Real property (inherited) (Chapters 14, 23), 18, 45, 57, 62, 64, 72, 148, 156, 197, 198–200, 203, 213–16, 218, 224–25, 227, 230–33, 237–38, 241–42, 254, 271, 276, 279, 280, 290–91, 310, 314, 317–18, 362, 365, 367–69, 374, 378, 382–83, 386–87, 403, 408, 411, 421, 426, 430, 432, 434, 446, 449, 480, 493–95, 503, 505, 510, 552, 555–57, 574, 576, 578, 586, 594, 597, 602, 612, 622, 628, 632, 641–42, 646, *672*, 686, 766, 770, 775–77, 782–83, 788–89, 791–92, 863, 913, 930–31, 1025, 1055, 1073–74, 1089–91, 1094–98, 1100, 1144, 1166, 1207, 1209, 1229, 1251, 1259, 1269, 1290, 1305, 1309, 1321, 1326, 1356–58, 1389, 1417, 1435–36, 1439, 1443, 1452, 1456, 1462, 1469, 1500, 1526, 1529, 1536, 1548, 1578, 1581, 1593, 1602, 1617, 1629, 1639, 1644, 1722, 1763–64, 1791, 1818, 1823, 1867, 1870, 1916, 1931, 1971–74, 1977, 1980–81. *See also* Realty

Realty (Chapters 14, 23), 461–65, 467, 472,
474–75, 477, 479–81, 483, 487, 493–96,
499, 501–3, 505, 517, 670, *672–73*, 67–76,
678–81. *See also* Real property
Recall from memory, 15, 42, 131, 283, *1150–53*,
1158, 1164, 1168, 1192, 1200, 1203, 1208, 1226,
1233, 1270, 1521, 1818, 1826, 1876–77, 1894–
95, 1901, 1916
Reclamation (Chapter 53), 1420, 1535, 1561,
1577, *1582–90*, 1592, 1782, 1787–89
Record (written), 24, 36, 93, 211, 261, 1023,
1092, 1250, 1254, 1256, 1532, 1888–89
Recourse, 649, 665, 1131–33, 1152, 1163, 1165,
1349, 1397, 1410, 1530, 1580, 1926
Redeem (Chapter 44), 403, 487–88, 505, 552,
555, 603, 1138, 1356, 1358–61, *1363–71*, 1373,
1379–1403, 1405–12, 1414–1504, 1553–54,
1686, 1820. *See also* Redemption
Redemption (Chapter 44), 79, 297, 403, 505,
555, 613, 1290, 1356–63, 1369, 1371–72, 1377–
78, 1381, 1384, 1387–95, 1397, 1399, 1401,
1404–7, 1409, 1411, 1414, 1417, 1555, 1820,
1822. *See also* Redeeem
Reimburse, reimbursement, 90, 398, 459,
1111, 1117, 1142, 1284, 1308–9, 1312–13, 1316,
1318, 1327, 1329, 1337, 1663. *See also* Repay;
Make good
Relief (for fief), *762–66*, 1104, 1494, 1578–79,
1893, 1917–18. *See also* Inheritance tax
Religious house (Chapter 46), 137, 168, 178,
262, 314, 316, 322, 325, 332, 338, 700, 1439,
1454, 1462–66, 1469–73, 1476, 1517, 1529,
1531, 1578–79, 1616–17, 1641, 1644
Rent (Chapter 38), 28, 230, 286, 317, 444,
467, 658, 672, 679, 680–81, 688–90, 693–
95, 698, 703–4, 755, 782, 862–63, 894, 972–
73, 975, 977, 1009, 1016, 1018–19, 1021,
1064–65, 1074, *1121–28*, 1130–36, 1138–42,
1144, 1305, 1351, 1390, 1412, 1439, 1443, 1452,
1457, 1459, 1461, 1487, 1529, 1547, 1618, 1938
Repay, 449, 813, 1351, 1397, 1455, 1599, 1907.
See also Reimburse; Make good
Repute, reputation, 15–16, 19, 25–26, 29–30,
34, 38, 47, 52, 213, 422, 549, 634, 804, 815,
913, 926, 937, 940–42, 985, 991, 1046, 1076,
1078, 1113, 1136, 1187, 1189, 1197, 1205, 1223,
1258, 1354, 1601, 1634, 1721, 1815, 1949, 1982
Reseise, reseisin, 59, 61, 64, 73, 76–79, 82,
205, 237, 853, 902, 903, 904, 1325, 1419, 1650
Restitution, 53, 368, 382, 396–97, 404, 408,
412, 419, 426, 449, 554, 700, 730, 735, 747,

799, 804, 841, 879, 986, 996, 1009, 1117–18,
1299, 1390, 1404–5, 1561, 1928
Right, 29, 78, 125, 166, 196, 198, 200, 203, 213,
216, 226, 233–34, 248, 250, 262, 281, 294,
314–15, 363, 386, 391, 401, 414, 424, 433,
446–48, 450–52, 454, 456, 460, 466, 469,
472–73, 476–78, 485, 487, 503, 514, 520, 522,
533, 552, 555, 566, 570–71, 573, 594, 596, 601–
2, 612–13, 644, 647, 649, 658–60, 672, 674,
689–90, 693, 696, 698–700, 718, 723, 735,
751, 803, 813, 835, 886, 912, 928, 948, 988,
1025, 1033, 1053, 1074, 1103–5, 1116, 1166,
1172, 1175, 1218–19, 1238, 1251, 1286, 1343,
1359, 1361, 1363, 1369, 1383, 1386, 1398–99,
1402, 1405–6, 1408, 1414, 1417, 1419, 1422,
1425, 1428, 1445, 1450, 1457, 1467, 1469,
1470, 1472, 1482, 1496, 1500, 1504, 1508,
1517, 1518, 1525, 1536, 1550–51, 1555, 1572, 1577,
1616–17, 1619, 1624–25, 1650, 1662, 1665–68,
1671, 1686–88, 1715, 1755, 1787, 1818, 1822–23,
1825, 1834–35, 1850, 1858, 1861, 1879, 1892–
93, 1898, 1940, 1944, 1970–71
Robber, 327, 330, 741, 985, 1413, 1772, 1901
Robbery, 207, 330, 996

Safekeeping (Chapter 36), *1105*, 1107–8, 1110,
1113–14, 1122, 1135, 1138, 1527, 1540, 1544,
1595, 1604, 1662, 1772–73
Sales tax, *767*, 782, 788–89, 792, 864, 1133, 1379,
1398–99, 1414, 1454, 1494, 1531, 1578–81
Seal, 52, 140, 144–45, 165, 211, 297–98, 371,
426, 588, 807, 915, 1074–76, 1078–79, 1084–
85, 1092, 1094, 1097–99, 1104, 1202–3,
1214–16, 1225, 1250, 1254, 1269, 1280, 1284,
1386, 1429, 1827, 1877, 1916
Secular court, 140, 311, 313, 315–16, 318, 321–
22, 333, 337, 340–44, 347, 353, 357–61, 376,
397, 428, 443, 578, 586–89, 592, 599, 989,
1092, 1136, 1197, 1204, 1211, 1221–22, 1292,
1308, 1316, 1321–22, 1334, 1337–38, 1340,
1348, 1350, 1352, 1354, 1356, 1616, 1622, 1626,
1709, 1800–1801, 1878–79, 1909, 1911, 1913,
1925–26, 1932. *See also* Ecclesiastical court
Secular judge, 311, 315, 321, 347, 353, 1092, 1137,
1926. See also *Bailli*; Ecclesiastical judge;
Provost
Security, 161, 246, 422–23, 441–42, 511–14,
520, 538, 542, 548–49, 572–73, 614–15, 632,
638, 687, 695, 740, 776, 872–75, 975, 990,
1019, 1021, 1024, 1030–31, 1047, 1064–65,
1090, 1108, 1132–34, 1136–37, 1321, 1338,

1397, 1420, 1527, 1544, 1576, 1580, 1583–84, 1586, 1591, 1596–1600, 1607, 1611, 1906–7, 1930–31, 1977–80

Seisin, 64, 74, 197, 199, 206, 210, 224, 237, 246, 276, 291, 361, 518, 587, 699, 902–4, 1219–20, 1359, 1367, 1369, 1371–75, 1379, 1389, 1398–99, 1412–14, 1416, 1443–44, 1459, 1531, 1597, 1915–16. *See also* Ownership

Seize, seizure (Chapter 51), 19, 76, 321, 367, 373, 376, 483–84, 514, 523, 551, 688, 694, 703–4, 795, 799, 804, 862, 876, 963, 1018, 1045, 1131, 1133–35, 1398, 1419–22, 1447, 1522, 1533–34, 1536–38, 1540, 1545, 1547, *1556–57*, 1560–63, 1565–67, 1569–70, 1576–78, 1582–86, 1588–90, 1592–93, 1595, 1597, 1601, 1604–5, 1649, 1662, 1732, 1779, 1782, 1788, 1789, 1864. *See also* Confiscate

Serf (Chapter 45), 13, 187, 365, 812, 973, 1030, 1176, 1209, 1259, 1270, 1331, 1418, 1424–25, 1431–42, 1445–50, *1452–59*, 1500–1501, 1578, 1687, 1799, 1823

Serious crime (Chapter 30), 85, 121, 160, 187, 212, 221, 227, 242, 297, 304, 341, 352, 355, 411, 560, 619, 701, 803, *824*, 924, 992, 1046, 1182, 1186, 1229, 1236, 1243, 1286, 1293, 1332–33, 1353, 1534–37, 1539, 1554, 1563, 1571, 1573, 1575, 1585, 1601, 1622, 1625, 1629, 1638, 1642, 1649, 1656–60, 1673, 1691, 1698, 1710, 1746, 1748, 1751, 1764, 1848, 1873, 1891, 1901. *See also* Crime; Offense

Serjeanty, 386

Service, 18–9, 21, 60, 124, 166, 177, 185, 195, 376, 386, 418, 514, 525–26, 792, 794–801, *805–6, 812–13*, 817–18, 820–22, 877, 886, 991, 1003, 1009, 1060, 1071, 1109, 1190, 1288, 1438, 1446, 1497, 1529, 1597, 1687, 1725, 1738, 1866, 1868–69, 1893, 1981

Sharecrop, sharecropper, 449, 541, 789, 852, 894–95, 899, 1134, 1439, 1443, 1459, 1461, 1487, 1547

Sharp practice, 123, 129, 522, 541, 592, 694, 1070, 1103, 1113, 1117, 1142, 1245, 1362, 1405, 1414, 1416, 1430, 1575, 1596–97, 1604, 1657, 1670, 1826, 1940. *See also* Fraud; Trick

Sovereign, 24, 36, 44, 51, 65, 67, 72, 100, 120, 137, 172, 192, 214, 227, 246, 265, 289, 295, 297–98, 573, 624, 637, 663–64, 666, 669, 691–92, 729–30, 742, 755, 922, 931, 986, 996, 1036, *1042–45*, 1074, 1076, 1078–79, 1092, 1094, 1103, 1268, 1283, 1286, 1293, 1347, 1423, 1437, 1440, 1443, 1445–46, 1454,

1466–67, 1471, 1527, 1536, 1586, 1592, 1659, 1662, 1692–93, 1695–96, 1698, 1704, 1710, 1718, 1726, 1732, 1734–35, 1737, 1740, 1776, 1780, 1785, 1789, 1802, 1806, 1825, 1827, 1866, 1877, 1897, 1901. *See also* Baron; King

Steal, 210, 326, 711, 813, 832, 835, 935, 939, 942–43, 945, 947–49, 996, 1023, 1105, 1111, 1113, 1354, 1576, 1815, 1960. *See also* Theft; Thief; Larceny

Sub-fief (Chapter 47), 60, 67, 77, 80, 82, 322, 343, 471, 497, 788, 1044, *1477–79*, 1483–86, 1489–91, 1494, 1586, 1917–18, 1971

Substitute, 152, 1713, 1795, 1810, 1813, 1834–35, 1838, 1841, 1849–50. *See also* Champion

Summon (Chapter 2), 43, 53, *57–60*, 62–72, 80–87, 91–98, 100–101, 103–4, 109–11, 119–24, 128, 136, 210, 214, 237, 267, 297, 305–6, 308, 314, 322, 357–58, 360, 376, 483, 486, 588, 793, 795, 797, 854–56, 867, 901, 917, 922–24, 959, 961, 974, 976, 981, 987–88, 1017, 1022, 1027, 1044–45, 1074–75, 1078, 1102, 1115, 1253, 1310–11, 1318, 1329, 1343–45, 1347, 1372, 1374, 1389, 1391–92, 1400, 1419–21, 1438, 1470, 1545, 1576–77, 1583, 1592, 1610, 1649, 1665, 1684, 1695, 1698–99, 1701, 1726–27, 1731, 1734, 1739, 1775, 1785, 1788–89, 1813, 1869–70, 1887, 1909, 1926, 1932, 1956, 1981

Surety, suretyship (Chapter 43), 64, 70, 90, 219, 274, 301, 558–59, 695, 712, 776, 873, 874, 920, 990, 1005, 1019, 1021, 1024, 1026, 1030, 1039, 1104, 1131, 1134, 1179, 1212, 1263, 1296, *1308–23*, 1325–36, 1341, 1343–50, 1356, 1389, 1397, 1413, 1535, 1580, 1585, 1590–91, 1596, 1615, 1755, 1763, 1766, 1789, 1873, 1926

Surtax, 704–5, 782, 1581

Tax, 346, 571, 620, 646, 659, 698, 705, 977, 1457, 1463, 1514, 1525, 1526, 1529

Tenancy, 723, 972–74, 976, 1045, 1439, 1443, 1687, 1791. *See also* Tenant

Tenant, 233, 299, 303, 308, 694, 703–4, 723, 755, 761, 766, 778, 786, 862, 893–96, 899, 907–8, 963, *972–77*, 1045, 1132, 1343, 1443–44, 1459, 1461, 1530–31, 1687, 1742, 1786, 1791. *See also* Tenancy

Testify, testimony (Chapter 40), 52, 87, 94, 187, 212, 234, 258, 292, 333, 371, 405, 426, 568, 586–89, 618, 658, 815, 820, 855, 869, 907, 913, 929, 992, 1047, 1073, 1092, 1100, 1153,

Testify (*cont.*)
1155, 1157, 1170–87, 1196–1200, 1202, 1204–7, 1209–11, 1213–16, 1221–22, 1224–25, 1227–28, 1230–36, 1239, 1245, 1251–52, 1257, 1259–60, 1270, 1386, 1396, 1428, 1472, 1566, 1601, 1605, 1675, 1742, 1761–62, 1764–68, 1784, 1786, 1837, 1877, 1881, 1891, 1894, 1902

Theft, 212, 925, 927, 940, 1189, 1935. *See also* Larceny; Thief

Thief, 327, 906, 928, 939–40, 946, 950–51, 953, 980, 1023, 1565, 1570. *See also* Larceny; Theft

Toll, 346, 659, 672, 719, 791, 891–93, 897, 912

Townsman, 843, 1450, 1497–99, 1520, 1671–72, 1898

Traitor, 327, 846, 885, 1207, 1772, 1901

Treachery, 826–27, 992, 1629, 1675, 1680, 1689, 1698, 1704, 1746, 1772–73. *See also* Treason

Treason, 36, 207, 212, *824*, 923, 1572, 1642. *See also* Treachery

Trick, 19, 163, 221, 514, 541, 592, 694, 815, 1046, 1049, 1076. *See also* Fraud; Sharp practice

Trickery, 1118, 1245, 1339, 1347, 1356, 1379, 1396, 1524, 1596–97, 1840

Trickster, 894

Truce (Chapter 50), 299, 300, 303, 825, 827, 839, 887, 996, 1537, 1546–48, 1655, 1669, 1681, *1690–1707*, 1726, 1746, 1872

Tutor (Chapter 17), 266, 552, 568, *570–72*, 574–77

Unchallenged (tenure of land), 554, 722, 979–82, 1824, 1826

Usage, 722, 751, 1202, 1314, 1510, 1819

Usury (Chapter 68), 1000, 1103, *1921–29*, 1931–32, 1934–38

Valid (witness), 405, 426, 1046, 1075, *1184*, 1200, 1204, 1224, 1227, 1230–34, 1245, 1251, 1877–78

Villeinage (Chapters 14, 23), 62, 241, 343, 386, 452, 461, *466–67*, 475, 499, 502, 504, 511–13, 516, 533–34, 537, 557, 564, 602, 630, 638, 761, 766–68, 789, 792, 864–66, 907–8, 1018, 1131, 1398, 1443, 1446, 1459–61, 1469, 1481, 1487, 1489, 1502, 1529–31, 1549, 1552–53, 1578, 1581, 1786, 1791. *See also* Fief

Wager of battle (Chapter 64), 24, 36, 93, 121, 212, 227, 233–34, 293, 340, 619, 919, 923,

926, 929, 940, 985, 993, 1046, 1148, 1163, 1167, 1174, 1184, 1192, 1209, 1222, 1229, 1244, 1251, 1259, 1333, 1353, 1427–29, 1431, 1471, 1532, 1535, 1585, 1642, 1656, 1658, 1682, 1709–10, 1712, 1720–24, 1734, 1747–51, 1755–58, 1761–68, 1772–73, 1780–81, 1801, 1809–30, 1832, 1836–38, 1846, 1872, 1874, 1888–89, 1894, 1901, 1905

War (Chapter 59), 65, 105, 590, 603, 640, 797, 858, 887, 986, 996, 1034, 1107, 1115, 1180, 1187, 1278, 1347, 1354, 1453, 1510, 1514, 1546, 1628, 1655, 1662, 1664–65, 1667–79, 1681–91, 1693, 1699, 1702–3, 1809, 1811, 1872, 1903, 1940–41

Warranty, warrantee, warrantor, 231, 254, 433, 449, 482, 497, 558–59, 711, 739–41, 799, 952, 980, 998, *1008–13*, 1015, 1017, *1046–49*, 1070–73, 1088, 1091, 1094, 1097, 1104, 1108, 1116, 1133, 1310, *1347–48*, 1382, 1409, 1421, 1423, 1580, 1593, 1970, 1972, 1978

Weight (Chapter 26), 743, 760, 773, 835

Widow, 90, 319, 442–43, 445–46, 448–49, 454, 456–59, 585, 599, 614, 617, 643, 674, 1054, 1175, 1322, 1334, 1435

Will: discretion, 26, 38, 51, 295, 1604, 1659, 1740–41, 1764–65, 1901 (*see also* Discretion); testament (Chapter 12), 91, 199, 214, 274, 295, 320–21, 361–65, 368, *371–417*, 419, 420–29, 456, 474, 503, 505, 518, 547, 597, 612, 669, 676, 680, 776, 1025, 1133, 1204, 1218, 1417, 1447, 1456, 1531, 1543, 1549, 1576, 1617, 1659, 1696, 1821–22, 1928, 1971, 1975

Witness (Chapter 40), 27, 101, 140, 211–12, 226–27, 233–34, 237, 239, 247, 258, 292–93, 304, 342, 405, 426, 556, 563, 568, 588, 593, 619, 759, 814, 816, 827, 868, 908–9, 992, 1026, 1041, 1046, 1075, 1078, 1092, 1145, *1149*, 1152–53, 1155, 1163–64, 1170–72, 1174, *1182–86*, 1188, 1190, 1192, 1194, 1196, 1200, 1202–5, 1207, 1209, 1216, 1219–37, 1239–41, 1244–45, 1247–48, 1251–52, 1255–70, 1273–74, 1276, 1281–82, 1289, 1302, 1338, 1349, 1428, 1431, 1433, 1565, 1567, 1589, 1601, 1605, 1636–37, 1656, 1724, 1727, 1761–62, 1764–68, 1815–16, 1818, 1820, 1823–24, 1827, 1837, 1876–78, 1881, 1891, 1894, 1902

Woman, women, 49, 55, 71, 90, 103, 116, 168, 190, 202, 246, 306, 313, 334–37, 366, 382, 387, 436–38, 444–45, 449, 456, 472, 490, 502, 510, 522, 536, 544–46, 548, 560, 579, 581–86, 590–91, 594, 597–601, 615, 617–18,

622, 628, 630, 632, 677, 719, 815, 821, 829,
863, 925–31, 933–34, 971, 993, 1054, 1061,
1137, 1159, 1175, 1188–89, 1197, 1211, 1259,
1287–88, 1330, 1335–36, 1378, 1410, 1434,
1438, 1441–42, 1445, 1452, 1455–56, 1500,
1504, 1572, 1576, 1599–1600, 1606, 1618,
1626–34, 1636, 1638–40, 1642, 1662, 1688,
1713, 1717, 1795–96, 1813–14, 1822, 1841, 1867,
1901, 1928, 1943, 1950, 1956, 1963, 1974
Write, written, writing (Chapter 35), 27, 38,
44, 52, 92–93, 131, 154, 169, *201*, 211, 238,

259–261, 264, 297, 342, 347, 396, 405, 426,
550, 568, 669, 696–97, 806–7, 816, 915,
1023–24, 1055, 1064, *1073–75*, 1078–80,
1082–1101, 1103–4, *1147*, 1166, 1172, 1201–4,
1213, 1214, 1215–16, 1221, 1223, 1225, 1227,
1230, 1235, 1240, 1245, 1247, 1249, 1254–56,
1260, 1280, 1284, 1296, 1304, 1310, 1316, 1386,
1429, 1433, 1445, 1538, 1565, 1604, 1827, 1863,
1877–78, 1916, 1926, 1980, 1982
Wrong (to be righted in will), 368, *382*, 396,
412, 426, 1928

University of Pennsylvania Press
MIDDLE AGES SERIES
Edward Peters, General Editor

Books in the series that are out of print are marked with an asterisk.

F. R. P. Akehurst, trans. *The* Coutumes de Beauvaisis *of Philippe de Beaumanoir.* 1992
David Anderson. *Before the Knight's Tale: Imitation of Classical Epic in Boccaccio's* Teseida. 1988
Benjamin Arnold. *Count and Bishop in Medieval Germany: A Study of Regional Power, 1100–1350.* 1991
J. M. W. Bean. *From Lord to Patron: Lordship in Late Medieval England.* 1990
Uta-Renate Blumenthal. *The Investiture Controversy: Church and Monarchy from the Ninth to the Twelfth Century.* 1988
Daniel Bornstein, trans. *Dino Compagni's Chronicle of Florence.* 1986
Betsy Bowden. *Chaucer Aloud: The Varieties of Textual Interpretation.* 1987
James William Brodman. *Ransoming Captives in Crusader Spain: The Order of Merced on the Christian-Islamic Frontier.* 1986
Otto Brunner (Howard Kaminsky and James Van Horn Melton, eds. and trans.). *Land and Lordship: Structures of Governance in Medieval Austria.* 1991
Robert I. Burns, S.J., ed. *Emperor of Culture: Alfonso X the Learned of Castile and His Thirteenth-Century Renaissance.* 1990
David Burr. *Olivi and Franciscan Poverty: The Origins of the* Usus Pauper *Controversy.* 1989
Thomas Cable. *The English Alliterative Tradition.* 1991
Leonard Cantor, ed. *The English Medieval Landscape.* 1982*
Anthony K. Cassell and Victoria Kirkham, eds. and trans. *Diana's Hunt. Caccia di Diana. Boccaccio's First Fiction.* 1991
Brigitte Cazelles. *The Lady as Saint: A Collection of French Hagiographic Romances of the Thirteenth Century.* 1991
Willene B. Clark and Meradith T. McMunn, eds. *Beasts and Birds of the Middle Ages: The Bestiary and Its Legacy.* 1989
G. G. Coulton. *From St. Francis to Dante: Translations from the Chronicle of the Franciscan Salimbene (1221–1288).* 1972*
Richard C. Dales. *The Scientific Achievement of the Middle Ages.* 1973
Charles T. Davis. *Dante's Italy and Other Essays.* 1984
George T. Dennis, trans. *Maurice's Strategikon: Handbook of Byzantine Military Strategy.* 1984*
Katherine Fischer Drew, trans. *The Burgundian Code: The Book of Constitutions or Law of Gundobad and Additional Enactments.* 1972
Katherine Fischer Drew, trans. *The Laws of the Salian Franks.* 1991.

Katherine Fischer Drew, trans. *The Lombard Laws*. 1973

Nancy Edwards. *The Archaeology of Early Medieval Ireland*. 1990

Margaret J. Ehrhart. *The Judgment of the Trojan Prince Paris in Medieval Literature*. 1987

Patrick J. Geary. *Aristocracy in Provence: The Rhône Basin at the Dawn of the Carolingian Age*. 1985

Julius Goebel, Jr. *Felony and Misdemeanor: A Study in the History of Criminal Law*. 1976*

Avril Henry, ed. *The Mirour of Mans Saluacioune: A Middle English Translation of* Speculum Humanae Salvationis. 1987

J. N. Hillgarth, ed. *Christianity and Paganism, 350–750: The Conversion of Western Europe*. 1986

Richard C. Hoffmann. *Land, Liberties, and Lordship in a Late Medieval Countryside: Agrarian Structures and Change in the Duchy of Wrocław*. 1990

Robert Hollander. *Boccaccio's Last Fiction: "Il Corbaccio."* 1988

Edward B. Irving, Jr. *Rereading* Beowulf. 1989

C. Stephen Jaeger. *The Origins of Courtliness: Civilizing Trends and the Formation of Courtly Ideals, 939–1210*. 1985

William Chester Jordan. *The French Monarchy and the Jews: From Philip Augustus to the Last Capetians*. 1989

William Chester Jordan. *From Servitude to Freedom: Manumission in the Sénonais in the Thirteenth Century*. 1986

Ellen E. Kittell. *From* Ad Hoc *to Routine: A Case Study in Medieval Bureaucracy*. 1991

Alan C. Kors and Edward Peters, eds. *Witchcraft in Europe, 1100–1700: A Documentary History*. 1972

Barbara M. Kreutz. *Before the Normans: Southern Italy in the Ninth and Tenth Centuries*. 1991

Jeanne Krochalis and Edward Peters, ed. and trans. *The World of Piers Plowman*. 1975

E. Ann Matter. *The Voice of My Beloved: The Song of Songs in Western Medieval Christianity*. 1990

María Rosa Menocal. *The Arabic Role in Medieval Literary History*. 1987

A. J. Minnis. *Medieval Theory of Authorship*. 1988

Lawrence Nees. *A Tainted Mantle: Hercules and the Classical Tradition at the Carolingian Court*. 1991

Lynn H. Nelson, trans. *The Chronicle of San Juan de la Peña: A Fourteenth-Century Official History of the Crown of Aragon*. 1991

Charlotte A. Newman. *The Anglo-Norman Nobility in the Reign of Henry I: The Second Generation*. 1988

Thomas F. X. Noble. *The Republic of St. Peter: The Birth of the Papal State, 680–825*. 1984

Joseph F. O'Callaghan. *The Cortes of Castile-León, 1188–1350*. 1989

William D. Paden, ed. *The Voice of the Trobairitz: Perspectives on the Women Troubadours*. 1989

Kenneth Pennington. *Pope and Bishops: The Papal Monarchy in the Twelfth and Thirteenth Centuries*. 1984*

Edward Peters. *The Magician, the Witch, and the Law*. 1982

Edward Peters, ed. *Christian Society and the Crusades, 1198–1229.* Sources in Translation, including The Capture of Damietta by Oliver of Paderborn. 1971

Edward Peters, ed. *The First Crusade: The Chronicle of Fulcher of Chartres and Other Source Materials.* 1971

Edward Peters, ed. *Heresy and Authority in Medieval Europe.* 1980

Edward Peters, ed. *Monks, Bishops, and Pagans: Christian Culture in Gaul and Italy, 500–700.* 1975*

Clifford Peterson. *Saint Erkenwald.* 1977*

James M. Powell. *Anatomy of a Crusade, 1213–1221.* 1986

Donald E. Queller. *The Fourth Crusade: The Conquest of Constantinople, 1201–1204.* 1977*

Michael Resler, trans. *EREC by Hartmann von Aue.* 1987

Pierre Riché (Jo Ann McNamara, trans.). *Daily Life in the World of Charlemagne.* 1978

Jonathan Riley-Smith. *The First Crusade and the Idea of Crusading.* 1986

Joel T. Rosenthal. *Patriarchy and Families of Privilege in Fifteenth-Century England.* 1991

Barbara H. Rosenwein. *Rhinoceros Bound: Cluny in the Tenth Century.* 1982

Steven D. Sargent, ed. and trans. *On the Threshold of Exact Science: Selected Writings of Anneliese Maier on Late Medieval Natural Philosophy.* 1982

Robert Somerville and Kenneth Pennington, eds. *Law, Church, and Society: Essays in Honor of Stephan Kuttner.* 1977*

Sarah Stanbury. *Seeing the Gawain-Poet: Description and the Act of Perception.* 1991

Susan Mosher Stuard, ed. *Women in Medieval History and Historiography.* 1987

Susan Mosher Stuard, ed. *Women in Medieval Society.* 1976

Ronald E. Surtz. *The Guitar of God: Gender, Power, and Authority in the Visionary World of Mother Juana de la Cruz (1481–1534).* 1990

Patricia Terry, trans. *Poems of the Elder Edda.* 1990

Frank Tobin. *Meister Eckhart: Thought and Language.* 1986

Ralph V. Turner. *Men Raised from the Dust: Administrative Service and Upward Mobility in Angevin England.* 1988

Harry Turtledove, trans. *The Chronicle of Theophanes: An English Translation of anni mundi 6095–6305 (A.D. 602–813).* 1982

Mary F. Wack. *Lovesickness in the Middle Ages: The Viaticum and Its Commentaries.* 1990

Benedicta Ward. *Miracles and the Medieval Mind: Theory, Record, and Event, 1000–1215.* 1982.

Suzanne Fonay Wemple. *Women in Frankish Society: Marriage and the Cloister, 500–900.* 1981

This book has been set in Linotron Galliard. Galliard was designed for Mergenthaler in 1978 by Matthew Carter. Galliard retains many of the features of a sixteenth century typeface cut by Robert Granjon but has some modifications that give it a more contemporary look.

Printed on acid-free paper.